SQL Server 2000 XML Distilled

Kevin Williams
Daryl Barnes
Bryant Likes
Stephen Mohr
Paul Morris
Andrew Novick
Andrew Polshaw
Simon Sabin
Jeni Tennison

Curlingstone Publishing Ltd. ®

SQL Server 2000 XML Distilled

© 2002 Curlingstone Publishing Ltd.

All rights reserved. No part of this book may be reproduced, stored in a retrieval system, or transmitted in any form or by any means, without the prior written permission of the publisher, except in the case of brief quotations embodied in critical articles or reviews.

The authors and publisher have made every effort in the preparation of this book to ensure the accuracy of the information. However, the information contained in this book is sold without warranty, either express or implied. Neither the authors, Curlingstone Publishing Ltd., nor its dealers or distributors will be held liable for any damages caused or alleged to be caused either directly or indirectly by this book.

Published by Curlingstone Publishing Ltd.,
Arden House, 1102 Warwick Road,
Acocks Green, Birmingham, B27 6BH, UK.
Printed in the United States
ISBN 1-904347-08-8

Trademark Acknowledgements

Curlingstone has endeavored to provide trademark information about all the companies and products mentioned in this book by the appropriate use of capitals. However, Curlingstone cannot guarantee the accuracy of this information.

Credits

Authors
Kevin Williams
Daryl Barnes
Bryant Likes
Stephen Mohr
Paul Morris
Andrew Novick
Andrew Polshaw
Simon Sabin
Jeni Tennison

Managing Editor
Fiona McParland

Commissioning Editors
Timothy Briggs
Sarah Larder

Technical Editors
Sarah Larder
Gareth Oakley
Craig Weldon

Indexer
Bill Johncocks

Proofreaders
Pauline Briggs
Katrina Hands

Technical Reviewers
Joshua Allen
Daryl Barnes
Paul Bausch
Michael Corning
Louis Davidson
Bruno Denuit
Sreekanth Gongalareddy
Terry Hickman
Mark Horner
Ramesh S. Mani
Paul Morris
Baya Pavliashvili
Rogerio Saran

Project Managers
Sarah Larder
Fiona McParland

Production Manager
Zuned Kasu

Cover Design
Dawn Chellingworth
Corey Stewart

Figures
Rachel Taylor
Pip Wonson

Production Project Coordinator
Pippa Wonson

About the Authors
Kevin Williams

Kevin Williams is a software architect, technical author, and technology trainer living and working in the bucolic environs of the eastern panhandle of West Virginia, a Washington, DC suburb. He is a founder of Blue Oxide Technologies (http://www.blueoxide.com), an XML and XML web services software company. Over the last thirteen years he has architected and implemented software and Web solutions for clients in financial services, healthcare, communications, manufacturing, and government.

His latest efforts include the creation of XML design collaboration and registry software. Although he holds a BSc in Electrical Engineering from Virginia Polytechnic Institute and State University (Virginia Tech), it shouldn't be held against him. Computer science has always been his primary love from the time he first hand-assembled 6502 code on his Atari 400 at the tender age of 12. Kevin may be reached at kevin@blueoxide.com

Kevin Williams contributed Chapters 3, 6, 7, 9, 11, and 14.

Daryl Barnes

Daryl has worked in IT for over 12 years, and he has experienced the Finance, Pharmaceuticals, Logistics, Manufacturing, and Entertainment industries in his career.

He has an MSc from the London School of Economics in Analysis, Design and Management of Information Systems, and a BSc(Hons) in Business Information Technology. Daryl is currently working as a Technical Architect for a major bank in Zurich, Switzerland, but he is really only in Switzerland for the mountains and the skiing.

To Charlotte and Eve, you are my life; the rest is just a smokescreen.

Daryl Barnes contributed Chapters 1 and 17.

Bryant Likes

Bryant Likes is Microsoft's MVP for SQL Server XML and the creator of the http://www.sqlxml.org/ web site, which is the number one for solving SQLXML problems. Bryant has been developing applications that use SQLXML since its first release. He is currently attending California State University Northridge, where he is working on a Bachelor of Science in Information Systems.

To my Dad
I would like to thank my beautiful fiancée for all her support while I was writing this book. I am also indebted and offer many thanks to the wonderful editors at Curlingstone Publishing, who helped me through the writing of this book. I could not have done it without them.

Bryant Likes contributed Chapters 2, 8, and 15.

Stephen Mohr

Stephen Mohr is a senior software systems architect with Omicron Consulting and XMLabs in Philadelphia, USA. He has over twelve years experience developing software and systems for various platforms. Currently focusing on XML and related technologies as they apply to web applications, he has research interests in distributed computing and artificial intelligence. Stephen holds BS and MS degrees in computer science from Rensselaer Polytechnic Institute.

Stephen Mohr contributed Chapter 16.

Paul Morris

Paul is a database architect and consultant based in South West London, UK. He has over fifteen years experience in IT, the last ten immersed in Microsoft technologies. He specialises in designing and building e-commerce solutions for clients of all sizes. Currently, he is Database Architect for http://www.Totaljobs.com, a leading e-recruitment provider.

He is a Microsoft Certified Database Administrator (MCDBA), solution developer (MSCD), and systems engineer (MCSE+I).

Paul Morris contributed Chapters 4 and 5.

Andrew Novick

Andrew Novick develops applications as consultant, project manager, and President of Novick Software. His firm specializes in implementing solutions using the Microsoft tool set: SQL Server, ASP, ASP.Net, Visual Basic and VB.Net. 2002 marks his 31st year of computer programming, starting in High School with a PDP-8 and moving on to a degree in Computer Science, an MBA, and then programming mainframes, minicomputers and, for the last 16 years, PCs. When not programming he enjoys coaching Little League baseball, woodworking, mowing the lawn, and the occasional movie with his wife. He can be found on the web at http://www.NovickSoftware.com or by e-mail at anovick@NovickSoftware.com.

I would like to dedicate my chapters in this book to my wife Ulli. She has always supported me in whatever path I've chosen. I'd also like to thank the many clients whose interesting problems have given me a fun career. Finally, I'd like to thank Tim Briggs and Sarah Larder at Curlingstone who gave me my first book assignment and who have been supportive and professional throughout.

Andrew Novick contributed Chapters 12, 13, and Appendix C.

Andrew Polshaw

Andrew Polshaw, a Mathematics and Philosophy graduate, has been an IT enthusiast most of his life, and works for Wrox Press as an editor for their Visual Basic .NET Handbook series. While working there, he has been exposed to numerous programming languages, database systems, and ways to work with both. His programming experience and his interest in databases, mean that he has a natural interest in XML Schema, and has edited and written on many texts produced by Wrox on this topic.

Outside of work, he lives in Staffordshire, England, has an interest in folk music, history, and cheesy TV programmes, like Buffy the Vampire Slayer. He lives close to the Peak District, UK, and likes walking in the hills whenever he can.

To my wife and love, Lee, who knows of everything I could write here. Life is never dull with you around.

Andrew Polshaw contributed Appendix B.

Simon Sabin

Simon Sabin is a Consultant for CMG (http://www.cmg.com), an international services and solutions company. Since graduating from Nottingham University, he has worked on developing solutions with Microsoft technologies in the insurance, utilities, and HR services sectors. He specializes in the performance analysis and tuning of n-tier systems, focusing on the database and database interaction.

To Rachel, for persevering while I wrote this on holiday.

Simon Sabin contributed Chapter 10.

Jeni Tennison

Jeni is an independent consultant on XML, XSLT, XML Schema, and related technologies based in Nottingham, England. She has a background in knowledge engineering: her PhD was on developing ontologies collaboratively over the web. Her interest in representing information led to XML, the requirement to support different views of information to XSLT, and the definition of ontologies to XML Schema. She is one of the founders of the EXSLT initiative and author of *XSLT & XPath: On The Edge* (HungryMinds, ISBN 0764547763) and *Beginning XSLT* (Wrox Press, ISBN 1861005946). She was recently awarded the ActiveState 2002 Activator's Choice Award for XSLT Programming.

Jeni Tennison contributed Appendix A.

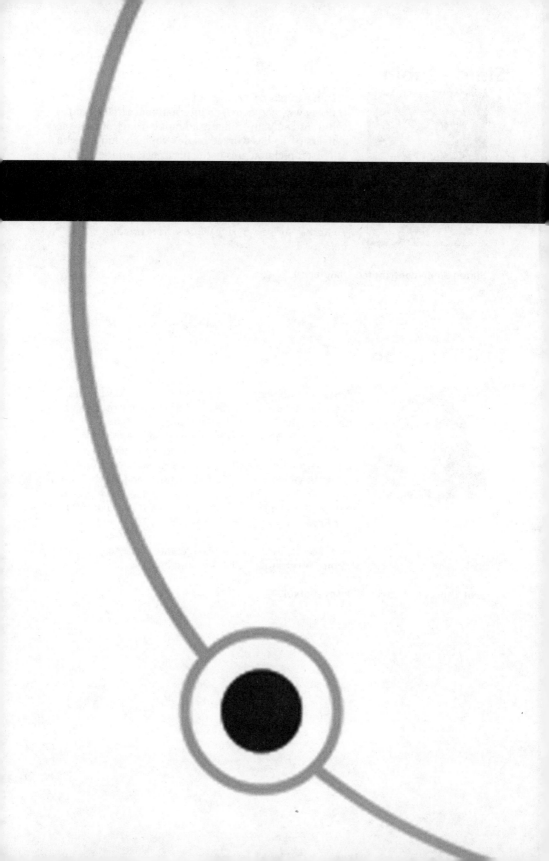

Table of Contents

Introduction   1

What Does This Book Cover?   1
What You Need to Use This Book   4
Source Code   5
Conventions   5
Customer Support   5
    Errata   6
    E-mail Support   6

Chapter 1: SQL Server, XML, and the DBA   9

Data Based Computing   10
    The Success of Relational Databases   10
    The Success of the Web   11
    XML – The Next Step   12
        System Interoperability and Data Interchange in an n-tier Environment   13
        Web Services   13

What Aspects of XML are Relevant to Databases?   13

XML and Relational Structures   17
    Relational Structures   17
    XML Structures   17
        Storing XML in Relational Structures   18
        Storing Relational Data Using XML   18

Mapping XML and Relational Data   18

The Main Uses of XML Structures   19
    XML for Messaging – The Other Application Wants XML   19
    XML as Document – Markup Based Document Objects   20
    XML for Presentation – The Browser Wants Markup   20

An Architectural View   20
    Different Approaches to the Problem   21
        XML End-to-End   21
        Relational End-to (near the)-end   23
        Ad Hoc   24
        Take a Step Back   25
    Which Approach?   27

Summary   28

Table of Contents

Chapter 2: Architecture and Setup — 31

Architecture Overview — 31
- Architecture of SQL Server 2000 XML — 32
  - FOR XML Queries — 32
  - OPENXML — 33
- Architecture of SQLXML — 34
  - HTTP Access — 34
  - XDR Schemas — 35
  - XML Templates — 36
  - XML Bulk Load — 37
  - Updategrams — 38
  - Client-side XML — 38
  - .NET Managed Classes — 39
  - DiffGrams — 40
  - XML Schemas — 40
  - Web Services — 41
- Putting it All Together — 41
  - Where SQLXML Fits With .NET/DNA — 42

Installation of SQLXML — 42
- Requirements — 42
- Installing SQLXML 3.0 — 43

Creating SQLXML Virtual Directories — 44
- General Tab — 45
- Security Tab — 46
- Data Source Tab — 47
- Settings Tab — 48
- Virtual Names Tab — 50
- Advanced Tab — 51
- Upgrade to Version 3 Tab — 52
- Test Your Setup — 52
- Registry Settings — 53
- Security Considerations — 53
  - URL Queries — 54
  - Types of Authentication — 54
  - Other Security Issues — 54
- Troubleshooting — 54

Debugging Tools — 56
- SQL Profiler — 56
- IIS Logging — 56
- Query Analyzer — 56

Summary — 57

Chapter 3: Mapping SQL Server to XML — 59

Considerations When Mapping Data — 59
- Standards Support — 59
- Transmission — 61
- Presentation — 62
- Archival — 63

Table of Contents

XML Schemas vs. XML-Data Reduced Schemas	**64**
Equivalent XML Datatypes	**65**
Design Approach	**74**
Identification of Relevant Information	74
Design of XML Document Overall Structure	75
Sequence, Choice, or All?	75
Understanding Foreign Key Relationships	76
Proper Usage of ID-IDREF Relationships	77
Handling "Dangling" Elements	78
Mapping Column Values	78
Converting Data Types	79
Handling Constraints	79
Include or Exclude Identifiers	80
Handling NULL Values	81
Implementation	**81**
Using an XML View to Create the XML Document	82
Using FOR XML EXPLICIT to Create the XML Document	82
Inventory Example	**82**
Design Goals	82
Identifying the Relevant Information	83
Designing the Document Structure	83
Mapping the Column Values	85
A FOR XML EXPLICIT Query Mapping the Data to XML	86
Summary	**89**

Chapter 4: FOR XML   91

Comparison of Server-Side and Client-Side XML Processing	**92**
FOR XML Query Results	**93**
Server-Side XML Processing	**94**
SQL Limitations	95
Security Considerations	95
Performance Implications	96
FOR XML RAW	96
XMLDATA	98
BINARY BASE64	98
FOR XML AUTO	99
ELEMENTS	103
FOR XML EXPLICIT	104
Directives	110
Client-Side XML Processing	**117**
RAW	118
NESTED	118
EXPLICIT	119
Ways of Using Client-Side FOR XML	119
Summary	**119**

iii

Table of Contents

Chapter 5: URL Queries and Template Queries — 121

URL Queries — 121
- Security Considerations — 122
- Setting up the Environment — 123
- Usage — 123
  - Data Modification — 125
  - Executing Stored Procedures — 125
  - Using Stylesheets — 127
  - Content Types — 130

Template Queries — 132
- Usage Guidelines — 132
- Security Considerations — 133
- Setting up the Environment — 133
  - Template and XSL Stylesheet Caching — 134
- Usage — 135
  - Stored Procedures — 136
  - Parameterizing Queries — 136
  - Using Multiple Queries — 138
  - Using Output Parameters — 140
  - Using Stylesheets — 140
  - XPath Queries — 141
  - Other Options — 141
  - Posting Templates — 142

Summary — 143

Chapter 6: Annotating XML Schemas — 145

Why Annotate XML Schemas? — 145

XML Schemas vs. XDR Schemas — 146

The XML Schema Annotation Namespace — 146

Annotation Mechanisms — 147
- Mapping Complex Elements to SQL Server Tables — 147
- Mapping Attributes to SQL Server Columns — 148
- Mapping Text-only Elements to SQL Server Columns — 149
- Defining Unmapped XML Elements — 150
- Excluding XML Elements From the Mapping — 151
- Specifying Relationships Between Two SQL Tables — 152
- Filtering the Data in an XML Document — 155
- Specifying Unique Keys in an XML Document — 157
- Creating ID-IDREF Relationships in XML Schemas — 159
- Escaping Invalid XML Characters in XML Schemas — 161
- Mapping Binary Large Objects (BLOBs) — 162
- Specifying Identity Columns in an XML Schema — 165
- Specifying a GUID in an XML Schema — 166
- Limiting Recursion Depths in XML Schemas — 167

Summary — 168

Chapter 7: XML Views — 173

The What and Why of XML Views — 173

Creating an XML View — 174
Annotating an Existing XDR or XML Schema — 175
Modeling Tables and Columns in XML Views — 175
Modeling Joins in XML Views — 177

Accessing Data Through an XML View — 180
Accessing Data Using URLs — 180
Accessing Data Using Templates — 180

Examples — 181
Simple Example — 181
Layering an XML View Over a SQL Server View — 183

Summary — 185

Chapter 8: XPath Queries — 187

Overview of XPath — 187

Setting up the Sample — 188
Set up a Schema Mapping — 188
Create the Sample Schema — 189

From T-SQL to XPath — 190
SELECT — 190
FROM — 190
  Namespaces — 191
WHERE — 193
  XPath Data Types — 195
  XPath Operators — 198
  XPath Functions — 198

Using XPath Queries — 199
XPath Queries in a URL — 199
XPath Queries in Templates — 199
  Using Parameters — 201
XPath Queries in ADO — 202
XPath Queries in the Managed Classes — 202

Performance Considerations — 202
Tuning XPath Using SQL Profiler — 202
Recursive Queries — 203

Security Issues — 207
Who Has Access to the Data? — 207
Can the Data be Changed? — 207
Other Methods — 208

Limitations — 208

Summary — 210

Table of Contents

Chapter 9: Mapping XML to SQL Server — 213

Things to Consider — 213
Loading Persistent Data — 213
Loading Temporary Data for Manipulation — 215
Inserts or Updates? — 217

Equivalent SQL Data Types — 219
Types to Avoid in XML Data Destined for SQL Server — 223

Design Approach — 224
Mixed-mode Documents — 224
Identification of Relevant Information — 225
Design of the Overall Relational Structure — 226
    Handling Child Elements — 226
    Handling ID-IDREF Relationships — 231
    Handling ID-IDREFS Relationships — 233
Mapping Data Points — 235
    Converting Data Types — 237
    Creating Constraints Based on XML Schema Constraints — 237
    Modeling Enumeration Constraints — 238
    Creating Record Identifiers — 239

Example — 239
Design Goals — 241
Identifying the Relevant Information — 241
Designing the Tables — 241
Mapping the Column Values — 242

Summary — 244

Chapter 10: OPENXML — 247

Introduction — 247

Parsing an XML document with OPENXML — 248
Parsing Example — 250
    Namespaces — 252

OPENXML Function Syntax — 253
TableName — 253
SchemaDeclaration — 255
    XML Document Example — 256
rowpattern — 258
    Restricting Results — 258
    Set Operations in the rowpattern — 260
OPENXML Flags — 262
    Consumed Data — 264
Column Patterns — 265
    Specifying metaproperties — 266

Combining with Other Tables — 267

Using XML Data to Modify Tables — 271

Using XML Meta Data — 279
Simple Edge Table — 280
Edge Table with DTD or Inline Schema — 282

Performance — 283
Memory — 283
Timing — 284
IO — 285

Limitations — 286
Updating Documents — 286
Caching and Statistics — 286
Whitespace and Escaped Characters — 286
Multi-Valued Attributes — 287

Summary — 287

Chapter 11: Updategrams — 291

What are Updategrams? — 292
Driving Updategrams with an Annotated Schema — 295
Default Mapping in Updategrams — 297
Inserting Data with an Updategram — 298
Inserting Multiple Rows — 301

Deleting Data with an Updategram — 302
Deleting Multiple Rows — 303

Updating Data with an Updategram — 304
Explicitly Relating Records — 306
Explicitly Relating Before and After — 307

Multiple Actions Within One Updategram — 307
Capturing Identity Values for Inserted Records — 311
Inverse Relationships in an Updategram — 315
Creating GUIDs as Part of an Updategram — 317
Generating Updategrams "on-the-fly" — 318
Applying Updategrams to a Database — 319
Applying an Updategram Using HTTP — 319
Applying an Updategram from a URL — 320
Applying Updategrams from Templates — 320
Applying an Updategram Directly Using HTTP Post — 322
Applying an Updategram Using ADO — 323

Summary — 324

Table of Contents

Chapter 12: SQLXML Bulk Load — 327

Overview — 328
Creating the Schema — 330
Sample Script — 335
Properties of the SQLXMLBulkLoad Object — 336
Providing Connection information — 336
Table Creation and Deletion — 338
Error Handling — 339
Optimization — 340
Transaction Management — 341
Control over Data Loading — 342
- CheckConstraints — 342
- IgnoreDuplicateKeys — 343
- KeepIdentity — 343
- KeepNulls — 343
- XMLFragment — 344

Completing the Script and Running it in DTS — 344
Loading Multiple Tables — 348
Loading From a Stream Instead of a File — 354

Differences from Other Bulk Load Interfaces — 356
Comparison to Updategrams — 358
Comparison to OPENXML — 358

Summary — 359

Chapter 13: Programmatic Access with SQLXML — 363

Programming XML with ADO — 365
Extended Properties of the ADO Command Object — 368
- XML Root — 369
- NameSpaces — 369
- Output Encoding — 370
- Base Path — 370
- Mapping Schema — 371
- XSL — 371
- SS STREAM FLAGS — 374
- Output Stream — 375

Querying with Templates — 375
Querying Using XPath and a Mapping Schema — 377
SQLXMLOLEDB Provider and Client-Side Processing — 381
- FOR XML NESTED — 383
- Coding for Client-Side XML — 383
- Querying Stored Procedures to Get XML — 384
- Letting ADO Create the XML — 385
Using ADO and a Stored Procedure with OPENXML — 388

Programming XML with ADO.NET — 389
Executing a FOR XML Query With SqlCommand — 390
Saving ADO.NET Datasets as XML — 392

SQLXML Managed Classes	393
SqlXmlCommand	394
Properties of SqlXmlCommand	395
Methods of SqlXmlCommand	400
SqlXmlParameter	401
SqlXmlAdapter	402
DiffGrams	**404**
Summary	**412**

Chapter 14: Web Services in SQL Server 2000 — 415

What is a Web Service?	415
Setting up a SQL Server 2000 Web Service With SQLXML 3.0	**416**
The Sample Database	416
Creating the SOAP Virtual Name	418
Exposing Stored Procedure Functionality as a Web Service	419
Output Options	420
XML Objects	421
DataSet Objects	422
Error Mechanisms	423
Stored Procedure Return Codes	423
SOAP Faults	423
Exposing UDF Functionality as a Web Service	423
Consuming Services Through Visual Studio.NET	**424**
Further SQL Server 2000 Web Service Topics	**426**
UDDI Registries	426
Web Service Security/Authentication	427
Shortcomings of SQL Server Web Services	427
Microsoft Specific	427
No Control Over Return Values	428
Wrapping Services with .NET Services	428
Summary	**430**

Chapter 15: Case Study: Detecting Web Site Clients — 433

Benefits and Drawbacks of the Methods	434
Basic Detection	**434**
Client Detection Using SQLXML	**435**
Client-Side Scripting	435
Server-Side Scripting	435
The Solution to SQLXML Client Detection	435
The SQLXML Virtual Directory	436
Creating the XML Templates	436
Creating Client Detection Code	439
Drawbacks to Client Detection in SQLXML	443

Table of Contents

Client Detection Using the SQLXML Managed Classes — 444
Visual Studio.NET and the .NET Framework — 444
Creating the Project — 444
ASP.NET Browser Detection — 445
SQLXML Managed Classes — 446
Plugging in our SQLXML Templates — 447
Advantages to Using ASP.NET Client Detection — 450

Client Detection Using SQLXML and ADO — 451
Using Classic ADO — 451
ASP Browser Detection — 453
Advantages to Using ASP Client Detection — 454

Summary — 454

Chapter 16: Case Study: BizTalk Integration — 457

Software You Will Need — 458
HR and Departmental Databases — 459
HR Database — 459
Department Database — 461
SQLXML Configuration — 461

Ideal Business Process — 462
Advantages — 463
Security Ramifications — 463

BizTalk Primer — 464
First Problem — 464
Revised Business Process — 465

BizTalk Messages — 465
New Employee — 465
Updategrams — 469

HR Orchestration Schedule — 473
HR Business Process — 474
Updategram Component — 474
HR Messaging Implementations — 476
HR Data Flow — 480
BizTalk Messaging Configuration — 481

Department Phone List Schedule — 485
Department Business Process — 485
Department Messaging Implementations — 486
Department Data Flow — 487
BizTalk Messaging Configuration — 488

Testing the System — 489

Assessing the System — 490
Performance — 490
Security — 491

Summary — 492

Chapter 17: The Future - Emergent Technologies — 495

ISO SQL/XML Working Draft (or SQLX) — 496

Oracle 9i Release 2 (9.0.2) — 496
Oracle and XML Support — 497
What's so Good About the Native xmltype? — 497
And What's So Good About the Integrated Support for XML Schema? — 498
What About These Integrated Functions? — 499
Oracle and XQuery — 500
Oracle Summary — 500

W3C XQuery — 500
XQuery Working Draft — 500
XQuery and XPath 2.0, XSLT and XPath 1.0 and 2.0 — 501
XQuery Overview — 501
Basic Syntax — 502
FLoWeR – or FOR LET WHERE RETURN — 503
FLoWeR and SQL — 505
Joins — 505
If…Then…Else — 507
Core Functions — 507
Data Types and Validation — 508
XQuery Future – In the Pipeline — 508
XQuery Summary — 508

Microsoft Next Steps — Yukon — 509

So What Does all This Mean? — 510

Appendix A: XPath Reference — 513

XPath Data Model — 514
Node Types — 516
Node Properties — 516
Data Types — 518

Location Paths — 521
Absolute and Relative Location Paths — 521
Steps — 522
Axes — 522
Node Tests — 525
Abbreviations — 527
Predicates — 527

Variables — 529

Operators — 530
Arithmetic Operators — 530
Comparisons — 531
Logical Operators — 533
Node-Set Operators — 533

Functions — 534

XPath 2.0 and XQuery — 552
XPath 2.0 — 552
XQuery 1.0 — 555

Appendix B: XML Schema Reference — **559**

Namespaces for XML Schema — **559**

XML Schema Elements — **560**
Global Attributes — 560
<xsd:schema> — 561
<xsd:element> — 562
<xsd:group> — 566
<xsd:attribute> — 568
<xsd:attributeGroup> — 569

Defining and Constraining Types — **570**
<xsd:simpleType> — 572
<xsd:complexType> — 573
Simple Type Restrictions — 575
Complex Type Restrictions — 582

Relationships and Null Fields — **585**
<xsd:unique> — 586
<xsd:key> — 589
<xsd:keyref> — 590

Namespaces — **591**
form Attribute — 591

Importing Schemas — **593**
<xsd:include> — 593
<xsd:redefine> — 593
<xsd:import> — 594

Documentation — **594**
<xsd:documentation> — 594
<xsd:appinfo> — 595

Varying XML Content — **595**
<xsd:any> — 596
<xsd:anyAttribute> — 597

The XML Schema Instance Namespace — **597**

References — **599**

Appendix C: A Tool for XML Queries — **601**

Why is a Query Tool Useful? — **601**

The Query Tool — **603**

Index — **609**

Table of Contents

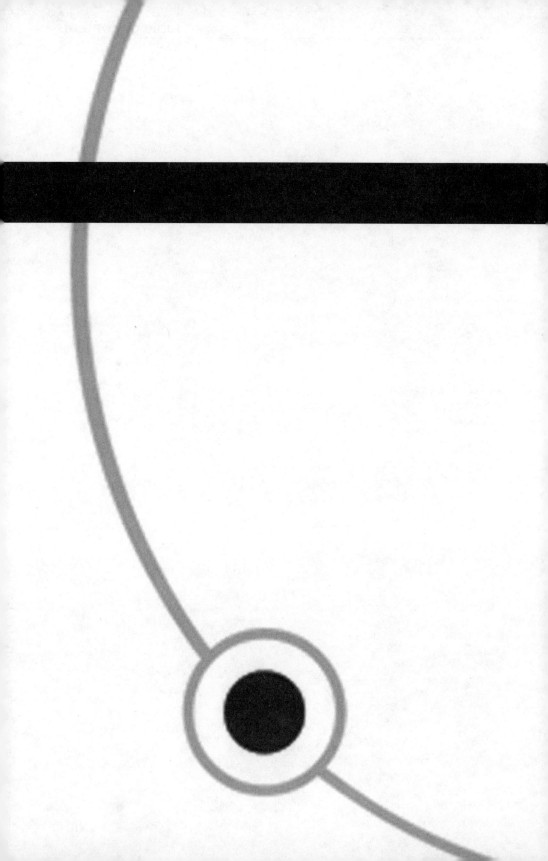

Introduction

This book will act as your guide to Microsoft's latest tools for working with the XML standards and SQL Server 2000. It assumes that you have SQL Server experience and are already familiar with the XML standards themselves, but want to know how to work with them to make SQL Server data available to applications as XML, or safely take XML data into SQL Server databases. If you are working with SQL Server, and being asked to provide data as XML, or take data from XML, then this book is for you.

The features of each of SQL Server's XML technologies are introduced in turn, alongside practical working examples to reinforce what you are learning. The security and performance implications of using each feature are considered in context, so this book will also act as a reference when you come to implement XML solutions for real.

> *As we have said, the basics of XML and its associated standards are not covered here. For background information on XML, we recommend Beginning XML, 2nd Edition (Wrox Press, ISBN: 1861005598).*

What Does This Book Cover?

The chapters of this book don't form a continuous narrative, so feel free to read each as a discrete entity. Cross-references are provided in each chapter, where appropriate, allowing you to read up on related material elsewhere in the book.

Here's a look at what each of the chapters covers:

Introduction

Chapter 1 – SQL Server, XML, and the DBA

Why do we want to get XML in and out of our database anyway? Which XML standards are relevant? How does this all relate to the DBA? Chapter 1 explains all about web services, document creation, the increasing role of XML in the data transport world, and how SQL Server can bring security, integrity, and scalability to the party. We recommend best practices to bear in mind whilst you are reading the rest of the book, and when implementing solutions that include XML.

Chapter 2 – Architecture and Setup

Before you start working with SQL Server 2000 XML, you need to know how to install and set up the various tools required. Here we explain the XML features of SQL Server 2000 and SQLXML 3.0 SP1, as well as how to get them up and running. Many of these features rely on the use of Internet Information Services virtual directories, so we conclude with a section on how to set them up, along with how to troubleshoot them if you encounter problems.

Chapter 3 – Mapping SQL Server to XML

SQL Server databases have a relational format. XML has a hierarchical format. In this chapter, we see how to create mappings between the data types and structures of each, using XML schemas to act as the go between.

Chapter 4 – FOR XML

One of the easiest to use new features of SQL Server 2000 is the FOR XML clause that can be appended at the end of T-SQL queries, enabling the query to return XML rather than a resultset. Here, we see how to use this clause and its various options, using Query Analyzer.

Chapter 5 – URL Queries and Template Queries

We have a new method of returning data in SQL Server 2000: SQLXML 3.0's URL and template query mechanisms. Here we continue using FOR XML to illustrate these new methods, as well as discussing their security implications. URL queries are further developed, showing how simply a data driven web site can be created, without knowledge of ADO or ADO.NET.

Chapter 6 – Annotating XML Schemas

Building on the schemas we learned to build in Chapter 3, we now learn how to annotate them. Annotated XML schemas map schema elements and attributes directly to tables and fields within a database. These annotated schemas are used in many of the other processes we see in the book, such as XML views, Updategrams, DiffGrams and XML Bulk Load.

Chapter 7 – XML Views

Using SQL Server views, we can hide our raw data from the outside world and query solely against the view. With XML views, we can do a similar thing. We see how to produce a view of the data in a database that can be queried as if it were an existing XML document.

Chapter 8 – XPath Queries

XPath is XML's current query language. We initially compare its queries with equivalent T-SQL queries, to help you grasp more quickly how they work to return data as XML from XML views. This chapter then introduces XPath querying both via URLs and via templates, so you can compare and contrast the two methods in terms of ease of use, performance, and security.

Chapter 9 – Mapping XML to SQL Server

In Chapter 3, we saw how to map data from a database to an XML document. In this chapter we take the opposite approach, showing how appropriate SQL Server structures can be modeled from the information in XML data structures, enabling XML data to be stored effectively in SQL Server.

Chapter 10 – OPENXML

As `FOR XML` allows us to return an XML document from SQL Server data, so another T-SQL feature, `OPENXML`, allows us to return a SQL Server rowset from an XML document. This capability allows us to transfer the data in an XML document straight into SQL Server for storage and manipulation. We look at using this feature, as well as the implications of its use like preparation, memory use, and identity columns.

Chapter 11 – Updategrams

Updategrams take SQL Server's XML support a step further than with `OPENXML`. Now, we don't even need to use T-SQL, as we can update, delete, and insert data in an XML format into our database over the web. We also discuss the security implications of using Updategrams to modify data in your database.

Chapter 12 – SQLXML Bulk Load

You will probably be familiar with SQL Server's BCP (Bulk Copy Program) that is used to copy large datasets from one location to another. SQLXML 3.0 introduces the XML Bulk Load feature, enabling us to upload and store large amounts of data from XML documents into SQL Server tables, in much the same way as BCP. This chapter gives you all the information you need to use it effectively.

Chapter 13 – Programmatic Access with SQLXML

Most of this book discusses XML support in SQL Server 2000, but does not delve into implementing this support programmatically. In Chapter 13 we resolve that, with examples in both VB 6/ADO and VB.NET/ADO.NET. We feature returning XML from templates, from XPath queries, from stored procedures that nominally return a dataset; we see how to parse XML on both the server and client side, how to store XML in a stream or file, and discuss DiffGrams (a sort of Updategrams-lite) and the various options available to configure your XML output from code.

Chapter 14 – Web Services in SQL Server 2000

Web services are an emerging technology. They have been creating quite a buzz, as, using an XML-based SOAP transport protocol, they allow true interoperation between methods and components coded on different platforms. SQL Server 2000 is in on the web services act, and your stored procedures and user-defined functions can be exposed in a new way to the outside world. We show you how to set up SQL Server web services, and consume them from a .NET project.

Introduction

Chapter 15 - Case Study: Detecting Web Site Clients

A case study that shows how SQLXML 3.0 can be used to detect different client browsers accessing a web site, and return appropriately styled HTML for those browsers. It contrasts three methods: using SQLXML alone, using it with ASP.NET, and using it with ASP with ADO.

Chapter 16 - Case Study: BizTalk Integration

A case study showing how to integrate SQL Server 2000 and Biztalk Server 2002, using XML structures as the messaging mechanism between them. The messages are passed over HTTP, meaning that this can be done using a bare minimum of custom programming.

Chapter 17 - The Future - Emergent Technologies

Our final chapter takes a glimpse into the future of database vendor support for existing and emerging XML standards, such as XQuery. We talk about the likely forthcoming XML features of Yukon (the next version of SQL Server), and compare this to what Oracle is offering its users.

Appendices

Three appendices are included:

- Appendix A is a reference to the features available within the current XPath 1.0 Recommendation, and goes on to look at what may change in the next Recommendation. XPath 2.0 is discussed in terms of how it will interact with another forthcoming standard, XQuery.

- Appendix B is a reference to the features available within the current XML Schema Recommendation.

- Query Analyzer produces some pretty badly formatted XML results from queries. Appendix C solves this by introducing a neat tool for executing queries to produce usefully formatted XML results. You can use this tool with a lot of the examples throughout the book, and indeed will find it valuable in your further investigations of SQL Server's XML support. This tool is included in the code download for this book.

What You Need to Use This Book

The following software is required:

- SQL Server 2000
- SQLXML 3.0, Service Pack 1. Chapter 2 explains how to download and install this.
- Microsoft SOAP Toolkit 2.0 to enable the web services features of SQLXML 3.0, SP1
- Internet Information Services (IIS). This is installed automatically with SQLXML 3.0, SP1.
- MSXML 4. This is installed automatically with SQLXML 3.0, SP1.

❑ Internet Explorer 5.0 or above.
❑ A text editor, such as Notepad.

In the chapters that involve programmatic access, we also use:

❑ Visual Studio 6 and Visual Basic 6
❑ Visual Studio .NET, Visual Basic .NET, and C#.
❑ ASP and ASP.NET

The case study in Chapter 16 requires Biztalk Server 2002.

Source Code

The complete source code from the book is available for download at http://www.curlingstone.com/.

Conventions

To help you understand what's going on, and in order to maintain consistency, we've used a number of conventions throughout the book:

When we introduce new terms, we **highlight** them.

> These boxes hold important information.

Advice, hints, and background information are presented like this.

Words that appear on the screen in menus like the **File** or **Window** menu are in a similar font to what you see on screen. URLs are also displayed in this font.

In the book text, we use a fixed-width font when we talk about databases, fields, values, elements, attributes, and other objects that may appear in code. Take, for example, the `Customer` table and the `<Invoice>` element.

Example code is shown like this:

```
In our code examples, the code foreground style shows new,
important, pertinent code.
  Code background shows code that's less important in the present
  context, or code that has been seen before.
```

Customer Support

We always value hearing from our readers, and we want to know what you think about this book: what you liked, what you didn't like, and what you think we can do better next time. You can send us your comments by e-mail to feedback@curlingstone.com. Please be sure to mention the book title in your message.

Introduction

Errata

We've made every effort to make sure that there are no errors in the text or in the code in this book. However, no one is perfect and mistakes do occur. If you find an error in one of our books, like a spelling mistake or a faulty piece of code, we would be very grateful for feedback. By sending in errata you may save a future reader hours of frustration, and of course, you will be helping us provide even higher quality information. Simply e-mail the information to support@curlingstone.com, your information will be checked and if correct, posted to the errata page for that title and used in subsequent editions of the book.

To see if there are any errata for this book on the web site, go to http://www.curlingstone.com/, and locate the book through our title list.

E-mail Support

If you wish to directly query a problem in the book with an expert who knows the book in detail then e-mail support@curlingstone.com. A typical e-mail should include the following things:

- The **title of the book**, **last four digits of the ISBN**, and **page number** of the problem in the Subject field.
- Your **name**, **contact information**, and the **problem** in the body of the message.

We *won't* send you junk mail. We need the details to save your time and ours. When you send an e-mail message, it will go through the following chain of support:

- Customer Support – Your message is delivered to our customer support staff, who are the first people to read it. They have files on most frequently asked questions and will answer anything general about the book or the web site immediately.
- Editorial – Deeper queries are forwarded to the technical editor responsible for that book. They have experience in all the topics discussed, and are able to answer detailed technical questions on the subject.
- The Author – Finally, in the unlikely event that the editor cannot answer your problem, he or she will forward the request to the author. We do try to protect the author from any distractions to their work; however, we are quite happy to forward specific requests to them. All Curlingstone authors help with the support on their books. They will e-mail the customer and the editor with their response, and again all readers should benefit.

The Curlingstone support process can only offer support to issues that are directly pertinent to the content of our published title.

Introduction

Daryl Barnes

- Data Based Computing
- What Aspects of XML are Relevant to Databases?
- XML and Relational Structures
- Mapping XML and Relational Data
- The Main Uses of XML Structures
- An Architectural View
- Summary

1

SQL Server, XML, and the DBA

Some of the reasons you have bought this book may include:

- ❑ You need to return queries on SQL Server relational data in an XML format
- ❑ You want to store XML data in SQL Server
- ❑ You want to find out more about SQL Server's XML capabilities in general

But you may well be wondering why data needs to be transmitted in an XML format at all, when relational datasets offer a mechanism for presenting data to the end user or system that works well? You would be right to wonder.

Why change? Why invest all this time in recreating and optimizing the whole storage and retrieval mechanism, when a perfectly good system exists already? Well, as we shall see, the data format that the end application or system needs is changing (for all the right reasons).

Whatever the reason for your interest, this book will help by providing you with a thorough grounding in the different capabilities offered by SQL Server 2000 to provide XML to applications, end users, or other systems, and also to store XML data in your SQL Server instance.

This first chapter provides you with an overview of where the need for XML as a data format comes from, and its main uses from a DBA's viewpoint, so that you can best decide how to implement an XML solution that's right for you.

This chapter is structured as follows:

- ❑ *Data Based Computing*. A look at what's driving the integration of relational databases and the web, and how XML fits in.
- ❑ *What Aspects of XML are Relevant to Databases?* A brief overview of XML standards relevant to this book.

Chapter 1

- *XML and Relational Structures*. Assuming that you have at least a basic appreciation of these structures, this section will highlight the different uses of each.
- *The Main Uses of XML Structures*. Consideration will be given to just why XML is becoming critical to today's IT environment.
- An *Architectural View* (or a different approach to the same problem). This sub-section will provide different ways to look at the 'bigger picture' and understand the bigger forces at work

Let's now move on to the first of these sections.

Data Based Computing

In order to understand the approach to using relational data and XML advocated by Microsoft and covered in this book, we need to take a short look at the history of **data based** (rather than **database**) computing.

Throughout the evolution of data based computing there have been (at least) four constants:

- Data needs to be stored somewhere in a structured, readily retrievable way
- Data must be presented somehow (electronically or on paper) in a semi-structured way
- Data must somehow be extracted, transmitted, and transformed between its persisted storage location and its presentation location
- All of the above must work optimally at each stage, without losing flexibility

These constants say nothing about the actual data or any relations it may have internally; it's assumed that they will be captured. Instead, they refer more to the environment data must exist and operate in to be considered "a working solution".

The Success of Relational Databases

Relational databases have been a huge success. At the present time, they offer support for:

- Many thousands of concurrent users
- Terabytes of data
- Storage of almost any data type you can mention
- Relational and analytical models of data
- Querying data in an ad hoc and flexible manner
- Security, both authentication and authorization
- Programming within the database

SQL Server, XML, and the DBA

- Network connectivity to applications and other databases allowing efficient data retrieval
- Tools to develop, manage, and report on huge amounts of data

Relational databases do well on every one of these four constants, SQL Server among them. There's no compelling reason to change from the relational model as the primary store for structured data.

The Success of the Web

The Web application architecture is basically the latest in a series of computer architectures:

- The computer is the platform – data is shared within a computer, whether mainframe or PC.
- The operating system is the platform – data is shared between networked computers running the same operating system.
- The application or database is the platform – data is shared between databases from the same manufacturer, and between relational databases using data connectivity tools.
- The Web is the platform – data is shared between all sorts of data stores using standard protocols, languages, and discovery mechanisms implemented on all platforms, and supported by all applications.

Each level increases the amount of data that can be shared, expands the audience who can use that data, and simplifies the provision of the pieces that make up the system.

Data-driven web applications have been the making of the commercial web. The now "classic" web application consists of data stored in a database, processing done either within the database or on a web server, and presentation as semi-structured HTML documents over HTTP to a web browser:

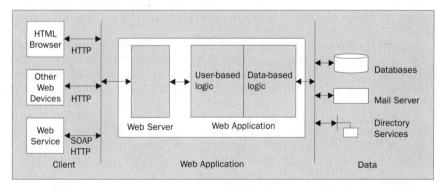

The main change in this approach, compared to client-server, is that the browser does not work in the same way as the client GUI. It doesn't understand a `DataSet` object natively; it has to be converted to HTML in order to work. Something fundamental has happened here. In the past the `Recordset` was the means of communication; the database knew how to give a `Recordset`, the client application knew how to process it.

11

Chapter 1

What is clear is that HTML and browsers work. They allow easy rendition of both documents and data, and provide a solid framework for interoperability of a myriad different applications, with different native backgrounds. It is also clear that the potential end user community is now global and not limited to clients that have the right software installed. Sorry to all those in IT security for throwing down this gauntlet, but this is the new challenge.

It is also clear that HTML isn't optimal. Hence the creation, and ongoing momentum of standards generated by the W3C, to enhance and enrich what functionality is available in a browser (XML, XHTML, XSLT, XPath, and so on).

XML – The Next Step

Most of the web applications to date create documents for humans to read. But the principles of web applications, central data store, closely-tied business logic, and loosely-coupled communication between authenticated clients and URL-based services, can be applied to client-server computing to:

- Make more pieces of the system generic and thus reduce "re-coding the wheel".
- Expand the audience of applications and users who can consume that data.

XML and other Internet technologies provide the future format for data moving over the Web. The pieces of this puzzle are:

- TCP/IP – the network extends everywhere – the medium for conversation.
- HTTP/SOAP – the protocol for sharing documents – the conversation.
- XML – the language of languages that can be shared. The data is 'readable', and can't be lost in proprietary formats – the language of the conversation.

Why are the relational database giants slugging it out in a war over their XML support? The reason is that the closer the interaction between the source of the data, the database, and the format in which the data is transferred, the better.

Until this point it has been application developers who have had to consider the best way of turning relational data into HTML or XML. In the Microsoft world, ADO does this very effectively; as does ADO.NET, which provides rich XML functionality for free, but such functionality is gradually reaching into the database. SQL Server has offered functionality to allow retrieval as XML from relational data as an add-on to Version 7, with fuller support in SQL Server 2000, and much more promised in Yukon (see Chapter 17). So where do you do the conversion? Indeed, do you store data as XML in the first place in order to enhance performance? Do you offer a dataset following an URL query of the data? It's a question you can no longer ignore. It depends upon the application, as we shall see.

This applies to traditional client-server systems too, where the need to make the application as flexible as possible means that the web is used to link rich clients and server applications. Whilst ADO, OLE DB, and ODBC formerly offered the cleanest mechanism for supplying data to a Windows forms application, this *may* no longer be the case. Again, it depends upon the application. We'll see more of this in Chapter 13 on .NET

SQL Server, XML, and the DBA

System Interoperability and Data Interchange in an n-tier Environment

Vendors have realized the potential for the use of XML as a base structure to provide cross communication between different systems. First XML-RPC, then SOAP have been released, which provide communication directly by file transfer as recommended, over HTTP, or through SMTP. This opens up the standard presentation tier, using HTTP as a sound base for cross communication.

So just when you thought you had enough to be getting on with, there is another massive area to understand, which I am sure will dominate the evolution of IT architectures and environments for many years to come. That area is **web services**.

Web Services

Though not directly an evolution of the n-tier architecture, web services represent the next step in IT thinking. Web services are all about software as service; that is, rather than simply offer data to a web browser, why not offer (or expose) methods and business logic functionality? Web services utilize SOAP and WSDL to expose functionality to a consumer. As long as the consumer understands the WSDL, they can query the web service. In terms of n-tier architecture, web services can be incorporated into both the presentation tier and the business tier (or, as we shall see in Chapter 14, the data tier).

In terms of the constants we talked about, web services should be seen as another way to make the data available either for presentation, or for distributed interoperability.

In summary, the following worlds have been converging:

- Multi-user databases, with a central data store, central data-specific processing, and great concurrency.
- Internet networking protocols that allow for platform-independent access to data.
- Client-server models allowing a division of processing.
- Distributed data, allowing clients to query multiple databases and combine information from different sources.
- Interaction between platforms, necessitating platform independent data that can be worked with on any of the platforms involved, and shared between them.

What Aspects of XML are Relevant to Databases?

The following figure is a high level overview of the many XML standards and their purposes:

Chapter 1

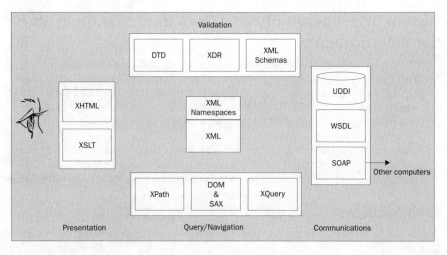

We'll follow this with a table to summarize the nature of these standards. It is not meant to be definitive (importantly it doesn't talk about versions): more a general overview of the XML standards discussed in this book:

XML Target Area	Name	Description and URL
Core	XML	Simply put, XML on its own is no more than a standard format for representing data. **Well-formed XML** conforms to the XML Recommendation. XML specifies how to represent elements and attributes, how elements nest, and what elements may contain. http://www.w3.org/XML/
Core	XML Namespaces	Namespaces are used to identify the uniqueness of an XML element. For example: `<xsl:stylesheet version="1.0" xmlns:xsl="http://www.w3.org/1999/XSL/Transform">` ties any XML element preceded by `xsl:` to the XSL standard. http://www.w3.org/TR/REC-xml-names/

SQL Server, XML, and the DBA

XML Target Area	Name	Description and URL
Querying/ Navigation	DOM parser (Document Object Model)	A method of reading and manipulating an XML document which works by creating a virtual tree structure in memory. DOM APIs exist for most platforms. http://www.w3.org/DOM/
Querying/ Navigation	XPath	XPath provides a mechanism to interrogate an XML document. http://www.w3.org/TR/xpath
Querying/ Navigation	XQuery	XQuery expands upon the interrogative nature of XPath and introduces a complete query language structure, similar to SQL, but for XML documents. http://www.w3.org/TR/xquery/
Validation	DTD (Document Type Definition)	An early SGML-based method which allows the definition of an XML document structure. An XML document which conforms to the structure defined in a DTD is said to be **valid**. http://www.w3.org/TR/REC-xml#dt-doctype
Validation	XDR (XML-Data Reduced) Schema	An early approach by Microsoft to define a validation mechanism which can allow the definition of datatypes as well as XML document structure. Similar to the final World Wide Web Consortium(W3C) XML Schema Recommendation. http://www.w3.org/TR/1998/NOTE-XML-data/
Validation	XML Schema	A W3C Recommendation which allows the definition of datatypes as well as XML document structure. http://www.w3.org/XML/Schema

Table continued on following page

Chapter 1

XML Target Area	Name	Description and URL
Presentation	XHTML (Extensible HTML)	An evolution of HTML which defines standard document types and module structures for more rigid implementation of a browser page. An XHTML document is an XML document. http://www.w3.org/TR/xhtml1/
Presentation	XSLT (Extensible Stylesheet Language for Transformations)	XSLT provides a transformation mechanism which is used to convert XML to other formats (including XML). In the context of HTML creation, an XSLT stylesheet provides the presentation information to be applied to the XML content. A transformation API is used to merge the XML and XSLT stylesheet. http://www.w3.org/TR/xslt
Presentation	XSL	XSL is the overall term used to encapsulate the XSLT and XSL:FO (a document presentation technology) vocabularies. http://www.w3.org/TR/xsl/
Communication**	XML-RPC (XML Remote Procedure Call)	XML-RPC is basically the use of XML to define the request/response mechanism for a method call and response over a network (LAN, WAN, or Internet). It is the precursor to SOAP. http://www.xmlrpc.com/
Communication	SOAP (Simple Object Access Protocol)	SOAP is an evolution of XML-RPC and provides a low level XML structure for method call/response. As a protocol, it is richer than XML-RPC and offers asynchronous calls, error handling, and data typing (using XML Schema in SOAP 1.2). SOAP is the bedrock of web services. http://www.w3.org/2002/ws/

XML Target Area	Name	Description and URL
Communication	WSDL (Web Service Description Language)	WSDL is an XML vocubulary that is used to describe web services. It describes the "rules of engagement" for a web service. A WSDL file can be read by a web service creation mechanism in order to understand what methods are available to be consumed. http://www.w3.org/TR/wsdl
Communication	UDDI (Universal, Description, Discovery and Integration)	UDDI is a repository-based registry service for looking up web services. http://www.uddi.com/

**All XML-based communication protocols are typically used over HTTP and offer easy interoperability between disparate systems.

If many of these standards and Recommendations are new to you, you might like to refer to *Beginning XML, 2nd Edition* (Wrox Press, ISBN 1861005598) for good introductory information.

XML and Relational Structures

Let's now take a brief look at the main similarities and differences between the two different data structures, to get a feel for the areas they work in, and the areas where they are not optimal.

Relational Structures

Within SQL Server, a data item, for example a customer name, is stored as a field, within a record, within a table, and it conforms to a defined data type. It is indexed as appropriate, and because of its status in the database (that is, as part of the customer record), it can be extracted via any route using SQL, as long as a relationship exists. SQL Server databases are optimized for the storage and retrieval of such data items and, because they sit within a SQL Server database, they dwell in a secure, versioned, and administered environment.

XML Structures

Let's consider the same data item (customer name) within an XML document. It is stored as an element (or an attribute), it is a child of a parent element, and it can conform to a defined data type (using XML Schema). Because of its status in the XML tree, it can be extracted using XPath. The security of the XML document depends upon where it is stored: NT file security, third party application, web server, or SQL Server. Did I say SQL Server? I did.

Chapter 1

Storing XML in Relational Structures

An XML document is just a string, right? Therefore, it makes common sense to store my XML in SQL Server as a string (or for bigger documents, a BLOB). That way, I can let my customer name data item enjoy all of the benefits of SQL Security. There are issues here though:

- How do I retrieve my customer name?
- How can I use SQL to access XML?
- How do I add a customer?
- How can I update or delete it?

Logically, it would seem that the best way is to extract the XML document and stream it through an XML parser; then query it with XPath. The performance hit of this is large and anyway, what if I wanted to cross query an XML document with a relational dataset? You can begin to see the complexity behind this, and also see why SQL Server 2000 needs to offer different approaches to solve the problem.

Storing Relational Data Using XML

Relational data is just data, right? Just put a few tags around it and call it XML? Right, but wrong. If your goal is to duplicate a relational data set as XML then, in all seriousness, why not just keep it as relational data? XML is hierarchical by nature (cynics may refer back to how mainframes used to store data), which means that it is not meant be structured relationally.

XML documents match how human logic works; they are designed to be human readable. Everything in this world has a natural logical tree structure to it; basic scientific classification is designed around hierarchies. However, XML documents don't yet offer the flexibility for querying that relational datasets do, so the solution is to use both formats appropriately.

The remainder of this chapter will offer some ideas to help you decide when each is appropriate; the most important thing to realize here being that it is by no means as simple as it first appears.

Mapping XML and Relational Data

Mapping one relational data structure to another is relatively straightforward, as is mapping one XML structure to another. Each environment has its own tools and mechanisms to allow for internal mapping, but cross mapping is an issue. The SQL Server 2000 XML tools available offer help with this cross mapping, but the following must be considered:

- Do not expect a one-to-one mapping or, if you do, examine why you're not sticking with relational datasets.
- Instances of the same element are allowed in XML. Consider as an example a database table where you define one customer name field; if it were appropriate to have many customer name fields, you would add another table with a foreign key. In XML you do not have to do this; the `<CustomerName>` element can be duplicated many times as shown below:

```
<Customer_Details>
    <CustomerName>Ran Hawthorn</CustomerName>
    <CustomerName>Ralph Brown</CustomerName>
    <CustomerName>Fred Simmons</CustomerName>
</Customer_Details>
```

- Once you have decided upon your mapping to XML, you must be aware that you have effectively 'set in stone' that the XML document structure is no longer relational, which has its own implications. This means that you lose all the benefits of storing data relationally, but your data is now more portable.
- XML is designed to be human readable; many physical database field names are not. To what degree do you support the goal of XML to be human readable? The level of importance will depend on how your XML is going to be used. If it is destined to be consumed by another system, then this will not be a major concern.
- When converting XML structures to relational structures, consideration must be given to the resultant physical database structure. If it is a new database, then that's not really a problem, but what if you have to transform the data into an existing database structure? Perhaps some intermediate tables are required.

All of this might lead you to wonder why we shouldn't just have the whole end-to-end as either XML or relational, but for the reasons we have discussed it isn't as easy as that.

The Main Uses of XML Structures

Up to this point in the chapter, we have focused on trying to understand the precursors to web based development, application interoperability, and data interchange, and have started to consider the concept of a different type of approach. We have also looked at the complexity of relational and XML structured data mapping. Let us now look at the uses of XML in a little more detail to understand the main concepts involved.

XML for Messaging – The Other Application Wants XML

With the advent of distributed computing, the question has always been how to communicate. TCP/IP at the network level is now mostly standard. There is general agreement on using HTTP/HTML for the presentation of document-structured data.

For distributed object computing, COM/MTS, DCOM, COM+, or .NET Remoting exist for the Microsoft environment, and CORBA and IIOP exist for the heterogeneous environment. The advent of object based computing has resulted in a set of common object based approaches to solving problems irrespective of native environment. This means that if a common message format exists then, in theory, it is fairly straightforward to cross communicate between different native environments. XML-RPC, and latterly SOAP and web services, offer this facility.

XML as Document – Markup Based Document Objects

This is not a book about document management, but some of you may well have heard talk of storing document structured information (that is, not data tables) relationally. Much of this has come about because document management systems offer similar data storage and retrieval mechanisms to traditional database management systems. Document management systems also allow the storage of document 'objects' in XML format. So, the lines are blurring between documents and data, and the beauty of it all is that, at last, a similar base format is being used.

XML for Presentation – The Browser Wants Markup

Browsers love markup, in fact it is what they do; they take a HTML file and render it to the screen. OK, there are other mechanisms to allow non-HTML functionality (ActiveX, applets, Flash, audio/video streaming, and so on) but markup is preferred. The main reason is that HTTP and HTML are non-vendor specific standards based mechanisms, which provide a common approach to working with or viewing data. HTML itself is a limited tag set offering fairly simple functionality. The standards bodies (W3C in particular) acknowledge this; initiatives such as Dynamic HTML, Cascading Style Sheets, and XHTML, address the issue in great detail.

HTML is perceived by many as a solution of the past but a problem of the future. If you look at a typical HTML file, you will see information content blindly mixed up with presentation formatting (not to mention the whole swathes of script that can sometimes be found interspersed). The major XML based initiative XSL addresses this very issue by separating content from presentation, allowing us to transform XML into HTML, or any other format of our choice, for display. The key is to realize that XML is here to stay in terms of browser markup, and that is a good thing.

An Architectural View

If you think about it, XML only makes sense when viewed architecturally (OK, that's my opinion but I believe it!). What really matters is the end-to-end performance of an application and, sorry to use a cliché, getting the right data in the right format at the right time. That means not viewing each part of the chain as a separate entity requiring a separate solution. If, for example, the end application doesn't use or remotely want, XML, then why on earth provide XML as an output format? I have actually witnessed this happening more than once. Conversely, if the end application works with a markup focus, why force the poor application developer to use only relational datasets?

SQL Server, XML, and the DBA

To be honest, the debate about where to process what, and how, is as old as the hills. For example, depending upon whom you speak to, you will get a different answer every time about where business processing should occur. Should it be in a stored procedure, or COM component, or raw SQL in an ASP page? The arbitrator in me suggests that the best approach is the one that makes common sense given the budget, size, and experience of the project team. Understand the alternatives, but choose the most appropriate technology on a case-by-case basis.

The rest of this book gives you a detailed view on the SQL Server 2000 methods currently available for handling XML. Try to think of what follows as looking at software development as a design problem, where the problem could be solved with the use of SQL Server 2000 XML tools; *not* the other approach of "We've got these tools, where shall we use them?"

Different Approaches to the Problem

This subsection aims to provide you with some answers and give you some guidelines. It also provides you with an architectural view of what is going on, so that you can best decide on an approach that is right for you. It will do this by talking about four likely paths that organizations will take in trying to solve the problems we have discussed, and will address them in terms of SQL Server 2000.

Here are our four likely paths:

1. XML end-to-end
2. Relational, end-to (near the)-end
3. Ad-hoc, just do it and see where we get
4. Let's take a step back before we decide

We will focus on five main areas of each solution:

- **Performance** – what sort of end-to-end performance will we achieve, from a user's perspective?
- **Volumes** – what volumes of data are expected to flow both in and between tiers?
- **Security** – what security is applied to the data in terms of authorization and authentication?
- **Scalability** – how is the system able to handle expected volumes over time? Is it expandable?
- **Future proofing** – how easy will it be to manage any new design requirements that may follow?

XML End-to-End

If you were to implement this solution using SQL Server 2000, the following would provide a typical approach:

- The XML documents would be stored as BLOBs.

- In order to extract the information, you would use SQL to extract the BLOB and then parse it using an MSXML parser.
- You could then apply an XSLT stylesheet to the XML document to render it within a browser.
- The XML document could be queried using XPath (using the MSXML API).
- The XML document could also be manipulated using the MSXML Document Object Model (DOM).
- Finally, the XML Document could then be persisted as a BLOB again, using a SQL UPDATE.

The first major question to ask is: if the relational database already exists and is stable and reliable, does it makes any sense at all to initiate a complete upheaval in order to get the data stored as XML? If the solution were a brand new one, native XML databases could be an option but you would need to consider the viability of any vendor, and decide whether the content of the application really justifies full XML end-to-end.

If we now consider this approach against the five main areas:

- **Performance** – For small systems, where the developer knowledge sits firmly outside SQL Server 2000, this could provide an acceptable solution. For medium to large-scale operations the performance of this type of application is non-comparable to existing relational methods. Having said that, this approach could be appropriate for certain parts of the application. For example, if the XML document was a set of reference data that could sit on the web server and only get updated once a week.
- **Volumes** – The MSXML parser could handle large volumes in terms of manipulating the XML document using the DOM, before it is persisted back to SQL Server. It is important to consider, however, that whilst an XML document exists in the DOM it is effectively 'in memory' and not persisted securely. Most DBAs wouldn't see the logic in not using SQL Server transactions to conduct this type of operation.
- **Security** – From a DBA's perspective (especially if the DBA is responsible for the data), any data that is handled outside the DBMS is non-supported. The answer then, as to whether it makes sense in terms of security to handle critical data in this manner, is no.
- **Scalability** – SQL Server is very efficient at handling many BLOBs and simple SQL to update and retrieve them, so this approach is easily scalable. Looking at the end-to-end view, however, it can be seen that this is not the optimal approach.
- **Future proofing** – Imagine that you are a DBA and you manage 15 different applications (in terms of the database) and they are all structured this way; you have no control over the data except to consider it as a BLOB. It would make reporting a real headache and all the years of handling structured relational data, such that it is easily readable and updateable now and in the future, would appear to have been in vain.

In summary, this approach may be suitable for smaller applications, but for larger ones other approaches should be considered.

SQL Server, XML, and the DBA

Relational End-to (near the)-end

I call this approach the 'Reluctant Codd Approach', where DBAs see any use of XML as an erosion of the great relational world. I know I hit a spot with that comment because I know many DBAs.

Typically, this solution would utilise an existing, stable SQL Server database that performs well, and any existing applications would be thoroughbred in terms of their use of ODBC, OLE DB, and ADO. The application developers would be proficient at using ADO `Recordsets` or `DataSets`, and also readily able to use the MSXML API. They would be looking to move to ADO.NET in the near future.

- The XML data would be stored relationally just as it always has been.
- Standard SQL stored procedures, or embedded SQL in COM components, would be used to extract the `Recordsets` or `DataSets`.
- The application developer would create the required XML by turning the `Recordset` into an XML document, using the MSXML API, or ADO/ADO.NET methods for persisting XML.
- An XSLT stylesheet could be applied to the XML document in order to render it within a browser.
- The XML document could be queried using XPath (using the MSXML API).
- There would be no manipulation of the XML document because all data manipulation happens using SQL through ADO, OLE DB, ODBC, or stored procedures.

Considering this approach against the five main areas:

- **Performance** – From a DBA's perspective, there is no performance hit. SQL Server is running optimally. The additional performance hit happens outside in the application where ADO recordsets are manipulated and MSXML API is used to create the XML documents.
- **Volumes** – One could validly argue that the optimal way to insert, update, and delete records is to use tried and tested mechanisms; so the use of ADO, OLE DB, ODBC, or stored procedures is no bad thing. For high volume reads, though, where the output is required as XML, the application would suffer terribly, especially in an environment where the XML is generated on the fly.
- **Security**
- – The security is handled by tried and trusted mechanisms and the data is secure, *but* all the XML documents external to the database are not covered. OK, you can say that the root data is fully secure within the database, but what about when the data extracted from the database is only half of the XML document? For example, the other half could be data that defines the XML document structure, or a key component of it, and it might not be backed up. Even worse, the XML document might be visible to someone who shouldn't see it.
- **Scalability** – Again, the classic SQL Server application approach is highly scalable; but as the volume of XML documents that the application is creating increases, so does the processing overhead at run time. The scalability of this approach will be questioned for this reason.

Chapter 1

- **Future proofing** – This is a main area where thought needs to be given. We have established that XML is here to stay, and that its use is going to grow and grow. Thought needs to be given to the viability of forcing every application to create its XML documents outside the database. Given that XML documents are going to become more and more prolific, there needs to be a push to get them stored natively within a highly secure environment.

In summary, this approach is just a manifestation of classic n-tier application design. It does not really address the issues of the ever-growing demand for XML. Whether another solution is needed will depend on how critical XML is to your application.

Ad Hoc

Before you read any further I have to tell you that this is the nightmare scenario. Unfortunately, it is also the most likely path for many organisations.

> Probably many of the terms used are new to the reader; this book covers them in great detail, so don't worry. Come back to this section once you have considered the rest of this book and you will appreciate even more the potential for confusion and performance problems.

Typically the solution utilises one or more existing SQL Server databases and, just like any organization I have ever worked in, there are more than a few inspired application developers and/or DBAs involved. By inspired, I mean that they readily try new technologies and approaches. This in itself is not bad, but it is one thing to try out new approaches, and another to use them wherever possible in a live environment. Good planning and design becomes an afterthought (not to mention actually documenting an application). It is fair to say that deadlines and bad management practices can also heavily influence this.

- Some applications (or parts of applications) would store XML documents as BLOBs; some would maintain the relational storage of the data, to be converted to XML at runtime. Other applications (or parts of applications) would make use of OPENXML in order to provide a relational view of an XML document. Many would focus their efforts on keeping the data relationally but using SQLXML to retrieve it as XML that matches a predefined schema (good schema creation is another story). Another application could use URL based queries directly. Finally, some applications would continue to use ADO XML functionality to extract XML from a relational source.

- Application developers would then use the MSXML API to parse the XML document before use. Perhaps some would retrieve the data as XML using XPath queries on SQL Server, thereby not needing to use MSXML at all. XSLT could be applied appropriately to any XML document, but where should the XSLT file be stored? After all, it is only an XML document, perhaps a BLOB, in SQL Server or cached on the web server.

- In terms of updating SQL Server, many applications would use the Updategram functionality. Others would use the SQLXML bulk load facility. The remainder would use the classic relational mechanisms.

SQL Server, XML, and the DBA

Considering this approach against the five main areas, it is fair to say the following:

- **Performance, Volumes, Security, Scalability** – Because SQL Server 2000 tools have been used (in places) it would be fair to say that the retrieval of XML documents could perform well and be a scalable solution. Volumes and security could have been handled properly, but without an end-to-end view it is hard to say anything concretely.
- **Future proofing** – It should be fairly obvious that the many approaches, used in the many different possible ways, probably do not make any solution future proof. Just consider the data itself for example. Some would be held relationally, some as XML, some would be persisted in the database, and some outside. This would be really ugly.

In summary, this solution isn't a solution at all. It is a badly managed approach that results in loss of control, inability to plan any future application development, and no overall view of the environment. This approach is not recommended, so let's move on to look at one that is.

Take a Step Back

This solution uses the opposite approach to the previous solution, starting at the front end rather than the back end. There are four main types of XML document used here:

- **Document-focused** – The XML produced relates directly to a human readable flow of information; for example, a company report where the report paragraphs are stored in a database.
- **Data-focused** – The XML produced is an XML representation of basic tabular data; for example, sales figures by region for a report.
- **Document and data focused** – A combination of both of the above.
- **A system XML file that is used by the application** – An XSLT stylesheet, for example.

Storage

All the documents above are XML based, but the difference is in the way they naturally fit (or not) into a relational structure, and the issue is whether it makes sense to pull them apart to store them. For example, it probably would not make sense to store an XSLT file in anything other than a BLOB, as it would only be used as a whole. For performance reasons, it may not make sense to store it in SQL Server at all, and instead keep it cached on the web server.

> As a general rule, the more data-centric an XML document is, the more it makes sense to store it relationally.

Data stored relationally could then be extracted using the SQLXML 3.0 Managed Classes, or the FOR XML (AUTO or EXPLICIT) functionality.

> Conversely, the more document-centric an XML document, the more it makes sense to store it as XML.

If the document is hardly ever manipulated, or the majority is not touched when retrieving it, then storing it as a BLOB, or on a file system and using OPENXML to put the data in the database if you wanted to manipulate it, makes sense.

The next chapter explains exactly what each of the new technologies mentioned above are, and how they fit into SQL Server architecture.

Retrieval

This basically comes down to how it is best to persist the (document- or data-centric) document combined with the performance required for output.

If the document stored is data-centric (that is, held in SQL Server relationally), and the speed of the output requirement is not critical, then any of the SQLXML methods for retrieval would make sense, depending upon how formal you want the XML to be (FOR XML RAW, for example, is not 'beautiful' XML). If the requirement is for XML documents that contain different data, then use of the XPath query mechanisms should be considered.

For critical output, **pre-fetching** must be considered. Pre-fetching could mean that XML documents are persisted on the web server as part of a daily batch run, or SQLXML routines update a BLOB field on occasion with an XML document.

> The more critical the retrieval performance required, the safer it is to pre-fetch as XML or store as XML.

Updates

This is perhaps the hardest area to decide upon, given the relative performance of pure SQL Server data processes against the XML routines.

It all depends on the amount of XML that is contained in your application. If your application is purely XML structures on the front end, and it is not critical (let's face it, most applications aren't that critical), then the use of Updategrams, OPENXML, or SQLXML Bulk Load should be considered as an alternative to using the MSXML API and ADO connections.

> If performance isn't critical, and your application has a logical mix of XML on the front end and relational data on the back, then the SQL Server 2000 XML update mechanisms make sense.

Interoperability

This may seem glaringly obvious, but it is important to consider an application alongside any other applications it might interface with.

SQL Server, XML, and the DBA

> **If the interoperating applications are mainly relational, then it is completely sensible to keep the interfaces relational.**

Another important factor to consider is that it may make sense to design an application so that it has many possible end-to-end views in order to match the end systems. For example, an XML interface for one part, and relational for another. The key is to be aware of where you are using what, and why.

To summarize this solution, we will consider this approach against our five main areas:

- **Performance** – It should now be clear that end-to-end performance is what counts, and the type of XML document required has a large impact upon the best approach. It is no longer relevant to just benchmark against traditional retrieval methods when the use of XML is vital at the front end.

- **Volumes** – The volumes involved generally dictate how optimal the XML handling should be. For small applications, it could well make sense to just use ADO and the MSXML API, but for generic data loads, the SQLXML Bulk Load facility is appropriate.

- **Security** – Anything that occurs within an IIS and SQL Server environment can only be as secure as the administrators can make it. Common sense applies when considering what data to make available over the Internet. For example, I would not be happy exposing any highly secret corporate data via a URL query to all Internet users.

- **Scalability** – Because an application will be defined by the type of XML document it processes (data- or document-centric), scalability should be a fairly straightforward consideration. If, for example, the right decision is made in the short term about processing a data-centric XML document using Updategrams, then this decision could be expected to scale, as long as the XML document types remain constant.

- **Future proofing** – as a concept, future proofing is all about planning. By planning an implementation, as this subsection highlights, you will be aware of what is being used and why. That logical approach will then show itself throughout your SQL Server implementation, when you come to create another application.

Which Approach?

The aim of this architectural section was to show you that it is vital to consider your approach end-to-end. If you only see the database end, it is easy to assume that the application developer is doing the right thing at the other end, only to find out (or perhaps not find out!) that the performance of the application has been hit massively.

The first two approaches show what it is like to ignore completely the fact that SQL Server 2000 has tried to provide solutions for the handling of XML. Hopefully, by virtue of the fact that you are reading this book, you will appreciate that they are two extremes. The approach you really have to try and avoid is the third one. If this chapter has persuaded you to give the last one a try, then it has been successful.

Summary

In this chapter we have considered a great deal, with the goal of understanding at a high level the main factors that need to be considered by a DBA who is required to expose or store XML using SQL Server 2000:

- We considered the evolution of the n-tier architecture in order to try and establish where XML came from, and why it is important today, given its use for web presentation, application interoperability, and data interchange.

- We got a feel for the relevant XML standards and mechanisms appropriate to this book.

- We looked at XML structures and relational structures, to establish the main differences.

- XML structures and their main uses were shown to give a feel for their relevance in today's IT environment.

- Finally, and very importantly, we took an architectural view to try and gather an overall appreciation of the end-to-end use of XML.

In the next chapter we will take a look at how Microsoft has implemented functionality both within SQL Server itself, and via the SQLXML 3.0 add in, to allow us to work with XML.

Bryant Likes

- Architecture Overview
- Architecture of SQL Server 2000 XML
- Architecture of SQLXML
- Installation of SQLXML
- Requirements
- Creating SQLXML Virtual Directories
- Summary

2

Architecture and Setup

With the release of SQL Server 2000, Microsoft introduced built-in XML support, as opposed to the add-on available with SQL Server 7. Since that point, Microsoft has provided three updates in the form of SQLXML web releases. In this chapter, we will look at the XML features of both SQL Server 2000 and the SQLXML web releases. We will start by looking at where the features can be found and how each of these features works. Next, we will look at how all the features work together. We will also install SQLXML 3.0 and configure it for use throughout the rest of the book. Once we have gone over the basics, we will look at security and how to troubleshoot virtual directories. After this chapter you should have a basic understanding of what XML features Microsoft has provided in SQL Server, the features added by SQLXML, and how they can be used.

Architecture Overview

Microsoft's approach to providing XML support in SQL Server 2000 comes in two parts. The first is the XML support that is built into SQL Server 2000. These features are updated with SQL Server 2000 service packs, rather than web releases, and will most likely not see any upgrades until the next version of SQL Server (currently codenamed Yukon).

The second part of the XML support is the SQLXML web releases. These releases are a type of add-on for SQL Server 2000 and provide a lot of missing functionality. This approach works because XML standards are moving at a very rapid pace, much faster than the releases of the database software. By having these add-on packs, Microsoft is able to keep SQL Server 2000 reliable, but at the same time up-to-date with the current XML technologies.

> *You can read more about current XML standards at*
> *http://www.w3.org/XML/*

Besides SQL Server itself and the SQLXML web releases, another important part of Microsoft's SQL Server XML strategy is the Microsoft XML Parser (MSXML), now known as Microsoft XML Core Services (though using the same acronym of MSXML). MSXML is Microsoft's XML parsing engine, used in many of the SQL Server XML and SQLXML features, and also updated via web releases. It is currently in version 4.0 (Service Pack 1) and can be downloaded at
http://msdn.microsoft.com/downloads/default.asp?url=/downloads/sample.asp?url=/msdn-files/027/001/766/msdncompositedoc.xml.

The continued upgrades of MSXML have contributed greatly to the SQLXML web releases by improving the speed and the features of SQLXML.

The diagram below outlines the SQL Server XML and SQLXML features:

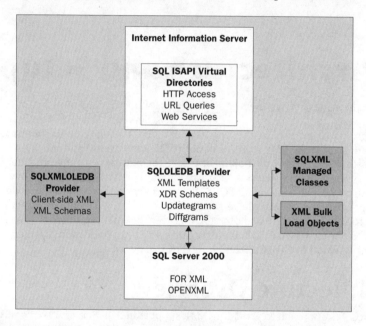

Architecture of SQL Server 2000 XML

There are two XML features that are built into SQL Server 2000:

- FOR XML queries
- OPENXML

FOR XML Queries

Prior to SQL Server 2000, creating an XML document from SQL Server data was not a trivial task, especially if you wanted your XML data in a specific format. There were ways to get XML out of SQL Server in 6.5 and 7.0 with the XML technology preview and the Save method of ADO Recordsets, but neither of these was integrated with SQL Server itself. Microsoft changed this with the release of SQL Server 2000, where you can use what is called a FOR XML query to generate XML.

Architecture and Setup

While a simple T-SQL query in SQL Server returns a rowset (a set of records), FOR XML queries return data in XML format. This means that you can no longer use a Recordset object to loop through the returned rowset. Instead, we now have a stream of data being returned. While each row in the rowset has the same structure, streaming data may combine several data structures where each piece might be different in structure. To deal with the streamed data, we can now use ADO Stream objects to load the data into an XML parser like MSXML, or use ADO.NET to load the data into a Dataset, or we can use a variety of other methods to deal with the returned XML.

There are three modes you can use within SQL Server to extract data in XML format: AUTO, RAW, and EXPLICIT. The different modes are used to handle different methods of formatting the resulting XML. These modes, and how they are used, are discussed in Chapter 4.

OPENXML

OPENXML is another built-in XML technology, and is the reverse of the FOR XML clause. Whereas FOR XML turns a rowset into an XML document, OPENXML turns an XML document into a rowset. This allows us to get XML into SQL Server by using two stored procedures: sp_xml_preparedocument and sp_xml_removedocument.

OPENXML uses MSXML to parse an XML document using the sp_xml_preparedocument stored procedure. This document is then stored in memory and can be accessed in T-SQL as if it were a table by using the OPENXML keyword. Once the XML document is no longer needed, sp_xml_removedocument must be called to remove the document from memory. The memory that is used by OPENXML is up to one-eighth of the memory that is allocated to SQL Server. It is important to note that this is only up to one-eighth in total and not one-eighth per document. If you try to exceed this amount of memory you will get an out of memory error. The one-eighth is a fixed amount and cannot be changed; however, this shouldn't be a problem since large XML documents can be imported using XML Bulk Loading, which we will look at in a later section.

The following diagram shows this process in action:

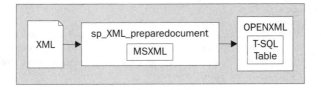

OPENXML is covered in detail in Chapter 10.

Now we've finished looking at the built-in XML features of SQL Server 2000, let's move on to the additional functionality made available in the SQLXML add-on.

33

Chapter 2

Architecture of SQLXML

At the time of writing, the most recent version of SQLXML is Version 3.0, Service Pack 1. This version includes all of the features of previous versions along with some new ones. These features are listed below:

Feature	Location	Introduced
FOR XML	SQL Server	SQL Server 2000 (7.0 add-on)
OPENXML	SQL Server	SQL Server 2000
XDR schemas	SQLOLEDB provider	SQL Server 2000
XML templates	SQLOLEDB provider	SQL Server 2000
HTTP access	SQL ISAPI	SQL Server 2000
XML Bulk Load	COM object	XML for SQL Web Release 1 (WR1)
Updategrams	SQLOLEDB provider	XML for SQL WR1
Client-side XML	SQLXMLOLEDB provider	SQLXML 2.0
Managed Classes	.NET Class	SQLXML 2.0
DiffGrams	SQLOLEDB provider	SQLXML 2.0
XML schemas	SQLXMLOLEDB provider	SQLXML 2.0
Web services	SQL ISAPI	SQLXML 3.0

We've already discussed the first two features, which are part of SQL Server XML. All the features listed above from XDR Schemas onwards have either been introduced or enhanced by one of the SQLXML releases (formerly called XML for SQL Web Releases). So, for example, even if you only want to use XDR schemas (available in SQL Server 2000), you should still install the latest version of SQLXML, since XDR schemas have been improved in SQLXML 3.0.

HTTP Access

SQL Server 2000 has HTTP access built in, but this is not enabled by default. HTTP access can be used to get XML both into and out of SQL Server. It is configured through the use of the **Virtual Directory Management** (**VDM**) tool included with SQL Server 2000.

> Note that the VDM has been upgraded with each SQLXML release.

HTTP access is accomplished with the use of an **Internet Server API** (**ISAPI**) **Dynamic Link Library** (**DLL**) called the SQL ISAPI (named Sqlis3.dll in SQLXML 3.0).

Architecture and Setup

The VDM tool is used to configure a special Internet Information Server (IIS) virtual directory that can interact with SQL Server 2000, and is found under the Microsoft SQL Server program group as **Configure SQL XML Support in IIS**, or under the SQLXML 2.0 or 3.0 program group as **Configure IIS Support**. This tool is the only way to configure SQLXML virtual directories.

> Note that even though you can see the directories in other tools like the IIS Management Tool, changing the directory's settings with these can create problems. We'll look in more detail at this in the 'Troubleshooting' section at the end of this chapter.

There are several ways to get XML out of SQL Server using the HTTP access:

- **URL queries** – URL queries are SQL statements that are passed in using a URL. These statements have the same limitation as that of the templates, namely only being able to return a single result per query.
- **XML templates** – These can be mapped to a virtual name. This mapping is accomplished with the VDM tool and will be covered in the setup portion of this chapter.
- **Schema** (either XDR or XML) – Schemas can also be mapped to a virtual name. When the schema is then accessed, using its mapped URL, an XPath query can be appended to the URL to run specific queries against it. You can read more about XPath queries in Chapter 8.

XDR Schemas

XML-Data Reduced (**XDR**) schemas are used in Microsoft SQL Server to describe and constrain the structure and valid data types of an XML document. SQL Server uses annotations in these schemas to map tables and fields to XML elements and attributes. The data types can also be declared as SQL data types, such as int, varchar, datetime, allowing you to specify what type of data the column will store. The result is an XML document as a view of your data that can be queried using XPath (a query language used with XML). In other words, SQL Server takes the XDR schema and transforms it into a query, which is then run to generate the XML document. This method enables you to retrieve data from SQL Server as XML without using any T-SQL. Since XDR schemas are part of the SQLOLEDB provider, they can be used either with Microsoft **ActiveX Data Objects** (**ADO**), or any other client that uses the SQLOLEDB provider. The diagram below shows how schemas are handled through either an HTTP request from IE or through an ADO command:

Chapter 2

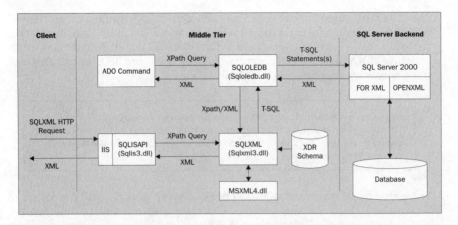

When the HTTP request is made against an XDR schema, IIS passes the call to the SQLISAPI. This then sends an XPath query to SQLXML. SQLXML uses MSXML to load the schema. It then uses the schema to generate T-SQL statements, in the form of FOR XML EXPLICIT queries. The T-SQL is passed to SQLOLEDB and then to SQL Server. SQL Server returns XML, which is passed all the way back to the client.

ADO commands that use XDR schemas take a slightly different path. ADO sends the XPath query to SQLOLEDB. SQLOLEDB then passes the XPath to SQLXML, where the schema is parsed with MSXML and the T-SQL statements are generated. The T-SQL is then passed back to SQLOLEDB, which passes it to SQL Server. The XML that is returned by SQL Server is passed to the client through SQLOLEDB.

Since the release of SQL Server 2000, XDR has been replaced by the **XML Schema** Recommendation from the W3C, which has now been accepted as an industry-wide standard (http://www.w3.org/TR/xmlschema-0/). For this reason, it is recommended that you use XML schemas instead of XDR schemas, since XDR schemas are likely to be deprecated in the future. You can read more about this in Chapter 6.

XML Templates

XML templates are XML documents that can have SQL statements or XPath queries embedded in them, and are very useful for getting XML out of SQL Server. These XML documents are passed to the SQLOLEDB provider, which parses the documents, executes the SQL statement or XPath query, and then returns the resulting XML. Here is an example of a simple XML template:

```
<root xmlns:sql="urn:schemas-microsoft-com:xml-sql">
    <sql:query>
        SELECT * FROM employees
        FOR XML AUTO
    </sql:query>
</root>
```

Architecture and Setup

In between the `<sql:query>` tags you can include any valid T-SQL statement, with the restriction that the query must return a single row with only one field, or the query must use the `FOR XML` clause. This is because the results are returned as an XML document.

XML templates can also have parameters that allow you to pass in values, much like a stored procedure. How the values are passed in depends on the method you're using to send the template to the `SQLOLEDB` provider. If you're using ADO, you can use ADO parameters to pass them in. If you've mapped the template to a virtual name, then you can use standard URL parameters. Mapping templates will be explained when we set up the sample virtual directory later in the chapter. The following diagram outlines how XML templates are processed as HTTP request or ADO commands:

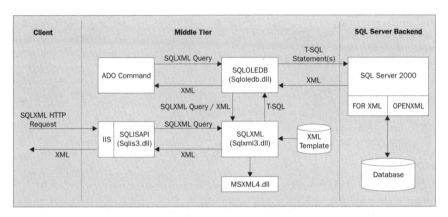

XML templates are processed is very similar way to XDR schemas. SQLXML is what interprets the template by using MSXML to parse it. It then creates T-SQL statements that are passed to `SQLOLEDB` and then on to SQL Server.

XML Bulk Load

XML Bulk Load is similar to `OPENXML` in that it allows you to import XML into SQL Server. However, it differs from `OPENXML` in several ways. First, XML Bulk Load is geared toward larger XML documents. It is a bulk insert utility and functions much like SQL Server's BCP utility but instead of a comma-delimited file, you use an XML document. So, just as you wouldn't use BCP to insert a few records into SQL Server, neither would you use XML Bulk Load to insert a few records. Rather, it is used for situations where you have a large number of records that you want to insert into the database. A second difference is that, unlike `OPENXML`, you can use XML Bulk Load to insert data into multiple tables. The final difference is that an XML bulk load is performed through a COM object that is included with SQLXML (it is not included with SQL Server 2000). The COM object uses an XML schema or an XDR schema to parse an XML document or fragment, and then loads it into the database using the bulk insert statement.

Chapter 2

The XML Bulk Load COM object is located in the `xblkld3.dll` in SQLXML 3.0 and `xblkdl2.dll` in SQLXML 2.0. XML Bulk Load uses MSXML 4 to parse both the XML data file and the XDR or XML schema. It then uses the SQL annotations on the schema to generate the T-SQL statements, which are passed to SQL Server using SQLOLEDB. This T-SQL includes a `Bulk Insert` statement to insert the data into the database.

Updategrams

Updategrams are another way of getting XML data into SQL Server. They are XML documents that include before and after representations of your data. These XML documents can be passed to the SQLOLEDB provider using ADO, stored as XML templates, or posted to a SQLXML virtual directory. Here is an example of what these documents look like:

```
<ROOT xmlns:updg="urn:schemas-microsoft-com:xml-updategram">
    <updg:sync [mapping-schema= "AnnotatedSchemaFile.xml"] >
        <updg:before>
            ...
        </updg:before>
        <updg:after>
            ...
        </updg:after>
    </updg:sync>
</ROOT>
```

Each `sync` block is considered a transaction, and can contain multiple `before` and `after` pairs. The XML contained in the `before` and `after` blocks is mapped to SQL Server tables and fields using either an XDR or an XML schema. Updategrams are very useful for inserting, updating, or deleting records.

Updategrams are executed in the same way as XML templates. They can be utilized either through ADO or through HTTP requests. The Updategram is interpreted by SQLXML using MSXML to generate T-SQL statements, which are then passed to SQL Server.

Client-side XML

Another SQLXML specific feature is client-side FOR XML queries. This feature reduces the load on the server by allowing the XML to be generated on the client. This doesn't mean that the client ever sees the results before they are transformed; rather the results look the same but the processing occurs in the client tier instead of the server tier. The following diagram shows how this works when a HTTP request for a template uses client-side FOR XML:

Architecture and Setup

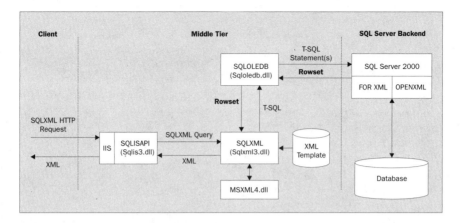

As we can see, everything proceeds in the same manner as a server-side FOR XML template with the exception of what is returned by SQL Server. Instead of returning XML, SQL Server returns a rowset. This rowset is passed through SQLOLEDB to SQLXML, where it is then turned into XML. This XML is then passed out to the client.

Client-side FOR XML can also be done via ADO and it is handled in the same manner. For ADO to use client-side FOR XML, it must use the SQLXMLOLEDB provider, which references SQLXML. So the SQLXML query is passed to SQLXML straight from ADO instead of coming through the SQLOLEDB provider as it does in server-side FOR XML.

Client-side FOR XML is done using the FOR XML clause, but it is slightly different. The three modes of client-side FOR XML are RAW, NESTED, and EXPLICIT. RAW and EXPLICIT we've seen before in the server side, but NESTED is a new mode. NESTED is similar to AUTO, but differs in that it handles the XML formatting on the client side. This means you can add FOR XML NESTED to the end of a stored procedure call and it will format the results as XML. It also allows you to use the FOR XML clause on queries that use the GROUP BY clause that is not supported by FOR XML AUTO. There are a few other differences, which will be covered in detail in Chapter 4. Client-side XML is supported in the SQLXML virtual directories, XML templates, the SQLXML Managed Classes, and the SQLXMLOLEDB provider.

.NET Managed Classes

The SQLXML Managed Classes bring many of the features of SQLXML to the .NET environment. Using the SQLXML Managed Classes, you can execute XML templates and Updategrams, run XPath queries against XML or XDR schemas, and make use of client-side XML. The Managed Classes are really just a COM interop wrapper for SQLXMLOLEDB. Below is a diagram of how this works:

Chapter 2

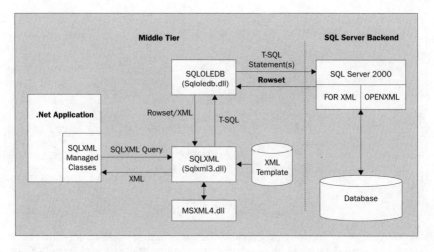

The SQLXML Managed Classes (`Microsoft.Data.SqlXml.dll`) connect to SQLXMLOLEDB through a COM interop object. The SQLXML query is passed to SQLXMLOLEDB, which uses MSXML to parse the query and generate T-SQL. The T-SQL is passed to SQL Server through SQLOLEDB. SQL Server then returns either XML if it is server-side processing, or a rowset if it is client-side processing. In both cases XML is returned to the Managed Classes by SQLXMLOLEDB.

DiffGrams

DiffGrams are not specific to SQLXML, but were introduced with the Microsoft .NET Framework. They are used to get XML data into SQL Server, and are similar to Updategrams in that they do this with a before and after snapshot of your data. They can be used to INSERT, UPDATE, or DELETE records from the database. Since they are built into the SQLOLEDB provider, they can be accessed through ADO or the .NET Managed Classes. When they are executed they are interpreted by SQLXML or SQLXMLOLEDB, which creates T-SQL code to execute. DiffGrams are more useful in a .NET context, since they can be created dynamically by DataSets.

XML Schemas

XML schemas work the same way as XDR schemas, in that the server processes them and creates a FOR XML EXPLICIT query. The use of XML schemas goes far beyond SQLXML. XML schemas are used in the Microsoft .NET Framework as well as many other applications, such as MSXML, to validate that XML conforms to a specific format. It is important to note that SQLXML does not use XML schemas in this manner. Rather, SQLXML only uses XML schemas to get data into or out of SQL Server and does not validate that the data conforms to the XML schema. You can perform this validation yourself using a tool like MSXML, but SQLXML does not do it for you.

Architecture and Setup

Web Services

One of the most useful features is the web service (SOAP) support. This feature allows you to expose stored procedures, user-defined functions (UDF), and XML templates through a web service (we'll learn more about them in Chapter 14). Your stored procedure, UDF, or XML template can then be programmed against with any tool that supports SOAP, such as the Microsoft SOAP Toolkit or Visual Studio .NET. This provides the benefits of creating web services without having to write any code. The web service uses the SOAP Toolkit to process the incoming SOAP messages and then formats the message into T-SQL. This is then sent to the SQL Server where it is processed and returned as XML. This XML is then returned or formatted as an ADO.NET dataset and sent back as a SOAP message.

Putting it All Together

Now that we've briefly looked at all the features of SQL Server XML and SQLXML, we need to start putting them together. In this section, we'll look at how these features interact, and how they fit with Microsoft's DNA and .NET Framework. After reading this section you should have a general idea of how you can start using these features.

To understand the interactions between the features, take a look at the following overview diagram:

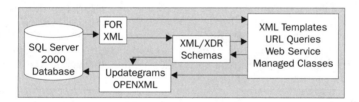

Note that this diagram is not comprehensive since, for example, XML templates can run stored procedures that directly update the database, and FOR XML *queries can be run without using a template, URL query, web service, or a managed class.*

FOR XML queries are the basis for getting XML out of SQL Server. Even if you use XML or XDR schemas, you're still using FOR XML (if indirectly). This is why it is important to have a good understanding of how FOR XML works. Even if you only plan to use the schemas, being able to debug them requires looking at and understanding FOR XML queries. So, whenever we are retrieving data from SQL Server as XML, we will be tapping into FOR XML in some way.

Getting XML into SQL Server is another story. To do this, we can use updategrams, OPENXML, diffgrams, or XML Bulk Load. It is important to note that each of these features, with the exception of OPENXML, uses XML or XDR schemas to translate the XML into SQL Server tables. Which method you choose to use will depend on several factors, such as how much data you plan to insert, whether you need to be able to update records, how much control you want over the format of the XML, as well as other factors which were discussed in broad terms in the previous chapter.

41

Chapter 2

Where SQLXML Fits With .NET/DNA

SQLXML fits in well with either Microsoft DNA architecture or the Microsoft .NET Framework. Using SQLXML with Microsoft DNA is accomplished by using the SQLOLEDB provider or the SQLXMLOLEDB provider with ADO. With SQLOLEDB and ADO you can use XML templates, Updategrams, FOR XML queries, and XDR schemas. With SQLXMLOLEDB you get all the benefits of the SQLOLEDB provider with the addition of XML schemas, templates, and client-side XML. ADO also makes use of the caching features of SQLXML which speeds up performance. ADO isn't the only way to make use of SQLXML in .NET; using SQLXML virtual directories you can access SQL Server data using MSXML and HTTP. Additionally, there are the XML Bulk Load components, which can also be used in the COM environment.

SQLXML also fits with the Microsoft .NET Framework via the SQLXML Managed Classes. With the managed classes you can make use of all the SQLXML features that are available via the SQLOLEDB and the SQLXMLOLEDB providers. In addition, since SQLXML 3.0 adds support for web services, you can easily program against them using the .NET Framework.

Installation of SQLXML

Now that we've looked at the features of SQLXML and how they are related, let's go ahead and install the latest release of SQLXML, which is SQLXML 3.0, Service Pack 1. In this next section, we will walk through the installation of SQLXML, configuring a virtual directory, and testing the setup to make sure it's working. Once we are finished with this section, you should have a working virtual directory, which you can use to test the examples that are found throughout the book.

> In order to view the examples in this section you need to use Internet Explorer (IE) 5 or greater. The URLs are not encoded, which makes them easier to read; but in browsers other than IE they may not work. IE also supports enhanced viewing of XML documents, which is helpful.

Requirements

The following are required before you can install SQLXML:

- ❑ Microsoft Windows 98, Millennium, NT 4.0, 2000, or XP
- ❑ SQL Server 2000 Client Tools – You must have the SQL Server 2000 client tools in order to install SQLXML, since SQLXML uses SQL-DMO to connect to SQL Server. Without the client tools installed, you won't have access to SQL-DMO. The current licensing policy also means that even if you're just creating a set up that will connect to a SQL Server database on another machine, you still need to have the SQL Server 2000 client tools installed.
- ❑ MDAC 2.6 or 2.7 – If you've installed SQL Server 2000 you should already have this.

Architecture and Setup

- Windows Installer 2.0 – The Windows Installer runs the installation program. If you don't have this you can download it from http://www.microsoft.com/downloads/release.asp?releaseid=32832&NewList=1.
- SOAP Toolkit 2.0 (Service Pack 2) – This is required if you wish to use the web services (SOAP) features of SQLXML. It is a very simple install, so I would recommend installing it before SQLXML so that you can try out the web service features. It can be downloaded at http://msdn.microsoft.com/downloads/default.asp?URL=/code/sample.asp?url=/msdn-files/027/001/580/msdncompositedoc.xml.

Note that SOAP Toolkit 3.0 is available, but at the time of going to press, Microsoft has not tested SQLXML 3.0 with SOAP Toolkit 3.0.

- Microsoft .NET Framework – This is required if you want to use the SQLXML Managed Classes. This install is a bit more involved that the SOAP Toolkit, though still straightforward. Once you have installed this you can run programs that have been developed in .NET. The Framework RTM can be downloaded from http://msdn.microsoft.com/net (for free, like the other downloads) and is 21 MB. Note that it is installed by default if you have a copy of Visual Studio .NET.

Having checked off this list, you can download the SQLXML installation from http://msdn.microsoft.com/sqlxml. If you do end up installing SQLXML without the .NET Framework, you will have to reinstall it after installing the Framework to get the Managed Classes to work. It's also worth mentioning here that if you do ever have to reinstall SQLXML you won't lose all your settings.

If you have previously installed other versions of SQLXML, you can install SQLXML 3.0 alongside them; previous versions will not be overwritten. However, before you can make use of the new features and improvements in SQLXML 3.0, you will need to upgrade your virtual directory to Version 3. More details on this are given in the *Creating SQLXML Virtual Directories* section.

Installing SQLXML 3.0

To install SQLXML, just run the install program. While you can choose the components you need, it is recommended that you just install everything since you may decide to use more features as you go.

Once you have clicked through the starting screen, you will come across the licence agreement and, on accepting that, you will reach the **Choose Setup Type** screen. **Install Now** installs SQLXML with all the features. Clicking **Customize** takes you to the next screen, shown below. Installing all the features and the documentation requires approximately 1MB, and, since you have to configure things like URL access, there are really no security issues to consider. So the easiest route is to just install everything, even if you don't plan on using it right away.

Chapter 2

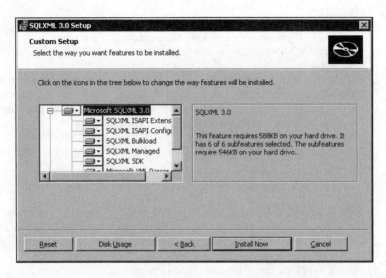

This screen has been expanded to show all the possible features that can be installed. Here is a short description of each feature:

- **SQLXML ISAPI Extension** – This is the ISAPI extension that provides HTTP support.
- **SQLXML ISAPI Configuration** – This is the configuration tool that is used to configure the ISAPI extension.
- **SQLXML Bulkload** – This installs the COM objects that allow you to run XML Bulk Loading.
- **SQLXML Managed** – This is the SQLXML Managed Classes, which are only available if you have the .NET SDK installed.
- **SQLXML SDK** – The SQLXML Software Developer's Kit is really just two files, which are only needed if you're developing in C++.
- **Microsoft XML Parser 4.0** – This feature should not be disabled since MSXML 4.0 is required in order for SQLXML to work.
- **SQLXML Documentation** – This is the SQLXML help file, essential to anyone working with SQLXML, and takes up 436 KB of disk space. The documentation is a very useful resource for learning about the features in SQLXML, but if you're just installing this on a server then you probably don't need it.

Once the install begins running it should be very quick, and on completion you can start working with virtual directories right away. The virtual directories are what we will use to test many of the features of SQLXML.

Creating SQLXML Virtual Directories

It is fairly easy to create a SQLXML virtual directory with the management tool. This is the tool that you will always use when creating or making changes to SQLXML virtual directories. Begin by starting the SQLXML Virtual Directory Management Tool. It is under Start | Programs | SQLXML 3.0 | Configure IIS Support.

Architecture and Setup

You will need to have at least one web site running on the machine that you are using. To create a new virtual directory, click **Action | New | Virtual Directory**. This should bring up the **New Virtual Directory Properties** dialog. This dialog is the same dialog as the one for editing the properties of existing virtual directories. Let's take this opportunity to create a new virtual directory, looking at each of the tabs on this dialog in turn.

General Tab

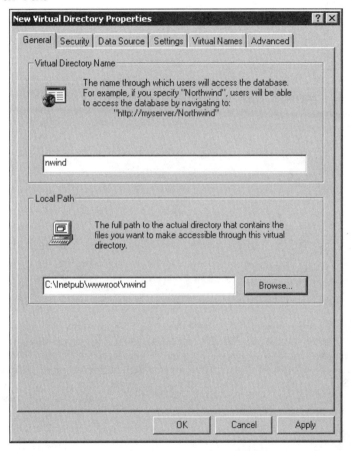

This tab is used to specify the name of your virtual directory and to define the path to it (it can also be a UNC (Universal/Uniform Naming Convention)path if you are running IIS and SQL Server on separate servers). In this example, we will be using the Northwind sample database, so we will name our virtual directory nwind. This means that, when we finish, you should be able to access this virtual directory at **http://localhost/nwind**. Make sure the nwind folder exists before browsing to it, since the management tool does not allow you to create the directory, and only lets you browse to existing directories.

Security Tab

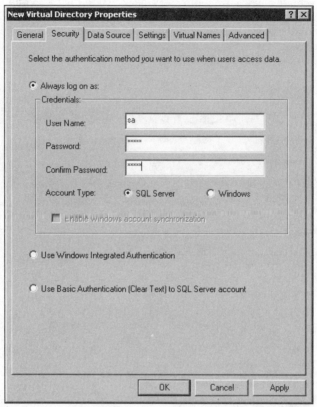

On this tab, we configure database connection. Quite a few problems can stem from these settings. Using **Always log on as** security grants anonymous access to anyone who wants to access your virtual directory, using either a SQL Server account or a Windows account. If you use a SQL Server account, make sure that your SQL Server is using SQL Server and Windows Authentication. If your server is running in Windows only mode, then a SQL Server account won't work here.

Using the other two options require the user to send their credentials with the request. **Windows Integrated Authentication** is the most secure method of the three, but users will not be able to view anything unless they are on the same LAN and have the proper credentials. **Basic Authentication** requires the user to enter their SQL Server username and password and they are sent as clear text, which isn't a very secure method.

The type of authentication you select will be based on your needs. Some sites, such as http://sqlxml.org/, need to allow anonymous users to access them. Other sites, such as intranets, need to keep anonymous users out. For our example, we will use the **Always log on as** setting with the sa user account. This is the method that is the easiest to set up, requiring no knowledge of Windows users or domains, but is not recommended for a production system.

Architecture and Setup

Data Source Tab

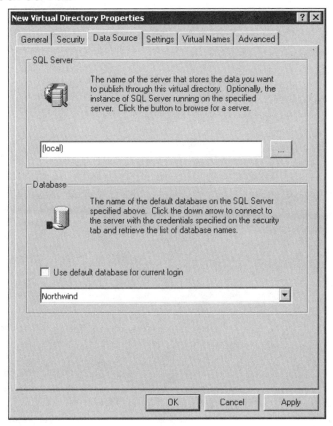

This tab is used to select the server and database that you want to connect to. Once you select the server you want to connect to, the list of databases will be populated based on the logon information specified on the **Security** tab. For our example, we should be able to use the local SQL Server, which is input as (local) as shown in the screenshot. If you are connecting to another server, be sure to specify the correct server name instead of (local). We will be using the Northwind sample database, so also make sure that you select this database from the list of databases in the dropdown.

47

Settings Tab

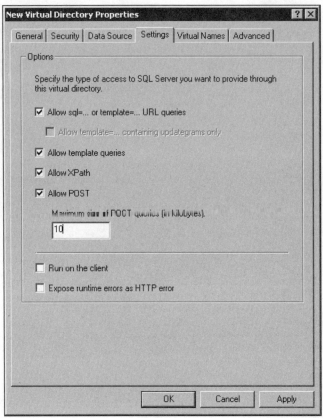

This tab is perhaps the most important one. Allow sql= or template= URL queries is a good feature when testing SQLXML, but this should **never** be left checked on a system that is accessible via the Internet. If this is left checked, especially if anonymous access is being used, you could end up with some very unpleasant results. As an illustration, try creating a table called test then dropping it with a URL query to see how much of a potential problem this feature creates:

http://localhost/nwind?sql=drop table test

The Allow template queries and Allow XPath checkboxes are not as dangerous, and in fact are necessary if you want to take full advantage of SQLXML. The Allow POST just turns on the POST method for sending HTTP requests. This is no different from allowing POST requests on any IIS server. SQLXML even allows you to limit the amount of data that can be posted. The maximum size should be set somewhere close to how much data you expect to be sending. If you're using a form with two text fields, you don't need to set this to 100 KB. If you do set this to a small amount, make sure you make a note of it so that you don't run into problems down the road if you increase the amount of data that is posted.

Architecture and Setup

Checking **Expose runtime errors as HTTP error** is a useful feature for handling errors if you're using another application to connect to SQL Server via HTTP. Normally, when you have an error in your query, such as SELECT * FROM employees FOR XML ATUO (notice AUTO is misspelled), SQLXML will return HTTP/1.1 200 OK and the error will be returned in the body of the response. When you check the **Expose runtime errors...** checkbox, SQLXML will instead return HTTP/1.1 512 Runtime error.

Checking the **Run on the client** checkbox will force the client-side XML to be always on. This means that you don't have to specify the `client-side-xml` attribute in templates. However, be aware that **all** FOR XML AUTO queries will still run on the server. This is a fairly common misunderstanding.

> **Client-side XML does not support the** AUTO **mode of** FOR XML. **So, if you turn on client-side formatting and run** FOR XML AUTO **queries in the URL, they will still be formatted on the server. Instead you should use** FOR XML NESTED.

For our example, we are going to turn on URL queries, template queries, XPath, and POST. Once we have verified that the virtual directory is working properly, we will turn off URL queries. If you don't plan on using this test directory until later, leave the URL queries unchecked. I would recommend turning this on when you need to test something, and then immediately turning it off when you're done.

Chapter 2

Virtual Names Tab

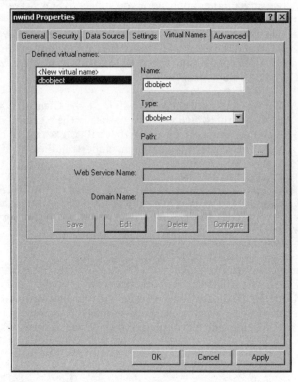

Virtual names are what we use to reference folders in SQLXML. A virtual name is a mapping between a physical folder and folder name that will be specified in the URL. There are four types of mappings: dbobject, schema, template, and soap.

dbobject mappings are for accessing specific objects in the database. The most useful way this feature can be used is to access binary data, such as images, directly in the browser. To create this mapping you just give it a virtual name and select the dbobject type. Once you have done this, you can use the mapped virtual name to access any object in the database. You can now access images through a URL with this method using the dbobject mapping. For our example, we will create a dbobject mapping called dbobject, as shown in the previous screenshot. After clicking **Save**, you can click **Apply**, which will allow you to test this out:

http://localhost/nwind/dbobject/employees[@EmployeeID='9']/@Photo

You should see an image in your browser, as long as you have everything configured correctly. However, this also creates a potential security issue since we can use this to access any object in the database:

http://localhost/nwind/dbobject/employees[@EmployeeID='9']/@firstname

Architecture and Setup

So, Microsoft recommends that you do not use this feature, especially if you have sensitive information stored in your tables. While this may seem like a useless feature, it makes sense if you don't have sensitive information in your database. The sqlxml.org database is a good example of this: all the data in the database is public, so it doesn't matter if someone looks through every field of every table.

The **schema** and **template** mappings are used to map to directories that contain your schemas and templates respectively. In previous versions of SQLXML, you could map to specific templates instead of entire directories, but Microsoft changed this with SQLXML 3.0.

The **soap** mapping is used to create a web service. Once you have created the mapping, you need to click the **Configure** button, which will allow you to add stored procedures and templates to the web service.

Both web services and schemas are covered in greater detail later in the book.

Advanced Tab

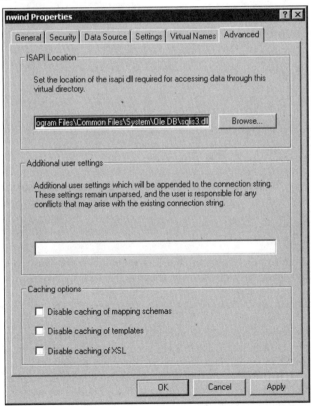

This tab is used to specify various other settings, most of which you are unlikely to use. Changing the ISAPI location will cause your virtual directory to quit working if you specify an incorrect location or the wrong SQLXML ISAPI. For SQLXML 3.0, the correct ISAPI is the `sqlis3.dll` as shown in the screenshot.

Chapter 2

If you are using the VDM tool to access a remote server, this field will be blank with SQLXML 3.0. With SQLXML 2.0 it won't be blank, but it might contain the wrong path. In both cases, you will need to enter the correct path, which is the location where the `sqlis3.dll` (SQLXML 3.0) or `sqlis2.dll` (SQLXML 2.0) files reside.

Caching gives SQLXML quite a boost and we do not recommended that you turn it off. According to an article on MSDN (http://msdn.microsoft.com/library/en-us/dnsql2k/html/sqlxml_OptimPerformance.asp), turning on caching gives about a 40% performance boost. However, when you are developing SQLXML applications, it might be useful to turn this off if you need to make sure you're not getting cached versions of your files.

Upgrade to Version 3 Tab

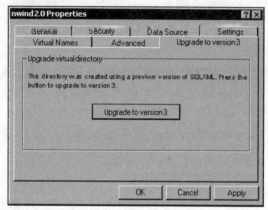

This only appears if you have setup a virtual directory using an older version of SQLXML. You can leave this directory as the older version, or upgrade it to SQLXML 3.0. Note that you won't get the benefits of SQLXML 3.0 until you click this upgrade button.

Test Your Setup

Once you have completed setting up the virtual directory, you can test it to see if it is working. To do this, open the following URL in your browser:

http://localhost/nwind?sql=select * from customers for xml auto&root=root

If everything is set up correctly, you should get XML showing up in your browser. Go ahead and try a few more URL queries to get an idea of how they work (these are covered in much more detail in Chapter 5). The `root` parameter is used to specify a document root for the XML document that is returned. If you this parameter, the document will not be a valid XML document. If your queries don't work, you can skip down to the *Troubleshooting* section, which will help you get it all working.

> When you are done testing your virtual directory, make sure you turn off URL queries.

Registry Settings

There are five different registry settings that can be changed in order to tweak the performance of SQLXML. Microsoft has listed four of them in the documentation (in contrast to earlier versions), omitting the `XSLCacheSize` registry key. SQLXML does not create all of these keys when it is installed, so if you decide to change their settings you will have to create them. As an example, for SQLXML 2.0 the location will be `Client\SQLXML2\`.

> Only edit the registry if you understand what you're doing and that you are doing so at your own risk.

The first three registry keys deal with caching. By default, the cache size is 31 files for each of the settings. This means that you can have 31 different templates, 31 different XML or XDR schemas, and 31 XSL files cached in memory at the same time. For many applications this will be plenty. However, if you have more than 31 of any of the above, you will most likely want to increase the corresponding registry setting. The maximum number you can set these to is 128 files. Remember that these files are stored in memory; so the higher the number, the more memory is required:

- `HKEY_LOCAL_MACHINE\SOFTWARE\Microsoft\MSSQLServer\Client\SQLXML3\TemplateCacheSize`
- `HKEY_LOCAL_MACHINE\SOFTWARE\Microsoft\MSSQLServer\Client\SQLXML3\SchemaCacheSize`
- `HKEY_LOCAL_MACHINE\SOFTWARE\Microsoft\MSSQLServer\Client\SQLXML3\XSLCacheSize`

The next registry key is the `NumThreads` key. This specifies how many threads SQLXML will use. The maximum is 256 and the default setting is two times the number of processors plus one. So, if you have a single processor machine, that would be three threads:

- `HKEY_LOCAL_MACHINE\SOFTWARE\Microsoft\MSSQLServer\Client\SQLIS3\NumThreads`

The `MaxRequestQueueSize` is the number of requests that can be queued up before the server will start returning server too busy errors:

- `HKEY_LOCAL_MACHINE\SOFTWARE\Microsoft\MSSQLServer\Client\SQLIS3\MaxRequestQueueSize`

Security Considerations

For many DBAs, the very idea of connecting IIS to SQL Server is a terrifying thought. However, SQLXML can be configured to be very secure. The fact that it can be potentially dangerous is offset by the fact that it can also be very useful, just like driving a car or flying in an airplane. In this section, we will briefly cover some of the important security issues that you should keep in mind when working with SQLXML.

URL Queries

As mentioned earlier, URL queries pose a serious security problem. You should never leave this enabled on a server that is accessible by anonymous users. No one should really have access to this feature except those who are working on the development of the database. Users could easily execute something without realizing what they are really doing (you'll remember the query that dropped our test table earlier). So this should mostly be turned off, even if the server is only accessible to users on your LAN. It should only be turned on for testing and, once testing is completed, it should be turned off again.

Types of Authentication

Also, be careful with your authentication. If you set things up so that users always log on as sa and you have also created a dbobject mapping, be aware that every field and record in the database is now viewable by anyone who can figure out the structure of your data. If you have sensitive information in your database, this could create a serious security issue. Be aware that if you are using the **Use Basic Authentication** option on the **Security** tab, then your SQL Server usernames and passwords are being sent with only base64 encoding, which is easy to decode. Microsoft recommends using Secure Sockets Layer (SSL) security if you decide to use basic authentication.

Other Security Issues

One of the keys to successfully using SQLXML is always to be as specific as possible about the actions you wish to carry out over the Internet. If you create a schema and allow Updategrams to be posted, be aware that users can read and write any of the data that is viewable in the schema. This is a good reason why you should always use templates with parameters whenever possible, since this allows you to specify which fields you want to be read-only, and which fields users should be able to write to. You can also include your own authentication with this type of method.

Troubleshooting

If your SQLXML virtual directory is not working, you can run through the following section to determine what the problem is and how to fix it. First, try running through steps one through four which will help you verify that your SQLXML is set up properly. Step five lists problems that occur with properly set up virtual directories. The final section lists some debugging tools, which are essential when trying to debug a SQLXML problem.

Step 1—Turn off Friendly Error Messages in Internet Explorer

IE has a feature that hides HTTP error messages. This is a nice feature for people who would only get confused by these messages. However, when you're working with SQLXML or any other web technology, you need to see error messages. To turn this feature off go to **Tools | Internet Options | Advanced**. Uncheck **Show friendly HTTP error messages**. Once you have done this, you should get a more detailed message, which will help point you to the real problem.

Architecture and Setup

Step 2—Verify That IIS is Working Properly

The next step is to make sure that IIS is actually working. The easiest method to check your IIS setup is to open http://localhost in the browser. If you can't connect to the local web server, then make sure that you have installed IIS and that it is running. If you're having problems with IIS, skip down to the section on *Debugging Tools*, which gives a quick explanation on how to use IIS logging to debug your IIS problems.

Step 3—Use a New Virtual Directory

Many of the problems that occur with SQLXML virtual directories are caused by editing their properties with a tool other than the SQLXML VDM. If you use the IIS management tool to edit the setting of a virtual directory, you can break it. To rule out these types of problem, make sure you create a new virtual directory as shown earlier in the chapter. If you can get the new virtual directory to work but are having problems with an older one, try deleting the old one and then recreating it.

Step 4—Run the Version Test

If your virtual directory does not have URL queries turned on, go ahead and turn them on to run this test. Once you are done with the test, you can turn them back off. When you have turned them on, open the following URL in your browser:

http://localhost/nwind?sql=select @@version

When this query runs, you should see something similar to the following in your browser:

Microsoft SQL Server 2000 - 8.00.534 (Intel X86) Nov 19 2001 13:23:50
Copyright (c) 1988-2000 Microsoft Corporation Developer Edition on Windows NT 5.1 (Build 2600:)

If you do, then your virtual directory is working. When you are done with this test, make sure you turn URL queries off again. If you get an error at this point skip down to *Debugging Tools* and take a look at IIS logging and SQL Trace.

Step 5—Other SQLXML Problems

If you're using a template or schema, make sure that you have mapped the folder as the correct type. Double-check the virtual name that you chose and make sure you are using that name in the URL. Check to make sure that all other files that are referenced, such as XSL files, are using the correct paths. Also, make sure your template is using the correct namespace (urn:schemas-microsoft-com:xml-sql).

If you're still having trouble getting things going, head over to the Microsoft SQLXML newsgroup, which is a great resource for solving any SQLXML problem It and can be found at:

news://msnews.microsoft.com/microsoft.public.sqlserver.xml

55

Chapter 2

Debugging Tools

Here we list and describe some debugging tools that will help you to debug any SQLXML problems that you may encounter.

SQL Profiler

This program allows you to run a trace that will let you see everything that is passed into SQL Server. This is very useful for debugging SQLXML problems. If you try to open an URL and nothing shows up in the SQL trace, then the problem isn't with SQL Server. If nothing is showing up in the trace then you should move on to check the IIS logs. SQL Profiler is also helpful for debugging XML and XDR schemas, since it allows you to see the FOR XML EXPLICIT query that is generated by the schema.

You can see the profiler in use doing just this in Chapter 8.

IIS Logging

IIS logging is turned on by default, but if not, you can check in the IIS management tool by looking at the properties of your web site. The IIS logs are found in the LogFiles folder, which is in the system32 folder. Each web site will have its own folder in the LogFiles folder. In each folder you will find a number of log files, and on opening up the most recent file in Notepad, you should see some requests. For instance, for each URL query that you tried to run you should see something like the following:

    23:32:26 127.0.0.1 GET /nwind 200
    23:48:14 127.0.0.1 GET /nwind 200

If you don't see any activity, then your requests are not being passed to IIS. Make sure that IIS is installed and running.

Query Analyzer

Query Analyzer is a great tool for looking into SQLXML problems. If you're trying to run an URL query and it isn't working, try running the same SQL statement in Query Analyzer. This is useful, because often the initial error message can be obscured by subsequent errors. For example, if SQLXML is returning an XML document, the XML document might not be well-formed if an error occurred while running the T-SQL that produced it. However, you will only see the error message about the badly formed XML, which isn't really the problem.

Summary

In this chapter we have taken an overview of the XML support provided both within SQL Server and within the SQLXML web releases. Our focus was on the SQLXML web releases, looking at what features are contained within the latest release, and what benefits they provide for the developer or DBA.

We then moved on to look at installing SQLXML, including security considerations, and we set up a SQLXML virtual directory, which will be used in the examples found in several of the subsequent chapters. Our final section looked at the tools available for debugging any problems you may encounter in using a virtual directory.

Don't forget to turn off those URL queries before moving on to consider how we can map data from a database to XML, which is the topic of the next chapter.

Kevin Williams

- Considerations When Mapping Data
- XML Schemas vs. XML-Data Reduced Schemas
- Equivalent XML Datatypes
- Design Approach
- Implementation
- Inventory Example
- Summary

3

Mapping SQL Server to XML

In this chapter, we'll be taking a look at some techniques used to map data from a SQL Server database to XML. We'll see how SQL Server data types map to XML Schema datatypes, and how we can best represent complex relationships in our relational database within a hierarchical XML document. Finally, we'll see examples of extracting data from the database using SELECT FOR XML EXPLICIT and we'll then run through a case study that puts it all together.

Considerations When Mapping Data

Before beginning the XML document design process, we need to examine the business requirements driving the design and take them into account. In any XML analysis process, it's critically important to make sure you have a comprehensive understanding of the role the created XML document is to play in your system architecture. Will the document be used to drive presentation, or will it be used to share information with other companies? Does the document need to be standalone, or can it rely on other information being available? Depending on the role the extracted XML document is to play in our overall design, we can make some immediate decisions up front that will help govern the approach we take to our XML document design.

Standards Support

The most obvious consideration is standards support. If the XML design needs to support a particular standard (such as ebXML, or simply an agreed-upon document structure used to share data between applications), the extracted data must be shaped to fit the standard. This can influence relatively major decisions, such as whether to use elements or attributes for data, as well as minor decisions, such as the unit types, or data points, for individual values represented in the document (for example, does a particular value represent meters or feet?).

Chapter 3

It would generally be a mistake, however, to design your relational database to directly support these kinds of standards. Since standards are by their very nature generic, they are typically very good for flexible data transmission, but very bad for relational databases that support transactional systems directly. The relational database should be designed with the highest-volume operations in mind, which are typically the transactions that populate the database in the first place. A mapping process (either XSLT, a SQL Server view, or a stored procedure) can then transform the information in the database into the form required by the standard.

Let's look at an example. Say that you are designing a real estate site for potential real estate buyers to get information about properties that match their needs. You might have a table called `Property` that describes the information about each property that looks something like the following:

```
CREATE TABLE Property (
  propertyID int IDENTITY,
  address1 varchar(100),
  address2 varchar(100) NULL,
  city varchar(50),
  state char(2),
  postalCode varchar(10),
  lotSize float, /* this is in square feet */
  appraisedValue float)
```

After a while, your company decides to enter into an agreement with a partner firm (say a lender). You want to be able to exchange information about the property by transferring XML documents back and forth. The partner already has systems in place to support a particular XML format for properties that is somewhat normalized, uses different names and units, and looks like this:

```
<Property>
  <lot>1.52</lot>
  <apprValue>585000.00</apprValue>
  <Address>
      <street>762 Evergreen Terrace</street>
      <city>Springfield</city>
      <state>Va</state>
      <zip>25241</zip>
  </Address>
</Property>
```

Instead of reengineering your existing system to match this standard (and going through a costly redesign and recode effort), it will typically make more sense to use an XML view (see Chapter 7) or a FOR XML EXPLICIT query to modify the shape of the document to match the desired output. The following FOR XML EXPLICIT query would do this for us in our example:

```
SELECT 1 AS Tag,
    NULL AS Parent,
    NULL AS [Address!2!street!element],
    NULL AS [Address!2!city!element],
```

Mapping SQL Server to XML

```
        NULL AS [Address!2!state!element],
        NULL AS [Address!2!zip!element],
        'property' + CONVERT(varchar, propertyID)
        AS [Property!1!propertyID],
        CONVERT(decimal(9,2), lotSize / 43560)
        AS [Property!1!lot!element],
        CONVERT(decimal(9,2), appraisedValue)
        AS [Property!1!apprValue!element]
        FROM Property
UNION ALL
SELECT 2 AS Tag,
        1 AS Parent,
        address1 AS [Address!2!street!element],
        city AS [Address!2!city!element],
        state AS [Address!2!state!element],
        postalCode AS [Address!2!zip!element],
        'property' + CONVERT(varchar, propertyID) AS
[Property!1!propertyID],
            NULL AS [Property!1!lot!element],
            NULL AS [Property!1!apprValue!element]
            FROM Property
    ORDER BY [Property!1!propertyID], [Address!2!street!element]
```

Don't worry about the details of this query at present: FOR XML is covered in detail in the next chapter. For now, it is enough to understand that this query allows us to extract data from the database, and produce XML in the format we require for passing to our partner.

This approach may not work in a situation where most of the information manipulated by the system is arriving in the XML form mentioned above, since performance will suffer as documents are transformed to the native representation. In this case, you can consider retrofitting the code, but be aware that any reengineering effort has time and money costs associated with it.

Transmission

If one of the expected uses of the created XML document instances is to transmit data between systems, then many of the same concerns apply as if you were designing to a particular standard. In many cases, the systems participating in the data transaction already expect the information to be serialized to a particular XML format; in this case, you should handle the design process using the guidelines mentioned in the previous section. Also, issues of data security and privacy arise when transmitting XML data, particularly to partners outside your enterprise. Assuming for the moment that the transmission channel itself is secure (see **http://www.w3.org/Encryption/** for more details regarding new standards for document signature and encryption), there are concerns about the use of the information once it reaches the trading partner. Is any of the data that could possibly be transmitted sensitive? Do any of the data (especially inscrutable values like identifiers) lose their meaning once they leave your enterprise?

Often, the best approach when designing XML documents for transmission is to step into the shoes of the programmers who will be consuming the document. Does the document provide them with everything they need to take action? Is the document self-contained, or does it rely on external information, such as additional descriptive documents (for looking up identification codes) to clarify the data?

Here's an example. Say you are a widget manufacturer and you want to transmit your catalog information to one of your trading partners. You might have a Part table in your database that looks like this:

```
CREATE TABLE Part (
   partCode int,
   sizeCode tinyint,
   colorCode tinyint,
   description varchar(200))
```

However, your trading partner isn't going to know what sizeCode 157 is, necessarily, or colorCode 23. Instead, you should think about creating enumerated values in your XML documents that explain these fields in human-readable terms:

```
<Part
   partID="part217"
   size="2-inch"
   color="Blue"
   description="Threaded widgets" />
```

This will make the document a bit larger, but it may be worth it to make development turnaround and maintenance quicker and easier. This also fits well with the "make the document self-contained" rule; in other words, that the document contains all of the information necessary to completely describe the various elements in the document.

Presentation

When using XML documents to drive a presentation layer (such as an XSL transform to HTML or WML), the first and foremost consideration needs to be the information to be shown by the presentation layer. While your XML document shouldn't contain specific formatting instructions (part name is bold, part price is a column in a table, and so on), it should be organized in such a way that it supports the presentation layer well. This can include:

- Serializing content in the right order.
- Ensuring that the units on the data points are right before styling for presentation. Since XSLT is not good at performing arithmetic expressions, we should make sure that, if appropriate, our lot size is expressed in acres rather than square feet at document creation time.
- Aggregating data up or pushing data down (repeating it) in the XML hierarchy.

The reasoning behind this is simply that SQL Server is generally good at manipulating the structure of a relational data hierarchy, while XSLT isn't. Typically, this means that you should get the data as close to the presentation form as possible, and make the XSLT be responsible only for adding the formatting tags and other structural information. It follows from this approach that, rather than trying to drive several different presentation structures from the same XML document, you should instead be willing to create a different XML document to support each presentation structure (here, we're talking about business structure, not destination platform). Doing so ensures that you take advantage of SQL Server's strong data manipulation facilities and don't rely on the relatively computationally expensive XSLT to handle the restructuring and manipulation of your data. The additional benefit is that you only create data in the XML document that you need; if you try to share XML documents across presentation structures then you end up eating up processor time and bandwidth serializing data that you won't necessarily use.

For example, in the real estate system we mentioned, we might want to have two presentation structures: one that lists all of the properties in a particular postal code, and another that lists detailed information about a single property. The temptation might be to export all the data for all the properties in a particular postal code; or, even worse, to export all the data for all the properties in the system. This would enable the same XML document to drive more than one presentation structure, and might at first glance seem to be a better approach. However, the list of properties will likely only include the most basic information about the property, such as its address, the list price, size in square feet, and so on. If we serialize all the property information (down to whether the property has a vacuum cleaner or not) into the XML document, we have wasted a great number of SQL Server cycles and parse cycles just to acquire, then discard, all that information (not to mention the extra memory footprint required to parse the document). Similarly, if we choose to use the same document to drive our detail screen, then we need to discard the information for all the properties other than the one selected.

A better approach would be to create two different XML documents, each of which contains just the data required to drive the particular presentation layer with which it is associated. This allows us to avoid the serialization of data that we don't need, and shape the data as precisely as possible to make our styling task as easy as possible.

Archival

Unlike SQL Server database dumps or flat file exports, XML archive documents can be accessed via a broad range of software, making them very useful in a business environment. When designing XML documents for archiving, the key consideration is the usefulness of the archived data. When the irate customer calls five years from now demanding to know how many two-inch blue grommets they've ordered since 1997, you want to be able to access the information as easily as possible. This has a couple of implications for design.

First, it's important that XML documents used for archival purposes be as complete as possible. As we all know, systems change, internal identifiers change, and personnel change; so when archived information needs to be retrieved, it shouldn't rely on external information to be interpreted.

Second, the XML archive should be designed to directly support the way the archive will be accessed. This may entail storing information more than one way. For example, it may be common for your customers to request summary information over a particular time period (how many grommets did I order last year?), but much less common to request detailed information (how many grommets did I order on January 12th to be delivered to our Birmingham plant?). A good archival strategy in this case might be to archive the data two different ways: summarized into XML documents by customer by month, stored in a quickly accessible form (such as on optical media), and detailed by invoice (stored offline on tape backup). Once information has been persisted to XML it is notoriously difficult to manipulate, especially when aggregation across documents or similar functionality is required; so it always makes sense to store the data in the form that best supports the anticipated archival access pattern. When designing an archival strategy, you should try to forecast these requirements and design your storage structures accordingly.

XML Schemas vs. XML-Data Reduced Schemas

In this chapter (and throughout this book), we are choosing to focus on the use of the XML Schema document definition language for the creation of XML document structures. Many implementations already use a document definition language known as **XML-Data Reduced**, or **XDR**. This language was developed by Microsoft for use with its BizTalk Server, and has been in use since before the XML Schema specification was promoted to Recommendation status. The XDR specification is gradually being phased out by Microsoft in favor of the XML Schema Recommendation, which it helped to develop.

So which of these two should you use? Unless you have some prior reason not to, you should definitely use XML schemas, due to their good cross-sectional support (as opposed to XDR schemas), and XDR schemas are likely to be deprecated over time. The primary reason not to move to XML schemas would be if you have existing XDR schemas in production, or if you need to maintain compatibility with other systems that rely on them.

For new development, you should try to use XML schemas rather than XDR schemas if at all possible. If you have to create XDR schemas for legacy reasons, the techniques covered in this chapter will work equally well for the creation of XDR schemas; only the specific syntax will be different.

> You can find more information about XML schemas in Appendix B and at http://www.w3.org/XML/Schema. Chapter 6 explains how to annotate them for use with relational databases.

Mapping SQL Server to XML

Equivalent XML Datatypes

Before we dive into the design approach we're going to use when moving data from a relational database to XML, we first need to take a look at the built-in types in SQL Server and how they map to XML Schema datatypes. It's important that schemas generated from a relational database are strongly typed if they are to be used to bring information into the database; this guarantees that information stored in an XML instance conforming to the schema will also conform to the rules governing the database content. The following table summarizes which datatypes in the XML Schema Recommendation correspond to SQL Server data types:

SQL Server data type	Equivalent XML Schema datatype
bigint	long
int	int
smallint	short
tinyint	byte
bit	boolean
decimal(p, s) numeric(p, s)	decimal with restrictions (see below)
money	decimal with restrictions (see below)
smallmoney	decimal with restrictions (see below)
float(n)	double with restrictions (see below)
real	float with restrictions (see below)
datetime	dateTime with restrictions (see below)
smalldatetime	dateTime with restrictions (see below)
char	string with restrictions (see below)
varchar	string with restrictions (see below)
text	string with restrictions (see below)
nchar	string with restrictions (see below)
nvarchar	string with restrictions (see below)
ntext	string with restrictions (see below)
binary	base64Binary or hexBinary (see below)
varbinary	base64Binary or hexBinary (see below)
image	base64Binary or hexBinary (see below)

Table continued on following page

Chapter 3

SQL Server data type	Equivalent XML Schema datatype
sql_variant	string (see below)
timestamp	string (see below)
uniqueidentifier	string with restrictions (see below)

Now let's consider some specific issues you need to keep in mind when moving data programmatically between these various data types.

In the following examples, you'll see several XML Schema elements and attributes, denoted by the xsd: *namespace prefix, in action. This prefix is used to denote the* XMLSchema *namespace, described in Appendix B.*

decimal/numeric

When using the decimal or numeric SQL Server data types, you need to include restrictions on the decimal datatype in your XML schema. Specifically, you need to set the totalDigits restriction to be the total number of digits allowed in the decimal, and the fractionDigits to be the number of places beyond the decimal point. Here are a couple of examples:

```
InterestRate decimal(5,2)
```

maps to:

```
<xsd:element name="interestRate">
  <xsd:simpleType>
    <xsd:restriction base="xsd:decimal">
      <xsd:totalDigits value="5" />
      <xsd:fractionDigits value="2" />
    </xsd:restriction>
  </xsd:simpleType>
</xsd:element>
```

and:

```
AreaInSquareFeet decimal(7,0)
```

maps to:

```
<xsd:element name="areaInSquareFeet">
  <xsd:simpleType>
    <xsd:restriction base="xsd:decimal">
      <xsd:totalDigits value="7" />
      <xsd:fractionDigits value="0" />
    </xsd:restriction>
  </xsd:simpleType>
</xsd:element>
```

money

In the case of the `money` SQL Server type, we need to put some restrictions on the XML `decimal` type to ensure that the allowable values match what is allowed by `money`. Specifically, we need to constrain both the precision and scale, as well as the maximum and minimum values allowed. For this, as for many SQL Server types, you would be well served to create your own complex types by restriction in your XML document, and reuse them as necessary. Take the following example:

```
AppraisedValue money
```

that maps to:

```xml
<xsd:element name="appraisedValue">
  <xsd:simpleType>
    <xsd:restriction base="xsd:decimal">
      <xsd:totalDigits value="19" />
      <xsd:fractionDigits value="4" />
      <xsd:minInclusive value="-922337203685477.5808" />
      <xsd:maxInclusive value="922337203685477.5807" />
    </xsd:restriction>
  </xsd:simpleType>
</xsd:element>
```

For the sake of brevity, we can create a named simple type, in this case effectively a user-defined datatype that we can reuse:

```xml
<xsd:simpleType name="money">
    <xsd:restriction base="xsd:decimal">
      <xsd:totalDigits value="19" />
      <xsd:fractionDigits value="4" />
      <xsd:minInclusive value="-922337203685477.5808" />
      <xsd:maxInclusive value="922337203685477.5807" />
    </xsd:restriction>
</xsd:simpleType>
<xsd:element name="appraisedValue" type="money" />
```

You can read more about simple and complex types in Appendix B.

smallmoney

Like `money`, `smallmoney` requires us to restrict the XML Schema type `decimal` to ensure that we don't permit a value that SQL Server can't store. For example, in the case of the SQL field:

```
MonthlyPayment smallmoney
```

the appropriate XML schema declaration is this:

```xml
<xsd:simpleType name="smallmoney">
   <xsd:restriction base="xsd:decimal">
      <xsd:totalDigits value="10" />
      <xsd:fractionDigits value="4" />
      <xsd:minInclusive value="-214748.3648" />
      <xsd:maxInclusive value="214748.3647" />
   </xsd:restriction>
</xsd:simpleType>
<xsd:element name="monthlyPayment" type="smallmoney" />
```

float

The `float` data type in SQL Server turns out to be one of the more problematic data types to map to XML. This is because the closest XML Schema datatype (`double`) has a mantissa (number of significant figures) that is fixed at 53 bits, leaving 11 bits for the exponent; on the other hand, the `float` datatype can take a parameter that allows the number of bits in the mantissa to be finely controlled. Also, the range of the exponent in the XML Schema representation is -1075 to 970, while the `float` datatype can potentially allow exponents to be much higher (as many as 39 depending on the number of bits allocated to the exponent). This restriction will only affect your data mapping if you are working with extremely large numbers or extremely small numbers. If this is an absolute need, you can always map the data field to `string`, but you run the risk, for example, of a valid document asserting that the number of hydrogen atoms in the universe is "purple". Under other circumstances, you can simply map directly to the `double` type.

Here's an example:

```
runTimeInSeconds float
```

maps to:

```xml
<xsd:element name="interestRate" type="xsd:double" />
```

real

Like the `float` data type, the `real` data type doesn't have a direct match in XML Schemas but the closest match is the `float` datatype in the XML Schema Recommendation (getting confused yet?) The number of bits in the mantissa is the same (24) and, while the exponents may not map directly, it will only be an issue if you are working with extremely large or extremely small numbers (see the discussion of the float data type above). Otherwise, mapping `real` to `float` works just fine:

```
pi real
```

maps to:

```xml
<xsd:element name="pi" type="xsd:float" />
```

Mapping SQL Server to XML

datetime

The `datetime` SQL Server type maps directly to the `dateTime` XML Schema data type. There are a couple of things to watch for, though:

- you will probably want to add restrictions to the `dateTime` declaration, as it permits dates that fall outside the normal `datetime` range. For example, `dateTime`s in an XML schema allow dates prior to January 1, 1753.
- when creating XML documents with `dateTime` elements or attributes, the `datetime` needs to be formatted as follows:

    CCYY-MM-DDThh:mm:ss[.sss]

followed by an optional Z for Greenwich Mean Time or time zone offset in the form [+|-]hh:mm. If you are using XML Views or FOR XML EXPLICIT to extract the data from the database, SQL Server handles this conversion for you:

```
ApplicationReceivedDate datetime
```

maps to:

```
<xsd:simpleType name="sqldatetime">
    <xsd:restriction base="xsd:dateTime">
        <xsd:minInclusive value="1753-01-01T00:00:00" />
        <xsd:maxInclusive value="9999-12-31T23:59:59" />
    </xsd:restriction>
</xsd:simpleType>
<xsd:element name="applicationReceivedDate"
             type="sqldatetime" />
```

smalldatetime

The `smalldatetime` data type also maps to the `dateTime` XML Schema type; in this instance, the restrictions are simply more stringent:

```
PaymentDueDate smalldatetime
```

maps to:

```
<xsd:simpleType name="smalldatetime">
    <xsd:restriction base="xsd:dateTime">
        <xsd:minInclusive value="1900-01-01T00:00:00" />
        <xsd:maxInclusive value="2079-06-06T23:59:00" />
    </xsd:restriction>
</xsd:simpleType>
<xsd:element name="applicationReceivedDate"
             type="smalldatetime" />
```

Note that if a value is stored with seconds, `smalldatetime` will discard them when the value is moved to SQL Server. If this really bothers you, you can add a regular expression restriction that prevents seconds from being included in the value, but that goes beyond the scope of our discussion here.

char

The simplest way to represent a fixed-length character string in an XML schema is by using a `string` value with the `length` restriction set. This ensures that exactly that many characters will appear in the element or attribute's value. For example, the following field:

```
PostalCode char(10)
```

maps to:

```
<xsd:element name="postalCode">
  <xsd:simpleType>
    <xsd:restriction base="xsd:string">
      <xsd:length value="10" />
    </xsd:restriction>
  </xsd:simpleType>
</xsd:element>
```

varchar

Like `char`, `varchar` maps to the `string` XML Schema type; however, instead of using the `length` restriction, we use the `maxLength` restriction:

```
Name varchar(50)
```

maps to:

```
<xsd:element name="name">
  <xsd:simpleType>
    <xsd:restriction base="xsd:string">
      <xsd:maxLength value="50" />
    </xsd:restriction>
  </xsd:simpleType>
</xsd:element>
```

text

Fields with the `text` data type are like fields with the `varchar` data type, except that the maximum length is fixed at 2,147,483,647 bytes. We can represent this the same way we did `varchar` (except that in this example, we'll create a simple type with the appropriate length restriction):

```
OtherInfo text
```

Mapping SQL Server to XML

maps to:

```
<xsd:simpleType name="text">
    <xsd:restriction base="xsd:string">
        <xsd:maxLength value="2147483647" />
    </xsd:restriction>
</xsd:simpleType>
<xsd:element name="otherInfo" type="text" />
```

nchar, nvarchar, ntext

These Unicode representations of text are handled much like their `text` counterparts, except that the `ntext` data type has a maximum length of 1,073,741,823 characters.

> Note that XML Schema doesn't have specific types for 8-bit character sets and 16-bit character sets; instead, the allowable characters in an element or attribute are governed by the encoding on the document.

This means that if you want to serialize Unicode strings to an XML document, you need only to ensure that the encoding of the target document will allow those strings to be properly represented there. If you use `FOR XML EXPLICIT` or an XML view to extract the data, this will be handled for you.

binary

Since binary content may contain values that do not conform to the XML encoding type, or may contain codes that are interpreted as markup, it's important to change the binary content to a form that can peacefully exist inside an XML instance. In this regard you have a couple of choices for serializing binary content in an XML document. One choice is to hex-encode the content; when you do this, each byte of the content is represented as a two-byte hex code (from 00 to FF) in the resulting XML. If you prefer, you can base-64 encode the byte content; in this encoding, each three bytes in the source are represented as four bytes in the resulting XML document.

> *In base-64 encoding: each 24-bit sequence is split into four six-bit sequences and then mapped onto a string of 64 printable characters (the alphabet upper and lower case, the ten digits, the minus sign and the underscore) and those four characters are serialized to the destination document.*

Base-64 encoding is always the better choice from a serialized length perspective, since the resulting string in bytes is 133% of the original size, versus 200% for hex encoding. But if the receiving system cannot understand base-64 encoding, then hex encoding may be your only choice. A base-64 encoded binary field is represented with the XML Schema type `base64Binary`, while a hex-encoded binary field is represented by `hexBinary`.

71

Chapter 3

Here's an example:

```
PublicKey binary(15)
```

maps to:

```xml
<xsd:element name="publicKey">
  <xsd:simpleType>
    <xsd:restriction base="xsd:base64Binary">
      <xsd:length value="20" />
    </xsd:restriction>
  </xsd:simpleType>
</xsd:element>
```

or:

```xml
<xsd:element name="publicKey">
  <xsd:simpleType>
    <xsd:restriction base="xsd:hexBinary">
      <xsd:length value="30" />
    </xsd:restriction>
  </xsd:simpleType>
</xsd:element>
```

> Note that the `length` constraint maps to the number of encoded characters in the target string, not the number of bytes in the original binary value! This is important to keep in mind when designing structures to hold binary information.

varbinary

Like `binary`, `varbinary` can be encoded either using `base64Binary` or `hexBinary` on the XML schema side. As with `varchar`, however, we need to restrict the `maxLength` of the binary, not just the `length`:

```
AccessValue varbinary(200)
```

maps to:

```xml
<xsd:element name="publicKey">
  <xsd:simpleType>
    <xsd:restriction base="xsd:base64Binary">
      <xsd:maxLength value="268" />
    </xsd:restriction>
  </xsd:simpleType>
</xsd:element>
```

Mapping SQL Server to XML

Don't be confused by the length attribute here; in base-64 encoding, each three characters in the source document are mapped to four characters in the destination document. If the length of the original document isn't exactly divisible by three, then it is padded with blank information to make the bit count exactly 24 at the end of the encoding process. The resulting encoding length must actually accommodate 201 characters, not 200; hence the 268 declared for the length in this case.

image

The `image` SQL Server type is like the `text` SQL Server type, in that it allows binary strings up to a particular maximum size to be created. Again, we can emulate this using either `base64Binary` or `hexBinary` with a `maxLength` restriction imposed:

```
RealtorImage image
```

maps to:

```
<xsd:simpleType name="image">
    <xsd:restriction base="xsd:base64Binary">
        <xsd:maxLength value="2863311532" />
    </xsd:restriction>
</xsd:simpleType>
<xsd:element name="realtorImage" type="image" />
```

sql_variant

Assuming that you've managed to create a structure that includes the `sql_variant` type (which of course you should be trying to avoid at all costs because it is runtime-typed), there's no simple way to represent it in an XML Schema. While field declarations are strongly typed, there's no mechanism provided to assign a data type directly to a value; so the best you can do is set it to be the XML Schema type `string`. Unfortunately, this means you won't be able to tell the difference between the `integer` 17, the `float` 17, and the `string` 17.

timestamp

This data type in SQL Server is represented internally by an eight-byte binary value. However, when SQL Server exposes it either through FOR XML EXPLICIT or via an XML View, it will be converted to an eight-byte integral value. To represent this properly in your XML document, you should then use the XML Schema type `long`. Here's an example:

```
LastUpdated timestamp
```

maps to:

```
<xsd:element name="lastUpdated" type="xsd:long" />
```

uniqueidentifier

Finally, SQL Server provides a way to automatically create or store **Globally Unique Identifiers** (**GUID**s) in your XML documents. These always take the form:

NNNNNNNN-NNNN-NNNN-NNNN-NNNNNNNNNNNN

where each N is a hex digit from 0 to F (note that the hyphens actually appear in the field, and are a part of the globally unique identifier). These can be represented in an XML schema by using the `string` datatype with some restrictions, including a regular expression restriction, as in the following example:

```
ObjectId uniqueidentifier
```

maps to:

```
<xsd:simpleType name="uniqueidentifier">
    <xsd:restriction base="xsd:string">
        <xsd:length value="36" />
        <xsd:pattern value="[0-9A-F]{8}-[0-9A-F]{4}-[0-9A-F]
                            {4}-[0-9A-F]{4}-[0-9A-F]{12}" />
    </xsd:restriction>
</xsd:simpleType>
<xsd:element name="objectId" type="uniqueidentifier" />
```

Now that we know how to represent all of the possible SQL Server data types in corresponding XML Schema datatypes, let's see how we approach framing the rest of the XML schema structure.

Design Approach

A design methodology for deriving appropriate XML schemas from SQL Server structures consists of several steps. First, we need to identify the relevant information in the database: what pieces of information need to be represented in our XML document? This will depend largely on the purpose of the document, as we stated earlier in the chapter. Second, we need to shape the overall structure of the document, building our elements and relationships to accurately reflect the relationships between the information in the source database. Finally, we need to map the actual columns into their appropriate elements, based on the data type mappings we just established in the previous section. Let's take a look at each step in this process in turn.

Identification of Relevant Information

First, we need to identify what pieces of information need to be represented in the XML document. This analysis takes place at a column level, rather than at a row level, since we're interested in what kind of information will appear in the document. Row-level decisions for the inclusion or exclusion of data are made when each document is created, and determine which specific instances of that information occur.

We've already seen some criteria for making these decisions, such as whether the document is to be used for presentation purposes, and what information appears in the presentation layer that needs to be provided? If the document is used archivally, what information will be relevant to the retrieval process later?

Once the analysis has been performed on the source database and the columns containing information to be included have been identified, the next step is to decide how the overall element structure in the document will look.

Design of XML Document Overall Structure

The first step is to identify the root element for the structure. Loosely speaking, this is the table in the relational database that most closely corresponds to the information type you are representing in your document. For example, if you were designing an XML document to support a property detail page in a real estate system, you might choose the `Property` table as your starting point. If your XML design were intended to archive information about a borrower, you would choose the `Borrower` table as your starting point. Note that this doesn't have to correspond to a single row; it's perfectly permissible to create an XML document that contains, for example, information about all properties in a particular postal code. If you choose to do this, however, you'll simply need to create an additional root element that will contain each of the properties. For example, the following document would support a single property definition:

```
<property>
    ... property information ...
</property>
```

Whereas this example would support multiple Property definitions within a single document:

```
<properties>
  <property>
     ... property information ...
  </property>
  <property>
     ... property information ...
  </property>
  ...
</properties>
```

Once you've established this starting point, you will move through the relational structure to determine the other structural elements that need to appear in the XML document, as we'll see a little later.

Sequence, Choice, or All?

One decision that needs to be made at this point is whether the content of elements in the created XML document will be organized using the `<xsd:sequence>`, `<xsd:choice>`, or `<xsd:all>` model groups.

Since we are mapping from a relational database, the answer is clearly based on the restrictions imposed by the XML Schema Recommendation. The `<xsd:all>` model group does not allow multiple instances of elements to appear; so if we wanted to model one invoice with several line items, we could not use `<xsd:all>` to do so. Similarly, the `<xsd:choice>` model group only allows us to include one item from a list of possible items, which is not appropriate for our purposes. Therefore, our model groups will always be described in terms of `<xsd:sequence>` model groups (Remember that in an `<xsd:sequence>` group, each declared sub-element must be satisfied and in the order given).

If you choose to use elements to model data points (we'll learn more about this in the *Mapping Column Values* section below), you can include the data point elements in an `<xsd:all>` model group, rather than an `<xsd:sequence>` model group, since data points won't appear more than once. The `<xsd:all>` model group is acceptable for these purposes, since it allows you to include the actual data points in any order you like while ensuring that the structural elements themselves would still be ordered. In our examples, we'll be using the `<xsd:sequence>` model group exclusively.

Understanding Foreign Key Relationships

In SQL Server, a foreign key relationship is simply a way of representing, through data, a one-to-one or one-to-many relationship between two tables. The foreign key itself does not indicate the cardinality of the relationship; rather, the logical model of your database (you do have a logical model, don't you?) should indicate this. Foreign key relationships are **directed**; that is, the order in which they are examined matters. For example, in the following relationship (which is one-to-many in our logical model):

```
CREATE TABLE Invoice (
   invoiceID int identity,
   customerName varchar(200))

CREATE TABLE LineItem (
   lineItemID int identity,
   invoiceID int
     FOREIGN KEY REFERENCES Invoice(InvoiceID),
   partName varchar(100))
```

the relationship can be said to be one-to-many when moving from `Invoice` to `LineItem`, or many-to-one when moving from `LineItem` to `Invoice`. This becomes important when we start to lay out our XML structure.

To determine which elements need to appear inside other elements, we need to "walk the structure". This means we need to start at the table that corresponds to our root element, which will either be represented as the root element of our XML structure, or one element down (if it may appear more than once) and, traversing relationships through the tree, create an element for every table that includes columns we're interested in. (If this sounds a little confusing, don't worry; the example at the end of the chapter will make it crystal clear).

Mapping SQL Server to XML

For each relationship that gets traversed in this way, we need to determine its cardinality and create the appropriate structure in XML. If the relationship is one-to-one or one-to-many, then the relationship will be represented in the XML document as a parent/child relationship. If the relationship is many-to-one (remember, the direction of the evaluation matters!), then we represent the relationship using an `IDREF` attribute, which we'll learn about next.

Proper Usage of ID-IDREF Relationships

The `ID-IDREF` relationship in XML is a way to relate two XML elements without requiring them to be ancestors or descendants of one another. This allows relationships that are more complex than simple hierarchies to be correctly represented. For example, say we have the following element structure:

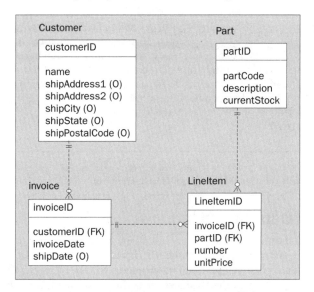

Say that we have decided that the document needs to represent a single customer's order history, including detailed information about all of the customer's invoices. We start at the `<customer>` element (since it best corresponds to the information we are trying to convey). We then navigate to the `<invoice>` element; since this is one-to-many, we can represent `<invoice>` as a sub-element of `<customer>`. The same applies for the invoice-lineItem relationship, namely that `<lineItem>` should be a child of `<invoice>`. However, when we try to navigate from `<lineItem>` to `<part>`, that relationship is many-to-one, since one part may appear in many Line items. We shouldn't represent this using another parent/child relationship since, if the customer has ordered the same part on all twelve orders they have ever placed, the part information would have to be repeated twelve times! Instead, we need to include the `<part>` elements somewhere else, and then use an `IDREF` attribute to reference those elements:

```
<customer>
  <invoice>
    <lineitem partIDREF="p1" />
```

77

```
            <lineitem partIDREF="p2" />
        </invoice>
        <part partID="p1" />
        <part partID="p2" />
    </customer>
```

Unfortunately, relationships expressed this way tend to be computationally expensive. If you are parsing a document like this using the DOM, it must navigate through the entire list of elements looking for one with an `ID` attribute that matches the `IDREF` attribute given, which is slightly slower than providing the information as a direct child of the parent element. With a streaming parser like SAX or the .NET `XmlTextReader`, the problem's even worse; if the `partIDREF` happens to reference a `partID` that's already been streamed through the parse window, then the software driving the parser will either need to cache this information for later use (defeating the whole purpose of the small-footprint streaming XML parser) or parse the document again. Either way, performance will suffer significantly. Another approach to these sorts of issues is to actually repeat the part information in each line item where it should appear, though this will increase the document size and hence the parse times and memory footprints. However, this is an acceptable solution if the system that is reading the document doesn't care that the blue widgets on invoice 1 and the blue widgets on invoice 2 are the "same" widgets (that is, if it doesn't need to correlate the two).

> Only use `IDREF` pointers if they are the only way you can represent important relationships in your XML documents.

Handling "Dangling" Elements

You'll notice that we put the `<part>` elements directly in the root of the `<customer>` element in our document structure. This is a decision that needs to be made whenever there are **dangling elements**, that is, elements that are only pointed to, and never explicitly declared as the children of other elements. After all, the elements need to appear in our structure somewhere! Usually, the best approach is to include them in the root element of the structure, but they can be included anywhere you like in the document.

Even though we used `ID` and `IDREF` values in our example, we could also have used the XML Schema-only concept of `<xsd:key>` and `<xsd:keyref>` values. These field types roughly correspond to `ID` and `IDREF`, and may be used to represent complex relationships in a similar fashion to `ID` and `IDREF`. However, if the designed structure needs to be backward compatible to DTDs, then you should use `ID` and `IDREF` attributes to make this connection.

Mapping Column Values

Now that we have derived the element structure representing the shape of our XML document, we need to add the data points to it. This means we need to take those columns we identified in the first step of this process, use the data type derivation process we discussed earlier, and produce XML content that can be added to our skeleton XML document structure.

First, though, we need to decide whether elements or attributes will be used to represent our individual points of information. This is a subject that's been covered extensively in other places, so it will suffice to say here that, when working with data, attributes have several advantages over elements for data points:

- Documents using attributes are smaller than documents using elements.
- Attributes are not constrained to appear in any particular order, while elements can be.
- Documents using attributes are easier to parse with processing technologies like the DOM or SAX, since attributes are associated directly with the element to which they belong, and require one less tree node traversal to access than elements.

There are only a couple of reasons you might want to use elements to represent data rather than attributes. If you are designing your XML document to conform to a particular standard or platform that requires that data points be stored as elements, then that may influence your decision. Also, if you happen to have information that needs to be annotated (such as a monetary value with a currency type), you may need to use elements (because you can't annotate attributes with attributes). Some arguments would have it that using elements instead of attributes to represent data points makes the schema easier to extend, but the reality is that any schema change is going to require code changes regardless of whether an element value is extended or an attribute value is added.

You can read more about annotating schemas in Chapter 6.

The techniques we have learned in this chapter are equally applicable to data stored as elements and data stored as attributes; the simple types are then applied to element or attribute declarations as appropriate.

Converting Data Types

Next, we take each column that we want to represent in an XML document and map it to the appropriate XML Schema datatype, using the guidelines that we laid out earlier in the chapter. Whether we are using elements or attributes for our data points, we create simple types for each column and set the element or attribute's type appropriately.

Handling Constraints

If you have check constraints on your columns in SQL Server, you may be able to model those appropriately in the XML schema document. Specifically, check constraints will allow you to accurately model minima or maxima you place on fields. For example, given the following SQL:

```
CREATE TABLE employee (
  salary decimal(9, 2)
  CHECK (salary > 10000 AND salary < 300000))
```

Chapter 3

You can implement this by adding `<minExclusive>` and `<maxExclusive>` restrictions to your declaration in the XML schema:

```
<xsd:element name="salary">
  <xsd:simpleType>
    <xsd:restriction base="xsd:decimal">
      <xsd:totalDigits value="5" />
      <xsd:fractionDigits value="2" />
      <xsd:minExclusive value="10000" />
      <xsd:maxExclusive value="300000" />
    </xsd:restriction>
  </xsd:simpleType>
</xsd:element>
```

Unfortunately, more complex check constraints cannot be modeled directly in XML schemas; if you need to enforce these, your code will have to do so when you import the data.

Include or Exclude Identifiers

Another question has to be addressed at this point in the design. Most likely, your SQL Server tables include integer columns (perhaps `IDENTITY` columns) that uniquely identify records in each table. Should these identifiers be included in your XML schema design? Generally, the answer is no; remember that the rule of thumb is that the XML document should be complete and stand alone, and keys from the relational database usually aren't appropriate. An exception might be if you are integrating systems that all understand a particular set of keys, such as multiple applications that all run on the same SQL Server database backbone. In this case, it might make sense to include the keys.

A separate issue is whether the values should be included as `ID` attributes on your created elements. You should typically only include these attributes when you need to; that is, when you have an `IDREF` attribute elsewhere in the design that points to the element in question (as the result of walking a many-to-one relationship). Bear in mind, however, that two conditions need to be satisfied with `ID` attributes: they must be unique across an entire document, and they must begin with a letter or an underscore. With these guidelines in mind, then, one approach to creating usable `ID` attributes is to prefix the integer key with the name of the table, like this:

```
<customerData>
  <customer customerID="customer1" />
  <customer customerID="customer2" />
  <part partID="part1" />
  <part partID = "part3" />
</customerData>
```

Mapping SQL Server to XML

That way, the ID values won't collide (except in the case where you have tables with the same names, but different numeric suffixes, in your database), and the ID values will satisfy XML's constraints for those values. Of course, if you are creating structures that do not need to be backward compatible with DTDs and have chosen to use `<xsd:key>` and `<xsd:keyref>` to represent these relationships, you may use any key value you like (Chapter 6 has more details on this).

Handling NULL Values

The XML Schema Recommendation provides a mechanism to explicitly express NULL values in a document. By declaring an element with the attribute `nillable`, an instance can use the `xsi:nil` attribute (from the XML Schema instance namespace - see Appendix B for more on this) to indicate that the element's value is actually NULL. Here's an example. Say we have the following table:

```
CREATE TABLE customer (
  customerFax varchar(15) NULL)
```

We can create a `nillable` field in our XML schema with this declaration:

```
<xsd:element name="customerFax" nillable="true">
  <xsd:simpleType>
    <xsd:restriction base="xsd:string">
      <xsd:maxLength value="15" />
    </xsd:restriction>
  </xsd:simpleType>
</xsd:element>
```

We then represent a NULL value in our document using `xsi:nil`, as in this example:

```
<customerFax xsi:nil="true"
    xmlns:xsi="http://www.w3.org/2001/XMLSchema-instance" />
```

Note that the explicit NULL declaration only works for elements, not attributes (since you can't associate an attribute with another attribute). When SQL Server exports a NULL value using FOR XML EXPLICIT or an XML View as an attribute, it simply omits the attribute from the generated XML altogether. Programmatically, this is no different from providing an empty string for the value. Unless you have a serious need to disambiguate a NULL value from an empty string (for example, to make the distinction on a middle name between "none" and "not provided"), you should avoid using this technique (and stick to attributes for data values).

Implementation

Finally, let's take a look at a couple of ways we can extract the data from our existing relational database into our new XML form. We won't dwell on this too much, since both XML Views and FOR XML EXPLICIT will be covered in much greater detail in later chapters; but the examples should be enough to give you an idea of how easy it is to generate XML from the database.

Chapter 3

Using an XML View to Create the XML Document

You can extract the data from the database using an annotated XML schema document. This allows you to apply XPath expression against the data as if it were exported in an XML schema form, either through the HTTP access to SQL Server or via ADO.NET. We'll learn more about using XML Views in Chapter 7.

Using FOR XML EXPLICIT to Create the XML Document

You can also use FOR XML EXPLICIT to synthesize the document from a specialized rowset generated by a query. Building up the rowset by performing a UNION together several different queries, then sorting the results so that the records appear in the rowset in the proper order, typically does this. We'll learn more about FOR XML EXPLICIT in Chapter 4.

Inventory Example

Let's take a look at an example that applies all of the techniques we've learned in this chapter. For this example, we will be working from an inventory database that has the following structure:

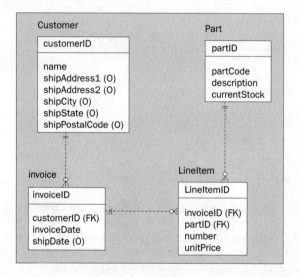

The DDL create script for this sample database can be found in the code download for this chapter, available at http://www.curlingstone.com/.

Design Goals

For the purposes of this example, we'd like to create an XML document to drive a transmission layer; in other words, an XML document that we can use to send information to other systems. We have identified a business need to generate customer invoice histories in XML to send electronically to our customers. Each invoice history should provide a detailed accounting of every invoice for a particular customer.

Mapping SQL Server to XML

Identifying the Relevant Information

First, we need to identify which pieces of information should be included in the document. We will include the customer name (but not the shipping address), as a check to make sure the customer has received the proper invoice history. We will then include the invoice date and the ship date for all invoices, as well as the number, price, part code, and description of each part ordered on that invoice. The following diagram shows the columns we are interested in (the relevant columns have asterisks next to them):

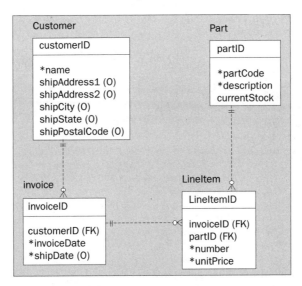

Designing the Document Structure

Next, let's go through the process of designing the document structure. Since we're conveying information about a single customer, it makes sense for us to use `<customer>` as our root element (and starting table in the design process):

```
<xsd:schema xmlns:xsd="http://www.w3.org/2001/XML-Schema">
    <xsd:element name="Customer" />
</xsd:schema>
```

Next, we have to walk through the relationships between the tables that contain data that will appear in our document. Starting from the `Customer` table, we walk through the relationship to the `Invoice` table. This relationship is one-to-many, so we add an `<Invoice>` child element to our `<Customer>` element:

```
<xsd:schema xmlns:xsd="http://www.w3.org/2001/XML-Schema">
    <xsd:element name="Customer">
        <xsd:complexType>
            <xsd:sequence>
                <xsd:element ref="Invoice" maxOccurs="unbounded" />
            </xsd:sequence>
        </xsd:complexType>
```

83

Chapter 3

```
    </xsd:element>
    <xsd:element name="Invoice" />
</xsd:schema>
```

From `Invoice`, we walk through the relationship to `LineItem`. This relationship is also one-to-many, so we create a `<LineItem>` child element as part of `<Invoice>`:

```
<xsd:schema xmlns:xsd="http://www.w3.org/2001/XML-Schema">
    <xsd:element name="Customer">
        <xsd:complexType>
            <xsd:sequence>
                <xsd:element ref="Invoice" maxOccurs="unbounded" />
            </xsd:sequence>
        </xsd:complexType>
    </xsd:element>
    <xsd:element name="Invoice">
        <xsd:complexType>
            <xsd:sequence>
                <xsd:element ref="LineItem"
                             minOccurs="1"
                             maxOccurs="unbounded" />
            </xsd:sequence>
        </xsd:complexType>
    </xsd:element>
    <xsd:element name="LineItem" />
</xsd:schema>
```

Finally, we walk through the relationship between `LineItem` and `Part`. However, this relationship is many-to-one (remember that it is walked from `LineItem` to `Part`), so we should use a pointing relationship to indicate which `<Part>` elements are related to which `<LineItem>` elements. Since `<Part>` elements will only be pointed to, we'll add them as children of our root (`<Customer>`) element:

```
<xsd:schema xmlns:xsd="http://www.w3.org/2001/XML-Schema">
    <xsd:element name="Customer">
        <xsd:complexType>
            <xsd:sequence>
                <xsd:element ref="Invoice" maxOccurs="unbounded" />
                <xsd:element ref="Part" maxOccurs="unbounded" />
            </xsd:sequence>
        </xsd:complexType>
    </xsd:element>
    <xsd:element name="Invoice">
        <xsd:complexType>
            <xsd:sequence>
                <xsd:element ref="LineItem" minOccurs="1"
                                            maxOccurs="unbounded" />
            </xsd:sequence>
        </xsd:complexType>
    </xsd:element>
    <xsd:element name="LineItem">
```

Mapping SQL Server to XML

```
      <xsd:complexType>
        <xsd:attribute name="partIDREF" type="xsd:IDREF" />
      </xsd:complexType>
    </xsd:element>
    <xsd:element name="Part">
      <xsd:complexType>
        <xsd:attribute name="partID" type="xsd:ID" />
      </xsd:complexType>
    </xsd:element>
</xsd:schema>
```

Now that we've got the element structure framed, we need to add the values that we identified in the previous section.

Mapping the Column Values

We have previously identified the following columns as information that belongs in our XML document:

```
Customer.name varchar(100)
Invoice.invoiceDate datetime
Invoice.shipDate datetime
LineItem.number smallint
LineItem.unitPrice smallmoney
Part.partCode char(10)
Part.description varchar(100)
```

Using our mapping table from before, we convert each of these to the appropriate XML Schema datatype. For restricted datatypes that we plan to reuse, we'll create `<xsd:simpleType>`s that contain the appropriate information. Each column is then added as an attribute at the appropriate place in the document structure. The completed schema specification for this document looks like this:

```
<xsd:schema xmlns:xsd="http://www.w3.org/2001/XML-Schema">
  <xsd:element name="Customer">
    <xsd:complexType>
      <xsd:sequence>
        <xsd:element ref="Invoice" maxOccurs="unbounded" />
        <xsd:element ref="Part" maxOccurs="unbounded" />
        <xsd:attribute name="name" type="varchar100" />
      </xsd:sequence>
    </xsd:complexType>
  </xsd:element>
  <xsd:element name="Invoice">
    <xsd:complexType>
      <xsd:sequence>
        <xsd:element ref="LineItem" minOccurs="1"
                                    maxOccurs="unbounded" />
        <xsd:attribute name="invoiceDate" type="sqldatetime" />
        <xsd:attribute name="shipDate" type="sqldatetime" />
      </xsd:sequence>
    </xsd:complexType>
```

```xml
    </xsd:element>
    <xsd:element name="LineItem">
      <xsd:complexType>
        <xsd:attribute name="partIDREF" type="xsd:IDREF" />
        <xsd:attribute name="number" type="xsd:short" />
        <xsd:attribute name="unitPrice" type="smallmoney" />
      </xsd:complexType>
    </xsd:element>
    <xsd:element name="Part">
      <xsd:complexType>
        <xsd:attribute name="partID" type="xsd:ID" />
        <xsd:attribute name="partCode" type="char10" />
        <xsd:attribute name="description" type="varchar100" />
      </xsd:complexType>
    </xsd:element>
    <xsd:simpleType name="varchar100">
      <xsd:restriction base="xsd:string">
        <xsd:maxLength value="100" />
      </xsd:restriction>
    </xsd:simpleType>
    <xsd:simpleType name="char10">
      <xsd:restriction base="xsd:string">
        <xsd:length value="10" />
      </xsd:restriction>
    </xsd:simpleType>
    <xsd:simpleType name="smallmoney">
      <xsd:restriction base="xsd:decimal">
        <xsd:totalDigits value="10" />
        <xsd:fractionDigits value="4" />
        <xsd:minInclusive value="-214748.3648" />
        <xsd:maxInclusive value="214748.3647" />
      </xsd:restriction>
    </xsd:simpleType>
    <xsd:simpleType name="sqldatetime">
      <xsd:restriction base="xsd:dateTime">
        <xsd:minInclusive value="1753-01-01T00:00:00" />
        <xsd:maxInclusive value="9999-12-31T23:59:59" />
      </xsd:restriction>
    </xsd:simpleType>
</xsd:schema>
```

Now that we've defined our XML schema for the target XML document we can use it for any number of purposes. It can be annotated to allow XML Views against the database, it can be shared with trading partners to let them know how exported information from the system will appear, and so on. To see an example, let's take a look at a query that extracts a document in this form from the database using FOR XML EXPLICIT.

A FOR XML EXPLICIT Query Mapping the Data to XML

We'll cover FOR XML EXPLICIT in the next chapter, so don't worry too much about the details here; but the following query extracts a document from our database in the format we defined:

Mapping SQL Server to XML

```sql
SELECT
  1 AS Tag,
  NULL AS Parent,
  Customer.customerID AS [Customer!1!customerID!hide],
  Customer.name AS [Customer!1!Name],
  NULL AS [Invoice!2!invoiceID!hide],
  NULL AS [Invoice!2!InvoiceDate],
  NULL AS [Invoice!2!ShipDate],
  NULL AS [Part!3!partID!hide],
  NULL AS [Part!3!partID],
  NULL AS [Part!3!partCode],
  NULL AS [Part!3!description],
  NULL AS [LineItem!4!lineItemID!hide],
  NULL AS [LineItem!4!partIDREF],
  NULL AS [LineItem!4!number],
  NULL AS [LineItem!4!unitPrice]
FROM Customer
WHERE Customer.customerID = 1
UNION ALL
SELECT
  2 AS Tag,
  1 AS Parent,
  Invoice.customerID AS [Customer!1!customerID!hide],
  NULL AS [Customer!1!Name],
  Invoice.invoiceID AS [Invoice!2!invoiceID!hide],
  Invoice.invoiceDate AS [Invoice!2!InvoiceDate],
  Invoice.shipDate AS [Invoice!2!ShipDate],
  NULL AS [Part!3!partID!hide],
  NULL AS [Part!3!partID],
  NULL AS [Part!3!partCode],
  NULL AS [Part!3!description],
  NULL AS [LineItem!4!lineItemID!hide],
  NULL AS [LineItem!4!partIDREF],
  NULL AS [LineItem!4!number],
  NULL AS [LineItem!4!unitPrice]
FROM Invoice
WHERE Invoice.customerID = 1
UNION ALL
SELECT DISTINCT
  3 AS Tag,
  1 AS Parent,
  Invoice.customerID AS [Customer!1!CustomerID!hide],
  NULL AS [Customer!1!Name],
  NULL AS [Invoice!2!invoiceID!hide],
  NULL AS [Invoice!2!InvoiceDate],
  NULL AS [Invoice!2!ShipDate],
  NULL AS [Part!3!partID!hide],
  'part' + CONVERT(varchar, Part.partID) AS [Part!3!partID],
  Part.partCode AS [Part!3!partCode],
  Part.description AS [Part!3!description],
  NULL AS [LineItem!4!lineItemID!hide],
  NULL AS [LineItem!4!partIDREF],
  NULL AS [LineItem!4!number],
  NULL AS [LineItem!4!unitPrice]
FROM Invoice, LineItem, Part
```

Chapter 3

```
     WHERE Invoice.customerID = 1
       AND Invoice.invoiceID = LineItem.invoiceID
       AND LineItem.partID = Part.partID
     UNION ALL
     SELECT
       4 AS Tag,
       2 AS Parent,
       Invoice.customerID AS [Customer!1!customerID!hide],
       NULL AS [Customer!1!Name],
       Invoice.invoiceID AS [Invoice!2!invoiceID!hide],
       NULL AS [Invoice!2!InvoiceDate],
       NULL AS [Invoice!2!ShipDate],
       NULL AS [Part!3!partID!hide],
       NULL AS [Part!3!partID],
       NULL AS [Part!3!partCode],
       NULL AS [Part!3!description],
       LineItem.lineItemID AS [LineItem!4!lineItemID!hide],
       'part' + CONVERT(varchar, LineItem.partID) AS
     [LineItem!4!partIDREF],
       LineItem.number AS [LineItem!4!number],
       LineItem.unitPrice AS [LineItem!4!unitPrice]
     FROM Invoice, LineItem
     WHERE Invoice.customerID = 1
       AND Invoice.invoiceID = LineItem.invoiceID
     ORDER BY [Customer!1!name] DESC,
              [Invoice!2!invoiceID!hide] DESC,
              [Part!3!partID!hide],
              [LineItem!4!lineItemID!hide]
     FOR XML EXPLICIT
```

Using the sample data we added earlier, this SELECT generates the following XML document:

```
<Customer Name="Kevin Williams">
  <Invoice InvoiceDate="2002-06-06T00:00:00"
        ShipDate="2002-07-01T00:00:00">
   <LineItem partIDREF="part1" number="8" unitPrice="0.4000"/>
   <LineItem partIDREF="part3" number="22" unitPrice="0.6000"/>
  </Invoice>
  <Invoice InvoiceDate="2002-05-06T00:00:00"
        ShipDate="2002-06-01T00:00:00">
   <LineItem partIDREF="part1" number="17" unitPrice="0.3500"/>
   <LineItem partIDREF="part2" number="39" unitPrice="0.2500"/>
  </Invoice>
  <Part partID="part2" partCode="Q2653R" " description="1-inch widgets"/>
  <Part partID="part3" partCode="A3834G" " description="1-inch grommets"/>
  <Part partID="part1" partCode="X1726Y" " description="2-inch grommets"/>
</Customer>
```

Note that, if you're running this example in SQL Server's Query Analyzer, you'll need to tweak the settings to see the entire result. To do this you need to access the Tools | Options | Results tab, where you can change the output method to text and increase the maximum number of characters per column. Alternatively, to make the result clearer, you can choose to save it to a file and then open it in Internet Explorer to see the internal structure. Appendix C also provides a tool to help format the results of queries in a manner friendlier to the user.

Mapping SQL Server to XML

Writing FOR XML EXPLICIT queries can tend to be a bit cumbersome for complex documents, and a good alternative might be to use an XML View, discussed in Chapter 7.

Summary

In this chapter, we've taken a look at some best practices for designing XML documents to hold existing relational data. We've seen that, from an analysis perspective, you need to take into account the following:

- Whether the document needs to comply with any particular standard or standards.
- If the document is to be used for transmission, what information is in the agreed-upon transmission format.
- If the document is to be used for presentation, what information actually needs to be present (in other words, what information will appear in the presentation layer?)
- If the document is to be used for archiving, what information is germane to the archival retrieval process (and what information is necessary to make the archive atomic and complete)?

We've also seen how SQL Server data types map to XML Schema datatypes, and exposed some not-so-obvious gotchas (such as the allowable date ranges for SQL Server's `datetime` type and XML Schema's `dateTime` type being significantly different). Finally, we took a look at the creation of an XML structure for a particular business need, including shaping the element structure and adding all of the attributes to represent the column values. With this library of tips at your disposal, you'll find that creating XML schemas to store data from the relational database is no trouble at all.

Paul Morris

- Comparison of Server-Side and Client-Side XML Processing
- FOR XML Query Results
- Server-Side XML Processing
- Client-Side XML Processing
- Summary

4

FOR XML

In this chapter we'll take a practical look at the extensions to the SELECT statement that were introduced into SQL Server in the SQL Server 2000 release, namely the various flavors of FOR XML. These are:

- RAW
- AUTO
- EXPLICIT

These are all processed by SQL Server itself on the server side. We'll then cover the new client-side options that were introduced in the SQLXML 2.0 release and then further enhanced in release 3.0:

- RAW
- NESTED
- EXPLICIT

Finally, in this chapter we also look at the security implications and performance trade offs of using FOR XML as opposed to straight SELECT statements feeding Recordsets to ADO.

> FOR XML is complementary to the OPENXML statement that we discuss in Chapter 10, in that it is used to retrieve data where OPENXML is used to maintain it.

Chapter 4

Comparison of Server-Side and Client-Side XML Processing

With **server-side** FOR XML all the processing is carried out within SQL Server 2000. That is, the query is executed and then the XML formatting is carried out prior to anything being sent back to the client. It is sent back as a single column rowset. Once back at the client the XML can either be transformed via an XSLT stylesheet or by streaming using ADO.

This method of processing has two advantages:

❑ You only have to maintain a single installation, so you only have to install updates to SQLXML in one place.

❑ You know that the results will be consistent.

The down-side of this is that SQL Server has the overhead of processing all the XML formatting on top of the actual queries. This is fine as long as your server has enough spare processing capacity to do this but, if not, you may wish to consider using client side.

Server-side, there are two ways that the processing can be carried out. The first, as the diagram below shows, uses the SQLOLEDB library that ships with the SQL Server 2000 release:

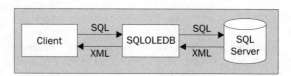

With the release of SQLXML 3.0, you also have the option of using the SQLXMLOLEDB library in addition to the SQLOLEDB one, as shown in the next diagram. By default you use the original method in SQL Server, but you can access this new method by setting the SQLXML version on the connection object if you are accessing the data programmatically.

Programmatic Access with SQLXML is the subject of Chapter 13.

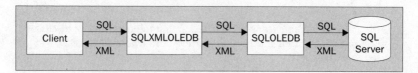

With **client-side** FOR XML, which was introduced in SQLXML 2.0, the SQL query part of the request is executed within SQL Server and the rowset is returned to the requesting client to do the XML formatting:

FOR XML

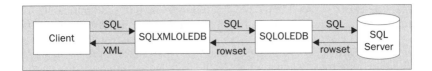

This has several advantages over server-side XML processing:

❑ It reduces the load on the machine hosting SQL Server by allowing it to concentrate purely on retrieving the data rather than having to worry about formatting it.

❑ It allows other databases servers, such as older versions of SQL Server or any other database that provides an OLEDB interface, to be queried and have their results returned as XML.

❑ It allows stored procedures that were written without reference to FOR XML to be used to return XML.

As all the security is determined when the query is run, there isn't anything additional to worry about when using client-side over server-side. The only real drawback of using it is that you lose some of the central control and simplicity of having all the query defined in one place within SQL Server itself. By this I mean that, with server-side XML processing, you would write the query as a stored procedure and the FOR XML is all included within it. With client-side, this method isn't available to you as the query will be stored outside of SQL Server in, say, a template. This can make it more difficult to determine what is affected if you need to make a change to the database schema later.

FOR XML Query Results

Before we move on to looking more closely at server-side FOR XML, we need to take a slight detour to see how we can run the queries we'll see in this chapter and view their results.

The queries here are run in SQL Server's Query Analyzer. Here are some typical results, with Query Analyzer set to view them as text:

93

XML_F52E2B61-18A1-11d1-B105-00805F49916B is the column name. It usually gets in the way and it can be eliminated by turning off Query Analyzer's **Print Column Headers** option. Also, in order to view the results optimally, it is best to configure Query Analyzer to show the results as text rather than a grid and also to increase the **Maximum characters per column** value to a very large value; with a maximum of 8192. This can be done by choosing **Options** from the **Tools** menu and going to the **Results** tab.

As you can see the result we have returned from our query isn't even well formed XML, so if we wanted to display this in, for example Internet Explorer (IE), we'd need to add a root element to these results. Viewing XML in IE allows us to see its structure more easily, as it is formatted into separate lines per element, and the hierarchy is indicated.

Unless otherwise stated, all the results of queries shown in IE in this chapter have had a <root> element added to the output, which has been copied and pasted from Query Analyzer into a separate file. To achieve the same results, you will need to do the same each time, or view the results files from the code download. Also note that unfortunately with large sets of data, Query Analyzer sometimes puts in extra line breaks that invalidate the XML. You may need to remove these as well. This is purely a problem with Query Analyzer and doesn't otherwise affect the functionality of FOR XML.

> *Please also note: in Appendix C, we show you how to install a tool that uses ADO to pass FOR XML and other SQLXML queries to SQL Server, and pass the results back to be formatted in one of two ways: as text, and in an IE browser window). The tool has an option to add a root element to the returned XML automatically if your query won't otherwise include one in the result. You could use this tool to display the results of the queries in this and every other chapter.*

> You can download all the queries, and the resulting XML files with <root> elements added, for this chapter from
> **http:\\www.curlingstone.com**.

Server-Side XML Processing

There are three different flavors of the FOR XML clause available on the server-side, as we saw in the introduction to this chapter: RAW, AUTO and EXPLICIT.

- ❑ RAW - an easy way to return an XML fragment to an application that requires a rowset, but doesn't care about the XML semantics or formatting. By returning a single column rowset, you allow a certain degree of platform independence, as you are not forced into using an ADO Resultset.

- ❑ AUTO - This is one up from RAW. It provides an easy and automatic way to create an XML document to return to a client that supports simple hierarchies.

FOR XML

It uses the relationships as defined by the JOINs within the query to determine the hierarchy of the XML. AUTO shows its strengths when used in conjunction with templates and XSLT stylesheets to return formatted results to the client very quickly. Its usefulness can soon become limited however, as its structure maps directly onto the database schema. We'll show you ways to get around this, but it can quickly begin to feel like you are shoehorning a solution.

❑   EXPLICIT is where you'll end up once you need to do more serious business logic and formatting of the XML hierarchies. EXPLICIT can very easily create extremely long and complicated SQL statements, so you may also wish to consider using a combination of AUTO and XML Views (discussed in Chapter 7) or templates (discussed in the next chapter).

Before we move on to delve deeper into each of these in turn, we need to take a quick look at some of the wider considerations that apply on the server-side:

SQL Limitations

There is a major limitation to the SQL statements that you construct using AUTO and EXPLICIT. You can't use the GROUP BY clause and, as a side affect of this, aggregate functions (SUM, COUNT, and so on) are not available either.

> *It is possible to get around this limitation by creating sub queries or views that contain the aggregate expressions to build virtual tables and using these to SELECT against. However, there can be a performance penalty in doing this, so check the query plan carefully to see how costly it is.*

Security Considerations

FOR XML is run as part of a SELECT statement or stored procedure, and hence within SQL Server's security context. This means that for a SELECT statement you need to have SELECT permissions on the tables or views that are referenced within the query, just as you would if you weren't using FOR XML. The same applies for a stored procedure – you need to have execute permission on the stored procedure in order to run it.

This makes it nice and simple to use and there aren't any security concerns with actually running these queries. As we'll see in the next chapter, the real concerns arise over where you run them, and who can see the results.

Conversely though, as the security is the same as for a standard SELECT or stored procedure, you don't have any control over stopping the use of FOR XML. As an example, if your server was already heavily loaded and you wanted to stop developers adding to the problem by using unoptimized FOR XML, the only way to do it would be by policing the code that is put onto it.

95

Chapter 4

Performance Implications

Using FOR XML on the server-side causes very little overhead to SQL Server, and I have successfully used it in cases with thousands of active users.

As with any SQL query, performance is governed by what the query is actually doing. As long as you follow the normal, common sense rules of optimizing the query and only returning the data that you need, both in terms of columns and rows of data, you will almost certainly see little or no difference in performance.

The only slight consideration to be aware of is that the XML documents returned are much bigger than the standard results that SQL Server would return because they contain all of the XML meta data as well as the data extracted from the database. If you are returning a large XML rowset from a query, with many columns and long column names, there can be much more data to transmit over the network to the client.

FOR XML RAW

In its simplest form, the SQL statement using the FOR XML clause takes the form of:

```
SELECT columnlist
FROM table
FOR XML RAW [,XMLDATA] [,BINARY BASE64]
```

With RAW mode, SQL Server uses a generic name of row for the element name and takes the names of the columns, or the alias names given to them in the query, to make the attribute names with the results. The XML returned is not well formed unless just one row is retrieved because there is no top-level (root) element returned.

So, taking a simple example of returning a list of employees from the Northwind Employees table, we would construct our query like this:

```
SELECT EmployeeID, LastName, FirstName
FROM Employees
FOR XML RAW
```

> **Please note:** all examples in this chapter use the Northwind sample database supplied with SQL Server 2000.

Here are the results of our example, with a <root> element added and displayed in IE:

FOR XML

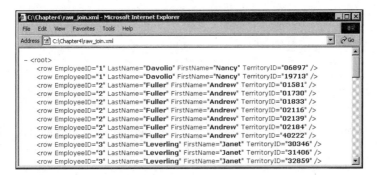

We can also perform JOINs within the SQL statement, but with RAW this doesn't have any effect on the structure of the XML that is output. So, if we JOIN the previous query with the EmployeeTerritories table using the statement below:

```
SELECT Employees.EmployeeID, LastName, FirstName, TerritoryID
FROM Employees
JOIN EmployeeTerritories
ON Employees.EmployeeID = EmployeeTerritories.EmployeeID
FOR XML RAW
```

we get the following XML rowset (minus the <root> element, of course):

As you can see, there is no hierarchy to the XML and each employee is repeated once for each territory, so a lot of data is repeated.

Each of the attributes uses the column name but you can change these names by using column aliases in the normal way. Every column must have a name, so if you are returning computed values or aggregates these must be aliased, otherwise you'll see error 6809:

Server: Msg 6809, Level 16, State 1, Line 1
Unnamed column or table names cannot be used as XML identifiers. Name unnamed columns using AS in the SELECT statement.

97

Chapter 4

XMLDATA

The next option when using FOR XML RAW is to use the XMLDATA argument. This returns an XML schema as part of the results, which is quite useful if you want to quickly generate a schema to use with XPath queries or XML Views, as you'll see in later chapters.

The XMLDATA argument is placed directly following FOR XML RAW, as shown in the query below:

```
SELECT EmployeeID, LastName, FirstName
FROM Employees
FOR XML RAW, XMLDATA
```

As you can see from the output, when viewed in IE, the schema is prefixed to the returned data:

You'll notice that the schema is given a name, in this case **Schema1**. Each time you run the query, this is incremented by one. If you want to reset this for any reason, you'll need to close the connection and open a new one.

BINARY BASE64

Finally, you may also use the BINARY BASE64 argument. This is used to encode any binary data you wish to return in BASE64 format. It goes in the same place in your query as XMLDATA (and can be used at the same time as XMLDATA if required) as shown below:

```
SELECT EmployeeID, Photo
FROM Employees
WHERE EmployeeID = 1
FOR XML RAW, BINARY BASE64
```

FOR XML

This returns the Photo binary data for the first employee:

This argument must be used if binary data is being returned, and you'll see the error 6829 in Query Analyzer (shown below), if you attempt to do so without specifying it:

Server: Msg 6829, Level 16, State 1, Line 1
FOR XML EXPLICIT and RAW modes currently do not support addressing binary data as URLs in column 'Photo'. Remove the column, or use the BINARY BASE64 mode, or create the URL directly using the 'dbobject/TABLE[@PK1="V1"]/@COLUMN' syntax.

> There is a third argument available with FOR XML – ELEMENTS. However this argument is only available when using AUTO mode and is discussed later in the chapter.

FOR XML AUTO

As with the RAW option, using AUTO is pretty straightforward as it doesn't allow us to control our desired output any more closely, although the depth of the results is different. It takes the form of:

```
SELECT columnlist
FROM table
FOR XML AUTO [,XMLDATA] [,ELEMENTS] [,BINARY BASE64]
```

With AUTO mode, SQL Server uses table names (or their aliases) to form the element names. As with RAW mode, the column names (or their aliases) make up the attribute names. The ordering of the columns within the SELECT list is used to determine the hierarchy of the returned XML. This means that, where tables have been JOINed within the query, the columns that are listed first will form the parent elements and the subsequent columns will form sub-elements of this.

Chapter 4

Where possible within this section, we'll use the same queries as with FOR XML RAW, so that you can easily compare and contrast the results. So, let's start off with a simple SELECT query:

```
SELECT EmployeeID, LastName, FirstName
FROM Employees
FOR XML AUTO
```

The XML returned (with a `<root>` element added) looks like:

```
- <root>
    <Employees EmployeeID="1" LastName="Davolio" FirstName="Nancy" />
    <Employees EmployeeID="2" LastName="Fuller" FirstName="Andrew" />
    <Employees EmployeeID="3" LastName="Leverling" FirstName="Janet" />
    <Employees EmployeeID="4" LastName="Peacock" FirstName="Margaret" />
    <Employees EmployeeID="5" LastName="Buchanan" FirstName="Steven" />
    <Employees EmployeeID="6" LastName="Suyama" FirstName="Michael" />
    <Employees EmployeeID="7" LastName="King" FirstName="Robert" />
    <Employees EmployeeID="8" LastName="Callahan" FirstName="Laura" />
    <Employees EmployeeID="9" LastName="Dodsworth" FirstName="Anne" />
  </root>
```

which at first glance looks identical to the FOR XML RAW output. The only difference is that, instead of using the generic name of `<row>` to name the element used for each row of data, the table name is used to give the name, so in this case we get `<Employees>`.

> **Please note:** since XML is case sensitive the elements and attributes of the output inherit the case of column and table names in the query. This means that if you execute two queries that only differ in the case used for the column name, SELECT EmployeeID ... FOR XML and SELECT employee id... FOR XML, they will return element names that also differ in case.

If you want to change the name used within the XML elements you can do this by aliasing the table within the query. For example, we could alias the Employees table to Employee to make it sound more grammatically correct if we wanted.

Following from the simple query, we can also use JOINs within FOR XML AUTO queries as below:

```
SELECT Employees.EmployeeID, LastName, FirstName, TerritoryID
FROM Employees
JOIN EmployeeTerritories
ON Employees.EmployeeID = EmployeeTerritories.EmployeeID
FOR XML AUTO
```

FOR XML

The XML hierarchy is created automatically in the results of this query, so whereas in the previous RAW version we saw all the <Employees...> data repeated, we now see it just once, with the territory information listed as sub-elements within:

The main thing to remember is that the ordering of the columns in the SELECT statement makes all the difference here. The columns that will form the attributes of the parent element need to be listed before the child column, so in this case all the columns from Employees are listed before the TerritoryID. If we swapped them around we get a very different set of XML returned with the TerritoryID forming the parent instead:

```
SELECT TerritoryID, Employees.EmployeeID, LastName, FirstName
FROM Employees
JOIN EmployeeTerritories
ON Employees.EmployeeID = EmployeeTerritories.EmployeeID
FOR XML AUTO
```

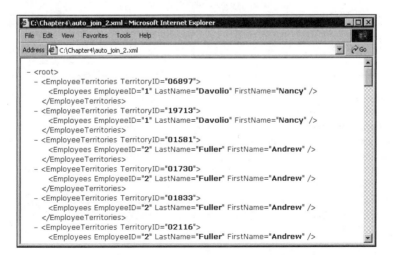

101

Chapter 4

So far, this has all been pretty straightforward, but unfortunately we've seen all the control over the structure of the XML that we have. Say we need to JOIN three tables together, but want the second two tables in the query to form the same sub-element within the parent? You may need to do this to use a pre-written XSLT stylesheet, or because the data more naturally fits this hierarchy. In this situation we might try to get our desired result using the following query (in the hope that we would return <Territories> elements, with two attributes, TerritoryID and TerritoryDescription, contained within an <Employees> element):

```
SELECT TOP 5 Employees.EmployeeID, LastName, FirstName,
EmployeeTerritories.TerritoryID, TerritoryDescription
FROM Employees
JOIN EmployeeTerritories
ON Employees.EmployeeID = EmployeeTerritories.EmployeeID
JOIN Territories
ON EmployeeTerritories.TerritoryID = Territories.TerritoryID
FOR XML AUTO
```

However, the resulting XML has a hierarchy three levels deep, with the EmployeeTerritories data forming its own element, as we can see:

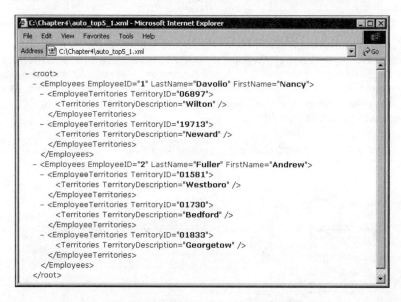

There isn't any way to directly control this behavior within the syntax of the statement itself when using FOR XML AUTO. The only real way to have any influence on the results is to be careful which column is returned. By changing the TerritoryID so it comes from Territories instead of EmployeeTerritories we can achieve the desired result, with both columns from Territories forming attributes of the <Territories> element:

```
SELECT TOP 5 Employees.EmployeeID, LastName, FirstName,
Territories.TerritoryID, TerritoryDescription
FROM Employees
```

FOR XML

```
JOIN EmployeeTerritories
ON Employees.EmployeeID = EmployeeTerritories.EmployeeID
JOIN Territories
ON EmployeeTerritories.TerritoryID = Territories.TerritoryID
FOR XML AUTO
```

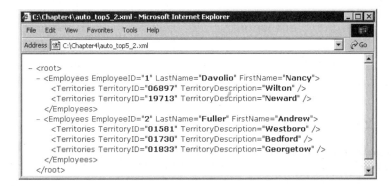

Once you have come up against these limitations in the level of control you can have over the formatting of the returned structure, or you need to use aggregate expressions, you really need to start using FOR XML EXPLICIT. Before we get onto this, there is one more option that we can use with FOR XML AUTO – the ELEMENTS parameter.

ELEMENTS

The ELEMENTS parameter can only be used with FOR XML AUTO and changes the returned XML from being attribute-based to being elements-based. This allows applications that are expecting the XML to come back as elements rather than attributes to still use FOR XML queries. So if we go back to our original query and add in this parameter:

```
SELECT EmployeeID, LastName, FirstName
FROM Employees
FOR XML AUTO, ELEMENTS
```

we see a very different set of results, with each column from the table forming its own element:

103

We can see that instead of returning the columns as attributes within an element of the table name, they have been returned as sub-elements contained within the table named element. Having this parameter available gives us additional flexibility in how we return the data so that applications that require the XML to be element-centric can be used. With FOR XML AUTO at least, the use of elements is an all or nothing affair. You can either return every column as an element or every column as an attribute – you can't specify which you would like one particular column to be. To be able to do this, you need to use FOR XML EXPLICIT.

> *When deciding on whether you need to use attributes or elements, it's always a good idea to look at the schema used by the destination application.*

FOR XML EXPLICIT

With FOR XML EXPLICIT our queries take on a whole new dimension and will almost certainly rank amongst the longest queries that you'll ever need to write with SQL Server. However, the ability to produce XML constructed exactly as you want it easily offsets this complexity.

When using FOR XML EXPLICIT, you are responsible for ensuring that the XML is well-formed, so two additional columns must be added to the front of the query that will be used by SQL Server itself. You also need to use a separate SELECT for each level of the hierarchy, then UNION the SELECT results together. These steps ensure that the query is in a suitable format for the meta data Universal Table, with details on the desired hierarchical structure, element, and attribute names in its columns. SQL Server then uses this table to construct the returned XML.

The two meta data columns that need to be supplied at the front are:

- **Tag**: This is essentially the level that the element will appear in within the hierarchy, taking integer values starting from 1 for the top level.
- **Parent**: This contains the Tag number of the element that this element will appear under within the hierarchy. If this element is at the top level, then there won't be a value, so you will normally see a NULL value put in here, though you can also use 0.

Rather than try and confuse things further, let's get straight in and show an example of this by querying out the names of the employees from the Northwind Employees table. Under normal circumstances, it would be very rare to see this query as you can achieve the same effect with much less work by using FOR XML AUTO:

```
SELECT  1 AS Tag,
        NULL AS Parent,
        EmployeeID AS [Employees!1!EmployeeID],
        LastName AS [Employees!1!LastName],
        FirstName AS [Employees!1!FirstName]
FROM Employees
FOR XML EXPLICIT
```

FOR XML

As you can see, as well as adding the two extra columns to the front, we also need to alias the names of the other columns as well. This takes the form of:

```
[elementname]!TagNumber[!AttributeName][!Directive]
```

Using this syntax, we also have the ability to set the level within the hierarchy for each attribute and to change its name as well.

We'll come to [!Directive] later on in this section.

Running this query gives the following results (you'll need to add the `<root>` element again to view this in IE). So far, this hasn't gained us anything over our first FOR XML AUTO query:

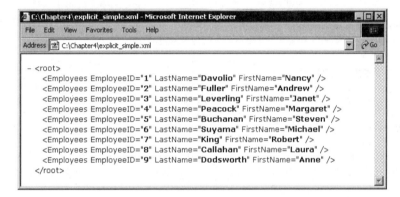

Things begin to get more interesting when we want to start adding in extra elements within the hierarchy. Rather than using a JOIN to put the data together as we did with FOR XML AUTO, we use a UNION to combine the statements together. This allows us to have much more flexibility within the individual statements:

```
SELECT    1 AS Tag,
          NULL AS Parent,
          ProductID AS [Products!1!ProductID],
          ProductName AS [Products!1!ProductName],
          NULL AS [Suppliers!2!SupplierID],
          NULL AS [Suppliers!2!SupplierName]
FROM Products
WHERE ProductID < 10

UNION ALL

SELECT    2 AS Tag,
          1 AS Parent,
          ProductID,
          NULL,
          Suppliers.SupplierID,
          CompanyName
FROM Products
```

105

Chapter 4

```
       JOIN Suppliers
       ON Products.SupplierID = Suppliers.SupplierID
       WHERE ProductID < 10

       ORDER BY [Products!1!ProductID], [Suppliers!2!SupplierID]
       FOR XML EXPLICIT
```

To do this we create the definition of the Universal Table within the first SELECT statement, to return a list of products (I've restricted it to those with an ProductID of less than 10 for brevity) and two columns at the end for which each product's supplier is:

```
       SELECT    1 AS Tag,
                 NULL AS Parent,
                 ProductID AS [Products!1!ProductID],
                 ProductName AS [Products!1!ProductName],
                 NULL AS [Suppliers!2!SupplierID],
                 NULL AS [Suppliers!2!SupplierName]
       FROM Products
       WHERE ProductID < 10
```

Here we have defined that the top-level element is <Products> and the second level is <Suppliers>. To achieve this we have to add in an extra column for each one that will be supplied by the subsequent query or queries.

Within the second SELECT statement, we need to supply the key to the parent element, along with the values that will go into this level of the hierarchy:

```
       SELECT    2 AS Tag,
                 1 AS Parent,
                 ProductID,
                 NULL,
                 Suppliers.SupplierID,
                 CompanyName
       FROM Products
       JOIN Suppliers
       ON Products.SupplierID = Suppliers.SupplierID
       WHERE ProductID < 10
```

Finally, it is also very important to put an ORDER BY clause into the statement, otherwise we could end up with all the Products records returned first followed by all the Suppliers records:

```
       ORDER BY [Products!1!ProductID], [Suppliers!2!SupplierID]
```

If we hadn't included this clause, our result would be wrong, as you can see from the following screenshot. Without the ORDER BY, all the suppliers have been placed as child elements of the last <Products> element, which is incorrect:

FOR XML

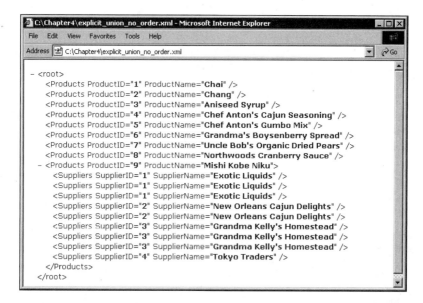

Once the correct ordering is used, we get the following, correct XML returned:

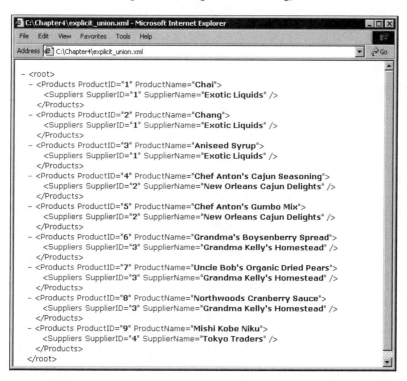

We can also add in additional elements under the <Products> element, so for example we could also return the Categories information for each product, by altering our query like so:

```
SELECT    1 AS Tag,
          NULL AS Parent,
          ProductID AS [Products!1!ProductID],
          ProductName AS [Products!1!ProductName],
          NULL AS [Suppliers!2!SupplierID],
          NULL AS [Suppliers!2!SupplierName],
          NULL AS [Category!3!CategoryID],
          NULL AS [Category!3!CategoryName]
FROM Products
WHERE ProductID < 10

UNION ALL

SELECT    2 AS Tag,
          1 AS Parent,
          ProductID,
          NULL,
          Suppliers.SupplierID,
          CompanyName,
          NULL,
          NULL
FROM Products
JOIN Suppliers
ON Products.SupplierID = Suppliers.SupplierID
WHERE ProductID < 10

UNION ALL

SELECT    3 AS Tag,
          1 AS Parent,
          ProductID,
          NULL,
          NULL,
          NULL,
          Categories.CategoryID,
          CategoryName
FROM Products
JOIN Categories
ON Products.CategoryID = Categories.CategoryID
WHERE ProductID < 10

ORDER BY [Products!1!ProductID], [Suppliers!2!SupplierID],
[Category!3!CategoryID]
FOR XML EXPLICIT
```

> Note that as we are peforming a UNION on the three parts of the query together we need to pad each one out with NULL columns in order for them to be compatible. We could also have used UNION instead of UNION ALL and this would have only returned unique rows from each query rather than all rows as here.

FOR XML

In the following screenshot, we can see that a `<Category>` element, with the appropriate attributes has been added to our results:

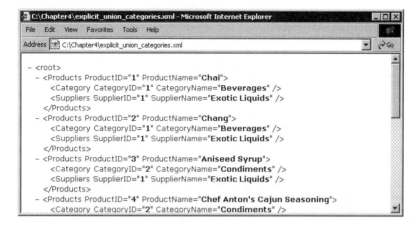

As you can see, even though we are still only producing a relatively simple set of XML result, our query is already starting to get quite large.

As with all the examples in this chapter, no top-level element is returned to make the XML well-formed. This isn't a problem if you are using url or template queries (covered in the next chapter) or ADO (covered in Chapter 13), but sometimes you'll want to output this top-level element as well. This can be done quite easily in EXPLICIT mode by adding a level 1 tag above the actual query. We can alter our query from earlier that outputs all the employee names to automatically include a `<root>` element by doing this, like so:

```
SELECT   1 AS Tag,
         NULL AS Parent,
         NULL AS [root!1!root],
         NULL AS [Employees!2!EmployeeID],
         NULL AS [Employees!2!LastName],
         NULL AS [Employees!2!FirstName]

UNION ALL

SELECT   2,
         1,
         NULL,
         EmployeeID,
         LastName,
         FirstName
FROM Employees
FOR XML EXPLICIT
```

To give the root element a name other than `<root>`, just change the name in the third line.

109

Chapter 4

Directives

Now that we've shown all the fun of how to code up the statements, let's return to the `Directives` that we mentioned earlier. There are quite a few of these and they allow us to have even more control over how we see the data being returned.

Directive	Description
element	Returns the column as an element rather than the default attribute.
hide	Hides the column from the XML results.
xmltext	Used to decode the contents of the column back into XML if it contains XML tags within the data.
xml	Returns the column as an element rather than an attribute (which is the default behaviour) but unlike the element directive, it doesn't encode.
cdata	This wraps the column within a CDATA section.
ID, IDREF and IDREFS	Used to define the key and referencing attributes when using XMLDATA.

Let's take a closer look at the properties of each directive in turn.

element

This allows you to return individual columns of the query as sub-elements rather than attributes. As with the `ELEMENTS` argument we saw earlier with `AUTO` mode, this gives you the flexibility of formatting the XML document for applications that require element-centric rather than attribute-centric XML. To illustrate this we'll go back to our simple first query again and add the `element` directive to the `LastName` and `FirstName` columns:

```
SELECT    1 AS Tag,
          NULL AS Parent,
          EmployeeID AS [Employees!1!EmployeeID],
          LastName AS [Employees!1!LastName!element],
          FirstName AS [Employees!1!FirstName!element]
FROM Employees
FOR XML EXPLICIT
```

As you can see in the screenshot, this returns the value of each column it is specified on as a sub-element:

FOR XML

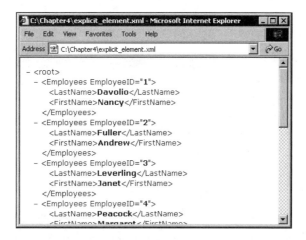

hide

The `hide` directive allows a column to be used within the query, but not to show up in the resulting XML. This might sound like an odd thing to want to do at first but it can come in very handy if you want to order the data by a field that won't be returned.

For example, say we wanted to return a list of products as we did earlier, but order them so that the ones with the most stock appeared first. If we didn't actually want the stock units to appear in our output XML, we could use the following query:

```
SELECT    1 AS Tag,
          NULL AS Parent,
          ProductID AS [Products!1!ProductID],
          ProductName AS [Products!1!ProductName],
          UnitsInStock AS [Products!1!UnitsInStock!hide],
          NULL AS [Suppliers!2!SupplierID],
          NULL AS [Suppliers!2!SupplierName]
FROM Products
WHERE ProductID < 10

UNION ALL

SELECT    2 AS Tag,
          1 AS Parent,
          ProductID,
          NULL,
          UnitsInStock,
          Suppliers.SupplierID,
          CompanyName
FROM Products
JOIN Suppliers
ON Products.SupplierID = Suppliers.SupplierID
WHERE ProductID < 10

ORDER BY [Products!1!UnitsInStock!hide],
[Products!1!ProductID], [Suppliers!2!SupplierID]
FOR XML EXPLICIT
```

111

Chapter 4

This query returns our products (and their suppliers) in descending order of stock level, without showing the figures:

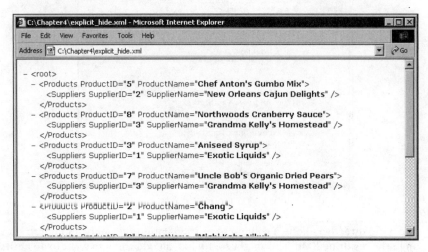

xmltext

When using constructs such as OPENXML (see Chapter 10) or XML Bulk Load (see Chapter 12) to load data into SQL Server, it is quite common to put any unmapped attributes into an overflow column rather than throw them away and have them lost. The xmltext directive allows you to get these fragments back out again from these overflow columns (or any other column that has XML encoded data in it for that matter) and re-integrate them into the results of the query.

To illustrate this, we need to amend the Northwind Employees table to add an extra column to hold this overflow data, and then populate it. First, run the following ALTER TABLE statement to add the column:

```
ALTER TABLE Employees
ADD XMLOverFlow varchar(200) NULL
```

and then the following update statement to populate the column for the first employee:

```
UPDATE Employees
SET XMLOverFlow = '<Personnel Salary="50000"
NextPromotion="2003"/>'
where EmployeeId = 1
```

We then have two options for how we retrieve this data. Firstly we can select the column back and name the alias as we have seen previously:

```
SELECT  1 AS Tag,
        NULL AS Parent,
        EmployeeID AS [Employees!1!EmployeeID],
        LastName AS [Employees!1!LastName],
```

FOR XML

```
            FirstName AS [Employees!1!FirstName],
            XMLOverflow AS [Employees!1!PrivateData!xmltext]
FROM Employees
WHERE EmployeeID = 1
FOR XML EXPLICIT
```

This returns the overflow data as attributes within a sub-element. So, here we named the attribute `PrivateData` and this is a sub-element of `<Employees>`:

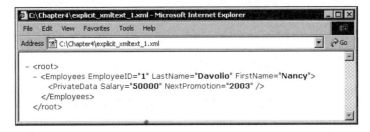

The other option is to leave the name out entirely, by using two exclamation marks to indicate the missing name:

```
SELECT     1 AS Tag,
           NULL AS Parent,
           EmployeeID AS [Employees!1!EmployeeID],
           LastName AS [Employees!1!LastName],
           FirstName AS [Employees!1!FirstName],
           XMLOverflow AS [Employees!1!!xmltext]
FROM Employees
WHERE EmployeeID = 1
FOR XML EXPLICIT
```

This returns the overflow data as extra attributes of the `<Employees>` element:

xml

The `xml` directive works in the same way as the `element` directive but with one difference – the `element` directive escapes the data whereas the `xml` directive does not. This is useful if the data is in a format such as HTML or XML that contains tags, which could interfere with the structure of the returned XML.

We just created the `XMLOverflow` column that contains XML within it. If we return this using the `element` directive, then we see that the data is returned with the relevant characters escaped (such as < being replaced with <):

113

Chapter 4

```
SELECT    1 AS Tag,
          NULL AS Parent,
          EmployeeID AS [Employees!1!EmployeeID],
          XMLOverflow AS [Employees!1!Overflow!element]
FROM Employees
WHERE EmployeeID = 1
FOR XML EXPLICIT
```

```
<root>
  <Employees EmployeeID="1">
    <Overflow><Personnel Salary="50000" NextPromotion="2003"/></Overflow>
  </Employees>
</root>
```

However, if we use the xml directive instead, it is returned exactly as it is stored within the column:

```
SELECT    1 AS Tag,
          NULL AS Parent,
          EmployeeID AS [Employees!1!EmployeeID],
          XMLOverflow AS [Employees!1!Overflow!xml]
FROM Employees
WHERE EmployeeID = 1
FOR XML EXPLICIT
```

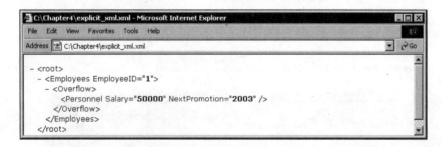

```
<root>
  <Employees EmployeeID="1">
    <Overflow>
      <Personnel Salary="50000" NextPromotion="2003" />
    </Overflow>
  </Employees>
</root>
```

Unfortunately, apart from the slight change in the bolding of the text, it's hard to see the difference between the two in black and white, so you'll just have to run these for yourselves; but with the elements directive, the column is just treated as a string of text – IE is translating the encoded characters back within the string for display purposes. This is the actual XML that is returned:

<Employees EmployeeID="1"><Overflow><Personnel Salary="50000" NextPromotion="2003"/></Overflow></Employees>

whereas the xml directive returns the data just as it is stored so, in this case where the column actually contains an XML fragment, it is output just like any other attribute. Note that if this were not the case, you could end up with XML was not well formed.

FOR XML

cdata

The `cdata` directive outputs the column as a CDATA section within the XML document and, like `xml`, allows the output of data that contains markup language that could interfere with the XML structure. The difference with `cdata` is that this is done without it being interpreted by the XML parser.

So, if we wanted to avoid any ambiguity in how the data is interpreted in the previous example, we could code the query using a `cdata` directive rather than using `xml` or `elements`:

```
SELECT    1 AS Tag,
          NULL AS Parent,
          EmployeeID AS [Employees!1!EmployeeID],
          XMLOverflow AS [Employees!1!!cdata]
FROM Employees
WHERE EmployeeID = 1
FOR XML EXPLICIT
```

As you can see, the tags for a CDATA block have been added:

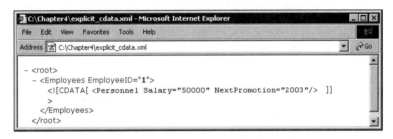

As a CDATA section doesn't have an attribute name, you must not attempt to specify one within the query.

ID, IDREF, and IDREFS

The ID, IDREF, and IDREFS directives are used in conjunction with the XMLDATA parameter to enable links within the XML document. As we saw earlier in the chapter, the XMLDATA argument tells SQL Server to output a schema definition along with the XML document. These directives are used to feed the key and referencing attributes of the document into this schema definition (for a detailed discussion on how ID and IDREF interact see Chapter 3). If the XMLDATA parameter is not used, then ID and IDREF or IDREFS are ignored.

> The IDREF and IDREFS directives are used in exactly the same way to provide a link back to IDs. The only difference is that IDREFS is used when we want to refer to a list of ID attributes, rather thank just one.

If you want to think of this in relational terms, then think of the ID being the primary key and the IDREF a foreign key to it. The following code shows ID and IDREF in action in a query designed to extract all the people who directly report to employee 2:

Chapter 4

```
SELECT    1 AS Tag,
          NULL AS Parent,
          EmployeeID AS [Manager!1!EmployeeID!ID],
          LastName AS [Manager!1!LastName],
          FirstName AS [Manager!1!FirstName],
          NULL AS [SubOrdinate!2!ManagerID!IDREF],
          NULL AS [SubOrdinate!2!SubOrdinateID],
          NULL AS [SubOrdinate!2!SubOrdinateLastName],
          NULL AS [SubOrdinate!2!SubOrdinateFirstName]
FROM Employees
WHERE EmployeeID = 2
UNION ALL
SELECT    2,
          1,
          NULL,
          NULL,
          NULL,
          ReportsTo,
          EmployeeID,
          LastName,
          FirstName
FROM Employees
WHERE ReportsTo = 2
FOR XML EXPLICIT, XMLDATA
```

In the first highlighted line, we have defined the EmployeeID as an attribute of the <Manager> element, called EmployeeID and set this to be the ID:

Then, in the second highlighted line we set the ManagerID attribute of the <Subordinate> element to be the IDREF. In the third highlighted line, we have returned the ReportsTo column as the ManagerID.

As you can see from the results below, the schema is returned first and then within this the EmployeeID attribute has been set with dt:type="id" and the ManagerID has been set with dt:type="idref":

FOR XML

```
C:\Chapter4\explicit_ID-IDREF.xml - Microsoft Internet Explorer
File  Edit  View  Favorites  Tools  Help
Address  C:\Chapter4\explicit_ID-IDREF.xml

- <root>
  - <Schema name="Schema1" xmlns="urn:schemas-microsoft-com:xml-data" xmlns:dt="urn:schemas-microsoft-com:datatypes">
    - <ElementType name="Manager" content="mixed" model="open">
        <AttributeType name="EmployeeID" dt:type="id" />
        <AttributeType name="LastName" dt:type="string" />
        <AttributeType name="FirstName" dt:type="string" />
        <attribute type="EmployeeID" />
        <attribute type="LastName" />
        <attribute type="FirstName" />
      </ElementType>
    - <ElementType name="SubOrdinate" content="mixed" model="open">
        <AttributeType name="ManagerID" dt:type="idref" />
        <AttributeType name="SubOrdinateID" dt:type="i4" />
        <AttributeType name="SubOrdinateLastName" dt:type="string" />
        <AttributeType name="SubOrdinateFirstName" dt:type="string" />
        <attribute type="ManagerID" />
        <attribute type="SubOrdinateID" />
        <attribute type="SubOrdinateLastName" />
        <attribute type="SubOrdinateFirstName" />
      </ElementType>
    </Schema>
  - <Manager xmlns="x-schema:#Schema1" EmployeeID="2" LastName="Fuller" FirstName="Andrew">
      <SubOrdinate ManagerID="2" SubOrdinateID="1" SubOrdinateLastName="Davolio" SubOrdinateFirstName="Nancy" />
      <SubOrdinate ManagerID="2" SubOrdinateID="3" SubOrdinateLastName="Leverling" SubOrdinateFirstName="Janet" />
      <SubOrdinate ManagerID="2" SubOrdinateID="4" SubOrdinateLastName="Peacock" SubOrdinateFirstName="Margaret" />
      <SubOrdinate ManagerID="2" SubOrdinateID="5" SubOrdinateLastName="Buchanan" SubOrdinateFirstName="Steven" />
      <SubOrdinate ManagerID="2" SubOrdinateID="8" SubOrdinateLastName="Callahan" SubOrdinateFirstName="Laura" />
    </Manager>
  </root>
```

That about wraps up the various flavors of server side FOR XML. We've discussed the three options, RAW, AUTO and EXPLICIT and have shown how to use each of them.

We'll now turn our attention to the client-side version of FOR XML.

Client-Side XML Processing

Firstly, we need to understand exactly what is meant by the label client-side. It means that the part of the query that does the XML processing does not happen within SQL Server itself. So the client could either be a middle tier object or an application the client computer.

By moving the FOR XML client side, we move processing off SQL Server to free up some resources. Doing this also allows us to make use of existing stored procedures that don't permit FOR XML by wrapping the query with FOR XML on the client side. There is an example of doing this in the *NESTED* section, a little further on.

As we discussed in the previous section, there are no security considerations in using FOR XML other than requiring the normal SELECT permissions on the objects referenced by the query or EXECUTE permissions for a stored procedure. Again, security comes into play in how you implement the processes that make the calls to the queries. That is, are they restricted to just running the queries we define or can they run any SQL statement that we throw at them? We'll see more on the difference between the two methods in the next chapter, with templates and URL queries.

Chapter 4

Unless the SQL Server is extremely busy, you will likely see no difference in performance between using client-side and server-side FOR XML unless you are returning large amounts of data from a query, in which case client-side may be slightly quicker because less data needs to be transported across the network. Gaining the best performance really comes down to processing in the most appropriate place for your architecture.

Unlike on the server-side, we can't just fire up Query Analyzer and run client-side queries directly within it. We need to use one or more of URL queries, templates, SQLXMLOLEDB or the SQLXML Managed Classes in order to make use of the client-side queries.

> There is more on URL queries and templates in the next chapter. SQLXMLOLEDB and the SQLXML Managed Classes are discussed in Chapter 13.

Like the server-side processing that we've seen in this chapter up to now, there are three flavors of the FOR XML clause that can be used on the client-side:

RAW

This behaves in an identical manner to the server side FOR XML RAW, so the details are the same as those given earlier in the chapter.

NESTED

This maps to the FOR XML AUTO on the server side but with some differences:

- One of the major limitations of AUTO is that you can't do any aggregations or use the GROUP BY clause. With NESTED you can use them:

```
SELECT CustomerID, COUNT(*) AS NoOrders
FROM Orders
GROUP BY CustomerID
HAVING COUNT(*) > 20
FOR XML NESTED
```

- FOR XML NESTED always uses the names of the base table to populate the element names. This overrides any aliasing that you do within the query or views that you reference.

- With FOR XML NESTED you can't have multiple statements executed at the same time returning multiple rowsets. That is, each query must return just a single XML fragment.

- You can use the FOR XML NESTED to format the results of a stored procedure that doesn't return XML. You can do this by calling the stored procedure in the normal way and appending FOR XML NESTED to the end of it. If we take the stored procedure [Ten Most Expensive Products] that ships with the Northwind database we can wrap this with FOR XML NESTED as opposite:

FOR XML

```
EXECUTE [Ten Most Expensive Products] FOR XML NESTED
```

Further examples using FOR XML NESTED *are given in Chapter 13.*

EXPLICIT

Client-side FOR XML EXPLICIT maps directly to the server-side FOR XML EXPLICIT.

Ways of Using Client-Side FOR XML

There are several ways to use client-side FOR XML queries:

- **URL Queries**. These are discussed in the next chapter. URL queries allow you to open your SQL Server up via HTTP and put SQL statements directly within the URL. To allow client-side queries to be run, you set up the virtual directory in the usual way but make sure that the **Run on the client** option is ticked on the **Settings** tab of the Virtual directory's properties.
- **Templates**. Again, these are discussed fully in the next chapter. Within the template, you specify the `client-side-xml` attribute in the query tag to have a value of 1.
- **SQLXMLOLEDB Provider**. This interface allows the client side XML to be executed via ADO and is discussed in Chapter 13.
- **SQLXML Managed Classes**. These were introduced new in SQLXML 3.0 and provide .NET support for client-side queries. Again, these are discussed in Chapter 13.

Summary

In this chapter we've covered server-side FOR XML syntax in detail, and discussed the differences when using the client-side version. Future chapters will show more practical use of client-side FOR XML as its supporting technologies are discussed.

We've discussed the three forms of the server-side option: RAW, AUTO, and EXPLICIT and the three counterparts on the client-side: RAW, NESTED, and EXPLICIT. RAW and EXPLICIT map across the two versions and AUTO and NESTED are very similar with a few exceptions such as NESTED allowing aggregations and making it possible to execute stored procedures that don't support returning XML.

In the next chapter we move on to URL and template queries where we show how to make practical use of the server side statements.

Paul Morris

- URL Queries
- Security Considerations
- Setting up the Environment
- Usage
- Template Queries
- Usage Guidelines
- Security Considerations
- Setting up the Environment

5

URL Queries and Template Queries

In this chapter we'll introduce the use of **URL queries** and **templates**. URL queries, just as the name suggests, allow us to insert a SQL query statement directly into an URL. While this can be a great tool, it has limitations that we'll also examine.

Templates provide us with similar functionality to URL queries, but abstract away the SQL statements from the user of the web page, thereby removing one of the major concerns about URL queries, namely security. We'll show you how to create templates for simple queries, complex queries, and stored procedures. We'll then take a look at how to format the output using XSLT stylesheets.

URL Queries

URL queries are an elegant way of empowering client-side web development with access to database functionality without either relying on or even having to know proprietary database access technologies such as ADO or ADO.NET.

Using URL queries, we can perform everything from a simple `SELECT` statement returned as XML, right through to using an XSLT stylesheet to format the query result. As a result it is possible to code up the whole of a web site using just URL queries. This would be great for something like an intranet site that was used for displaying management reports.

In Chapter 2 we saw how to set up a virtual directory in order to link a web site to a SQL Server. URL queries are run against such directories to return data from the database to the browser. Once you have a working virtual directory with the **Allow URL queries** option ticked in the **Options** tab, you are ready to go. We'll step through how to set up the virtual directory for the URL queries in this chapter shortly, in the section *Setting up the Environment*.

Chapter 5

Security Considerations

The major drawback of URL queries is the fact that the query is displayed to the user because they can see the URL. Unless you are very careful in the way you configure your security within SQL Server, the server will be open to all kinds of abuse. A simple query such as:

http://localhost/urlquery?sql=select+*+from+employees+where+employeeid+=+1+for+xml+auto

returns the details of one of the people in the Employees table in the Northwind database and seems fairly harmless:

<employees EmployeeID="1" LastName="Davolio" FirstName="Nancy" Title="Sales Representative" TitleOfCourtesy="Ms." BirthDate="1948-12-08T00:00:00" HireDate="1992-05-01T00:00:00" Address="507 - 20th Ave. E. Apt. 2A" City="Seattle" Region="WA" PostalCode="98122" Country="USA" HomePhone="(206) 555-9857" Extension="5467" Photo="dbobject/employees[@EmployeeID='1']/@Photo" Notes="Education includes a BA in psychology from Colorado State University in 1970. She also completed "The Art of the Cold Call." Nancy is a member of Toastmasters International." ReportsTo="2" PhotoPath="http://accweb/emmployees/davolio.bmp" />

However, if we then alter this URL just as any user could, we can make it much more interesting:

> **Warning: Please don't try running the next query example! It's just shown here to illustrate why you need to be careful with your security.**

http://localhost/urlquery?sql=drop+database+Northwind

This query would drop our database.

As you can see there is definite potential for wreaking havoc if you don't set up your SQL Server in a very secure manner. For this reason, the use of URL queries is probably best restricted to intranet applications where you know who the users are, and have given minimal read-only access to just the objects that are required to run the queries.

At this point you're probably wondering, "why would I ever consider using URL queries?" Well, configured securely, they do provide a very elegant way of producing a set of reporting web pages without having to know ASP or ADO, that is – they empower the DBA.

As we learned in Chapter 2, Windows Integrated Authentication is the strongest security mode we can use on our virtual directories. This means that people using the URL query will log into the database as themselves. They can only do this once they have already logged into the Windows network, so typically this means that it is only suitable for an intranet environment. This is more secure than having them use a generic account, which is what would happen if you used the first option on the Security tab – **Always logon as**. For Internet use, you'll need to fall back to using the **Always logon as** option, but remember that this isn't recommended.

URL Queries and Template Queries

By using Windows Integrated Authentication, you can easily restrict the queries to certain users within the organization by setting up a role, assigning the users to it, and then giving this role either EXECUTE permissions on the stored procedures or SELECT permissions on the tables. It even allows you to set up multiple roles and assign different permissions if you want to restrict some of the more sensitive queries to a select group of users.

Finally, by using this method, you can track exactly who did what query or attempted to do their own queries, so you have a full audit trail.

Using the **Always log on as** option, you are restricted to using one role and lose the ability to have an audit trail, but if you can live with this, there is less administration work to do because you only have to set up one account within the role rather than maintain a changing list of users.

Setting up the Environment

As we've already described how the virtual directories work and all the options that can be set to configure them, we won't go over that all again here. We'll just run through the small part that's needed to run the examples given in this chapter:

- From within the IIS Virtual Directory Management for SQLXML 3.0 console, right click on the **Default Web Site** and choose **New | Virtual Directory**.
- On the **General** tab of the Virtual Directory Management tool, enter `urlquery` for the **Virtual Directory Name** and choose a local path.
- On the **Security** tab, choose a method of connecting to the database. If your server is configured to allow Windows Integrated Authentication, then choose this for added security.
- On the **Data Source** tab, select the server that you want to connect to, as well as the `Northwind` database that we will use for all the examples.
- Finally, on the **Settings** tab, make sure that the **Allow URL queries** option is checked (it won't be by default).

That's all there is to it, so press **OK** to close the dialog box and we're ready to begin.

Usage

The general form for accessing the server using URL queries is:

```
http://webservername/virtualrootname?{sql=sqlquery}
[&param=value[&param=value]..n]
```

where:

- `webservername` is either the IP address or the DNS server name pointing to the web server.
- `virtualrootname` is the name given to the virtual directory when creating it in the IIS Virtual Directory Management tool.

123

- ❏ &param takes a value from **contenttype**, **outputencoding**, **root** and **xsl**. We'll discuss each of their uses as we go through the chapter.

To run a query we need to pass it to the URL that we have just configured, in this case:

http://localhost/urlquery?

The SQL statement we pass to the URL needs to be in the form:

sql=*sql statement*

There are a couple of initial things to watch out for. The first is that an URL can't have any spaces in it, so we have to replace these with a +.

> *If you were using this in conjunction with ASP and were dynamically creating the URLs for the queries, you could use the Server.URLEncode() method to do this.*

The second is that the SQL statement must use the FOR XML syntax as part of the query. This can be any of the three forms (RAW, AUTO or EXPLICIT) that we described in detail in the previous chapter, although it would be very unusual to see EXPLICIT used in this instance due to the complexity of writing it within the URL.

In the first example we saw at the beginning of this chapter, we just returned a single row of data without a top-level element. This is because FOR XML (as we saw in the last chapter) doesn't return one. As the result isn't well-formed, it cannot be displayed in IE. To get around this we need to use the **root** parameter in our URL query. For example, to return the names of all the people from the Employees table within an <Employees> top-level element, we would use the following URL:

http://localhost/urlquery?sql=select+EmployeeId,LastName,FirstName+from+employees+for+xml+auto**&root=Employees**

which returns the following results:

```
<?xml version="1.0" encoding="utf-8" ?>
- <Employees>
    <employees EmployeeId="1" LastName="Davolio" FirstName="Nancy" />
    <employees EmployeeId="2" LastName="Fuller" FirstName="Andrew" />
    <employees EmployeeId="3" LastName="Leverling" FirstName="Janet" />
    <employees EmployeeId="4" LastName="Peacock" FirstName="Margaret" />
    <employees EmployeeId="5" LastName="Buchanan" FirstName="Steven" />
    <employees EmployeeId="6" LastName="Suyama" FirstName="Michael" />
    <employees EmployeeId="7" LastName="King" FirstName="Robert" />
    <employees EmployeeId="8" LastName="Callahan" FirstName="Laura" />
    <employees EmployeeId="9" LastName="Dodsworth" FirstName="Anne" />
  </Employees>
```

URL Queries and Template Queries

Data Modification

As well as standard `SELECT` queries we can also issue data modification statements such as:

http://localhost/urlquery?sql=update+Employees+set+TitleOfCourtesy+=
+'Lady'+where+EmployeeId=9

This doesn't return any results, so at first it doesn't look like anything has happened. However, if we run a `SELECT` statement afterwards we can see that the `UPDATE` has been successful, and employee 9's `TitleOfCourtesy` is now `Lady` rather than `Ms`:

> *I'm running these as a user with system administrator privileges within SQL Server. You'll need to have at least update permissions on the `Employees` table for this to work.*

```
<?xml version="1.0" encoding="utf-8" ?>
- <Employees>
    <employees EmployeeId="1" TitleOfCourtesy="Ms." />
    <employees EmployeeId="2" TitleOfCourtesy="Dr." />
    <employees EmployeeId="3" TitleOfCourtesy="Ms." />
    <employees EmployeeId="4" TitleOfCourtesy="Mrs." />
    <employees EmployeeId="5" TitleOfCourtesy="Mr." />
    <employees EmployeeId="6" TitleOfCourtesy="Mr." />
    <employees EmployeeId="7" TitleOfCourtesy="Mr." />
    <employees EmployeeId="8" TitleOfCourtesy="Ms." />
    <employees EmployeeId="9" TitleOfCourtesy="Lady" />
  </Employees>
```

Executing Stored Procedures

In addition to running SQL statements, we can also execute stored procedures. There are two methods of doing this: either use `EXEC` to run the procedure as you would from within Query Analyzer, or use the ODBC call syntax. Both these ways of calling stored procedures provide the same functionality, so your decision on which to use really comes down to which set of the syntax you know best and are most comfortable with. Let's take a look at each method now.

Using Exec

Unfortunately the `Northwind` sample database doesn't include any stored procedures that return XML, so we'll need to create one that does. This stored procedure, `Ten Least Expensive Products`, does as its name suggests and returns the cheapest products from the `Northwind Products` table:

```
CREATE PROCEDURE [Ten Least Expensive Products] AS
SET ROWCOUNT 10
SELECT ProductName, UnitPrice
FROM Products
ORDER BY UnitPrice
FOR XML AUTO
GO
```

We can run this stored procedure using the URL:

http://localhost/urlquery?sql=exec+[Ten+Least+Expensive+Products]&root=ProductList

The following results will be returned:

```
<?xml version="1.0" encoding="utf-8" ?>
- <ProductList>
    <Products ProductName="Geitost" UnitPrice="2.5" />
    <Products ProductName="Guaraná Fantástica" UnitPrice="4.5" />
    <Products ProductName="Konbu" UnitPrice="6" />
    <Products ProductName="Filo Mix" UnitPrice="7" />
    <Products ProductName="Tourtière" UnitPrice="7.45" />
    <Products ProductName="Rhönbräu Klosterbier" UnitPrice="7.75" />
    <Products ProductName="Tunnbröd" UnitPrice="9" />
    <Products ProductName="Teatime Chocolate Biscuits" UnitPrice="9.2" />
    <Products ProductName="Zaanse koeken" UnitPrice="9.5" />
    <Products ProductName="Rogede sild" UnitPrice="9.5" />
  </ProductList>
```

Using this syntax, we can just as easily call a stored procedure that takes parameters as input. As an example, let's create a stored procedure called XML Sales By Year, which is identical to the Sales By Year stored procedure included as part of the Northwind database, with the exception that it returns the results as XML:

```
CREATE PROCEDURE [XML Sales By Year]
    @Beginning_Date DateTime,
    @Ending_Date DateTime
AS
    SELECT  Orders.ShippedDate,
            Orders.OrderID,
            "Order Subtotals".Subtotal,
            DATENAME(yy,ShippedDate) AS Year
    FROM    Orders
    INNER JOIN  "Order Subtotals"
        ON      Orders.OrderID = "Order Subtotals".OrderID
        WHERE   Orders.ShippedDate Between @Beginning_Date And
@Ending_Date
    FOR XML AUTO
GO
```

We can run it using positional parameters:

http://localhost/urlquery?sql=exec+[XML+Sales+by+Year]+**'1+Jan+1998','31+Dec+1998'**&root=Sales

or named parameters:

URL Queries and Template Queries

http://localhost/urlquery?sql=exec+[XML+Sales+by+Year]+**@Beginning_date ='1+Jan+1998',@Ending_date='31+Dec+1998'**&root=Sales

The latter produces a longer URL but is useful if there are optional parameters for the stored procedure that you want to omit.

Using ODBC Call Syntax

The second method we could use is the ODBC call syntax. To run the previous two stored procedures we would use the following URL queries:

For the ten least expensive products:

http://localhost/urlquery?sql={call+[Ten+Least+Expensive+Products]}&root= ProductList

For XML Sales by Year:

http://localhost/urlquery?sql={call+[XML+Sales+by+Year]}+'1+Jan+1998','31+D ec+1998'&root=Sales

or named argument:

http://localhost/urlquery?sql={call+[XML+Sales+by+Year]}+@Beginning_date= '1+Jan+1998',@Ending_date='31+Dec+1998'&root=Sales

Using Stylesheets

In addition to enabling us to return XML to IE, URL queries also allow the passing of an XSL stylesheet within the URL to format the results. This is done by specifying the **xsl** parameter in the query.

To illustrate this, we'll take the `Ten Least Expensive Products` query that we used earlier and add some formatting to it. First we need to define the stylesheet:

```
<?xml version='1.0' encoding='UTF-8'?>
<xsl:stylesheet
    xmlns:xsl="http://www.w3.org/1999/XSL/Transform"
    version="1.0">
  <xsl:template match = '/'>
    <HTML>
      <HEAD>
        <TITLE>Northwind Management Reports</TITLE>
          <STYLE>th { background-color: #AAAEEE }</STYLE>
      </HEAD>
      <BODY>
        <TABLE border='1' style='width:300;'>
          <TR><TH colspan='2'>
              Ten Least Expensive Products</TH></TR>
          <TR><TH >Product Name</TH><TH>Unit Price</TH></TR>
          <xsl:for-each select = 'ProductList/Products'>
            <TR>
              <TD><xsl:value-of select = '@ProductName' /></TD>
```

127

```
                <TD><xsl:value-of select = '@UnitPrice' /></TD>
            </TR>
        </xsl:for-each>
        </TABLE>
    </BODY>
    </HTML>
  </xsl:template>
</xsl:stylesheet>
```

For information on how to create your own XSL stylesheets, please see Beginning XML, 2nd Edition, Wrox Press (ISBN: 1861005598).

Save this to a file named `products.xsl` (or extract it from the code download) and put it into the folder that the virtual directory we created earlier points to. We can then apply this stylesheet to the results of our query by adding the `xsl` parameter to the end of the URL:

http://localhost/urlquery?sql=exec+[Ten+Least+Expensive+Products]&root=ProductList&xsl=products.xsl

This produces a nicely formatted web page:

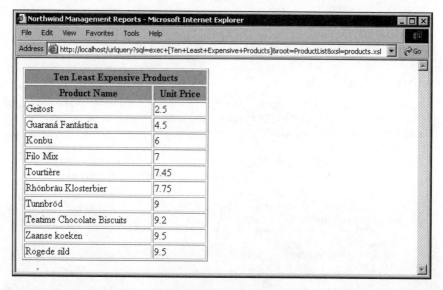

We could enhance this further by adding in hyperlinks back to a main page so that a whole web site could be produced. We could create a simple home page, as shown below, and put this under the IIS `wwwroot` folder as `default.htm`. This home page includes a hyperlink that uses our URL query to bring back the formatted list of the ten least expensive products:

```
<HTML>
    <HEAD>
        <title>Northwind Management Reports</title>
```

URL Queries and Template Queries

```
    </HEAD>
    <BODY>
      <B> Northwind Traders Management Reports</B><P>
      <A HREF="/urlquery?sql=exec+[Ten+Least+Expensive+Products]
           &root=ProductList&xsl=products2.xsl">
           Ten Least Expensive Products
      </A>
    </BODY>
</HTML>
```

Here is what it looks like:

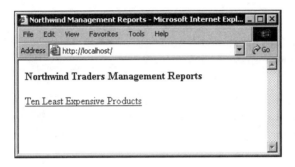

If we modify our original XSL stylesheet (and save it as products2.xsl), we can add a link back to the home page on our product details page, and begin to build a workable site:

```
<?xml version='1.0' encoding='UTF-8'?>
<xsl:stylesheet
xmlns:xsl="http://www.w3.org/1999/XSL/Transform"

version="1.0">
  <xsl:template match = '/'>
    <HTML>
      <HEAD>
        <TITLE>Northwind Management Reports</TITLE>
          <STYLE>th { background-color: #AAAEEE }</STYLE>
      </HEAD>
      <BODY>
        <TABLE border='1' style='width:300;'>
          <TR><TH colspan='2'>
              Ten Least Expensive Products</TH></TR>
          <TR><TH >Product Name</TH><TH>Unit Price</TH></TR>
          <xsl:for-each select = 'ProductList/Products'>
            <TR>
              <TD><xsl:value-of select = '@ProductName' /></TD>
              <TD><xsl:value-of select = '@UnitPrice' /></TD>
            </TR>
          </xsl:for-each>
        </TABLE>
        <P>
```

129

Chapter 5

```
            <A HREF=".."> Return to home page </A>
         </P>
      </BODY>
   </HTML>
 </xsl:template>
</xsl:stylesheet>
```

Our product details page now look like this:

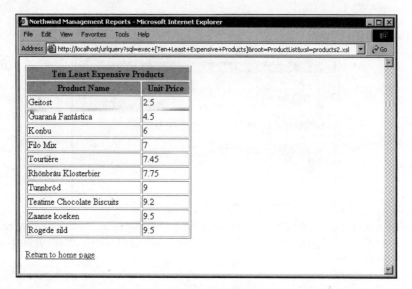

Obviously, you could add all kinds of fancy graphics and layout to these pages but we're just trying to show the possibilities here.

Content Types

You can also change the content type of the output. XML aware browsers like IE, automatically detect the content type and display it accordingly. The default type is text/xml when xsl isn't specified or text/html when it is. It is only necessary to override these defaults if you need the browser to recognize a different content type.

To specify a content type, you put it as an extra parameter (**contenttype**) on the URL just as we've done with the root and xsl parameters. The following example overrides IE's text/xml default by specifying text/html for the result instead:

http://localhost/urlquery?sql=exec+[Ten+Least+Expensive+Products]
&contenttype=text/html

At first this looks like it doesn't do anything because the browser doesn't recognize the result as valid HTML, but if you view the source of the page, you'll see that the XML has been returned as a fragment, without a root element. To make this display as HTML, add a root parameter to the query:

http://localhost/urlquery?sql=exec+[Ten+Least+Expensive+Products]
&contenttype=text/html&root=ProductList

URL Queries and Template Queries

Using Special Characters

Some characters that you would use within a SQL statement aren't valid within an URL. We've already seen this where we've replaced spaces with +. There are other characters that you'll commonly need to replace, such as the wildcards that are used in the LIKE clause. If we wanted to return all employees whose first name began with A using a normal SQL statement, we'd use LIKE 'A%'. % is a special character used within URLs to encode values, and cannot be used for any other purpose. We therefore need to replace it with characters that will be recognized as the appropriate wildcard (that is, we need to **escape** it).

In this case we can replace it with %25. Once we have done this, our query is:

http://localhost/urlquery?sql=select+firstname,lastname+from+employees+where +firstname+like+'**A%25**'+for+xml+auto&root=employees

which returns:

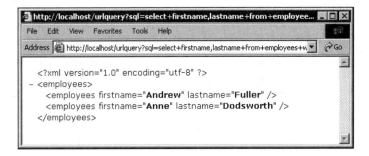

The list of special characters and their appropriate replacements is:

Special Character	Replacement Value
+	%20
/	%2F
?	%3F
%	%25
#	%23
&	%26

charset

This parameter allows you to specify a particular character set for the returned XML to override the default of UTF-8. So, for example, if you wanted to specify that it was Windows Traditional Chinese you would append the following to the end of the URL:

&_charset_=Windows-950

For a list of appropriate character set encodings, please see:
http://www.devsphere.com/mapping/docs/guide/encodings.html

Template Queries

Template queries provide similar functionality to URL queries. The most significant advantage of using templates over URL queries is that everything is abstracted away from the user. Apart from the name of the template, they are given no information about which tables are in the database or which fields they contain. In fact, they can't even tell whether there is a query to SQL Server going on behind the scenes or not because all they see is the name of the XML file.

Template queries also overcome one of the other major pitfalls of URL queries – security. Users are prevented from altering the query as they don't ever get to see it. This is similar to the way that a stored procedure abstracts the query from the user. There is no direct access to the database, thus preventing users from running their own, potentially dangerous queries against it.

A template is an XML file stored within the virtual directory that can contain one or more queries, or statements to run stored procedures. They can also contain references to XSL stylesheets for formatting the results.

As with URL queries, using templates is also a very elegant way of producing a set of web pages with access to database functionality without either relying on or even having to know proprietary data access technologies such as ADO or ADO.NET, or web technologies like ASP, ASP.NET or JSP.

In the following sections we'll show the use of templates to:

- Run standard SELECT statements
- Execute stored procedures
- Parameterize queries
- Pass parameters to stored procedures
- Run multiple queries or stored procedures within a single template
- Apply stylesheets to the template results

Usage Guidelines

As templates remove most of the security concerns of URL queries, they can be considered for use in a much wider set of applications. This includes Internet as well as intranet use, although there are some limitations that you should be aware of.

Using templates gives us flexibility in querying and formatting the results, but for complex requirements where there is a lot of user interaction with the pages alternatives should be considered. ASP, and especially ASP.NET, are likely to provide an easier to develop, more supportable application, as well as allowing richer business logic to be implemented.

In reality, you might consider a mixed environment as this can work very well. As the DBA you could set up a series of templates to give access to the database for producing reports, providing parameters to these templates that could then be programmed against by developers using ASP or ASP.NET.

URL Queries and Template Queries

In terms of performance, you're likely to see little difference between these two query methods, although templates may be marginally quicker. Installing the SQLXML onto a web server that is separate from the SQL Server allows you to use technologies such as Network Load Balancing to scale out onto multiple web servers as required to get extra capacity.

Security Considerations

Templates are set up using virtual directories, as with URL queries. You should still be very careful to only give the account that is set here the minimum permissions it needs to run the queries within the templates.

The recommendation is to use a Windows account to access the database using Windows Authentication. You can do this either by using the account the user accesses the web page with, or by setting up a single account for all access. The decision on which you use really depends on what you are trying to achieve.

User-by-user access allows more granular control over which templates each user can employ. This can be accomplished by restricting access to particular database objects account-by-account, or by creating roles that group the access to particular sets of templates. However, using a single account can be simpler to administer if everybody is to have the same privileges. It also takes away the worry that somebody may have additional access given to them through a separate application and hence be given extra permissions that you don't know about.

Templates are normally stored within the virtual directory to be executed on the server side, but there is also the option of allowing templates to be posted from the client. Doing this enables a user or application to create a template and upload it to the web server to run it.

> Use of the posting option should be considered carefully as it gives the user the potential to run any query in the same way that we demonstrated with URL queries at the beginning of this chapter. For example, you could post a template that had a query in it to delete all the rows from a table or even to delete an entire database.

Template posting is discussed further in the *Posting Templates* section at the end of this chapter.

Setting up the Environment

To enable our templates to be used correctly, we need to set up a virtual directory that will host them appropriately. This is a similar process to the one we stepped through for URL queries, except that this time we set the virtual name type to `template`. What follows is a list of the steps needed to prepare a virtual directory for the examples in this chapter.

- ❑ From within the IIS Virtual Directory Management for SQLXML 3.0 console, right-click on the **Default Web Site** and choose **New | Virtual Directory** from the **Action** menu.

Chapter 5

- On the **General** tab of the Virtual Directory Management tool, enter `templates` for the **Virtual Directory Name** and choose a local path.
- On the **Security** tab, choose a method of connecting to the database. If your server is configured to allow Windows Integrated Authentication, then choose this for added security.
- On the **Data Source** tab, select the server that you want to connect to. In this case we'll use the `Northwind` database for all the examples, so select this database.
- Finally, on the **Virtual Names** tab, we need to define where the templates will be stored. Click **New** and create a new virtual name called `template`, choose the `template` type, and select the folder that you specified on the **General** tab. Apart from this step, the process is identical to setting up a virtual directory for URL query access.
- Click **OK** to save all this and the virtual directory is now ready for use.

Template and XSL Stylesheet Caching

There were a couple of other options that we could have altered that are located in the bottom third of the **Advanced** tab:

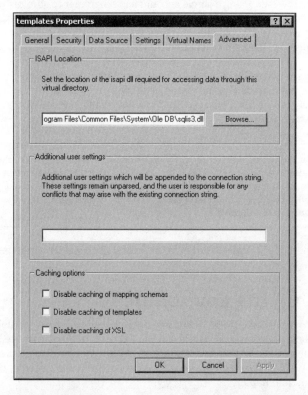

These are to disable the caching of templates and/or XSL stylesheets. By default these are un-checked, meaning that the caching is enabled. This enhances performance, as they don't need to be loaded from disk each time they are used by the web server.

URL Queries and Template Queries

Even with caching enabled, the database query within the template is still run each time. It's purely the template that is cached and not its results.

With caching enabled, there is a significant performance increase for templates that are used a lot. The cache is kept up to date automatically as each time the template is used the modification timestamp of the cached version is checked against the version in the file system.

Normally you won't want to change this option except in two circumstances:

- ❏ This is a development environment and you are constantly changing the files. There isn't much point in enabling caching then.
- ❏ You have a huge number of files that are being used, and caching consumes a large amount of server memory that you decide is better used for something else

Usage

In its simplest form there is very little work that needs to go into creating a template to run a SQL query:

```
<ROOT xmlns:sql="urn:schemas-microsoft-com:xml-sql" >
   <sql:query>
      SELECT FirstName, LastName FROM Employees FOR XML AUTO
   </sql:query>
</ROOT>
```

Our `employees.xml` template consists of two elements: **<ROOT>** and **<sql:query>**.

The <ROOT> element can be given any name you wish and contains the XML namespace for Microsoft SQL. This namespace defines the set of valid XML tags that are allowed within the template. As we'll see shortly, it is also possible to include details of an XSL file to use to format the results in this element.

The <sql:query> element is where we do most of the work though. As its name indicates, this is where we put our SQL statements.

To use this template, save it as `employees.xml` in the `template` folder we defined earlier. Then use the following URL:

http://localhost/templates/template/employees.xml

where `templates` is the name of the virtual directory and `template` is the virtual name we created within it.

Chapter 5

This query produces the following list of employees in XML format:

```
- <ROOT xmlns:sql="urn:schemas-microsoft-com:xml-sql">
    <Employees FirstName="Nancy" LastName="Davolio" />
    <Employees FirstName="Andrew" LastName="Fuller" />
    <Employees FirstName="Janet" LastName="Leverling" />
    <Employees FirstName="Margaret" LastName="Peacock" />
    <Employees FirstName="Steven" LastName="Buchanan" />
    <Employees FirstName="Michael" LastName="Suyama" />
    <Employees FirstName="Robert" LastName="King" />
    <Employees FirstName="Laura" LastName="Callahan" />
    <Employees FirstName="Anne" LastName="Dodsworth" />
  </ROOT>
```

Stored Procedures

We can call a stored procedure from within the `<sql:query>` element. To run the Ten Least Expensive Products stored procedure we created earlier, we need the following template (`leastexpensiveproducts.xml`):

```
<Products xmlns:sql="urn:schemas-microsoft-com:xml-sql" >
   <sql:query>
      exec [Ten Least Expensive Products]
   </sql:query>
</Products>
```

which produces the same result as running this stored procedure in an URL query did before:

```
- <Products xmlns:sql="urn:schemas-microsoft-com:xml-sql">
    <Products ProductName="Geitost" UnitPrice="2.5" />
    <Products ProductName="Guaraná Fantástica" UnitPrice="4.5" />
    <Products ProductName="Konbu" UnitPrice="6" />
    <Products ProductName="Filo Mix" UnitPrice="7" />
    <Products ProductName="Tourtière" UnitPrice="7.45" />
    <Products ProductName="Rhönbräu Klosterbier" UnitPrice="7.75" />
    <Products ProductName="Tunnbröd" UnitPrice="9" />
    <Products ProductName="Teatime Chocolate Biscuits" UnitPrice="9.2" />
    <Products ProductName="Zaanse koeken" UnitPrice="9.5" />
    <Products ProductName="Rogede sild" UnitPrice="9.5" />
  </Products>
```

Parameterizing Queries

Let's consider cases where we want to make a query more generic. For example, rather than returning all the employees as we did in our simple query template, what if we wanted to just bring back those employees within an alphabetical range? We need to use a new element for this, `<sql:header>`. This element allows us to define one or more parameters for the template.

URL Queries and Template Queries

Each parameter is contained within its own **<sql:param>** element within <sql:header>. Parameters have two parts: the first is the name of the parameter and the second the default value. This is optional, so if you don't want to set a default, just leave the second part blank:

```
<sql:param name='StartLetter'></sql:param>
```

Here is a parameterized template (rangedemployees.xml) that includes A and Z as the default values for its parameters:

```
<ROOT xmlns:sql="urn:schemas-microsoft-com:xml-sql" >
   <sql:header>
      <sql:param name='StartLetter'>A</sql:param>
      <sql:param name='EndLetter'>Z</sql:param>
   </sql:header>
   <sql:query>
   SELECT FirstName, LastName
      FROM Employees
      WHERE LEFT(LastName,1)
         BETWEEN @StartLetter
         AND @EndLetter
   FOR XML AUTO
   </sql:query>
</ROOT>
```

To use these parameters as you would any other variable within the query, you take the name and put an @ at the front of it. To use the template you can either make use of the default parameter values and call it this way:

http://localhost/templates/template/rangedemployees.xml

or pass in the parameters in the form:

http://localhost/templates/template/rangedemployees.xml?**StartLetter=P&EndLetter=S**

which gives these results:

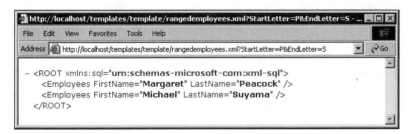

We can call a stored procedure that takes parameters in the same way (salesbyyear.xml):

```
<ROOT xmlns:sql="urn:schemas-microsoft-com:xml-sql" >
   <sql:header>
      <sql:param name='StartDate'>1 Jan 1998</sql:param>
      <sql:param name='EndDate'>31 Dec 1998</sql:param>
   </sql:header>
   <sql:query>
      exec [XML Sales by Year]
         @Beginning_date=@StartDate,@Ending_date=@EndDate
   </sql:query>
</ROOT>
```

By passing parameters in the URL that calls this template, we can restrict the results to be returned to February rather than the whole year:

http://localhost/templates/template/salesbyyear.xml?
StartDate=1998-02-01&EndDate=1998-02-28

Using Multiple Queries

In the same way that we can put more than one query into a batch using Query Analyzer, we can also put multiple queries (or stored procedures) into a template. We can do this in two ways, either by putting multiple statements within a single <sql:query> element, or by including multiple <sql:query> elements and putting a single statement into each one.

The following template (employeesterritories.xml) includes two SQL statements in one <sql:query> element:

```
<ROOT xmlns:sql="urn:schemas-microsoft-com:xml-sql" >
   <sql:query>
      SELECT EmployeeID, FirstName, LastName
         FROM Employees
         FOR XML AUTO
      SELECT EmployeeID, TerritoryID
         FROM EmployeeTerritories
         FOR XML AUTO
   </sql:query>
</ROOT>
```

We can call it using:

http://localhost/templates/template/employeesterritories.xml

URL Queries and Template Queries

and return the following results:

```
- <ROOT xmlns:sql="urn:schemas-microsoft-com:xml-sql">
    <Employees EmployeeID="1" FirstName="Nancy" LastName="Davolio" />
    <Employees EmployeeID="2" FirstName="Andrew" LastName="Fuller" />
    <Employees EmployeeID="3" FirstName="Janet" LastName="Leverling" />
    <Employees EmployeeID="4" FirstName="Margaret" LastName="Peacock" />
    <Employees EmployeeID="5" FirstName="Steven" LastName="Buchanan" />
    <Employees EmployeeID="6" FirstName="Michael" LastName="Suyama" />
    <Employees EmployeeID="7" FirstName="Robert" LastName="King" />
    <Employees EmployeeID="8" FirstName="Laura" LastName="Callahan" />
    <Employees EmployeeID="9" FirstName="Anne" LastName="Dodsworth" />
    <EmployeeTerritories EmployeeID="1" TerritoryID="06897" />
    <EmployeeTerritories EmployeeID="1" TerritoryID="19713" />
    <EmployeeTerritories EmployeeID="2" TerritoryID="01581" />
    <EmployeeTerritories EmployeeID="2" TerritoryID="01730" />
```

Having multiple `<sql:query>` tags is just as simple (employeeterritories2.xml):

```
<ROOT xmlns:sql="urn:schemas-microsoft-com:xml-sql" >
  <sql:query>
    SELECT EmployeeID, FirstName, LastName
      FROM Employees
      FOR XML AUTO
  </sql:query>
  <sql:query>
    SELECT EmployeeID, TerritoryID
      FROM EmployeeTerritories
      FOR XML AUTO
  </sql:query>
</ROOT>
```

and returns exactly the same results.

So what is the practical difference between them? The statements within each `<sql:query>` element are sent to SQL Server as a single query batch, and therefore form a single transaction. This means that the statements can pass information between themselves. Because of this, it is more usual to put all the statements within a single `<sql:query>` element.

However, there are some SQL statements that cannot be put into the same batch, so if you were doing something unusual (for a template anyway), like dropping and recreating a stored procedure, you would need to put the DROP and CREATE statements into separate `<sql:query>` elements.

> **Note: It is not recommended practice to use templates for any form of database administration**

139

Chapter 5

Using Output Parameters

As we said, we can pass values between statements within a single `<sql:query>` tag. One way of doing this is by using the value of an OUTPUT parameter from a stored procedure as we'll see in the following example. Create this stored procedure (TopProduct) that returns the product ID of the best selling product:

```
CREATE PROCEDURE TopProduct
   @ProductID int OUTPUT
AS

SELECT TOP 1 @ProductID = ProductID
FROM [Order Details]
GROUP BY ProductID
ORDER BY SUM(Quantity) DESC
```

This can be used in the following template (topproduct.xml) to return the product ID that is then used to return details about this product.

```
<ROOT xmlns:sql="urn:schemas-microsoft-com:xml-sql" >
   <sql:query>
      DECLARE @ProductID int
      EXEC TopProduct @ProductID = @ProductID OUTPUT
      SELECT ProductID, ProductNAME FROM Products
         WHERE ProductID = @ProductID FOR XML AUTO
   </sql:query>
</ROOT>
```

Using Stylesheets

We can format the results using an XSL stylesheet just as we did with URL queries. If we copy the products.xsl stylesheet we created previously into our templates directory, we can map it into our template (leastexpensiveproductsxsl.xml) by adding the sql:xsl= to the <ROOT> tag:

```
<Products xmlns:sql="urn:schemas-microsoft-com:xml-sql"
   sql:xsl='products.xsl' >
   <sql:query>
      EXEC [Ten Least Expensive Products]
   </sql:query>
</Products>
```

We can then call this using:

http://localhost/templates/template/leastexpensiveproductsxsl.xml?contenttype=text/html

Note that we have had to add the contenttype parameter to the end of the URL in order to make this work. Otherwise IE adopts its default behavior and treats the result as XML rather than HTML because of its file extension.

We could also have specified the XSL stylesheet within the URL rather than inside the template, like this:

140

URL Queries and Template Queries

http://localhost/templates/template/leastexpensiveproducts.xml?xsl=products.xsl

This second method has the advantage that you can use different stylesheets with the same template, so you can do things like branding the page in different ways, or aim the results at different platforms such as PDAs or WAP phones as well as normal web browser. For example, you could invoke the template dynamically using ASP and within the ASP detect the browser type and alter the XSL filename accordingly. You can see this in action in Chapter 15.

XPath Queries

XPath is used in conjunction with a mapping schema (XML or XDR) to query the database. The mapping schema cross references the XML elements and attributes to tables and columns within the database. XPath queries are then used to make queries against this schema.

You can use the `<sql:xpath-query>` element within templates to reference a schema and specify your XPath query. The query is run when you call the template. Using XPath within templates is covered Chapter 8, *XPath*.

Other Options

There are a few little-used settings that can be used within templates, which allow the use of features that wouldn't otherwise be available.

is-xml

This attribute can be specified within a `<sql:param>` element to define what is being passed into the parameter. It can take a value of 0 or 1. The default is 1 if no value is specified.

1 means that the value being passed into the parameter is treated as XML, so any special coding is translated before use. If you don't want this functionality then you need to set this attribute to 0 as we have done in the fragment below:

```
<sql:header>
  <sql:param name='ProductDescription'
             is-xml='0'></sql:param>
</sql:header>
```

In this case, the product description might contain HTML tags that you wished to preserve rather than having them translated to XML.

sql:nullvalue

It isn't possible to pass a NULL value into a parameter from the URL, as any value that is passed is treated as a string. The **sql:nullvalue** attribute on the `<sql:header>` element allows you to define a special value that will indicate to the template that you want to pass a NULL value. Here's an example where we specify NULLValue as the value we will pass when we want NULL:

Chapter 5

```
<sql:header sql:nullvalue='NULLValue'>
  <sql:param name='ProductID'> </sql:param>
</sql:header>
```

You can then call this from the URL by passing in the parameter value as:

…?ProductID=NULLValue

to have the parameter produce `ProductID=NULL`

client-side-xml

This was discussed fully in Chapter 4, but just to recap: SQLXML 3.0 introduced the option of having the XML formatting carried out on the client rather than the server. This allows work to be offloaded from SQL Server onto the web server in order to free up processing under heavy loads. To use this option, change the `<sql:query>` element as below:

```
<sql:query client-side-xml;='1'>
```

Posting Templates

As well as using pre-configured templates stored within the virtual directory, it is also possible to create a template dynamically in an application on a client and then use `HTTP POST` to upload it to the web server for running. By default this option is not enabled for a virtual directory.

Allowing this option to be turned on brings up exactly the same security implications as we discussed at the beginning of this chapter for URL queries. Unless the user's security permissions within SQL Server are carefully restricted to allow read access to only those objects they need, you are providing an open invitation for people to run whatever SQL statements they want on your server. Therefore, it isn't recommended that this option be turned on except in an environment used exclusively for development, or a small intranet where you know exactly who the users are.

> *The code download contains a fragment of Visual Basic code (`VB_Posting.txt`) to illustrate how you might build the template string and then use the `xmlHttp` object to post it to a virtual directory.*

Summary

In this chapter we have shown how to use URL queries to put a SQL statement directly into the URL to execute and return either XML or, with the use of an XSL stylesheet, a formatted web page.

We then went on to show how templates enhance the security of URL queries by allowing you to abstract away from the user the details of the query. We showed how to call simple queries and stored procedures, how to pass parameters into them, and then how to use XSL to format the results.

Finally, we showed how it is possible to use your own dynamic template by posting it to the server rather than using one that is pre-stored.

Kevin Williams

- Why Annotate XML Schemas?
- XML Schemas vs. XDR Schemas
- The XML Schema Annotation Namespace
- Annotation Mechanisms
- Summary

6

Annotating XML Schemas

In this chapter, we're going to learn about annotating XML schemas with information about a SQL Server database. These annotations serve to indicate how relational data maps onto the hierarchical contents of an XML schema, and vice-versa. Our focus here is on the methods of annotation; we will see how XML schema annotations are applied in other chapters of this book.

Why Annotate XML Schemas?

SQL Server 2000 and the SQLXML 3.0 library use annotated XML schemas for a number of purposes. Since a typical XML document will not have the same shape as the tables and foreign key relationships in the corresponding SQL Server database, the various XML technologies included in SQL Server 2000 and SQLXML 3.0 require additional information to determine how one form maps onto the other. There are several different technologies in SQL Server 2000 and SQLXML 3.0 that rely on annotated XML schemas to correctly interpret data in one form and return it in another, and we'll take a quick look at them here. You can find further details on each of these technologies later in this book.

- ❑ **Updategrams** – Updategrams are a SQLXML 2.0+ technology that can be used to update a database with information found in an XML document. Updategrams can either be run implicitly or explicitly. In the implicit case, each complex element in an Updategram corresponds to a table in the database, and each simple element or attribute corresponds to a column in the database. In the explicit case, the mapping between the SQL Server tables and the XML constructs is defined in an annotated XML schema document. We'll learn more about Updategrams in Chapter 11.

- ❑ **DiffGrams** – DiffGrams are similar to Updategrams, except that DiffGrams can be used to describe the current state of an ADO.NET `DataSet` (including the current and original states of records that have not yet been committed to the underlying database), as well as apply an update to the database. Like Updategrams,

- **XML Bulk Load** – XML Bulk Load is a COM object included with SQLXML version 2.0+ that allows XML data to be quickly loaded into SQL Server tables. It tends to perform much better than either Updategrams or an INSERT command in conjunction with OPENXML. When a call is made to the bulk load object to load a particular XML document into the database, you must also provide the annotated XML schema document that defines the mapping from the XML format to the SQL Server format. XML bulk load is covered in more depth in Chapter 12.

- **XML Views** – XML views, in contrast to all the other technologies listed above, manipulate data in the other direction since they are used to expose data in a SQL Server database as if it were XML. XPath expressions can then be used against these XML views to return XML fragments (similar to applying T-SQL against traditional database views). Since XML views can take the form of templates, they can be accessed through HTTP as well as through more standard mechanisms (such as ADO). We'll learn more about XML views in the next chapter.

XML Schemas vs. XDR Schemas

Annotated schemas have been in SQLXML since before the World Wide Web Consortium promoted the XML Schema specification to Recommendation status. As a result, SQLXML provides support for the annotation of both XDR and XML schemas (formerly known as XSD). This support is still provided so that if you usually work with XDR schemas (for example, if you have a heavy legacy investment in BizTalk schemas, which use XDR), you can annotate those in the same way you would annotate an XML schema.

In this chapter, we'll describe how annotation mechanisms apply to XML schema definitions, but these annotation mechanisms can equally well be applied, in most cases, to XDR schemas. Where the mechanisms we describe do not map directly to XDR schemas, we'll indicate that in the text.

> *A comprehensive reference to XML Schema elements and attributes is provided in Appendix B. Mapping SQL Server data types to XML Schema datatypes was covered in Chapter 3.*

The XML Schema Annotation Namespace

XML schema annotations have their own namespace – urn:schemas-microsoft-com:mapping-schema. All annotation declarations must appear in this namespace. By convention, we'll use the sql: prefix in this chapter for the XML Schema namespace.

Annotating XML Schemas

Annotations appear as attributes added to the declarations for the elements, attributes, or types they are annotating. For example, the following relation annotation associates the table `Customer` with the `<customer>` XML element in this schema:

```
<xsd:schema xmlns:xsd="http://www.w3.org/2001/XMLSchema"
        xmlns:sql="urn:schemas-microsoft-com:mapping-schema">
  <xsd:element name="customer" sql:relation="Customer">
    <xsd:complexType>
      <xsd:attribute name="customerName" type="xsd:string" />
    </xsd:complexType>
  </xsd:element>
</xsd:schema>
```

Annotation Mechanisms

In this section, we'll introduce the most common annotation attributes; more information about how these attributes impact the various data manipulation technologies (outlined earlier) will be provided in the chapters discussing them in further detail.

For all of the following examples, we'll be using this sample SQL Server structure (which is the Inventory database created in the final example in Chapter 3):

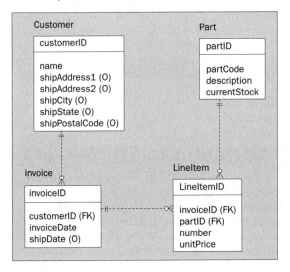

Mapping Complex Elements to SQL Server Tables

The first step in annotating an XML schema is to define how elements in the schema map to elements in our relational database. Adding the **sql:relation** attribute to elements with complex types in our XML schema does this. For example, let's say we had the following schema that describes a particular customer in our database:

147

Chapter 6

```xml
<xsd:schema xmlns:xsd="http://www.w3.org/2001/XMLSchema">
  <xsd:element name="dataCustomer">
    <xsd:complexType>
      <xsd:attribute name="customerName" type="xsd:string" />
    </xsd:complexType>
  </xsd:element>
</xsd:schema>
```

We add the `sql:relation` attribute to the element declaration for customer, to assert that each `<dataCustomer>` complex element in our XML document corresponds to a row in the `Customer` SQL Server table:

```xml
<xsd:schema xmlns:xsd="http://www.w3.org/2001/XMLSchema"
            xmlns:sql="urn:schemas-microsoft-com:mapping-schema">
  <xsd:element name="dataCustomer" sql:relation="Customer">
    <xsd:complexType>
      <xsd:attribute name="customerName" type="xsd:string" />
    </xsd:complexType>
  </xsd:element>
</xsd:schema>
```

> *As a brief reminder here, note that table and column names are case sensitive in XML.*

If this mapping is omitted for a particular element, the various mapping technologies assume that a table with the same name as the element, but without a `sql:relation` attribute, contains the data for that element. In our example, if we omit the `sql:relation` attribute, it is assumed that there exists a table called `dataCustomer` in our database, corresponding to this element. It's also possible for you to indicate, through another attribute (**sql:is-constant**) in the mapping schema namespace, that a particular element or attribute does not have a corresponding table or column in the SQL Server database – we'll see how this is done later in the chapter.

Mapping Attributes to SQL Server Columns

Attribute values are mapped to SQL Server columns using the **sql:field** attribute on the attribute declaration in the XML schema. The combination of `sql:relation` and `sql:field` provides a complete mapping between the attribute values in the XML schema and the columns in the database. For example, we can map the `customerName` attribute in our previous sample schema by adding a `sql:field` attribute to its declaration:

```xml
<xsd:schema xmlns:xsd="http://www.w3.org/2001/XMLSchema"
            xmlns:sql="urn:schemas-microsoft-com:mapping-schema">
  <xsd:element name="dataCustomer" sql:relation="Customer">
    <xsd:complexType>
      <xsd:attribute name="customerName" type="xsd:string"
                     sql:field="name" />
    </xsd:complexType>
  </xsd:element>
</xsd:schema>
```

Annotating XML Schemas

Now, when the various technologies move information between XML and SQL Server or SQL Server and XML, the parser has enough information to know that the `customerName` attribute on the `<dataCustomer>` element maps to the `name` column of the `Customer` table in the database.

As with `sql:relation`, omitting `sql:field` implies that the SQL Server column has the same name as the attribute; so here it would imply that the column in the `Customer` table was called `customerName`. Often, the accidental omission of a `sql:relation` or `sql:field` annotation can create unexpected results when trying to use the annotated schema, so this is a good place to start looking if there are problems. We can also include the `sql:relation` field on an attribute; if provided, this indicates that the attribute maps to a different table than the overall element itself.

Mapping Text-only Elements to SQL Server Columns

Mapping simple-content elements (elements that contain data points) to SQL Server columns uses the same mechanism as attribute mapping. In other words, you can simply add the `sql:field` attribute to the simple element declaration to indicate with which column in the mapped table it corresponds. Let's say that we chose to use simple elements rather than attributes to represent our data points in our (as yet unannotated) XML schema:

```
<xsd:schema xmlns:xsd="http://www.w3.org/2001/XMLSchema">
  <xsd:element name="dataCustomer">
    <xsd:complexType>
      <xsd:sequence>
        <xsd:element name="customerName" type="xsd:string" />
      </xsd:sequence>
    </xsd:complexType>
  </xsd:element>
</xsd:schema>
```

We add the `sql:field` attribute to the element declaration for `<customerName>`, to assert that the value of this element is mapped to the `name` column in the `Customer` table in our database:

```
<xsd:schema xmlns:xsd="http://www.w3.org/2001/XMLSchema"
            xmlns:sql="urn:schemas-microsoft-com:mapping-schema">
  <xsd:element name="dataCustomer" sql:relation="Customer">
    <xsd:complexType>
      <xsd:sequence>
        <xsd:element name="customerName" type="xsd:string"
                     sql:field="name" />
      </xsd:sequence>
    </xsd:complexType>
  </xsd:element>
</xsd:schema>
```

As with the attribute mapping, omitting the `sql:field` attribute on an element with a simple type implies that the name of the field is the same in both the XML schema and the SQL Server table. We can also include the `sql:relation` field on simple type elements; if provided, this indicates that the simple type element maps to a different table than the overall element itself. If you don't want an attribute or an element with a simple type to be mapped to the SQL Server tables, there's a mechanism, the **`sql:mapped`** annotation, that we'll see more about later.

Defining Unmapped XML Elements

In many cases, you may need to generate XML elements that do not correspond to any particular tables in the SQL Server database (but that you still want to appear in your XML documents). Here's an example. Say you want to create an XML document that contains information about all the customers in your database. Simply mapping the Customer table to the <customer> XML element isn't sufficient; a generated document would look something like this:

```
<customer customerName="Kevin Williams" />
<customer customerName="Joe Somebody" />
<customer customerName="Fred Nobody" />
```

This isn't a well-formed XML document because there's no root element. To create a root element, we can declare it in our XML schema and add the **`sql:is-constant`** attribute (with a value of 1 signifying True) to the element declaration. The mapping will recognize that the element needs to be created at the appropriate location in the element hierarchy. The declaration would look something like this:

```
<xsd:schema xmlns:xsd="http://www.w3.org/2001/XMLSchema"
            xmlns:sql="urn:schemas-microsoft-com:mapping-schema">
   <xsd:element name="customerList"
                sql:is-constant="1">
      <xsd:complexType>
         <xsd:sequence>
            <xsd:element name="dataCustomer"
                         maxOccurs="unbounded"
                         sql:relation="Customer">
               <xsd:complexType>
                  <xsd:attribute name="customerName"
                                 sql:field="name" />
               </xsd:complexType>
            </xsd:element>
         </xsd:sequence>
      </xsd:complexType>
   </xsd:element>
</xsd:schema>
```

Annotating XML Schemas

A sample document for this schema would look like this:

```
<customerList>
  <customer customerName="Kevin Williams" />
  <customer customerName="Joe Somebody" />
  <customer customerName="Fred Nobody" />
</customerList>
```

The `sql:is-constant` attribute can also be used to add container elements around lists of other elements; for example, if you wanted to group together all of the `<Part>` definitions in the document into a `<PartList>` element.

Excluding XML Elements From the Mapping

If you want to indicate that a particular element or attribute is not mapped to a SQL Server table or column, and in addition you don't want it to appear in any XML document derived from that data using this mapping, you would use the `sql:mapped` attribute. By setting this attribute to 0 (or the string `false`), you can specify that the element or attribute will be ignored altogether in the mapping process. This is useful if you need to annotate an XML schema that is being used to validate other XML documents. Let's say we have the following XML schema declaration:

```
<xsd:schema xmlns:xsd="http://www.w3.org/2001/XMLSchema">
  <xsd:element name="dataCustomer">
    <xsd:complexType>
      <xsd:attribute name="customerName" type="xsd:string" />
      <xsd:attribute name="customerSSN" type="xsd:string" />
    </xsd:complexType>
  </xsd:element>
</xsd:schema>
```

If we choose to discard the `customerSSN` (it is not relevant to the SQL structure onto which we are mapping), we can exclude it using the `sql:mapped` attribute:

```
<xsd:schema xmlns:xsd="http://www.w3.org/2001/XMLSchema"
            xmlns:sql="urn:schemas-microsoft-com:mapping-schema">
  <xsd:element name="dataCustomer"
               sql:relation="Customer">
    <xsd:complexType>
      <xsd:attribute name="customerName"
                     type="xsd:string"
                     sql:field="name" />
      <xsd:attribute name="customerSSN"
                     type="xsd:string"
                     sql:mapped="false" />
    </xsd:complexType>
  </xsd:element>
</xsd:schema>
```

So how do we choose when to use `sql:mapped` or `sql:is-constant`? Here are some guidelines:

- sql:is-constant can only be specified for elements with a complex type (in other words structural elements). For such structural elements, you should use sql:is-constant when you need to create an element in the resulting XML structure that does not exist in the SQL Server schema.
- If you want to ignore an element with a simple type or an attribute in the mapping, you need to specify sql:mapped="false". In the case of complex types, you should also use sql:mapped to indicate that an element in the XML structure should be completely ignored (both from the perspective of the SQL Server database and any XML structures derived from it), other than the case stated in the bullet point above.

> In XDR schemas, the sql:mapping attribute is called map-field.

Specifying Relationships Between Two SQL Tables

When you are mapping more than one table in your SQL Server database to your XML structure, you need some way of specifying how the data in the SQL Server database is related (if they are related at all). This enables the **serializer** – that part of the XML engine responsible for creating XML documents from the relational database contents – to associate the proper records together in parent/child relationships (in the case of XML document creation), or to properly interpret the parent-child relationships (in the case of a database modification, such as an Updategram). Let's see an example. Say we want to create a document from our database that looks like this:

```xml
<customerHistory>
  <customer name="Kevin Williams">
    <invoice invoiceDate="2002-03-14" shipDate="2002-04-17" />
    <invoice invoiceDate="2002-04-19" shipDate="2002-05-22" />
  </customer>
  <customer name="Fred Nobody">
    <invoice invoiceDate="2002-06-01" shipDate="2002-06-15" />
    <invoice invoiceDate="2002-07-01" shipDate="2002-07-07" />
  </customer>
</customerHistory>
```

The XML schema for this document looks like this:

```xml
<xsd:schema xmlns:xsd="http://www.w3.org/2001/XMLSchema">
  <xsd:element name="customerHistory">
    <xsd:complexType>
      <xsd:sequence>
        <xsd:element name="customer" maxOccurs="unbounded">
          <xsd:complexType>
            <xsd:sequence>
              <xsd:element name="invoice"
                           maxOccurs="unbounded">
                <xsd:complexType>
                  <xsd:attribute name="invoiceDate"
                                 type="xsd:dateTime" />
```

Annotating XML Schemas

```
                    <xsd:attribute name="shipDate"
                                   type="xsd:dateTime" />
                  </xsd:complexType>
                </xsd:element>
              </xsd:sequence>
            </xsd:complexType>
          </xsd:element>
        </xsd:sequence>
      </xsd:complexType>
    </xsd:element>
</xsd:schema>
```

To assert the relationship between the <customer> and <invoice> elements, we need to add a **<sql:relationship>** element to the **<xsd:appinfo>** element inside the **<xsd:annotation>** element in our XML schema.

You may not be familiar with these XML schema elements – they are used to add outside information to a schema document, and are typically used for documentation purposes. These elements should be added either for the XML schema itself (for a relationship that is named, and then referenced by name later), or in the <xsd:annotation> element for the child element in the relationship (by convention, for an unnamed relationship). The relationship needs to have four attributes (five, including the name attribute, if it is named):

- ❏ **parent** contains the name of the SQL Server table that is the parent of the relationship
- ❏ **child** contains the name of the SQL Server table that is the child
- ❏ **parent-key** contains the name of the SQL Server column that is the primary key of the parent
- ❏ **child-key** contains the name of the foreign key in the child table that relates back to the primary key of the parent.

Let's look at a couple of examples.

To specify a named relationship between <customer> and <invoice>, we add the following to our XML schema declaration:

```
<xsd:schema xmlns:xsd="http://www.w3.org/2001/XMLSchema"
            xmlns:sql="urn:schemas-microsoft-com:mapping-schema">
  <xsd:annotation>
    <xsd:appinfo>
      <sql:relationship name="CustomerInvoiceRelation"
                        parent="Customer"
                        parent-key="customerID"
                        child="Invoice"
                        child-key="customerID" />
    </xsd:appinfo>
  </xsd:annotation>
    <xsd:element name="customerHistory"
                 sql:is-constant="1">
      <xsd:complexType>
        <xsd:sequence>
```

153

```
            <xsd:element name="customer"
                         maxOccurs="unbounded"
                         sql:relation="Customer">
              <xsd:complexType>
                <xsd:sequence>
                  <xsd:element name="invoice"
                               maxOccurs="unbounded"
                               sql:relation="Invoice"
                               sql:relationship="CustomerInvoiceRelation">
                    <xsd:complexType>
                      <xsd:attribute name="invoiceDate"
                                     type="xsd:dateTime"
                                     sql:field="invoiceDate" />
                      <xsd:attribute name="shipDate"
                                     type="xsd:dateTime"
                                     sql:field="shipDate" />
                    </xsd:complexType>
                  </xsd:element>
                </xsd:sequence>
              </xsd:complexType>
            </xsd:element>
          </xsd:sequence>
        </xsd:complexType>
      </xsd:element>
    </xsd:schema>
```

Now, when this XML schema is used to map data between an XML document and the SQL Server tables, the **mapper** – that part of the XML engine responsible for decomposing the XML document and turning it into SQL Server rows – will be able to establish the proper relationship between the various database records.

We could also choose to specify the relationship within an element so that it can be used only by that element, rather than establishing and naming it at the top for use with any element within the schema. The following schema specifies the relationship this way:

```
<xsd:schema xmlns:xsd="http://www.w3.org/2001/XMLSchema"
            xmlns:sql="urn:schemas-microsoft-com:mapping-schema">
  <xsd:element name="customerHistory"
               sql:is-constant="1">
    <xsd:complexType>
      <xsd:sequence>
        <xsd:element name="customer"
                     maxOccurs="unbounded"
                     sql:relation="Customer">
          <xsd:complexType>
            <xsd:sequence>
              <xsd:element name="invoice"
                           maxOccurs="unbounded"
                           sql:relation="Invoice">
                <xsd:annotation>
                  <xsd:appinfo>
```

```xml
                        <sql:relationship
                                    name="CustomerInvoiceRelation"
                                    parent="Customer"
                                    parent-key="customerID"
                                    child="Invoice"
                                    child-key="customerID" />
                    </xsd:appinfo>
                </xsd:annotation>
                <xsd:complexType>
                    <xsd:attribute name="invoiceDate"
                                   type="xsd:dateTime"
                                   sql:field="invoiceDate" />
                    <xsd:attribute name="shipDate"
                                   type="xsd:dateTime"
                                   sql:field="shipDate" />
                </xsd:complexType>
            </xsd:element>
          </xsd:sequence>
        </xsd:complexType>
      </xsd:element>
    </xsd:sequence>
  </xsd:complexType>
</xsd:element>
</xsd:schema>
```

> In XDR schemas, the parent, child, parent-key, and child-key attributes are called key-relation, foreign-relation, key, and foreign-key respectively.

Filtering the Data in an XML Document

When you are mapping data from a SQL Server database to an XML document, you may want to filter the rows that appear in the created document. This is especially useful if there are specialized structures in the XML that correspond to general structures in the database. As an example, let's imagine that we had created these two tables in a database:

```
CREATE TABLE Customer (
    customerID int IDENTITY PRIMARY KEY NOT NULL,
    customerName varchar(50) NOT NULL)
GO

CREATE TABLE Address (
    addressID int IDENTITY NOT NULL,
    customerID int FOREIGN KEY REFERENCES Customer (customerID)
    NOT NULL,
    addressType tinyint NOT NULL,
    address1 varchar(100) NOT NULL,
    address2 varchar(100) NOT NULL,
    city varchar(50) NOT NULL,
    state char(2) NOT NULL,
    zip varchar(10) NOT NULL)
GO
```

Chapter 6

Customers may have multiple addresses in this database and the `addressType` specifies the type of the address. It contains 1 for a billing address and 2 for a shipping address. However, we want to generate an XML document that looks like this:

```xml
<customerList>
   <customer name="Kevin Williams">
      <shipAddress address1="742 Evergreen Terrace"
                   city="Springfield"
                   state="VA"
                   zip="24601" />
   </customer>
   <customer name="Fred Nobody">
      <shipAddress address1="100 Main Street"
                   city="Somewheresville"
                   state="VA"
                   zip="25678" />
   </customer>
</customerList>
```

In the resulting document, we are only interested in the addresses that have a 2 in the `addressType` column.

We can restrict the data by adding the **sql:limit-field** and **sql:limit-value** attributes to the element declaration that corresponds to that address. Here's an example of a schema, annotated to only return shipping addresses:

```xml
<xsd:schema xmlns:xsd="http://www.w3.org/2001/XMLSchema"
        xmlns:sql="urn:schemas-microsoft-com:mapping-schema">
   <xsd:element name="customerList"
                sql:is-constant="1">
      <xsd:complexType>
         <xsd:sequence>
            <xsd:element name="customer"
                         maxOccurs="unbounded"
                         sql:relation="Customer">
               <xsd:complexType>
                  <xsd:sequence>
                     <xsd:element name="shipAddress"
                                  maxOccurs="unbounded"
                                  sql:relation="Address"
                                  sql:limit-field="addressType"
                                  sql:limit-value="2">
                        <xsd:annotation>
                           <xsd:appinfo>
                              <sql:relationship
                                     name="CustomerShipAddressRelation"
                                     parent="Customer"
                                     parent-key="customerID"
                                     child="Address"
                                     child-key="customerID" />
```

Annotating XML Schemas

```
              </xsd:appinfo>
            </xsd:annotation>
            <xsd:complexType>
              <xsd:attribute name="address1"
                             type="xsd:string"
                             sql:field="address1" />
              <xsd:attribute name="city"
                             type="xsd:string"
                             sql:field="city" />
              <xsd:attribute name="state"
                             type="xsd:string"
                             sql:field="state" />
              <xsd:attribute name="zip"
                             type="xsd:string"
                             sql:field="zip" />
            </xsd:complexType>
          </xsd:element>
        </xsd:sequence>
      </xsd:complexType>
    </xsd:element>
  </xsd:sequence>
 </xsd:complexType>
 </xsd:element>
</xsd:schema>
```

Between `sql:limit-field`, `sql:limit-value`, and `sql:mapped` (which we discussed earlier), you can control both the rows and the columns of information that are returned as part of a resulting XML document.

Specifying Unique Keys in an XML Document

When annotating an XML schema with information about a SQL Server database, you should always provide information about which fields in the database tables make a particular record unique. This allows the mapper to correctly identify records that are being updated or deleted, as well as to order the data properly when it is retrieved from the database so that the XML generated is correct. This is done using the **sql:key-fields** attribute on each element with complex type. You should be sure to add these declarations to every complex type element in your schema. For example, given our customer invoice example from earlier in the chapter:

```
<customerHistory>
  <customer name="Kevin Williams">
    <invoice invoiceDate="2002-03-14" shipDate="2002-04-17" />
    <invoice invoiceDate="2002-04-19" shipDate="2002-05-22" />
  </customer>
  <customer name="Fred Nobody">
    <invoice invoiceDate="2002-06-01" shipDate="2002-06-15" />
    <invoice invoiceDate="2002-07-01" shipDate="2002-07-07" />
  </customer>
</customerHistory>
```

157

We need to indicate which fields in our database make our customer records (`customerID`) and invoice records (`invoiceID`) unique. After annotating our schema from before with this information, it now looks like this:

```
<xsd:schema xmlns:xsd="http://www.w3.org/2001/XMLSchema"
        xmlns:sql="urn:schemas-microsoft-com:mapping-schema">
  <xsd:annotation>
    <xsd:appinfo>
      <sql:relationship name="CustomerInvoiceRelation"
                        parent="Customer"
                        parent-key="customerID"
                        child="Invoice"
                        child-key="customerID" />
    </xsd:appinfo>
  </xsd:annotation>
  <xsd:element name="customerHistory"
               sql:is-constant="1">
    <xsd:complexType>
      <xsd:sequence>
        <xsd:element name="customer"
                     maxOccurs="unbounded"
                     sql:relation="Customer"
                     sql:key-fields="customerID">
          <xsd:complexType>
            <xsd:sequence>
              <xsd:element name="invoiceID"
                           maxOccurs="unbounded"
                           sql:relation="Invoice"
                           sql:relationship="CustomerInvoiceRelation"
                           sql:key-fields="invoiceID">
                <xsd:complexType>
                  <xsd:attribute name="invoiceDate"
                                 type="xsd:dateTime"
                                 sql:field="invoiceDate" />
                  <xsd:attribute name="shipDate"
                                 type="xsd:dateTime"
                                 sql:field="shipDate" />
                </xsd:complexType>
              </xsd:element>
            </xsd:sequence>
          </xsd:complexType>
        </xsd:element>
      </xsd:sequence>
    </xsd:complexType>
  </xsd:element>
</xsd:schema>
```

The `sql:key-fields` annotation may also be used to indicate that a particular table has a compound key by setting its value to be a whitespace-separated list of field names.

Creating ID-IDREF Relationships in XML Schemas

As shown in other chapters, there are some relationships that are too complex to be represented by simple containment. We need to use attributes of type `ID` and `IDREF` to represent theses relationships. The XML Schema annotation language provides some functionality to make this an easier process. Take the following example XML document, which we might want to create from our database:

```xml
<customer name="Kevin Williams">
  <invoice shipDate="2002-06-03">
    <lineItem quantity="7" price="0.45" partID="part1" />
    <lineItem quantity="13" price="0.25" partID="part2" />
  </invoice>
  <invoice shipDate="2002-07-01">
    <lineItem quantity="6" price="0.45" partID="part1" />
    <lineItem quantity="12" price="0.15" partID="part3" />
  </invoice>
  <part partID="part1" description="2 inch grommet" />
  <part partID="part2" description="1 inch grommet" />
  <part partID="part3" description="1 inch widget" />
</customer>
```

The following XML schema describes this document:

```xml
<xsd:schema xmlns:xsd="http://www.w3.org/2001/XMLSchema">
  <xsd:element name="customer">
    <xsd:complexType>
      <xsd:sequence>
        <xsd:element name="invoice">
          <xsd:complexType>
            <xsd:sequence>
              <xsd:element name="lineItem">
                <xsd:complexType>
                  <xsd:attribute name="quantity"
                                 type="xsd:short" />
                  <xsd:attribute name="price" type="xsd:float" />
                  <xsd:attribute name="partID" type="xsd:IDREF" />
                </xsd:complexType>
              </xsd:element>
            </xsd:sequence>
            <xsd:attribute name="shipDate" type="xsd:dateTime" />
          </xsd:complexType>
        </xsd:element>
        <xsd:element name="part">
          <xsd:complexType>
            <xsd:attribute name="partID" type="xsd:ID" />
            <xsd:attribute name="description"
```

```
                        type="xsd:string" />
        </xsd:complexType>
      </xsd:element>
    </xsd:sequence>
    <xsd:attribute name="customerName" type="xsd:string" />
  </xsd:complexType>
</xsd:element>
</xsd:schema>
```

As part of the schema mapping for this document, we create the ID and IDREF values using the **sql:prefix** attribute:

```
<xsd:schema xmlns:xsd="http://www.w3.org/2001/XMLSchema"
            xmlns:sql="urn:schemas-microsoft-com:mapping-schema">
  <xsd:element name="customer"
               sql:relation="Customer">
    <xsd:complexType>
      <xsd:sequence>
        <xsd:element name="invoice"
                     sql:relation="Invoice">
          <xsd:annotation>
            <xsd:appinfo>
              <sql:relationship parent="Customer"
                                parent-key="customerID"
                                child="Invoice"
                                child-key="customerID" />
            </xsd:appinfo>
          </xsd:annotation>
          <xsd:complexType>
            <xsd:sequence>
              <xsd:element name="lineItem"
                           sql:relation="LineItem">
                <xsd:annotation>
                  <xsd:appinfo>
                    <sql:relationship parent="Invoice"
                                      parent-key="invoiceID"
                                      child="LineItem"
                                      child-key="invoiceID" />
                  </xsd:appinfo>
                </xsd:annotation>
                <xsd:complexType>
                  <xsd:attribute name="quantity"
                                 type="xsd:short"
                                 sql:field="number" />
                  <xsd:attribute name="price"
                                 type="xsd:float"
                                 sql:field="unitPrice" />
                  <xsd:attribute name="partID"
                                 type="xsd:IDREF"
                                 sql:field="partID"
                                 sql:prefix="part" />
                </xsd:complexType>
              </xsd:element>
```

Annotating XML Schemas

```
        </xsd:sequence>
        <xsd:attribute name="shipDate" type="xsd:dateTime" />
      </xsd:complexType>
    </xsd:element>
    <xsd:element name="part"
                 sql:relation="Part">
      <xsd:complexType>
        <xsd:attribute name="partID"
                       type="xsd:ID"
                       sql:field="partID"
                       sql:prefix="part" />
        <xsd:attribute name="description"
                       type="xsd:string"
                       sql:field="description" />
      </xsd:complexType>
    </xsd:element>
  </xsd:sequence>
  <xsd:attribute name="customerName"
                 type="xsd:string"
                 sql:field="name" />
  </xsd:complexType>
 </xsd:element>
</xsd:schema>
```

When the document is generated by the mapping, the value in the ID column (an integer value) will be prefixed with the string "part" to ensure that the generated IDs conform to the XML rules (as a reminder, they must begin with a letter, a hyphen, or an underscore).

Note that one problem with this approach is that there is no restriction on the parts being returned; so, if you choose to return a specific customer, you will retrieve all of the parts in the entire database (and not just the parts that that customer has ordered). You can avoid this by pre-selecting only the appropriate parts (perhaps by using a view or a temporary table which is then annotated).

Escaping Invalid XML Characters in XML Schemas

XML documents prohibit the literal use of certain characters in element values. Specifically, the characters involved in markup itself (<, >, and &), as well as quotation marks (", ') are not allowed. To correctly represent values in the database that may potentially include these markup characters, you can specify the **sql:use-cdata** attribute on a simple type element declaration with a value of 1 (or true). When this is specified, the element contents in the serialized XML document will be surrounded with a CDATA block, effectively escaping all of the invalid characters. For example, if we have the following table in the database:

```
CREATE TABLE SampleXML (
    TheXmlString varchar(8000) NOT NULL)
```

161

we know that this column may contain markup characters. To map it, we indicate that the appropriate element in the XML schema needs to be escaped with a `CDATA` block:

```
<xsd:schema xmlns:xsd="http://www.w3.org/2001/XMLSchema"
            xmlns:sql="urn:schemas-microsoft-com:mapping-schema">
  <xsd:element name="sampleXMLStrings"
               sql:is-constant="1">
    <xsd:complexType>
      <xsd:sequence>
        <xsd:element name="sampleXMLString"
                     sql:relation="SampleXML">
          <xsd:complexType>
            <xsd:sequence>
              <xsd:element name="escapedXML"
                           type="xsd:string"
                           sql:field="TheXmlString"
                           sql:use-cdata="1" />
            </xsd:sequence>
          </xsd:complexType>
        </xsd:element>
      </xsd:sequence>
    </xsd:complexType>
  </xsd:element>
</xsd:schema>
```

When this mapping is used to extract data from the database, the resulting document looks like this:

```
<sampleXMLStrings>
 <sampleXMLString>
  <escapedXML>
   <![CDATA[<foo>This is sample XML</foo>]]>
  </escapedXML>
 </sampleXMLString>
 <sampleXMLString>
  <escapedXML>
   <![CDATA[He drove to <city>Houston</city>]]>
  </escapedXML>
 </sampleXMLString>
</sampleXMLStrings>
```

This way, an XML parser can correctly interpret the apparent markup characters as literal text, and correctly read the values in the `<escapedXML>` elements.

Mapping Binary Large Objects (BLOBs)

When mapping binary large object data in SQL Server (`image`, `binary`, or `varbinary` types) to XML schemas, the contents of the BLOB are typically returned as base-64 encoded streams of data. For example, using the following table:

Annotating XML Schemas

```
CREATE TABLE Customer (
  name varchar(50) NOT NULL,
  picture image NOT NULL)
```

an XML schema that maps to it might look like this:

```
<xsd:schema xmlns:xsd="http://www.w3.org/2001/XMLSchema"
            xmlns:sql="urn:schemas-microsoft-com:mapping-schema">
  <xsd:element name="customerImages"
               sql:is-constant="1">
    <xsd:complexType>
      <xsd:sequence>
        <xsd:element name="customer"
                     sql:relation="Customer">
          <xsd:complexType>
            <xsd:sequence>
              <xsd:element name="customerName"
                           type="xsd:string"
                           sql:field="name" />
              <xsd:element name="customerPicture"
                           type="xsd:base64Binary"
                           sql:field="picture" />
            </xsd:sequence>
          </xsd:complexType>
        </xsd:element>
      </xsd:sequence>
    </xsd:complexType>
  </xsd:element>
</xsd:schema>
```

When this mapping is applied to the data, the following document is the result:

```
<customerImages>
 <customer>
  <customerName>Kevin Williams</customerName>
  <customerPicture>1H7w3Euy8Un7n-h2nfi...</customerPicture>
 </customer>
 <customer>
  <customerName>Joe Nobody</customerName>
  <customerPicture>U32JuHyGpoDoin8SJ2j...</customerPicture>
</customerImages>
```

This demonstrates the default handling for binary large objects; they are returned embedded directly into the XML document. However, it may be advantageous to return a URL reference to the image instead. This results in a much smaller document size (a quicker return time), as well as a document that is easier to style into a more usable form, such as XHTML. To do this, we simply add the **sql:encode** attribute with a value of url:

```
<xsd:schema xmlns:xsd="http://www.w3.org/2001/XMLSchema"
            xmlns:sql="urn:schemas-microsoft-com:mapping-schema">
```

Chapter 6

```
            <xsd:element name="customerImages"
                        sql:is-constant="1">
        <xsd:complexType>
          <xsd:sequence>
            <xsd:element name="customer"
                         sql:relation="Customer">
              <xsd:complexType>
                <xsd:sequence>
                  <xsd:element name="customerName"
                               type="xsd:string"
                               sql:field="name" />
                  <xsd:element name="customerPicture"
                               type="xsd:base64Binary"
                               sql:field="picture"
                               sql:encode="url" />
                </xsd:sequence>
              </xsd:complexType>
            </xsd:element>
          </xsd:sequence>
        </xsd:complexType>
      </xsd:element>
</xsd:schema>
```

When this schema is used to extract the data, this is the result:

<customerImages>
 <customer>
  <customerName>Kevin Williams</customerName>
  <customerPicture>
   customer/Customer[@customerID="1"]/picture
  </customerPicture>
 </customer>
 <customer>
  <customerName>Joe Nobody</customerName>
  <customerPicture>
   customer/Customer[@customerID="2"]/picture
  </customerPicture>
 </customer>
</customerImages>

This XML document can then easily be styled to produce an XHTML document that contains `img` URL references to the customer images. The URL provided by SQL Server when the annotated schema is used to access the database (as with an XML View) can then be used to query the database directly and return the unencoded form of the BLOB. In the preceding example, for instance, the picture of the customer with `customerID` of 1 may be found at:

http://IISServer/VirtualRoot/customer/Customer[@customerID="1"]/picture

and this URL can be used as the `href` attribute on an `img` element.

Specifying Identity Columns in an XML Schema

If you are inserting records into a table that contains an `identity` column (an automatically incremented, automatically generated key), you can govern the behavior of that column using the **sql:identity** attribute. For example, let's say you are using Updategrams to insert records into a table with the following structure:

```
CREATE TABLE Customer (
  customerID INT IDENTITY NOT NULL,
  name varchar(100) NOT NULL)
```

In the XML schema mapping, you can choose to indicate how the `customerID` field will be handled. If you set the `sql:identity` attribute to `ignore`, then SQL Server decides what value belongs in the identity column, namely either the existing value on an update, or a newly-generated key on an insert. A mapping (that we will call `ourMapping.xsd`) would look like this:

```
<xsd:schema xmlns:xsd="http://www.w3.org/2001/XMLSchema"
            xmlns:sql="urn:schemas-microsoft-com:mapping-schema" >
  <xsd:element name="customer"
               sql:relation="Customer">
    <xsd:complexType>
      <xsd:attribute name="customerID"
                     type="xsd:integer"
                     sql:field="customerID"
                     sql:identity="ignore" />
      <xsd:attribute name="customerName"
                     type="xsd:string"
                     sql:field="name" />
    </xsd:complexType>
  </xsd:element>
</xsd:schema>
```

When an Updategram like the one below is submitted against this schema, the mapper will automatically generate the `customerID` for the inserted record:

```
<ROOT xmlns:updg="urn:schemas-microsoft-com:xml-updategram">
  <updg:sync mapping-schema="ourMapping.xsd">
    <updg:after>
      <customer customerName="Kevin Williams" />
    </updg:after>
  </updg:sync>
</ROOT>
```

If this Updategram included children of the `<customer>` element, the generated ID would be used to set the foreign keys of the child elements as well.

165

On the other hand, a specific value can be forced for the identity column using `sql:identity="useValue"`. If this is specified, then the mapper will rely on a particular value being passed in for the identity column (and, like any other primary key, the mapper will return an error if the value already exists in the table). So for this example mapping:

```
<xsd:schema xmlns:xsd="http://www.w3.org/2001/XMLSchema"
            xmlns:sql="urn:schemas-microsoft-com:mapping-schema">
   <xsd:element name="customer"
                sql:relation="Customer">
      <xsd:complexType>
         <xsd:attribute name="customerID"
                        type="xsd:integer"
                        sql:field="customerID"
                        sql:identity="useValue" />
         <xsd:attribute name="customerName"
                        type="xsd:string"
                        sql:field="name" />
      </xsd:complexType>
   </xsd:element>
</xsd:schema>
```

an Updategram needs to specify a particular value for the `customerID`, as follows:

```
<ROOT xmlns:updg="urn:schemas-microsoft-com:xml-updategram">
   <updg:sync mapping-schema="ourMapping.xsd">
      <updg:after>
         <customer customerID="17"
                   customerName="Kevin Williams" />
      </updg:after>
   </updg:sync>
</ROOT>
```

The value 17 will then be assigned to the `customerID` value in the inserted record, regardless of what other values are already in the column. If the value 17 already exists, then the Updategram will return an error.

> Note that the `sql:identity` attribute is not available for XDR schemas.

Specifying a GUID in an XML Schema

The **sql:guid** attribute is similar to the `sql:identity` column, in that it allows a mapping schema to dictate whether a **Globally Unique Identifier (GUID)** should be generated for a particular column value when Updategrams or DiffGrams are applied against a database. By setting the `sql:guid` attribute value to generate, the mapper will automatically create a new GUID for the inserted record. So, for example, if we take this mapping schema:

Annotating XML Schemas

```
<xsd:schema xmlns:xsd="http://www.w3.org/2001/XMLSchema"
            xmlns:sql="urn:schemas-microsoft-com:mapping-schema">
  <xsd:element name="customer"
               sql:relation="Customer">
    <xsd:complexType>
      <xsd:attribute name="customerGUID"
                     type="xsd:string"
                     sql:field="customerID"
                     sql:guid="generate"/>
      <xsd:attribute name="customerName"
                     type="xsd:string"
                     sql:field="name" />
    </xsd:complexType>
  </xsd:element>
</xsd:schema>
```

and use the Updategram shown below to apply it, the mapper generates a new GUID for the inserted record and stores it in the `customerGUID` column:

```
<ROOT xmlns:updg="urn:schemas-microsoft-com:xml-updategram">
  <updg:sync mapping-schema="ourMapping.xsd">
    <updg:after>
      <customer customerName="Kevin Williams" />
    </updg:after>
  </updg:sync>
</ROOT>
```

> Note that the `sql:guid` attribute is not available when mapping XDR schemas.

Limiting Recursion Depths in XML Schemas

When using an XPath query to access SQL Server data mapped by an XML schema, it is important to guard against possible infinite recursion. This case can occur if your database contains either circular joins (a table's primary key is another table's foreign key, and vice-versa) or self joins (a table contains a foreign key that is related to its own primary key). The deeper the allowed tree structure (in other words, the deeper the recursion), then the slower XPath queries against that data will run (since the internal implementation of XPath queries involves their transformation into `FOR XML EXPLICIT` queries). In the following example, the `Partner` table contains a self-join:

```
CREATE TABLE Partner (
  partnerID int IDENTITY PRIMARY KEY NOT NULL,
  partnerName varchar(100) NOT NULL,
  preferredpartnerID int FOREIGN KEY REFERENCES Partner
(partnerID) NOT NULL)
```

167

Chapter 6

If an infinite recursion state exists in the table, such as if partner 1 is the preferred partner of partner 2, and vice-versa, then the following XML document would be created:

```
<Partner partnerID="1" partnerName="Foo Industrial Steel">
  <Partner partnerID="2" partnerName="Bar Machine Shop">
    <Partner partnerID="1" partnerName="Foo Industrial Steel">
      <Partner partnerID="2" partnerName="Bar Machine Shop">
        ...
```

This is obviously unacceptable, since the information is not usable in this form; and once the recursion reaches 500 levels, the mapper will return an error. Instead, we can set a maximum level of recursion using `sql:max-depth`. If we set this value to 2, then the following document is created instead:

```
<Partner partnerID="1" partnerName="Foo Industrial Steel">
  <Partner partnerID="2" partnerName="Bar Machine Shop" />
</Partner>
```

This is obviously a much more sensible document to work with (and will be generated much more quickly by the mapper).

> The `sql:max-depth` attribute is not available when annotating XDR schemas.

Summary

In this chapter, we've learned the basics of annotating XML schema documents using the SQL Server schema annotation language. The following table summarizes the various annotations and their purpose (note that some of these are covered in the chapters where they are the most relevant):

Annotation	Description	Available in XDR?
`sql:relation`	Maps an XML element to a database table.	Yes
`sql:field`	Maps an XML text element or attribute to a database column.	Yes
`sql:is-constant`	Creates an XML element that appears in the output, but does not map to any table.	Yes
`sql:mapped`	Allows XML elements or attributes to be excluded from the mapping.	Available as `map-field`

Annotating XML Schemas

Annotation	Description	Available in XDR?
`sql:relationship`	Specifies relationships between XML elements.	Available, but uses different attributes: `key-relation, foreign-relation, key ,foreign-key`
`sql:limit-field` `sql:limit-value`	Allows the restriction of rows returned based on a particular column value.	Yes
`sql:key-fields`	Allows unique keys to be specified for a table.	Yes
`sql:prefix`	Used to create `ID`, `IDREF`, and `IDREFS` values by prepending values with a string.	Yes
`sql:use-cdata`	Indicates that specific values are to be wrapped in CDATA blocks in generated XML.	Yes
`sql:encode`	Allows a URI reference to a BLOB to be returned in the XML, rather than the encoded BLOB itself.	Available as `url-encode`
`sql:overflow-field`	Identifies the database column that contains overflow (unmapped) XML data.	Yes
`sql:inverse`	Used by Updategrams to invert relationships between SQL Server and XML schemas.	No
`sql:hide`	Used to omit particular elements and attributes from generated XML.	No
`sql:identity`	Used to govern how an `IDENTITY` column in the database will be affected by an Updategram or DiffGram.	No
`sql:guid`	Used to govern how a GUID column in the database will be affected by an Updategram or DiffGram.	No

Table continued on following page

169

Chapter 6

Annotation	Description	Available in XDR?
`sql:max-depth`	Used to specify the maximum level of recursion that will be pursued in a database (in the case of a circular join or a self-join).	No

Learning how to annotate XML schemas effectively is a key skill in effective use of the other technologies available as part of SQL Server 2000 and SQLXML 3.0, such as XML Views, Updategrams, DiffGrams, and XML bulk loads. We'll see more specific implementations of XML schema annotations in later chapters that describe these technologies in more depth, including the following chapter on XML views.

Annotating XML Schemas

Kevin Williams

- The What and Why of XML Views
- Creating an XML View
- Accessing Data Through an XML View
- Examples
- Summary

7

XML Views

In this chapter, we'll take a look at the XML view mechanism provided by SQL Server 2000. The XML view mechanism is analogous to the SQL Server view mechanism. In a plain SQL Server view, data from one or more tables is transformed into a different form; in an XML view, one or more tables are made accessible as an XML structure. You can then use XPath expressions to access the data in the tables as if they were in an XML document.

> *This chapter shows some simple examples of using XPath queries in SQLXML, but this topic is covered in detail in the next chapter. A complete reference for the W3C XPath 1.0 Recommendation is also included in Appendix A.*

Subjects we'll cover in this chapter include:

- ❑ When to use XML views instead of other SQL Server XML technologies, such as FOR XML EXPLICIT
- ❑ Modeling table joins as part of an XML view
- ❑ Accessing the data in an XML view
- ❑ Layering an XML view over a SQL view

The What and Why of XML Views

First, let's take a closer look at how XML views work, and how they compare to the other technologies available for accessing SQL Server data as XML.

XML Views rely on annotated XML schemas, which we discussed in the previous chapter. To create an XML view, you simply annotate an XML schema that has the proper structure and contents along with the appropriate information to map it to the existing SQL Server database. This annotated schema can then be specified either as part of a template or as a schema virtual object.

Chapter 7

We'll see examples of both later in the chapter. Once you have specified the location of the annotated schema, you can either include the query in the template, or as part of the URL itself to access parts of the returned table structure.

XML views are particularly useful if you have an existing XML schema and want to extract data quickly from your database in XML form. This is similar to creating SQL Server views and then running queries against them. By using XML views and SQL Server views together, you can easily expose data in your database as XML in a tightly controlled fashion (as opposed to allowing FOR XML EXPLICIT calls directly against the database, which can result in significant performance problems if the user issues a poorly-formed query) .

> Note that XML views can be used only to read data, not write it; if you want to write XML data into your SQL Server database, you should consider using OPENXML (Chapter 10), Updategrams (Chapter 11), SQLXML Bulk Load (Chapter 12), or DiffGrams through ADO.NET (discussed in Chapter 13) to do so.

When you create an annotated schema and then designate it as an XML view, either by setting it up as a schema object or part of a template, SQL Server effectively writes the FOR XML EXPLICIT expression for you, building the XML structure up from the specified element, attribute, and relationship mappings provided in the annotations. This can be convenient if you need to get a mapping up and running quickly, since creating FOR XML EXPLICIT expressions by hand tends to be fairly cumbersome (as we discussed in Chapter 4). Annotations don't give you the same level of granular control over the creation of the XML structure as you have with FOR XML EXPLICIT but, if you are performing a simple mapping of the information from your tables into XML, an XML view might be the easiest solution for generating the information in that form.

However, with this convenience come some limitations, which we'll look at now. First, since the information contained in views must be accessed through XPath expressions, it is difficult to perform any sort of sophisticated manipulation of the information (such as pivoting relationships or selecting distinct groups of data). Furthermore, XML views only support a subset of the XPath 1.0 language, as we'll see in the next chapter.

With SQLXML's current support for XPath, our ability to manipulate an XML document's contents through expressions is significantly limited. However, first creating a SQL Server view, and then creating the XML view using the SQL Server view as a source can overcome many of these limitations. We'll see an example of that later in the chapter.

Creating an XML View

Creating an XML view is straightforward. First, you need to annotate an XML schema with the structure you wish the XML data to take, in the same way as we saw in the previous chapter.

As a reminder:

- Elements are mapped to tables using the `sql:relation` annotation
- Data elements or attributes are mapped to columns using the `sql:field` annotation
- Relationships between the data in the SQL Server database are specified using the `sql:relationship` annotation

These three annotations are sufficient to create many views, but there are others you can use to better control the exact information returned (such as `sql:is-constant` to create elements that do not correspond directly to relational tables, or `sql:limit-field` and `sql:limit-value` to restrict the allowable values returned as part of the XML document).

Annotating an Existing XDR or XML Schema

As we already know, XDR schemas are being superseded by XML schemas, which are now supported in SQLXML. If you have legacy XML structures designed in the XDR form (such as BizTalk schemas), you can annotate them and make them into views. However, Microsoft has said that it is phasing out XDR in favor of XML Schema, so you should create new annotated schemas as XML schemas. All the examples in this chapter will use XML schemas. To learn more about the differences between XDR and XML schema annotations, please see the previous chapter.

Modeling Tables and Columns in XML Views

The first step in annotating an XML schema for use as part of an XML view, is to map each piece of information that will appear in the generated XML structure to the corresponding piece of information in the SQL Server database. Remember that tables (modeled with `sql:relation`) map directly to elements; so if you specify that a particular element in your structure is represented in the database by a table, then for each record in that table one element will appear in the resulting document. Let's take a look at a quick example. Let's say you had the following table in the database:

```
CREATE TABLE Customer (
    customerID int IDENTITY PRIMARY KEY,
    name varchar(100) NOT NULL,
    address1 varchar(50) NOT NULL,
    address2 varchar(50) NULL,
    city varchar(50) NOT NULL,
    state char(2) NOT NULL,
    postalCode varchar(10) NOT NULL)
```

You might want to create the following XML schema that equates to it:

```
<xsd:schema xmlns:xsd="http://www.w3.org/2001/XMLSchema">
  <xsd:element name="Customer">
    <xsd:complexType>
```

```
            <xsd:attribute name="customerName"
                           type="xsd:string"
                           use="required" />
            <xsd:attribute name="address1"
                           type="xsd:string"
                           use="required" />
            <xsd:attribute name="address2"
                           type="xsd:string" />
            <xsd:attribute name="city"
                           type="xsd:string"
                           use="required" />
            <xsd:attribute name="state"
                           type="xsd:string"
                           use="required" />
            <xsd:attribute name="zip"
                           type="xsd:string"
                           use="required" />
        </xsd:complexType>
    </xsd:element>
</xsd:schema>
```

Note that the schema seems to specify that only one customer can appear in the document, but the XML view engine will return multiple instances of the root element if multiple rows associated with that element appear in the table. To annotate this schema (Customer.xsd), we simply add sql:relation and sql:field annotations wherever they are appropriate:

```
<xsd:schema xmlns:xsd="http://www.w3.org/2001/XMLSchema"
            xmlns:sql="urn:schemas-microsoft-com:mapping-schema">
    <xsd:element name="Customer"
                 sql:relation="Customer">
        <xsd:complexType>
            <xsd:attribute name="customerName"
                           type="xsd:string"
                           use="required"
                           sql:field="name"/>
            <xsd:attribute name="address1"
                           type="xsd:string"
                           use="required"
                           sql:field="address1"/>
            <xsd:attribute name="address2"
                           type="xsd:string"
                           sql:field="address2" />
            <xsd:attribute name="city"
                           type="xsd:string"
                           use="required"
                           sql:field="city" />
            <xsd:attribute name="state"
                           type="xsd:string"
                           use="required"
                           sql:field="state" />
            <xsd:attribute name="zip"
```

```
                    type="xsd:string"
                    use="required"
                    sql:field="postalCode" />
    </xsd:complexType>
  </xsd:element>
</xsd:schema>
```

Since we are only modeling one table in our resulting XML document, we don't need to worry about modeling joins, so this is all that is needed. XPath queries against this view will now return information as if the `Customer` table were actually a set of `<Customer>` elements. For example, let's say we have a customer called Kevin Williams in our database; if we use the following XPath query against this view:

```
Customer/[@customerName='Kevin Williams]
```

the following output will be returned:

```
<Customer customerName="Kevin Williams"
         address1="100 Main Street"
         city="Springfield"
         state="VA"
         zip="10298" />
```

Next, let's take a look at how relationships are modeled in XML views.

Modeling Joins in XML Views

Joins between tables are modeled in XML views using the `sql:relationship` annotation. If you are modeling multiple tables in your XML view, it is critical that you include the correct `sql:relationship` annotation, otherwise the XML view will not know how to relate the elements it creates from the various tables. Let's extend our previous example. Say we have the following `Customer` and `Invoice` tables in our database:

```
CREATE TABLE Customer (
    customerID int IDENTITY PRIMARY KEY,
    name varchar(100) NOT NULL,
    address1 varchar(50) NOT NULL,
    address2 varchar(50) NULL,
    city varchar(50) NOT NULL,
    state char(2) NOT NULL,
    postalCode varchar(10) NOT NULL)
GO

CREATE TABLE Invoice (
    invoiceID int IDENTITY PRIMARY KEY,
    customerID int FOREIGN KEY REFERENCES Customer (customerID),
    invoiceDate datetime NOT NULL,
    invoiceAmount decimal(9,2) NOT NULL)
GO
```

We want to create a simple hierarchical structure in our XML view, where each `<Customer>` element contains the proper `<Invoice>` elements for that customer:

```xml
<xsd:schema xmlns:xsd="http://www.w3.org/2001/XMLSchema">
  <xsd:element name="Customer">
    <xsd:complexType>
      <xsd:sequence>
        <xsd:element name="Invoice">
          <xsd:complexType>
            <xsd:attribute name="date"
                           type="xsd:dateTime" />
            <xsd:attribute name="amount"
                           type="xsd:decimal" />
          </xsd:complexType>
        </xsd:element>
      </xsd:sequence>
      <xsd:attribute name="customerName"
                     type="xsd:string"
                     use="required" />
      <xsd:attribute name="address1"
                     type="xsd:string"
                     use="required" />
      <xsd:attribute name="address2"
                     type="xsd:string" />
      <xsd:attribute name="city"
                     type="xsd:string"
                     use="required" />
      <xsd:attribute name="state"
                     type="xsd:string"
                     use="required" />
      <xsd:attribute name="zip"
                     type="xsd:string"
                     use="required" />
    </xsd:complexType>
  </xsd:element>
</xsd:schema>
```

In addition to adding the `sql:relation` and `sql:field` mappings (similar to the previous example), we now need to assert the relationship between the Customer and Invoice tables. We do so by adding a `<sql:relationship>` element as an annotation on the schema itself (`CustomerInvoice.xsd`):

```xml
<xsd:schema xmlns:xsd="http://www.w3.org/2001/XMLSchema"
            xmlns:sql="urn:schemas-microsoft-com:mapping-schema">
  <xsd:annotation>
    <xsd:appinfo>
      <sql:relationship name="CustomerInvoice"
            parent="Customer"
            parent-key="customerID"
            child="Invoice"
            child-key="customerID" />
```

XML Views

```
        </xsd:appinfo>
     </xsd:annotation>
     <xsd:element name="Customer"
                  sql:relation="Customer">
        <xsd:complexType>
           <xsd:sequence>
              <xsd:element name="Invoice"
                           sql:relation="Invoice"
                           sql:relationship="CustomerInvoice">
                 <xsd:complexType>
                    <xsd:attribute name="date"
                                   type="xsd:dateTime"
                                   sql:field="invoiceDate" />
                    <xsd:attribute name="amount"
                                   type="xsd:decimal"
                                   sql:field="invoiceAmount" />
                 </xsd:complexType>
              </xsd:element>
           </xsd:sequence>
           <xsd:attribute name="customerName"
                          type="xsd:string"
                          use="required"
                          sql:field="name"/>
           <xsd:attribute name="address1"
                          type="xsd:string" use="required"
                          sql:field="address1"/>
           <xsd:attribute name="address2"
                          type="xsd:string"
                          sql:field="address2" />
           <xsd:attribute name="city"
                          type="xsd:string"
                          use="required"
                          sql:field="city" />
           <xsd:attribute name="state"
                          type="xsd:string"
                          use="required"
                          sql:field="state" />
           <xsd:attribute name="zip"
                          type="xsd:string"
                          use="required"
                          sql:field="postalCode" />
        </xsd:complexType>
     </xsd:element>
</xsd:schema>
```

Asserting that the `Customer` and `Invoice` tables are related through the `customerID` column in both tables allows the XML view engine to associate invoices with customers properly.

Now that we have the XML view, we need some way to apply an XPath expression against it to return results. Let's see how this can be done.

Chapter 7

Accessing Data Through an XML View

As we've mentioned previously in the chapter, there are really two ways in which data that is mapped to an XML view may be accessed. The first is to create an XML template that contains both the XML view schema object and the XPath expression associated with the template. This mechanism is the best to use if you want to prevent users from running any XPath expression they like against the view. If you want to leave it open to the user, on the other hand, you can create an XML schema object in IIS for the annotated schema, and then include the XPath expression in the URL used to reference that schema object.

Accessing Data Using URLs

To publish an XML view as a schema that allows any XPath expression to be used against it in the URL of an HTTP accessor (such as a browser), you must create a schema object in a SQL Server virtual directory for the database in which it resides that corresponds to the annotated schema you have created. This can be done by launching Configure IIS Support from the SQLXML 3.0 menu, going to the Virtual Names panel for the SQL Server virtual directory for your database, and adding a virtual name with type schema (there's an example of how to do this in the next chapter). Placing annotated XML schemas or templates in that directory makes them available through HTTP, as we'll see in our examples.

Once you have published the XML view (and set the permissions on the virtual directory to allow XPath expressions as part of the URL), you can specify the XPath to the data you want as part of an HTTP request.

The URL takes the following form:

```
http://{server}/{SQLServerRoot}/{schemaObject}/{schemaFile}/
{XpathExpression}
```

For example, if we had created a SQL Server root called Customer and a schema object called views on the local machine, and saved our previous example annotated customer schema as Customer.xsd, the following URL would return all the information about all customers who are in the state of Virginia:

http://localhost/Customer/views/Customer.xsd/Customer[@state='VA']

To exert better control over what XPath expressions are used to query the system, we can use an XML template with the expression built right in, as we'll see now.

Accessing Data Using Templates

XML views can also be accessed through XML templates. In these templates the structure for the resulting XML is provided in the form of an XML schema, as well as the exact XPath expression used to extract the information from the database. A sample XML template document would look something like this:

XML Views

```
<Customers xmlns:sql="urn:schemas-microsoft-com:xml-sql">
  <sql:xpath-query mapping-schema="Customer.xsd">
    Customer
  </sql:xpath-query>
</Customers>
```

This template references an annotated schema XML view stored as a schema virtual object in a virtual directory. It is also possible to save the schema as part of the template itself; that is, to have an inline schema. This second method is not recommended if you need to be able to reuse your schema.

XML view templates can be used in the same way as the templates we created in Chapter 5. There are examples of accessing XML view templates of both types in the next chapter.

To recap:

- ❑ Saving the XML view as a schema object gives the user the greatest degree of freedom, since they can use any XPath expression on the view to govern the data returned.
- ❑ Saving the XML view as a schema referenced through a template prevents the user from running any random XPath expression they like, as the actual expression used is part of the template itself. In this approach, the annotated XML schema is stored in a separate file.
- ❑ If you choose to use inline schemas (rather than keeping them separate), you won't be able to reuse the schema file. Any other template that wants to use the same annotated schema will also have to include it.

Examples

Now, let's take a look at a couple of examples. They will use both what we have learned about XML views in this chapter, and the annotation mechanisms we learned in the previous chapter. If you see any unfamiliar annotations you should check back.

Simple Example

In this example, we're going to revisit our `Customer` table. Say we have a table in our database called `Customer` that has the following structure:

```
CREATE TABLE Customer (
    customerID int NOT NULL,
    name varchar(100) NOT NULL,
    address1 varchar(50) NOT NULL,
    address2 varchar(50) NULL,
    city varchar(50) NOT NULL,
    state char(2) NOT NULL,
    postalCode varchar(10) NOT NULL)
```

Our business requirement is to offer the ability to retrieve the customer ID, name, and city for a given state. We choose to do so through an XML view. Our resulting XML structure should look something like the following:

```
<CustomerList>
  <Customer name="Kevin Williams" city="Springfield" />
  <Customer name="Fred Nobody" city="Alexandria" />
</CustomerList>
```

The XML schema structure for the desired XML looks like this:

```
<xsd:schema xmlns:xsd="http://www.w3.org/2001/XMLSchema">
  <xsd:element name="CustomerList">
    <xsd:complexType>
      <xsd:sequence>
        <xsd:element name="Customer" maxOccurs="unbounded">
          <xsd:complexType>
            <xsd:attribute name="name"
                           type="xsd:string"
                           use="required" />
            <xsd:attribute name="city"
                           type="xsd:string"
                           use="required" />
          </xsd:complexType>
        </xsd:element>
      </xsd:sequence>
    </xsd:complexType>
  </xsd:element>
</xsd:schema>
```

When we start to annotate this schema, the first thing we notice is that the `<CustomerList>` element doesn't correspond directly to any element in the database. We need to use the `sql:is-constant` annotation to indicate that this element should be created when the structure is generated. Our annotated XML schema (`Customer2.xsd`) then looks like the following:

```
<xsd:schema xmlns:xsd="http://www.w3.org/2001/XMLSchema"
            xmlns:sql="urn:schemas-microsoft-com:mapping-schema">
  <xsd:element name="CustomerList"
               sql:is-constant="1">
    <xsd:complexType>
      <xsd:sequence>
        <xsd:element name="Customer"
                     maxOccurs="unbounded"
                     sql:relation="Customer">
          <xsd:complexType>
            <xsd:attribute name="name"
                           type="xsd:string"
                           use="required"
                           sql:field="name"/>
            <xsd:attribute name="city"
```

XML Views

```
                    type="xsd:string"
                    use="required"
                    sql:field="city" />
            </xsd:complexType>
          </xsd:element>
        </xsd:sequence>
      </xsd:complexType>
    </xsd:element>
</xsd:schema>
```

If we assume that our server is behind a firewall, and that we trust all the users who will be accessing the machine, we can decide to specify the schema in the schema virtual directory, and access it using an XPath expression in the URL. The following URL returns all the customers who live in Springfield:

http://localhost/Customer/schema/Customer2.xsd/CustomerList/Customer[@city='Springfield']

If we didn't trust the users who would be accessing the machine, we would want to lock down their ability to use *ad hoc* XPath expressions against our XML view. We would accomplish this by embedding both the allowed XPath expression and a reference to the annotated schema in a template, and then we would only expose the template in the SQL Server virtual directory, thus preventing the users from trying to apply unexpected XPath expressions to the view.

Now, let's take a look at a way we can create more complex behaviors from XML views.

Layering an XML View Over a SQL Server View

As we mentioned earlier, we can create an XML view that maps to a SQL Server view, instead of tables in a database. In this example, we have a classic OLTP to OLAP scenario. In an existing database, we have a transaction table that tracks which IP addresses have accessed our server and which resources they have retrieved. We'd like to build an XML document from this that summarizes, for each IP address, how many page hits the IP address has had. Since we don't have this table in reality, we'll need to create it. The DDL looks like this:

```
CREATE TABLE Accesses (
    IPAddress varchar(15) NOT NULL,
    Resource varchar(255) NOT NULL,
    accessedAt datetime NOT NULL)
```

The behavior we're looking for here is more complex than we'd be able to produce with simple XPath processing (especially the limited form of XPath supported by XML views). To summarize the data without consuming any additional space in the database, we'll first create a view on the `Accesses` table that summarizes them for each IP address. We'll call the view `AccessView`. The view creation script looks like this:

183

Chapter 7

```
CREATE VIEW AccessView
AS
SELECT IPAddress, COUNT(*) AS AccessCount
FROM Accesses
GROUP BY IPAddress
GO
```

Now, for the purposes of annotated XML schemas (at least as far as XML views are concerned), we can treat this view as if it were a table. We want our output document to look like this:

```
<Statistics>
  <User IPAddress="127.0.0.1" hits="17" />
  <User IPAddress="192.168.0.1" hits="13" />
</Statistics>
```

so the XML schema is as follows.

```
<xsd:schema xmlns:xsd="http://www.w3.org/2001/XMLSchema">
  <xsd:element name="Statistics">
    <xsd:complexType>
      <xsd:sequence>
        <xsd:element name="User" maxOccurs="unbounded">
          <xsd:complexType>
            <xsd:attribute name="IPAddress"
                           type="xsd:string"
                           use="required" />
            <xsd:attribute name="hits"
                           type="xsd:integer"
                           use="required" />
          </xsd:complexType>
        </xsd:element>
      </xsd:sequence>
    </xsd:complexType>
  </xsd:element>
</xsd:schema>
```

We now need to map it to our `AccessView` SQL Server view. This is a fairly straightforward mapping, though we need to create the `<Statistics>` element using `sql:is-constant` when we annotate the schemas, like this:

```
<xsd:schema xmlns:xsd="http://www.w3.org/2001/XMLSchema"
            xmlns:sql="urn:schemas-microsoft-com:mapping-schema">
  <xsd:element name="Statistics"
               sql:is-constant="1">
    <xsd:complexType>
      <xsd:sequence>
        <xsd:element name="User"
                     maxOccurs="unbounded"
                     sql:relation="AccessView">
          <xsd:complexType>
            <xsd:attribute name="IPAddress"
```

XML Views

```
                            type="xsd:string"
                            use="required"
                            sql:field="IPAddress" />
            <xsd:attribute name="hits"
                            type="xsd:integer"
                            use="required"
                            sql:field="AccessCount" />
          </xsd:complexType>
        </xsd:element>
      </xsd:sequence>
    </xsd:complexType>
  </xsd:element>
</xsd:schema>
```

We can now issue an URL query against the XML view to retrieve our information as XML:

http://localhost/Customer/views/AccessSchema.xsd/Statistics

This query returns a `<User>` element for every user in the SQL Server view, wrapped in the `<Statistics>` element that is the root of the document produced by our XML view.

Using XML views in conjunction with SQL Server views in this way gives you the greatest control over the resulting XML document. If you need to do any sort of manipulation of your data, you should try to take care of it from within a SQL Server view (letting the relational database do what it's best at), and use the XML view only for the generation of the appropriate XML structure.

Summary

In this chapter, we've seen some examples of XML views at work. XML views are particularly useful when:

❏ You need to retrieve data from the database (they cannot be used to update data)

❏ Your requirements aren't especially complex (no sophisticated manipulation of the data structure is required)

❏ You want to expose the data as XML through an HTTP interface

❏ The structures are so complex that writing a `FOR XML EXPLICIT` query directly will be too time-consuming

In addition, we've seen how SQL Server views can be used in conjunction with XML views to provide a greater level of functionality. If you have a more sophisticated structure that you need to build (such as elements appearing according to complex conditions, recursive structures, or other higher-level constructs), then you may have to resort to building your queries using `FOR XML EXPLICIT` (as discussed in Chapter 4).

The next chapter goes on to examine more deeply how we can submit XPath queries against our database to produce results in XML format.

185

Bryant Likes

- Overview of XPath
- Setting up the Sample
- From T-SQL to XPath
- Using XPath Queries
- Performance Considerations
- Security Issues
- Limitations
- Summary

8

XPath Queries

As we learned in the last chapter, XPath is the query language used with XML documents. In this chapter, we will take a look at XPath from a T-SQL viewpoint and how to use it to get data out of SQL Server. Once we have a basic understanding of XPath, we will explore the different ways it can be used with SQL Server. Finally, we will look at the performance implications of XPath queries, as well as any security issues that they create. When you are done with this chapter, you should be able to create your own XPath queries and put them to use in a secure way.

Overview of XPath

XPath is a query language that is specified by the World Wide Web Consortium (W3C) and is in version 1.0 of the specification at the time of writing. XPath is used not only in SQL Server but also in many other XML technologies, like XSLT, XPointer, and XQuery. The primary purpose of XPath is to address the different parts of an XML document. In other words, XPath allows you to reference elements within an XML document, just as T-SQL allows you to reference tables and columns with the SELECT statement.

> Please note: SQLXML 3.0 does not support the full set of XPath 1.0 functionality. A list of unsupported features is given at the end of the chapter.

As we saw in the preceding chapter, by creating XML views of our data using XML or XDR schemas, we are allowing users to view our SQL data as XML. Often, the whole XML document created with the view is not needed all at once. For example, if we create a document that contains all the orders in the database, we may only want one single order, or orders placed by a certain customer, rather than every order.

Chapter 8

XPath in SQLXML makes this possible by allowing us to run queries against XML or XDR schemas, either in a URL, through a template, or programmatically using ADO or the SQLXML Managed Classes.

To gain an understanding of how XPath queries work, we will be setting up an annotated XML schema and creating an XML view from it. This will allow us to run XPath queries in the URL against this schema. We'll use these URL queries to learn about how XPath works and how it relates to SQL Server. We'll also be using the SQL Profiler utility to run SQL traces. These will allow us to look at what is going on inside SQL Server when we use XPath queries, enabling us to look at the FOR XML EXPLICIT coding that these queries create, and how we can tune them to get the best performance.

Setting up the Sample

In order to learn about XPath, we'll need to have an XML view to run XPath queries against. To do this, we will use the SQLXML virtual directory that we setup in Chapter 2. Once you have completed that setup, follow the steps below to add a simple XML schema, providing us with the XML view we need.

Set up a Schema Mapping

We need to create a new folder to hold our schemas and then create a mapping to the folder, as we saw previously in Chapter 5. Open up the folder that your virtual directory points to and add a new folder in it called `schemas`. Next, using the SQLXML virtual directory management tool, open the `nwind` virtual directory, and go to the **Virtual Names** tab. Here is a screenshot of how this will look:

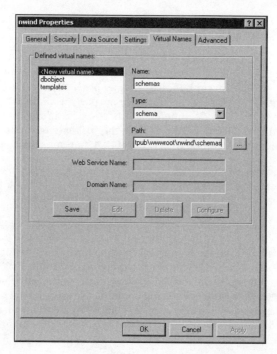

188

XPath Queries

In the **Name** field, type `schemas` and in the **Type** field, select `schema`. Use the browse button next to the **path** field to browse to the new folder you created, which is called `schemas`. Once you have these filled in hit the **Save** button and then **OK** and close the management tool.

Create the Sample Schema

The next step is to create the sample XML schema that maps to our `Northwind` tables (`Customers` and `Orders`) joined on `CustomerID`. Here is the schema that we will be using for our examples in this chapter:

```
<xsd:schema
  xmlns:xsd="http://www.w3.org/2001/XMLSchema"
  xmlns:sql="urn:schemas-microsoft-com:mapping-schema">

<xsd:annotation>
 <xsd:appinfo>
  <sql:relationship name="CustOrders"
           parent="Customers"
           parent-key="CustomerID"
           child="Orders"
           child-key="CustomerID" />
 </xsd:appinfo>
</xsd:annotation>

<xsd:element name="root" sql:is-constant="1">
 <xsd:complexType>
  <xsd:sequence>
    <xsd:element name="Customer" sql:relation="Customers">
     <xsd:complexType>
      <xsd:sequence>
       <xsd:element name="Order"
                    sql:relation="Orders"
                    sql:relationship="CustOrders" >
          <xsd:complexType>
             <xsd:attribute name="OrderID" />
             <xsd:attribute name="CustomerID" />
          </xsd:complexType>
       </xsd:element>
      </xsd:sequence>
        <xsd:attribute name="CustomerID" />
        <xsd:attribute name="ContactName" />
    </xsd:complexType>
   </xsd:element>
  </xsd:sequence>
 </xsd:complexType>
</xsd:element>

</xsd:schema>
```

Save the schema as `orders.xsd` and place it in the `schemas` folder. You're now ready to begin using XPath.

Chapter 8

From T-SQL to XPath

Since this book assumes you have a good understanding of T-SQL, we'll use the T-SQL SELECT statement as our starting point for learning XPath.

SELECT

The SELECT clause is probably the first T-SQL statement you learn since it allows you to choose which columns of a table you want to return, among other things. With XPath you don't get this option. If you think of each XML element as a table, and the attributes as columns, then an XPath query would be like a SELECT * statement. When an element is returned, it is returned as a whole (including its attributes and child elements). This is one of the most confusing features of XPath for those who are used to T-SQL.

FROM

As with T-SQL, we need to be able to choose where we return our results from. Not only does the XPath query return the entire element, all of the element's children are returned as well. The most basic query you can run is to select the <root> element, which returns the entire document along with it. To do this with our sample XML schema, we can use the following URL query:

http://localhost/nwind/schemas/orders.xsd/root

The results of this URL query are shown below. You can see the three elements that we defined in our schema: <root>, <Customer>, and <Order>:

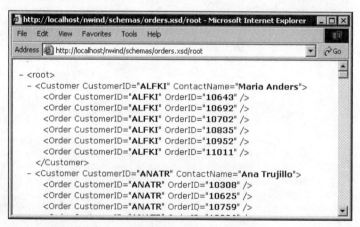

If you don't get similar results, try running through the troubleshooting section of Chapter 2.

As you can see, we selected the <root> element and got not only the <root> element but all of the <root> element's children as well. However, if we try to select the next level down, the <Customer> elements, using a query like this:

XPath Queries

http://localhost/nwind/schemas/orders.xsd/root/Customer

we get an error returned from Internet Explorer. It states **The XML page cannot be displayed**, and:

Only one top level element is allowed in an XML document. Error processing resource 'http://localhost/nwind/schemas/orders.xsd/root/Customer'. Line 1, Position 327

For an XML document to be valid, it must have only one root node. Our query tried to return all the `<Customer>` elements, but omitted the root node. Without the root node, the result is an invalid XML document. To remedy this, we can specify that SQLXML should add a root node for us. To do this we use the following URL query:

http://localhost/nwind/schemas/orders.xsd/root/Customer?root=root

The results should be the same as our first query.

Next let's go down one more level to the `<Order>` element:

http://localhost/nwind/schemas/orders.xsd/root/Customer/Order?root=root

The results of this query should be the root node with every single order in the database as a child, as shown below:

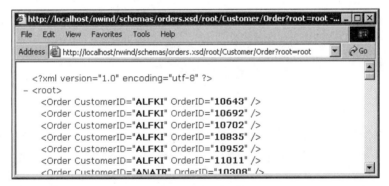

So from these queries we can see there is a path in the XML document itself. The `<root>` element is our starting point and then we traverse through each parent until we get to the child we want. This is pretty different from the T-SQL SELECT statement. Not only do you get all the columns from the table, but you also get all the columns plus all the related tables as child elements.

Namespaces

In our XML schema, we can specify namespaces that can be applied to the entire document or just to certain elements. This helps to distinguish between different XML declarations. For example, you might have two types of order, one for products and one for services; to distinguish between each `<order>` element you could use a namespace in the form of `prd:order` and `srv:order`. This would allow you to validate both XML structures against different schema declarations.

191

Chapter 8

This makes our XPath a little trickier. We not only have to specify the correct name of the element we want, but we also have to specify the element's namespace. To explore how this works, let's create another schema. Below is the code for this schema, which uses a slightly different format from our first one. To simplify the schema, we've removed the `<root>` element. We're also declaring our elements as types instead of declaring them inline. The most important thing to take note of is our new namespace, which we've declared as `urn:mycompany:Services`. This has been set as the target namespace so now, when we refer to our elements and types, we must prefix them with this namespace:

```xml
<xsd:schema
  xmlns:xsd="http://www.w3.org/2001/XMLSchema"
  xmlns:sql="urn:schemas-microsoft-com:mapping-schema"
  xmlns:srv="urn:mycompany:Services"
  targetNamespace="urn:mycompany:Services">

<xsd:annotation>
  <xsd:appinfo>
    <sql:relationship name="CustOrders"
           parent="Customers"
           parent-key="CustomerID"
           child="Orders"
           child-key="CustomerID" />
  </xsd:appinfo>
</xsd:annotation>

<xsd:element name="Customer"
             type="srv:CustomerType"
             sql:relation="Customers"/>
<xsd:element name="Order"
             type="srv:OrderType"
             sql:relation="Orders"
  sql:relationship="CustOrders" />

  <xsd:complexType name="OrderType">
  <xsd:attribute name="OrderID"/>
  <xsd:attribute name="CustomerID"/>
  </xsd:complexType>

  <xsd:complexType name="CustomerType">
  <xsd:sequence>
    <xsd:element ref="srv:Order"/>
  </xsd:sequence>
  <xsd:attribute name="CustomerID"/>
  <xsd:attribute name="ContactName"/>
  </xsd:complexType>

</xsd:schema>
```

Save this file as `srvorder.xsd` in our `schemas` directory.

By adding the `targetNamespace` attribute, we are giving the elements in our schema a specific namespace. This means that the elements in the resulting document will have a namespace prefix that maps to the `urn:mycompany:Services` namespace, as a direct result of our declaration of those elements within that namespace.

XPath Queries

If you run any of the earlier XPath queries on our new schema, you will find that they no longer work. For them to work, we have to add the namespace prefix to our XPath query and declare it in our URL as follows:

http://localhost/nwind/schemas/srvorder.xsd/**srv:**Customer?namespaces= **xmlns:srv='urn:mycompany:Services'**&root=root

With this query we are now asking for the `<Customer>` elements that have a prefix that maps to the `urn:mycompany:Services` namespace. The results of this query are as follows:

Notice that each of the elements is prefixed with `y0`, which maps to the `urn:mycompany:Services` namespace. The prefix is generated programmatically to avoid duplication, which is why the `srv` prefix that we declared in our schema isn't seen in the results here.

WHERE

None of this would be worth much if we didn't have some way to specify which pieces of data we wanted, like the T-SQL WHERE clause. To specify the WHERE condition in an XPath query, we use what is called a **predicate**. To see what this looks like, we'll select all the orders that have a `CustomerID` of `VINET`, using the highlighted predicate:

http://localhost/nwind/schemas/orders.xsd/root/Customer/**Order[@CustomerID= 'VINET']**?root=root

This XPath query is equivalent to `SELECT * FROM Orders WHERE CustomerID='VINET'`. Notice that to specify that `CustomerID` is an attribute, as declared in our schema, we prefix it with the `@` symbol. If we omitted the `@` symbol, then the query would look for all `<order>` elements that have a child element named `<CustomerID>` with a value of `VINET`.

Here are the results when we correctly specify the `<CustomerID>` as an attribute:

193

Chapter 8

```
<?xml version="1.0" encoding="utf-8" ?>
- <root>
    <Order CustomerID="VINET" OrderID="10248" />
    <Order CustomerID="VINET" OrderID="10274" />
    <Order CustomerID="VINET" OrderID="10295" />
    <Order CustomerID="VINET" OrderID="10737" />
    <Order CustomerID="VINET" OrderID="10739" />
  </root>
```

What if we also want information from the Customer table? To get this, we can specify the predicate on the <Customer> element instead of the <Order> element:

http://localhost/nwind/schemas/orders.xsd/root/**Customer[@CustomerID='VINET']**

Notice that we don't have the <Order> element in our XPath; this gives us all the customer information in addition to all the orders as shown below:

```
- <Customer CustomerID="VINET" ContactName="Paul Henriot">
    <Order CustomerID="VINET" OrderID="10248" />
    <Order CustomerID="VINET" OrderID="10274" />
    <Order CustomerID="VINET" OrderID="10295" />
    <Order CustomerID="VINET" OrderID="10737" />
    <Order CustomerID="VINET" OrderID="10739" />
  </Customer>
```

In this case, since there was only one customer returned, the XML was valid, and we didn't need to specify the root parameter. If there were more than one customer returned, the XML would be invalid if we didn't include it in our query.

Note that you can specify a predicate on any of the elements in the XPath, and indeed specify a predicate on a predicate. Consider the following URL query:

http://localhost/nwind/schemas/orders.xsd/root/
Customer[Order[@CustomerID='VINET']]

This query is asking for all the <Customer> elements that have an <Order> element, with a CustomerID attribute that equals VINET.

> **It is very important to understand the flow of XPath.**

Here is one XPath query that returns results that you might not expect:

http://localhost/nwind/schemas/orders.xsd/root/Customer[Order[@OrderID='10739']]

XPath Queries

This query returns the same results as the previous one. You might expect that it would return only the `<Order>` with an `OrderID` equal to `10739`, but this isn't the case; it returns all the orders. To understand why this is so, we need to look carefully at what the XPath is asking for. This XPath says 'give me all the `<Customer>` elements that have an `<Order>` element with an `OrderID` attribute that equals `10739`'. Notice that we are only asking for the `<Customer>` element, not the `<Order>` element. Since this is the case, we get the `<Customer>` element that has this `<Order>` element. However, that same `<Customer>` element also has all the other elements tied to it as well, so we get all of them.

XPath Data Types

Since XML documents are plain text, how do we differentiate between different data types? With XML Schema this is done through the `type` attribute, and in XDR with the `sql:datatype` attribute. Without these declared types, SQL Server will assume that everything is a `nvarchar(4000)`. To see this in action, start the SQL Profiler, which is found under the SQL Server programs group, and run a trace. To start a trace, open the SQL Profiler, click **File | New | Trace**, specify the server you want to connect to, and then on the **Events** tab remove everything except **SQL:BatchCompleted**. This latter setting is simply to reduce the load on your server. You can then click the **Run** button and open the following URL in your browser:

http://localhost/nwind/schemas/orders.xsd/root/Customer/Order[@OrderID='10739']

> Note that you must be a member of the SYSADMIN role in order to run a trace

In IE you will see the following XML:

Back in SQL Profiler, you should see an entry generated that starts out as **select 1 as Tag**. Copy the text of this entry and paste it into SQL Query Analyzer. This is the `FOR XML EXPLICIT` query that was generated by our XPath query. If you look at the `WHERE` clause you will see the following:

```
WHERE  _Q1.A1 IS NOT NULL AND
   (CONVERT(nvarchar(4000),_Q1.A1,126) = N'10739')
   and _Q2._TBAAMMFEBA=_Q1._TCAAMMFEBA
```

Notice that SQL Server is converting our `OrderID` value to a `nvarchar` value. To see how data types work, we'll modify our XML schema to use the `type` attribute on the `OrderID` attribute. Find the `OrderID` attribute in the schema `orders.xsd`, which is shown below:

195

Chapter 8

```
<xsd:element name="Order" sql:relation="Orders"
    sql:relationship="CustOrders" >
  <xsd:complexType>
     <xsd:attribute name="OrderID"/>
     <xsd:attribute name="CustomerID"/>
  </xsd:complexType>
</xsd:element>
```

Once you have found the highlighted line, modify it to include the type attribute as follows:

```
<xsd:attribute name="OrderID" type="xsd:integer"/>
```

Now repeat the steps as before, running the same URL that we opened above, and again copy the traced results into Query Analyzer. They look pretty much the same, except now SQL Server is doing two conversions instead of one:

(CONVERT(nvarchar(4000),CONVERT(float(53),_Q1.A1),0) = N'10739'

As you can see, the value is first converted to a float and then to a nvarchar. Our aim is to eliminate the type conversions, so adding an extra conversion isn't really what we want. The problem is that we are specifying that our attribute is an xsd:integer, but then we are passing in a string in the XPath. To avoid all these extra conversions, which can impair performance, we need to specify in the XPath that our OrderID value is a number. To do this we use the number() function, which is shown below. Notice the @OrderID value is encapsulated in the XPath number() function:

http://localhost/nwind/schemas/orders.xsd/root/Customer/Order[@OrderID=**number('10739')**]

With this XPath query we'll get the results we want:

(CONVERT(float(53),_Q1.A1) = CAST(10739.000000000000000 AS float(53)))

> Note that we could also get the same results by omitting the quotes around the OrderID, which would also specify that the ID is a number.

Now we're comparing both numbers as float values, instead of nvarchar values. Since the OrderID field is an integer value, this is an appropriate comparison. To understand how mapping from XPath translate to XML and XDR schemas, you can refer to the table opposite:

XPath Queries

XPath function	XML Schema data type	XDR data type	SQL Server conversion used
None	Not specified	Not specified	No conversion used
	`base64Binary`	`bin.base64`	
	`hexBinary`	`bin.hex`	
Boolean (OrderID)	`boolean`	`boolean`	CONVERT(bit, OrderID)
Number (OrderID)	`decimal`	`number`	CONVERT(float (53), OrderID)
	`integer`	`int`	
	`float`	`float`	
	`byte`	`i1`	
	`short`	`i2`	
	`int`	`i4`	
	`long`	`i8`	
	`float`	`r4`	
	`double`	`r8`	
	`unsignedByte`	`ui1`	
	`unsignedShort`	`ui2`	
	`unsignedInt`	`ui4`	
	`unsignedLong`	`ui8`	
String (OrderID)	`id, idref, idrefs`	`id, idref, idrefs`	CONVERT (nvarchar(4000), OrderID, 126)
	`entity, entities`	`entity, entities`	
	`notation`	`enumeration`	
	`nmtoken`	`notation`	
	`nmtokens`	`nmtoken`	
	`dateTime`	`nmtokens`	
	`string`	`char`	
	`anyURI`	`dateTime`	
		`dateTime.tz`	
		`string`	
		`uri`	
		`uuid`	

Table continued on following page

197

Chapter 8

Path function	XML Schema data type	XDR data type	SQL Server conversion used
None	`decimal`	`fixed14.4`	CONVERT(money, OrderID)
`String (OrderID)`	`date`	`date`	LEFT(CONVERT(nvarchar(4000), OrderID, 126), 10)
`String (OrderID)`	`time`	`time,` `time.tz`	SUBSTRING(CONVERT(nvarchar(4000), OrderID, 126), 1 + CHARINDEX(N'T', CONVERT(nvarchar(4000), OrderID, 126)), 24)

XPath Operators

SQLXML supports all the XPath operators such as +, -, *, and so on, which can be used in performing calculations. For example, if we wanted to find all the orders that have an `OrderID` greater than 11,000, we could use the greater than operator as follows:

http://localhost/nwind/schemas/orders.xsd/root/Customer/Order[@OrderID>11000]?root=root

This is an example of a relational operator (<, <=, >, >=). We can also make use of Boolean operators (AND, OR) to combine predicates as follows:

http://localhost/nwind/schemas/orders.xsd/root/Customer/Order[@OrderID>11000 **or** @OrderID<10100]?root=root

This query will give us all orders that have an `OrderID` greater than 11,000 or an `OrderID` that is less than 10,100. To see a full list of these operators and what they do, take a look at Appendix A.

XPath Functions

The XPath 1.0 Recommendation also provides us with functions, such as `number()`, `boolean()`, and `string()` that we've already seen. These three functions will be the most useful when dealing with XPath queries that run against SQL Server, since they allow you to convert values to the appropriate data type. You should note however, that some of the other more useful XPath functions, such as `contains()`, which can be used like the SQL WHERE clause, aren't currently supported in SQLXML. We'll consider how to get round this in the *Limitations* section later in this chapter.

For more on XPath functions, please see Appendix A.

Using XPath Queries

In the previous section, we looked how the XPath queries work and what they look like. There are several ways that you can implement XPath queries, and in this section we will look at how you can use them in your applications.

XPath Queries in a URL

This one should need no introduction, since this is what we have been doing in the first half of the chapter. With this method you create an XML schema, create a virtual mapping, and then use a URL to retrieve your data. This can be done with a browser, as in our examples, or it can be done programmatically with components like MSXML.

There are two main problems with using URL access. The first is that if you use URL access, then the FOR XML EXPLICIT that the schema generates will be generated each time this URL access occurs. This can cause considerable slowing down of performance. The second problem is one with security, since you're exposing the entire schema, leaving anyone who can figure out your schema capable of accessing any of the data it maps to. This may not be desirable, but it can't be prohibited with XML schema URL access.

To avoid these problems, you should put your XPath queries into templates, use ADO to run the XPath, or use the SQLXML Managed Classes to run the XPath. URL queries are very useful for developing and testing XML schemas; they also function well as training tools, which could be used when explaining your XML schemas to developers, for example.

> *You should also be aware that the very nature of URLs means that certain XPath expressions either will not work, or will not work as you expect. The XPath abbreviations . . and // may be ignored by the browser or be converted. For example, a query like* `order.xsd//Customers` *may be converted to* `order.xsd/Customers`, *which will give entirely different results.*

XPath Queries in Templates

There is an easy solution that can be used to solve the performance problem, and part of the security problem, which is to put your XPath query into a template. Since the generated FOR XML EXPLICIT query will get cached along with the template, you will see a big performance boost in comparison to running URL queries. In addition, by placing your XPath query in a template, you limit what data the user can access, although they still have URL access to the data. To test this out, we need to configure a mapping to a `templates` virtual folder. Go ahead and create a folder named `templates` in the `WWWroot` folder of your web site. Once you have done that, use the virtual directory management tool to open the SQLXML `nwind` virtual directory that we configured in Chapter 2. Go to the **virtual names** tab and fill it in as follows:

Chapter 8

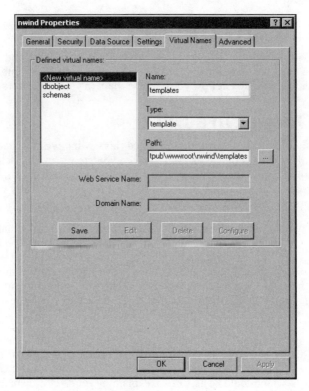

Once you have done this, hit the **Save** button.

The XML template we'll use in this case is called `orders.xml`, and should be saved in the `templates` folder. Please note that this won't work unless you have the `orders.xsd` schema in the `schemas` folder that we configured earlier in the chapter. Here is the `orders.xml` template:

```
<ROOT xmlns:sql='urn:schemas-microsoft-com:xml-sql'>
<sql:header>
  <sql:param name="CustomerID"/>
</sql:header>
<sql:xpath-query mapping-schema='../schemas/orders.xsd'>
   /root/Customer[@CustomerID=$CustomerID)]
</sql:xpath-query>
</ROOT>
```

As we saw in Chapter 5, we use the `<sql:xpath-query>` element to enclose our XPath query. We use a parameter (`$CustomerID`) in this template, as a way of passing in values to the XPath query. You should also note the use of the `mapping-schema` attribute, used to define the schema that we are going to execute the XPath query against. Once this has been set up you can test out the template by opening the following URL:

http://localhost/nwind/templates/orders.xml?CustomerID=VINET

XPath Queries

The results of running the template using the URL are as follows:

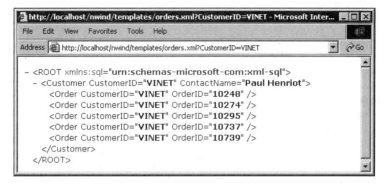

Notice that you should get a fairly quick response from the server, especially after the first time you run it. This is because, as we mentioned above, SQLXML is caching the FOR XML EXPLICIT query that is generated by the XPath query. The template is having SQLXML load up the XML schema and is then running the XPath query against it.

> *Please note: when running XPath queries from within a template, you will need to escape characters, such as ? and &, that may form part of your query. This is because the template is an XML file. See the Using Special Characters section of Chapter 5 for more on this.*

Using Parameters

The example above used the CustomerID parameter in the template. Parameters are passed in to the template as strings and are then referenced in the XPath as a variable. XPath variables are declared in the <sql:header> section of the template within <sql:param> elements, as we learned in Chapter 5. Without XPath variables, you would only be able to create static templates. You can read more about XPath variables in Appendix A.

> *Note that if you use a parameter then you need to remember the rules that apply: if you are using a number, you should use the number() function in the XPath query, which is located in the template itself.*

You can also use parameters in URL queries, by using the XPath variable and passing the parameter in the same way that you pass parameters for templates. An example of this is as follows:

http://localhost/nwind/schemas/orders.xsd/root/Customer[@CustomerID=$CustomerID]?CustomerID=VINET

201

XPath Queries in ADO

With ADO, you can use XPath queries without using the SQLXML virtual directories. This can be done either by directly querying the XML schema with an XPath query, or by passing in a template to the ADO Command object. To utilize either of these methods, you need to use the SQLXMLOLEDB provider in your connection string. You can find examples of how this is done in Chapter 13.

By using ADO, you get both performance benefits and tighter security than URL queries allow, since you can run checks in your code to make sure someone isn't accessing data they shouldn't have access to. This gives application programmers much more control, and doesn't expose important details about the underlying data structure.

XPath Queries in the Managed Classes

You can also use XPath queries with the Managed Classes. Just as with ADO access, this can be done by directly querying the schema with an XPath query, or by passing in an XML template like the one we created. To see examples of how this is done, take a look at Chapter 13.

Performance Considerations

While we have seen how XPath queries allow us to query a database as if it were an XML document, the direct benefits of this need to be weighed against the issue of performance. There is no question that a standard T-SQL query will always beat an XPath query in terms of speed. XPath queries have to do a lot of extra work in order to even generate the T-SQL that gets the results, not to mention the extra work to format the results as XML. All this added work does slow things down. However, the fact that you can return your results in XML format by running queries using XPath makes the performance price worth the cost. By returning the data as XML, the results can be exchanged over the Internet and be interpreted by any client that understands XML; thus avoiding the need to pass data into a middle-tier to be formatted for output to the presentation layer. Producing XML data also enables easy passing of results between different platforms, as long as the user is capable of interpreting XML.

Tuning XPath Using SQL Profiler

The most essential tool when tuning XPath queries is SQL Profiler, since you can go behind the scenes to see what SQL Server is doing with your query, as we did earlier in the chapter. You may often be surprised at how your data is being retrieved. To get the best performance out of your XPath queries, you will often need to run them through and catch the T-SQL using SQL Profiler. You can then check to make sure the SQL being generated is efficient.

The first thing to check is whether or not the correct data types are being used in the query. If your column is an integer, make sure the comparison isn't done as a string comparison. This is the most common type of tuning that is done using SQL Profiler. Use the table we saw earlier in the chapter to figure out what type of schema elements you should be using, and what XPath function you can use to create that type.

XPath Queries

The way your tables are joined together will affect performance just as it does in normal T-SQL queries, so you should check your data types here too. Since you are still joining tables using SQL Server, the same rules apply as with T-SQL. You should also check the data type on any sql:limit-field annotations you may have. All of these can slow down your XML schema if you're not careful.

> **Remember that you get a big performance gain when you put your XPath query in a template. Sometimes this might not be possible right from the start, but once you figure out what data needs to be exposed, the best option is always to put it into a template.**

Recursive Queries

With SQLXML 3.0, Microsoft allowed what is called a **recursive query** (or **self-join**), where you join a table to itself. You can specify this type of join in an XML schema using the sql:max-depth annotation that we saw in Chapter 6. This specifies how many times the table should be joined to itself. Incorporating this method can be very useful for things like menus or organizational charts, where each item in the table may have child items in the same table.

While this feature is useful for getting recursive XML out of SQL Server, the overhead to use it is way too high. Even if you only specify a max-depth of six or so, your query may still run slowly. To see why, run a SQL trace and take a look at the T-SQL that is generated. You will see that for each level of max-depth that you specify, another self-join is created. So even though this feature may be very useful, it's probably not worth the price you will pay in performance. A much easier solution, performance wise, is to return the data unjoined and then use an XSL transformation to join the data.

To demonstrate this, we need to create a table and fill it with some sample data. Run the following T-SQL against the Northwind database so that we can use the virtual directory we already created to run this sample:

```
CREATE TABLE menus (
    menuID int NOT NULL,
    parentID int NULL,
    Title varchar(50) NOT NULL,
    URL varchar(256) NULL
)

GO

ALTER TABLE menus ADD CONSTRAINT PK_menus primary key clustered
(
    menuID
)
```

Once you have successfully created the menus table go ahead and run the T-SQL below to add the sample data:

```
INSERT INTO menus VALUES (1000, null, 'Root Menu', null)
INSERT INTO menus VALUES (1001, 1000, 'Group 1', null)
INSERT INTO menus VALUES (1002, 1000, 'Group 2', null)
INSERT INTO menus VALUES (1003, 1001, 'Group 1 - item 1', null)
INSERT INTO menus VALUES (1004, 1001, 'Group 1 - item 2', null)
INSERT INTO menus VALUES (1005, 1002, 'Group 2 - item 1', null)
INSERT INTO menus VALUES (1006, 1002, 'Group 2 - item 2', null)
INSERT INTO menus VALUES (1007, 1000, 'Group 3', null)
INSERT INTO menus VALUES (1008, 1007, 'Group 3 - item 1', null)
INSERT INTO menus VALUES (1009, 1007, 'Group 3 - item 2', null)
INSERT INTO menus VALUES (1010, 1008, 'Group 3 - item 1 -
                    subitem 1', 'http://www.dell.com')
INSERT INTO menus VALUES (1011, 1008, 'Group 3 - item 1 -
                    subitem 2', 'http://msdn.microsoft.com')
INSERT INTO menus VALUES (1012, 1009, 'Group 3 - item 2 -
                    subitem 1', 'http://www.msn.com')
INSERT INTO menus VALUES (1013, 1009, 'Group 3 - item 2 -
                    subitem 2', 'http://www.microsoft.com')
```

For our first example, we'll create an XML schema with a recursive relationship, save it as a schema virtual object, and then test it out with XPath queries in the URL. Create the following schema and save it in the schemas folder as rmenu.xsd:

```
<xsd:schema
  xmlns:xsd="http://www.w3.org/2001/XMLSchema"
  xmlns:dt="urn:schemas-microsoft-com:datatypes"
  xmlns:sql="urn:schemas-microsoft-com:mapping-schema">
  <xsd:annotation>
    <xsd:appinfo>
      <sql:relationship name="MenuLevels"
           parent="menus"
           parent-key="menuID"
           child="menus"
           child-key="parentID" />
    </xsd:appinfo>
  </xsd:annotation>

  <xsd:element name="menu" type="menuType"
                          sql:relation="menus"
                          sql:key-fields="menuID"
                          sql:limit-field="parentID" />

  <xsd:complexType name="menuType">
    <xsd:sequence>
      <xsd:element name="menu" type="menuType"
                              sql:relation="menus"
                              sql:key-fields="menuID"
                              sql:relationship="MenuLevels"
                              sql:max-depth="6" />
```

XPath Queries

```
        </xsd:sequence>
        <xsd:attribute name="menuID" type="xsd:ID" />
        <xsd:attribute name="Title" type="xsd:string"/>
        <xsd:attribute name="URL" type="xsd:string"/>
    </xsd:complexType>


</xsd:schema>
```

This schema can be queried using the following XPath query:

http://localhost/nwind/schemas/rmenu.xsd/menu?root=root

that should give you the following results:

This method works well for small resultsets, like the one in this example, but when you get larger amounts of data with more complex structures, such as multiple tables, it quickly becomes very inefficient. You can see why if you run a SQL trace and look at the very complex FOR XML EXPLICIT query that is generated. To get around this problem, we can remove the relationship in the schema and create the recursion using XSL instead. In this example, we're going to use what is called an **inline** schema. What this means is that instead of creating a separate schema file for the example, we'll simply put the schema in the template being using to call the XPath. The template with the inline schema embedded in it, which should be saved to the templates folder in your nwind directory as menus.xml, is as follows:

205

```
<ROOT xmlns:sql='urn:schemas-microsoft-com:xml-sql'
    sql:xsl="menus.xsl">
<xsd:schema xmlns:xsd='http://www.w3.org/2001/XMLSchema'
        xmlns:ms='urn:schemas-microsoft-com:mapping-schema'
        id='menuSchema' sql:is-mapping-schema='1'>

  <xsd:element name="menus">
    <xsd:complexType>
      <xsd:attribute name="menuID" type="xsd:ID"/>
      <xsd:attribute name="parentID" type="xsd:integer"/>
      <xsd:attribute name="Title" type="xsd:string"/>
      <xsd:attribute name="URL" type="xsd:string"/>
    </xsd:complexType>
  </xsd:element>

</xsd:schema>
<sql:xpath-query mapping-schema='#menuSchema'>
    /menus
</sql:xpath-query>
</ROOT>
```

> Note that although inline schemas in templates can be useful, this method has a disadvantage: the annotated schema is only available to the template that houses it, which prevents us from being able to reuse it for other templates or queries.

The ID on the `<xsd:schema>` element is used to reference the schema in the `mapping-schema` attribute. We prefix the ID with the # symbol to signify that the schema is an inline schema. Then we use the `sql:xsl` attribute to tell SQLXML that we want to use the following XSL file to modify our results. Save the XSL file below as menus.xsl in your templates folder:

```
<?xml version="1.0"?>
<xsl:stylesheet
xmlns:xsl="http://www.w3.org/1999/XSL/Transform" version="1.0">

<xsl:template match="/">
    <root>
    <xsl:apply-templates select="ROOT/menus[not(@parentID)]"/>
    </root>
</xsl:template>

<xsl:template match="menus">
    <xsl:variable name="ID" select="@menuID"/>
    <menu>
    <xsl:attribute name="Title">
      <xsl:value-of select="@Title"/>
    </xsl:attribute>
    <xsl:if test="@URL">
      <xsl:attribute name="URL">
        <xsl:value-of select="@URL"/>
```

```
            </xsl:attribute>
        </xsl:if>
        <xsl:apply-templates select="../menus[@parentID=$ID]"/>
    </menu>
</xsl:template>

</xsl:stylesheet>
```

This XSL document takes our flat XML result from the XPath query and adds the recursion. The result is the same result that we got when we used the `rmenu.xsd` schema and can be viewed by opening the following URL:

http://localhost/nwind/templates/menus.xml

So, by using XSL we can generate the same recursive XML without having the high overhead costs.

Security Issues

Of course, with XPath queries there are security issues, but they are really tied to the methods used to run the XPath rather than to XPath itself. For example, if you create a mapping to a schema and allow anonymous access, then anyone who can figure out your schema can get access to your data. This is really a security issue with how your directory has been setup and not with XPath queries *per se*. When looking at security in terms of XPath queries, there are really two questions you need to ask:

Who Has Access to the Data?

This depends on your security setup. If you're using virtual directories, then the security that you set up on the virtual directory itself is the security that is on the schema. So, if you give everyone access to the directory, you're giving everyone access to the schema. For information on how to secure virtual directories refer back to Chapter 2 and Chapter 5.

As we discussed above, you should use templates for providing access to your schemas whenever possible, as opposed to URL queries, since this means that users can only perform the queries that you specify in your templates, rather than being able to access all the data.

Can the Data be Changed?

The data can be viewed, but it can't be changed, unless you allow Updategrams to be posted. This becomes especially dangerous since the user now knows the format of the data and can use an Updategram to delete, modify, or add data. This is all the more reason not to allow Updategrams to be posted. For more information on Updategrams and how they can be used safely, take a look at Chapter 11.

Chapter 8

Other Methods

Microsoft also recommends that you use aliases, rather than actual table names, in your schemas. This prevents users from being able to find out the structure of your database, which in turn could be used to exploit other security holes.

Using these methods, you can keep your data secure while making use of XML and XDR schemas to expose your data as an XML document. End users will be able to make use of the XML without having to fully understand SQL Server or the actual data structures, and your data will remain secure.

Limitations

As we mentioned earlier, SQL Server does not support the entire XPath 1.0 Recommendation. The following features are *not* supported by in XPath queries on XML views in SQL Server 2000:

- Certain axes (ways of selecting other nodes in an XPath expression with a particular relation to the current node). Only the `attribute`, `child`, `parent`, and `self` axes are supported. As a result, SQL Server XPath expressions can only move up and down the node tree in single steps, not along sibling relations or rapidly up and down the tree.
- Numeric-valued predicates. This means that any XPath expression that relies on a numeric-valued predicate (such as a quick test to determine if a value is not zero) needs to be changed to perform an explicit boolean test.
- The `mod` and `unary -` arithmetic operators.
- Node functions, including `position()`.
- Many string functions: `starts-with()`, `substring()`, `substring-before()`, `substring-after()`, `string-length()`, `normalize()`, `translate()`, or the big two: `concat()` and `contains()`.
- The numeric functions `sum()`, `floor()`, `ceiling()`, and `round()`.

If some of these terms, operators and functions are unfamiliar to you, please see Appendix A.

Let's take a look now at how we can work around one of these limitations; namely, not being able to use the `postion()` function. This function is used for returning elements that are in a certain position, like elements 1 through 5. If this function was supported in SQLXML 3.0, then we might use a query like this:

http://localhost/nwind/schemas/orders.xsd/root/Customer[position() < 5]

This URL query is asking for all the `<Customer>` elements that have a position that is less than 5. As you can see, this function would be very useful for paging through result sets, especially very large ones. However, if you try to run this query, you will get an error similar to the following:

XPath Queries

HResult: 0x80004005
Source: Microsoft XML Extensions to SQL Server
Description: XPath: the position() function is not supported

So how can we get around this limitation? There are a couple of methods, and your choice of which to use depends mostly on the size of the XML document generated by your schema.

The method we'll look at here is really useful if you don't have a large XML result, as it returns the entire XML document and then uses XSLT to do the paging. The XML template below uses an XPath query to retrieve customer information, while the XSLT stylesheet deals with splitting the XML results into multiple pages. You should save this template in your `templates` directory as `paged.xml`:

```
<ROOT xmlns:sql='urn:schemas-microsoft-com:xml-sql'
  sql:xsl="paged.xsl">
  <sql:header>
    <sql:param name="page">1</sql:param>
    <sql:param name="size">5</sql:param>
  </sql:header>
  <sql:query>
    <![CDATA[select '<page>' + @page + '</page>' + '<size>' +
        @size + '</size>' ]]>
  </sql:query>
  <sql:xpath-query mapping-schema='../schemas/orders.xsd'>
      /root/Customer
  </sql:xpath-query>
</ROOT>
```

Next we need the XSL document that we'll use to transform the resulting XML into paged data. The XSL file does this by using the `$page` and `$size` parameters that are passed in to it. Based on these parameters, the XSLT returns only the customers that fit on the specific page. This file is called `paged.xsl`, and can be found in the code download. Download it and save it in the `templates` directory too.

You can test this out with the following URL:

http://localhost/nwind/templates/paged.xml?page=1&size=5

Which should give you these results:

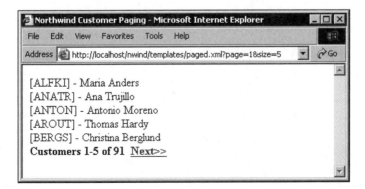

This method is very useful since it doesn't send all the results down to the client, but instead filters out the required data first with the XSL, using the $page and $size parameters we pass in. In this case, we use a page value of 1 and a size value of 5. However, if you have a very large XML document, this solution might not be the optimum one to use, since the XSL file will have to work through many values to filter out the required results. Because of this you should use a stored procedure instead of the XPath query.

Summary

In this chapter we looked at how XPath queries relate to SQL queries. We ran through how to query a schema virtual object using Xpath, and then considered how we could modify basic XPath queries by using parameters, namespaces, and predicates to return specific results. Once we built a basic understanding of how XPath queries work, we looked at how to make them perform better and what security issues they create. We saw that, whenever possible, you should include your XPath queries in a template rather than a URL query to maximize their performance, and minimize the related security issues. We ended by considering some of the limitations of SQLXML, in terms of XPath functionality that isn't supported. Having reached the end of this chapter you should now understand how to query your database as if it were an XML document.

XPath Queries

Kevin Williams

- Things to Consider
- Equivalent SQL Data Types
- Design Approach
- Example
- Summary

9

Mapping XML to SQL Server

In this chapter, we will take a look at some techniques that we can use to create SQL Server database structures to store data from an XML document. Topics we'll be discussing include:

- ❑ Understanding the role of the SQL Server tables to be created
- ❑ Mapping XML data types to SQL Server
- ❑ Handling mixed-mode documents
- ❑ Mapping elements to tables
- ❑ Mapping data elements or attributes to columns
- ❑ Mapping child relationships to foreign key relationships
- ❑ Mapping ID-IDREF relationships to foreign key relationships
- ❑ Creating primary keys for created tables

Things to Consider

Often, keeping data in an XML form is not enough. In order to perform higher-level manipulation of the data, it can be useful to move the information into a relational structure, such as a set of SQL Server tables. As with converting SQL Server structures to XML structures, we need to think about how the resulting tables and columns will be used. Understanding the business role played by these structures will help us understand how we should approach the design process. Let's take a look at some of the ways XML data can be used in a relational database, and how each influences the design process.

Loading Persistent Data

The first reason we might want to design SQL Server tables for an existing XML document is to store transient data – such as data that is received via a transaction in XML – in a persistent fashion.

Chapter 9

For example, we might want to load transaction data submitted as XML documents into an OLTP (Online Transaction Processing) database for further processing. In this case, we should design our tables to represent just that portion of the incoming XML document that we will need to manipulate later. For example, say we had the following XML structure:

```xml
<invoice>
   <totalAmount>19.40</totalAmount>
   <invoiceDate>2002-08-21</invoiceDate>
   <customerName>John Q. Public</customerName>
   <lineItem>
      <itemName>Grommets</itemName>
      <quantity>37</quantity>
      <price>0.20</price>
   </lineItem>
   <lineItem>
      <itemName>Widgets</itemName>
      <quantity>12</quantity>
      <price>1.00</price>
   </lineItem>
</invoice>
```

We might want to load this data into a SQL Server database so that we can track the total amount that has been invoiced to each customer at any given time. To do this, we don't actually need the specific line item information, so we can discard it when creating our SQL Server tables. Remember, there's no rule set in stone about how data needs to move between XML and SQL Server. Instead, we use our best judgment based on the current (*and anticipated*) business requirements, and the security and performance requirements on the database.

A sample SQL Server structure to hold this data might look something like this:

```sql
CREATE TABLE Invoice (
invoiceID int IDENTITY PRIMARY KEY,
customerName varchar(100) NOT NULL,
invoiceDate DATETIME NOT NULL,
invoiceAmount decimal(9,2) NOT NULL)
```

In many cases, it makes sense to reorganize the data in the actual SQL Server tables. The most common reason for this (although there are others) is the granularity of the documents – in some cases, the contents of the XML document may not exactly reflect the relational structures we want to capture. For example, say we were importing the previous invoice XML document. In this case, however, we may want to be able to accurately model the relationship between invoices and customers, to easily capture the various invoices for a single customer. To achieve this, we should move the customer information out into a separate table:

```sql
CREATE TABLE Customer (
customerID int IDENTITY PRIMARY KEY,
customerName varchar(100) NOT NULL)
```

Mapping XML to SQL Server

```
CREATE TABLE Invoice (
invoiceID int IDENTITY PRIMARY KEY,
customerID int FOREIGN KEY REFERENCES Customer(customerID),
invoiceDate DATETIME NOT NULL,
invoiceAmount decimal(9,2) NOT NULL)
```

Of course, loading documents into this table structure will be a little more complex – we'll need to determine whether the customer referenced in the XML document already exists (probably through the use of `customerName` as an alternate key) and then either insert a record into the `Customer` table or use the `customerID` of the existing record as the value of the `customerID` foreign key in the `Invoice` table. We'll take a closer look at inserting and updating records later in this section.

Loading Temporary Data for Manipulation

We may also want to load data temporarily from an XML document for manipulation. This is common when we need to perform arithmetic processing of the XML document's contents, such as aggregating data from multiple documents or performing sophisticated arithmetic calculations using that data. In this case, it's less important that we tune our SQL Server tables to our business requirements – after all, the temporary information in the database will be discarded after it has been processed.

> When working with XML documents and SQL Server tables, our mantra should always be this: perform the processing where it makes the most sense. Computationally expensive manipulation of data (such as aggregation or arithmetic manipulation) should be performed on the data platform best suited to it, in other words, the SQL Server platform.

Here's an example; say we are receiving the following XML document that represents a single transaction:

```xml
<invoice>
   <invoiceDate>2002-08-21</invoiceDate>
   <customerName>John Q. Public</customerName>
   <lineItem>
      <itemName>Grommets</itemName>
      <quantity>37</quantity>
      <price>0.20</price>
   </lineItem>
   <lineItem>
      <itemName>Widgets</itemName>
      <quantity>12</quantity>
      <price>1.00</price>
   </lineItem>
</invoice>
```

215

Chapter 9

Note that this is the same as our previous example, except that the total invoice amount isn't provided – we will need to have that calculated at some point during the load process. We would like to use this invoice to populate a table that looks like the following:

```
CREATE TABLE TotalInvoice (
   totalInvoiceID int IDENTITY PRIMARY KEY,
   customerName varchar(100) NOT NULL,
   totalAmount decimal(9,2) NOT NULL)
```

To do this, we need to determine the total invoice amount by summing up the quantity multiplied by the price for each line item in the invoice. It makes more sense to perform this processing in SQL Server, rather than trying to perform it against the XML document directly. We create the following structure:

```
CREATE TABLE TempInvoice (
   invoiceID int IDENTITY PRIMARY KEY,
   customerName varchar(100))

CREATE TABLE TempLineItem (
   lineItemID int IDENTITY PRIMARY KEY,
   invoiceID int FOREIGN KEY REFERENCES TempInvoice(invoiceID)
     ON DELETE CASCADE,
   quantity int NOT NULL,
   price decimal(5,2) NOT NULL)
```

Note that we've discarded the `<invoiceDate>` and `<itemName>` elements, as we don't need them for the business process we need to perform. We then create a stored procedure that updates the `TotalInvoice` table with the data from the `TempInvoice` and `TempLineItem` tables and then discards the temporary records:

```
CREATE PROC sp_UpdateTotalInvoice (@invoiceID int)
AS
BEGIN

DECLARE @TotalInvoiceID int

SELECT @TotalInvoiceID = invoiceID
FROM TempInvoice, TotalInvoice
WHERE TempInvoice.invoiceID = @invoiceID
  AND TempInvoice.customerName = TotalInvoice.customerName

IF (@TotalInvoiceID IS NULL)
BEGIN
  INSERT TotalInvoice (customerName, totalAmount)
  SELECT TempInvoice.customerName, 0
    FROM TempInvoice
    WHERE TempInvoice.invoiceID = @invoiceID
  SELECT @TotalInvoiceID = @@IDENTITY
END

DECLARE @invoiceTotal decimal(9,2)

SELECT @invoiceTotal = SUM(quantity * price)
FROM TempLineItem
WHERE TempLineItem.invoiceID = @invoiceID
```

Mapping XML to SQL Server

```
UPDATE TotalInvoice
SET totalAmount = totalAmount + @invoiceTotal
WHERE totalInvoiceID = @TotalInvoiceID

DELETE TempInvoice
WHERE invoiceID = @invoiceID

END
```

This stored procedure processes one document at a time – if you wanted to perform the processing in batch, there are other approaches that would work better (such as a XML Bulk Load, followed by a stored procedure that process all the data at once). Note that we're applying the same good design practices here as we would to any other kind of code – there's nothing magical about XML that requires that well-tuned design go out the window. We discard the information we don't need, add only the information we do, and perform the computationally expensive processing on the best platform for it – SQL Server.

Inserts or Updates?

As we alluded to earlier in this section, the issue of inserting and updating records can be a real headache when moving data from XML to SQL Server because XML documents are designed to be self-contained (that is, each XML document contains all the information necessary to describe the data inside it). We will often have information repeated from document to document that we may not want to insert repeatedly into a normalized database . For example, take our invoice sample XML document from the previous section:

```xml
<invoice>
  <invoiceDate>2002-08-21</invoiceDate>
  <customerName>John Q. Public</customerName>
  <lineItem>
    <itemName>Grommets</itemName>
    <quantity>37</quantity>
    <price>0.20</price>
  </lineItem>
  <lineItem>
    <itemName>Widgets</itemName>
    <quantity>12</quantity>
    <price>1.00</price>
  </lineItem>
</invoice>
```

In this document, the `<customerName>` information will likely be redundant because, if an individual customer places more than one order, that customer's information will appear repeated across several invoice documents. However, we'd like to capture that relation in our database, so we move the `Customer` data out as before. This necessitates some code complexity: we need to determine whether the data about the customer being added already exists in the `Customer` table, or if we need to create a new record in that table for using the customer data from this invoice. While this issue is addressed to a certain extent by `OPENXML` (see Chapter 10), Updategrams (see Chapter 11) and DiffGrams (see Chapter 13), sophisticated behavior can be hard to create using these technologies.

Chapter 9

In some cases, procedural code – either as part of a SQL Server stored procedure or trigger, or as part of a VB/VC++/C# class – will be needed to make this determination before the structure can be accurately created. While this is a relatively simple problem in our simple example, more complex XML documents can compound the issue.

Fortunately, there is a formulaic approach we can take to identifying whether an INSERT or an UPDATE should be performed. The first step is to identify an alternate key for the table that will receive the INSERT or UPDATE. We need to do this because the odds are good that we'll be using our own identity column for the primary key in that table, and naturally the XML document isn't going to provide a value for that key (except in very specialized circumstances, such as a message passed between two systems that rely on the same keys to identify records). The alternate key must consist of one or more data fields provided in the XML document, otherwise we could never correctly identify whether an INSERT or an UPDATE needed to be performed (that is, we couldn't identify whether a particular record already existed or not). Once we have identified the alternate key, we need only to see whether a record with that alternate key already exists in the table to identify the record correctly. If it does, then we select the primary key from that row and use it as the foreign key in all of the child tables. If it does not, then we need to insert a record with the information provided in the XML document. The resulting identity value is then used as the foreign key in the child tables. The following stored procedure provides an example:

```
CREATE PROC sp_InsertOrUpdateCustomer (@customerName
varchar(100))
AS
BEGIN
  DECLARE @customerID int
  SELECT @customerID = customerID
    FROM Customer
    WHERE customerName = @customerName
  IF (@customerID IS NULL)
    BEGIN
      INSERT Customer (customerName) VALUES (@customerName)
      SELECT @customerID = @@IDENTITY
    END
  SELECT @customerID

END
GO
```

This stored procedure returns the customerID of either the created or the reused record, which can then be used to insert records into the child tables.

Now that we have an idea of how our XML document is to be moved into SQL Server from a business perspective, let's take a look at some specific technical issues we need to address before starting to create our structures.

Equivalent SQL Data Types

The datatypes allowed in XML Schema are more complete than those allowed in SQL Server. For example, XML Schema allows various restricted forms of integers, such as non-negative integers and non-positive integers. Fortunately, most (but not all, as we'll see a little later in the chapter) of these datatypes map directly to SQL Server data types. The following table lists all of the datatypes allowed in an XML schema, along with the best possible matches in SQL Server:

> *Please note: there is a reverse table showing the XML Schema equivalent for SQL Server data types in Chapter 3. XML Schema data types are also discussed in Appendix B.*

XML Schema type	SQL Server type	Comments
duration	datetime	The best way to store these is to map them onto a base datetime (say 1/1/1900); therefore, a duration of P5D (five days, using the XML duration syntax) would be stored as 1/6/1900. The duration may then be used by performing a datediff on this value and 1/1/1900.
dateTime	datetime	Datetime representations in XML schemas take the form YYYY-MM-DDTHH:MI:SS, which does not load directly into SQL Server. If you are decomposing the document manually (as opposed to using an XML-aware mechanism like Updategrams or XML Bulk Load), you must make sure to convert this to a SQL Server legal datetime before inserting it into the database.

Table continued on following page

Chapter 9

XML Schema type	SQL Server type	Comments
time	datetime	For this (and all the other) partial datetime formats, they can be stored as datetime with the non-specified portion of the datetime fixed. For example, a time of 03:00 might be represented in SQL Server as 1/1/1900 03:00. Performing a datepart on the specified partial date can then retrieve the time portion. If you don't need to store milliseconds, you can also use the smalldatetime data type to save a few bytes.
date	datetime	As time, but with the time portion set to 00:00:00.
gYearMonth	datetime	As time, but with the time portion set to 00:00:00 and the day set to 1.
gYear	datetime	As time, but with the time portion set to 00:00:00, the month set to 1, and the day set to 1.
gMonthDay	datetime	As time, but with the time portion set to 00:00:00 and the year set to 1900.
gDay	datetime	As time, but with the time portion set to 00:00:00, the month set to 1, and the year set to 1900.
gMonth	datetime	As time, but with the time portion set to 00:00:00, the day set to 1, and the year set to 1900.
boolean	bit	Straightforward conversion.

Mapping XML to SQL Server

XML Schema type	SQL Server type	Comments
base64Binary	image/varbinary	The value should be decoded first (many XML libraries, including web services created with .NET, will handle this decode automatically – the XmlTextReader class (see Chapter 13) provides a ReadBase64 method that handles this as well); if we know that the value will be less than 8000 bytes (this is typically not the case), we can use varbinary instead.
hexBinary	image/varbinary	The value should be decoded first; if we know that the value will be less than 8000 bytes (this is typically not the case), we can use varbinary instead.
float	real	Straightforward conversion.
double	float	Straightforward conversion.
anyURI	varchar/nvarchar	For this and all other string values, if the exact length is specified in the XML schema, we can use char instead of varchar; note that if the encoding of the XML document is UTF-16, we'll want to use nvarchar and nchar instead; and if the string allows (or we expect) values longer than 8000 characters (or 4000 for UTF-16), we should use text or ntext instead.
QName	varchar/nvarchar	As anyURI.
NOTATION	varchar/nvarchar	As anyURI.
string	varchar/nvarchar	As anyURI.
normalizedString	varchar/nvarchar	As anyURI.

Table continued on following page

Chapter 9

XML Schema type	SQL Server type	Comments
token	varchar/nvarchar	As anyURI.
language	varchar/nvarchar	As anyURI.
Name	varchar/nvarchar	As anyURI.
NCName	varchar/nvarchar	As anyURI.
ID	varchar/nvarchar	In most instances, if the ID has no intrinsic semantic value (and it usually won't), this will only be used to establish a relationship between two elements – see *Mapping Relationships*, later in the chapter.
IDREF	varchar/nvarchar	In practice, this value will never be mapped directly – see *Mapping Relationships*, later in the chapter.
IDREFS	varchar/nvarchar	In practice, these values will never be mapped directly – see *Mapping Relationships*, later in the chapter.
ENTITY	varchar/nvarchar	As anyURI.
ENTITIES	varchar/nvarchar	As anyURI.
NMTOKEN	varchar/nvarchar	As anyURI.
NMTOKENS	varchar/nvarchar	As anyURI.
decimal	decimal	Use the total digits constraining facet, if present in the source XML schema, as the precision; use the fraction digits constraining facet, if present in the source XML schema, as the scale; note that values may exceed the allowable range for SQL decimal values.
integer	bigint, int, smallint, tinyint	Use the data type that corresponds to the expected value space (see below).
NonPositive Integer	bigint, int, smallint	Use the data type that corresponds to the expected value space (see below).

Mapping XML to SQL Server

XML Schema type	SQL Server type	Comments
`long`	`bigint`	Straightforward conversion.
`NonNegativeInteger`	`bigint, int, smallint, tinyint`	Use the data type that corresponds to the expected value space (see below).
`negativeInteger`	`bigint, int, smallint`	Use the data type that corresponds to the expected value space (see below).
`int`	`int`	Straightforward conversion.
`unsignedLong`	`bigint`	Straightforward conversion.
`positiveInteger`	`bigint, int, smallint, tinyint`	Use the data type that corresponds to the expected value space (see below).
`short`	`smallint`	Straightforward conversion.
`unsignedInt`	`int`	Straightforward conversion.
`byte`	`smallint`	Straightforward conversion.
`unsignedShort`	`int`	Straightforward conversion.
`unsignedByte`	`tinyint`	Straightforward conversion.

Note that, for many of the mappings, the SQL Server allowable range of values is a superset of the values allowed in XML Schema. If we are moving information strictly from XML to SQL Server, this is OK – the values provided in the XML documents will always map into the appropriate SQL Server columns. However, if we need to extract the data as XML at some point, be aware that a value may have crept into a column that does not map to the value space of the XML schema – see Chapter 3 for more information on mapping data from SQL Server to XML.

Types to Avoid in XML Data Destined for SQL Server

There are certain types in the XML Schema Recommendation that present significant problems when mapping to SQL Server. In particular, the unbounded number types – `decimal`, `integer`, `nonPositiveInteger`, `nonNegativeInteger`, `negativeInteger`, and `positiveInteger` – cannot be accurately modeled in SQL Server.

223

Chapter 9

For example, if a value is specified as integer in the XML schema, any value will pass – including values that exceed even `bigint`'s capability to store them (a hundred thousand numeric digits in a row is a valid value for an element or attribute of type `integer`). When modeling these types, we'll need to use our best judgement based on the expected value space – sometimes, they need to be modeled with a character rather than numeric type. Often, XML schema designers who are unfamiliar with the better constrained types such as `int` and `long` select the `integer` type as default. Once we know the intended value space for the `integer`, pick the smallest SQL Server type that covers the value space and use that. For example, if a value is defined as `integer` but the known value space for that value is a range from 0 to 100, we can use a `tinyint` in the SQL Server representation.

Another potential problem is the `decimal` XML Schema type. Since it does not specify an upper limit for the total number of digits in the value, a `decimal` can potentially exceed both the value space and the precision space of the SQL Server `decimal` type. However, the good news is that this rarely happens in practice – decimal values are usually used to represent things such as currency values that easily fall within the SQL Server `decimal` value space. If we do come across a `decimal` whose value space exceeds that of the SQL Server `decimal` type, we may need to model the value as a `float` instead (and be aware that this may introduce rounding errors).

Design Approach

Now that we know how our XML Schema types map onto the SQL Server types, we can begin to design our SQL Server structures. Before we start, though, we need to address a particular type of document that doesn't map well at all onto SQL Server: the mixed-mode document.

Mixed-mode Documents

Mixed-mode documents, also known as **narrative documents** or **markup documents**, are XML documents that contain blocks of marked-up text. These blocks of marked-up text can be a real nightmare to model correctly in SQL Server. Let's take a look at an example. Say we have the following XML document:

```
<report>The subject, <subject>Kevin Williams</subject> lives at
<address>762 Evergreen Terrace</address> in the town of
<city>Springfield</city>. </report>
```

Here, our business case comes into play. Do we only want to capture the relevant information about the subject – the name, address, and city – or do we want to capture the actual narrative as it appeared? I'm going to go out on a limb here a little bit and assert that if the narrative is important, we should store it as a single XML BLOB, rather than trying to decompose it into text blocks and values (which can be difficult to model well in a relational database model).

224

Mapping XML to SQL Server

The reality is this: the text values that appear as part of the `<report>` element, but are not themselves further marked up, have no meaning outside the context of the `<report>` element itself. In other words, it doesn't make sense to pull the text elements apart. A possible representation of the report element in our database might look like this:

```
CREATE TABLE Report (
    reportText varchar(6000) NOT NULL,
    subjectName varchar(50) NOT NULL,
    address varchar(100) NOT NULL,
    city varchar(50) NOT NULL)
```

While this forces us to repeat data in our database, it saves us from some computationally-expensive processing where we would be forced to shred the report element text, store it in some sort of ordered representation in the database, and then reconstitute it whenever it was needed.

Of course, the better solution in this particular case is simply to not store the narrative portion of the text at all because it has no intrinsic value other than as a way to provide the individual data points we're interested in. We might want to simply use a table that contains just the values of interest:

```
CREATE TABLE Report (
    subjectName varchar(50) NOT NULL,
    address varchar(100) NOT NULL,
    city varchar(50) NOT NULL)
```

Let's now return to our discussion of the design approach we should generally take.

Identification of Relevant Information

Firstly, we need to identify which information in the XML document needs to be represented in our SQL Server tables. As we mentioned before, the driving factor here is the business case. What will the information be used for? Do we need to be able to recreate the original XML document from the stored information? Remember that less is more in this situation: we want to model just the information from the XML document that will satisfy the business need in the SQL Server database. This can entail discarding particular values or even entire subtrees of the XML document. We'll learn a little more about this later in the chapter.

If you need to persist XML documents for storage or archival purposes, then a hybrid approach is often the best solution. In this approach, you might store the XML documents in some URL-addressable location and then include a reference to that URL in data generated from that document. This provides the best of both worlds: it is easy access to the document in its original state, but we also get direct searching and aggregation capabilities that we can use on the data contained in the document. The obvious downside is the increased consumption of storage space to keep both the original document and the information indexed out of it.

225

Chapter 9

Design of the Overall Relational Structure

The next step is to design the overall shape of the SQL Server model. We know that we will be creating (generally) one element in our schema per complex element (one with subcontent) in our XML structure. However, there are some tricks to getting this right. Let's take a look at some common (and uncommon) situations that arise when designing the relationships between tables in our derived SQL Server structures.

Handling Child Elements

In most cases, we will want to model child elements as additional tables that are mapped back to the parent tables using a foreign key relationship. This approach is necessary when the child elements may appear more than once. For example, say we have the following XML structure:

```
<invoice customerName="Kevin Williams"
         invoiceDate="2002-08-22">
  <lineItem partName="Grommets" quantity="17" price="0.30" />
  <lineItem partName="Widgets" quantity="22" price="0.15" />
</invoice>
```

The XML schema for this document looks like this:

```
<xsd:schema xmlns:xsd="http://www.w3.org/2001/XMLSchema">
  <xsd:element name="invoice">
    <xsd:complexType>
      <xsd:sequence>
        <xsd:element ref="lineItem" maxOccurs="unbounded" />
      </xsd:sequence>
      <xsd:attribute name="customerName"
                     type="xsd:string"
                     use="required" />
      <xsd:attribute name="invoiceDate"
                     type="xsd:dateTime"
                     use="required" />
    </xsd:complexType>
  </xsd:element>
  <xsd:element name="lineItem">
    <xsd:complexType>
      <xsd:attribute name="partName"
                     type="xsd:string"
                     use="required" />
      <xsd:attribute name="quantity"
                     type="xsd:short"
                     use="required" />
      <xsd:attribute name="price"
                     type="xsd:decimal"
                     use="required" />
    </xsd:complexType>
  </xsd:element>
</xsd:schema>
```

Mapping XML to SQL Server

It makes sense in this case to model this XML structure as two separate tables, one for the invoice data and one for the line item data, related by a foreign key:

```
CREATE TABLE Invoice (
  invoiceID int IDENTITY PRIMARY KEY,
  customerName varchar(100) NOT NULL,
  invoiceDate datetime NOT NULL)

CREATE TABLE LineItem (
  lineItemID int IDENTITY PRIMARY KEY,
  invoiceID int FOREIGN KEY REFERENCES Invoice(invoiceID),
  partName varchar(50) NOT NULL,
  quantity smallint NOT NULL,
  price decimal(7,2) NOT NULL)
```

One-to-One Parent-Child Relationships

However, modeling child relationships as separate tables isn't always the best approach. For example, many XML documents model one-to-one relationships as child elements. This often occurs when a schema designer wants part of their specification to be compatible with some other standard, such as a particular address representation. Take for example the following document:

```
<invoice customerName="Kevin Williams"
         invoiceDate="2002-08-22">
  <address address1="762 Evergreen Terrace"
           city="Springfield"
           state="VA"
           zip="21892" />
  <lineItem partName="Grommets" quantity="17" price="0.30" />
  <lineItem partName="Widgets" quantity="22" price="0.15" />
</invoice>
```

The XML schema for this structure looks like this:

```
<xsd:schema xmlns:xsd="http://www.w3.org/2001/XMLSchema">
  <xsd:element name="invoice">
    <xsd:complexType>
      <xsd:sequence>
        <xsd:element ref="address" />
        <xsd:element ref="lineItem" maxOccurs="unbounded" />
      </xsd:sequence>
      <xsd:attribute name="customerName"
                     type="xsd:string"
                     use="required" />
      <xsd:attribute name="invoiceDate"
                     type="xsd:dateTime"
                     use="required" />
    </xsd:complexType>
  </xsd:element>
  <xsd:element name="address">
    <xsd:complexType>
      <xsd:attribute name="address1"
                     type="xsd:string"
                     use="required" />
      <xsd:attribute name="address2"
                     type="xsd:string" />
```

```
            <xsd:attribute name="city"
                           type="xsd:string"
                           use="required" />
            <xsd:attribute name="state"
                           type="xsd:string"
                           use="required" />
            <xsd:attribute name="zip"
                           type="xsd:string"
                           use="required" />
    </xsd:complexType>
  </xsd:element>
  <xsd:element name="lineItem">
    <xsd:complexType>
      <xsd:attribute name="partName"
                     type="xsd:string"
                     use="required" />
      <xsd:attribute name="quantity"
                     type="xsd:short"
                     use="required" />
      <xsd:attribute name="price"
                     type="xsd:decimal"
                     use="required" />
    </xsd:complexType>
  </xsd:element>
</xsd:schema>
```

In this case, the address information may not have any intrinsic value normalized out into a separate structure, since it will always be referenced in the context of a customer. For our design, since the relationship is known to be one-to-one, we can simply promote the address attributes into our `customer` table design:

```
CREATE TABLE Customer (
  customerID int IDENTITY PRIMARY KEY,
  name varchar(100) NOT NULL,
  address1 varchar(100) NOT NULL,
  address2 varchar(100) NULL,
  city varchar(50) NOT NULL,
  state char(2) NOT NULL,
  zip varchar(10) NOT NULL)
```

Of course, if we had some business reason to do so, we could keep the address information normalized out into its own table – but this leads to other problems, as we'll see in our next example.

Reuse of Element Types

The next things to watch out for when designing our relationships are element types that are reused in the XML structure. For example, let's say we had the following sample XML document that lists all the suppliers and all the customers for a given company:

```
<partners>
  <supplier name="Freds Grommets">
    <address address1="100 Main Street"
         city="Somewheretown"
         state="VA"
```

Mapping XML to SQL Server

```
              zip="26152" />
  </supplier>
  <customer name="Kevin Williams">
    <address address1="762 Evergreen Terrace"
             city="Springfield"
             state="VA"
             zip="21826" />
  </customer>
</partners>
```

In this document, the `<address>` element is being reused – it appears both as a child of the `<supplier>` element and a child of the `<customer>` element. The XML schema for this structure is the following:

```
<xsd:schema xmlns:xsd="http://www.w3.org/2001/XMLSchema">
  <xsd:element name="partners">
    <xsd:complexType>
      <xsd:sequence>
        <xsd:element ref="supplier" maxOccurs="unbounded"/>
        <xsd:element ref="customer" maxOccurs="unbounded" />
      </xsd:sequence>
    </xsd:complexType>
  </xsd:element>
  <xsd:element name="address">
    <xsd:complexType>
      <xsd:attribute name="address1"
                     type="xsd:string"
                     use="required" />
      <xsd:attribute name="address2"
                     type="xsd:string" />
      <xsd:attribute name="city"
                     type="xsd:string"
                     use="required" />
      <xsd:attribute name="state"
                     type="xsd:string"
                     use="required" />
      <xsd:attribute name="zip"
                     type="xsd:string"
                     use="required" />
    </xsd:complexType>
  </xsd:element>
  <xsd:element name="supplier">
    <xsd:complexType>
      <xsd:sequence>
        <xsd:element ref="address" />
      </xsd:sequence>
      <xsd:attribute name="name"
                     type="xsd:string"
                     use="required" />
    </xsd:complexType>
  </xsd:element>
  <xsd:element name="customer">
    <xsd:complexType>
      <xsd:sequence>
```

Chapter 9

```
            <xsd:element ref="address" />
        </xsd:sequence>
        <xsd:attribute name="name"
                       type="xsd:string"
                       use="required" />
    </xsd:complexType>
 </xsd:element>
</xsd:schema>
```

In this case, we have several choices we can make as to the correct modeling approach. One option would be to model the address information as its own element:

```
CREATE TABLE Supplier (
   supplierID int IDENTITY PRIMARY KEY,
   name varchar(100) NOT NULL)

CREATE TABLE Customer (
   customerID int IDENTITY PRIMARY KEY,
   name varchar(100) NOT NULL)

CREATE TABLE Address (
   addressID int IDENTITY PRIMARY KEY,
   address1 varchar(100) NOT NULL,
   address2 varchar(100) NULL,
   city varchar(50) NOT NULL,
   state char(2) NOT NULL,
   zip varchar(10) NOT NULL)
```

However, what foreign key do we add to the `Address` table? We could add both `supplierID` and `customerID` as foreign keys, allowing `NULL`s in each; or we could add a generic ID with a type indicator that specifies whether the ID is a `customerID` or `supplierID`, with a `CHECK` constraint that forces the ID to match an existing `ID` in the specified table. However, neither of these solutions is a good one from a reusability or a maintainability perspective. In this case, since the relationships are one-to-one, we can simply promote the address data elements into the appropriate structures:

```
CREATE TABLE Supplier (
   supplierID int IDENTITY PRIMARY KEY,
   name varchar(100) NOT NULL,
   address1 varchar(100) NOT NULL,
   address2 varchar(100) NULL,
   city varchar(50) NOT NULL,
   state char(2) NOT NULL,
   zip varchar(10) NOT NULL)

CREATE TABLE Customer (
   customerID int IDENTITY PRIMARY KEY,
   name varchar(100) NOT NULL,
   address1 varchar(100) NOT NULL,
   address2 varchar(100) NULL,
   city varchar(50) NOT NULL,
   state char(2) NOT NULL,
   zip varchar(10) NOT NULL)
```

Mapping XML to SQL Server

This avoids the problem of the foreign key entirely. If we want to keep the address information normalized into a separate table, we could avoid the foreign key problem by actually creating tables that reflect the context of the address: to wit, a `CustomerAddress` table and a `SupplierAddress` table:

```
CREATE TABLE Supplier (
  supplierID int IDENTITY PRIMARY KEY,
  name varchar(100) NOT NULL)

CREATE TABLE Customer (
  customerID int IDENTITY PRIMARY KEY,
  name varchar(100) NOT NULL)

CREATE TABLE CustomerAddress (
  addressID int IDENTITY PRIMARY KEY,
  customerID int FOREIGN KEY REFERENCES Customer(customerID),
  address1 varchar(100) NOT NULL,
  address2 varchar(100) NULL,
  city varchar(50) NOT NULL,
  state char(2) NOT NULL,
  zip varchar(10) NOT NULL)

CREATE TABLE SupplierAddress (
  addressID int IDENTITY PRIMARY KEY,
  supplierID int FOREIGN KEY REFERENCES Supplier(supplierID),
  address1 varchar(100) NOT NULL,
  address2 varchar(100) NULL,
  city varchar(50) NOT NULL,
  state char(2) NOT NULL,
  zip varchar(10) NOT NULL)
```

The one drawback to this design approach is that we now have two separate tables that represent the same information; however, if our business case doesn't require us to use the two together, this may be an acceptable solution.

Now that we have an idea of how to model parent-child relationships in XML, let's take a look at a trickier relationship and how it can be modeled: the `ID-IDREF` relationship.

Handling ID-IDREF Relationships

In XML, the `IDREF` type is used to relate one element to another when a parent-child relationship is not possible (such as in a more complex relationship, where a many-to-many relationship is expressed through a relating XML element). Fortunately, SQL Server allows this type of relationship to be easily modeled using foreign keys. Let's see an example. Say we had the following structure:

```xml
<invoices>
  <invoice customerName="Kevin Williams">
    <lineItem partIDREF="p187" quantity="17" price="0.30" />
    <lineItem partIDREF="p191" quantity="22" price="0.15" />
  </invoice>
  <part partID="p187" name="Grommets" />
  <part partID="p191" name="Widgets" />
</invoices>
```

Chapter 9

In this case, we are expressing a many-to-many relationship – each invoice may contain many parts, and each part may appear on many invoices – through a relating element (the `<lineItem>` element). We are doing so through a combination of a parent-child relationship (`<invoice>` to `<lineItem>`) and an ID-IDREF relationship (`<lineItem>` to `<part>`). The XML schema for this document looks like this:

```xml
<xsd:schema xmlns:xsd="http://www.w3.org/2001/XMLSchema">
  <xsd:element name="invoices">
    <xsd:complexType>
      <xsd:sequence>
        <xsd:element ref="invoice" maxOccurs="unbounded" />
        <xsd:element ref="part" maxOccurs="unbounded" />
      </xsd:sequence>
    </xsd:complexType>
  </xsd:element>
  <xsd:element name="invoice">
    <xsd:complexType>
      <xsd:sequence>
        <xsd:element ref="lineItem" maxOccurs="unbounded" />
      </xsd:sequence>
      <xsd:attribute name="customerName"
                     type="xsd:string"
                     use="required" />
    </xsd:complexType>
  </xsd:element>
  <xsd:element name="lineItem">
    <xsd:complexType>
      <xsd:attribute name="partIDREF"
                     type="xsd:IDREF"
                     use="required" />
      <xsd:attribute name="quantity"
                     type="xsd:short"
                     use="required" />
      <xsd:attribute name="price"
                     type="xsd:decimal"
                     use="required" />
    </xsd:complexType>
  </xsd:element>
  <xsd:element name="part">
    <xsd:complexType>
      <xsd:attribute name="partID"
                     type="xsd:ID"
                     use="required" />
      <xsd:attribute name="name"
                     type="xsd:string"
                     use="required" />
    </xsd:complexType>
  </xsd:element>
</xsd:schema>
```

Mapping XML to SQL Server

When modeling documents like this in SQL Server, it's important to remember that the `IDREF` type in XML Schema does not specify a particular type of element it references, it can reference any element with an attribute of type `ID`. However, typically we can determine from context what the `IDREF` may reference – in this case, `<part>` elements. We begin by modeling the parent-child relationships, discarding the root element because it simply wraps the data:

```
CREATE TABLE Invoice (
  invoiceID int IDENTITY PRIMARY KEY,
  customerName varchar(100) NOT NULL)

CREATE TABLE Part (
  partID int IDENTITY PRIMARY KEY,
  name varchar(50) NOT NULL)

CREATE TABLE LineItem (
  lineItemID int IDENTITY PRIMARY KEY,
  quantity smallint NOT NULL,
  price decimal(7,2) NOT NULL)
```

Next, we need to model the `ID-IDREF` relationship. To do this, we need to add a foreign key in the table that corresponds to the element that contains the `IDREF` attribute. This foreign key should reference the primary key of the table that corresponds to the element being pointed to:

```
ALTER TABLE LineItem
  ADD partID int FOREIGN KEY REFERENCES Part(partID)
```

Note that this can introduce the same sorts of complexities that other relationships introduce – such as our address problem from before, where there are two different tables (the `Supplier` table and the `Customer` table) that would need to be the target of the foreign key reference in the `Address` table. Similarly, there can be more than one element that is pointed to by a particular element type. In this case, using the techniques we described earlier (creating separate child tables or integrating the data points into the pointed-to element where possible) can produce good results.

Handling ID-IDREFS Relationships

The `ID-IDREFS` relationship is a bit trickier to model correctly in SQL Server. Since an `IDREFS` value contains multiple ID values separated by whitespace, what an `IDREFS` attribute really represents is a many-to-many join without the relating element. Let's take a look at an example. Say we had the following sample document:

```
<library>
  <author authorID="a1" name="Kevin Williams" />
  <author authorID="a2" name="David Hunter" />
  <author authorID="a3" name="Jonathon Pinnock" />
  <book title="Professional XML 2nd Edition"
        authorIDREFS="a1 a3" />
  <book title="Beginning XML 2nd Edition"
        authorIDREFS="a2 a3" />
</library>
```

Here, we see the implicit many-to-many relationship – each book may be written by many authors, and each author may write many books. The XML schema for this sample document looks like this:

```xml
<xsd:schema xmlns:xsd="http://www.w3.org/2001/XMLSchema">
  <xsd:element name="library">
    <xsd:complexType>
      <xsd:sequence>
        <xsd:element ref="author" maxOccurs="unbounded" />
        <xsd:element ref="book" maxOccurs="unbounded" />
      </xsd:sequence>
    </xsd:complexType>
  </xsd:element>
  <xsd:element name="author">
    <xsd:complexType>
      <xsd:attribute name="authorID"
                     type="xsd:ID"
                     use="required" />
      <xsd:attribute name="name"
                     type="xsd:string"
                     use="required" />
    </xsd:complexType>
  </xsd:element>
  <xsd:element name="book">
    <xsd:complexType>
      <xsd:attribute name="title"
                     type="xsd:string"
                     use="required" />
      <xsd:attribute name="authorIDREFS"
                     type="xsd:IDREFS"
                     use="required" />
    </xsd:complexType>
  </xsd:element>
</xsd:schema>
```

To model this correctly in SQL Server, we'll need to create a relating table to express the many-to-many relationship between `<book>` and `<author>`:

```sql
CREATE TABLE Author (
  authorID int IDENTITY PRIMARY KEY,
  name varchar(100) NOT NULL)

CREATE TABLE Book (
  bookID int IDENTITY PRIMARY KEY,
  title varchar(100) NOT NULL)

CREATE TABLE AuthorBook (
  authorID int FOREIGN KEY REFERENCES Author(authorID),
  bookID int FOREIGN KEY REFERENCES Book (bookID))
```

When we are importing the document, we tokenize the `IDREFS` value provided, that is, we split it up into a list of `IDREF` values. Then for each `IDREF` value, we add a row to the `AuthorBook` table that references both the `<book>` element we are parsing and the `<author>` element we created with the `authorID` provided. These imports can be performed using the technologies we'll see in the following chapters.

Mapping XML to SQL Server

Note that both `IDREF` and `IDREFS` are intended to show relationships between elements in a particular document – they have no meaning outside the context of that document. For example, it would be perfectly acceptable to receive this document:

```
<library>
   <author authorID="a1" name="Kevin Williams" />
   <book title="Professional XML 2nd Edition"
         authorIDREFS="a1" />
</library>
```

followed by this document:

```
<library>
   <author authorID="a1" name="David Hunter" />
   <book title="Beginning XML 2nd Edition"
         authorIDREFS="a1" />
</library>
```

We need to use caution in how we use the `ID` and `IDREF(S)` values – don't rely on them to be consistent over multiple documents, as XML only guarantees that `ID`, `IDREF`, and `IDREFS` values are distinct within a single document. Instead, use the values when we are parsing the document to ensure that the relationships we create from that document are internally consistent.

Now that we have created our document structure, we need to learn the specific methods for mapping the data points found in our XML document. We've seen some examples of this, but let's take a closer look.

Mapping Data Points

In our XML source document, data points (which we would like to map to columns) can appear in a couple of forms. The most common way data points will arrive is as text-only element values. Take, for example, the following XML:

```
<customer>
   <name>Kevin Williams</name>
   <shipMethod>UPS</shipMethod>
</customer>
```

In this example, the `<name>` element and the `<shipMethod>` element are data points. We would need to map these elements to columns in the appropriate table (here it would be the `Customer` table).

Data points can also appear in the XML document as attributes. Again, these are text-only values that need to be mapped to columns in the appropriate table in our SQL Server design. Consider this example:

```
<customer name="Kevin Williams" shipMethod="UPS" />
```

Here, the `name` and `shipMethod` attributes are data points that would be mapped to columns in the `Customer` table.

235

Chapter 9

There is one slightly more complex type of data point that can appear in our source XML documents: the **attributed data element**. Here's an example:

```
<invoice>
  <totalAmount currency="USD">172.00</totalAmount>
</invoice>
```

While relatively uncommon, this mechanism is sometimes used to indicate the units used for a particular value (such as the currency of the `<totalAmount>` data element in the example above). To model this in SQL Server, the best approach is to create a column whose name is some combination of the data element's name and the attribute's name. For example, we might model the preceding sample this way:

```
CREATE TABLE Invoice (
    invoiceID int IDENTITY PRIMARY KEY,
    totalAmount decimal(9,2) NOT NULL,
    totalAmountCurrency varchar(5) NOT NULL)
```

It's important to use this type of naming convention because attributes used this way will likely appear on more than one element. Take this example:

```
<invoice>
  <totalAmount currency="USD">172.00</totalAmount>
  <amountDue currency="USD">86.00</amountDue>
</invoice>
```

Here, we will have to give each of the columns a different name, based on the type of element it modifies:

```
CREATE TABLE Invoice (
    invoiceID int IDENTITY PRIMARY KEY,
    totalAmount decimal(9,2),
    totalAmountCurrency varchar(5),
    amountDue decimal(9,2),
    amountDueCurrency varchar(5))
```

Again, our business rules apply here. If we only care about the amount due, we don't bother mapping the total amount into our SQL Server database.

Converting Data Types

We saw a table earlier in the chapter that described how XML Schema datatypes map onto SQL Server data types. While this table shows only the SQL Server built-in data types, user-defined data types can also be modeled this way based on their base type. In our examples, we show particular constraints based on the assumed value space for values in the XML documents. Whenever possible, you should determine the actual value space for the element or attribute before adding this constraint; however, you may need to take your best guess if the value space for the XML document is not readily available.

Creating Constraints Based on XML Schema Constraints

If you want your SQL Server data to be constrained in exactly the same way as your XML data, you can do so by adding CHECK constraints to the columns you add to tables. For example, say we have the following XML schema:

```
<xsd:schema xmlns:xsd="http://www.w3.org/2001/XMLSchema">
   <xsd:element name="invoice">
     <xsd:complexType>
        <xsd:attribute name="priority"
                       type="Priority"
                       use="required" />
     </xsd:complexType>
   </xsd:element>
   <xsd:simpleType name="Priority">
     <xsd:restriction base="xsd:positiveInteger">
        <xsd:maxExclusive value="10" />
     </xsd:restriction>
   </xsd:simpleType>
</xsd:schema>
```

A sample document for this schema might look like this:

```
<invoice priority="7" />
```

In this case, the priority attribute must take a value between 1 and 10. We can model this in SQL Server this way:

```
CREATE TABLE Invoice (
  invoiceID int IDENTITY PRIMARY KEY,
  priority tinyint CHECK (priority>=1 AND priority<=10) NOT NULL)
```

However, this can introduce unnecessary processing time (slower inserts and updates) if you don't need to constrain the data. Since the value space for `tinyint` is a superset of the value space for our `priority` attribute, any data that is loaded from a valid XML document conforming to this schema will automatically be constrained according to our CHECK constraint. You should only use the CHECK constraint if you will be adding data to this table via other means (such as ADO inserts), but you still want it to conform to the specified constraints.

Chapter 9

Modeling Enumeration Constraints

There is a special kind of constraint that deserves a closer look: the **enumeration** constraint (also known as a set of lookup values in SQL Server). Here's an example XML schema that contains an enumeration constraint:

```
<xsd:schema xmlns:xsd="http://www.w3.org/2001/XMLSchema">
  <xsd:element name="invoice">
    <xsd:complexType>
      <xsd:attribute name="priority"
                     type="Priority"
                     use="required" />
    </xsd:complexType>
  </xsd:element>
  <xsd:simpleType name="Priority">
    <xsd:restriction base="xsd:string">
      <xsd:enumeration value="high" />
      <xsd:enumeration value="low" />
      <xsd:enumeration value="critical" />
    </xsd:restriction>
  </xsd:simpleType>
</xsd:schema>
```

A sample document for this schema would look something like this:

```
<invoice priority="high" />
```

Rather than carrying around the string in each Invoice row imported from a document, it makes sense to create a lookup table for this enumeration (and all others). This allows you to use a smaller representation in each row (in this case, a tinyint key), as well as providing a place for you to add descriptive information to each of the allowable enumerated types. For our example, we might create a SQL Server schema that looks like this:

```
CREATE TABLE PriorityLookup (
  priorityType int IDENTITY PRIMARY KEY,
  priorityValue varchar(10) NOT NULL,
  description varchar(200) NOT NULL)

CREATE TABLE Invoice (
  invoiceID int IDENTITY PRIMARY KEY,
  priorityType int FOREIGN KEY REFERENCES
  PriorityLookup(priorityType) NOT NULL)
```

As part of our SQL Server design step, then, we would create INSERT statements that populate the PriorityLookup table with the appropriate values:

```
INSERT PriorityLookup (priorityValue, description)
  VALUES ('high', 'High Priority')
GO
INSERT PriorityLookup (priorityValue, description)
```

Mapping XML to SQL Server

```
    VALUES ('low', 'Low Priority')
GO
INSERT PriorityLookup (priorityValue, description)
    VALUES ('critical', 'Critical Priority - Ship ASAP')
GO
```

Then, as we insert records into our `Invoice` table, we take the enumerated value provided in the `priority` attribute and look up the appropriate key in the `PriorityLookup` table; that value is then inserted into the `Invoice` table.

Creating Record Identifiers

In all of our examples, we've glossed over the way the primary keys are created. We've just assumed that the primary keys are identity columns added to each table we create. Let's take a look at why we need to do things this way.

XML documents are, for the most part, key-less – the relationship between the various elements is expressed through the parent-child relationships between them. ID values are really no better – as we've seen, these do not have to be consistent from document to document, so they cannot be used as identifiers in a system that must hold the data from multiple documents. The only safe approach we can take if no guaranteed unique key values are provided is to create our own primary key values. Since these key values are abstract (they are only used to represent the relationship between elements), it makes sense to create them as `IDENTITY` values.

Example

Let's take a look at a more complex example that pulls together the design techniques we've learned in this chapter. Let's say we have the following XML document that lists all the invoices placed in a particular time period, along with a list of warehouses that carry the parts ordered:

```
<invoices>
  <invoice customerName="Kevin Williams"
           orderDate="2002-08-22"
           shipMethod="UPS">
    <lineitem partIDREF="p1"
              quantity="17"
              price="0.30" />
    <lineitem partIDREF="p2"
              quantity="22"
              price="0.15" />
  </invoice>
  <part partID="p1"
        name="Grommets"
        warehouseIDREFS="w1">
  <part partID="p2"
        name="Widgets"
        warehouseIDREFS="w1 w2">
  <warehouse warehouseID="w1" name="Springfield" />
  <warehouse warehouseID="w2" name="Roanoke" />
</invoices>
```

Chapter 9

The XML schema for this document looks like this:

```xml
<xsd:schema xmlns:xsd="http://www.w3.org/2001/XMLSchema">
  <xsd:element name="invoices">
    <xsd:complexType>
      <xsd:sequence>
        <xsd:element ref="invoice" maxOccurs="unbounded"/>
        <xsd:element ref="part" maxOccurs="unbounded"/>
        <xsd:element ref="warehouse" maxOccurs="unbounded"/>
      </xsd:sequence>
      <xsd:attribute name="customerName"
                     type="xsd:string"
                     use="required"/>
      <xsd:attribute name="orderDate"
                     type="xsd:dateTime"
                     use="required"/>
      <xsd:attribute name="shipMethod"
                     type="ShippingMethod"
                     use="required"/>
    </xsd:complexType>
  </xsd:element>
  <xsd:element name="invoice">
    <xsd:complexType>
      <xsd:sequence>
        <xsd:element ref="lineItem" maxOccurs="unbounded"/>
      </xsd:sequence>
      <xsd:attribute name="partIDREF"
                     type="xsd:IDREF"
                     use="required"/>
      <xsd:attribute name="quantity"
                     type="xsd:short"
                     use="required"/>
      <xsd:attribute name="price"
                     type="xsd:decimal"
                     use="required"/>
    </xsd:complexType>
  </xsd:element>
  <xsd:element name="part">
    <xsd:complexType>
      <xsd:attribute name="partID"
                     type="xsd:ID"
                     use="required"/>
      <xsd:attribute name="name"
                     type="xsd:string"
                     use="required"/>
      <xsd:attribute name="warehouseIDREFS"
                     type="xsd:IDREFS"
                     use="required"/>
    </xsd:complexType>
  </xsd:element>
  <xsd:element name="warehouse">
    <xsd:complexType>
      <xsd:attribute name="warehouseID"
                     type="xsd:ID"
                     use="required"/>
      <xsd:attribute name="name"
                     type="xsd:string"
                     use="required"/>
    </xsd:complexType>
  </xsd:element>
  <xsd:simpleType name="ShippingMethod">
```

Mapping XML to SQL Server

```
    <xsd:restriction base="xsd:string">
      <xsd:enumeration value="UPS"/>
      <xsd:enumeration value="USPS"/>
      <xsd:enumeration value="FedEx"/>
    </xsd:restriction>
  </xsd:simpleType>
</xsd:schema>
```

In order to build a SQL Server schema for this XML document, we first need to understand what the purpose of the database will be.

Design Goals

In the enterprise model we have defined, the invoicing system creates a document conforming to this schema once a day. The document contains all the orders placed on that day. The data needs to be extracted from this document and used to populate a fulfillment system, which in turn will dispatch orders to the appropriate warehouses for fulfillment.

Identifying the Relevant Information

To fulfill the placed orders, we will need the majority of the information provided in the XML document. However, there are a couple of pieces of information that we can discard. First, we don't need the order date – it's irrelevant to the fulfillment system (the orders are filled on a first come, first served basis). Also, we don't care what price the customer had to pay for their grommets – all we care about from a fulfillment perspective is how many grommets they ordered.

Designing the Tables

First, we need to decide what tables belong in our structure. Since there are no one-to-one relationships in our source document, we conclude that we need four data tables: an `Invoice` table, a `LineItem` table, a `Part` table, and a `Warehouse` table.

```
CREATE TABLE Invoice (
  invoiceID int IDENTITY PRIMARY KEY)

CREATE TABLE LineItem (
  lineItemID int IDENTITY PRIMARY KEY)

CREATE TABLE Part (
  partID int IDENTITY PRIMARY KEY)

CREATE TABLE Warehouse (
  warehouseID int IDENTITY PRIMARY KEY)
```

> *Please note: we will be redefining these tables many times as we follow through the process of modeling our database schema appropriately. You may wish to wait until we have the final CREATE statement at the end of the example before you create the tables in a database.*

In addition, we see that we have a set of lookup values that we need to model (the `shipMethod`). We represent that using a `ShippingMethodLookup` table:

241

Chapter 9

```
    CREATE TABLE ShippingMethodLookup (
      shippingMethodType tinyint IDENTITY PRIMARY KEY,
      shippingMethodName varchar(5) NOT NULL,
      description varchar(100) NOT NULL)
    GO

    INSERT ShippingMethodLookup (shippingMethodName, description)
      VALUES ('UPS', 'United Parcel Service')
    GO
    INSERT ShippingMethodLookup (shippingMethodName, description)
      VALUES ('USPS', 'United States Postal Service')
    GO
    INSERT ShippingMethodLookup (shippingMethodName, description)
      VALUES ('FedEx', 'Federal Express')
    GO
```

Next, we need to establish the relationships between the tables. We see that the `<lineItem>` element is a child of the `<invoice>` element, so we modify the LineItem table accordingly:

```
    CREATE TABLE LineItem (
      lineItemID int IDENTITY PRIMARY KEY,
      invoiceID int FOREIGN KEY REFERENCES Invoice (invoiceID))
```

The `<part>` element is pointed to by the `<lineItem>` element using an ID-IDREF relationship, so we add that key to the `LineItem` table as well:

```
    CREATE TABLE LineItem (
      lineItemID int IDENTITY PRIMARY KEY,
      invoiceID int FOREIGN KEY REFERENCES Invoice (invoiceID),
      partID int FOREIGN KEY REFERENCES Part (partID))
```

The `<warehouse>` element is pointed to by the `<part>` element using an ID-IDREFS relationship. This is an implicit many-to-many relationship, so we add a relating table that relates parts and warehouses:

```
    CREATE TABLE PartWarehouse (
      partID int FOREIGN KEY REFERENCES Part(partID),
      warehouseID int FOREIGN KEY REFERENCES Warehouse
    (warehouseID))
```

We've established all the relationships present in our source XML document. The next step is to add the columns based on the data from the source document that we want to hang on to.

Mapping the Column Values

As we said before, we want to capture all the values except the `orderDate` and `price` information provided in the original document. Additionally, we can discard the `ID` and `IDREF(S)` attributes (as they are only used to relate two elements). Mapping all the other columns to our SQL Server data model gives us this:

Mapping XML to SQL Server

```
CREATE TABLE ShippingMethodLookup (
  shippingMethodType tinyint IDENTITY PRIMARY KEY,
  shippingMethodName varchar(5),
  description varchar(100))
GO

INSERT ShippingMethodLookup (shippingMethodName, description)
  VALUES ('UPS', 'United Parcel Service')
GO
INSERT ShippingMethodLookup (shippingMethodName, description)
  VALUES ('USPS', 'United States Postal Service')
GO
INSERT ShippingMethodLookup (shippingMethodName, description)
  VALUES ('FedEx', 'Federal Express')
GO

CREATE TABLE Invoice (
  invoiceID int IDENTITY PRIMARY KEY,
  customerName varchar(100) NOT NULL,
  shippingMethodType tinyint FOREIGN KEY
    REFERENCES ShippingMethodLookup (shippingMethodType))

CREATE TABLE Part (
  partID int IDENTITY PRIMARY KEY,
  name varchar(100) NOT NULL)

CREATE TABLE LineItem (
  lineItemID int IDENTITY PRIMARY KEY,
  invoiceID int FOREIGN KEY REFERENCES Invoice (invoiceID),
  partID int FOREIGN KEY REFERENCES Part (partID),
  quantity smallint NOT NULL)

CREATE TABLE Warehouse (
  warehouseID int IDENTITY PRIMARY KEY,
  name varchar(100) NOT NULL)

CREATE TABLE PartWarehouse (
  partID int FOREIGN KEY REFERENCES Part(partID),
  warehouseID int FOREIGN KEY REFERENCES Warehouse
(warehouseID))
```

And that's it – we've successfully created a SQL Server structure that captures the information we need from the source XML document. We could now use an Updategram, a DiffGram, a stored procedure using `OPENXML`, or parser code such as DOM or SAX to insert the data. Of course, we still need to worry about inserts vs. updates – based on the alternate keys such as the part names – but the individual implementation is up to the reader.

Chapter 9

Summary

In this chapter, we've seen some techniques for creating SQL Server data structures to hold XML data. We've seen how business case factors should be accounted for when creating these structures, and when it's safe to discard information. We've also learned how to model parent-child and `ID-IDREF` relationships in SQL Server, as well as how XML Schema datatypes map onto SQL Server. The important thing to bear in mind when designing SQL Server tables to hold your XML data is that nothing is set in stone: use the design that best suits your business case and processing requirements.

In the following chapters, we'll learn how to take a newly created SQL Server model and populate it using the technologies built into SQL Server 2000 and SQLXML 3.0.

Mapping XML to SQL Server

Simon Sabin

- Parsing an XML document with OPENXML
- OPENXML Function Syntax
- Combining with Other Tables
- Using XML Data to Modify Tables
- Using XML Meta Data
- Performance
- Limitations
- Summary

10

OPENXML

As we have seen in the preceding chapters, SQL Server 2000 introduced a number of new features to enable us to use XML. One of the most important of these new features is OPENXML. OPENXML can be considered as the opposite of the FOR XML clause. While FOR XML can be used to return an XML document from SQL Server OPENXML is used to obtain a rowset of data from an XML document. In this chapter we will consider:

- ❑ Preparing an XML document for use with OPENXML
- ❑ Returning a rowset using OPENXML function syntax
- ❑ Using complex expressions to filter the rowset returned
- ❑ Combining XML data with existing relational tables
- ❑ Modifying database tables using XML data
- ❑ Using XML meta data to determine document structure
- ❑ Performance issues and limitations in using OPENXML

Introduction

OPENXML allows us to use the data in an XML document as if it were any other table, view or rowset function in the database. This gives us a very powerful tool to insert, update and delete multiple rows of data, in multiple tables, with one stored procedure call. The power of OPENXML comes from its flexibility in where and how it can be used. Unlike the other new XML features in SQL 2000, OPENXML and FOR XML are both T-SQL extensions, and so don't require any external application, like SQLXML or IIS, in order to work.

In considering whether to use OPENXML rather than other XML functionality, the normal questions that arise with respect to data access need to be answered:

- ❑ Are you happy putting processing in the database?

Chapter 10

- Are there the skills in your company?
- Are you saving one record, multiple records or hierarchies?
- Do you prefer simpler database code or data access code?

If you have an application that holds data in the middle tier in XML, then it would be very simple to pass this document to the database in one call to save the data. You only require one stored procedure call per type of document you wish to save, which reduces your data access code but makes your stored procedures more complex. Looking at the new data access mechanisms in ADO.NET the situation becomes more complex, with enhanced XML support and the ability to reduce data access code. You can read more about this in the article titled *Performance Comparison: Data Access Techniques* on http://msdn.microsoft.com/library/default.asp?url=/library/en-us/dnbda/html/bdadotnetarch031.asp.

Examples of where OPENXML can be used include:

- Importing data that does not require business validation
- Returning data from a table based on a list of values
- Loading of reference data
- Saving of hierarchical data, like orders and order details

Parsing an XML document with OPENXML

The following diagram shows the process of parsing XML with OPENXML in SQL Server.

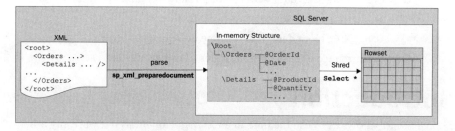

First, an in-memory structure of the XML document needs to be created via the sp_xml_preparedocument system stored procedure. Note that the amount of memory that can be used up by XML documents parsed into memory is limited to one eighth of the total available memory, the implications of which we will discuss later. The parsed document is a tree representation of the nodes (elements, attributes, text, comments, and so on) in the XML document. The OPENXML function uses this parsed XML document to provide a rowset in a process known as **shredding**. A document can be shredded multiple times to provide different rowset representations. The rowset returned from OPENXML can be used in many ways, commonly in inserting data into a table.

OPENXML

If you have programmed with the MSXML `DomDocument`, then the preparation of the document using `sp_xml_preparedocument` is similar to the `LoadXML` method of the `DOMDocument`. The syntax for `sp_xml_preparedocument` is:

```
sp_xml_preparedocument @idoc OUTPUT [@xmltext]
[@xpath_namespaces]
```

This stored procedure takes the following arguments:

Argument	Description	Type
@idoc	The handle to the prepared XML document.	`integer`
[@xmltext]	The original XML document name. The MSXML parser parses this XML document.	`char`, `nchar`, `varchar`, `nvarchar`, `text`, or `ntext`
[@xpath_namespaces]	Specifies any namespaces that are to be used in any XPath expressions.	`char`, `nchar`, `varchar`, `nvarchar`, `text`, or `ntext`

`sp_xml_preparedocument` returns 0 if the document was parsed successfully and >0 if an error occurred.

When we have finished shredding a document, the parsed structure has to be removed from memory using the system stored procedure `sp_xml_removedocument`. The only other time a document is removed is when a connection is closed, or the MTS/COM+ resets a connection. The syntax in this case is very simple:

```
sp_xml_removedocument @idoc
```

Argument	Description	Type
@idoc	The handle to the prepared XML document	`integer`

`sp_xml_removedocument` returns 0 if the document was parsed successfully and >0 if an error occurred.

> Note that whenever a document is prepared and finished with, it must be removed using the `sp_xml_removedocument`. If this isn't done then the memory assigned for storing prepared documents will be used up. This is especially true in connection pooled environments when connections are not dropped, except when used with MTS or COM+.

249

Chapter 10

Parsing Example

The following is a basic example of preparing a document and then removing it, and can be found in the code download as `OPENXML-sp_xml_preparedocument-BasicExample.sql`. We are not yet using any data or objects from a particular database so this example can be run on any database.

```
Declare @idoc    int
Declare @sXML    varchar(1000)
Declare @Result  int

SET @sXML =
'<Root>
  <Customers CustomerID="ALFKI" CompanyName="Alfreds
Futterkiste" ContactName="Maria Anders" >
    <Orders OrderID="10643" EmployeeID="6"
            OrderDate="1997-08-25" />
    <Orders OrderID="10692" EmployeeID="4"
            OrderDate="1997-10-03" />
    <Orders OrderID="10702" EmployeeID="4"
            OrderDate="1997-10-13" />
    <Orders OrderID="10835" EmployeeID="1"
            OrderDate="1998-01-15" />
    <Orders OrderID="10952" EmployeeID="1"
            OrderDate="1998-03-16" />
  </Customers>
</Root>'

EXEC @result = sp_xml_preparedocument @idoc OUTPUT, @sXML

IF @result = 0
  BEGIN
    SELECT @idoc "DocumentId"
    EXEC sp_xml_removedocument @idoc
  END
ELSE
  SELECT 'Document failed to parse'
```

The first section of the example declares the variables we need, and creates the XML document we are going to prepare. While all the examples in this chapter will be pure T-SQL, in practice most people will use stored procedures, passing the XML document as a parameter. This simplifies the steps required to use the XML document for the application developers, and enables you to secure the use of `OPENXML` to particular stored procedures.

```
Declare @idoc    int
Declare @sXML    varchar(1000)
Declare @Result  int

SET @sXML =
'<Root>
  <Customers CustomerID="ALFKI"
             CompanyName="Alfreds Futterkiste"
             ContactName="Maria Anders" >
```

```
        <Orders OrderID="10643" EmployeeID="6"
                OrderDate="1997-08-25" />
        <Orders OrderID="10692" EmployeeID="4"
                OrderDate="1997-10-03" />
        <Orders OrderID="10702" EmployeeID="4"
                OrderDate="1997-10-13" />
        <Orders OrderID="10835" EmployeeID="1"
                OrderDate="1998-01-15" />
        <Orders OrderID="10952" EmployeeID="1"
                OrderDate="1998-03-16" />
    </Customers>
</Root>'
```

If you are building XML documents in T-SQL, then because local variables can't be of text data type you are restricted to using only 8000 characters (4000 for Unicode). If you want to use more characters than this, there is a trick you can use involving the EXECUTE statement. The code for this is included in the code download as OPENXML-sp_xml_preparedocument-TipForLargeXML.sql.

The `sp_xml_preparedocument` procedure is then executed, passing in the XML document. This is parsed, the in-memory structure created, and the handle to the document returned through the `@idoc` parameter:

```
EXEC @result = sp_xml_preparedocument @idoc OUTPUT, @sXML
```

This document handle can be used within the context of the connection it was created in, until the document is explicitly removed using `sp_xml_removedocument`. When a connection to the server is closed, all documents prepared in it are removed from memory. In a COM+ environment when a pooled ADO connection is reopened, a system stored procedure `sp_reset_connection` is executed on the connection which also clears any documents from memory. This does not occur with normal pooled connections.

> **A document prepared in one connection can't be used in another connection.**

In this example, after we have tried to prepare the document, we test to see if the document prepared successfully and then remove it (as we aren't doing anything further with it in this case):

```
IF @result = 0
  BEGIN
    SELECT @idoc "DocumentId"
    EXEC sp_xml_removedocument @idoc
  END
ELSE
  SELECT 'Document failed to parse'
```

The intention of this is to catch the errors that the MSXML parser raises when it checks that the document is a well-formed, valid XML file. If you remove all but the opening `<Root>` tag from the preceding example (OPENXML-sp_xml_preparedocument-ErrorHandling.sql):

Chapter 10

```
Declare @idoc     int
Declare @sXML     varchar(1000)
Declare @Result   int

SET @sXML =
'<Root>'

EXEC @result = sp_xml_preparedocument @idoc OUTPUT, @sXML

IF @result = 0
  BEGIN
    SELECT @idoc "DocumentId"
    exec sp_xml_removedocument @idoc
  END
ELSE
  SELECT 'Document failed to parse'
```

The document will fail to parse, but the SELECT statement informing you of this won't be executed. An error like this will occur instead:

Server: Msg 6603, Level 16, State 1, Procedure sp_xml_preparedocument, Line 16
XML parsing error: Element was not closed.

This shows us that this type of error must be handled by the calling code (such as C# or VB.NET for example) rather than T-SQL contained within the stored procedure. In other words, if you write a stored procedure to perform the processing, any clean up code that you write at the end of it won't be called. This is a problem if you have created temporary tables, which would have been dropped at the end of the T-SQL statement, as nothing following the prepare statement will be executed if the document preparation fails. Note that if the removing of a document fails, the error can be caught and handled in T-SQL. This should only occur if you try and remove a document that doesn't exist.

Namespaces

If you wish to use namespaces in your document, then you have to declare them by using the xpath_namespace parameter within the sp_xml_preparedocument procedure. As with all XML documents, you have to specify the namespace in the XML document itself; if you don't then the document preparation will fail.

To assist in processing your XML document, Microsoft has created metaproperties, the use of which we'll discuss in detail later in this Chapter. These metaproperties all belong to the urn:schemas-microsoft-com:xml-metaprop namespace and by default have a prefix of mp. This metaproperties namespace doesn't need to be declared in order to be used, and is always valid irrespective of what namespaces are defined in the XML document or the xpath_namespace parameter. Note that you must declare the metaproperties namespace if you want to use the mp prefix for a different namespace.

OPENXML Function Syntax

Once the document is prepared, you can use the document handle along with the `OPENXML` command to return a rowset. The syntax for the use of `OPENXML` is as follows:

```
OPENXML (@idoc ,rowpattern [, flags])
[WITH (SchemaDeclaration | TableName)]
```

Argument	Description	Type
@idoc	Handle to the prepared XML document.	`integer`
rowpattern	Dictates what rows are returned in the rowset. This supplies a path to a node (element or attribute) that serves as a starting point for all XPath queries. This allows you to refer to all parts of the XML document in the schema declaration.	`char`, `nchar`, `varchar`, `nvarchar`, `text`, or `ntext`
[Flags]	Determine how elements and attributes are interpreted.	`byte`

The `WITH` clause is used to control what columns are returned in the rowset. The values it can take are described in the following sections:

TableName

If a `tablename` is specified, then the child attributes or elements of the rowset will be based on the columns of a database table; that is, each column in the database table will be mapped to an XML element or attribute of the XML element specified in the `rowpattern`. Whether attributes or elements are mapped, depends upon the `flags` setting used in the `OPENXML` clause.

There are however some restrictions:

- ❑ The matching of columns to elements is case sensitive.
- ❑ If the table specified has non-nullable columns, the corresponding element or attribute in the document must exist or an error will occur and the entire code will halt.
- ❑ Identity columns are not mapped.

While the latter might appear to be a serious flaw, what it allows you to do is perform a statement like:

```
SELECT *
  FROM OPENXML (....)
  WITH MyTableWithIdentity
  INTO MyTableWithIdentity
```

Chapter 10

In other words, if you are performing an update using `OPENXML`, and require the primary key column as an identity, then you have to use a `SchemaDeclaration` to return an identity column. If you're dealing with hierarchical data, then to be able to use the `tablename` clause, you need to repeat the foreign key data from the parent element on the child element. This means that you can't use a document like this where the `CustomerID` is only held on the `<Customers>` element:

```
<Root>
  <Customers CustomerID="ALFKI"
             CompanyName="Alfreds Futterkiste">
    <Orders OrderID="10643" OrderDate="25 Aug 1997" />
    <Orders OrderID="10692" OrderDate="03 Oct 1997" />
  </Customers>
</Root>
```

Instead of this, you need to use a document where the `CustomerID` is repeated on the `<Orders>` elements, such as the following:

```
<Root>
  <Customers CustomerID="ALFKI"
             CompanyName="Alfreds Futterkiste">
    <Orders OrderID="10643" CustomerID="ALFKI"
            OrderDate="25 Aug 1997"/>
    <Orders OrderID="10692" CustomerID="ALFKI"
            OrderDate="03 Oct 1997" />
  </Customers>
</Root>
```

If we use the above two XML documents with the `SELECT` statement:

```
SELECT CustomerId, OrderDate
  FROM OPENXML (@idoc ,'/Root/Customers/Orders')
  WITH Orders
```

then we get the following results:

CustomerID	OrderDate
NULL	1997-08-25 00:00:00.000
NULL	1997-10-03 00:00:00.000

CustomerID	OrderDate
ALFKI	1997-08-25 00:00:00.000
ALFKI	1997-10-03 00:00:00.000

OPENXML

You can generate these results by running the OPENXML-WithTable.sql script from the code download.

As you can see, the `CustomerID` is `NULL` in the first result set because it is not on the `<Orders>` element. Note that, if you are repeating the `CustomerID` on the child elements, you will need to be careful that the data is correct. In the following example, the `OrderID` on the second `<OrderDetails>` element isn't the same as its parent `<Orders>` element, and this is likely to cause problems:

```
<Order OrderID="1" />
  <OrderDetails OrderID="1" ProductID="1" />
  <OrderDetails OrderID="2" ProductID="1" />
</Order>
```

SchemaDeclaration

Using a `SchemaDeclaration` opens up the full power of OPENXML. This allows you to configure the names of your columns, the data types, and where in the XML document the data comes from. The following are examples of situations where a `SchemaDeclaration` is required:

- Returning data from different levels of the document
- Changing the names of attributes or elements
- Casting to specific data types
- Returning metaproperties
- Overriding the flags setting

The syntax for a declaration is as follows:

```
ColName ColType [ColPattern | MetaProperty][, ColName ColType
[ColPattern | MetaProperty]...]
```

Argument	Description	Type
ColName	The column name in the rowset. Maximum 128 characters. Can use quoted identifiers for names including invalid characters. Can't be a variable.	n/a
ColType	The SQL data type of the column in the rowset. In cases where this differs from the underlying XML data type of the attribute (default string), automatic type coercion will occur. Can't be a variable.	n/a

Table continued on following page

Chapter 10

Argument	Description	Type
[ColPattern]	XPath string that describes what XML value should be used for the column. If this isn't specified, the default mapping (as specified by flags) takes place. Specifying a ColPattern overrides the flags setting for that column.	char(8000), nchar(4000), varchar(8000), nvarchar(4000)

The following points should be taken into account:

❑ If you declare a column in your rowset with a user-defined data type then it must exist for every element, since an implicit NOT NULL is being applied.

❑ Do not declare columns as timestamp or rowversion. Use bigint (int is not large enough to hold a full range of timestamps). Conversion from the XML string to a timestamp data type does not produce the correct results. This mirrors the automatic conversion to bigint when returning data using FOR XML AUTO or RAW (see OPENXML-TimestampIssue.sql).

XML Document Example

Throughout this chapter we will look at a number of examples. They will all use the following XML document BaseData.xml, which you can find in the code download for this chapter:

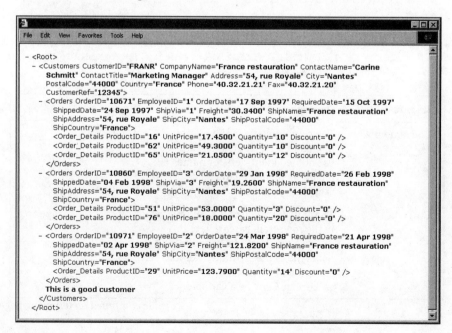

OPENXML

The examples will assume both that the document has been prepared using sp_xml_preparedocument and the document handle is @idoc, using the same code as in the sp_xml_preparedocument example above.

Using the document above and a simple OPENXML statement, we can return a basic rowset (OPENXML-BasicSelect.sql). Remember that this is a generic example, since we haven't specified a particular database:

```
SET @sPath = '/Root/Customers/Orders'

SELECT *
  FROM OPENXML (@idoc, @sPath)
  WITH (OrderID    int
       ,OrderDate  datetime
       ,EmployeeID int)
```

Firstly we define the XPath we are to use for the rowpattern. Here we are asking for all <Orders> elements that are children of <Customers> elements, which themselves are children of a <Root> element, which is at the root of the document.

You can read more about XPath queries in Chapter 8

We then specify that we want three columns, OrderID, OrderDate and EmployeeID. As we haven't specified any column patterns, these will be mapped using the flags parameter of the OPENXML clause. Since we haven't specified a value for flags the default attribute of centric mapping is used. In other words, in our present example the server looks for attributes of each of the <Orders> elements with the names OrderID, OrderDate, and EmployeeID. The example returns the following rowset:

OrderID	OrderDate	EmployeeID
10671	1997-09-17 00:00:00.000	1
10860	1998-01-29 00:00:00.000	3
10971	1998-03-24 00:00:00.000	2

In this example we have shown that the rowpattern doesn't have to be specified as a literal string: it can be a local variable, unlike the column names or column data types, which can't. If we had used a literal string the example would have looked like:

```
SELECT *
  FROM OPENXML (@idoc, '/Root/Customers/Orders')
  WITH (OrderID    int
       ,OrderDate  datetime
       ,EmployeeID int)
```

257

Chapter 10

rowpattern

The `rowpattern` parameter determines the rows of the returned rowset, and can be any XPath query that returns a set of XML nodes. Elements and attributes are both types of nodes, so `/Root/Customers/Orders` and `/Root/Customers/Orders/@OrderID` are valid rowpatterns. It is less common to use attributes in a `rowpattern` parameter, since this complicates the column patterns required to map columns.

> In the previous example we used a `rowpattern` of `/Root/Customers/Orders`. Note that we could have written this as `//Orders` or `//*[name()="Orders"]`.

It is worth noting that the number of rows in the returned rowset will be the number of nodes returned by the rowpattern, so it is crucial to use the correct `rowpattern`. If we're using a `SchemaDeclaration` we can always return data from different levels of the document by using a `ColPattern`.

Restricting Results

Since the `rowpattern` can be any XPath statement, it is possible to filter data to restrict the results returned. The following are some examples of filtering:

Rowpattern	Description
`//Customers[1]/Orders`	Orders of the first Customer in the document
`//Customers[count(Orders)>4]`	All Customers with four or more orders
`//Orders[@EmployeeID=3]`	All Orders with `EmployeeID` 3
`/Root/Customers[@ContactName]`	Customers who are children of the `<root>` element where the `ContactName` is specified (NOT NULL)
`/Root/Customers[Orders]`	Customers who are children of the `<root>` element and have at least one `<Orders>` element
`/Customers/Orders[../@Country = @ShipCountry]`	Orders where the `ShipCountry` is the same as the `Country` of the Customers

> Note that all comparisons are either string or integer based, which means that comparisons of dates, like `@datecol < '1/1/2001'` don't work as expected.

OPENXML

If you need to filter the data returned by OPENXML then if possible it should be done using the rowpattern rather than in the WHERE clause. To understand why, consider the following example. The first code listing here shows the filtering included in the WHERE clause:

```
SELECT *
  FROM OPENXML (@idoc, '/Root/Customers/Orders/Order_Details')
    WITH (CompanyName varchar(100) '../../@CompanyName'
         ,ProductID    int
         ,UnitPrice    money
         ,Quantity     int
         ,Discount     real)
  WHERE Quantity < 3
```

The second code listing shows the filtering being done with the rowpattern:

```
SELECT *
  FROM OPENXML (@idoc,
'/Root/Customers/Orders/Order_Details[@Quantity<3]')
    WITH (CompanyName varchar(100) '../../@CompanyName'
         ,ProductID    int
         ,UnitPrice    money
         ,Quantity     int
         ,Discount     real)
```

If you run the example file (OPENXML-FilteringData.sql) and command SET STATISTICS TIME ON in Query Analyzer, you will see that the first example takes approximately twice the time of the latter. This is because, when using the WHERE clause, the database engine has to build the full rowset and then filter the data, whereas when using the rowpattern parameter the rowset is built directly from the filtered data produced by the XPath query. The difference increases as the number of columns in the rowset increases and the number of rows being filtered out increases. We'll see more details on this in the *Performance* section later in this chapter.

While XPath allows you to use grouping functions, the parser used by SQL Server (MSXML2) only supports the count() function. This can still be useful. Imagine, for example, that you only want to return order information where the order has more than two order details. This can be accomplished using our example document as follows:

```
SELECT Orders.*
  FROM (SELECT CustomerId, OrderID
    FROM OPENXML (@idoc,
'/Root/Customers/Orders/Order_Details')
        WITH (OrderID     int '../@OrderID'
                    ,CustomerID  char(5)
'../../@CustomerID')
        GROUP BY CustomerId, OrderID
          HAVING COUNT(*) > 2) LargeOrders
  JOIN OPENXML (@idoc, '/Root/Customers/Orders')
        WITH (CompanyName varchar(100) '../@CompanyName'
```

```
             ,CustomerID   char(5)  '../@CustomerID'
             ,OrderID      int
             ,OrderDate    datetime) Orders ON Orders.OrderID =
                                        LargeOrders.OrderId
                                        AND Orders.CustomerID
                                        = LargeOrders.CustomerId
```

We use a derived table based on the <OrderDetails> elements, to find the relevant orders and then join back to a rowset of all the orders to get the rowset we want. If we use a `rowpattern` parameter, and include the `count()` function, then we can simplify this to:

```
SELECT *
  FROM OPENXML (@idoc,
'/Root/Customers/Orders[count(Order_Details)>2]')
  WITH (CompanyName varchar(100)  '../@CompanyName'
       ,OrderID      int
       ,OrderDate    datetime)
```

Looking at the performance of these two queries, by using the T-SQL command SET STATISTICS TIME ON in Query Analyzer, we can see that the former takes 3ms and the latter takes 1ms. As with the previous example the performance difference increases as the number of columns increases and the number of rows being filtered out increases.

> If you need to filter the data returned by OPENXML then if possible it should be filtered using XPath in the `rowpattern` you use rather than in the WHERE clause.

Set Operations in the rowpattern

The `rowpattern` property can also be extended to use set operations, such as UNION, which can be used to return the combination of two data sets. The benefit of performing set operations in the `rowpattern` is that it reduces the number of OPENXML clauses, simplifying your code. There is also a performance advantage when you are dealing with larger volumes of data. The downside is that the only set operation is |, which is the equivalent of UNION ALL.

In this example (OPENXML-Set operators.sql), we want to return all the company names from the <Shippers> and <Customers> elements. If we use the following document:

```
<root>
  <Customers CompanyName="Alfreds Futterkiste"/>
  <Customers CompanyName="Ana Trujillo Emparedados y helados"/>
```

```
    <Customers CompanyName="Antonio Moreno Taquería"/>
    <Customers CompanyName="Around the Horn"/>
    <Shippers CompanyName="Speedy Express"/>
    <Shippers CompanyName="United Package"/>
    <Shippers CompanyName="Federal Shipping"/>
</root>
```

then the code we require is as follows:

```
SELECT CompanyName
  FROM OPENXML (@i, '//Customers|//Shippers')
        WITH (CompanyName varchar(100))

SELECT CompanyName
  FROM OPENXML (@i, '//Customers')
        WITH (CompanyName varchar(100))
UNION ALL
SELECT CompanyName
  FROM OPENXML (@i, '//Shippers')
        WITH (CompanyName varchar(100))

EXEC sp_xml_removedocument @i
```

The first `SELECT` statement uses the set based functionality of XPath in the rowpattern, returning all the `<Customers>` and `<Shippers>`:

```
SELECT CompanyName
FROM OPENXML (@i, '//Customers|//Shippers')
    WITH (CompanyName varchar(100))
```

The second uses a standard `UNION ALL` clause, requiring that two `OPENXML` calls are made:

```
SELECT CompanyName
FROM OPENXML (@i, '//Customers')
    WITH (CompanyName varchar(100))
UNION ALL
SELECT CompanyName
FROM OPENXML (@i, '//Shippers')
    WITH (CompanyName varchar(100))
```

Chapter 10

If we look at the query execution plan in Query Analyzer, we see that the second method has twice the cost of the first:

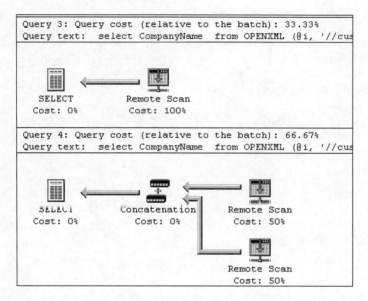

However, if you look at the actual time taken for the query they are almost identical. The point here is not to trust the query plan figures when using OPENXML, since a fixed cost of 3.36 and an estimated rowcount of 10,000 are always associated with an OPENXML call. This can understandably cause the Optimizer to avoid choosing the best query plan. We will see more about this in the *Performance* section below.

In this basic example there is little performance difference between the two options. However, when the example is extended to more columns and rows (OPENXML-Set operators2.sql) and joining to tables then the code is simpler and the performance better when using the XPath set functionality.

OPENXML Flags

Before we proceed any further we need to understand the use of the flags property in the OPENXML command. The flags property is a byte, dictating how SQL Server should map data in the XML document to the columns specified in the WITH clause, when a column pattern is not specified.

If you have used XML before you will know that the data in an XML document can be held two ways, either between the tags of an element or as attributes of the element. The former is **element-centric**:

```
<Customer >
   <Name>James Smith</ Name>
</Customer>
```

and the latter **attribute-centric**:

```
<Customer Name="James Smith" />
```

These are the possible values for the `flags` property:

Value	Definition
0	Default attribute-centric.
1	Attribute-centric.
2	Element-centric.
3	Combined attribute and element-centric. First an attribute is looked for, and then an element.
8	Dictates that consumed data (columns already mapped) are not output for columns with a column pattern of mp:xmltext.
9	Combination of 8 and 1.
10	Combination of 8 and 2.
11	Combination of 8 and 3.

The values 3, 9, 10 and 11 are combinations of 1,2, and 8. When you specify 3 (1 combined with 2) then the server will, when mapping the columns, first look for attributes, and then elements. This does of course have a performance impact if your XML data is mainly element-centric, because an attribute is looked for first. In the code download there is a script that shows the performance of each option (`OPENXML-FlagsPerformance.sql`). Although not a very thorough test, it shows that option 1 and 2 are similar in performance when used for the appropriate type of document. When they are combined, however, and option 3 is specified, the time taken for the `OPENXML` command increases by 50% when the XML data is element-centric. This is due to having to do two searches for each column in the rowset. Remember the flag setting does not apply if you explicitly define a column pattern.

> **Element-centric files are approximately twice the size of attribute-centric ones. Using the combined element and attribute-centric flags setting (3) is significantly slower than using the appropriate specific flag (2) for element-centric files.**

One of the major things I have learnt in using XML is that standards are essential. Given the performance and size implications above, I suggest that you implement a standards policy for the XML that you write. This should require that, unless for some specific reason, all documents should be attribute-centric.

Chapter 10

Consumed Data

The `mp:xmltext` metaproperty returns the XML of the element/attribute returned by the `rowpattern`. The default for this property is to return all of the XML; if, however, you specify a `flags` property of 8 then any elements/attributes that you return in your rowset are not returned by this metaproperty. To illustrate this run the `OPENXML-Flag8.sql` script.

If you had an element:

```
<Customers CustomerID="ALFKI" CompanyName="Alfreds Futterkiste"
           ContactName="Maria Anders"
           CustomerRef="123ABCD"      />
```

and your `SchemaDeclaration` was:

```
WITH (CustomerID    varchar(10)
    , CompanyName   varchar(100)
    , ContactName   varchar(100)
    , extra         varchar(200) '@mp:xmltext')
```

then without flag 8 you would see:

CustomerID	Company Name	Contact Name	Extra
ALFKI	Alfreds Futterkiste	Maria Anders	\<Customers CustomerID="ALFKI" CompanyName="Alfreds Futterkiste" ContactName="Maria Anders" CustomerRef="123ABCD" />

With flag 8 you would see:

CustomerID	Company Name	Contact Name	Extra
ALFKI	Alfreds Futterkiste	Maria Anders	\<Customers CustomerRef="123ABCD"/>

This allows you to save data that may be passed to you, which you either don't have columns for, or aren't interested in. If you then export data as XML you can include this data using the `xmltext` directive and `FOR XML EXPLICIT` (see Chapter 4 for more details on this).

OPENXML

Column Patterns

In the examples so far, we have used a `SchemaDeclaration` to define the rowset, and haven't used any column patterns. It is more than likely that most of your OPENXML statements will require columns that have column patterns specified. This will be the case if you need to:

- Use a different name for an XML attribute or element
- Map to a value that is not an attribute or element of the node selected by the rowset
- Use namespaces
- Use a metaproperty

The rules governing the column pattern are that it must return an XML node (element or attribute), use one of the supported XPath functions, or return a metaproperty. It is valid to perform filtering in your expressions, so long as the result still conforms to the previous rule. For a comprehensive reference on XPath see Appendix A.

This example shows some of the different things you can do in your column patterns:

```
SELECT *
FROM OPENXML (@idoc, '/Root/Customers')
WITH (CustomerID  char(5)      '@CustomerID'
     ,SumbitDate  datetime     '../@SubmitDate'
     ,OrderID     int          'Orders[1]/@OrderID'
     ,Information varchar(100) 'text()'
     ,PrefCol     char(12)
'Orders[1]/@*[name()=../../@ColumnOUTPUT]/text()'
     )
```

The output should be:

Customer ID	SubmitDate	Order ID	Information	PrefCol
ALFKI	2002-08-01 00:00:00.000	10643	This is a very good customer	1997-08-25

We have specified five different column patterns in this example. The first one '@CustomerID' maps to the CustomerID attribute of the <Customers> element. This is one of the simplest and most used column patterns. The second '../@SubmitDate' returns an attribute from the parent element, and is generally used to return the primary key of the parent element. The third column pattern 'Orders[1]/@OrderID' uses a more complex XPath expression in returning an attribute of a specific child of the main element (<Customers>). Orders[1] and indicates that we want the first of the <Orders> elements, while /@CustomerID indicates that we want the CustomerID attribute of this first Order; if there is no such <Orders> element, then this will be NULL.

265

Chapter 10

The fourth, `'text()'`, shows the use of one of the supported functions. This returns the text of the main element. The use of `'.'` as the column pattern would achieve the same goal. The final column pattern displays the real power of XPath and what can be done if you put your mind to it. What this returns is the column specified in the `ColumnOutput` attribute of the main `<Customers>` element. This shows that you could configure what data is output in the XML itself!

Specifying metaproperties

We have already briefly mentioned metaproperties, without going into exactly what they are. Metaproperties provide access to properties of the XML document nodes. These properties don't exist in the physical document text, but are provided with OPENXML and all belong to the metaproperties namespace (urn:schemas-microsoft-com:xml-metaprop), which by default has the prefix **mp**. It is assumed in the following list of metaproperties that the namespace prefix hasn't been changed from this default:

Metaproperty attribute	Description
@mp:id	This is an identifier, for the node, generated when the document is parsed and is guaranteed to be unique across the document nodes (element, attribute, and so on). This ID will always refer to the same node until the document is reparsed. Root nodes have an ID of **0** and the parent ID is NULL.
@mp:localname	This returns the local part of the name of the node. So an element of "ns:surname" will return "surname".
@mp:namespaceuri	Returns the namespace URI of the current element. If the node does not have a namespace this will be NULL.
@mp:prefix	Returns the namespace prefix of the current node. If no prefix is present (NULL) and a URI is given, it indicates that the specified namespace is the default namespace. If no URI is given, no namespace is attached.
@mp:prev	Returns XML ID of the previous sibling that has the same parent element. For the first sibling this is NULL.
@mp:xmltext	This returns the XML text of the node. As discussed earlier, the `flags` setting dictates the behavior of this property.

> Note that you can't reference these metaproperties in any XPath navigation, so `'../@mp:id'` and `'Orders[1]/@mp:xmltext'` are invalid.

If you want to return the metaproperty of a parent element then you need to use one of the following metaproperties:

Parent metaproperty attribute	Description
@mp:parentid	Corresponds to ../@mp:id
@mp:parentlocalname	Corresponds to ../@mp:localname
@mp:parentnamespaceuri	Corresponds to ../@mp:namespaceuri
@mp:parentprefix	Corresponds to ../@mp:prefix

Metaproperties are essential in the saving of hierarchical data, the @mp:id and @mp:parentid metaproperties allow us to extract the different levels of the hierarchy and relate the results back together.

Combining with Other Tables

So far we have only looked at the basics of using OPENXML. In real applications it is more likely that you will want to combine the OPENXML rowset with other rowsets (tables, views, subqueries, and so on). In this way we can accomplish more complex tasks such as inserting data based on the XML and other tables, update data, join to reference data tables to convert descriptions into foreign keys, and return data based on a list of values in our XML document. We can enhance our diagram of the OPENXML world as follows:

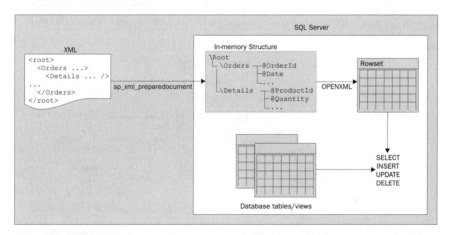

In the example below, we return a full rowset of orders information from the Northwind database, based on an XML list of OrderIDs passed in. Unlike other solutions to the problem of selecting data based on a list of values, this does not require dynamic SQL or a mechanism to tokenize the string. This also removes the security issue of using dynamic SQL, in that you only have to give the user access to the stored procedures, rather than the underlying tables.

Chapter 10

The example file `OPENXML-ReturnOrderBasedOnList.sql` uses this XML document:

```
'<Root >
    <Orders OrderID="10643" />
    <Orders OrderID="10835" />
    <Orders OrderID="10952" />
</Root>'
```

and this code:

```
SELECT Orders.*, Details.*
  FROM OPENXML (@hdoc, '/Root/Orders')
          WITH (OrderID int) OrderList
    JOIN Northwind.dbo.Orders Orders ON Orders.OrderId =

OrderList.OrderId
    JOIN Northwind.dbo.[Order Details] Details
      ON Details.OrderId = Orders.OrderId
```

The XML we use has three `OrderID`s specified, and the `SELECT` statement returns all the orders and order details data for those `OrderID`s specified. This all looks straightforward until you look at the query plan that is produced. With a standard `Northwind` database the query plan looks like this:

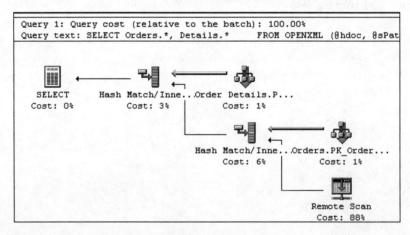

However, when you load more data into the database (say >1000 Orders, as can be done using the VB Performance test application available in the code download) the plan starts to look more worrying:

OPENXML

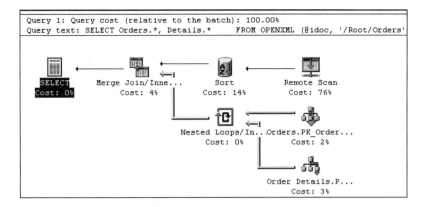

Looking at the statistics for this query, which returns five rows, we see a lot of IO:

Table 'Order Details'. Scan count 1270, logical reads 2621, physical reads 0, read-ahead reads 0.
Table 'Orders'. Scan count 1, logical reads 32, physical reads 0, read-ahead reads 0.

The problem here is that the data in the XML document is not being used to filter the query, even though there are only three rows in it. This is because the OPENXML is considered to be a remote scan, so SQL Server doesn't know what data will be returned from the OPENXML statement until it is actually performed. Consequently it uses the information on the statistics from the other two tables in the query and assigns a cost of 3.36 and an estimated rowcount of 10,000 to the OPENXML statement. There are a couple of ways to get round this:

❑ Force a JOIN mechanism using a hint
❑ Store results in a table variable or temporary table

The first solution is to force the JOIN mechanism, by replacing the JOIN with an INNER LOOP JOIN as follows:

```
SELECT Orders.*, Details.*
  FROM OPENXML (@hdoc, @sPath)
       WITH (OrderID int) OrderList
  INNER LOOP JOIN Orders Orders ON Orders.OrderId =
OrderList.OrderId
  INNER JOIN [Order Details] Details
    ON Details.OrderId = Orders.OrderId
```

Using this (OPENXML-JoinToTable.sql) reduces the IO to:

Table 'Order Details'. Scan count 3, logical reads 7, physical reads 0, read-ahead reads 0.
Table 'Orders'. Scan count 3, logical reads 6, physical reads 0, read-ahead reads 0.

269

This is the simplest solution, forcing the compiler to perform a nested loop between the OPENXML rowset and the Orders table. In the example this gives an excellent result performance-wise, due to the small number of OrderIDs in the document. However, if the document were to contain 20% of the total OrderIDs possible, then forcing a looping join is likely to perform worse. The use of join hints also causes a warning to be generated on the connection, so you will need to ensure that your application is not treating these as errors.

The next solution is to store the results of the OPENXML in a table, whether a variable, temporary, or standard table, and then use this populated table in the query as follows:

```
DECLARE @OrderList TABLE (OrderId int)
INSERT INTO @OrderList
SELECT OrderId
  FROM OPENXML (@idoc, '/Root/Orders')
       WITH (OrderID int) OrderList

SELECT Orders.*, Details.*
  FROM @OrderList OrderList
  INNER JOIN Northwind.dbo.Orders Orders
    ON Orders.OrderId = OrderList.OrderId
  JOIN Northwind.dbo.[Order Details] Details
    ON Details.OrderId = Orders.OrderId
```

This uses the following IO:

Table '#7962BF4A'. Scan count 0, logical reads 4, physical reads 0, read-ahead reads 0.
Table 'Worktable'. Scan count 1, logical reads 5, physical reads 0, read-ahead reads 0.
Table 'Order Details'. Scan count 3, logical reads 7, physical reads 0, read-ahead reads 0.
Table 'Orders'. Scan count 3, logical reads 6, physical reads 0, read-ahead reads 0.
Table '#7962BF4A'. Scan count 1, logical reads 1, physical reads 0, read-ahead reads 0.

This has the benefit that the Server can generate statistics for the data and hopefully produce the optimal plan without the need for hints. You do, however, have the IO overhead of writing the data to disk, the overhead of having a second statement, and the added complexity of having to create a table, populate it (and drop it if it is a temporary table). Having said that, this solution allows for any future optimizations of the compiler and is also of benefit if you will be using the OPENXML rowset more than once. This is therefore the recommended solution.

> Statistics are not created for OPENXML rowsets as they are treated as remote data. Query plans need to be analyzed closely. It's recommended that you do not join directly to an OPENXML rowset since not having an optimal query plan will cause excessive IO due to the reading of more data than necessary from the joined tables.

Using XML Data to Modify Tables

So far we have seen how we can return data from an XML document. The next extension of this is to modify (insert, update, and delete) data in the database with the data from the document. As we have just seen you don't get the best performance if you join directly from `OPENXML` to a document, so we should use intermediate temporary tables or table variables whenever possible. `INSERT`s can use `OPENXML` directly but `UPDATE`s and `DELETE`s should be performed using these tables as you would normally.

A basic example (`OPENXML-BasicInsert.sql`) of inserting data from our example document is as follows:

```
INSERT INTO Orders (
  CustomerID, EmployeeID, OrderDate, RequiredDate, ShippedDate,
  ShipVia
  )
SELECT CustomerID, EmployeeID, OrderDate, RequiredDate,
ShippedDate, ShipVia
  FROM OPENXML (@idoc, '/Root/Customers/Orders')
  WITH (CustomerID   nchar(5) '../@CustomerID'
      , EmployeeID   int
      , OrderDate    datetime
      , RequiredDate datetime
      , ShippedDate  datetime
      , ShipVia      int)
```

This will result in three rows being inserted into the `Orders` table. There are two points overlooked in this example:

❑ The identity values generated for the `OrderID` aren't returned to the client.

❑ Our example document also contains `Order Details` data that has not been saved.

The first of these points is solved in simple cases if we only save one order at a time by using the `SCOPE_IDENTITY()` function. If, however, we want to insert more than one `Orders` record then we have to use a combination of T-SQL calls. To illustrate this consider the following example, which can be found in the `OPENXML-MultipleInsertsWithIdentity.sql` file:

```
DECLARE @Orders TABLE
        (OrderID        int IDENTITY(1,1)
        ,CustomerID     nchar(5)       NULL
        ,EmployeeID     int            NULL
        ,OrderDate      datetime       NULL
        ,RequiredDate   datetime       NULL
        ,ShippedDate    datetime       NULL
        ,ShipVia        int            NULL)

INSERT @Orders    (CustomerID, EmployeeID, OrderDate
                , RequiredDate, ShippedDate, ShipVia)
    SELECT CustomerID, EmployeeID, OrderDate
        , RequiredDate, ShippedDate, ShipVia
```

Chapter 10

```
            FROM OPENXML (@idoc,'//Orders')
                 WITH ( CustomerID nchar(5) '../@CustomerID'
                       ,EmployeeID int
                       ,OrderDate   datetime
                       ,RequiredDate datetime
                       ,ShippedDate datetime
                       ,ShipVia      int)

SET TRANSACTION ISOLATION LEVEL SERIALIZABLE
BEGIN TRANSACTION

SELECT @maxOrderId = MAX(OrderID)
  FROM Northwind.dbo.Orders (UPDLOCK)

SET IDENTITY_INSERT Northwind.dbo.Orders ON

INSERT INTO Northwind.dbo.Orders
      (OrderId
    , CustomerID
    , EmployeeID
    , OrderDate
    , RequiredDate
    , ShippedDate
    , ShipVia)
SELECT @maxOrderId + OrderId
    , CustomerID
    , EmployeeID
    , OrderDate
    , RequiredDate
    , ShippedDate
    , ShipVia
  FROM @orders

COMMIT TRANSACTION

SELECT Customers.*, Orders.*
  FROM OPENXML(@idoc, '//Customers')
       WITH (CustomerID nchar(5)) Customers
  JOIN Northwind.dbo.Orders Orders
   ON Orders.CustomerId=Customers.CustomerId
 WHERE Orders.OrderID IN (SELECT @maxOrderId +OrderId FROM
@Orders)
     FOR XML AUTO
```

The first stage of this is to declare a local variable to hold the orders we want to INSERT and then populate it:

```
    DECLARE @Orders TABLE
            (OrderID         int IDENTITY(1,1)
            ,CustomerID      nchar(5)      NULL
            ,EmployeeID      int           NULL
            ,OrderDate       datetime      NULL
            ,RequiredDate    datetime      NULL
            ,ShippedDate     datetime      NULL
            ,ShipVia         int           NULL)

    INSERT @Orders    (CustomerID, EmployeeID, OrderDate
```

OPENXML

```
            , RequiredDate, ShippedDate, ShipVia)
SELECT CustomerID, EmployeeID, OrderDate
    , RequiredDate, ShippedDate, ShipVia
    FROM OPENXML (@idoc,'//Orders')
        WITH ( CustomerID nchar(5) '../@CustomerID'
                ,EmployeeID   int
                ,OrderDate    datetime
                ,RequiredDate datetime
                ,ShippedDate  datetime
                ,ShipVia      int)
```

The `OrderID` column is not the true `OrderID` but a pseudo value used to uniquely identify each order being saved. This value, combined with the current maximum `OrderID` value, will be used as the final `OrderID` inserted into the table.

To obtain the maximum `OrderID` we perform a simple SQL statement. To ensure that this is still the maximum when we perform the `INSERT` we set the transaction isolation level to serializable. An update lock is also placed on the `SELECT` statement to ensure that when two different processes call they don't deadlock each other.

```
SET TRANSACTION ISOLATION LEVEL SERIALIZABLE
BEGIN TRANSACTION

SELECT @maxOrderId = MAX(OrderID)
   FROM Northwind.dbo.Orders (UPDLOCK)
```

We now have all the information we want and so the `INSERT` is executed and the transaction committed. The `IDENTITY_INSERT` setting for the table has to be turned on as we are setting the value of the identity column.

```
SET IDENTITY_INSERT Northwind.dbo.Orders ON

INSERT INTO Northwind.dbo.Orders
        (OrderId
        , CustomerID
        , EmployeeID
        , OrderDate
        , RequiredDate
        , ShippedDate
        , ShipVia)
SELECT @maxOrderId + OrderId
        , CustomerID
        , EmployeeID
        , OrderDate
        , RequiredDate
        , ShippedDate
        , ShipVia
    FROM @orders

COMMIT TRANSACTION
```

Chapter 10

The final statement in the example returns the XML document to the client with the newly generated `OrderIDs`:

```
SELECT Customers.*, Orders.*
  FROM OPENXML(@idoc, '//Customers')
       WITH (CustomerID nchar(5)) Customers
  JOIN Northwind.dbo.Orders Orders ON
Orders.CustomerId=Customers.CustomerId
  WHERE Orders.OrderID IN (SELECT @maxOrderId +OrderId FROM
@Orders)
    FOR XML AUTO
```

So we have corrected the first flaw in our `INSERT` example. We now need to look at how we save the `Order Details`. To achieve this we have to use a couple of the metaproperties mentioned earlier, namely `@mp:id` and `@mp:parentid` to return the ID of the current and parent elements respectively. Extracting these values from the XML document, when we populate our table variables, allows us to relate the order details records to the correct orders record.

The example of this (`OPENXML-InsertHierarchicalData.sql`) simply takes the previous example and adds an extra column to the `@Orders` table variable, populating it using the `@mp:id` metaproperty. This `INSERT` statement is then executed after the `Orders` have been inserted:

```
INSERT INTO Northwind.dbo.[Order Details]
SELECT @MaxOrderId + O.OrderId, od.ProductId, od.UnitPrice,
       od.Quantity, od.Discount
  FROM OPENXML (@idoc , '//Orders/Order_Details')
       WITH ( ProductID   int
            , UnitPrice   money
            , Quantity    smallint
            , Discount    real
            , ParentId    bigint '@mp:parentid') od
  JOIN @Orders O  ON O.id = od.ParentId
```

The key here is that we join back to the `@Orders` table variable to obtain the `OrderID` for the `Orders` record. A slightly more complex solution (`OPENXML-InsertHierarchicalDataPerformance.sql`) uses another table variable to store the `Order Details` to avoid the `JOIN` between the `OPENXML` function and the `@Orders` table, which as we have seen doesn't produce the best performance.

So we now have a means to `INSERT` a hierarchy of `Orders` and `Order Details` into the database from a single document. We can extend this to consider the saving of a hierarchy to the database, whether it be inserted, updated or deleted. If we look at the example of saving an order, including its detail records into the `Northwind Orders` and `Order Details` tables, then the steps required are:

OPENXML

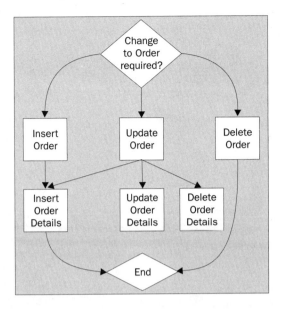

There is one aspect that we have to consider and that is how we identify which route(s) through the flow we need to follow and how specifically we identify when we need to delete data. Options for this include:

❑ Query the database to see if a record (Orders or Order Details) exists. If it does update it; if not insert it.

❑ Assume the XML document will contain all orders for a client and so any orders that exist in the database but not in the document should be deleted.

❑ Use a status attribute on the document, which informs us of the status of the record.

In the example included in the code download for this chapter (OPENXML-SaveHierarchy.sql) we have a status attribute on each element. The code for the solution is shown below, and is the combination of all we have learnt so far in using OPENXML:

```
PRINT 'Get data from XML Document'

INSERT INTO @Orders (OrderID
            ,CustomerID
            , EmployeeID
            , OrderDate
            , RequiredDate
            , ShippedDate
            , ShipVia
            , Freight
            , ShipName
            , ShipAddress
            , ShipCity
```

275

```
                        , ShipRegion
                        , ShipPostalCode
                        , ShipCountry
                        , Status
                        , xmlid  )
SELECT OrderId, CustomerID
                , EmployeeID
                , OrderDate
                , RequiredDate
                , ShippedDate
                , ShipVia
                , Freight
                , ShipName
                , ShipAddress
                , ShipCity
                , ShipRegion
                , ShipPostalCode
                , ShipCountry
                , Status
                , xmlid
    FROM OPENXML (@idoc,'//Orders')
         WITH ( OrderID      int
               ,CustomerID nchar(10)
               ,EmployeeID int
               ,OrderDate   datetime
               ,RequiredDate datetime
               ,ShippedDate datetime
               ,ShipVia     int
               ,Freight     money
               ,ShipName    nvarchar(80)
               ,ShipAddress nvarchar(120)
               ,ShipCity    nvarchar(30)
               ,ShipRegion  nvarchar(30)
               ,ShipPostalCode nvarchar(20)
               ,ShipCountry  nvarchar(30)
               ,Status      char(1)
               ,xmlid       int   '@mp:id')

    INSERT INTO @OrderDetails
    SELECT *
      FROM OPENXML (@idoc , '//Orders/Order_Details')
           WITH ( OrderId    int '../@OrderID'
                 ,ProductID  int
                 ,UnitPrice  money
                 ,Quantity   smallint
                 ,Discount   real
                 ,Status     char(1)
                 ,xmlParentId int '@mp:parentid')

SET TRANSACTION ISOLATION LEVEL SERIALIZABLE
```

OPENXML

```
PRINT 'Have to specify UPDLOCK to ensure queries don''t block each

other'
SELECT @maxOrderId = MAX(OrderID)
  FROM Northwind.dbo.Orders (UPDLOCK)

UPDATE @Orders
   SET OrderId = @maxOrderId + PseudoOrderId
 WHERE status = 'I'

SET IDENTITY_INSERT Northwind.dbo.Orders ON
PRINT 'INSERT Orders'
INSERT INTO Orders (OrderId
                  , CustomerID
                  , EmployeeID
                  , OrderDate
                  , RequiredDate
                  , ShippedDate
                  , ShipVia
                  , Freight
                  , ShipName
                  , ShipAddress
                  , ShipCity
                  , ShipRegion
                  , ShipPostalCode
                  , ShipCountry   )

SELECT  OrderID, CustomerID
                  , EmployeeID
                  , OrderDate
                  , RequiredDate
                  , ShippedDate
                  , ShipVia
                  , Freight
                  , ShipName
                  , ShipAddress
                  , ShipCity
                  , ShipRegion
                  , ShipPostalCode
                  , ShipCountry
  FROM @orders
 WHERE status = 'I'
SET IDENTITY_INSERT Northwind.dbo.Orders OFF

PRINT 'UPDATE Orders'
UPDATE Orders SET
        CustomerID      = NewOrders.CustomerID
      , EmployeeID      = NewOrders.EmployeeID
      , OrderDate       = NewOrders.OrderDate
      , RequiredDate    = NewOrders.RequiredDate
      , ShippedDate     = NewOrders.ShippedDate
      , ShipVia         = NewOrders.ShipVia
      , Freight         = NewOrders.Freight
      , ShipName        = NewOrders.ShipName
```

```
         , ShipAddress    = NewOrders.ShipAddress
            , ShipCity       = NewOrders.ShipCity
            , ShipRegion     = NewOrders.ShipRegion
            , ShipPostalCode = NewOrders.ShipPostalCode
            , ShipCountry    = NewOrders.ShipCountry
      FROM @Orders AS NewOrders
      WHERE NewOrders.OrderID = Orders.OrderID
        AND NewOrders.status = 'U'

PRINT 'INSERT order Details'

INSERT INTO dbo.[Order Details]
SELECT O.OrderId, od.ProductId, od.UnitPrice, od.Quantity,
       od.Discount
  FROM @OrderDetails od
  JOIN @Orders         O  ON od.xmlParentid = o.xmlid
 WHERE od.status = 'I'

PRINT 'UPDATE order details'

UPDATE dbo.[Order Details] SET
       UnitPrice = NewOrderDetails.UnitPrice
      ,Quantity  = NewOrderDetails.Quantity
      ,Discount  = NewOrderDetails.Discount
  FROM @OrderDetails NewOrderDetails
 INNER JOIN dbo.[Order Details]
       ON [Order Details].OrderID   = NewOrderDetails.OrderID
       AND [Order Details].ProductID =
NewOrderDetails.ProductID
  WHERE NewOrderDetails.status = 'U'

PRINT 'Delete order details'
DELETE FROM dbo.[Order Details]
  FROM @OrderDetails OD
 INNER JOIN dbo.[Order Details]
       ON OD.ORderId = dbo.[Order Details].OrderId
       AND OD.ProductID = dbo.[Order Details].ProductId
  WHERE OD.status = 'D'

PRINT 'Delete orders'
DELETE FROM dbo.[Orders]
  FROM @Orders O
 INNER JOIN dbo.[Orders]
       ON O.ORderId = dbo.[Orders].OrderId
  WHERE O.status = 'D'

SELECT 1 Tag, NULL Parent
       ,xmlid            "Orders!1!id!hide"
       ,OrderID          "Orders!1!OrderID"
       ,CustomerID       "Orders!1!CustomerID"
       ,EmployeeID       "Orders!1!EmployeeID"
       ,OrderDate        "Orders!1!OrderDate"
       ,RequiredDate     "Orders!1!RequiredDate"
       ,ShippedDate      "Orders!1!ShippedDate"
       ,ShipVia          "Orders!1!ShipVia"
       ,Freight          "Orders!1!Freight"
       ,ShipName         "Orders!1!ShipName"
       ,ShipAddress      "Orders!1!ShipAddress"
       ,ShipCity         "Orders!1!ShipCity"
       ,ShipRegion       "Orders!1!ShipRegion"
```

OPENXML

```
            ,ShipPostalCode   "Orders!1!ShipPostalCode"
            ,ShipCountry      "Orders!1!ShipCountry"
            ,''               "Orders!1!Status"
            , NULL             "OrderDetails!2!ProductID"
            , NULL             "OrderDetails!2!Quantity"
            , NULL             "OrderDetails!2!UnitPrice"
            , NULL             "OrderDetails!2!Discount"
            , NULL             "OrderDetails!2!Status"
    FROM @Orders
    WHERE status IN ('I','U','')
    UNION ALL
    SELECT 2,1
            , xmlparentId, NULL, NULL, NULL, NULL, NULL, NULL, NULL,
            , NULL, NULL, NULL, NULL, NULL, NULL, NULL, NULL
            , ProductID
            , Quantity
            , UnitPrice
            , Discount
            , ''
    FROM @OrderDetails
    WHERE status IN ('I','U','')
    FOR XML EXPLICIT
```

This example has been incorporated into two test applications that show the performance difference of saving a hierarchy by using OPENXML or by singleton stored procedures calls for each element in an XML document. Both applications test the same thing but one is written in VB and the other in VB.NET.

The results of the tests show that, when run on the same machine, OPENXML does not come close to the use of stored procedures. However, when the overhead of a network is introduced the results become more comparable as the number of rows being modified increases. The main benefit of using OPENXML is that only one stored procedure is used to save the whole hierarchy, returning the new XML.

You can test this yourself using the code available in the download. The files to look for are in the folders OPENXML-VB performance test and OPENXML-VB.Net performance test.

Using XML Meta Data

It is likely that for the majority, if not all, of the time you will be processing documents of a known structure. There may be times that you wish to examine or process a document of an unknown format, or want to do some processing with the document that OPENXML doesn't support (see the *Multi-Valued Attributes* below). When you don't specify a WITH clause with an OPENXML statement, the rowset returned is called an **edge table**. It gets this name because, in this table format, every edge in the parsed XML document tree maps to a row in the rowset. This edge table contains all the data and structure from the XML document, but in a tabular form. Each column in the edge table is one of the metaproperties detailed earlier, with the exception of the xmltext metaproperty. The format of the edge table is as follows:

279

Chapter 10

Column name	Data type	Description
id	bigint	The unique ID of the document node. The root element has an ID value of 0.
parentid	bigint	Identifies the parent of the node. A node at the top level of an XML document has a parentid that is NULL.
nodetype	int	An integer denoting the node type as one of the following: 1 = Element node 2 = Attribute node 3 = Text node.
localname	nvarchar	The local name of the element or attribute, which is NULL if the DOM object has no name.
prefix	nvarchar	The namespace prefix of the node name.
namespaceuri	nvarchar	The namespace URI of the node (NULL if no namespace is present).
datatype	nvarchar	The data type of the element or attribute row inferred from the inline DTD or inline schema.
prev	bigint	The XML ID of the previous sibling element.
text	ntext	Contains the attribute value or the element content in text form

As you can see, all the information you need regarding the document is in the edge table.

Simple Edge Table

Using the following simple XML document:

```
<Root>
   <Shippers ShipperID="1"
           CompanyName="Speedy Express"
           Phone="555-9831"/>
   <Shippers ShipperID="2"
           CompanyName="United Package"
           Phone="555-3199"/>
   <Shippers ShipperID="3"
           CompanyName="Federal Shipping"
           Phone="555-9931"/>
</Root>
```

OPENXML

We can return the edge table by not specifying a WITH clause on the OPENXML function:

```
SELECT *
  FROM OPENXML (@idoc ,'/Root/Shippers')
```

which gives us the edge table below:

id	parent id	node type	localname	prev	text
2	0	1	Shippers		
3	2	2	ShipperID		
14	3	3	#text		1
4	2	2	CompanyName		
15	4	3	#text		Speedy Express
5	2	2	Phone		
16	5	3	#text		(503) 555-9831
6	0	1	Shippers	2	
7	6	2	ShipperID		
17	7	3	#text		2
8	6	2	CompanyName		
18	8	3	#text		United Package
9	6	2	Phone		
19	9	3	#text		(503) 555-3199
10	0	1	Shippers	6	
11	10	2	ShipperID		
20	11	3	#text		3
12	10	2	CompanyName		
21	12	3	#text		Federal Shipping
13	10	2	phone		
22	13	3	#text		(503) 555-9931

Please note - this table omits the prefix, namespaceuri, and datatype columns that are returned, but contain no data.

281

Chapter 10

This edge table can be used to determine the structure of the document and create a table to store the results, or to determine how many elements there were in a document. To get the number of elements you could use:

```
SELECT Count(*)
  FROM OPENXML(@idoc, '//@*')
       WITH (id int)
```

or use the edge table:

```
SELECT Count(*)
  FROM OPENXML(@idoc, '')
 WHERE nodetype = 2
```

To find all references to France using T-SQL you could use:

```
SELECT Text
  FROM OPENXML(@idoc,
'//@*[contains(text(),"France")]|//*[contains(text(),"France")]
')
       WITH (Text text 'text()')
```

We could also do it this way with the edge table:

```
SELECT Text
  FROM OPENXML(@idoc, '')
 WHERE nodetype = 3
   AND text LIKE '%France%'
```

Edge Table with DTD or Inline Schema

The following code displays the use of an inline XDR schema. This gives the benefit of the edge table having datatypes specified. The same is also true if we use an inline DTD. You can generate an inline schema using the XMLDATA clause of FOR XML, which is what I did to produce the following document:

```
<Root>
    <Schema name="Schema3"
     xmlns="urn:schemas-microsoft-com:xml-data"
     xmlns:dt="urn:schemas-microsoft-com:datatypes">
        <ElementType name="Northwind.dbo.order_x0020_details"
                     content="empty" model="closed">
            <AttributeType name="OrderID" dt:type="i4"/>
            <AttributeType name="ProductID" dt:type="i4"/>
            <AttributeType name="UnitPrice"
                           dt:type="fixed.14.4"/>
            <AttributeType name="Quantity" dt:type="i2"/>
            <AttributeType name="Discount" dt:type="r4"/>
            <attribute type="OrderID"/>
            <attribute type="ProductID"/>
            <attribute type="UnitPrice"/>
```

OPENXML

```
                <attribute type="Quantity"/>
                <attribute type="Discount"/>
        </ElementType>
    </Schema>
    <Northwind.dbo.order_x0020_details
      xmlns="x-schema:#Schema3" OrderID="10248" ProductID="11"
      UnitPrice="14.0000" Quantity="12"
      Discount="0.0000000e+000"/>
    <Northwind.dbo.order_x0020_details
      xmlns="x-schema:#Schema3" OrderID="10248" ProductID="42"
      UnitPrice="9.8000" Quantity="10"
      Discount="0.0000000e+000"/>
</Root>
```

We can use a very basic query to get the edge table:

```
SELECT id
     , parentid
     , nodetype
     , CAST(localname as varchar(20)) localname
     , CAST(datatype as varchar(10)) datatype
     , CAST(text as varchar(20)) text
FROM OPENXML (@idoc ,'')
```

The edge table returned (not shown as it is very large) will now include the datatypes for the columns in the main document and the meta data for the schema, in addition to the types of data we returned in our simple edge table in the last section.

If there is an inline schema, then the document will be validated against it during parsing.

Performance

Now that we can parse the document, it is good to understand how this impacts on the server resources.

Memory

As we stated earlier in the chapter the MSXML parser uses one-eighth of the total memory available for SQL Server. The question we need to consider here is what exactly determines the total memory available. Testing indicates that this is a combination of the total memory configured for the server and the physical memory available to SQL Server when it starts up. Note that this is a server limit and doesn't take into account how the server is configured for memory. This may be an issue if you are using multiple instances and wish to configure each with a distinct set of memory.

Chapter 10

The download code for this chapter contains a file (OPENXML-sp_xml_preparedocument-MemoryProof.sql) to test how many documents a server can have parsed at one time. Running this shows that there is a static memory overhead of ~30Kb for each document prepared in SQL Server. This is irrespective of the size of the XML document.

The following calculation shows the number of documents you can have prepared at any one time per Gb.

- Each document consumes = 30KB.
- MSXML can use 1/8 of available memory => 8x30Kb = 240Kb = Available memory required to hold one document.
- For 1 Gb we can prepare = 1,000,000/240 ~ 4000 documents.

> This clearly shows that if you have a high user volume system, using OPENXML is not an option for all database interaction. The use of OPENXML should be considered carefully and only used where it has the most benefit.

While the memory used is not related to the size of the document, the tests I carried out here couldn't find the maximum size of a document the server could process. The server ground to a halt before an error was raised (document exceeded 100Mb), suggesting that very large documents should not be handled in this way. This becomes more relevant when returning the data using OPENXML.

Timing

The graphs below show the relative timing of parsing a document and returning a rowset. The code used to obtain the figures is available in the code download as OPENXML-PerformanceNodeTest.sql and OPENXML-sp_xml_preparedocument-MaximumDocumentSize.sql. The graphs clearly show that there is a linear relationship between the time taken to parse a document and the number of elements and the size of the document. There appears to be a fixed overhead for the number of elements, increasing with the number of elements:

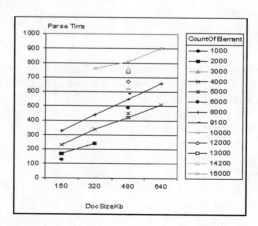

OPENXML

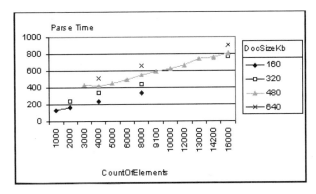

The performance of using OPENXML is directly related to the number of columns and rows in your rowset. There is a standard overhead for returning a rowset, which increases almost linearly with the number of columns being returned and the number of rows in the rowset. This table shows the results from the OPENXML-PerformanceNodeTest.sql code. Each test has been run 100 times and the results show the total duration and the average duration per execution.

Description	Duration	Iterations	Average
1 Column not used	793	100	7.930
2 Columns not used	770	100	7.700
1 Column used	1163	100	11.630
1 Column used and returned	1340	100	13.400
2 Columns used and returned	1593	100	15.930
3 Columns used and returned	1870	100	18.700
3 Columns 10 rows	683	100	6.830
3 Columns 20 rows	893	100	8.930
3 Columns 30 rows	1130	100	11.300

It can be seen from rows 1 and 2 that even if you declare a column in the schema declaration, if it's not used in the query then this column doesn't increase the timing of the query.

IO

The preparing of documents has no significant IO usage, as the documents are in-memory. You should note that, when joining to other tables, not having an optimal query plan will cause excessive IO because we read more data than necessary from the joined tables.

Chapter 10

During the stress testing of the performance of `sp_xml_preparedocument` I occasionally encountered fatal exceptions, although these only caused the connection to fail. However, you are strongly advised not to run these files on your production servers.

Limitations

So you now know what a powerful feature `OPENXML` is. However, there are some things that it can't do, and we will cover these now.

Updating Documents

As we have discussed, the `OPENXML` mechanism creates static memory structure of the XML document. Currently there is no mechanism to update the document for returning to the calling process. The knock-on effect of this is that if rows are inserted into a table with an identity or default values, there is no mechanism for putting these generated values back in the document.

Where I see the use of `OPENXML` having the greatest benefit is in the saving of hierarchical data. With a good application design, the restriction on updating the document may not be a problem, as we saw in the examples above.

Caching and Statistics

When SQL Server compiles the execution plan for a statement involving `OPENXML`, it treats the data from `OPENXML` as data from a remote source. If you have used `OPENROWSET` or `OPENQUERY` then you will be familiar with this. The issue here is that SQL Server doesn't have any knowledge of the data in the remote source and so statistics don't get created for the XML documents when used with `OPENXML`. This results in query plans that are very inefficient when joining tables together, if hints are not supplied. It is therefore better to populate a table from `OPENXML` and then use that table, especially if the same XML rowset is to be used more than once.

Whitespace and Escaped Characters

Whitespace refers to characters such as spaces, linefeeds and carriage returns. You need to be aware that what you put into an XML document might not be what you get out of it because of the way that the parser handles whitespace. Usually when programming with the parser, you can configure how whitespace is handled. Unfortunately with SQL Server this is not exposed to you, and so you have to accept the default mechanism. This can be summarized as follows:

- Whitespace is stripped from the start and end of all values (whether attribute or element-centric).
- Carriage returns are replaced by linefeeds except where a linefeed follows, in which case the carriage return is just removed.

OPENXML

This is shown in the code download `OPENXML-Whitespace.sql`. If you wrap your data in `CDATA` sections then this removes the issue of whitespace being stripped from the start and end, but does not help with carriage returns and line feeds.

Certain characters are illegal in the text of XML elements and attributes, such as &, <, >, ', ', ", and &quote;. These may only be used in their escaped versions: &, <, and >. Thankfully the XML parser does this for you automatically, so there is no need for lots of replace functions. You may now be thinking that you could escape your whitespace to stop it being removed. Unfortunately the parser does the escape character replacement before it strips the whitespace.

Multi-Valued Attributes

In XML schemas you can have references between elements using `ID`, `IDREF` and `IDREFS`, as we have seen in previous chapters. The last of these, the `IDREFS`, is a multi-valued attribute that references multiple elements with the associated `ID` values. The following document shows a `<Customers>` element that has a `ProductsBought` attribute containing the `ID` values of the `<Products>` that customer has bought:

```
<Root>
    <Customers CustomerID="ALFKI" ProductsBought="1 2 5" />
    <Customers CustomerID="ALFKI" ProductsBought="3 4 5" />
    <Products ProductID="1" ProductName="Lemonade" />
    <Products ProductID="2" ProductName="Strawberry Mousse" />
    <Products ProductID="3" ProductName="Chicken Nuggets" />
    <Products ProductID="4" ProductName="Mashed potatoes" />
    <Products ProductID="5" ProductName="Cheesy peas" />
</Root>
```

Unfortunately there is no straightforward mechanism in `OPENXML` for combining the data to return all customers and the products they have bought. A work around to achieve this requires the use of an edge table and some cursor operations in order to build up the result set.

Summary

In the course of this chapter we have seen how to parse an XML document to provide an in-memory structure for the `OPENXML` function to shred and return a rowset from. We have considered how to manipulate the results returned in the rowset through the use of arguments such as `TableName`, `rowpattern`, `SchemaDeclaration`, `flags`, column pattern, and metaproperties.

We moved on to look at how to combine `OPENXML` rowsets with other database tables, and how to use `OPENXML` data to modify existing database records. We also saw how we could use `OPENXML` to generate information in the form of meta data about XML documents.

Chapter 10

We rounded off the chapter with a look at the performance issues you may have to consider in using OPENXML, and some of the limitations you need to be aware of. We saw that OPENXML enables you to reduce the amount of code in the data calling layer of your applications. It also allows you, if you use stored procedures for all data access, to reduce the number of stored procedures in the database. These are of course minor compared with what is normally the main issue, performance. Since OPENXML is a rowset function the optimizer has no knowledge at compile time of the data that is to be returned. In addition there are no indexes to use, as the rowset is generated each time. Furthermore, the data is not cached resulting in the same performance hit each time OPENXML is used, meaning that table variables should be used whenever possible.

The main point is that OPENXML has its benefits but each use should be fully evaluated to ensure that the mechanism of use won't result in both your server and the application grinding to a halt. For small applications where top end performance is not crucial, or situations that occur infrequently, OPENXML can be very useful.

OPENXML

Kevin Williams

- What are Updategrams?
- Driving Updategrams with Annotated Schemas
- Default Mapping
- Inserting, Updating and Deleting Data
- Multiple Actions Within One Updategram
- Capturing Identity Values for Inserted Records
- Inverse Relationships
- Generating Updategrams "on-the-fly"
- Applying Updategrams to a Database

11

Updategrams

In this chapter, we're going to take a look at the Updategram technology provided as part of the SQLXML library. Updategrams are XML messages that describe a set of records in the database that are to be added, updated, or removed. In this chapter, we'll cover:

- How Updategrams work
- Inserting, deleting, and updating data with Updategrams
- Performing complex transactions with Updategrams
- Passing parameters using Updategrams
- Capturing identity values in Updategrams
- Inverse relationships in an Updategram
- Creating GUIDs from Updategrams
- Creating 'on-the-fly' Updategrams using XSLT
- Applying an Updategram to a database using a variety of methods

As you'll see, we're going to cover the basics of Updategrams before we look at how we actually apply them. The code for every example you'll see along the way is included in the code download for the chapter, and you can try the examples as we go. If you would like to do this, open the download code for this chapter, unzip it, and follow the instructions in README.txt. This file gives instructions on how to set yourself up to run the majority of Updategrams in this chapter as XML templates.

The chapter uses two tables, Customer and Invoice, in the initial examples - you might like to refer to the following create script (tableCreation.sql) to see the structure we're working with:

Chapter 11

```
CREATE TABLE Customer (
  customerID int PRIMARY KEY NOT NULL,
  customerName varchar(100) NOT NULL,
  address1 varchar(100) NOT NULL,
  address2 varchar(100) NULL,
  city varchar(50) NOT NULL,
  state char(2) NOT NULL,
  postalCode varchar(10) NOT NULL)

CREATE TABLE Invoice (
  invoiceID int PRIMARY KEY NOT NULL,
  customerID int REFERENCES Customer (customerID)
    ON DELETE CASCADE
    ON UPDATE CASCADE,
  invoiceDate datetime NOT NULL,
  invoiceAmount decimal(9,2) NULL)
```

What are Updategrams?

Updategrams are specially formatted XML documents that describe how rows are to be added to or deleted from a SQL Server database. They do this by providing a description of the database state before and after the changes are applied. Updategrams map the information in an XML structure onto a relational database structure (either directly or through an annotated XML schema, as we'll see later). The elements and attributes that make up an Updategram are found in the Updategram namespace: urn:schemas-microsoft-com:xml-updategram. As always, you can use whatever prefix you want to identify elements and attributes in the Updategram namespace; however, by convention the prefix updg: is used.

To see how to run Updategrams, go to the end of the chapter.

For reference, here is a table of all the elements and attributes in the Updategram namespace, along with a brief description of each (we'll delve into these more fully later in the chapter):

Name	Element or Attribute	Purpose
`<sync>`	Element	Appears as a child of the root element of the Updategram. Represents a single database transaction.
`<before>`	Element	Appears as the optional first child of the `<sync>` element. Contains the state of the data prior to the modification; used to verify information before performing an update or delete.
`<after>`	Element	Appears as the optional second child of the `<sync>` element (after a `<before>` element, if present). Contains the state of the data after the modification has been performed.

Table continued on following page

Updategrams

Name	Element or Attribute	Purpose
`mapping-schema`	Attribute	Appears as an optional attribute of either the root element or the `<sync>` element. Declares an annotated schema to be used as the mapping schema for a particular Updategram.
`<header>`	Element	Appears as an optional child of the root element, but before any `<sync>` elements. This is a container element used to hold any declared parameters for the Updategram.
`<param>`	Element	Appears as an optional child of the `<header>` element. Declares a parameter for the Updategram.
`name`	Attribute	Appears as a required attribute of the `<param>` element. Specifies the name of the parameter of the Updategram.
`at-identity`	Attribute	Appears as an optional attribute of any element in the `<after>` element. Associates a created identity value for an inserted or updated record with a placeholder value (to be used with the `returnid` attribute, or to assign foreign keys on child records).
`guid`	Attribute	Appears as an optional attribute of any element in the `<after>` element. Creates a placeholder for a generated GUID that can be used to update fields in the database (by referring to the placeholder value). Can be returned using `returnid`.
`returnid`	Attribute	Appears as an optional attribute of the `<after>` element. Contains a whitespace-separated list of the values generated by `at-identity` and `guid` that are to be returned to the caller.

Here is an example of an Updategram:

```
<ROOT xmlns:updg="urn:schemas-microsoft-com:xml-updategram">
   <updg:sync>
      <updg:before>
         <Customer customerID="1" name="Kevin Williams" />
      </updg:before>
      <updg:after>
         <Customer customerID="1" name="Kevin B. Williams" />
      </updg:after>
   </updg:sync>
</ROOT>
```

Note that the Updategram has a <ROOT> element – the name of this element can be whatever you want but, by convention, the element name ROOT is used. Inside the <ROOT> element, there are one or more **<updg:sync>** blocks. Each <updg:sync> block represents one single transaction to be applied against the database. This means that, should an <updg:sync> block contain more than one modification (say, an UPDATE and an INSERT), should any one of the operations fails, the entire set of operations specified in that <updg:sync> block is rolled back. It is much as though the information in the <sync> block is being transformed into INSERT, UPDATE, and DELETE statements, and then being applied inside a BEGIN TRAN - ROLLBACK TRAN - COMMIT TRAN block.

Inside each <updg:sync> element, there must appear either an **<updg:before>** element, an **<updg:after>** element, or both. The <updg:before> element indicates the state of the information of the database before the transaction is applied; the <updg:after> element indicates the state of the information after the transaction is applied. By using the <updg:before> and <updg:after> elements in various combinations, we can insert, update, or delete records in the database.

In the next example, two separate transactions to update data in the Customer database are being performed:

```
<ROOT xmlns:updg="urn:schemas-microsoft-com:xml-updategram">
  <updg:sync>
    <updg:before>
       <Customer customerID="1" name="Kevin Williams" />
    </updg:before>
    <updg:after>
       <Customer customerID="1" name="Kevin B. Williams" />
    </updg:after>
  </updg:sync>
  <updg:sync>
    <updg:before>
       <Customer customerID="2" name="Joe Somebody" />
    </updg:before>
    <updg:after>
       <Customer customerID="2" name="Joseph Somebody" />
    </updg:after>
  </updg:sync>
</ROOT>
```

We'll learn more about applying multiple transactions from a single Updategram later.

For Updategrams to correctly identify records in the database tables, they need to know how those records are related – what the primary and foreign keys are, how the names in the Updategram map to the table and column names in the XML database, and so on. This is accomplished by associating the Updategram with an XML View – a mapping of an XML structure to a database structure (we learned about XML views in Chapter 7). Let's take a look at how this is done using annotated XML schema views.

Driving Updategrams with an Annotated Schema

When using an Updategram to update a database, typically (but not always, as we'll see) you need to associate the Updategram with an annotated schema. The annotated schema provides information about how the elements and attributes in the Updategram correspond to tables and columns in the SQL Server database. The other important feature provided by the annotated schema is information about the primary keys of each table, and how they relate to the foreign keys in other tables. As we will see later in this chapter, we can perform some fairly sophisticated database changes when the Updategram processor knows about how the tables are related in the database.

To specify an annotated schema for an Updategram, you simply specify the URL for that schema in the **mapping-schema** attribute of the `<updg:sync>` element to which it applies. Let's say that we have the following annotated XML schema called `customerSchema.xml` describing the relationship between `Customer` and `Invoice`:

```
<xsd:schema xmlns:xsd="http://www.w3.org/2001/XMLSchema"
            xmlns:sql="urn:schemas-microsoft-com:mapping-schema">
  <xsd:element name="Customer"
               sql:relation="Customer"
               sql:key-fields="customerID">
    <xsd:complexType>
      <xsd:sequence>
        <xsd:element name="Invoice"
                     maxOccurs="unbounded"
                     sql:relation="Invoice"
                     sql:key-fields="invoiceID">
          <xsd:annotation>
            <xsd:appinfo>
              <sql:relationship
                  parent="Customer"
                  parent-key="customerID"
                  child="Invoice"
                  child-key="customerID" />
            </xsd:appinfo>
          </xsd:annotation>
          <xsd:complexType>
            <xsd:attribute name="invoiceID"
                           sql:field="invoiceID"
                           type="xsd:integer" />
            <xsd:attribute name="invoiceDate"
                           sql:field="invoiceDate"
                           type="xsd:dateTime" />
          </xsd:complexType>
        </xsd:element>
```

Chapter 11

```
            </xsd:sequence>
            <xsd:attribute name="customerID"
                           sql:field="customerID"
                           type="xsd:integer" />
            <xsd:attribute name="name"
                           sql:field="customerName"
                           type="xsd:string" />
        </xsd:complexType>
    </xsd:element>
</xsd:schema>
```

The following Updategram (Nested.xml) references the specified XML schema:

```
<ROOT xmlns:updg="urn:schemas-microsoft-com:xml-updategram">
    <updg:sync mapping-schema="customerSchema.xml">
        <updg:before>
            <Customer customerID="1" />
        </updg:before>
        <updg:after>
            <Customer customerID="1" name="Kevin B. Williams">
                <Invoice invoiceID="1" invoiceDate="2002-06-17" />
                <Invoice invoiceID="2" invoiceDate="2002-07-12" />
            </Customer>
        </updg:after>
    </updg:sync>
</ROOT>
```

This Updategram instructs the database to update the name of the customer with customerID of 1 to be Kevin B. Williams, and to add two invoice records related to that customer. Because the <Invoice> elements are nested inside the <Customer> element, the processor infers that there is a foreign key in the Invoice table pointing back to the primary key of the Customer table; and to determine what those key fields are, the Updategram engine uses the annotated schema.

There are a couple of important things to note about the annotated schema. Firstly, the relationship between the Customer and the Invoice tables is explicitly specified using the <sql:relationship> element (found inside the <Invoice> element declaration's annotation block). This informs the Updategram processor that Invoice is related to Customer through the foreign key customerID. Secondly, the key fields for both Invoice and Customer are specified using the sql:key-fields attribute. This enables the Updategram processor to identify when records are being updated, as opposed to inserted, by examining the key fields provided in the element in the <updg:before> and <updg:after> sections of the Updategram, and using that information to uniquely identify distinct rows in the database tables.

Note also, that the annotated schema is specified as an attribute of the <updg:sync> element. This makes it possible to perform two updates in a single Updategram that rely on two different annotated schemas to correctly identify records in the database:

Updategrams

```
<ROOT xmlns:updg="urn:schemas-microsoft-com:xml-updategram">
  <updg:sync mapping-schema="customerSchema.xml">
    <updg:before>
      <Customer customerID="1" />
    </updg:before>
    <updg:after>
      <Customer customerID="1" name="Kevin B. Williams">
        <Invoice invoiceID="1" invoiceDate="2002-06-17" />
        <Invoice invoiceID="2" invoiceDate="2002-07-12" />
      </Customer>
    </updg:after>
  </updg:sync>
  <updg:sync mapping-schema="partSchema.xml">
    <updg:after>
      <Part partID="1" partName="2 inch grommets" />
    </updg:after>
  </updg:sync>
</ROOT>
```

If a single mapping schema is to be used for the entire Updategram, you can add the attribute to the root element; every updg:sync transaction will then use the same mapping schema.

Later in the chapter, when we discuss the various kinds of manipulation possible with Updategrams, we'll take a closer look at some of the ramifications of the annotated schema declaration and how they affects the way Updategrams are processed.

Default Mapping in Updategrams

It's also possible to execute an Updategram that does not explicitly reference a mapping schema. In this case, the element and attribute names in the Updategram must exactly match the table and column names in the database; this is known as "implicit" or "default" mapping. Text-only elements and attributes are mapped to columns with the same name, and structural elements are mapped to tables with the same name. Updategrams that do not contain a reference to a mapping schema can only be used for simple modifications to the database. For instance, the following schemaless Updategram (Insert2.xml) inserts a new record into the Customer table:

```
<ROOT xmlns:updg="urn:schemas-microsoft-com:xml-updategram">
  <updg:sync>
    <updg:after>
      <Customer customerID="2"
                customerName="William Kevins"
                address1="92 Deciduous Avenue"
                city="Perth"
                state="WA"
                postalCode="27651" />
    </updg:after>
  </updg:sync>
</ROOT>
```

Chapter 11

In this case, a record is inserted into a table called Customer in the SQL Server database that has columns called customerID, customerName, address1, city, state, and postalCode. Note that using name or zip will not work as it did in Insert1.xml, as we are not using an annotated schema to map columns. If the table or column names do not match, or if the Customer table contains other required columns that are not specified in the Updategram, the Updategram will fail and an error will be returned. While it is possible to issue Updategrams this way, for the greatest control and flexibility you should always specify a schema for each <updg:sync> element in an Updategram (or at the root level).

It's worth taking a quick look at an example of an Updategram error here, because its structure is a little surprising:

```
<ROOT xmlns:updg="urn:schemas-microsoft-com:xml-updategram">
  <?MSSQLError HResult="0x80040e2f" Source="Microsoft OLE DB
    Provider for SQL Server" Description=
    "The statement has been terminated."?>
  <?MSSQLError HResult="0x80040e2f" Source="Microsoft OLE DB
    Provider for SQL Server" Description="Cannot insert
    duplicate key row in object 'Customer' with unique index
    'IDX_Customer_CustomerID'."?>
</ROOT>
```

If you're not familiar with those tags starting with a question mark, don't be worried; most XML developers don't work with them much either. They're called **processing instructions**, and they effectively provide information to a parser telling it how to interpret a document it has received. Fortunately, the DOM, SAX (or XmlTextReader), and XSLT all allow processing instructions to be intercepted and handled; so your code can detect the presence of these processing instructions in the returned XML structure and act accordingly. Note that when a parser interprets a processing instruction, it returns everything after the leading tag as a single string; so you'll have to parse that value to obtain the Hresult code, source, and description for each error encountered.

Inserting Data with an Updategram

Inserting data into the database with an Updategram is straightforward. To insert rows, simply add elements to the <updg:after> element in the Updategram, and omit the <updg:before> element (or if you are combining this insertion with other operations, do not specify a record with a matching identifier in the <updg:before> element). For example, suppose we have the following table definition in our database (if you have run tableCreation.sql already you do not need to run it again):

```
CREATE TABLE Customer (
  customerID int PRIMARY KEY NOT NULL,
  customerName varchar(100) NOT NULL,
  address1 varchar(100) NOT NULL,
  address2 varchar(100) NULL,
  city varchar(50) NOT NULL,
  state char(2) NOT NULL,
  postalCode varchar(10) NOT NULL
```

Updategrams

The following Updategram (`Insert1.xml`) would insert a new customer:

```xml
<ROOT xmlns:updg="urn:schemas-microsoft-com:xml-updategram">
  <updg:sync mapping-schema="customerSchema.xsd">
    <updg:after>
      <Customer customerID="1"
                name="Kevin B. Williams"
                address1="762 Evergreen Terrace"
                city="Springfield"
                state="VA"
                zip="27651" />
    </updg:after>
  </updg:sync>
</ROOT>
```

This is the annotated schema (`customerSchema.xsd`) associated with the Updategram:

```xml
<xsd:schema xmlns:xsd="http://www.w3.org/2001/XMLSchema"
            xmlns:sql="urn:schemas-microsoft-com:mapping-schema">
  <xsd:element name="Customer"
               sql:relation="Customer"
               sql:key-fields="customerID">
    <xsd:complexType>
      <xsd:attribute name="customerID"
                     sql:field="customerID"
                     type="xsd:integer"
                     use="required" />
      <xsd:attribute name="name"
                     sql:field="customerName"
                     type="xsd:string"
                     use="required" />
      <xsd:attribute name="address1"
                     sql:field="address1"
                     type="xsd:string"
                     use="required" />
      <xsd:attribute name="address2"
                     sql:field="address2"
                     type="xsd:string" />
      <xsd:attribute name="city"
                     sql:field="city"
                     type="xsd:string"
                     use="required" />
      <xsd:attribute name="state"
                     sql:field="state"
                     type="xsd:string"
                     use="required" />
      <xsd:attribute name="zip"
                     sql:field="postalCode"
                     type="xsd:string"
                     use="required" />
    </xsd:complexType>
  </xsd:element>
</xsd:schema>
```

Chapter 11

Note that our schema allows us to map table and column names to elements and attributes (in this case, the `zip` attribute in the Updategram maps to the `postalCode` column in the `Customer` table).

We can also specify that element values are to be used for the individual data fields. The following example (`Insert3.xml`) uses elements with text values for the Updategram:

```
<ROOT xmlns:updg="urn:schemas-microsoft-com:xml-updategram">
    <updg:sync mapping-schema="customerElementSchema.xsd">
        <updg:after>
            <Customer>
                <customerID>3</customerID>
                <name>Bert T. Vogts</name>
                <address1>52 Hampden Terrace</address1>
                <city>Greentown</city>
                <state>FL</state>
                <zip>27651</zip>
            </Customer>
        </updg:after>
    </updg:sync>
</ROOT>
```

In this case, the mapping schema (`customerElementSchema.xsd`) would look like the following:

```
<xsd:schema xmlns:xsd="http://www.w3.org/2001/XMLSchema"
            xmlns:sql="urn:schemas-microsoft-com:mapping-schema">
    <xsd:element name="Customer"
                 sql:relation="Customer"
                 sql:key-fields="customerID">
        <xsd:complexType>
            <xsd:sequence>
                <xsd:element name="customerID"
                             sql:field="customerID"
                             type="xsd:integer" />
                <xsd:element name="name"
                             sql:field="customerName"
                             type="xsd:string" />
                <xsd:element name="address1"
                             sql:field="address1"
                             type="xsd:string" />
                <xsd:element name="address2"
                             sql:field="address2"
                             type="xsd:string"
                             minOccurs="0" />
                <xsd:element name="city"
                             sql:field="city"
                             type="xsd:string" />
                <xsd:element name="state"
                             sql:field="state"
                             type="xsd:string" />
                <xsd:element name="zip"
                             sql:field="postalCode"
                             type="xsd:string" />
            </xsd:sequence>
        </xsd:complexType>
    </xsd:element>
</xsd:schema>
```

Inserting Multiple Rows

It is also possible to insert multiple rows at once with a single Updategram. To do so, simply include an element in the `<updg:after>` element of the Updategram for each new row to be added. The following Updategram (`MultiInsert.xml`) inserts three records into the `Customer` table:

```
<ROOT xmlns:updg="urn:schemas-microsoft-com:xml-updategram">
   <updg:sync mapping-schema="customerSchema.xsd">
      <updg:after>
         <Customer customerID="4"
                   name="Kevin B. Williams"
                   address1="762 Evergreen Terrace"
                   city="Springfield"
                   state="VA"
                   zip="27651" />
         <Customer customerID="5"
                   name="Joe Q. Somebody"
                   address1="100 Main Street"
                   city="Somewheretown"
                   state="VA"
                   zip="21827" />
         <Customer customerID="6"
                   name="James X. Anybody"
                   address1="200 Elm Street"
                   city="Anywhereville"
                   state="VA"
                   zip="29377" />
      </updg:after>
   </updg:sync>
</ROOT>
```

Because all three `<Customer>` elements appear within a single `<updg:sync>` element, the three updates are treated together as a single transaction. This means that if any one of the inserts fails (for example, if there is a customer 3 in the database already), all of them will be rolled back and none of the customer rows will be inserted. To make the three insertions individual transactions, you simply need to move each `<Customer>` element into its own `<updg:sync>` element:

```
<ROOT xmlns:updg="urn:schemas-microsoft-com:xml-updategram">
   <updg:sync mapping-schema="customerSchema.xsd">
      <updg:after>
         <Customer customerID="7"
                   name="Kevin B. Williams"
                   address1="762 Evergreen Terrace"
                   city="Springfield"
                   state="VA"
                   zip="27651" />
      </updg:after>
   </updg:sync>
```

```
         <updg:sync mapping-schema="customerSchema.xsd">
            <updg:after>
               <Customer customerID="8"
                         name="Joe Q. Somebody"
                         address1="100 Main Street"
                         city="Somewheretown"
                         state="VA"
                         zip="21827" />
            </updg:after>
         </updg:sync>
         <updg:sync mapping-schema="customerSchema.xsd">
            <updg:after>
               <Customer customerID="9"
                         name="James X. Anybody"
                         address1="200 Elm Street"
                         city="Anywhereville"
                         state="VA"
                         zip="29377" />
            </updg:after>
         </updg:sync>
</ROOT>
```

In this case, each insertion will be treated as a separate transaction.

> When records are inserted with an Updategram, all of the normal table constraints apply. Therefore, if a column that is not nullable does not have a value supplied in the Updategram, the Updategram will fail; similarly, if a value is provided that does not correspond to the column type in the target table, the Updategram will fail.

Deleting Data with an Updategram

To delete data with an Updategram, specify information about the deleted record in the `<updg:before>` block but omit the entire `<updg:after>` block. Or if other operations are being performed in the same `<updg:sync>` block, omit the element with the same key in the `<updg:after>` block. The record specified by `<updg:before>` must correspond exactly to one row in the table, and should be identified using at least a primary or alternate key to the table. For example, the following Updategram (`Delete1.xml`) deletes the customer with a `customerID` of 4 from the database (these examples use the `customerSchema.xsd` schema declaration from the previous section):

```
<ROOT xmlns:updg="urn:schemas-microsoft-com:xml-updategram">
   <updg:sync mapping-schema="customerSchema.xsd">
      <updg:before>
         <Customer customerID="4" />
      </updg:before>
   </updg:sync>
</ROOT>
```

Updategrams

If (for example) the `customerName` column is an alternate key to the `Customer` table, you can also issue the following Updategram (`Delete2.xml`) to delete the customer:

```xml
<ROOT xmlns:updg="urn:schemas-microsoft-com:xml-updategram">
    <updg:sync mapping-schema="customerSchema.xsd">
        <updg:before>
            <Customer name="Bert T. Vogts" />
        </updg:before>
    </updg:sync>
</ROOT>
```

However, if there are multiple rows in the `Customer` table that match the information specified in the `<Customer>` element, the Updategram will fail.

The preceding Updategrams perform **optimistic deletions**; that is, they delete the row regardless of the other information found in the row, as long as the key value provided matches. If you want to ensure that the information hasn't been modified between the time the row was identified and the time of deletion, you can provide all the information for the row in the element (`Delete3.xml`):

```xml
<ROOT xmlns:updg="urn:schemas-microsoft-com:xml-updategram">
    <updg:sync mapping-schema="customerSchema.xsd">
        <updg:before>
            <Customer
                customerID="7"
                name="Kevin B. Williams"
                address1="762 Evergreen Terrace"
                city="Springfield"
                state="VA"
                zip="27651" />
        </updg:before>
    </updg:sync>
</ROOT>
```

In this case, the Updategram processor will check to make sure that the row exactly matches the fields specified in the `<updg:before>` element before the deletion is performed. If another user has updated the information since the row was initially retrieved, the deletion will fail. A **pessimistic delete** operation, such as this one, is appropriate when you want to ensure that a record hasn't been updated since it was read (as in a multiple-user editing system); in single-user systems or other controlled environments, an optimistic delete will do the trick.

Deleting Multiple Rows

As with inserts, we can perform multiple deletions in a single Updategram. To perform the deletions as part of a single transaction, include all of them in the same `<updg:sync>` element:

Chapter 11

```xml
<ROOT xmlns:updg="urn:schemas-microsoft-com:xml-updategram">
    <updg:sync mapping-schema="customerSchema.xsd">
        <updg:before>
            <Customer customerID="8" />
            <Customer customerID="9" />
        </updg:before>
    </updg:sync>
</ROOT>
```

Or, to make them individual transactions, break them out into individual `<updg:sync>` elements:

```xml
<ROOT xmlns:updg="urn:schemas-microsoft-com:xml-updategram">
    <updg:sync mapping-schema="customerSchema.xsd">
        <updg:before>
            <Customer customerID="2" />
        </updg:before>
    </updg:sync>
    <updg:sync mapping-schema="customerSchema.xml">
        <updg:before>
            <Customer customerID="5" />
        </updg:before>
    </updg:sync>
    <updg:sync mapping-schema="customerSchema.xml">
        <updg:before>
            <Customer customerID="6" />
        </updg:before>
    </updg:sync>
</ROOT>
```

Updating Data with an Updategram

To update information in the database using an Updategram, simply specify both the `<updg:before>` and `<updg:after>` elements. For example, the following Updategram (`Update1.xml`) updates the name of the customer with customerID 1:

```xml
<ROOT xmlns:updg="urn:schemas-microsoft-com:xml-updategram">
    <updg:sync mapping-schema="customerSchema.xsd">
        <updg:before>
            <Customer customerID="1" />
        </updg:before>
        <updg:after>
            <Customer
                customerID="1"
                name="Kevin Y. Williams" />
        </updg:after>
    </updg:sync>
</ROOT>
```

Updategrams

Note that this update will be applied regardless of whether or not the row in the `Customer` table has been changed since the last time it was accessed. To perform a more pessimistic update, we can (as with deletions) provide more information in the `<updg:before>` element (Update2.xml):

```
<ROOT xmlns:updg="urn:schemas-microsoft-com:xml-updategram">
  <updg:sync mapping-schema="customerSchema.xsd">
    <updg:before>
        <Customer customerID="1"
                  name="Kevin Y. Williams"
                  address1="762 Evergreen Terrace"
                  city="Springfield"
                  state="VA"
                  zip="27651" />
    </updg:before>
    <updg:after>
      <Customer customerID="1"
                name="Kevin B. Williams" />
    </updg:after>
  </updg:sync>
</ROOT>
```

In this case, all the information in the row will be matched against the information provided in the `<updg:before>` element before the update is applied.

Note that the `customerSchema.xsd` annotated schema specifies that the `customerID` is the primary key for the `Customer` table. This information is used by the Updategram processor to identify corresponding records in the `<updg:before>` and `<updg:after>` elements, to pair them up for updates. Make sure your primary keys match up. Suppose we issued the following Updategram (Update3.xml) instead:

```
<ROOT xmlns:updg="urn:schemas-microsoft-com:xml-updategram">
  <updg:sync mapping-schema="customerSchema.xsd">
    <updg:before>
        <Customer customerID="1" />
    </updg:before>
    <updg:after>
      <Customer customerID="2"
                name="Joe Q. Somebody"
                address1="100 Main Street"
                city="Somewheretown"
                state="VA"
                zip="21827" />
    </updg:after>
  </updg:sync>
</ROOT>
```

This Updategram would be treated as a single deletion (of the customer with `customerID` of 1) and a single insertion (of the customer with `customerID` of 2).

> **For updates, it's vitally important that the elements in the `<updg:before>` block match up with elements in the `<updg:after>` block.**

It's also important to provide the `sql:key-fields` annotation in the annotated schema; without it, the processor cannot determine when an update is being performed (as opposed to a delete-insert pair), and thus may inadvertently lose some information (because of a cascade delete constraint or update triggers).

Explicitly Relating Records

If you have not specified a mapping schema, or the mapping schema does not define the primary keys for records, you can explicitly relate the records in the update using the `updg:id` attribute. Records identified with the `updg:id` attribute in both the `<updg:before>` and `<updg:after>` elements are assumed to be a pair constituting a single update operation. For example, in the following Updategram (Relate1.xml), `updg:id` is used to pair multiple `Customer` records together (if you are trying out the code, you will need to run Insert1.xml again first to repopulate the database):

```
<ROOT xmlns:updg="urn:schemas-microsoft-com:xml-updategram">
  <updg:sync mapping-schema="customerSchema.xsd">
    <updg:before>
      <Customer updg:id="c1"
                customerID="1" />
      <Customer updg:id="c2"
                customerID="2" />
    </updg:before>
    <updg:after>
      <Customer updg:id="c1"
                name="Kevin B. Williams" />
      <Customer updg:id="c2"
                zip="23579" />
    </updg:after>
  </updg:sync>
</ROOT>
```

Note that we didn't need to specify the `customerID` attribute in the `<updg:after><Customer>` elements; the elements are related back to the `<updg:before>` elements by the matching `updg:id` values. This Updategram updates the name of the customer with `customerID=1` to be `Kevin B. Williams` and the zip of the customer with `customerID=2` to be `23579`.

> Whether you choose to specify the `updg:id` value directly or rely on the annotated schema to inform the Updategram of these relations is up to you – I prefer to do both, just to make sure that there are no unintended consequences when the Updategram is applied.

Explicitly Relating Before and After

If you prefer, you can instead explicitly relate before and after records. This is done by including multiple `<updg:before>` and `<updg:after>` elements within a single `<updg:sync>` element. When you do this, each pair of `<updg:before>` and `<updg:after>` elements is treated as a set. For example, the following Updategram (`Relate2.xml`) explicitly relates the two updates from the previous example:

```
<ROOT xmlns:updg="urn:schemas-microsoft-com:xml-updategram">
  <updg:sync>
    <updg:before>
       <Customer customerID="1" />
    </updg:before>
    <updg:after>
       <Customer customerName="Kevin B. Williams" />
    </updg:after>
    <updg:before>
       <Customer customerID="2" />
    </updg:before>
    <updg:after>
       <Customer postalCode="12345" />
    </updg:after>
  </updg:sync>
</ROOT>
```

Note that we don't have to specify `updg:id` here, as there is only one possible record in each `<updg:before>` and `<updg:after>` pair that can be processed. The Updategram processor knows that the name update in the first pair corresponds to the customer with a `customerID` of 1, and the `postalCode` update in the second pair corresponds to the customer with a `customerID` of 2.

As with insertions and deletions, all operations that take place within a single `<updg:sync>` element are treated as a single transaction. To apply these updates as separate transactions, move them into individual `<updg:sync>` elements.

Multiple Actions Within One Updategram

The real power of Updategrams lies in their ability to easily insert or update multiple records in the database in one transaction. Let's take a look at a slightly more complex example. Say you had the following table definitions in your database (`tableCreation.sql`):

```
CREATE TABLE Customer (
   customerID int PRIMARY KEY NOT NULL,
   customerName varchar(100) NOT NULL,
   address1 varchar(100) NOT NULL,
   address2 varchar(100) NULL,
   city varchar(50) NOT NULL,
```

Chapter 11

```
    state char(2) NOT NULL,
    postalCode varchar(10) NOT NULL)

CREATE TABLE Invoice (
    invoiceID int PRIMARY KEY NOT NULL,
    customerID int REFERENCES Customer (customerID)
      ON DELETE CASCADE
      ON UPDATE CASCADE,
    invoiceDate datetime NOT NULL,
    invoiceAmount decimal(9,2) NOT NULL)
```

We would like to be able to insert records into both the Customer and Invoice tables in one Updategram; we plan to represent the relationship between Customer and Invoice using a parent-child relationship. The first step is to create the appropriate annotated XML schema for the Updategram structure we want to use (customerSchema2.xsd):

```
<xsd:schema xmlns:xsd="http://www.w3.org/2001/XMLSchema"
            xmlns:sql="urn:schemas-microsoft-com:mapping-schema">
  <xsd:element name="Customer"
               sql:relation="Customer"
               sql:key-fields="customerID">
    <xsd:complexType>
      <xsd:sequence>
        <xsd:element name="Invoice"
                     maxOccurs="unbounded"
                     sql:relation="Invoice"
                     sql:key-fields="invoiceID">
          <xsd:annotation>
            <xsd:appinfo>
              <sql:relationship parent="Customer"
                                parent-key="customerID"
                                child="Invoice"
                                child-key="customerID" />
            </xsd:appinfo>
          </xsd:annotation>
          <xsd:complexType>
            <xsd:attribute name="invoiceID"
                           sql:field="invoiceID"
                           type="xsd:integer" />
            <xsd:attribute name="invoiceDate"
                           sql:field="invoiceDate"
                           type="xsd:dateTime" />
            <xsd:attribute name="invoiceAmount"
                           sql:field="invoiceAmount"
                           type="xsd:decimal" />
          </xsd:complexType>
        </xsd:element>
      </xsd:sequence>
      <xsd:attribute name="customerID"
                     sql:field="customerID"
                     type="xsd:integer" />
```

Updategrams

```
            <xsd:attribute name="name"
                           sql:field="customerName"
                           type="xsd:string" />
            <xsd:attribute name="address1"
                           sql:field="address1"
                           type="xsd:string"
                           use="required" />
            <xsd:attribute name="address2"
                           sql:field="address2"
                           type="xsd:string" />
            <xsd:attribute name="city"
                           sql:field="city"
                           type="xsd:string"
                           use="required" />
            <xsd:attribute name="state"
                           sql:field="state"
                           type="xsd:string"
                           use="required" />
            <xsd:attribute name="zip"
                           sql:field="postalCode"
                           type="xsd:string"
                           use="required" />
        </xsd:complexType>
    </xsd:element>
</xsd:schema>
```

Note that we have specified the relationship between the `Customer` table and the `Invoice` table using the `<sql:relationship>` element. We have also indicated which fields are the key fields in both the `Customer` and `Invoice` tables.

The following Updategram (`MultiAction1.xml`) inserts a `Customer` and a pair of `Invoices` using our schema:

```
<ROOT xmlns:updg="urn:schemas-microsoft-com:xml-updategram">
    <updg:sync mapping-schema="customerSchema2.xsd">
        <updg:after>
            <Customer customerID="3"
                      name="Kevin B. Williams"
                      address1="762 Evergreen Terrace"
                      city="Springfield"
                      state="VA"
                      zip="27651">
                <Invoice invoiceID="1"
                         invoiceDate="2002-06-17"
                         invoiceAmount="182.22" />
                <Invoice invoiceID="2"
                         invoiceDate="2002-07-12"
                         invoiceAmount="201.47" />
            </Customer>
        </updg:after>
    </updg:sync>
</ROOT>
```

Chapter 11

Because information about the relationship between `Customer` and `Invoice` is specified in the mapping schema, the Updategram processor determines that it needs to set the `customerID` on the inserted `Invoice` rows to match the `customerID` specified for the `Customer` being inserted. This Updategram inserts a single row into the `Customer` table, and two rows into the `Invoice` table related to the initial customer.

While the behavior of Updategrams is straightforward for inserts and deletions, for updates a little more care is required. Say that we have a customer with `customerID` of 3 already in the database, and that customer has invoices 1 and 2 associated with it. What happens when the following Updategram (`MultiAction2.xml`) is executed?

```
<ROOT xmlns:updg="urn:schemas-microsoft-com:xml-updategram">
    <updg:sync mapping-schema="customerSchema2.xsd">
      <updg:before>
        <Customer customerID="3" />
      </updg:before>
      <updg:after>
        <Customer customerID="3"
                  name="Kevin B. Williams"
                  address1="762 Evergreen Terrace"
                  city="Springfield"
                  state="VA"
                  zip="27651">
           <Invoice invoiceID="3"
                    invoiceDate="2002-08-22"
                    invoiceAmount="104.33" />
        </Customer>
      </updg:after>
    </updg:sync>
</ROOT>
```

You might think that the set of `Invoice` rows associated with the customer would be deleted and replaced with the new set of `Invoice` rows, but that's not the case. Instead, this Updategram updates the `Customer` data based on the `<Customer>` element provided, and then inserts invoice 3 and associates it with this customer. If you want to replace all the `Invoice` records (assuming you have the foreign key in `Invoice` set to `ON DELETE CASCADE`), you can do so by splitting the update up into a delete followed by an insert (`MultiAction3.xml`):

```
<ROOT xmlns:updg="urn:schemas-microsoft-com:xml-updategram">
    <updg:sync mapping-schema="customerSchema2.xsd">
      <updg:before>
        <Customer customerID="3" />
      </updg:before>
      <updg:after>
      </updg:after>
      <updg:before>
      </updg:before>
      <updg:after>
```

```
            <Customer customerID="3"
                    name="Kevin B. Williams"
                    address1="762 Evergreen Terrace"
                    city="Springfield"
                    state="VA"
                    zip="27651">
                <Invoice invoiceID="3"
                        invoiceDate="2002-08-22"
                        invoiceAmount="104.33" />
            </Customer>
        </updg:after>
    </updg:sync>
</ROOT>
```

The first `<updg:before>` and `<updg:after>` will be treated as a single operation. Since the `<updg:after>` in the first pair is empty, the operation will be treated as a deletion. In this case, the customer with `customerID` of 1 will be deleted, and the ON DELETE CASCADE constraint will cause all of the Invoice rows associated with `customerID` 1 to be deleted as well. Next, the second pair is processed. Since the `<updg:before>` in the second pair is empty, the second operation is treated as an insertion. The customer with `customerID` 1 is inserted back into the database, and then the single invoice row provided is associated with that customer. This shows how structured information in an Updategram is transformed into parent-child relationships in the resulting data.

Note that there is a slight performance hit when using Updategrams rather than direct T-SQL commands or ADO record methods. This is because the processor must read the Updategram and the annotated schema (if one is provided) and convert the XML payloads into INSERT, UPDATE, and DELETE statements that will then be applied to the database. However, in most cases this performance hit is minimal compared to the time required to actually modify the data.

Capturing Identity Values for Inserted Records

In our examples so far, we've been using manually created primary keys; however, most database tables have auto generated identity columns for primary keys. Updategrams provide a mechanism for using the identity value created during the row creation process.

We can change our table definitions slightly to include auto generated identity columns, for the following examples (`recreateTables.sql`):

```
DROP TABLE Invoice
DROP TABLE Customer
GO

CREATE TABLE Customer (
    customerID int PRIMARY KEY IDENTITY NOT NULL,
```

Chapter 11

```
            customerName varchar(100) NOT NULL,
            address1 varchar(100) NOT NULL,
            address2 varchar(100) NULL,
            city varchar(50) NOT NULL,
            state char(2) NOT NULL,
            postalCode varchar(10) NOT NULL)

         CREATE TABLE Invoice (
            invoiceID int PRIMARY KEY IDENTITY NOT NULL,
            customerID int REFERENCES Customer (customerID)
              ON DELETE CASCADE
              ON UPDATE CASCADE,
            invoiceDate datetime NOT NULL,
            invoiceAmount decimal(9,2) NOT NULL)
```

If you have properly defined the key fields in the annotated XML Schema associated with your Updategram, the Updategram processor will create the identity value for the inserted `Customer` row. The main difference is that you do not supply the value for the inserted row in the Updategram. In order for this to work properly, we need to modify the annotated schema slightly (`customerSchema3.xsd`):

```xml
<xsd:schema xmlns:xsd="http://www.w3.org/2001/XMLSchema"
            xmlns:sql="urn:schemas-microsoft-com:mapping-schema">
  <xsd:element name="Customer"
               sql:relation="Customer"
               sql:key-fields="customerID">
    <xsd:complexType>
      <xsd:sequence>
        <xsd:element name="Invoice"
                     maxOccurs="unbounded"
                     sql:relation="Invoice"
                     sql:key-fields="invoiceID">
          <xsd:annotation>
            <xsd:appinfo>
              <sql:relationship parent="Customer"
                                parent-key="customerID"
                                child="Invoice"
                                child-key="customerID" />
            </xsd:appinfo>
          </xsd:annotation>
          <xsd:complexType>
            <xsd:attribute name="invoiceID"
                           sql:field="invoiceID"
                           type="xsd:integer"
                           sql:identity="ignore" />
            <xsd:attribute name="invoiceDate"
                           sql:field="invoiceDate"
                           type="xsd:dateTime" />
            <xsd:attribute name="invoiceAmount"
                           sql:field="invoiceAmount"
                           type="xsd:decimal" />
```

Updategrams

```xml
            </xsd:complexType>
          </xsd:element>
        </xsd:sequence>
        <xsd:attribute name="customerID"
                       sql:field="customerID"
                       type="xsd:integer"
                       sql:identity="ignore" />
        <xsd:attribute name="name"
                       sql:field="customerName"
                       type="xsd:string" />
        <xsd:attribute name="address1"
                       sql:field="address1"
                       type="xsd:string"
                       use="required" />
        <xsd:attribute name="address2"
                       sql:field="address2"
                       type="xsd:string" />
        <xsd:attribute name="city"
                       sql:field="city"
                       type="xsd:string"
                       use="required" />
        <xsd:attribute name="state"
                       sql:field="state"
                       type="xsd:string"
                       use="required" />
        <xsd:attribute name="zip"
                       sql:field="postalCode"
                       type="xsd:string"
                       use="required" />
      </xsd:complexType>
    </xsd:element>
</xsd:schema>
```

The `sql:identity` attribute on the `customerID` attribute declaration in the `Customer` table and the `invoiceID` attribute declaration in the `Invoice` table instruct the Updategram processor to ignore any value provided by the Updategram, and instead to generate a new identity value according to SQL Server's identity rules.

The following Updategram (`Identity1.xml`) inserts a new customer and a pair of invoices, as in the previous section, using the annotated schema shown above:

```xml
<ROOT xmlns:updg="urn:schemas-microsoft-com:xml-updategram">
   <updg:sync mapping-schema="customerSchema3.xsd">
     <updg:after>
       <Customer
           updg:at-identity="x"
           name="Kevin B. Williams"
           address1="762 Evergreen Terrace"
           city="Springfield"
           state="VA"
           zip="27651">
         <Invoice
            customerID="x"
```

313

```
                invoiceDate="2002-06-17"
                invoiceAmount="182.22" />
         <Invoice
                customerID="x"
                invoiceDate="2002-07-12"
                invoiceAmount="201.47" />
      </Customer>
    </updg:after>
  </updg:sync>
</ROOT>
```

Note that we have to use the **updg:at-identity** attribute to ensure that the created identity value is propagated downward into the related tables – the processor is not able to capture this identity value directly. This attribute assigns the created identity value to a placeholder (in this case, "x"), which can then be used to set the foreign key value in the child tables.

When this Updategram is applied, the `customerID` and `invoiceID` values are automatically generated by the Updategram processor. Also, the `customerID` foreign key value in the `Invoice` rows is set to match the value created for the customer rows (because it is captured using `updg:at-identity`).

If you use `updg:at-identity` to catch the created identity value for a particular row, you can use the **updg:returnid** attribute on the `<updg:after>` element to specify that you would like the identity values that were created to be returned in response to the Updategram. This makes it possible for code to remember the ID of a created row (for use in a later update, perhaps). Consider the following example:

```
<ROOT xmlns:updg="urn:schemas-microsoft-com:xml-updategram">
  <updg:sync mapping-schema="customerSchema2.xsd">
    <updg:after updg:returnid="insertedCustomerID
                               firstInvoiceID secondInvoiceID">
      <Customer updg:at-identity="insertedCustomerID"
                name="Kevin B. Williams"
                address1="762 Evergreen Terrace"
                city="Springfield"
                state="VA"
                zip="27651">
         <Invoice updg:at-identity="firstInvoiceID"
                invoiceDate="2002-06-17"
                invoiceAmount="182.22" />
         <Invoice updg:at-identity="secondInvoiceID"
                invoiceDate="2002-07-12"
                invoiceAmount="201.47" />
      </Customer>
    </updg:after>
  </updg:sync>
</ROOT>
```

When this Updategram is processed, it will return the following XML result:

```
<ROOT xmlns:updg="urn:schemas-microsoft-com:xml-Updategram">
  <returnid>
    <insertedCustomerID>2</insertedCustomerID>
    <firstInvoiceID>3</firstInvoiceID>
    <secondInvoiceID>4</secondInvoiceID>
  </returnid>
</ROOT>
```

This result can then be processed, and the inserted identity values extracted from it for further processing later.

Inverse Relationships in an Updategram

Sometimes you may encounter a relationship in an Updategram that is reversed; that is, the parent-child relationship in the Updategram is in the opposite direction from the relationship in the database. For example, take the `Customer` and `Invoice` tables defined previously. However, our invoicing system might already have the information represented starting at the invoice level, with the `<Customer>` element as a child of `<Invoice>`. We might want to issue an Updategram (Inverse.xml) that looks like the following:

```
<ROOT xmlns:updg="urn:schemas-microsoft-com:xml-updategram">
    <updg:sync mapping-schema="customerSchema4.xsd">
      <updg:after>
          <Invoice customerID="x"
                   invoiceDate="2002-06-17"
                   invoiceAmount="182.22">
              <Customer updg:at-identity="x"
                        name="Kevin B. Williams"
                        address1="762 Evergreen Terrace"
                        city="Springfield"
                        state="VA"
                        zip="27651" />
          </Invoice>
      </updg:after>
    </updg:sync>
</ROOT>
```

In this case, the `<Customer>` information is a child of the `<Invoice>` information; but in our database, the `Customer` information is the parent of the `Invoice` information, which is reflected in the schema we need to use. To handle this Updategram properly, we need a new annotated XML schema, with the parent-child relationship reversed. It also includes the **sql:inverse** attribute in the `<sql:relationship>` element (call it `customerSchema4.xsd`):

Chapter 11

```xml
<xsd:schema xmlns:xsd="http://www.w3.org/2001/XMLSchema"
            xmlns:sql="urn:schemas-microsoft-com:mapping-schema">
  <xsd:element name="Invoice"
               sql:relation="Invoice"
               sql:key-fields="invoiceID">
    <xsd:complexType>
      <xsd:sequence>
        <xsd:element name="Customer"
                     sql:relation="Customer"
                     sql:key-fields="CustomerID">
          <xsd:annotation>
            <xsd:appinfo>
              <sql:relationship parent="Invoice"
                                parent-key="customerID"
                                child="Customer"
                                child-key="customerID"
                                inverse="true" />
            </xsd:appinfo>
          </xsd:annotation>
          <xsd:complexType>
          <xsd:attribute name="customerID"
                         sql:field="customerID"
                         type="xsd:integer"
                         sql:identity="ignore" />
          <xsd:attribute name="name"
                         sql:field="customerName"
                         type="xsd:string" />
          <xsd:attribute name="address1"
                         sql:field="address1"
                         type="xsd:string"
                         use="required" />
          <xsd:attribute name="address2"
                         sql:field="address2"
                         type="xsd:string" />
          <xsd:attribute name="city"
                         sql:field="city"
                         type="xsd:string"
                         use="required" />
          <xsd:attribute name="state"
                         sql:field="state"
                         type="xsd:string"
                         use="required" />
          <xsd:attribute name="zip"
                         sql:field="postalCode"
                         type="xsd:string"
                         use="required" />
          </xsd:complexType>
        </xsd:element>
      </xsd:sequence>
      <xsd:attribute name="invoiceID"
                     sql:field="invoiceID"
                     type="xsd:integer"
                     sql:identity="ignore" />
```

Updategrams

```
        <xsd:attribute name="invoiceDate"
                       sql:field="invoiceDate"
                       type="xsd:dateTime" />
        <xsd:attribute name="invoiceAmount"
                       sql:field="invoiceAmount"
                       type="xsd:decimal" />
    </xsd:complexType>
  </xsd:element>
</xsd:schema>
```

By specifying the `sql:inverse` attribute as True in the relationship, we are indicating that the relationship needs to be inverted before the information is inserted into the database. When this Updategram is applied, the processor will first insert a record into the Customer table, and then into the Invoice table (with the customerID set to the appropriate value for the inserted record).

> Note that care has to be taken when issuing Updategrams this way – for example, if the customer already exists this Updategram will create a new customer with a different `customerID`.

Creating GUIDs as Part of an Updategram

If you want to create a Globally Unique Identifier, or GUID, for a record, you can do so in an Updategram using the **updg:guid** attribute. You might want to use a GUID when you have a piece of information that needs to retain its own unique identity no matter where it appears (as opposed to a simple identity key, which only ensures uniqueness on a particular table). When you specify this attribute on an element, you indicate that a GUID should be created and assigned to the placeholder defined in the attribute. You can then use that value in the actual attributes of the element being inserted. Let's see an example. Suppose you had the following table in your database (Handler.sql):

```
CREATE TABLE Handler (
   handlerGUID uniqueidentifier PRIMARY KEY NOT NULL,
   handlerName varchar(100) NOT NULL)
```

To insert a new row into the Handler table, you could use the following Updategram (Guid.xml):

```
<ROOT xmlns:updg="urn:schemas-microsoft-com:xml-updategram">
  <updg:sync>
    <updg:after>
      <Handler updg:guid="createdGUID"
               handlerGUID="createdGUID"
               handlerName="CustomerHandler" />
    </updg:after>
  </updg:sync>
</ROOT>
```

The GUID will be automatically created and inserted into the new Handler row.

317

Chapter 11

Like `updg:at-identity`, using `updg:return-id` can return the value created by `updg:guid`. For example, if we change the Updategram (`Guid2.xml`) as follows:

```
<ROOT xmlns:updg="urn:schemas-microsoft-com:xml-updategram">
  <updg:sync>
    <updg:after updg:returnid="createdGUID">
      <Handler updg:guid="createdGUID"
               handlerGUID="createdGUID"
               handlerName="CustomerHandler" />
    </updg:after>
  </updg:sync>
</ROOT>
```

When the Updategram is applied now, the following response will be returned:

```
<ROOT xmlns:updg="urn:schemas-microsoft-com:xml-Updategram">
  <returnid>
    <createdGUID>F00DIBAD-8F7D-2A33-87DC17F9C98A</createdGUID>
  </returnid>
</ROOT>
```

Generating Updategrams "on-the-fly"

One useful technique when working with Updategrams is to create them as needed. Since Updategrams are XML, if the source of the information for an Updategram is also available as XML, it may make sense to create the Updategram using a technology like XSLT. Let's take a look at an example. Say we have a web service that inserts a customer. It delivers the following message fragment as part of its SOAP payload (`Fragment.xml`):

```
<NewCustomer>
  <name>Kevin R. Williams</name>
  <address1>762 Evergreen Terrace</address1>
  <city>Springfield</city>
  <state>VA</state>
  <zip>12345</zip>
</NewCustomer>
```

For more on web services and SOAP, see Chapter 14.

We know from the preceding discussion that we'd like to have a document that looks like the following:

```
<ROOT xmlns:updg="urn:schemas-microsoft-com:xml-updategram">
  <updg:sync mapping-schema="customerElementSchema.xsd">
    <updg:after>
      <Customer>
        <customerID>4</customerID>
        <name>Kevin R. Williams</name>
        <address1>762 Evergreen Terrace</address1>
        <city>Springfield</city>
        <state>VA</state>
        <zip>12345</zip>
```

```
            </Customer>
          </updg:after>
      </updg:sync>
</ROOT>
```

Using an XSLT stylesheet (`style.xslt`), we can easily transform the first form into the second:

```
<xsl:stylesheet
    xmlns:xsl="http://www.w3.org/1999/XSL/Transform"
                                                    version="1.0">
    <xsl:template match="NewCustomer">
    <ROOT xmlns:updg="urn:schemas-microsoft-com:xml-updategram">
        <updg:sync mapping-schema="customerElementSchema.xsd">
          <updg:after>
            <Customer>
                <name><xsl:value-of select="name" /></name>
                <address1><xsl:value-of select="address" />
                </address1>
                <city><xsl:value-of select="city" /></city>
                <state><xsl:value-of select="state" /></state>
                <zip><xsl:value-of select="zip" /></zip>
            </Customer>
          </updg:after>
      </updg:sync>
</ROOT>
    </xsl:template>
</xsl:stylesheet>
```

Applying the XSLT to the incoming payload and then applying the resulting Updategram can result in less code than decomposing the incoming payload and translating it into T-SQL commands directly. We can plug these files into the application in Appendix C to see the transformation in action.

Applying Updategrams to a Database

We've spent most of the chapter discussing the creation of Updategrams. Next, let's see how these Updategrams may be applied against a database.

Applying an Updategram Using HTTP

Updategrams may be applied to a database using HTTP. To do so, you must first set up a virtual directory using the IIS Virtual Directory Management for SQL Server utility (see Chapter 2 for more information on how to do this). Any HTTP requests made to that virtual directory will be handled by the SQL ISAPI handler, and the Updategram will be applied against the database. In the case of a `POST` request, the Updategram must be sent in the body of the HTTP message, either "bare," or as a value in the form `template="..."`; in the case of a `GET` request, the Updategram appears in the URL as a filename or as a value in the form `http://localhost/VirDirName?template="..."`. This enables us to submit Updategrams either from an HTML form or directly. Let's look at examples of each.

Chapter 11

Applying an Updategram from a URL

Once our virtual directory is set up to accept URL queries, we can submit an Updategram as a whole URL. To do so, simply type the following URL query (URL.txt) as one continuous line into the address bar on your browser:

```
http://localhost/VirDirName?template=<ROOT
xmlns:updg="urn:schemas-microsoft-com:xml-updategram">
  <updg:sync>
    <updg:after>
      <Customer
        customerID="4"
        customerName="William Kevins"
        address1="92 Deciduous Avenue"
        city="Perth"
        state="WA"
        postalCode="27651" />
    </updg:after>
  </updg:sync>
</ROOT>
```

This will return the following in the browser, with the database being updated with the new customer record accordingly:

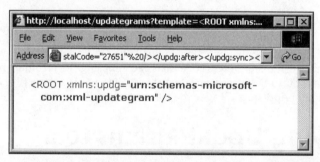

> Remember that allowing this to occur is extremely insecure. You should only allow URL queries to be used in an environment where you can be completely sure no one will use them maliciously, such as a firewall-protected intranet or on a well-secured development server. For more on this, see Chapter 5.

Applying Updategrams from Templates

A more secure approach to Updategrams is to store them on a web server as XML templates. These can then be run by users by either typing the URL into the browser, or from HTML links or buttons on forms. In this way, unscrupulous users can be prevented from applying unapproved Updategrams to a database.

To set up an Updategram as a template, simply store it as an XML file in a virtual directory with a virtual name configured to use the template type. You will also need to save your annotated schemas in the virtual directory to enable your Updategrams to work.

Updategrams

The instructions for running the Updategrams we've seen so far in the chapter are included in the README.txt file in the code download, along with all the Updategrams saved as XML files (ready to be used as templates), and the schemas.

Still more secure is to store Updategrams in the form of an XML template with parameters, and only allow the parameters themselves to be passed in over HTTP. Again, see Chapter 5 for examples of how to pass parameters into templates.

Applying Updategrams From HTML Forms

As well as running template Updategrams by typing in URLs in the browser, we can also run them from HTML forms. To apply an Updategram from an HTML form, the typical approach is to set the form action to call the template with the POST method.

> To do this you will need to ensure that your virtual directory has Allow Post checked. As we learned in Chapter 5, this has similar security implications to allowing URL queries, so posting should not be allowed in an insecure environment either.

The template may include parameter definitions; references to these parameters will be substituted for other values on the form when the `SQLISAPI.DLL` handler processes the form submission to the SQL Server virtual directory. For example, we might have the following HTML form (`Form.html`):

```html
<head>
    <title>Customer Name Update</title>
</head>
<body>
Provide the customer ID and the new name for the customer.
<form action="http://localhost/VirDirName/DirName/form.xml"
      method="POST">
    <b>Employee ID Number:</b>
    <input type="text" name="customerID" />
    <br />
    <b>New name:</b>
    <input type="text" name="customerName" />
    <input type="hidden" name="contenttype" value="text/xml">
        <p><input type="submit" /></p>
    </form>
</body>
</html>
```

that submits its values to the following Updategram, stored as a template alongside the `customerSchema2.xsd` schema we created earlier:

```xml
<ROOT xmlns:updg="urn:schemas-microsoft-com:xml-updategram">
    <updg:header>
        <updg:param name="customerID"/>
        <updg:param name="customerName" />
    </updg:header>
    <updg:sync mapping-schema="customerSchema2.xsd">
```

321

```
      <updg:before>
        <Customer customerID="$customerID" />
      </updg:before>
      <updg:after>
        <Customer customerID="$customerID"
                  name="$customerName" />
      </updg:after>
    </updg:sync>
</ROOT>
```

When this form is submitted from a browser to the template-enabled virtual directory, the Updategram looks for values for the two parameters `customerName` and `customerID` in the list of name-value pairs supplied with the form; it then takes those values and substitutes them into the Updategram. The Updategram is then applied against the database, updating the customer with the supplied ID to have the new name provided.

Note that you will have to allow nulls in all but `customerID` and `customerName` fields for this to work.

Applying an Updategram Directly Using HTTP Post

You can also apply an Updategram programmatically using `HTTP Post`. In this invocation method, the Updategram is simply passed as the body of an `HTTP Post` request that provides the `HTTP Post` enabled virtual directory of the database as the URL. To apply an Updategram against a virtual directory on `localhost` called `VirDirName`, you can issue the following `HTTP Post` request:

```
POST http://localhost/VirDirName HTTP/1.1
Content-Type: text/xml

<ROOT xmlns:updg="urn:schemas-microsoft-com:xml-Updategram">
  <updg:sync mapping-schema="customerSchema.xml">
    <updg:before>
      <Customer customerID="1" />
    </updg:before>
    <updg:after>
      <Customer customerID="1"
                name="Kevin B. Williams" />
    </updg:after>
  </updg:sync>
</ROOT>
```

When this request is processed by `SQLISAPI.DLL`, the customer with `customerID=1` is updated to reflect the new name provided for that customer.

The following VB code (`HttpPostUpdategram.vbp`) performs the `Http Post` submission using the `xmlHttp` object included with the MSXML libraries. In Visual Basic 6.0, open a new standard EXE, make a reference to `msxml3.dll`, and modify the following code to suit your server:

```
Private Sub Form_Load()
   Dim objHttp As New MSXML2.XMLHTTP
   Dim mydoc As New MSXML2.DOMDocument

Dim sUpdategram As String

sUpdategram = "<ROOT " & _
"xmlns:updg='urn:schemas-microsoft-com:xml-updategram'>"
sUpdategram = sUpdategram & "<updg:sync>"
sUpdategram = sUpdategram & "<updg:before>"
sUpdategram = sUpdategram & "<Customer "
sUpdategram = sUpdategram & "customerID='1' />"
sUpdategram = sUpdategram & "</updg:before>"
sUpdategram = sUpdategram & "<updg:after>"
sUpdategram = sUpdategram & "<Customer "
sUpdategram = sUpdategram & "customerID='1' "
sUpdategram = sUpdategram & "customerName=" & _
                            "'Kevin Q. Williams' />"
sUpdategram = sUpdategram & "</updg:after>"
sUpdategram = sUpdategram & "</updg:sync>"
sUpdategram = sUpdategram & "</ROOT>"

   ' Load the template into the document

   mydoc.loadXML sUpdategram

   ' Post the template
   objHttp.Open "POST", "http://localhost/VirDirName", False
   objHttp.setRequestHeader "Content-type", "application/xml"
   objHttp.send mydoc

   MsgBox objHttp.responseText

End Sub
```

Applying an Updategram Using ADO

An Updategram may also be applied directly against the database using ADO. To do so, we simply need to set the command dialect of our ADO Command object to be the MSSQLXML command dialect – this GUID has the value "{5d531cb2-e6ed-11d2-b252-00c04f681b71}" for MSXML 4.0. The following VB 6.0 code (`AdoUpdategram.vbp`) shows us how to apply an Updategram via ADO. if you create a Standard EXE yourself, remember to reference MSXML 3.0 and MDAC 2.7 in your project references:

```
Private Sub Form_Load()

   Dim cmd As New ADODB.Command
   Dim conn As New ADODB.Connection
   Dim strmIn As New ADODB.Stream
   Dim strmOut As New ADODB.Stream

   conn.Provider = "SQLOLEDB"
   conn.Open "server=(local); database=chapter11db;" & _
             "Integrated Security='SSPI';"
   conn.Properties("SQLXML Version") = "SQLXML.3.0"
   Set cmd.ActiveConnection = conn
```

Chapter 11

```
        strmIn.Open
        strmIn.WriteText "<ROOT " & _
"xmlns:updg='urn:schemas-microsoft-com:xml-updategram'>"
        strmIn.WriteText " <updg:sync>"
        strmIn.WriteText "   <updg:before>"
        strmIn.WriteText "    <Customer "
        strmIn.WriteText "       customerID='1' />"
        strmIn.WriteText "   </updg:before>"
        strmIn.WriteText "   <updg:after>"
        strmIn.WriteText "     <Customer"
        strmIn.WriteText "        customerID='1'"
        strmIn.WriteText "        customerName='Kevin Z. Williams' />"
        strmIn.WriteText "   </updg:after>"
        strmIn.WriteText " </updg:sync>"
        strmIn.WriteText "</ROOT>"

        cmd.Dialect = "{5d531cb2-e6ed-11d2-b252-00c04f681b71}"
        strmIn.Position = 0
        Set cmd.CommandStream = strmIn

        strmOut.Open
        strmOut.LineSeparator = adCRLF
        cmd.Properties("Output Stream").Value = strmOut
        cmd.Execute , , adExecuteStream
        strmOut.Position = 0
        Debug.Print strmOut.ReadText
        strmOut.Close
        strmIn.Close
        conn.Close

    End Sub
```

Once this is done, we can apply the Updategram as if it were any other SQL statement using the ADO objects.

You can read more about using ADO to apply Updategrams in Chapter 13.

Summary

In this chapter, we've taken a look at the Updategrams facility in SQLXML. We've seen how, in conjunction with annotated schemas, it is possible to make many database changes with a single Updategram. We've also seen how Updategrams may be used to insert, update, and delete records; and how they handle identity and globally unique identifier columns. If you are receiving data in an XML format (such as the payload of a SOAP message), you may find that converting the data to an Updategram using a technology like XSLT and applying it against the database results in shorter, more efficient code than decomposing the XML payload and issuing individual insert, update, and delete statements against the database.

Updategrams

Andrew Novick

- Overview
- Creating the Schema
- Sample Script
- Properties of the SQLXMLBulkLoad Object
- Completing the Script and Running it in DTS
- Differences from Other Bulk Load Interfaces
- Summary

12

SQLXML Bulk Load

`SQLXMLBulkLoad`, a part of SQLXML, is a standalone COM object providing an interface to SQL Server's bulk loading capability. The object loads data contained in XML files into SQL Server in a highly efficient manner, using the same mapping technology as the rest of the SQLXML components. This COM component has been available since SQLXML 1.0 and has been refined for SQLXML 3.0, which we will discuss in this chapter.

SQL Server has long provided a Bulk Load interface. You may already be familiar with `BCP` or the `BULK INSERT` statement in T-SQL. `SQLXMLBulkLoad` has many of the same capabilities, but exposes them to the programmer in a slightly different way. Being an ActiveX control, the interface to `SQLXMLBulkLoad` is through a script language or compiled program.

This chapter covers:

- ❑ The process of bulk loading data using `SQLXMLBulkLoad`.
- ❑ Creating the input data file.
- ❑ Creating the input schema.
- ❑ Coding a script to execute a bulk load.
- ❑ A detailed look at each property and how the properties are used together.
- ❑ Bringing the properties together and show a complete script running in **Data Transformation Services** (**DTS**).
- ❑ How `SQLXMLBulkLoad` compares to other Bulk Load interfaces.
- ❑ A comparison to Updategrams.
- ❑ A comparison to `OPENXML`.

Let's begin with an overview of `SQLXMLBulkLoad`.

Chapter 12

Overview

The following diagram shows how a SQLXML Bulk Load works:

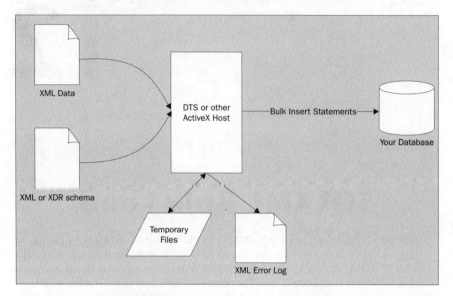

The objects in the diagram are:

- Everything starts with the **XML data** file. It contains the data that's going to be loaded into the SQL Server tables. It must conform to the XML Schema Recommendation.

- The **schema** is either an XML or an XDR annotated mapping schema that relates data in the XML file to the SQL Tables. While you may use either, XML schemas are becoming the schemas of choice and will be used throughout this chapter. Annotating XML schemas was covered in Chapter 6. There are a few annotations that are particularly relevant to SQLXMLBulkLoad. These are covered in this chapter.

- **DTS or other ActiveX Host** represents a program that's going to instantiate the SQLXMLBulkLoad component and execute it. More on your choice of hosts soon. The code must set all relevant properties then invoke the Execute method, passing the names of the XML schema file and XML file containing the data.

- When the bulk load is performed in transacted mode, SQLXMLBulkLoad uses the **Temporary Files** to store rows from each table before they are loaded into the database.

- During the course of the load, SQLXMLBulkLoad may produce error messages. These are saved to the **ErrorLogFile**, which is in an XML format.

- Finally, there is the database. The SQLXMLBulkLoad component communicates with the database using the same protocols that any ADO connection might use.

SQLXML Bulk Load

For the purpose of this chapter we'll be using VB Script that can be run in SQL Server DTS as an ActiveX Script Task. The same script could be run by the SQL Server Agent or by Windows Scripting Host. As an ActiveX component, SQLXMLBulkLoad can be used by any program that can host COM components, such as a compiled Visual Basic program, C++ program, or VBA application such as Microsoft Excel.

In this chapter there are two examples, one simple and the other more complex. Both examples are based on tables similar to the Customer and Invoice tables used in Chapters 6 and 7. As is common with Bulk Load, these are staging tables for the Customer and Invoice tables. Staging tables are used for quick loading, editing, and then migration to the production tables. They often have only a unique clustered index, if they have any indexes at all.

To start off the simple example, the following DDL script creates the BLCustomer and BLInvoice tables along with their relationship and a grant of all permissions to Public. You may want to adjust the permissions to suit your site:

```
CREATE TABLE BLCustomer (
    customerID int IDENTITY (1, 1) NOT NULL,
    name varchar (100) NULL ,
    address1 varchar (50) NULL ,
    address2 varchar (50) NULL ,
    city varchar (50) NULL ,
    state char (2) NULL ,
    postalCode varchar (10) NULL ,
    XMLOverflow varchar (2000) NULL ,
    CONSTRAINT PK_Customer PRIMARY KEY  CLUSTERED
    (customerID)  ON [PRIMARY]
) ON [PRIMARY]
GO

CREATE TABLE BLInvoice (
    customerID int NULL ,
    invoiceID int IDENTITY (1, 1) NOT NULL ,
    status char (1) NULL ,
    invoiceDate smalldatetime NOT NULL ,
    shipDate smalldatetime NULL ,
    invoiceAmount money NULL ,
    XMLOverFlow ntext NULL ,
    CONSTRAINT PK_BLInvoice PRIMARY KEY  CLUSTERED
    (invoiceID)  ON [PRIMARY]
) ON [PRIMARY] TEXTIMAGE_ON [PRIMARY]
GO

ALTER TABLE BLInvoice ADD
    CONSTRAINT FK_BLInvoice_BLCustomer FOREIGN KEY
        (customerID)
        REFERENCES [dbo].[BLCustomer] (customerID)
GO

GRANT REFERENCES , SELECT , UPDATE , INSERT , DELETE ON
BLCustomer TO public
GO

GRANT REFERENCES , SELECT , UPDATE , INSERT , DELETE ON
BLInvoice TO public
GO
```

Chapter 12

> You'll find the above script in the code download for this chapter (`TableCreationScript.sql`). To match the examples as closely as possible, create them in a database named `SQLXMLExamples`. If you'd prefer, they're already created in the `SQLXMLExamples_Data.MDF`, which can be attached to your server.

Let's say that we want to load an XML data file containing a customer list that the Marketing Department has exported from their Personal Information Manager (PIM), such as Microsoft Outlook or ACT. Receiving XML from a source that cannot be controlled is a common scenario for using `SQLXMLBulkLoad`. The following is the example file (`CustomerList.xml`):

```xml
<?xml version="1.0"?>
<CustomerList>
    <Customer customerID="1" customerName="Miles Archer"
        addressLine1="2345 Powell St."
        addressLine2="c/o Archer and Spade"
        addressLine3="Suite 200"
        city="San Francisco" state="CA" postalCode="99999"/>
    <Customer customerID="2"
        customerName="Herman Munster" taxid="213ABC"
        addressLine1="1313 Mockingbird Lane"
        city="Springfield" state="TX" postalCode="89823"/>
    <Customer customerID="3" customerName="Padme Amidala"
        addressLine1="Senate Office Building"
        city="Capitol City" state="NB"
        postalCode="NABOO-1234"/>
</CustomerList>
```

There are several differences between the XML schema implied by this data file, and both the database schema and the XML schema file that was used to extract data from the `Customer` table in Chapter 6. This is where the mapping schema and its annotations become important. The next section discusses the mapping. Following that, we'll start a script to do the bulk load.

Creating the Schema

The following schema was used to retrieve data from an XML View in Chapter 7:

```xml
<xsd:schema xmlns:xsd="http://www.w3.org/2001/XMLSchema">
    <xsd:element name="Customer">
        <xsd:complexType>
            <xsd:attribute name="customerName" type="xsd:string"
                           use="required" />
            <xsd:attribute name="address1" type="xsd:string"
                           use="required" />
            <xsd:attribute name="address2" type="xsd:string" />
            <xsd:attribute name="city" type="xsd:string"
                           use="required" />
            <xsd:attribute name="state" type="xsd:string"
                           use="required" />
            <xsd:attribute name="zip" type="xsd:string"
                           use="required" />
        </xsd:complexType>
    </xsd:element>
</xsd:schema>
```

SQLXML Bulk Load

To make this a realistic example of loading data into SQL Server, some simple changes are required. For starters, there are differences in field names. Most of the database columns in the example in Chapter 7 were mapped to XML fields with the same name. The XML data file above is different. For the address, the XML data file uses the names `addressLine1` and `addressLine2`, while the database and the XML schema shown above both use the names `address1` and `address2`. Another name difference is the use of the name `zip` instead of `postalCode`. In the original XML schema, `zip` became the attribute name when data was extracted. It's also the name used in the XML data file and it will have to be mapped back into `postalCode`.

To address the differences in names, annotations are added to the schema instructing it about the mapping between the XML data and the database. You'll recall that annotations are attributes added to schema elements from the namespace `schemas-microsoft-com:mapping-schema`. To add the namespace to our schema, a second `xmlns` attribute is added to the `<xsd:schema>` element at the root of the schema and it becomes:

```
<xsd:schema xmlns:xsd="http://www.w3.org/2001/XMLSchema"
    xmlns:sql="urn:schemas-microsoft-com:mapping-schema">
```

By convention this namespace is given the prefix `sql`. Once this namespace is part of the schema, annotations can be added to other schema elements to accomplish the renaming and other mapping tasks.

To map the address line elements to corresponding elements in the database, the `sql:field` attribute is added to the `<xsd:attribute>` element. The schema lines:

```
<xsd:attribute name="address1" type="xsd:string"
               use="required" />
<xsd:attribute name="address2" type="xsd:string" />
```

become:

```
<xsd:attribute name="addressLine1" type="xsd:string"
               sql:field="address1" use="required" />
<xsd:attribute name="addressLine2" type="xsd:string"
               sql:field="address2" />
```

A similar update to the `zip` field in the XML data allows it to be mapped to the `postalCode` field in the database and it becomes:

```
<xsd:attribute name="zip" type="xsd:string"
               sql:field="postalCode" use="required" />
```

When the schema was used to extract data, the `customerID` column was ignored because it wasn't necessary for the output. `customerID` is in the XML data file and it would be beneficial to use the same `customerID`s as the Marketing Department. This line adds it to the mapping:

```
<xsd:attribute name="customerID" type="xsd:ID"
               sql:field="customerID" use="required" />
```

Chapter 12

Notice that although all XML attributes are given as quoted strings, the `customerID` is treated as an ID using the attribute `type="xsd:ID"`. Later, this will be used by `SQLXMLBulkLoad` to create a Primary Key, if and when tables are created.

To make the XML data file well formed, `<CustomerList>` was used to provide a single root tag. `<CustomerList>` doesn't correspond to a database table; however, it can't be overlooked. If the XML schema doesn't define it, the entire input will be ignored when the bulk load is performed. Since `<CustomerList>` is an element, an `<xsd:element>` tag is needed and the `<Customer>` element becomes part of its type. The `<CustomerList>` element is given the attribute `sql:is-constant="true"` to signify that it's not mapped to any table. `is-constant` takes only 1 or true indicating a constant, and 0 or false indicating that it's not a constant. Here's the element:

```
<xsd:element name="CustomerList" sql:is-constant="true">
```

To complete the definition of `<CustomerList>`, `<xsd:complexType>` and `<xsd:sequence>` elements are needed around the definition of the `<Customer>` element, like this:

```
<xsd:element name="CustomerList" sql:is-constant="true">
   <xsd:complexType>
           <xsd:sequence>

   elements that can be in CustomerList go here...

           </xsd:sequence>
    </xsd:complexType>
</xsd:element>
```

Since `BLCustomer` and `BLInvoice` are staging tables, we might want to create them each time the Bulk Load is run. This has the advantage that the table is cleared of any prior results. This functionality will be covered later when discussing the `SchemaGen` property. For now, in the schema to support table creation, the `sql:datatype` annotation is added to each attribute or element that is mapped to a database column. The value of `sql:datatype` is a standard T-SQL data type. Here are two elements with `sql:datatypes` added:

```
<xsd:attribute name="customerID" type="xsd:ID"
  sql:field="customerID" sql:datatype="int" use="required" />
<xsd:attribute name="customerName" type="xsd:string"
  sql:field="name" sql:datatype="varchar(100)" use="required" />
```

One more change before producing a final XML schema. The input XML has a third address line for the first `<Customer>` with the attribute name `addressLine3`. There is also a `taxid` attribute for the second customer. For theb purposes of the example, assume that a decision has been made not to add extra fields to the database schema to support this information, but that the fields should be kept around in case they're needed in the future. To accommodate storage of XML that doesn't map to a column, `SQLXMLBulkLoad` provides for an overflow column.

SQLXML Bulk Load

The overflow column is created using the `sql:overflow-field` annotation on the element that corresponds to a table. Fields named `XMLOverflow` are in the `BLCustomer` and the `BLInvoices` table for this purpose. In the `BLCustomer` table I've used a `varchar(2000)` datatype for the `XMLOverflow` column to accommodate plenty of extra XML. If you let `SQLXMLBulkLoad` create the field during `SchemaGen`, it will create it as `ntext`. That will have virtually unlimited room, but is a very inefficient way to store a small amount of text.

Now add the `sql:overflow-field` annotation to the `<Customer>` element and it becomes:

```
<xsd:element name="Customer" sql:relation="BLCustomer"
             sql:overflow-field="XMLOverflow">
```

Note that I slipped in a change to the `sql:relation` attribute of the element above to map to the `BLCustomer` table.

Skipping ahead to the result, take a look at this query on the `XMLOverflow` column:

```
SELECT customerID, xmlOverflow from BLCustomer
GO
```

and the query result:

customerID	xmlOverflow
1	<Customer addressLine3="Suite 200"/>
2	<Customer taxid="213ABC"/>
3	NULL

The attributes that hadn't been defined in the mapping schema wind up in the `XMLOverflow` column. `SQLXMLBulkLoad` hasn't just dumped the attributes there, it has created a well-formed element. The overflow could someday be exported with other fields, or used as the input to `OPENXML` to recover the information it contains.

One of the beauties of XML as a data exchange format is that the sender can insert additional types of data, as elements or attributes, as it becomes available. The receiver doesn't have to process this new data because including extra elements or attributes doesn't break the transmission process. When the receiver later enhances the import process, the new data can be used.

Potentially, this opens a big hole in the process; the sender can be transmitting new data that the receiver is ignoring. While this might be OK, it might also indicate a breakdown in the specification process and the loss of valuable data. The overflow field provides protection against such possibilities and I recommend that it be used to guard against them.

Pulling together all the changes made since we last looked at the schema gives us a more complete schema that can be used for the `SQLXMLBulkLoad`:

Chapter 12

```xml
<?xml version="1.0"?>
<xsd:schema xmlns:xsd="http://www.w3.org/2001/XMLSchema"
            xmlns:sql="urn:schemas-microsoft-com:mapping-schema">
   <xsd:element name="CustomerList" sql:is-constant="true">
      <xsd:complexType>
         <xsd:sequence>
            <xsd:element name="Customer"
                         sql:relation="BLCustomer"
                         sql:overflow-field="XMLOverflow">
               <xsd:complexType>
                  <xsd:attribute name="customerID"
                                 type="xsd:ID"
                                 sql:field="customerID"
                                 sql:datatype="int"
                                 sql:identity="useValue"
                                 use="required" />
                  <xsd:attribute name="customerName"
                                 type="xsd:string"
                                 sql:field="name"
                                 sql:datatype="varchar(100)"
                                 use="required" />
                  <xsd:attribute name="addressLine1"
                                 type="xsd:string"
                                 sql:field="address1"
                                 sql:datatype="varchar(50)"
                                 use="required" />
                  <xsd:attribute name="addressLine2"
                                 type="xsd:string"
                                 sql:field="address2"
                                 sql:datatype="varchar(50)"/>
                  <xsd:attribute name="city" type="xsd:string"
                                 sql:field="city"
                                 sql:datatype="varchar(50)"
                                 use="required" />
                  <xsd:attribute name="state"
                                 type="xsd:string"
                                 sql:field="state"
                                 sql:datatype="char(2)"
                                 use="required" />
                  <xsd:attribute name="zip"
                                 type="xsd:string"
                                 sql:field="postalCode"
                                 sql:datatype="varchar(10)"
                                 use="required" />
               </xsd:complexType>
            </xsd:element>
         </xsd:sequence>
      </xsd:complexType>
   </xsd:element>
</xsd:schema>
```

Before you go too far with creating schemas, remember that, as with all XML, schemas are case-sensitive. This applies when names for elements or attributes in the XML are mapped by the schema. The element or attribute names used in the XML data file must be matched exactly by the element and attribute names (name attribute) in the schema. If the SQL Server is installed with a case-insensitive collating sequence, case-sensitivity does not extend to the sql:field or sql:relation annotations. Now that there is a XML data file and a XML schema, a script can be created and the data loaded.

Sample Script

There are many ways to host the `SQLXMLBulkLoad` object. Throughout this chapter we'll use VB Script as the programming language host for `SQLXMLBulkLoad`. Later, we'll show how a VB Script can be used in SQL Server DTS to execute the XML Bulk Load. A SQL Server Agent Job Step or Windows Scripting Host, available from Microsoft as a free extension to Windows, can also run VBScripts.

> Any Windows program that can create ActiveX objects can be used to run the `SQLXMLBulkLoad` object.

The script below is the minimum necessary to execute an XML Bulk Load:

In the next section, we'll discuss the properties that provide additional control over the XML bulk loading process.

```
' Sample VB Script for Bulk Loading
Dim objSQLXMLBL 'Bulk Load Object.

On Error Resume Next ' Handle errors in code

Set objSQLXMLBL = CreateObject _
("SQLXMLBulkLoad.SQLXMLBulkLoad.3.0")
ObjSQLXMLBL.ConnectionString="Provider=SQLOLEDB;Server=" & _
"(local);Database=SQLXMLExamples;Integrated Security=SSPI"

' Set other properties here…

objSQLXMLBL.Execute "c:\CustomerList.XSD",
"c:\CustomerList.xml"

If Err.Number <> 0 Then 'Pop up a message if there is an error
     Msgbox "Error " & Err.Number & " " & Err.Description
End If
Set objSQLXMLBL = Nothing ' Dispose of the Bulk Load object
```

The first parameter to execute is the path to the schema; the second parameter is the path to the XML data file. These are the only parameters. The `ConnectionString` property gives the object the information required to connect to the database. For illustration purposes, the example uses the database `SQLXMLExamples` that is assumed to be on a local server. Change the connection string to load into a different database or to use a SQL Server login. Also, be sure that the `CustomerList.XSD` and `CustomerList.xml` files are copied into the correct directory.

There are more properties to `SQLXMLBulkLoad` than just `ConnectionString`; they control how the object manages connections, creates and destroys tables, manages transactions, and performs the load. A realistic script will set many of these, although they all have defaults that may be adequate for a successful bulk load. We'll take a look at each of these properties before actually executing the script.

Chapter 12

Properties of the SQLXMLBulkLoad Object

There are 15 Properties to SQLXMLBulkLoad. We'll cover each group of parameters, roughly in the order in which they are logically addressed. Later we'll pull together a script that sets all the properties for our example. The examples that follow assume that objSQLXMLBL object has been created as in the line from the minimal script above:

```
Set objSQLXMLBL = CreateObject _
("SQLXMLBulkLoad.SQLXMLBulkLoad.3.0")
```

> When working with SQLXMLBulkLoad, it's a good idea to use the version-dependent PRODID. In this case it's "3.0". Otherwise, if for some reason a program installed an earlier version of SQLXMLBulkLoad after the version you wanted, the wrong version of the component will be run. These types of problems are difficult to track down.

Providing Connection information

Property	Type	Default	Usage
ConnectionCommand	ADODB.Command	Nothing	When a Command object is provided for connectivity. Used as an alternative to ConnectionString. Can use only when Transaction=True.
ConnectionString	String	Empty String	Provides the information for connecting to the database. Mutually exclusive with ConnectionCommand.

Database connection information is supplied either by setting the ConnectionString to a valid OLEDB connection string or by setting the ConnectionCommand object to an existing ADODB.Command object that has an open connection to the database. To use the ConnectionString property, code:

```
ObjSQLXMLBL.ConnectionString="Provider=SQLOLEDB;Server=" & _
"(local);Database=SQLXMLExamples;Integrated Security=SSPI"
```

The alternative to ConnectionString is ConnectionCommand. This involves creating an ADODB.Connection and an ADODB.Command object and assigning the Command to the ConnectionCommand property. ConnectionCommand can only be used when the Transaction property is True. By using a ConnectionCommand, the programmer gains control over whether the transaction is committed or rolled back. To use the ConnectionCommand, code:

SQLXML Bulk Load

```
Dim objSQLXMLBL ' Bulk Load Object.

Set objSQLXMLBL = CreateObject _
("SQLXMLBulkLoadLib.SQLXMLBulkLoad.3.0")

Dim objConn ' ADODB Connection for Bulk Loading
Dim objCmd  ' Command for Bulk Loading

Set objConn = CreateObject("ADODB.Connection")
ObjConn.Open "Provider=SQLOLEDB;Server=(local);" & _
            "Database=SQLXMLExamples;Integrated Security=SSPI"
Set objCmd = CreateObject("ADODB.Command")
Set objCmd.ActiveConnection = objConn '

objSQLXMLBL.ConnectionCommand = objCMD ' Let, not Set
                                       ' for Properties
objSQLXMLBL.Transaction = True ' Must use transaction with
                               ' ConnectionCommand

' Set other properties here...

objConn.BeginTrans

ObjSQLXMLBL.Execute "c:\CustomerList.XSD", _
"c:\CustomerList.xml"

' Commit only if there are no errors at all.
' Otherwise rollback.
If Err.Number = 0 Then
    objConn.CommitTrans
Else
    objConn.RollbackTrans
End If

Set objSQLXMLBL = Nothing ' free the object.
```

This example uses a very simple criterion, `Err.Number=0`, to decide if the transaction should be committed or rolled back. A more complex criterion could be used, including an examination of the `ErrorLogFile`.

In the line that assigns `objCMD` to the `ConnectionCommand`:

```
objSQLXMLBL.ConnectionCommand = objCMD ' Let, not Set
                                       ' for Properties
```

note that a `Let` assignment rather than a `Set` assignment is performed, even though an object is being assigned. That's the way the `ConnectionCommand` property works.

If both the `ConnectionString` property and the `ConnectionCommand` property are used, SQLXML uses the last one assigned.

Table Creation and Deletion

Property	Type	Default	Usage
BulkLoad	Boolean	True	Is a bulk load performed at all? When False, the bulk load is not performed. Only the schema operations are performed.
SchemaGen	Boolean	False	When True, tables are created to match those in the mapping schema.
SGDropTables	Boolean	False	When True, if there are existing tables with the same name as those about to be created, they are dropped.
SGUseID	Boolean	False	When True, the attribute in the mapping schema that has ID type is used as the primary key when tables are created.

SQLXMLBulkLoad can create tables based on the mapping schema before data is loaded. This group of options manages the table creation and deletion process. Creating tables is optional. Existing tables can be used without modification, if they're available.

The BulkLoad option governs whether a bulk load is performed at all. If set to False, only the table creation and deletion processes are performed; no data is loaded. The default for BulkLoad is True.

SchemaGen governs whether tables are created by SQLXMLBulkLoad. By default, SchemaGen is False and tables are not created. To create tables, code:

```
' create tables for schema generation.
ObjSQLXMLBL.SchemaGen = True
```

To create tables without loading data, code:

```
' create tables for schema generation.
ObjSQLXMLBL.SchemaGen = True
ObjSQLXMLBL.BulkLoad = False  ' Don't load the data,
                              ' just create the tables.
```

Either SchemaGen or BulkLoad must be True. When both are set to False, SQLXMLBulkLoad raises an error.

With SchemaGen set to True, SQLXMLBulkLoad won't create a table if it already exists; that is, unless SGDropTables is set to True. Then it will drop any existing tables with the same name. Of course, as the tables are dropped, any data in them is discarded. To request that tables are dropped before being created, code:

SQLXML Bulk Load

```
' create tables for schema generation.
ObjSQLXMLBL.SchemaGen = True
ObjSQLXMLBL.SGDropTables = True ' Drop existing tables before
                                ' creating them.
```

By default, when tables are created by `SQLXMLBulkLoad`, they're created without a primary key, without indexes, and without any relationships. If `SGUseID` is `True`, and there is an attribute on the mapping schema identified as an `ID` type, `SQLXMLBulkLoad` will create a primary key constraint on that column. Creating a primary key constraint on a new table creates it as a unique clustered index as well. Since the field is the primary key, it may not have `NULL` values. To create the primary key(s), code:

```
' create tables for schema generation.
ObjSQLXMLBL.SchemaGen = True
ObjSQLXMLBL.SGUseID = True ' Create PRIMARY KEY for ID type
                           ' columns.
```

While it's possible to bulk load into a SQL View on a single table, it's not possible to ask `SQLXMLBulkLoad` to create one; it will only create tables.

Earlier in the chapter, `sql:datatype` annotations were added to the schema. This was done so that when `SQLXMLBulkLoad` created the `BLCustomer` table it would know how to create it. If the annotations had not been part of the schema, the resulting table would be one you'd probably not want to use for long, due to the overhead of maintaining the `NVARCHAR(1000)` columns it creates. Here's a SQL Server diagram of the `BLCustomer` table, created from a XML schema similar to the one we saw before, but without `sql:datatype` annotations:

BLCustomer

Column Name	Condensed Type	Nullable
XMLOverflow	ntext	NULL
customerID	int	NOT NULL
state	nvarchar(1000)	NOT NULL
name	nvarchar(1000)	NOT NULL
address1	nvarchar(1000)	NOT NULL
address2	nvarchar(1000)	NULL
postalCode	nvarchar(1000)	NOT NULL
city	nvarchar(1000)	NOT NULL

The bottom line is: put in a `sql:datatype` for every field in your schemas.

Error Handling

Property	Type	Usage
`ErrorLogFile`	String	File to store errors and messages. The file is in XML format.

During the course of the bulk load, a variety of errors and messages can be produced. The `ErrorLogFile` property gives the name of the file that `SQLXMLBulkLoad` uses to store the error report and message. If `ErrorLogFile` is blank, messages are not logged. However, the error information may be available in the `Err` object. It's always a good idea to specify `ErrorLogFile`. The file is an XML file and we'll look at the format below.

The `ErrorLogFile` is created anew each time `SQLXMLBulkLoad` runs, so it's a good idea to give each log file a unique name. I usually build a name based on the date and time, as shown in this code:

```
' Full path and name to the XML error log for BulkLoad
Dim strErrorLogFile
Dim dtNow ' Current Date

dtNow = NOW ' Save the current date/time
strErrorLogFile = "c:\MyLogDirectory\BulkLoading-" & _
Year(dtNow) _
              & Month(dtNow) & "-" & Day(dtNow) & "T" _
              & Hour(dtNow) & "-" & Minute(dtNow) & "-" _
              & Second(dtNow) _
              & ".XML"

objSQLXMLBL.ErrorLogFile = strErrorLogFile
```

The user running the hosting program that executes the bulk load must have create and write authorization to the file. When running in a Visual Basic Executable, or another Windows program, this is the user that runs the program. When executed inside a DTS package, it's the SQL Server service account. If the `ErrorLogFile` is not specified, it's not created and any error information is lost.

Here's a sample `ErrorLogFile` created when I forgot to save the file `CustomerList.XML` to my hard disk before running the bulk load:

```
<?xml version="1.0"?>
<Result State="FAILED">
   <Error>
      <HResult>0x800C0006</HResult>
      <Description>
         <![CDATA[Schema: Cannot find the specified schema file
         'CustomerList.XML'.]]>
      </Description>
      <Source>Schema mapping</Source>
      <Type>FATAL</Type>
   </Error>
</Result>
```

Optimization

`SQLXMLBulkLoad` offers one option for optimizing the performance of the bulk load, `ForceTableLock`. When `True`, table locks will be taken out at the start of the loading process and not released until the load is complete. To request the use of just one table lock, set the `ForceTableLock` property to `True` as in this statement:

SQLXML Bulk Load

```
objSQLXML.ForceTableLock = True ' Lock for the full load
```

Using one table lock reduces the overhead for the usual locking that SQL Server Bulk Load performs. Normally, Bulk Load operations lock the table as rows are added and then release the lock after every insert. By using `ForceTableLock`, only one table lock is used.

The downside of locking the table for the entire load is that the data is unavailable to all database users until the load is complete. If the load takes an extended time, this could adversely effect usability. However, in many applications, the delay will be insufficient to warrant using `ForceTableLock`.

Transaction Management

Property	Type	Default	Usage
Transaction	Boolean	False	When True, the bulk load occurs in a single transaction. This cannot be used when loading bin.hex or bin.base64 data into binary or image columns.
TempFilePath	String		Path to a directory used to store the temporary files needed to support the transaction.

By default, `SQLXMLBulkLoad` doesn't run the bulk load in a transaction. If for any reason the bulk load were to fail in the middle of processing, incomplete results would be left in the database. This might make it difficult to just rerun the load.

An example of using the `Transaction` property was shown above in the section about `ConnectionCommand`. `Transaction=True` can be used with a `ConnectionString`. In this case, `SQLXMLBulkLoad` manages the transaction and rolls back the entire load, if there are any errors.

When executing with `Transaction=True`, `SQLXMLBulkLoad` stores all rows in temporary files before loading them, table by table, into the database. `TempFilePath` gives the directory where these files can be saved. Here's a sample of coding `Transaction` and `TempFilePath`:

```
oObjSQLXMLBL.Transaction=True
oObjSQLXMLBL.TempFilePath = "c:\Temp"
```

The user running the process hosting `SQLXMLBulkLoad` must have authorization to create and work with files in the directory, in the same way that this authority is needed for the `ErrorLogFile`. In a compiled environment, this is the user executing the compiled program. It could be the interactive user or a service account for a batch scheduler. If hosted in DTS, it's the SQL Server service account.

341

It almost goes without saying that there needs to be adequate space on the drive to hold the temporary files. They should be expected to be about the same size as the data in the original XML data file.

Control over Data Loading

Property	Type	Default	Usage
CheckConstraints	Boolean	False	When True, constraint checking is performed on Foreign key constraints and check constraints. When False, the checking of Foreign Key and Check Constraints is suppressed. Note that bulk load will fail if a foreign key is defined without the corresponding primary key being defined first.
IgnoreDuplicateKeys	Boolean	False	When True, duplicate keys won't stop the load.
KeepIdentity	Boolean	True	Don't assign a new id field. Similar to SET Identity_Insert ON.
KeepNulls	Boolean	False	Requests that NULL be inserted instead of the column default for any column that is not in the XML data.
XMLFragment	Boolean	False	Tells SQLXMLBulkLoad that the input is an XML fragment and not well-formed XML

This group of properties controls SQLXMLBulkLoad's behavior as it loads the data. These properties are independent of each other, so they'll be described individually.

CheckConstraints

CheckConstraints governs whether foreign key constraints and check constraints are checked as data is inserted into the table. By default, CheckConstraints is False, and only primary key and unique constraint checking is performed.

SQLXML Bulk Load

If `CheckConstraints` is set to `True`, constraints on individual fields, such as check constraints, are always checked. If a record fails to meet one of the constraints, an error is generated and the load fails.

Removing constraint checking will speed up a load. However, maintaining referential integrity becomes the responsibility of the programmer, not the database. It's most appropriate when a separate operation will complete the database. After such a procedure, it would be a good idea to run `DBCC CHECKCONSTRAINTS` on any tables that were loaded to ensure that all constraints have been satisfied.

IgnoreDuplicateKeys

Tells `SQLXMLBulkLoad` whether or not to stop if an attempt is made to insert a row with a duplicate key. When `IgnoreDuplicateKeys=True`, `SQLXMLBulkLoad` won't insert a duplicate record. However, it also won't consider the attempt to insert a duplicate record a fatal error.

When `True`, a commit statement is issued for every row inserted; this has a performance penalty.

`IgnoreDuplicateKeys` can only be used when `Transaction` is `False`. When `Transaction` is `True`, the load is performed using temporary files and duplicates cause an error.

KeepIdentity

When the input XML includes values for an identity column, `SQLXMLBulkLoad`'s default behavior is to use the identity value from the input. This works as if a `SET IDENTITY_INSERT table ON` statement were issued for the table before it was loaded. This behavior allows identity values to be inserted from the input instead of being assigned by SQL Server. The default value for `KeepIdentity` is `True`.

Setting `KeepIdentity` to `False` instructs `SQLXMLBulkLoad` to insert new identity values. All values for ID columns in the input are ignored. It's coded as follows:

```
ObjSQLXMLBL.KeepIdentity = False  ' Insert new identity values
```

Like other properties, there is only one setting for `KeepIdentity`. It applies to all tables that have columns with the attribute `xsd:type="id"` in the XML schema.

KeepNulls

When a column in an existing input table isn't included in the mapping schema, `SQLXMLBulkLoad` inserts the column's default value, if it has one. Setting `KeepNulls` to `True` tells SQL Server to insert `NULL` instead of the default value for the column. Of course, if the column doesn't allow `NULL` values, an error is generated and the row won't be inserted. `KeepNull` is a Boolean property that is `False` by default. To set it, code:

```
ObjSQLXMLBL.KeepNulls = True  ' Override defaults for unmapped
                              ' columns
```

Chapter 12

KeepNulls applies to all columns that are not present in the XML data. There is no way to set the behavior on a column-by-column basis.

XMLFragment

Well-formed XML has a root element. When XML is missing the root element, it's referred to as an **XML fragment**. You may have noticed that SQL Server doesn't always produce root elements. This is done so that XML fragments can be more easily combined. In order to parse the XML, SQL Server has to work with a fragment instead of well-formed XML. The XMLFragment property is set as in this example:

```
' XML file doesn't have a root tag pair
ObjSQLXMLBL.XMLFragment = True
```

If the <CustomerList> element in the example from the *Overview* section were removed, the XML data file would be a fragment.

Completing the Script and Running it in DTS

Now that we've prepared the XML data file, the XML schema, and know how to set all the desired properties of the SQLXMLBulkLoad object, we're ready to execute the loading of data.

To demonstrate how to run SQLXMLBulkLoad, we'll use DTS as the host for the VB Script. Using Enterprise Manager, create a new package by selecting the Data Transformation Services branch of the tree and right clicking to use the "New Package" menu. Then add an ActiveX Script task which you'll find in the Task menu. That's all that it takes. The package looks like the following:

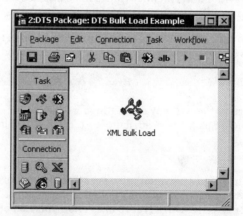

Of course, there could be other steps in the package. Good examples would be a File Transfer Protocol (FTP) task that downloaded the XML from the Internet before processing, or a Execute SQL Task that emptied staging tables.

DTS's editor for ActiveX Script tasks lets you write your script. Here's a screenshot showing the script editor as the script is being edited:

SQLXML Bulk Load

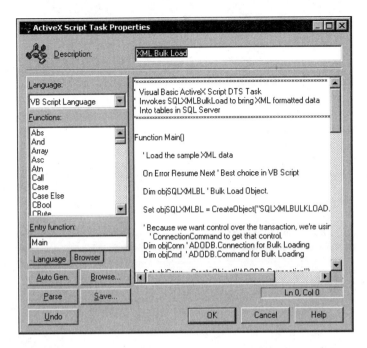

Personally, when I have to write such a VB Script, I write it and debug it in Visual Basic 6, then copy the result into the DTS script editor and remove any data types on the Dim statements. The debugging facilities are better in VB6 and the little extra effort required to copy the script is worth the trouble. However, there is a VB Script debugger that could be set up to ease the script-writing task. In Windows 2000 it's an optional Windows component, and in Windows NT it's in the Option Pack.

Here's the entire script:

```
'*****************************************************************
'   Visual Basic ActiveX Script DTS Task
'   Invokes SQLXMLBulkLoad to bring XML formatted data
'   Into tables in SQL Server
'*****************************************************************

Function Main()

    ' Load the sample XML data

    On Error Resume Next ' Best choice in VB Script

    Dim objSQLXMLBL ' Bulk Load Object.

    Set objSQLXMLBL = _
CreateObject("SQLXMLBULKLOAD.SQLXMLBulkLoad")

    ' Because we want control over the transaction, we're using
```

345

```
    ' the ConnectionCommand to get that control.
    Dim objConn   ' ADODB.Connection for Bulk Loading
    Dim objCmd    ' ADODB.Command for Bulk Loading

    Set objConn = CreateObject("ADODB.Connection")
    objConn.Open "Provider=SQLOLEDB;Server=(local);" _
            + "Database=Pubs;Integrated Security=SSPI"
    Set objCmd = CreateObject("ADODB.Command")
    Set objCmd.ActiveConnection = objConn

    objSQLXMLBL.ConnectionCommand = objCmd ' Let, not Set for
                                           ' Properties
    objSQLXMLBL.Transaction = True ' Required with
                                   ' ConnectionCommand
    ' Must have enough space.
    objSQLXMLBL.TempFilePath = "c:\Temp"

' Really do it, don't just create tables.
    objSQLXMLBL.BulkLoad = False
    objSQLXMLBL.SchemaGen = False ' Use original tables

    ' Create a named XML Error Log file
    ' so we may see any messages.
    ' Full path and name to the XML error log
    Dim strErrorLogFile
    Dim dtNow ' Current Date
    dtNow = Now ' Save the current date/time
    strErrorLogFile = "c:\Temp\BulkLoadLog " & _
Year(dtNow) & "-" & Month(dtNow) & "-" & Day(dtNow) & _
        "T" & Hour(dtNow) & "-" & Minute(dtNow) & "-" _
                            & Second(dtNow) & ".XML"
    objSQLXMLBL.ErrorLogFile = strErrorLogFile

    objSQLXMLBL.ForceTableLock = True ' For better performance.
    objSQLXMLBL.CheckConstraints = True ' Do the foreign key
                                        ' checking
    objSQLXMLBL.IgnoreDuplicateKeys = False ' In case of a
                                            ' mistake.
    ' This could result in duplicate entries.
    objSQLXMLBL.KeepIdentity = True ' The default we don't want
                                    ' new values
    objSQLXMLBL.KeepNulls = True ' Don't use column defaults

    objConn.BeginTrans  ' Start a transaction

   objSQLXMLBL.Execute "c:\CustomerList.XSD", _
"c:\CustomerList.xml"

    ' Commit only if there are no errors. Otherwise rollback.
```

SQLXML Bulk Load

```
       If Err.Number = 0 Then
           objConn.CommitTrans ' Finalize the result
           main = DTSTaskExecResult_Success ' Set task return code
       Else
           ' Save the error information so that it can be used after
           ' the transaction is rolled back. The Rollback may wipe
           ' out the error information.
           Dim nErr, strDesc, strSrc
           nErr = Err.Number
           strDesc = Err.Description
           strSrc = Err.Source

           objConn.RollbackTrans ' undo everything in the load

           msgbox "Error " & nErr & " " & sDesc & vbCRLF _
                 & "From " & sSrc & vbCrLf _
                 & "See ErrorLog in " & strErrorLogFile,, _
                 "Error in XML Bulk Load Task"

           main = DTSTaskExecResult_Failure ' Set task return code
       End If

       ' Close and clean up all COM objects.
       Set objCmd = Nothing
       objConn.Close ' Close before setting to Nothing
       Set objCmd = Nothing
       Set objSQLXMLBL = Nothing ' free the object.

End Function
```

Assigning the codes DTSTaskExecResult_Success or DTSTaskExecResult_Failure to Main sets the Task's return code. The return code can be used by DTS to branch to additional steps in the task.

The package is run by using the **Execute** command on the **Package** menu. If everything is right, we should see an alert box that says **Successfully completed execution of package**. SQLXML does not return an XML message on success, only on failure.

If, however, there had been a problem in the script, we would see an alert box like this:

In this particular case, both the BulkLoad property and the SchemaGen property had been set to False. The ErrorLogFile, after a little reformatting, looks like this:

347

Chapter 12

```
<?xml version="1.0"?>
<Result State="FAILED">
    <Error>
        <HResult>0x80070057</HResult>
        <Description><![CDATA[Bulkload or schemagen
                              option is required]]></Description>
        <Source>XML BulkLoad for SQL Server</Source>
        <Type>FATAL</Type>
    </Error>
</Result>
```

Our example runs successfully though, and we can run the following query to check out what has happened in the table:

```
SELECT customerID, left(name, 20) as [Name], xmloverflow
FROM BLCustomer
GO
```

Here are some of the results:

customerID	Name	xmloverflow
1	Miles Archer	`<Customer addressLine3="Suite 200"/>`
2	Herman Munster	`<Customer taxid="213ABC"/>`
3	Padme Amidala	NULL

Once the task is tested, you can run the DTS package whenever you have a new XML file to load. You might want to enhance the script with a `Dynamic Properties Task` that gets the name of the input file and stores it in a DTS global variable for use in the ActiveX task that does the bulk loading. For more information on coding SQL Server 2000 DTS, see *Professional SQL Server 2000 DTS*, ISBN 1861004419.

Loading Multiple Tables

One of the strengths of `SQLXMLBulkLoad` is that it can load more than one table at the same time. We'll do this with the `BLCustomer` and `BLInovice` tables created in the Overview section earlier. Here's a picture of what they look like:

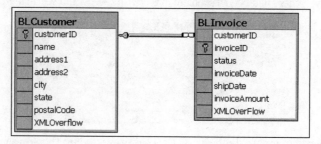

To load into both tables, the XML data file is expanded to include invoice information. Also, the root element has been changed to `<CustomerInvoices>`. You'll find the file `CustomerInvoices.XML` in the code download. Here's the new XML:

SQLXML Bulk Load

```xml
<?xml version="1.0"?>
<CustomerInvoices>
    <Customer customerID="1" customerName="Miles Archer"
            addressLine1="2345 Powell St."
            addressLine2="c/o Archer and Spade"
            addressLine3="Suite 200"
            city="San Francisco" state="CA" zip="99999">
        <Invoice date="2/12/1941" shipDate="2/14/1941"
                deliverTo="Miss Wonderly,
                1001 Coronet Apartments" />
        <Invoice date="4/19/1941" shipDate="4/21/1941" />
    </Customer>
    <Customer customerID="2" customerName="Herman Munster"
            taxid="213ABC"
            addressLine1="1313 Mockingbird Lane"
            city="Springfield" state="TX" zip="89823">
        <Invoice date="2/12/1965" shipDate="2/14/1965" />
        <Invoice date="12/19/1965" shipDate="12/24/1966" />
    </Customer>
    <Customer customerID="3" customerName="Padme Amidala"
            addressLine1="Senate Office Building"
            city="Capitol City" state="NB" zip="NABOO-1234">
        <Invoice date="5/19/2002" shipDate="5/31/2002" />
        <Invoice date="6/5/2002" shipDate="6/11/2002" />
    </Customer>
</CustomerInvoices>
```

Each `<Customer>` has `<Invoice>` elements that will be inserted into the `BLInvoice` table.

A few modifications were made to the `BLInvoice` table, when compared to the design of the `Inovice` table used in Chapter 6. The modifications make the table more useful, specifically:

- `Identity` has been added to the `invoiceID` column.
- The date fields have been turned into `smalldatetime`.
- The `XMLOverflow` field has been added to capture any extra XML.
- `NULL` or `NOT NULL` has been added to some of the columns to make that property explicit.

You've probably already executed the table creation script or attached the `SQLXMLExamples_Data.MDF` file. If not, this would be a good time to do this. See the *Overview* section for more information about the companion files.

Because of the relationship between `BLCustomer` and `BLInvoice`, `SQLXMLBulkLoad` may be able to create the tables, but it won't be able to drop and recreate them during a second run. That's because it isn't quite smart enough to know that it would have to drop the `BLInvoice` table before dropping `BLCustomer`.

Take a look at some of the `<Invoice>` elements such as these:

```
<Invoice invoiceDate="2/12/1941" shipDate="2/14/1941"
         deliverTo="Miss Wonderly,
         1001 Coronet Apartments" />
<Invoice invoiceDate="4/19/1941"
         shipDate="4/21/1941" />
```

You'll notice that they contain neither `customerID` nor `invoiceID`. Both will be inserted during the bulk load.

The XML schema must be enhanced to include the `<Invoice>` elements and to tell `SQLXMLBulkLoad` about the relationship between `BLCustomer` and `BLInvoice`. To start this off, the definition of the `<Invoice>` element would be:

```
<xsd:element name="Invoice"
             sql:relation="BLInvoice"
             sql:overflow-field="XMLOverFlow">
  <xsd:complexType>
    <xsd:attribute name="invoiceID"
                type="xsd:ID"
                sql:field="invoiceID"
                sql:datatype="int"/>
    <xsd:attribute name="status"
                type="xsd:string"
                sql:field="status"
                sql:datatype="char(1)"/>
    <xsd:attribute name="date"
                type="xsd:dateTime"
                sql:field="invoiceDate"
                use="required"
                sql:datatype="smalldatetime"/>
    <xsd:attribute name="shipDate"
                type="xsd:dateTime"
                sql:field="shipDate"
                sql:datatype="smalldatetime"/>
    <xsd:attribute name="amount"
                type="xsd:decimal"
                sql:field="invoiceAmount"
                sql:datatype="money" />
  </xsd:complexType>
```

To add the relationship information to the XML schema, an annotation element is added to the `<Invoice>` element:

```
<xsd:annotation>
  <xsd:appinfo>
    <sql:relationship parent="BLCustomer"
                      parent-key="customerID"
                      child="BLInvoice"
                      child-key="customerID" />
  </xsd:appinfo>
</xsd:annotation>
```

SQLXML Bulk Load

The final change is the name of the root element, which has changed from `<CustomerList>` to `<CustomerInvoices>`. Putting all these changes together, the complete schema (`CustomerInvoice.XSD`) becomes:

```xml
<?xml version="1.0"?>
<xsd:schema xmlns:xsd="http://www.w3.org/2001/XMLSchema"
    xmlns:sql="urn:schemas-microsoft-com:mapping-schema">
  <xsd:element name="CustomerInvoices" sql:is-constant="1">
   <xsd:complexType>
    <xsd:sequence>
    <xsd:element name="Customer"
                 sql:relation="BLCustomer"
                 sql:overflow-field="XMLOverflow">
      <xsd:complexType>
        <xsd:sequence>
          <xsd:element name="Invoice"
                       sql:relation="BLInvoice"
                       sql:overflow-field="XMLOverFlow">
            <xsd:annotation>
             <xsd:appinfo>
              <sql:relationship parent="BLCustomer"
                                parent-key="customerID"
                                child="BLInvoice"
                                child-key="customerID" />
             </xsd:appinfo>
            </xsd:annotation>
            <xsd:complexType>
              <xsd:attribute name="invoiceID"
                             type="xsd:ID"
                             sql:field="invoiceID"
                             sql:datatype="int"/>
              <xsd:attribute name="status" type="xsd:string"
                             sql:field="status"
                             sql:datatype="char(1)"/>
              <xsd:attribute name="date"
                             type="xsd:dateTime"
                             sql:field="invoiceDate"
                             use="required"
                             sql:datatype="smalldatetime"/>
              <xsd:attribute name="shipDate"
                             type="xsd:dateTime"
                             sql:field="shipDate"
                             sql:datatype="smalldatetime"/>
              <xsd:attribute name="amount"
                             type="xsd:decimal"
                             sql:field="invoiceAmount"
                             sql:datatype="money" />
            </xsd:complexType>
          </xsd:element>
        </xsd:sequence>
        <xsd:attribute name="customerID"
                       type="xsd:ID"
                       sql:field="customerID"
                       sql:datatype="int"
```

```
                           sql:identity="useValue"
                           use="required" />
         <xsd:attribute name="customerName"
                           type="xsd:string"
                           sql:field="name"
                           sql:datatype="varchar(100)"
                           use="required" />
         <xsd:attribute name="addressLine1"
                           type="xsd:string"
                           sql:field="address1"
                           sql:datatype="varchar(50)"
                           use="required" />
         <xsd:attribute name="addressLine2"
                           type="xsd:string"
                           sql:field="address2"
                           sql:datatype="varchar(50)"/>
         <xsd:attribute name="city"
                           type="xsd:string"
                           sql:field="city"
                           sql:datatype="varchar(50)"
                           use="required" />
         <xsd:attribute name="state"
                           type="xsd:string"
                           sql:field="state"
                           sql:datatype="char(2)"
                           use="required" />
         <xsd:attribute name="zip"
                           type="xsd:string"
                           sql:field="postalCode"
                           sql:datatype="varchar(10)"
                           use="required" />
       </xsd:complexType>
      </xsd:element>
     </xsd:sequence>
    </xsd:complexType>
   </xsd:element>
</xsd:schema>
```

Now, let's create a short VB Script (`CustomerInvoice.VBS`) to load it in DTS. Since the script doesn't use `SchemaGen`, be sure to remove any data from `BLInvoice` and `BLCustomer` before running it:

```
'******************************************************************
'   Visual Basic ActiveX Script DTS Task
'   Invokes SQLXMLBulkLoad to bring XML formatted data
'   from the CustomerInvoice.XML file.
'******************************************************************

Function Main()

    ' Load the sample XML data
```

SQLXML Bulk Load

```vbscript
    On Error Resume Next ' Best choice in VB Script

    Dim objSQLXMLBL ' Bulk Load Object.
    Set objSQLXMLBL =
CreateObject("SQLXMLBULKLOAD.SQLXMLBulkLoad")

    objSQLXMLBL.ConnectionString = _
        "Provider=SQLOLEDB;Server=(local);" _
      + "Database=SQLXMLExamples;Integrated Security=SSPI"

    objSQLXMLBL.Transaction = True
    objSQLXMLBL.TempFilePath = "c:\Temp" ' Must be space.
    objSQLXMLBL.keepnulls=False
    objSQLXMLBL.ignoreduplicatekeys=False
    objSQLXMLBL.CheckConstraints=False
    objSQLXMLBL.KeepIdentity=False

    ' Create a named XML Error Log file so we may see any
    'messages.
    Dim strErrorLogFile ' Full path & name to the XML error log
    Dim dtNow ' Current Date
    dtNow = Now ' Save the current date/time
    strErrorLogFile = "c:\Temp\BulkLoadLog " & _
                    Year(dtNow) & "-" _
                  & Month(dtNow) & "-" & Day(dtNow) & "T" _
                  & Hour(dtNow) & "-" & Minute(dtNow) & "-" _
                  & Second(dtNow) & ".XML"
    objSQLXMLBL.ErrorLogFile = strErrorLogFile

    objSQLXMLBL.ForceTableLock = True ' For better performance.

    objSQLXMLBL.Execute "c:\CustomerInvoices.XSD", _
"c:\CustomerInvoices.xml"

  ' Commit only if there are no errors. Otherwise rollback.
  If Err.Number = 0 Then
      main = DTSTaskExecResult_Success ' Set task return code
  Else
     msgbox "Error " & Err.Number & " " & _
            Err.Description & vbCRLF & "See ErrorLog in " & _
            strErrorLogFile,, "Error in XML Bulk Load Task"
     main = DTSTaskExecResult_Failure ' Set task return code
  End If

    Set objSQLXMLBL = Nothing ' free the object.

End Function
```

This script is a little shorter than the last one because the `ConnectionString` is used instead of the `ConnectionCommand`. This leaves the transaction control in the hands of `SQLXMLBulkLoad` component.

The resulting data in the `BLCustomer` table is the same as after the first example. This query shows the results in the `BLInvoice` table:

```
SELECT customerID, InvoiceID
            , Convert(char(11), InvoiceDate) AS Invoice
            , Convert(char(11),ShipDate) AS [Ship]
            , XMLOverflow AS Overflow
     FROM BLInvoice
GO
```

customerID	InvoiceID	Invoice	Ship	Overflow
1	7	Feb 12 1941	Feb 14 1941	<Invoice deliverTo="Miss
1	8	Apr 19 1941	Apr 21 1941	NULL
2	9	Feb 12 1965	Feb 14 1965	NULL
2	10	Dec 19 1965	Dec 24 1966	NULL
3	11	May 19 2002	May 31 2002	NULL
3	12	Jun 5 2002	Jun 11 2002	NULL

`CustomerIDs` have been assigned to the proper invoices and new `InvoiceIDs` generated, just as implied by the XML schema.

What `SQLXMLBulkLoad` does not do, but is often desirable, is to propagate newly assigned identity values from a parent to the corresponding field in the child. The parent ID fields must be in the input for loading multiple tables.

Loading From a Stream Instead of a File

The `Execute` method of `SQLXMLBulkLoad` can take a stream instead of a file name. This allows the XML to flow from an in-memory object into `SQLXMLBulkLoad` without being stored on disk. The .NET Framework makes extensive use of streams. For now we'll work with an `adodb.Stream` to create the XML and then hand it to `SQLXMLBulkLoad` in a two-step process.

For a scenario, assume that our company has just acquired Northwind traders. Wouldn't it be a good idea to add their customers to our customer database? To do so, we'll read their `Customer` table into a `Stream` and use it as input to `SQLXMLBulkLoad`. Northwind is one of SQL Server's sample databases. Here's a query that reads the first row of the data from `Northwind..Customer`:

```
SELECT top 1
       customerID AS NorthWind_CustomerID,
       CONVERT(varchar(100), CompanyName) AS CompanyName,
       CONVERT(varchar(60), Address) AS address1,
       CONVERT(varchar(50), City) AS city,
       CONVERT(char(2), left(Region,2)) AS state,
       CONVERT(varchar(10), PostalCode ) AS postalcode
    FROM Customers AS Customer
    FOR XML AUTO
```

SQLXML Bulk Load

There are a lot of practical issues with moving the data. Some of these issues have been handled in the query. For example, `Northwind..Customers.customerID` is a `nchar(5)` column which can't be converted into an `int` for use in `BLCustomer`. To handle this issue, the `customerID` is exported under the name `Northwind_CustomerID` and it will end up in the `XMLOverflow` column. The other columns are converted from their Unicode type, `nvarchar`, to `char` or `varchar` and truncated to the maximum length allowed in `BLCustomer`. This gets the data into better shape. Here's a sample of one row:

```
<Customer NorthWind_CustomerID="ALFKI"
          CompanyName="Alfreds Futterkiste"
          address1="Obere Str. 57" city="Berlin"
          postalcode="12209"/>
```

There are still two issues to handle in the schema. Earlier in this chapter the `CustomerList.XML` file was loaded using the `CustomerList.XSD` schema. The `customerID` attribute could be mapped to the `BLCustomer.customerID` column because it was an integer. Since `Northwind.customerID` is a character field we don't have an ID to work with. The solution is to remove the `<customerID>` element from the mapping schema entirely. Because `BLCustomer.customerID` has an `IDENTITY` property, a numeric ID will automatically be assigned.

Another problem is the availability of state elements in the source. Since `Northwind` has many international customers, many have a `NULL` Region code. The `CustomerList.XSD` requires a state, even though the state column does not. This is pretty easy to rectify; just remove the `use="required"` attribute from the `<state>` element, which becomes:

```
<xsd:attribute name="state"
               type="xsd:string"
               sql:field="state"
               sql:datatype="char(2)"/>
```

The complete XML schema (`NorthwindList.XSD`) is included in the code download.

To retrieve the data we'll use an `ADODB.Stream` object. There is a thorough discussion of using ADO and streams in the next chapter. For this chapter, a simple VB Script is used to construct the necessary stream:

```
Dim nwConn As adodb.Connection
Dim nwCmd As adodb.Command
Dim nsStrm As adodb.Stream

Set nwCmd = CreateObject("ADODB.Command")
Set nwConn = CreateObject("ADODB.Connection")
Set nwstrm = CreateObject("ADODB.Stream")

nwConn.Open "provider=SQLOLEDB;server=(local);" _
          + "database=Northwind;" _
          + "Integrated Security=SSPI"

Set nwCmd.ActiveConnection = nwConn
nwCmd.CommandText = _
```

Chapter 12

```
        " SELECT top 1" _
      + "    customerID AS NorthWind_CustomerID," _
      + "    CONVERT(varchar(100), CompanyName) AS CompanyName," _
      + "    CONVERT(varchar(60), Address) AS address1," _
      + "    CONVERT(varchar(50), City) AS city," _
      + "    CONVERT(char(2), left(Region,2)) AS state," _
      + "    CONVERT(VarChar(10), postalcode) AS postalcode" _
      + "  FROM Customers as Customer" _
      + "  FOR XML AUTO"

nwStrm.Open
nwStrm.LineSeparator = adCRLF
nwCmd.Properties("Output Stream").Value = nwstrm
nwCmd.Execute , , adExecuteStream ' Get the XML result
nwStrm.Position = 0 ' So it can be reread
```

Once the `Stream` is ready, it can be used in the `Execute` method as in this line:

```
objSQLXMLBL.Execute "c:\NorthwindList.XSD", nwStrm
```

The complete script is in the file `NorthwindList.vbs` in the companion materials. Be sure you change the database connection information and the location of files to match your computer.

Next up is a comparison of `SQLXMLBulkLoad` to traditional Bulk Load interfaces and to two XML facilities, Updategrams and `OPENXML`. These comparisons are made so that you have a basis for deciding when `SQLXMLBulkLoad` would work well and when another method might be better.

Differences from Other Bulk Load Interfaces

SQL Server has had bulk loading capability since the Sybase days. There is a variety of interfaces available for bulk loading of data. The original interface is the BCP utility, which is still available. SQL Server 7 introduced the `BULK INSERT` command, which allows for `BULK` operations to take place under the direction of T-SQL, in a stored procedure for example. There is also a DTS Bulk Load Task that makes automation of bulk loading simple. It's a different type of task from the ActiveX Script Task used above to implement `SQLXMLBulkLoad`. Finally, SQL-DMO has a COM interface that can be used to run bulk loading operations.

The traditional bulk load interfaces work by reading input files and loading each line of the file into a new row in a single target table or view. Options are available to specify the format of the input and to control the behavior of the load. Most of these options, or equivalent functionality, are available in SQLXML Bulk Load through the properties of the `SQLXMLBulkLoad` object. The options that are not available are covered in a table below.

Input files into the traditional bulk load interfaces are either text, or SQL Server's native Bulk Load format. The native format includes binary data that can be extraordinarily efficient. A `FORMATFILE` is needed to tell bulk load about the data types and precision of the input data.

SQLXML Bulk Load

In contrast to the traditional bulk load, SQLXML's bulk load reads a text file formatted as XML. An annotated XML or XDR schema is used to provide information about the data type of the input and the relationships between the elements. This is the biggest difference between the traditional Bulk Load and the SQLXML's version. A SQLXML Bulk Load file can contain data from multiple tables, and it uses the relationships between the tables to preserve referential integrity while performing the load. This greatly expands the capability of bulk load as seen in the previous section.

SQLXML Bulk Load doesn't do everything that can be done with other bulk load interfaces. For starters, it's input only; there is no bulk XML output option. For output, a template query with a `FOR XML` clause might suffice. There are also differences in the options that are available.

Our introduction mentioned that most of the options available in traditional bulk loading are available in SQLXML Bulk Load. Some options are not available and it's worthwhile knowing which ones they are. The options `DATAFILETYPE`, `CODEPAGE`, `FORMATFILE`, and `FIELDTERMINATOR` are superseded by the XML nature of the input file. The options that are neither available nor have equivalent functionality are:

Option	Description and Possible Work Around
FIRST_ROW	This option allows the load to begin with a particular record within the input. Work around this limitation by supplying only the records you want loaded in the XML file or by supplying the XML in a stream and positioning the stream where you want the load to start.
LAST_ROW	Similar to `FIRST_ROW`, this option allows the load to end with a particular record within the input. Work around this limitation by supplying only the records you want loaded in the XML file or stream.
MAXERRORS	Stops the bulk load when a certain number of errors have been encountered. There is no workaround.
FIRE_TRIGGERS	Can suppress firing of triggers. The only way to suppress the triggers is to disable them before the Bulk Load starts and then enable them after it ends.
KILOBYTES_PER_BATCH	The number of kilobytes of input between transactions. `SQLXMLBulkLoad` supports only one transaction or the use of implicit transactions. There is no workaround to this limitation.
ROWS_PER_BATCH	Number of rows of input between transactions. Similar to `KILOBYTES_PER_BATCH`. There is no workaround to this limitation.

Table continued on following page

Option	Description and Possible Work Around
ORDER	Tells SQL Server that the input data is ordered so that the load can be optimized. Loading the data either unordered, or in the order of the clustered index, is always fastest. There is no workaround to this limitation.

Comparison to Updategrams

SQLXML bulk load has some similar capabilities to the Updategram, and a little comparison might be useful. The similarities are:

- Both take XML input and change the database.
- Both can use XML schemas to provide direction to SQLXML about data types.

There are also differences such as:

- SQLXML Bulk Load is only for inserts. Updategrams handle updates and deletes as well.
- Because SQLXML uses SQL Server's bulk load capability, it can be much faster.
- Updategrams are pure XML and could be initiated on computers that do not run Windows or use the Intel 486 instruction set, such as a Pocket PC or a Macintosh. SQLXML Bulk Load is an ActiveX component, and must therefore be run on a Windows computer. Of course, any system can provide the XML data file to be loaded.
- Updategrams must follow the `schemas-microsoft-com:xml-updategram` schema syntax. The input file for `SQLXMLBulkLoad` follows a schema supplied when the bulk load runs. Therefore, when the format of the input is not under the control of the programmer loading the data, and thus cannot be in Updategram format, `SQLXMLBulkLoad` can accommodate the input.
- `SQLXMLBulkLoad` can be executed in one big transaction. Each Updategram is in its own transaction, although an updategram can perform multiple updates.

If the desired operation is for insert only, and it's possible to use SQLXML Bulk Load, then use it. However, many circumstances will dictate that it's not usable and Updategrams may be the better choice.

For more on Updategrams, please see Chapter 11.

Comparison to OPENXML

`SQLXMLBulkLoad` is an alternative to use of `OPENXML` for loading data from an XML file. While `OPENXML` can be used for additional purposes such as updating or deleting rows, they can both do data inserts, just in different ways. The similarities are:

- Both can be used to load data that is in XML format into SQL tables.
- Both can insert data into multiple tables from the same XML document while only parsing it once.

The differences are:

- `SQLXMLBulkLoad` does its parsing of the XML in the client application. Limited resources, such as memory and CPU that are consumed processing the XML, are taken from the client machine, saving server resources. `OPENXML` works inside the SQL Server and uses its memory and CPU.
- `SQLXMLBulkLoad` parses the XML on the fly as it adds rows to the SQL tables, or to its temporary tables, when using a transaction. This reduces memory requirements for `SQLXMLBulkLoad`. `OPENXML` parses the entire XML file before working with it, which may be prohibitive in consumption of memory.
- The way schema information is specified is different.

In general, if it's possible to use `SQLXMLBulkLoad`, it's preferable to `OPENXML` due to performance considerations.

For more on OPENXML, please see Chapter 10.

Summary

SQLXML Bulk Load adds significantly to the arsenal of XML tools. It does this by being able to load XML files through the high-speed bulk loading capability of SQL Server. When appropriate, this is the fastest way to get data stored as XML into a database.

SQL Server and Windows enforce their respective security requirements on the `SQLXMLBulkLoad` component. SQL Server enforces that the user executing the load must have access to the database and permissions to `SELECT` and `INSERT` into the tables being accessed. Windows enforces that the user running the program that executes the `SQLXMLBulkLoad` component must have permission to create any temporary files and the ErrorLogFile, when used. Nothing in `SQLXMLBulkLoad` enforces security on the XML. The XML could be from any source. You are responsible for verifying that the source is one you trust or for making your changes. Recently approved standards, such as XML-Signature, hold the promise of improved security implemented by standard tools. The tools to implement these standards are just emerging. For now, you're on your own and must implement security appropriate to your application.

In this chapter, we've discussed the process of implementing a `SQLXMLBulkLoad` including:

- Creating an annotated XML schema for use in the bulk load.
- Writing a VB Script to invoke the `SQLXMLBulkLoad` ActiveX component.
- Hosting the VB Script in a DTS package.

Chapter 12

To aid the process of deciding if it is appropriate to use SQLXML Bulk load, it's been compared to:

- Updategrams, which can also use XML to update a database.
- OPENXML, which does the XML parsing on the server.
- Traditional Bulk Load facilities of SQL Server, which take a different kind of input to perform the load.

When the data is XML and when it's possible to use SQLXMLBulkLoad, it is a more efficient choice than either Updategrams or OPENXML.

SQLXML Bulk Load

Andrew Novick

- Programming XML with ADO
- Programming XML with ADO.NET
- SQLXML Managed Classes
- DiffGrams
- Summary

13

Programmatic Access with SQLXML

So far, this book has discussed various ways to get XML data out of, or into, SQL Server. These methods have relied on either IIS and SQLXML 3.0, or have been done entirely within SQL Server itself, as in the case of SELECT statements with a FOR XML clause executed by the Query Analyzer. Generally, except for Chapter 11 where the SQLXMLBulkLoad object was used in a VBScript, there hasn't been much programming. This chapter takes XML access a step further, by showing how to use XML in programmatic interfaces to SQL Server.

There are many reasons for programmers to use XML with SQL Server. They boil down to this: under the circumstances, it's easier to communicate using XML than with other interfaces. This is often because the XML is needed to perform one of the functions of the program. Other than database access, a very common use of XML is within web programs, where the XML may be transformed using XSL into HTML for display on the browser, but there are other scenarios where it's useful:

❑ Constructing an XML document to be sent as the result of a web service method invocation.

❑ Retrieving hierarchal data as XML, because it can be conveniently stored in ASP session variables using MSXML's FreeThreadedDOMDocument object.

❑ Persisting Recordset (ADO) or DataSet (ADO.NET) to disk to use at a later date.

❑ Creating the XML data to be imported by SQLXML Bulk Load.

Microsoft has built XML capabilities into its newer tools, ADO and ADO.NET, and these are the interfaces that are covered in this chapter. In addition, the ADO.NET DiffGram format is covered. Specifically we touch on:

Chapter 13

- Programming SQLXML with ADO with all its properties.
- Using the SQLXMLOLEDB provider to implement client-side XML processing, including FOR XML NESTED queries.
- Sending XML to a stored procedure via ADO for use by OPENXML.
- Programming SQLXML with ADO.NET and the SQLXML Managed Classes.
- DiffGrams and how they're used by ADO.NET.

The choice between ADO and ADO.NET is usually dictated by the programming environment. ADO.NET is used with the .NET Framework, and ADO with COM-based programming languages and environments such as Visual Studio 6, VBScript, ASP, SQL Server DTS, and SQL Server's OPENROWSET. However, crossover between the two is possible. Through COM interop, ADO can be used in the .NET environment. This might commonly be done to port ADO using code from the COM environment to the .NET environment, or when a development staff just isn't yet comfortable with ADO.NET. Using ADO.NET in the COM environment is also possible, although I can't think why anyone would want to attempt it. Extensive coverage of .NET and COM interoperation can be found in the book *Professional Visual Basic Interoperability – COM and VB6 to .NET* (Wrox Press, ISBN 1861005652).

For our purposes, we'll use Visual Basic 6 and ADO and, when demonstrating the additional features of the new .NET framework, we'll use Visual Basic.NET.

Have you ever tried to execute a non-trivial FOR XML clause using Query Analyzer? The output formatting is hardly readable. Using techniques from this chapter, a useful tool for executing SQLXML queries can be built. This tool is described further in Appendix C. Once you're comfortable with the techniques described next, I suggest you load it up and try it out. It's available both as source code and as compiled version with a setup program, and makes the output of FOR XML much more readable, as well as a useful tool for running some of the code in this chapter.

To run the code in this chapter, you will need:

- Visual Basic 6.0 Professional
- ADO 2.7
- MSXML 4.0
- Visual Basic .NET
- SOAP Toolkit 2.0
- SQLXML 3.0 SP1

We use the Pubs database, as well as the SQLXMLExamples12 database developed in the previous chapter. A separate database with a 12 appended to the name has been provided to avoid any confusion caused by running the samples in Chapter 12. You'll need to attach the database to your server. Instructions are in the readme.txt file for this chapter. You might want to make a backup of Pubs as we make changes to it.

Programmatic Access with SQLXML

> The VB6 and VB.NET examples in this chapter are prepared for you to run as individual projects in the code download for this chapter.

Programming XML with ADO

ADO has been Microsoft's leading edge data access method for several years. It's a set of COM objects that provide a simple interface for reading all types of data, particularly data stored in relational databases. Since version 2.5, it's had the capability of working with SQL Server 2000 to exchange XML data. ADO's XML capability is independent of the SQLXML 3.0. The capability exists because ADO can request that SQL Server send XML results to ADO in a form that ADO can put into an `ADO.Stream` object. ADO streams contain text or binary data that can be read sequentially. Streams can also be used to send a SQLXML template to SQL Server.

Although many of the new features relating to Microsoft and XML are covered in this book, more details on this facility of ADO are given in Microsoft's `ADO260.CHM` help file. For a thorough explanation, you might want to take a look at *ADO 2.6 Programmers Reference*, (Wrox Press, ISBN 186100463X). The following is minimal code to retrieve the results of a FOR XML query using ADO. You'll find the code in the project `MinimalExample` in the code download:

```
Sub Main()
Dim objConn As ADODB.Connection
Dim objCMD As ADODB.Command   ' Command used to execute the query
Dim objResultStream As ADODB.Stream   ' Receives the XML result
On Error GoTo Handle_Error

' Create the ADODB.Connection and connect it
Set objConn = New ADODB.Connection
objConn.Open "Provider=SQLOLEDB;Server=(local);" & _
             "Database=Pubs;" & _
             "Integrated Security=SSPI"

    ' Create the Command and link to the Connection
Set objCMD = New ADODB.Command   ' Create the ADODB.COMMAND
' Attach the ADODB.Connection
Set objCMD.ActiveConnection = objConn

' T-SQL Query
objCMD.Dialect = "{C8B522D7-5CF3-11CE-ADE5-00AA0044773D}"

objCMD.CommandText = " SELECT au_id, au_fname, au_lname " _
                   & "    FROM Authors " _
                   & "    FOR XML RAW "
'CommandText is T-SQL SQL Statement
objCMD.CommandType = adCmdText
' Create output stream, open it, and associate with the Command
Set objResultStream = New ADODB.Stream
objResultStream.Open
```

365

```
    'Let for Properties
    objCMD.Properties("Output Stream") = objResultStream

        ' Run objCMD producing an output stream
    objCMD.Execute , , adExecuteStream
    ' Get all the text
    Debug.Print objResultStream.ReadText(adReadAll)
    Proc_Exit:
    Exit Sub
    Handle_Error:
    MsgBox "Error:" & CStr(Err.Number) & " " & Err.Description
    Resume Proc_Exit

    End Sub
```

The next couple of pages take the example apart line by line to show how it works.

For starters, objConn is an ADODB.Connection. It opens up the Pubs database on the local server, so you may have to change the connection string to get it to work on your system. If you're not using integrated security, add the clauses "User=<yourloginid>;Password=<yourpassword>" instead of "Integrated Security=SSPI":

```
    ' Create the ADODB.Connection and connect it
    Set objConn = New ADODB.Connection
    objConn.Open "Provider=SQLOLEDB;Server=(local);" & _
                 "Database=Pubs;" & _
                 "Integrated Security=SSPI"
```

Next an ADODB.Command object is created. Although there are other methods to execute SQL and retrieve data with ADO, only the Command object has support for getting XML. It's the Command object's support for the Dialect property and its ability to return its results as an ADODB.Stream object that are key:

```
    Set objCMD = New ADODB.Command  ' Create the ADODB.COMMAND
    ' Attach the ADODB.Connection
    Set objCMD.ActiveConnection = objConn
    ' T-SQL Query
    objCMD.Dialect = "{C8B522D7-5CF3-11CE-ADE5-00AA0044773D}"
```

The Dialect property is a string containing a GUID telling ADO the type of input the program is sending, so that ADO may query the database properly. In addition to traditional SQL queries, the other Dialects let the caller provide the query as an XML template or as an XPath query on a Mapping Schema. The list of valid dialects, and examples of how to use them are in section *Querying with Templates* and *XPath* sections later in this chapter. For now, the Dialect is set to the GUID for T-SQL queries.

Our next two lines provide the input to SQL Server in a traditional way:

```
        objCMD.CommandText = " SELECT au_id, au_fname, au_lname " _
                        & "      FROM Authors " _
                        & "      FOR XML RAW "
    'CommandText is T-SQL SQL Statement
    objCMD.CommandType = adCmdText
```

Programmatic Access with SQLXML

They set the `CommandText` property of the `Command` object to a T-SQL statement, and set the `CommandType` property to match. When a stored procedure is used, an alternative is to set `CommandText` to the name of a stored procedure and set `CommandType` to `adCmdStoredProc`.

SQL Server returns XML text rather than a `recordset` in response to a FOR XML query. To receive the results, ADO has the `ADODB.Stream` object implementing the COM `IStream` interface for manipulating text. These lines create the `Stream` and associate it with the `Command` object:

```
' Create output stream, open it, and associate with the Command
Set objResultStream = New ADODB.Stream
objResultStream.Open

'Let for Properties
objCMD.Properties ("Output Stream") = objResultStream
```

In addition to the `Public` properties of the `ADODB.Command` object, the object has a `Properties` collection holding properties that are specific to the OLEDB provider. `Output Stream` is one such property supported by SQLOLEDB. Note that even though the `objResultStream` variable is a COM object, the assignment is done without the `Set` statement.

The query is run by invoking the `Execute` method of the `Command` object:

```
' Run objCMD producing an output stream
objCMD.Execute , , adExecuteStream Debug.Print
```

The `adExecuteStream` option tells ADO that the results should be returned in the `Output Stream` instead of as a `Recordset`. For illustration purposes, the stream is sent to Visual Basic's debugging window. The debugging window isn't XML-friendly so I've captured the output and reformatted it to be easier to read:

```
<row au_id="409-56-7008" au_fname="Abraham" au_lname="Bennet"/>
<row au_id="648-92-1872" au_fname="Reginald" au_lname="Blotchet-Halls"/>
<row au_id="238-95-7766" au_fname="Cheryl" au_lname="Carson"/>
<row au_id="722-51-5454" au_fname="Michel" au_lname="DeFrance"/>
<row au_id="712-45-1867" au_fname="Innes" au_lname="del Castillo"/>
...
<row au_id="267-41-2394" au_fname="Michael" au_lname="O&apos;Leary"/>
<row au_id="672-71-3249" au_fname="Akiko" au_lname="Yokomoto"/>
```

In most respects, the result is valid XML. You might even notice that Mr. O'Leary's au_lname is given with the proper XML entity as `O&apos;Leary`. However, just as if the query had been executed in Query Analyzer, the result is an XML fragment, so it isn't well formed. ADO has a way to handle that problem with the `XML Root` extended property to be discussed next.

367

Extended Properties of the ADO Command Object

The ADO `Command` object exposes various COM properties, such as `CommandText`, and the new `Dialect` property. These allow the caller to provide settings that are used once the Execute method is invoked. In addition, ADO allows an OLE DB provider to support extended properties; these can be accessed using the `Command` object's `Properties` collection. The `Output Stream` property used in the previous example is one extended property.

`SQLOLEDB` adds a number of extended properties that can be used to work with XML output. In addition, SQLXML has another OLE DB provider, `SQLXMLOLEDB`, that adds an additional property to control the computer processing the XML; either the client running the program making the request, or the database server. `SQLXMLOLEDB` will be discussed later in this chapter in the section on client-side XML processing.

This table lists the extended properties that are relevant to working with XML:

Group	Property	Type	Use
XML Formatting	XML Root	String	Used to surround the XML fragment that SQL returns with a root element, to make well-formed XML.
	Namespaces	String	Gives the namespaces that are added to the output XML.
	Output Encoding	Boolean	UTF8, ASCII or Unicode.
Control Input Files	Base Path	String	The top-level path to the files referenced in other properties.
	Mapping Schema	Boolean	Points to an XML or XDR mapping schema that instructs ADO how to map between the relational database and XML.
	XSL	String	URL or file name of the XSLT that should be applied to the XML before producing the output.

Programmatic Access with SQLXML

Group	Property	Type	Use
	SS STREAM FLAGS	32 Bit Integer	Provides instructions to ADO about how to manage mapping schemas, XSLT, and templates specified by other properties.
Control Output	Output Stream	COM object implementing IStream	Provides the ADODB.Stream object to receive the output of the query.

XML Root

Normally, SQL Server returns an XML fragment instead of well-formed XML. XML fragments don't have a root tag, and so can't be loaded by the Microsoft XML parser. The XML Root property provides a way to specify a particular root element to surround SQL's XML fragment, turning it into well-formed XML. For example:

```
objCmd.Properties("XML Root") = "root"
```

or:

```
objCmd.Properties("XML Root") = "CustomerList"
```

Templates include a root, so you don't have to set the XML Root property when using a template. The same applies when using a mapping schema.

When a root is specified by any method, SQLXML adds the <?xml version="1.0"?> processing instruction.

NameSpaces

The NameSpaces property adds one or more namespaces to the root element of the XML result. They are used to differentiate element names from different XML vocabularies. Setting the Namespaces property allows the namespace to be used in the XPath query. For example, coding:

```
objCmd.Properties("NameSpaces") = _
"xmlns:rdf=""http://www.w3.org/TR/WD-rdf-syntax"""
```

would add the namespace to the root. Instead of:

```
<root>
```

The root element of the XML would be:

```
<root xmlns:rdf="http://www.w3.org/TR/WD-rdf-syntax">
```

Multiple namespaces can be inserted just by separating them with whitespace. So, if you code:

```
ObjCmd.Properties("NameSpaces") = _
"xmlns:rdf=""http://www.w3.org/TR/WD-rdf-syntax"" "_
& vbCRLF & vbTab & vbTab " " _
& "xmlns:myns=""http://www.myserver.com/myns"""
```

the result would be:

<root xmlns:rdf="http://www.w3.org/TR/WD-rdf-syntax"
    xmlns:myns="http://www.myserver.com/myns">

In fact, you can put almost anything in the namespaces and ADO puts it into the root element. If no root element is specified in the query, the namespaces are ignored by ADO and are lost.

Beware: the NameSpaces property is only available with the SQLXMLOLEDB provider discussed later in this chapter.

Output Encoding

The Output Encoding property specifies the encoding attribute that is inserted in the <?xml> processing instruction that begins an XML document. So if this statement is added to our program:

```
objcmd.Properties ("Output Encoding") = "Unicode"
```

The resulting <?xml> processing instruction, at the top of the returned XML document, would be:

<?xml version="1.0" encoding="Unicode">

Valid encodings are UTF8, ANSI, and Unicode.

Base Path

Specifying the Base Path allows other file references to be made relative to the Base Path, instead of by absolute reference. The path can be either a file path or a URL. This property then affects where mapping schema and XSL files are found. For example, coding:

```
ObjCmd.Properties ("Base Path") = "http://www.myserver.com/xml"
ObjCmd.Properties ("Mapping Schema") = "Catalog.xsd"
```

would cause ADO to look for http://www.myserver.com/xml/Catalog.xsd when it needed the mapping schema. URLs can't be used if the SS Stream Flag STREAM_FLAGS_DISALLOW_URL is set.

Similarly, coding:

```
objCmd.Properties ("Base Path") = "C:\XMLFiles\XSL"
objCmd.Properties ("XSL") = "Catalog2Table.xml"
```

tells ADO to use the file c:\XMLFiles\XSL\Catalog2Table.xml as the XSLT.

When a Base Path is specified, it is still possible to use absolute paths unless the STREAM_FLAGS_DISALLOW_ABSOLUTE_PATH flag of SS Stream Flags is Set.

Mapping Schema

The Mapping Schema property is used in coordination with the XPath query dialect. The schema file may be either an XDR or XML schema file. The Mapping Schema property specifies a file name or URL, pointing to the mapping schema used by the provider to translate the XPath command:

```
ObjCmd.Properties("mapping schema") = _
"c:\XMLFiles\Schema\CustomerInvoice.XSD"
```

Mapping schemas and XPath queries are covered in detail in the section *Querying Using XPath and a Mapping Schema* in a few pages. When not using an XPath query, the Mapping Schema is ignored.

XSL

On request, ADO will apply an XSLT stylesheet to the XML before it is returned to the caller. This can save an extra step of parsing the XML in order to apply the stylesheet. The most common use of XSL is to transform XML data into HTML for display. If the page is complete, the result can be sent to the browser without additional processing.

Once again using the Authors table from the Pubs SQL Server sample database, consider the following query:

```
SELECT * FROM Authors FOR XML AUTO, elements
```

This is an element-centric XML result that is easy to transform into a HTML page. Instead of the <row> elements with all the values as attributes that were retrieved with FOR XML RAW earlier in this chapter, the output contains the values within differentiated elements. Here's a fragment of the XML we'd return:

```
<?xml version="1.0"?>
<root>
<Authors>
  <au_id>172-32-1176</au_id>
  <au_lname>White</au_lname>
  <au_fname>Johnson</au_fname>
  <phone>408 496-7223</phone>
  <address>10932 Bigge Rd.</address>
  <city>Menlo Park</city>
```

```
      <state>CA</state>
      <zip>94025</zip>
      <contract>1</contract>
   </Authors>
   <Authors>
      <au_id>213-46-8915</au_id>
      <au_lname>Green</au_lname>
      <au_fname>Marjorie</au_fname>
      <phone>415 986-7020</phone>
      <address>309 63rd St. #411</address>
      <city>Oakland</city>
      <state>CA</state>
      <zip>94618</zip>
      <contract>1</contract>
   </Authors>
   <Authors>
      <au_id>238-95-7766</au_id>
...
```

The XSLT stylesheet to transform the above XML into a HTML page is in the file Authors2HTML.XSL in the code download. Here's the stylesheet:

```
<?xml version="1.0"?>
<xsl:stylesheet
  xmlns:xsl=http://www.w3.org/1999/XSL/Transform
  version="1.0">
<xsl:template match="/">
<html>
  <body>
    <h1>SQL-XML Demonstration</h1>
    <table title="Authors Table" border="1">
      <tr>
        <th>ID</th>
        <th>First Name</th>
        <th>Last Name</th>
      </tr>
      <xsl:for-each select="root/Authors">
        <xsl:sort select="au_lname"/>
        <tr>
          <td><xsl:value-of select="au_id"/></td>
          <td><xsl:value-of select="au_fname"/></td>
          <td><xsl:value-of select="au_lname"/></td>
        </tr>
      </xsl:for-each>
    </table>
  </body>
</html>
</xsl:template>
</xsl:stylesheet>
```

To associate the stylesheet with the ADO command object, add the code:

```
objCMD.Properties("XML Root") = "root"
objCmd.Properties ("XSL") = "c:\XMLFiles\Authors2HTML.XSL"
```

Programmatic Access with SQLXML

to `MinimalExample`. Also make sure that the `SELECT` statement reads:

```
SELECT * FROM Authors FOR XML AUTO, elements
```

The result, truncated after a few authors, is:

```
<html>
  <body>
    <h1>SQL-XML Demonstration</h1>
    <table title="Authors Table" border="1">
      <tr>
        <th>ID</th>
        <th>First Name</th>
        <th>Last Name</th>
      </tr>
      <tr>
        <td>409-56-7008</td>
        <td>Abraham</td>
        <td>Bennet</td>
      </tr>
...
```

When displayed as HTML it looks like this:

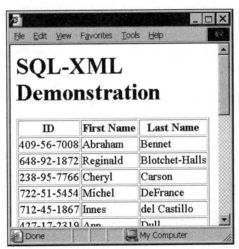

Output from an XSLT transformation does not have to be HTML or XML. XSL can transform the XML into any type of text. For a complete reference to XSLT, see *XSLT Programmer's Reference*, 2nd Edition (Wrox Press ISBN 1861005067).

In the example above, the stylesheet sorts the table by last name. The data could have been sorted by the SQL statement; instead, the sort task was moved to the client program. This moves the transform work from the server to the computer running the client program.

Processing an XSL stylesheet consumes CPU and memory. It always happens on the computer executing the ADO code, not on the server. The location of the XML processing can be important to the scalability of the application. Later on, the process of moving all the XML processing to the client program will be discussed.

373

Chapter 13

SS STREAM FLAGS

The SS STREAM FLAGS give the programmer control over various aspects of the input to ADO. Restrictions can be placed on the source of input files and the contents of templates. Also, the use of caching can be suppressed. This list of valid flags and their values is:

Constant	Value
STREAM_FLAGS_DISALLOW_URL	1
STREAM_FLAGS_DISALLOW_ABSOLUTE_PATH	2
STREAM_FLAGS_DISALLOW_QUERY	4
STREAM_FLAGS_DONTCACHEMAPPINGSCHEMA	8
STREAM_FLAGS_DONTCACHETEMPLATE	16
STREAM_FLAGS_DONTCACHEXSL	32

When used in code, the values are combined to produce the SS STREAM FLAGS attribute. Because each value is a binary order of magnitude, values can be combined with addition, or the bitwise 'or' operator. ADO doesn't provide constant values for the flags, so I've added constant declarations in the modSQLXMLConstants.bas module of the sample application. The constant declarations are:

```
' Constants for "SS Stream Flags",
' they can be combined by adding them
' together before setting the property.
Public Const STREAM_FLAGS_DISALLOW_URL As Long = 1
Public Const STREAM_FLAGS_DISALLOW_ABSOLUTE_PATH As Long = 2
Public Const STREAM_FLAGS_DISALLOW_QUERY As Long = 4
Public Const STREAM_FLAGS_DONTCACHEMAPPINGSCHEMA As Long = 8
Public Const STREAM_FLAGS_DONTCACHETEMPLATE As Long = 16
Public Const STREAM_FLAGS_DONTCACHEXSL As Long = 32
```

- STREAM_FLAGS_DISALLOW_URL is a security feature that prevents URLs from being used in a template to reference mapping schemas or XSL. This might be used in an object or subroutine that accepted a template for input to ADO. By setting this flag, URLs cannot be used for the Base Path, Mapping Schema or XSL properties.

- STREAM_FLAGS_DISALLOW_ABSOLUTE_PATH requires that the paths to files be given relative to the Base Path of the template. This prevents an arbitrary file from being specified.

- STREAM_FLAGS_DISALLOW_QUERY prevents a SQL query from being passed to SQL Server. When this is set, only XPath queries based on mapping schema are allowed.

Programmatic Access with SQLXML

The last three flags allow the suppression of the caching of three types of XML file: templates, mapping schema, and XSLT. XML files are cached by ADO in their parsed form, bringing a significant performance advantage. Even with the improvements in parsing speed made by MSXML 4, parsing text XML and constructing the DOM takes plenty of CPU cycles. However, it's a good idea to turn off caching during software development so that changes to the XML files can be used in processing.

Using the constants created above, the SS Stream Flags property could be set with this code:

```
ObjCMD.Properties("SS Stream Flags") = _
STREAM_FLAGS_DISALLOW_ABSOLUTE_PATH _
+ STREAM_FLAGS_DONTCACHEMAPPINGSCHEMA _
+ STREAM_FLAGS_DONTCACHETEMPLATE _
+ STREAM_FLAGS_DONTCACHEXSL
```

This statement prevents the use of absolute paths when specifying files such as the mapping schema or XSLT. Paths relative to the `Base Path` would have to be used instead. Also, all forms of caching are turned off.

Output Stream

The `output stream` was shown in the minimal example earlier. It lets the programmer provide the `ADODB.Stream` object, making it easier to work with the textual XML results provided by ADO. Here is a code fragment demonstrating use of "Output Stream":

```
Set objResultStream = New ADODB.Stream
objResultStream.Open
'Let for Properties
objCMD.Properties("Output Stream") = objResultStream
' Run objCMD producing an output stream
objCMD.Execute , , adExecuteStream
```

The first line creates the `ADO.Stream` object. Then we open it because you cannot use it without first calling the `Open` method. Next, the stream is associated with the `Command` by assigning it to the `Output Stream`. Finally, the `Command` is executed. The `adExecuteStream` property tells the `Command` that the results should be returned to the `Output Stream` instead of a `Recordset`.

That wraps up the properties. The next topic puts some of these properties to use in querying the database with templates, mapping schemas, and XPath expressions.

Querying with Templates

As mentioned earlier, the `ADODB.Command` object's `Dialect` property allows the use of both templates and XPath queries in addition to T-SQL. The template provided to ADO is the same as the templates discussed in Chapter 5. We can use all their capacities via ADO, such as:

375

Chapter 13

- Calling a stored procedure or parameterized query and providing the parameter values.
- Executing multiple queries and shaping the XML that surrounds the results.
- Executing a template residing at a URL or in a disk file.

Consider this simple template that you will find in the code download with the name `TemplateWith1Query.XML`:

```
<?xml version="1.0" ?>
<root>
<sql:query xmlns:sql='urn:schemas-microsoft-com:xml-sql'>
  SELECT * FROM authors FOR XML AUTO
</sql:query>
</root>
```

To use this template as input to the Command object, take a look at this fragment of code taken from the `TemplateExample` project:

```
...
      ' Constant for XML template query dialect
      Const DBGUID_MSSQLXML As String = _
              "{5D531CB2-E6ED-11D2-B252-00C04F681B71}"

      ' Create the template in a string
      strTemplate = "<?xml version=""1.0"" ?>" & vbCrLf _
      & "<root>" & vbCrLf _
      & "<sql:query xmlns:sql=" _
      & "'urn:schemas-microsoft-com:xml-sql'>" _
      & vbCrLf _
      & "SELECT * from authors for XML Auto" & vbCrLf _
      & "</sql:query>" & vbCrLf _
      & "</root>"

      ' Create the Command object and link it to our connection.
      Set objCmd = New ADODB.Command
      Set objCmd.ActiveConnection = objConn

      'Tell the Command that it's a template
      objCmd.Dialect = DBGUID_MSSQLXML

      objCmd.CommandText = strTemplate

      ' Create output stream, open it,
      ' and associate with the Command
      Set objResultStream = New ADODB.Stream
      objResultStream.Open
   'Let for Properties
      objCmd.Properties("Output Stream") = objResultStream
      'Run the command producing an output stream
      objCmd.Execute , , adExecuteStream
...
```

The template is put into a string and the string is assigned to the `Command`'s `CommandText`. Once the `Dialect` is set to `DBGUID_MSSQLXML`, we don't need to do anything else to provide the template to ADO.

While you might occasionally construct a template within code, what's really useful is to provide them in an input stream instead of as text. Using a `Stream` for input, the template can be a text file located on disk, the network, or on the web.

For example, this template (`TemplateWith2Queries.XML`) includes multiple queries:

```xml
<?xml version="1.0" ?>
<root>
  <Authors>
    <sql:query xmlns:sql='urn:schemas-microsoft-com:xml-sql'>
      SELECT * from authors for XML Auto
    </sql:query>
  </Authors>
  <Titles>
    <sql:query xmlns:sql='urn:schemas-microsoft-com:xml-sql'>
      SELECT * FROM titles FOR XML AUTO
    </sql:query>
  </Titles>
</root>
```

To create the input stream and load the file, I've coded the example project `TemplateFromFile` which you'll find in the code download. In the code behind the **Go** button, the key passage for using the input stream is:

```
' Create the input stream that will hold the
' Template or Command
Set objInputStream = New ADODB.Stream
objInputStream.Charset = "ASCII"
objInputStream.Open
objInputStream.LoadFromFile sFileName   ' Read the template
' Back to the beginning so it can be read.
objInputStream.Position = 0

' Associate input with Command
Set objCmd.CommandStream = objInputStream
```

This code sets up the stream, reads it from a file, and then associates the stream with the `Command` by assigning it to the `CommandStream` property. Notice that since `CommandStream` is a COM property with a specific object type, a `Set` is required. This is a little different from assigning the output stream to the `Properties`, collection where a `Let` is used and the Set keyword was omitted.

Querying Using XPath and a Mapping Schema

The last available query `Dialect` is XPath with a mapping schema. This is the most XML intensive of the query methods, and the target of the query is no longer SQL databases; it's the XML mapping schema.

Chapter 13

As the caller, you provide a mapping schema and an XPath query against that schema. Mapping schemas were covered earlier in Chapter 6. When a query is made using XPath and a mapping schema, SQLXML writes the FOR XML EXPLICIT query against the database tables to produce the XML for the result, as we saw in Chapter 8.

In Chapter 12 the `CustomerInvoices.XSD` schema was used to map XML into the `SQLXMLExamples` database. This schema joins the `Customer` and `Invoice` tables and maps column names as needed to match the XML available for bulk load. The schema was then used to bulk load an XML file into the database.

The same schema can also be used to retrieve XML. The `XpathExample` project illustrates how this works. It uses the `SQLXMLExamples12` database described at the start of this chapter.

> Because the schema is an XML schema as opposed to an XDR schema, it must use the `SQLXMLOLEDB` provider. The `SQLOLEDB` provider only supports XDR schema. `SQLXMLOLEDB` is discussed in detail in the next section, SQLXMLOLEDB Provider and Client-Side Processing.

The simplest of XPath queries asks for the root of the XML tree. In this case, it would be `<CustomerInvoices>`. To apply this query, the XPath query is placed in the `ADO.Command` object's `CommandText`, and the schema file is referenced in the `Mapping Schema` property. Before running the example, be sure to be connected to the correct database. When you're asked for the mapping schema, locate the `CustomerInovice.XSD` in this chapter's code download directory. Here's the code behind the **Go** button in the `XpathExample` project in the download:

```
Private Sub cmdGO_Click()

    ' Constant for XPath query dialect
    Const DBGUID_XPATH As String = _
                "{EC2A4293-E898-11D2-B1B7-00C04F680C56}"

    Dim objConn As ADODB.Connection
    Dim objCmd As ADODB.Command
' Receives the XML result
    Dim objResultStream As ADODB.Stream
    Dim sFileName As String
' When stream input is requested
    Dim objInputStream As ADODB.Stream
    ' Set up error handling for the Cancel button
    On Error GoTo User_Canceled
    comdlgXPath.CancelError = True

    ' Request a file
    comdlgXPath.ShowOpen
    sFileName = Trim$(comdlgXPath.FileName)
' can't do much with nothing
    If Len(sFileName) = 0 Then Exit Sub

' Handler for database operations
    On Error GoTo Handle_Error
```

```
    ' Create the Connection to SQLXMLExamples12
    Set objConn = New ADODB.Connection
    objConn.Open "Provider=SQLXMLOLEDB.3.0;" _
            & "Data Provider=SQLOLEDB;" _
            & "Server=(local);" _
            & "Database=SQLXMLExamples12;" _
            & "Integrated Security=SSPI"

    ' Create the Command and link it to the Connection
    Set objCmd = New ADODB.Command
    Set objCmd.ActiveConnection = objConn

' Tells the Command it's an XPath query
    objCmd.Dialect = DBGUID_XPATH
    objCmd.CommandText = "CustomerInvoices"

    objCmd.Properties("Mapping Schema") = sFileName

    ' Create output stream, open it,
    'and associate with the Command
    Set objResultStream = New ADODB.Stream
    objResultStream.Open
'Let for Properties
    objCmd.Properties("Output Stream") = objResultStream
' Run command to get an output stream
    objCmd.Execute , , adExecuteStream
    Debug.Print objResultStream.ReadText(adReadAll)

proc_exit:
    Exit Sub

Handle_Error:
    MsgBox "Error: " & Err.Number & " " & Err.Description
    Resume proc_exit

User_Canceled:
' Not a user cancel
    If Err.Number <> 32755 Then GoTo Handle_Error
    Resume proc_exit 'User canceled, just quit
End Sub
```

In the highlighted key lines, we can see that the `Dialect` is set, the XPath query is placed in the `CommandText`, and the `Mapping Schema` is set to the file name.

How about a more complex example? This next example returns all fields for all invoices in the state of California. In SQL, the query and results from the sample data are:

```
SELECT BLInvoice.*
FROM BLCustomer
Inner Join BLInvoice
ON BLCustomer.customerID = BLInvoice.CustomerID
WHERE BLCustomer.State='CA'
GO
```

Chapter 13

```
invoiceID  customerID  status  invoiceDate          shipDate ...
---------  ----------  ------  -------------------  ---------- ...
19         1           NULL    1941-02-12 00:00:00  1941-02-14 ...
20         1           NULL    1941-04-19 00:00:00  1941-04-21 ...
```

The equivalent XPath query is:

```
CustomerInvoices/Customer[@state='CA']/Invoice
```

When combined with a root of `<CAInvoices>`, which we saw how to do earlier by adding the line:

```
objCmd.Properties("XML Root") = "CAInvoices"
```

to the code, the result returned is:

```
<?xml version="1.0" encoding="utf-8" ?>
<CAInovices>
<Invoice date="1941-02-12T00:00:00" invoiceID="19" shipDate="1941-02-14T00:00:00" deliverTo="Miss Wonderly, 1001 Coronet Apartments" />
<Invoice date="1941-04-19T00:00:00" invoiceID="20" shipDate="1941-04-21T00:00:00" />
</CAInovices>
```

If you take a look at the first `<Invoice>`, you'll notice that the `deliverTo` attribute has been included in the result. `deliverTo` isn't a column in the `Invoices` table, nor is it referenced in the mapping schema; it was stored in the overflow field, `XMLOverflow`, by the Bulk Load run in Chapter 12. ADO extracted it and properly merged it with the other attributes of `<Invoice>`.

It's also instructive to take a look under the hood at what SQLXML must do to get this result. It starts by constructing a FOR XML EXPLICIT query to match the mapping schema, as we saw in Chapter 8.

Next, we might expect that the FOR XML query would pull over the entire `Customer` and `Invoice` join as XML, and then apply the XPath query on the client-side. Running a trace (listed in `trace.txt` in the download) on what actually happened revealed that this isn't the case. In fact, SQLXML converts the XPath expression into a WHERE clause, before sending the query to SQL Server; which is impressive because of the complexity involved in translating from one syntax to another. It also means that only the desired result is sent from the server to the client, minimizing network traffic.

Take a look at the lines at the bottom:

```
            WHERE _Q1.A6 IS NOT NULL
              AND (_Q1.A6 = N'CA')
              and _Q1._TBABEBNNDA=_Q2._TCABEBNNDA
```

SQLXML has converted the XPath expression into the WHERE clause before sending the query to SQL Server. Only the desired result is actually transmitted to the client program.

Programmatic Access with SQLXML

The level of sophistication on the part of SQLXML demonstrates the value of XPath with mapping schemas. The combination allows the developer to think in terms of the target XML and use an XML-oriented query syntax, XPath. SQLXML takes care of the hard part of converting that to a useful FOR XML EXPLICIT query.

Use of the FOR XML EXPLICIT query illustrates one of the drawbacks of this approach. The burden of creating a complex XML structure is placed on the computer hosting SQL Server. It's both CPU- and memory-intensive. The alternative is to process on the client-side, which is discussed next.

SQLXMLOLEDB Provider and Client-Side Processing

This diagram shows the components that process a FOR XML query made via ADO:

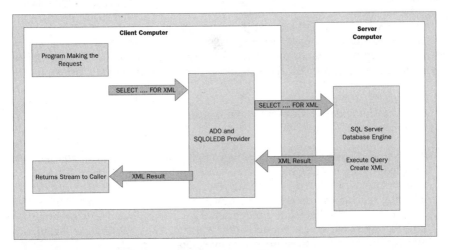

In this scenario, ADO and the SQLOLEDB provider are primarily conduits for the query. The hard part of retrieving the data and formatting it as XML is done by the SQL Server. In many circumstances, that's fine. However, when SQL Server resources are constrained, placing this burden on the SQL Server can be economically unattractive.

For example, what if the client computer is a member of a web farm of IIS servers? All the Web servers in the farm make requests from the same database. While it's possible to scale a SQL Server up, in processing power and CPUs, or out, via clustering, it's easier and cheaper to scale the web servers. IIS comes with Windows Server operating systems at no extra charge. SQL Server has charges for each additional CPU. There's also the matter of effort and complexity; adding servers in a web farm is easier, simpler, and usually cheaper than clustering SQL Server.

SQLXML addresses this concern with the option to move the processing of XML from the server to the client. Client-side processing of FOR XML queries was added in SQLXML 2.0. The OLE DB provider SQLXMLOLEDB does the work.

381

Chapter 13

The SQLXMLOLEDB provider uses the SQLOLEDB provider to retrieve rowsets from SQL Server. It does the XML formatting in the client application using the client computer's resources. This diagram shows how it works:

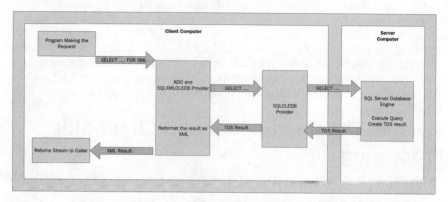

The arrows labeled **TDS Result** refer to **Tabular Data Stream**, the format SQL Server uses to communicate with SQLOLEDB and most other clients. The query that SQLXMLOLEDB sends to SQLOLEDB doesn't have the FOR XML clause. It's been stripped. The result is that the SQL Server does none of the XML formatting.

Once SQLOLEDB passes the rowset back to SQLXMLOLEDB, it turns it into XML and does the remainder of the requested processing, such as applying a XSL stylesheet, on the client.

Client-side processing also works when a mapping schema and an XPath query are used to create the SQL query. Take a look back at the big hairy FOR XML EXPLICIT query created by SQLXML when the CustomerInvoices.XSD mapping schema was used in the section above on *Querying Using XPath*. When ClientSideXML processing is requested, exactly the same query is sent by SQLXMLOLEDB with the exception of the FOR XML EXPLICIT clause. Again, this allows the SQL Server to return the smallest possible result.

There are some important differences between client and server-side processing that should be kept in mind. When using ClientSideXML:

- ❑ FOR XML NESTED is a new FOR XML clause, as we saw in Chapter 4.
- ❑ FOR XML AUTO queries cannot get client-side processing, although RAW and EXPLICIT can (see Chapter 4 for more on FOR XML RAW and EXPLICIT).
- ❑ GROUP BY queries can be used in FOR XML queries processed on the client.
- ❑ Only a single rowset can be requested. Multiple rowset queries, or stored procedures that return multiple rowsets, cannot be used and cause a run-time error.
- ❑ The FOR XML NESTED clause replaces FOR XML AUTO with some important differences. It's still possible to execute a FOR XML AUTO query via SQLXMLOLEDB, but it will be sent to the server.

Programmatic Access with SQLXML

FOR XML NESTED

In NESTED XML results, elements are always named after the base table that they came from. This occurs even if an alias is supplied or the query is against a view. The alias is ignored. This is done to facilitate retrieving XML for use in DiffGrams. The base table names are needed to create the updates.

Coding for Client-Side XML

To get client-side XML processing, start by using the SQLXMLOLEDB provider instead of SQLOLEDB. SQLXMLOLEDB needs an additional parameter, Data Provider, that must always be SQLOLEDB. There's a possibility that someday SQLXMLOLEDB may be able to perform XML queries against databases such as Access, Oracle, and MySQL, but that's not available now. Here's code to initialize a sample ConnectionString:

```
Dim objConn as ADODB.Connection
Set objConn = New ADODB.Connection

objConn.ConnectionString = "Provider=SQLXMLOLEDB;" _
  & "Data Provider=SQLOLEDB;Server=.;" _
  & "Database=Pubs;Integrated Security=SSPI"
```

Next, the ClientSideXML property is a Boolean that is set in this code:

```
Dim objCmd as ADODB.Command
Set objCmd = New ADODB.Command

objCmd.Properties("ClientSideXML") = True
...' Create the output stream and set other properties
objCmd.Execute ,,adExecuteStream
```

Client-side processing can also be requested in templates by using the client-side-xml attribute of the <sql:query> element as in this template:

```
<AuthorsList>
    <sql:query xmlns:sql='urn:schemas-microsoft-com:xml-sql'
               client-side-xml="1">
      SELECT Top 3
      au_id as ID
      , au_lname as Last
      , au_fname as First
      FROM Authors AuthorsAlias
      FOR XML NESTED
    </sql:query>
</AuthorsList>
```

The result of executing this template is:

```
<?xml version="1.0" encoding="utf-8" ?>
<AuthorsList>
<Authors ID="409-56-7008" Last="Bennet" First="Abraham" />
<Authors ID="648-92-1872" Last="Blotchet-Halls" First="Reginald" />
<Authors ID="238-95-7766" Last="Carson" First="Cheryl" />
</AuthorsList>
```

383

Chapter 13

The effects of the NESTED clause can be seen in the <Authors> elements. They're still called Authors even though an alias, AuthorsAlias, was provided. However, the column aliases, ID, Last, and First, were used.

Querying Stored Procedures to Get XML

One interesting option for stored procedures is to use client-side XML to turn their result into XML. This can be done without altering the stored procedure. Using this technique, the same stored procedure can be used for both XML and non-XML work.

Here's a sample stored procedure on the SQLXMLExamples12 database:

```
CREATE Procedure usp_CustomerInvoices (@State Char(2)) AS
SELECT Invoice.*
  FROM Customer
INNER JOIN Invoice
  ON Customer.customerID = Invoice.customerID
WHERE Customer.State=@State
```

The client-side query:

```
usp_CustomerInvoices 'CA' FOR XML NESTED
```

returns XML that is similar to the result when the XPath query:

```
CustomerInvoices/Customer[@state="CA"]/Invoice
```

was executed earlier using the mapping schema. Here's the result of the query:

```
<?xml version="1.0"?>
<root>
<BLInvoice customerID="1" invoiceID="1"
          invoiceDate="1941-02-12T00:00:00"
          shipDate="1941-02-14T00:00:00"
XMLOverFlow=
'<Invoice deliverTo="Miss Wonderly, 1001 Coronet Apartments"/>'/>
<BLInvoice customerID="1" invoiceID="2"
          invoiceDate="1941-04-19T00:00:00"
          shipDate="1941-04-21T00:00:00"/>
</root>
```

The only difference is in the treatment of the XMLOverFlow field. When the mapping schema was used to generate the XML query, ADO knew that XMLOverflow was from the sql:overflow-field annotation and used it to store any fields that hadn't been mapped. Without the mapping, XMLOverflow is treated as just another text field.

The code below is in the project ClientSideNestedQueryOnSP. As you can see, the query is a stored procedure that would normally return a recordset. In this case, the recordset is handed to SQLXMLOLEDB for ClientSideXML processing. The FOR XML NESTED clause is handled in the client computer, and the stored procedure does not have to be changed. Here's the code:

Programmatic Access with SQLXML

```vb
Sub Main()

    Dim objConn As ADODB.Connection
    Dim objCmd As ADODB.Command

' Receives the XML result
    Dim objResultStream As ADODB.Stream
    Dim sFileName As String

    On Error GoTo Handle_Error ' Handler for database
operations

    ' Create the Connection to SQLXMLExamples12
    Set objConn = New ADODB.Connection
    objConn.Open "Provider=SQLXMLOLEDB;Server=(local);" _
            & "Data Provider=SQLOLEDB;" _
            & "Database=SQLXMLExamples12;" _
            & "Integrated Security=SSPI"

    ' Create the Command and link it to the Connection
    Set objCmd = New ADODB.Command
    Set objCmd.ActiveConnection = objConn

    objCmd.CommandText = _
    "usp_CustomerInvoices 'CA' FOR XML NESTED"
    objCmd.CommandType = adCmdText

    ' Create output stream, open it,
    ' and associate with the Command
    Set objResultStream = New ADODB.Stream
    objResultStream.Open
    'Let for Properties
    objCmd.Properties("Output Stream") = objResultStream

    objCmd.Properties("XML Root") = "root"

    objCmd.Properties("ClientSideXML") = True
    ' Run cmd to get an output stream
    objCmd.Execute , , adExecuteStream
    Debug.Print objResultStream.ReadText(adReadAll)

proc_exit:
    Exit Sub

Handle_Error:
    MsgBox "Error: " & Err.Number & " " & Err.Description
    Resume proc_exit

End Sub
```

Letting ADO Create the XML

There's another way to get XML from ADO that doesn't depend on SQL Server at all. Since Version 2.1, ADO has been able to save its contents as XML. With the advent of Version 2.5, it can save its `Recordset` either to disk or to an `ADODB.Stream` object. The SQL query is a standard `SELECT` without any `FOR XML` clause. It works with all OLEDB providers, and therefore any database.

385

Chapter 13

The following example program is in the project `ADOcreatedXMLExample` in the chapter's code download. It uses the `Pubs` database and the `SQLOLEDB` provider:

```
Private Sub Main()
    Dim objConn As ADODB.Connection
    Dim objCmd As ADODB.Command
' Receives the XML result
    Dim objResultStream As ADODB.Stream
    Dim objRS As ADODB.Recordset
    Dim nRecords As Long

    On Error GoTo Handle_Error

    ' Create the Connection to Pubs
    Set objConn = New ADODB.Connection
    objConn.Open "Provider=SQLOLEDB;Server=(local);" _
                & "Database=Pubs;" _
                & "Integrated Security=SSPI"

    Set objCmd = New ADODB.Command
    Set objCmd.ActiveConnection = objConn

    objCmd.CommandText = "Select * from Authors"
    objCmd.CommandType = adCmdText

' Run cmd to get Recordset
    Set objRS = objCmd.Execute(nRecords)
    ' Create the stream
    Set objResultStream = New ADODB.Stream
    objResultStream.Open

' Save in the stream as XML
    objRS.Save objResultStream, adPersistXML
Debug.Print objResultStream.ReadText(adReadAll)

proc_exit:
    Exit Sub

Handle_Error:
    MsgBox "Error: " & Err.Number & " " & Err.Description
    Resume proc_exit

End Sub
```

Up to the point where the `Recordset` is persisted to the `Stream`, this is traditional ADO with no XML involved. These lines create the stream, and then have ADO save its internal representation to the Stream as XML:

```
' Create the stream
Set objResultStream = New ADODB.Stream
objResultStream.Open

' Save in the stream as XML
objRS.Save objResultStream, adPersistXML Debug.Print _
objResultStream.ReadText(adReadAll)
```

Programmatic Access with SQLXML

Once in the stream, it can be sent to any desired destination; in this case, the immediate window.

The result is pretty interesting. ADO uses several namespaces to define the schema, `rs` and `dt`. Then it creates an inline schema, `z`, which is included in the XML output. Finally, there's the data. You'll find the full XML file in the code download as `ADOFullXML.XML`. The following shows the results with some of the content removed from the middle:

```xml
<xml xmlns:s='uuid:BDC6E3F0-6DA3-11d1-A2A3-00AA00C14882'
     xmlns:dt='uuid:C2F41010-65B3-11d1-A29F-00AA00C14882'
     xmlns:rs='urn:schemas-microsoft-com:rowset'
     xmlns:z='#RowsetSchema'>
  <s:Schema id='RowsetSchema'>
    <s:ElementType name='row' content='eltOnly'>
      <s:AttributeType name='au_id' rs:number='1'
                       rs:writeunknown='true'>
        <s:datatype dt:type='string' rs:dbtype='str'
                    dt:maxLength='11' rs:maybenull='false'/>
      </s:AttributeType>
      <s:AttributeType name='au_lname' rs:number='2'
                       rs:writeunknown='true'>
        <s:datatype dt:type='string' rs:dbtype='str'
                    dt:maxLength='40' rs:maybenull='false'/>
      </s:AttributeType>
      <s:AttributeType name='au_fname' rs:number='3'
                       rs:writeunknown='true'>
        <s:datatype dt:type='string' rs:dbtype='str'
                    dt:maxLength='20' rs:maybenull='false'/>
      </s:AttributeType>
...

    </s:Schema>
    <rs:data>
      <z:row au_id='172-32-1176' au_lname='White'
             au_fname='Johnson' phone='408 496-7223'
             address='10932 Bigge Rd.' city='Menlo Park'
             state='CA' zip='94025' contract='True'/>
...

    </rs:data>
</xml>
```

ADO saves the schema information so that the `Recordset` can be recreated from this XML. In the section on ADO.NET later in this chapter, you'll see that it makes even more use of XML internally.

That wraps up the discussion of the details of programming ADO to retrieve XML. The example program in Appendix C pulls all the code together to make a useful tool for querying with XML. Next is a discussion of how to send XML to the server so that it can be used with `OPENXML`.

Chapter 13

Using ADO and a Stored Procedure with OPENXML

So far, we've retrieved XML with ADO in a variety of ways. You might also want to send XML to a database as data, either to store in a column, or to use as part of a stored procedure that uses `OPENXML`.

For the examples in this section, you'll find the code in the `SQLXMLOpenXMLExample project` in the code download. Once again the example uses the `Pubs` database.

The first example sends XML to a stored procedure in the `CommandText` of the `ADODB.Command` object. To start, add the stored procedure `usp_Update_AuthorNames` to the `Pubs` database. You'll find the file `Create usp_Update_AuthorNames.sql` in the same directory as the program. Here's the stored procedure:

```
CREATE PROC usp_Update_AuthorNames @AuthorData text
AS
    DECLARE @hDoc int
    exec sp_xml_preparedocument @hDoc OUTPUT, @AuthorData
    UPDATE Authors
        SET Authors.au_fname = XMLEmployee.au_fname,
            Authors.au_lname = XMLEmployee.au_lname
        FROM OPENXML(@hDoc, 'update/Authors')
            WITH Authors XMLEmployee
        WHERE Authors.au_id = XMLEmployee.au_id
    -- free any memory consumed by the document
        EXEC sp_xml_removedocument @hDoc
GO
```

The program reads the XML from a file, constructs an `exec` statement, and executes it. The stored procedure does the rest. Take a look at the program which is activated by the "**Execute with Inline XML**" button:

```
Private Sub cmdInLineXML_Click()
    'This example reads XML from a file, creates a SQL
    'command with the XML in the parameter of the SP and
    'executes it.
    Dim objCmd As ADODB.Command
    Dim strXML As String
' Asks for a file name using Common Dialog
    dlgFileName.ShowOpen
    strXML = FileGetContents(dlgFileName.FileName)
    Set objCmd = New ADODB.Command
    objCmd.ActiveConnection = "Provider=SQLOLEDB;" _
                & "Server=(local);" _
                & "Database=Pubs;Integrated Security=SSPI"
    ' The XML is part of the command text
    objCmd.CommandText = "exec usp_Update_AuthorNames '" _
                & Replace(strXML, "'", "''") & "'"

    objCmd.Execute ' Run the stored procedure.

End Sub
```

Programmatic Access with SQLXML

Of course, you'll need an XML file with the correct schema. In the **SQLXMLOpenXMLExample** directory you'll find the file `Example_AuthorUpdate.xml`:

```
<update>
    <Authors au_id="238-95-7766" au_lname="Ismore" au_fname="Les"/>
    <Authors au_id="427-17-2319" au_lname="More" au_fname="Bill"/>
</update>
```

Go ahead and press the **Execute with Inline XML** button, selecting the `Example_AuthorUpdate.xml` file to see it run. You can check the changes with the query:

```
SELECT au_lname, au_fname
       FROM Authors
       WHERE  au_id = '238-95-7766' OR au_id = '427-17-2319'
```

What we've built is kind of a private Updategram syntax. As long as the input XML matches what the `OPENXML` expects, everything works.

There's a second example in the same program that you can execute with the "**Execute with XML in a Parameter**" button, and a second XML file, `Example_AuthorUpdate_2.XML` for use with that example. It uses an ADO Parameter object to pass the XML to the stored procedure. I consider this a cleaner way to pass XML. Here's the main difference in the code:

```
' Tell ADO We're invoking a stored procedure
objCmd.CommandText = "usp_Update_AuthorNames"
objCmd.CommandType = adCmdStoredProc

' Create the parameter and set it's XML.
objCmd.Parameters.Refresh
objCmd.Parameters.Item(1).Value = objXMLDOM.xml
```

That wraps up the discussion of working with SQL Server, XML, and ADO. Next, on to the future and ADO.NET.

Programming XML with ADO.NET

The .NET Framework brings with it a new set of data access objects, ADO.NET. In many respects it's similar to ADO and the data access technologies that preceded it such as RDO and DAO. However, there are fundamental differences. Some of them are:

- The `DataSet` object is a virtual in-memory database. It and its component `DataTable` replace the `Recordset` object.
- There is increased flexibility, through the `DataAdapter` object, in controlling the SQL statements that ADO.NET uses to access SQL Server.
- ADO.NET's operation in much more disconnected from the database than ADO.

This section will show two ways of accessing XML with ADO.NET:

- Executing FOR XML queries with a SQLCommand Class.
- Creating ADO.NET DataSets and requesting ADO.NET's XML representation of the data.

Under the hood, ADO.NET makes extensive use of XML. In particular, it uses XML as its internal representation of data, as a method of persisting data to local files, and as the wire format when data is marshaled between components or across networks.

Executing a FOR XML Query With SqlCommand

The ADO.NET SqlCommand object is similar to the ADO Command object. Like ADO's Command object, it can be used to execute a SQL query. Once the query is executed, you can retrieve the XML using the ExecuteXMLReader method. The following Visual Basic .NET code is in the XMLTextReaderExample project in the code download:

```
Imports System                   ' Import statements bring in
Imports System.Data              ' namespaces so that complete object
Imports System.Data.SqlClient    ' namespaces dont need typed
Imports System.Xml               ' for each object reference

Module XMLTextReaderExample

    Sub Main()

        Dim objConn As New SqlConnection("Server=(local);" _
                & "Database=SQLXMLExamples12;" _
                & "Integrated Security=SSPI")
        objConn.Open()

        ' Create the SQL Command Object and the
        ' XMLTextReader from it.
        Dim objCmd As New SqlCommand( _
                "Select * FROM BLCustomer FOR XML RAW", objConn)
        Dim objXMLReader As XmlTextReader = _
        objCmd.ExecuteXmlReader()

        objXMLReader.MoveToContent() ' get to the beginning
        Do While objXMLReader.IsStartElement

            Console.WriteLine(objXMLReader.ReadOuterXml)

        Loop

        objXMLReader.Close()

        objConn.Close()
    End Sub

End Module
```

Programmatic Access with SQLXML

As with ADO, a connection to a database must be established to extract data. These lines create the `SqlConnection` object and open the connection. As described earlier, you must attach the SQLXMLExamples12 database, and you may have to change the connection string to get it to work on your system. Here's how the connection is established:

```
Dim objConn As New SqlConnection("Server=(local);" _
    & "Database=SQLXMLExamples12;" _
    & "Integrated Security=SSPI")
objConn.Open()
```

Notice how there is no `Provider` in the connection string. That's because the `SQLConnection` can only be used to connect to SQL Server 7.0+ (if you were using SQL Server 6.5, or other database like Oracle, you would have to use the less efficient OLE DB data provider). The `SQLConnection` object is part of the `System.Data.SQLClient` namespace imported at the top of the module. To make a connection to any database supported by `OLEDB`, use the `OLEDBConnection` object instead. It's included in the `System.Data.OLEDB` namespace.

Next, the `SQLCommand` is created and initialized with the SQL query:

```
Dim objCmd As New SqlCommand( _
"Select * FROM Customer FOR XML RAW", objConn)
```

The command is executed when the `ExecuteXmlReader` method is called. This method returns an `XmlReader` class. The `XMLReader` class is never instantiated; it's only available so that it can be inherited. You must use one of the classes that inherit from `XmlReader` to read the data. In this case, the `XmlTextReader` is used:

```
Dim objXMLReader As XmlTextReader = objCmd.ExecuteXmlReader()
```

The text reader interface to ADO.NET is for fast, forward-only reading and processing of XML. In the example, the XML is read and sent to the console window with this loop:

```
objXMLReader.MoveToContent()
Do While objXMLReader.IsStartElement

Console.WriteLine(objXMLReader.ReadOuterXml)
Loop
```

The XML result is displayed in the console window. You might want to set a break point at the line:

```
End Sub
```

so that the console window doesn't disappear before you can examine it.

Chapter 13

Saving ADO.NET Datasets as XML

This is only one of the ways to read XML with ADO.NET. The next method doesn't use SQL Server's XML Features. Just as in the earlier example, where ADO `Recordset` object saved its internal structure as XML, the ADO.NET `DataSet` object can do the same job, however, the data structure is different. This example shows how it's done. You'll find it as the `SQLXMLDataSetDemo` project in the code download:

```
Imports System
Imports System.Data
Imports System.Data.SqlClient

Module Module1
Sub Main()
        Dim objConn As New SqlConnection("Server=(local);" _
                                & "Database=Pubs;" _
                                & "Integrated Security=SSPI")
objConn.Open()
Dim objCmd As New SqlCommand( _
                            "SELECT * FROM Authors", objConn)
Dim objAdapter As New SqlDataAdapter(objCmd)
Dim objDataSet As New DataSet("AuthorList")
objAdapter.Fill(objDataSet, "Authors")
' Disconnect the connection, it's not needed anymore
objConn.Close()
objDataSet.WriteXml("c:\temp\SQLXMLDataSetDemo.XML" _
                    , XmlWriteMode.WriteSchema)
End Sub
End Module
```

The SQL query is a little different from the previous example, as it doesn't have a `FOR XML` clause. Once the `DataSet` is filled, the XML can be written to a file with the `WriteXml` method. Of course, it could also be sent to a `MemoryStream` object and worked with inside the program.

Using the `XmlWriteMode.WriteSchema` in the call to `WriteXml` requests that the schema be included in the result of the query. Here's part of the `SQLXMLDataSetDemo.XML` file. The schema is on top, followed by the data, truncated for display purposes. When you apply changes, be sure there are no lines between the end of the schema and the first `<author>`:

```
<?xml version="1.0" standalone="yes"?>
<AuthorList>
  <xs:schema id="AuthorList" xmlns=""
          xmlns:xs="http://www.w3.org/2001/XMLSchema"
          xmlns:msdata="urn:schemas-microsoft-com:xml-msdata">
    <xs:element name="AuthorList" msdata:IsDataSet="true">
    <xs:complexType>
    <xs:choice maxOccurs="unbounded">
    <xs:element name="Authors">
    <xs:complexType>
    <xs:sequence>
    <xs:element name="au_id" type="xs:string" minOccurs="0" />
    <xs:element name="au_lname" type="xs:string" minOccurs="0" />
```

Programmatic Access with SQLXML

```
        <xs:element name="au_fname" type="xs:string" minOccurs="0" />
        <xs:element name="phone" type="xs:string" minOccurs="0" />
        <xs:element name="address" type="xs:string" minOccurs="0" />
        <xs:element name="city" type="xs:string" minOccurs="0" />
        <xs:element name="state" type="xs:string" minOccurs="0" />
        <xs:element name="zip" type="xs:string" minOccurs="0" />
        <xs:element name="contract"
                    type="xs:boolean" minOccurs="0" />
      </xs:sequence>
     </xs:complexType>
    </xs:element>
   </xs:choice>
  </xs:complexType>
 </xs:element>
</xs:schema>
<Authors>
 <au_id>172-32-1176</au_id>
 <au_lname>White</au_lname>
 <au_fname>Johnson</au_fname>
 <phone>408 496-7223</phone>
 <address>10932 Bigge Rd.</address>
 <city>Menlo Park</city>
 <state>CA</state>
 <zip>94025</zip>
 <contract>true</contract>
</Authors>
<Authors>
 ...
</Authors>
</AuthorList>
```

Compare this to the XML produced by the ADO.Recordset in the earlier example. Microsoft has switched from using its own namespaces for defining the inline schema to using the W3C's schema. The results have also been switched from attribute-oriented to element-oriented XML.

While ADO can be persuaded to work with SQL Server to extract XML, SQLXML 3.0 added .NET classes to make the interface easier to program. That's the next subject.

SQLXML Managed Classes

The SQLXML Managed Classes are part of the SQLXML distribution. They are installed only if the .NET Framework is installed before SQLXML. There are three classes:

- SqlXmlCommand, which retrieves XML in a similar way to the ADO Command object.
- SqlXmlParameter, used to hold parameters to the SqlXmlCommand.
- SqlXmlAdapter, which allows you to retrieve a DataSet using various SQLXML methods, such as FOR XML clauses.

393

Chapter 13

To use the SQLXML Managed Classes in a Visual Studio.NET program, a reference to the `Microsoft.Data.SqlXml.dll` must be added to the project. This can be done with the **Add Reference** command on the **Project** menu. Once the reference is added, the line:

```
Imports Microsoft.Data.SqlXml
```

should be added to the program so that each reference in the code to something in that library doesn't have to have a fully qualified name.

We'll discuss each class in turn.

SqlXmlCommand

The `SqlXmlCommand` is a .NET class that allows a program to work with XML in a way nearly identical to the ADO `Command` object. It has a set of properties matching one-for-one with the properties and extended properties used in the earlier section of this chapter on ADO.

This minimal example, using the `Pubs` database, shows just how easy `SqlXmlCommand` can be to use. The code is in the project SQLXMLCommandDemo in the code download:

```
Imports System
Imports System.IO
Imports Microsoft.Data.SqlXml  ' The SQLXML Managed Classes

' This is an example of using the SqlXmlCommand object.
Module SQLXMLCommandDemo
Sub Main()
        Dim objCmd As New SqlXmlCommand("Provider=SQLOLEDB;" _
                        & "SERVER=(local);" _
                        & "Database=Pubs;" _
                        & "Integrated Security=SSPI")
objCmd.CommandType = SqlXmlCommandType.Sql
objCmd.CommandText = " SELECT au_id, au_fname, au_lname " _
                        & "    FROM Authors " _
                        & "    FOR XML RAW "

Dim objResultStream As MemoryStream = objCmd.ExecuteStream()

' The reader is needed for Dot NET Streams
' to retrieve the output
Dim objResultStreamReader As New StreamReader(objResultStream)

' Send all the XML to the console.
Console.Write(objResultStreamReader.ReadToEnd)

End Sub
End Module
```

Most of the properties and extended properties that were discussed in the section on ADO and its `Command` object also exist in `SqlXmlCommand`. The next section discusses the properties and how they might be used.

Programmatic Access with SQLXML

Properties of SqlXmlCommand

This table lists the properties of `SqlXmlCommand` and relates them to the matching property in `ADODB.Command`:

Group	Property	Corresponds to ADO Property	Usage
Command Input	CommandType	Command.Dialect	What type of input is in CommandText?
	CommandText	Command.CommandText	Holds the input query.
	CommandStream	Command.CommandStream	Provides the input when it's in a stream.
XML Formatting	RootTag	Command.Properties("XML Root")	Tag used to surround the XML fragment that SQL returns to make well-formed XML.
	Namespaces	Command.Properties("Namespaces")	Gives the namespaces that are added to the output XML.
	OutputEncoding	Command.Properties("Output Encoding")	UTF8, ASCII or Unicode.
Control Input Files	BasePath	Command.Properties("Base Path")	The top-level path to the files referenced in other properties.
	SchemaPath	Command.Properties("Mapping Schema")	Points to an XML or XDR mapping schema that instructs ADO how to map between the relational database and XML.

Table continued on following page

395

Group	Property	Corresponds to ADO Property	Usage
	`XslPath`	`Command.Properties("XSL")`	URL or file name of the XSL that should be applied to the XML before producing the output.
Client-Side Processing	`ClientSide XML`	`Command.Properties("ClientSideXML")`	Specifies that client-side XML be used instead of sending FOR XML.
No Analagous Property		`Command.Properties("SS STREAM FLAGS")`	Provides instructions to ADO about how to manage mapping schemas, XSLT, and templates specified by other properties.
		`Command.Properties("Output Stream")`	The output stream is no longer a property. In `SqlXmlCommand` it is the return value.

Many of these properties will be used in the examples that follow.

CommandType

Like `ADO.Command.Dialect`, this parameter tells the class what type of query is in the `CommandText`. Each type is a member of the `SqlXmlCommandType`. There are more values available than for the `Dialect` property, as shown in this table:

Programmatic Access with SQLXML

SqlXMLCommandType Value	Usage
SqlXmlCommandType.SQL	Executes a T-SQL query with a FOR XML clause.
SqlXmlCommandType.XPath	Executes an XPath query against a mapping schema.
SqlXmlCommandType.Template	Executes a template. The text of the template is in CommandText.
SqlXmlCommandType.TemplateFile	Executes a template that's in a file. The path to the file is in CommandText.
SqlXmlCommandType.UpdateGram	Executes an Updategram.
SqlXmlCommandType.DiffGram	Executes a DiffGram.

CommandText

When the input is provided as text, the CommandText property holds the query. Typical coding was shown in the above example program with the lines:

```
            Dim objCmd As New SqlXmlCommand("Provider=SQLOLEDB;" _
                            & "SERVER=(local);" _
                            & "Database=Pubs;" _
                            & "Integrated Security=SSPI")
objCmd.CommandType = SqlXmlCommandType.Sql
objCmd.CommandText = " SELECT au_id, au_fname, au_lname " _
                            & "    FROM Authors " _
                            & "    FOR XML RAW "
```

It's also possible to send a template in the CommandText, as we do here:

```
objCmd.CommandType = SqlXmlCommandType.Template
objCmd.CommandText = _
"<?xml version=""1.0"" ?>" & vbCrLf _
& "<root>" & vbCrLf _
& "   <sql:query xmlns:sql=" _
& "'urn:schemas-microsoft-com:xml-sql'>" _
& vbCrLf _
& "         SELECT * FROM authors FOR XML AUTO" & vbCrLf _
& "   </sql:query>" & vbCrLf _
& "</root>"
```

This code can be found as part of the SQLXMLCommandTemplate example project in the code download.

CommandStream

When using a long XML string as input to SqlXmlCommand, it's beneficial to put the input in a stream, and use the CommandStream property. For example:

Chapter 13

```
objCmd.CommandStream = New FileStream("PubsTemplate.xml" _
, FileMode.Open, FileAccess.Read)
objCmd.CommandType = SqlXmlCommandType.Template
```

This code can be found in the SQLCommandTemplateStream .NET example program in the code download. The PubsTemplate.XML file is located in the SQLCommandTemplateStream\bin subdirectory for this chapter.

RootTag

Unless a template or mapping schema is used, SQL Server returns a XML fragment. The RootTag property allows the addition of a root level element that makes the XML well-formed. For example, the line:

```
ObjCmd.RootTag = "authors"
```

adds an <authors> element which will be the root element of the resulting XML.

Namespaces

Adds the namespaces specified to the root element. This is useful when using XPath queries that use namespaces. For example, coding:

```
objCMD.NameSpaces = _
& "xmlns:rdf=""http://www.w3.org/TR/WD-rdf-syntax"""
```

would add the namespace to the root element. Instead of <authors>, the root element of the XML would be
<authors xmlns:rdf="http://www.w3.org/TR/WD-rdf-syntax">.
Multiple namespaces can be inserted just by separating them with whitespace.

OutputEncoding

The OutputEncoding property specifies the encoding attribute that is inserted in the <?xml> processing instruction at the start of an XML document. So if this statement is added to our program:

```
objcmd.OutputEncoding = "Unicode"
```

the result is that the <?xml> processing instruction in our resulting XML would be:

<?xml version="1.0" encoding="Unicode">

Other options are UTF-8 and ASCII.

BasePath

This property gives the directory used to locate a XSL file, mapping schema, or XML template.

Programmatic Access with SQLXML

SchemaPath

Gives the location of the mapping schema file when XPath queries are performed.

XSLPath

The path of the XSL file that is used to transform the XML result.

ClientSideXML

Running in the .NET Framework doesn't change the fact that formatting XML is work for SQL Server. The `ClientSideXml` property allows this work to be moved from the SQL Server to the client program. If you've skipped over section *SQLXMLOLEDB Provider and Client-Side Processing* earlier in the chapter, now would a good time to check it out. To request client-side processing, all that's required is to set the `ClientSideXml` property to `True`. Here's an example program that uses client-side processing. You'll find this code in the `SQLCommandClientSide` example project in the code download. The `CustomerInvoices.XML` file usually ends up in the \bin subdirectory of the project:

```
Imports System
Imports System.IO
Imports Microsoft.Data.SqlXml  ' The SQLXML Managed Classes

' This is an example of using the SqlXmlCommand object
' specifying client-side XML processing
Module SQLCommandClientSide
Sub Main()
        Dim objCmd As New SqlXmlCommand("Provider=SQLOLEDB;" _
                   & "SERVER=(local);" _
                   & "Database=SQLXMLExamples12;" _
                   & "Integrated Security=SSPI")
  objCmd.CommandText = "exec usp_CustomerInvoices ? " & _
                       "FOR XML NESTED"
objCmd.CommandType = SqlXmlCommandType.Sql
objCmd.ClientSideXml = True
objCmd.RootTag = "CustomerInovices"
objCmd.OutputEncoding = "ASCII"

' Create and initialize the parameter to the Stored Procedure.
Dim objParm As SqlXmlParameter = objCmd.CreateParameter
objParm.Name = "State"
objParm.Value = "CA"

' Create a stream to send the result to a file.
Dim objResultStream As New FileStream _
("CustomerInvoices.XML", FileMode.Create, FileAccess.Write)
objCmd.ExecuteToStream(objResultStream)
' You'll usually find the CustomerInvoices.XML file in the
' Bin subdirectory of the project.
End Sub
End Module
```

The line:

```
objCmd.ClientSideXml = True
```

makes the request for client-side processing. Notice that the `ConnectionString` does not include `SQLXMLOLEDB`. The managed class makes this substitution on its own.

Our `SqlXmlCommand` examples so far have used the `SqlXmlCommand.ExecuteStream` method to run the command. This last example uses one of the alternative methods, which are discussed next.

Methods of SqlXmlCommand

In place of the `ADODB.Command.Execute` method, there are several ways to run a command. Each executes the command but returns the results in a different way. The methods are listed in this table:

Method	Return Type	Usage
`ExecuteNonQuery()`	None	Executes the command, but does not return anything. An example is executing an updategram or a DiffGram that updates records but returns nothing.
`ExecuteStream`	`Stream`	Executes the command and returns a new stream.
`ExecuteToStream`	None	Executes the command and writes the query results to an existing stream. This method is useful when you have a stream to which you need the results appended (for example, to have the query results written to the `System.Web.HttpResponse.OutputStream`).
`ExecuteXmlReader()`	`XmlReader`	Executes the command and returns a new `XmlReader` such as `XmlTextReader`. You can use this method either to manipulate data in the `XmlReader` object directly or plug in the chainable architecture of `System.Xml`.

In the `ClientSideXml` example above, the `ExecuteToStream` method was used because a stream had already been created. This line created the stream:

Programmatic Access with SQLXML

```
' Create a stream to send the result to a file.
Dim objResultStream As New FileStream _
("CustomerInvoices.XML", FileMode.Create, FileAccess.Write)
The next line called ExecuteToStream:
objCmd.ExecuteToStream(objResultStream)
```

The XML results were written directly to the file as the command was executed. This type of overlapped work shows the potential for passing data from object to object efficiently with .NET streams.

In addition to methods for executing a command, `SqlXmlCommand` has two methods for working with parameters. These are useful when calling templates with parameters or stored procedures that take parameters. They are:

Method	Return Type	Usage
CreateParameter	SqlXmlParameter	Creates a new parameter.
ClearParameters	None	Clears the values of all parameters. Used when the SqlXmlCommand is being used for multiple calls.

`CreateParameter` was used in the `SQLCommandClientSide` example; it will be discussed further in the next section on the `SqlXmlParamater` object.

SqlXmlParameter

`SqlXmlParameter` is used when a `SqlXmlCommand` requires a data value to complete its SQL statement. The parameter is created by a call to `SqlXmlCommand.CreateParameter`, and the caller sets its value properties and name. The `SQLCommandClientSide` example above created a parameter and initialized it with this code:

```
' Create and initialize the parameter to the Stored Procedure.
Dim objParm As SqlXmlParameter = objCmd.CreateParameter
objParm.Name = "State"
objParm.Value = "CA"
```

The parameter value is substituted for the question mark in the SQL statement:

```
exec usp_CustomerInvoices ? FOR XML NESTED
```

The result is that `SqlXmlCommand` sends the statement:

```
exec sp_executesql
         N'exec usp_CustomerInvoices @P1 '
         , N'@P1 nvarchar(2)', N'CA'
```

401

Chapter 13

to SQL Server. `Sp_executesql` takes care of performing the parameter substitution. Remember, the `FOR XML NESTED` clause is for client-side processing. It has been stripped from the SQL, and is applied once SQL Server returns its results.

The `Name` property isn't really necessary in this case.

SqlXmlAdapter

There is one more SQLXML Managed Class, `SQLXMLAdpater`. It can be used to work with an ADO.NET `DataSet` in a way similar to the way `SQLAdapter` was used in the earlier `DataSet` example.

Adapters are responsible for orchestrating the movement of data between the command object, in this case `SqlXmlCommand`, and a `DataSet`. The command is responsible for writing the SQL and providing the results to the adapter. In the following example, the `SqlXmlCommand` uses an XPath query to retrieve the `Authors` table. You'll find the code in the `SQLXMLAdapterExample` project:

```
Imports System
Imports System.IO
Imports Microsoft.Data.SqlXml   ' The SQLXML Managed Classes

Module SQLXMLAdapterExample

    Sub Main()

        Dim objCmd As New SqlXmlCommand("Provider=SQLOLEDB;" _
                            & "SERVER=(local);" _
                            & "Database=Pubs;" _
                            & "Integrated Security=SSPI")

        objCmd.RootTag = "root"

        ' Set the XPath Query
        objCmd.CommandType = SqlXmlCommandType.XPath
        objCmd.CommandText = "Authors[au_lname != ""Novick""]"

        objCmd.SchemaPath = "Authors.XSD"  ' The schema file

        Dim objAdpt As New SqlXmlAdapter(objCmd)

        Dim objDS As New DataSet()

        objAdpt.Fill(objDS)

        Console.WriteLine("Original name 1st author is " _
                & objDS.Tables("Authors").Rows(0)("au_lname"))

        ' Get the first row of the Authors table
        Dim Row As DataRow = objDS.Tables("Authors").Rows(0)
        ' Change the first name to Novick
```

Programmatic Access with SQLXML

```
            Row("au_lname") = "Novick"

        ' The previous two lines could have been written as:
        ' objDS.Tables("Authors").Rows(0)("au_lname") = "Novick"

        objAdpt.Update(objDS)  ' Send the updates to the database

        Console.WriteLine("Update done.")

    End Sub

End Module
```

After the SQLXMLCommand object is created and its properties are set with the RootTag, XPath query, and schema file, the SqlXmlAdapter and DataSet are created and the adapter is used to fill the DataSet with the lines:

```
        Dim objAdpt As New SqlXmlAdapter(objCmd)

        Dim objDS As New DataSet()

        objAdpt.Fill(objDS)
```

When the objAdpt.Fill method is invoked, the SqlXmlAdapter uses the SQLXMLCommand to construct a SQL SELECT with a FOR XML EXPLICIT clause based on the mapping schema. That creates XML, which the SqlXmlAdapter uses to populate the DataSet. In this case, there is only one table in the DataSet, but there could be more.

DataSets are made up of a collection of DataTables, which are made up of a collection of DataRows, which contain the DataColumns holding the actual values. The next line creates a DataRow object that references the first row in the Authors DataTable:

```
        ' Get the first row of the Authors table
        Dim Row As DataRow = objDS.Tables("Authors").Rows(0)
```

Next, the value of the au_lname field in the row is set to "Novick":

```
    ' Change the first name to Novick
        Row("au_lname") = "Novick"
```

Finally, the SqlXmlAdapter is used to propagate the changes made to the DataSet back to the database:

```
        objAdpt.Update(objDS)  ' Send the updates to the database
```

403

The `SqlXmlCommand` will write the SQL to make the changes to the `DataSet`. When using the `SQLDataAdapter` and `SQLCommand` objects, programmers have the opportunity to construct the SQL exactly as they want, by creating `SQLCommand` objects for each database operation: `SELECT`, `INSERT`, `UPDATE`, and `DELETE`. That isn't the case with the `SQLXMLAdapter` which writes all the SQL for you, and does not require the creation of objects for every database operation.

The XPath query `Authors[au_lname != "Novick"]` limits the query results to authors whose name has not yet been changed to Novick. If you run the program enough times, all the authors will be named Novick, no rows are returned by the query, and the program fails.

The above example used a mapping schema and an XPath query to retrieve the data. It's also allowable to use any `SQLCommandType`, such as a SQL statement with a `FOR XML` clause, a template, an Updategram, or a Diffgram. What's required is that the query return XML. However, updates can be sent to the database only when using a mapping schema and XPath query.

Along with SQL, XPath, and templates, the `SQLXMLCommand` can take Updategrams and DiffGrams as their input. Updategrams are a type of template discussed in Chapter 11. Diffgrams are another way to update SQL Server with XML, and are the subject of the next section.

DiffGrams

During the discussion of ADO.NET, the fact that it made extensive use of XML as an internal format was mentioned. DiffGram is the internal format used by the ADO.NET `DataSet`. The format wasn't created as a convenient mechanism for humans to hand craft and send to SQL Server. The original intent of DiffGrams, and their primary use, is as a format for the .NET `DataSet` class to store and communicate data, state, and error information. I prefer using Updategrams where possible.

Every DiffGram is an XML template that follows the same layout:

```
<?xml version="1.0"?>
<diffgr:diffgram
xmlns:xsd="http://www.w3.org/2001/XMLSchema"
xmlns:msdata="urn:schemas-microsoft-com:xml-msdata"
xmlns:diffgr="urn:schemas-microsoft-com:xml-diffgram-v1">

<DataList>
... Elements for the new data
</DataList>
[<diffgr:before>
...Elements for the original data
</diffgr:before>]
[<diffgr:errors>
... Elements for error information
</diffgr:errors>]
</diffgr:diffgram>
```

Programmatic Access with SQLXML

A Diffgram starts with namespace references to three schemas in the top-level `<diffgr:diffgram>` element. This is then followed by an element with the new data. In the XML above, I've named this element `<DataList>`, but any name can be used for this element. That's followed by the `<diffgr:before>` element that gives the values before an update was applied. Finally, there is the `<diffgr:errors>` element, which contains error state information.

Since the .NET `DataSet` can save its internal state as a DiffGram, I wrote the example project `SQLDemoDiffGramWriter` to do just that:

```vb
Imports System
Imports System.Data
Imports System.Data.SqlClient
Imports Microsoft.Data.SqlXml
Imports System.IO

Module SQLDemoDiffGramWriter

    Sub Main()

        ' Create a Connection to the database
        Dim objConn As New SqlConnection("Server=(local);" _
                        & "Database=Pubs;" _
                        & "Integrated Security=SSPI")
        objConn.Open()

        Dim objCmd As New SqlCommand( _
                "Select Top 2 au_id, au_fname, au_lname " _
            & "   FROM Authors", _
                objConn)

        Dim objAdapter As New SqlDataAdapter(objCmd)
        Dim objDataSet As New DataSet("AuthorList")

        ' Execute the command to read the authors
        objAdapter.Fill(objDataSet, "Authors")

        Dim objTable As DataTable = _
objDataSet.Tables("Authors")

        ' Get a row object for the first row
        Dim dsRow As DataRow = objTable.Rows(0)

        dsRow("au_fname") = "Fred" ' Change the name to Fred

        ' Save the DataSet as a diffgram to a file.
        objDataSet.WriteXml("C:\Temp\SQLXMLDiffgram.XML", _
                XmlWriteMode.DiffGram)

        objConn.Close()

    End Sub

End Module
```

Chapter 13

The module reads the first two records from the `Authors` table into a `DataSet` with the lines:

```
Dim objCmd As New SqlCommand( _
            "Select Top 2 au_id, au_fname, au_lname " _
         & "   FROM Authors", _
            objConn)
Dim objAdapter As New SqlDataAdapter(objCmd)
Dim objDataSet As New DataSet("AuthorList")
objAdapter.Fill(objDataSet, "Authors")
```

It then makes one small change, by setting the `au_fname` field in row 0 to `Fred`:

```
Dim objTable As DataTable = objDataSet.Tables("Authors")
' Get a row object for the first row
Dim dsRow As DataRow = objTable.Rows(0)
dsRow("au_fname") = "Fred"
```

Finally, it uses the `DataSet`'s `WriteXml` method to write the file `c:\temp\SQLXMLDiffgram.XML`. Alternatively, you could use `objAdapter` to send changes to the `DataSet` directly to the database. Take a look at the resulting file shown below. Note that you may see slightly different rows, depending on how many changes have been made to your `Pubs` database:

This is `SQLXMLDiffgramBeforeUpdate.xml`:

```
<?xml version="1.0" standalone="yes"?>
<diffgr:diffgram
   xmlns:msdata="urn:schemas-microsoft-com:xml-msdata"
   xmlns:diffgr="urn:schemas-microsoft-com:xml-diffgram-v1">
   <AuthorList>
      <Authors diffgr:id="Authors1" msdata:rowOrder="0"
               diffgr:hasChanges="modified">
         <au_id>409-56-7008</au_id>
         <au_fname>Fred</au_fname>
         <au_lname>Bennet</au_lname>
      </Authors>

   ...

   </diffgr:before>
</diffgr:diffgram>
```

As you can see, it follows the standard DiffGram format. Instead of the element name `<DataList>` that was used above, the `DataSet` uses the `DataSet`'s name for the first subelement of the DiffGram. That element includes the rows of data. Had the `DataSet` contained multiple tables, the rows from one table would have followed the other.

Programmatic Access with SQLXML

Since the au_fname of Mr Bennet has changed, the updated data is in the first <Authors> element. The original values are in the <diffgram:before> element. This is the information that SQLDataAdapter needs when it is figuring out what changes to apply to the database. DiffGrams are a form of template, and they can be executed with the SqlXmlCommand class. However, executing one requires that a mapping schema be available. The project SQLXMLDiffgramUpdate shows how a DiffGram file created by the previous example can be applied to the database using a mapping schema. The file Authors.xsd, located in the \bin directory of the project, is the schema. The code to apply the DiffGram is short:

```
Imports System
Imports System.IO
Imports System.Data
Imports System.Data.SqlClient
Imports Microsoft.Data.SqlXml

Module SQLXMLDiffgramUpdate

    Sub Main()

        'Create a Command for the applying the Diffgram
        Dim objCmd As New SqlXmlCommand("PROVIDER=SQLOLEDB;" _
                        & "SERVER=(local);" _
                        & "DATABASE=Pubs;" _
                        & "INTEGRATED SECURITY=SSPI;")

        ' Load the Diffgram into the Command Stream
        objCmd.CommandStream = New _
FileStream("c:\temp\SQLXMLDiffgram.xml" _
            , FileMode.Open, FileAccess.Read)

        objCmd.CommandType = SqlXmlCommandType.DiffGram
        objCmd.SchemaPath = "Authors.xsd" ' in project's \bin

        objCmd.ExecuteNonQuery() ' run the query

    End Sub
End Module
```

The CommandStream is populated with the contents of the DiffGram that we wrote to c:\temp\SQLXMLDiffgram.XML in the previous example. The CommandType is set to DiffGram. The path to the mapping schema is set, and the ExecuteNonQuery method is used. This method executes the command but does not return a Stream. Then a miracle occurs! I've reformatted the SQL that performs the update, captured from the Profiler:

```
SET XACT_ABORT ON
BEGIN TRAN
DECLARE @eip INT, @r__ int, @e__ int
SET @eip = 0
```

Chapter 13

```
UPDATE Authors
SET au_fname=N'Fred'
WHERE  ( au_id=N'409-56-7008' )
AND    ( au_fname=N'Abraham' )
AND    ( au_lname=N'Bennet' ) ;

SELECT @e__ = @@ERROR, @r__ = @@ROWCOUNT
IF (@e__ != 0 OR @r__ != 1) SET @eip = 1
IF (@r__ > 1) RAISERROR ( N'SQLOLEDB Error Description:'
   ' Ambiguous update, unique identifier required '
   Transaction aborted ', 16, 1)
ELSE IF (@r__ < 1) RAISERROR ( N'SQLOLEDB Error Description:'
   ' Empty update, no updatable rows found '
   ' Transaction aborted ', 16, 1)
IF (@eip != 0)
ROLLBACK
ELSE COMMIT
SET XACT_ABORT OFF
```

Just the minimum SQL to perform the update, report errors, and rollback in case there was a runtime error or if more than one row was updated.

The DiffGram writes a WHERE clause that has every field in the data. If any of the fields, even one that is not being set, has changed, the UPDATE is not performed. I call this optimistic locking, although I've also seen it referred to as pessimistic. After all, no database locks have been held; in fact, weeks could have transpired between the time the DiffGram was generated and the time it was applied. It's your application's responsibility to handle these problems.

DiffGram INSERTs and DELETEs are applied the same way as the UPDATEs example above:

- ❏ A DataSet is created and filled using an adapter.
- ❏ Modifications are made to the DataTables in the DataSet.
- ❏ Changes to the DataSet are sent to the database by the adapter and command objects associated with it.

Let's tackle INSERTs first. The example program SQLXMLDiffgramInsert has the following code:

```
Imports System
Imports System.Data
Imports System.Data.SqlClient
Imports Microsoft.Data.SqlXml
Imports System.IO

Module SQLDemoDiffGramInsert

    Sub Main()

        Dim objCmd As New SqlXmlCommand("Provider=SQLOLEDB;" _
```

Programmatic Access with SQLXML

```
                            & "SERVER=(local);" _
                            & "Database=Pubs;" _
                            & "Integrated Security=SSPI")

        objCmd.RootTag = "root"

        ' Set the XPath Query
        objCmd.CommandType = SqlXmlCommandType.XPath
        objCmd.CommandText = "Authors"

    ' The schema file
        objCmd.SchemaPath = "Authors4Insert.XSD"

        Dim objAdpt As New SqlXmlAdapter(objCmd)

        Dim objDataSet As New DataSet("AuthorList")

        ' Execute the command to read the authors
        objAdpt.Fill(objDataSet)

        Dim objTable As DataTable = objDataSet.Tables("Authors")

        ' Delete the first row
        '       objTable.Rows(0).Delete()

        ' Get a row to insert, and fill it's fields
        Dim dsRow As DataRow = objTable.NewRow
        dsRow("au_id") = "999-99-9999" ' ID
        dsRow("au_fname") = "Andrew" ' first name
        dsRow("au_lname") = "Novick" ' Last name
        dsRow("contract") = 1 ' Has a contract
        objTable.Rows.Add(dsRow)

        ' Save the DataSet as a diffgram to a file.
        objDataSet.WriteXml("C:\Temp\SQLXMLDiffgramInsert.XML", _
                XmlWriteMode.DiffGram)

        objAdpt.Update(objDataSet)

    End Sub

End Module
```

It uses a `SqlXmlAdapter` and a `SqlXmlCommand` with an XPath query, `Authors`, and a mapping schema (`Authors4Insert.XSD`), to retrieve the data and populate the `DataSet`. This is the same type of code that was used in the `SQLXMLAdapterExample` project shown earlier, but there are a few changes.

The XPath Query was simplified to retrieve all the authors. If there are authors returned by SQL Server, the `SqlXmlAdapter` will not make an empty `DataTable` for `Authors`, and the line:

409

Chapter 13

```
Dim objTable As DataTable = objDataSet.Tables("Authors")
```

results in `objTable` being equal to nothing. The trick of specifying a `WHERE` clause of `1=2` when creating a `recordset` that's only going to be used for `INSERT`s won't work with the SQLXML Managed Classes.

Also note that a slightly different XML Schema file was used, `Authors4Insert.XSD`. It adds the contract column to the schema. Since the contract column doesn't have a default, it must be set by the `INSERT`. It wasn't in the `Authors.XSD` schema used earlier. The `Authors4Insert.XSD` has an element for the `contract` field, and is located in the `SQLXMLDiffGramInsert\bin` directory of the code download.

Before the updates are performed, the code writes the `DataSet` as a DiffGram to the file `c:\temp\SQLXMLDiffgramInserts.xml`. Take a look at the file, either in `c:\temp` or my copy in the code download directory. Most of the `<Authors>` have been removed to save space:

```xml
<?xml version="1.0" standalone="yes"?>
<diffgr:diffgram
  xmlns:msdata="urn:schemas-microsoft-com:xml-msdata"
  xmlns:diffgr="urn:schemas-microsoft-com:xml-diffgram-v1">
  <root>
    <Authors diffgr:id="Authors1" msdata:rowOrder="0">
      <au_id>172-32-1176</au_id>
      <au_fname>Johnson</au_fname>
      <au_lname>White</au_lname>
      <contract>1</contract>
    </Authors>

    ...

    <Authors diffgr:id="Authors24" msdata:rowOrder="23"
             diffgr:hasChanges="inserted">
      <au_id>999-99-9999</au_id>
      <au_fname>Andrew</au_fname>
      <au_lname>Novick</au_lname>
      <contract>1</contract>
    </Authors>
  </root>
</diffgr:diffgram>
```

The inserted `<Author>` is the last one with `diffgr:id="Authors24"`. The status as a newly inserted row is tracked by the `diffgr:hasChanges="inserted"` attribute on that row. There are no entries for it in `<diffgr:before>` or `<diffgr:after>`.

`DELETE`s are similar to `INSERT`s as seen in the project `SQLXMLDiffgramDelete`. Here's the code:

Programmatic Access with SQLXML

```vb
Imports System
Imports System.Data
Imports System.Data.SqlClient
Imports Microsoft.Data.SqlXml
Imports System.IO

Module SQLDemoDiffGramDelete

    Sub Main()

        Dim objCmd As New SqlXmlCommand("Provider=SQLOLEDB;" _
                            & "SERVER=(local);" _
                            & "Database=Pubs;" _
                            & "Integrated Security=SSPI")

        objCmd.RootTag = "root"

        ' Set the XPath Query
        objCmd.CommandType = SqlXmlCommandType.XPath
        objCmd.CommandText = "Authors[au_id = ""999-99-9999""]"

        objCmd.SchemaPath = "Authors.XSD" ' The schema file

        Dim objAdpt As New SqlXmlAdapter(objCmd)

        Dim objDataSet As New DataSet("AuthorList")

        ' Execute the command to read the authors
        objAdpt.Fill(objDataSet)

        Dim objTable As DataTable = objDataSet.Tables("Authors")

        ' Delete the first row
        objTable.Rows(0).Delete()

        ' Save the DataSet as a diffgram to a file.
        objDataSet.WriteXml("C:\Temp\SQLXMLDiffgramDelete.XML", _
                    XmlWriteMode.DiffGram)

        objAdpt.Update(objDataSet)

    End Sub

End Module
```

The line:

```
objTable.Rows(0).Delete()
```

deletes the first row. Again, a row must be retrieved in order for the SqlXmlAdapter to create the Authors DataTable in the DataSet. The DiffGram for the delete is in the file SQLXMLDiffgramDelete.XML:

411

Chapter 13

```xml
<?xml version="1.0" standalone="yes"?>
<diffgr:diffgram
   xmlns:msdata="urn:schemas-microsoft-com:xml-msdata"
   xmlns:diffgr="urn:schemas-microsoft-com:xml-diffgram-v1">
   <root />
   <diffgr:before>
      <Authors diffgr:id="Authors1" msdata:rowOrder="0">
         <au_id>999-99-9999</au_id>
         <au_fname>Andrew</au_fname>
         <au_lname>Novick</au_lname>
      </Authors>
   </diffgr:before>
</diffgr:diffgram>
```

The entire row to be deleted has been moved to the `<diffgr:before>` element and the `<AuthorsList>` is now omitted from the DiffGram.

The examples in this section have all used SQLXML Managed Classes to perform the updates. They work because the `DataSet` can persist its state as a DiffGram and that DiffGram can be applied to the database. However, this is not the conventional way to update a database from `DataSets`. The `System.Data.SQLClient` or `System.Data.OLEDB` namespaces contain adapters that can do the job with SQL statements, but that's just standard ADO.NET and doesn't involve SQLXML at all.

There's considerable overlap between the functionality available with a DiffGram and the functionality available with an Updategram. In general, Updategrams were intended to be crafted by programs that must communicate database changes and have them applied. The DiffGram is able to save the state of a `DataSet` and is best used as a way to persist `DataSets` and communicate them in an easily marshalable form.

Summary

While many SQLXML features are accessible through IIS or a SQL script, most of the work of using XML in a production application is conducted by a compiled program. This chapter has shown how to use SQL Server's XML features from programs to retrieve and update data.

The ADO interface has been the mainstay of Microsoft's data access technologies. Through its `Command` object, it provides methods for executing FOR XML queries, XPath queries, or templates. The XPath query with a mapping schema is particularly interesting, because of its ability to allow so much program logic to be expressed in XML syntaxes.

ADO.NET is the future of data access. While it's possible to use some XML features with standard ADO.NET objects, XML programming tasks are much easier with the SQLXML Managed Classes. They provide a direct interface to SQLXML features.

Finally, the DiffGram was discussed. It's another way to save database information and communicate changes back to the database via SQLXML. However, it is less functional than an Updategram, and not intended to replace it.

Programmatic Access with SQLXML

Kevin Williams

- What is a Web Service?
- Setting up a SQL Server 2000 Web Service With SQLXML 3.0
- Consuming Services Through Visual Studio.NET
- Further SQL Server 2000 Web Service Topics
- Summary

14

Web Services in SQL Server 2000

In this chapter, we'll take a look at the support for SOAP web services in SQL Server 2000 using SQLXML 3.0. This is an emerging technology, which, while rather rudimentary at this time, is set to become increasingly important in the future. In the course of this chapter we'll discuss:

- What a web service is.
- Setting up web service access in SQL Server 2000 with SQLXML 3.0.
- Exposing stored procedures as web services.
- Exposing UDFs (User Defined Functions) as web services.
- XML return mechanisms for SQL Server 2000 web services.
- Error handling mechanisms with SQL Server 2000 web services.
- Consuming a SQL Server 2000 web service.
- Limitations of SQL Server 2000 web services.
- Wrapping a SQL Server 2000 web service with a .NET web service.

What is a Web Service?

A web service (for the purposes of our discussion) is a way to exchange XML messages between a server and a client. The client creates a specially formatted XML message called a **SOAP** (Simple Object Access Protocol) **message** and transmits it to the server. The server then acts on that SOAP message (this could be anything, including modifying a database or sending a message to an operator) and responds with a SOAP message back to the client. Development platforms, like .NET or Java, provide built-in support for web services, allowing code to be written to create and access these services without needing to worry about the specific messages being sent back and forth.

Chapter 14

Web services have been hailed as the cross-platform remote procedure call (RPC) mechanism the industry has been waiting for, and, while still at an early stage, it's starting to look like it really will get the job done. RPC mechanisms, such as COM/DCOM or CORBA, allow either Microsoft or Java platforms to communicate with one another, but getting a Microsoft platform to communicate with a Java platform has been difficult until now.

There are several different technologies involved in creating a web service. Once a service has been created, information about that service is exposed as a WSDL (Web Service Definition Language) document. This is an XML document that specifies what the request and response SOAP messages look like, and any client application wishing to use the web service must refer to the web service's WSDL. When web services are created for SQL Server with SQLXML 3.0 IIS support, the support auto-generates these WSDL files for the services. Systems that understand WSDL can now read the file and understand how the messages need to be passed back and forth.

As we mentioned before, the actual messages sent back and forth between server and client are SOAP messages. Most of the newer development environments, such as Microsoft's .NET platform, provide support for web services and create SOAP messages behind the scenes.

> More information on WSDL and SOAP may be found at
> http://www.w3.org/TR/wsdl and http://www.w3.org/TR/SOAP
> respectively.

Setting up a SQL Server 2000 Web Service With SQLXML 3.0

With the introduction of the SQLXML 3.0, Microsoft has provided support for SOAP web services directly from SQL Server. As we'll see, this support allows us to create web services that run directly on the database server over HTTP, encapsulating stored procedures or user-defined functions with SOAP serialization and deserialization code. This eliminates the need to hand-code a middle-tier wrapper for the service. Unfortunately, the current implementation of web services in SQLXML 3.0 isn't especially flexible, as we'll see.

> **Please note: you must install Microsoft SOAP Toolkit 2.0 to enable the web services features of SQLXML 3.0. Please refer to Chapter 2 for more information on this.**

The Sample Database

To test the web service examples in this chapter, we'll create a sample database with a structure as shown below:

Web Services in SQL Server 2000

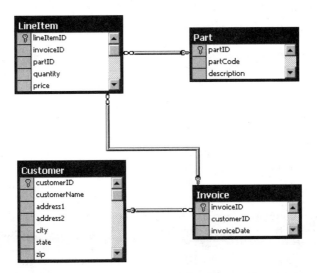

Note that the creation script for these tables is included in the code download for this chapter, available at *http://www.curlingstone.com*.

TableCreation.sql creates and populates these tables. It also creates three stored procedures that access the data:

```
CREATE PROC SelectCustomersByName (@namePart varchar(100))
AS
BEGIN

SELECT customerName, address1, address2, city, state, zip
FROM Customer
WHERE customerName LIKE '%' + @namePart + '%'

END
GO

CREATE PROC GetCustomerNameByID (@customerID int)
AS
BEGIN

SELECT CustomerName
FROM Customer
WHERE customerID = @customerID

END
GO

CREATE PROC GetInvoicesByBillingDate (@invoiceDate datetime)
AS
BEGIN
```

Chapter 14

```
        SELECT c.customerName, c.address1, c.address2, c.city, c.state,
        c.zip,
          i.invoiceDate, li.quantity, li.price, p.partCode,
          p.description
        FROM Customer c, Invoice i, LineItem li, Part p
        WHERE i.invoiceDate = @invoiceDate
          AND i.customerID = c.customerID
          AND li.invoiceID = i.invoiceID
          AND li.partID = p.partID

        END
        GO
```

The `SelectCustomersByName` stored procedure simply returns all the information in the `Customer` table for customers matching a specified string, while the `GetCustomerNameByID` stored procedure returns the name of a customer for a given Customer ID. The `GetInvoicesByBillingDate` stored procedure returns a list of all the invoices for a given date. We will see how to expose these stored procedures as web services as we move through the chapter.

Creating the SOAP Virtual Name

To expose SQL Server content as a web service, the first thing we need to do is create a SOAP virtual name on our SQL Server virtual directory (to learn more about setting up a SQL Server virtual directory under IIS, see Chapter 2). The code samples assume the following parameters for our virtual directory:

- ❑ **General** tab: **Virtual Directory Name:** `Customers`. **Local Path:** `C:\inetpub\wwwroot\Customers`.
- ❑ **Security** tab: **Always Log on as** `SQL Server Account type` (you will need to add your own logon details here).
- ❑ **Data Source** tab: select the SQL Server and the database against which you ran `TableCreation.sql`.
- ❑ **Settings** tab: Make sure the **Allow POST** checkbox is checked, as SOAP web service calls run over HTTP POST.
- ❑ **Virtual Name** tab: **Name:** `soap`. **Type:** `soap`. **Path:** `C:\inetpub\wwwroot\Customers`. The tab automatically fills in the **Web Service Name** and **Domain** textboxes. So long as you are running IIS on the same computer as SQL Server, then leave these boxes as they are; otherwise, change the **Domain** textbox to match your IIS Server.

> Note that if you are reusing a previously created virtual directory, template calls will be permitted if a virtual name of Type: `template` has previously been created. For security reasons, you may wish to only have a virtual name of Type: `soap` in this virtual directory.

418

Web Services in SQL Server 2000

Once you have done this, click **Save**:

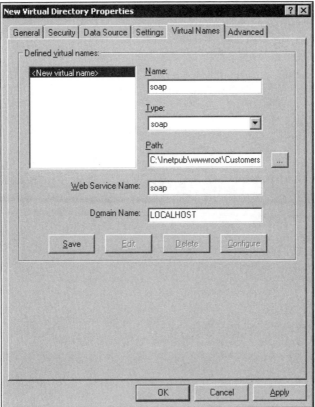

Exposing Stored Procedure Functionality as a Web Service

Even though we've got the virtual name set up, we still haven't actually exposed anything on our server as a web service yet. To do so, we need to configure a virtual name.

Click the **Configure** button on the **Virtual Names** tab. Ensure **Edit/New Mapping** is set to **SP**, **Formatting** is set to **Raw**, and **Output as** is set to **XML Object**. Click the ellipsis button next to **SP/Template** to bring up a list of stored procedures we can expose as web services. Click on **GetCustomerNameByID** and click **Save**. Repeat for **SelectCustomersByName** and **GetInvoicesByBillingDate**.

Click **OK** twice, and we have set up our web services.

> Note that we cannot set up a web service in this way for stored procedures that already return XML documents (through the use of `FOR XML`).

Chapter 14

If you look in the directory C:\Inetpub\wwwroot\Customers, you should see that the files soap.ssc (with configuration information for this virtual name) and soap.wsdl have been automatically created. You can call them up within your browser to see the contents. Type:

http://localhost/customers/soap?wsdl

in your browser. This should return the soap.wsdl file, which should look similar to the extract below (full sample included in download):

```
...
<wsdl:operation name="SelectCustomersByName">
<soap:operation
soapAction=
"http://LOCALHOST/Customers/soap/SelectCustomersByName"
style="document" />
<wsdl:input>
<soap:body use="literal" />
</wsdl:input>
<wsdl:output>
<soap:body use="literal" />
</wsdl:output>
</wsdl:operation>
</wsdl:binding>
<wsdl:service name="soap">
<wsdl:port name="SXSPort" binding="tns:SXSBinding">
<soap:address location="http://LOCALHOST/Customers/soap" />
</wsdl:port>
...
```

There are a couple of interesting things to note about the generated WSDL. First, the messages for each individual method are called (service name) and (service name)Response, respectively. Second, the content of the response message has the Microsoft-specific type sqlresultstream:SqlResultStream. As we'll discuss a little later in the chapter, all the various output mechanisms rely on Microsoft-specific result types for their output, making them less cross-platform compatible.

Another point to note is that you cannot return the file directly by typing http://localhost/customers/soap/soap.wsdl. If we want to test the web service, we need to create a SOAP message and submit it to this URI programmatically using HTTP POST. This is what we'll do in the section *Consuming Services Through Visual Studio.NET*, after a detour around the SQLXML 3.0 IIS supported output options.

Output Options

There are three different output methods supported by the SQLXML 3.0 SOAP mechanism. While we've already seen an example of one of them, the XML object, we can also return information serialized as Dataset objects. Let's see how these output methods differ.

Web Services in SQL Server 2000

XML Objects

The XML Objects output method returns the results as one or more XmlElement objects, one per resultset returned by the stored procedure or template. The XmlElement contents can then be used to drive a stylesheet or other XML processing engine. We have two row formatting options with this object, **Raw** and **Nested**. Let's take a look at each.

Raw

If the raw row formatting option is selected, the information will be returned as a series of row objects. Each row object will have further subelements corresponding to each column in the selected result, with the names matching those in the original SELECT statement. For example, if we call the GetInvoicesByBillingDate method for 8/5/2002 in our sample data with the formatting set to Raw, the following document is returned:

```xml
<SqlXml>
  <row>
    <customerName>Kevin Williams</customerName>
    <address1>762 Evergreen Terrace</address1>
    <city>Springfield</city>
    <state>VA</state>
    <zip>21602</zip>
    <invoiceDate>2002-08-05T00:00:00</invoiceDate>
    <quantity>22</quantity>
    <price>.30</price>
    <partCode>grom02</partCode>
    <description>2-inch grommets</description>
  </row>
  <row>
  ...
  </row>
</SqlXml>
```

We'll see how we actually perform the call to this service later in the chapter.

Note that the rows are returned "flat", that is, the record set that is returned is basically a two-dimensional, row-and-column dataset in XML form. While this format lends itself to automatic processing, a flattened dataset will repeat information and generally not provide the best form for manipulating that information in XML. Typically, we'll want a more normalized shape in our resultset, which can be achieved by setting the output format to Nested.

Nested

If we choose Nested as the output formatting method, then SQLXML 3.0 will format the resulting XML document based on the shape of the JOIN structure. Elements with foreign keys will be nested into the appropriate parent elements, resulting in the creation of an XML document that better supports typical XML operations, such as styling for presentation. SQL Server actually does a very good job of determining the resulting structure of the document based on the structure of the SELECT statement that creates the output for the stored procedure. For example, when running the GetInvoicesByBillingDate method again for 8/5/2002, with the method formatting set to Nested, the following output is returned:

Chapter 14

```
<SqlXml>
  <Customer>
    <customerName>Kevin Williams</customerName>
    <address1>762 Evergreen Terrace</address1>
    <city>Springfield</city>
    <state>VA</state>
    <zip>21602</zip>
    <Invoice>
      <invoiceDate>2002-08-05T00:00:00</invoiceDate>
      <LineItem>
        <quantity>22</quantity>
        <price>.30</price>
        <Part>
          <partCode>grom02</partCode>
          <description>2-inch grommets</description>
        </Part>
      </LineItem>
      <LineItem>
        <quantity>13</quantity>
        <price>.20</price>
        <Part>
          <partCode>spro02</partCode>
          <description>2-inch sprockets</description>
        </Part>
      </LineItem>
    </Invoice>
  </Customer>
  <Customer>
  ...
  </Customer>
</SqlXml>
```

As we can see, this format is much more like a 'traditional' XML document, with parents and children properly nested in the resulting structure. Unfortunately, we cannot use FOR XML to control the XML document that is generated by our stored procedure, since processing of the resultset takes place on the client rather than on the server. If we were to use FOR XML, the resulting document would be an encoded string that wouldn't be easy to work with. If we need a different structure from that created automatically by SQL Server, we can use a stylesheet to return the document in the desired format.

The benefit of using the XML Objects output method is that, by selecting **Nested** format, a structured response (one that shows the parent-child relationships between the data returned by the stored procedure) containing the results can be returned. However, if we want to consume the results using the data libraries in .NET, we have two further options for returning the results.

DataSet Objects

When we choose to format the results as DataSet objects, the SOAP mechanism will return a DataSet object for each resultset in the stored procedure or template. If the stored procedure has a return value, it will also be returned as one of these objects. These objects can be iterated through as if they were Datasets returned directly from SQL Server.

Single Dataset

If we choose to format the results as a single `Dataset` object, the SOAP mechanism will return a single `Dataset` object containing each of the resultsets in the stored procedure or template. If the stored procedure or template returns more than one resultset, they will be concatenated, producing unpredictable results. If you have more than one resultset, you should use the dataset objects option rather than the single dataset option. Again, the `Dataset` object can be iterated through as if it were a Dataset returned directly from SQL Server.

Error Mechanisms

There are several ways stored procedures and templates can return error and status codes to the client. Let's take a look at these mechanisms now.

Stored Procedure Return Codes

The SQLXML 3.0 libraries support return codes returned by stored procedures. When a stored procedure returns a value (apart from any records selected), it appears in the object array as a `<SqlResultCode>` element containing the four-byte integer return code. By iterating through the object array, the code can determine what objects represent resultsets and what objects represent return codes. For example, if we have a stored procedure returning two resultsets and one return code (and the output type is set to XML or `Dataset` objects), there will be three objects in the returned object array. The first two will represent the resultsets (as objects of the appropriate types), and the third will be a four-byte integer containing the return value.

SOAP Faults

On the configuration screen seen previously, we can select whether errors should be returned as SOAP faults or not. It is usually best to choose to return SOAP faults, as they will cause an exception to be thrown at the client, and the client can then handle the fault accordingly. If we choose not to return errors as SOAP faults, they will be returned instead as `SqlMessage` objects in the returned object array (in the case of stored procedures), or embedded `MSSqlError` elements in the returned XML document (in the case of templates). For example, say we have a stored procedure that returns two resultsets. If an error is encountered during the creation of the second resultset, the returned object array will have three objects: the first resultset, a `SqlMessage` object for the error encountered, and the four-byte integer return code for the stored procedure. Code that accesses this service will need to check the types of the items in the returned object array to determine if there was a critical failure in the execution of the stored procedure that prevented information from being returned. Note that this setting only applies to stored procedures or templates that are configured to return XML objects or `Dataset` objects; if the method returns a single `Dataset` object, errors encountered will always be returned as SOAP faults. User-defined functions with simple scalar return types also always return errors as SOAP faults.

Exposing UDF Functionality as a Web Service

To expose UDF functionality as a web service, all we have to do is add a UDF from the **SP/Template** list, just as with stored procedures. UDFs can be useful when creating web services directly from SQL Server as they allow simple values to be returned, as we will see later in the chapter.

Chapter 14

Consuming Services Through Visual Studio.NET

To finish this section off, let's see how a web service we have created can be consumed by a client. We will use Visual Studio .NET to code the client.

To access a SQLXML 3.0 web service method through a Visual Studio.NET application, we simply need to add it to the **Web References** section of our project as we would any other web service, by pointing to the WSDL for the service (specified using the virtual directory and virtual name we set up earlier in the chapter). This allows us to instantiate a service object proxy to make synchronous and asynchronous calls to the methods we have created. Let's walk through a quick example.

Start up Visual Studio.NET, and create a new C# Console Application project called SoapServiceTest.

Before we start writing code for our application, we need to add a Web reference to the service we created. Right-click on **References** in Solution Explorer, and select **Add Web Reference**. In the **Address** text box, type the URL of the service we created; for our example, it should be
`http://localhost/Customers/soap?wsdl`.

On hitting *Enter*, the WSDL for our service and our two methods will load in the listbox on the left, and the service will appear on the right:

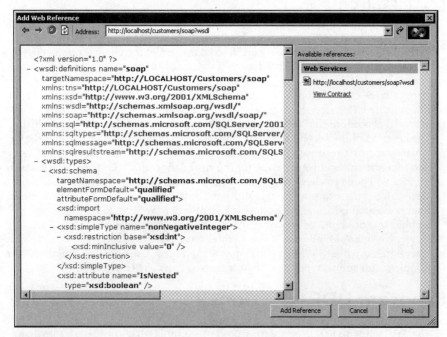

Click **Add Reference** to add a reference to this service to our project. We now have access to the `localhost.soap` object.

424

Web Services in SQL Server 2000

Note that if we aren't testing this code on our local machine, then it will be on the machine running SQL Server

Next, we'll add some test code to `Main()` to try out our web service. Paste the following code into the body of `Main()`, between the curly braces:

```
localhost.soap myService = new localhost.soap();
try
{
object[] response = myService.SelectCustomersByName("Kevin");
if (response[0].GetType().ToString() !=
"System.Xml.XmlElement")
{
// this may be an error (if SOAP Faults are turned off)
if(response[0].GetType().ToString() ==
"soapServiceTest.localhost.SqlMessage")
{
// this is an error returned by SQL Server
System.Console.WriteLine("A SqlMessage object was returned.");
    System.Console.WriteLine(((doc.SqlMessage)response[0])
.Message);
}
}
else
{
System.Console.WriteLine((
(System.Xml.XmlElement)response[0]).OuterXml);
}
}
catch (Exception e)
{
// this will be any SOAP fault thrown by the call
System.Console.WriteLine(e.Message);
System.Console.WriteLine("An exception was encountered.");
}
System.Console.ReadLine();
```

This code, along with instructions to run it, are included in `soapServiceText.txt`.

If we run the application just as it is, we should get the following result:

Note that the returned XML isn't formatted for readability. However, it can easily be used to drive an XSLT layer or some other mechanism.

425

Chapter 14

Now let's take a look at the way errors are returned. Make sure that **Return Errors as SOAP Faults** is still turned on for the `GetCustomersByName` virtual name, and then drop the stored procedure. If we run the program again (make sure you right-click on the web reference and select **Update Web Reference** first), we'll get the following output:

An exception was encountered.

Note that we don't bother to return the error message shown in the exception. That's because the web service support in Visual Studio.NET doesn't pass the details of the SOAP fault along in the exception it raises; the only message is that there was a runtime error. This is a good way to obfuscate the details of the system underneath because, as we'll see, returning the actual message from the server can give away clues as to the underlying database structure.

Go back and rebuild the `GetCustomersByName` stored procedure before turning off the SOAP fault support for the `GetCustomersByName` method. Now, save the method again, then drop the stored procedure again and run the sample code. This time, the result looks like this:

A SqlMessage object was returned.
Could not find stored procedure 'SelectCustomerByName'.

If we examine the structure of the `SqlMessage` object, we'll see that it provides a great deal of information about the exact nature of the SQL error generated. If we have systems outside our organization calling these services, we should take care to use SOAP faults to hide the actual underlying mechanisms that caused the errors.

Further SQL Server 2000 Web Service Topics

Now we have seen what web services are, and how to set up SQLXML 3.0 to provide them from SQL Server 2000, we will cover some of the other issues involved in using them.

UDDI Registries

An emerging standard for web service registries is the **UDDI** or Universal Discovery, Description, and Integration specification. UDDI registries can be used to store ontological information about web services such as:

- What company provides them?
- What do they do?
- Where can information about the service be discovered?

While these registries are still not being heavily used, in the future they will be the primary mechanism web service creators use to expose their services to potential clients.

Registering services created in SQLXML 3.0 in a UDDI registry is straightforward. Since these services create WSDL documents like any other service, when the service is registered with UDDI, this URL should be provided. Clients that find your service in the UDDI registry can then reference that WSDL document to find out how your service needs to be called, and call it as if it were any other web service. That's the beauty of web services; namely that the client doesn't need to worry about the specifics of your internal implementation, but only the way your implementation interfaces to the outside world.

Web Service Security/Authentication

Industry standards bodies are still working out web service security and authentication mechanisms. Since it's likely that highly sensitive information will need to be exchanged using web services in the future, it will be critically important for companies to be able to ensure that web service calls are secure. Until these mechanisms become final, however, there are a couple of approaches that you can take to secure your SQL Server web services. As these services are implemented as an ISAPI extension to IIS, you can take advantage of the same mechanisms IIS provides to secure other HTTP transactions, like HTML pages. For example, you can choose to expose the virtual directory you create for SQL Server through HTTPS. This will encrypt messages sent between SQL Server and clients, including the SOAP messages that make up web service calls. You can also add an authentication mechanism to the virtual directory, forcing users to pass authentication credentials along with the SOAP messages. These credentials are passed in the HTTP header when the SOAP request is received. If you are transmitting information that is at all sensitive, you should consider controlling access to your created services this way.

Shortcomings of SQL Server Web Services

As we mentioned earlier in the chapter, while it's nice to be able to access stored procedures directly as web services (without needing to write a middle layer in a language like C#, to wrap these stored procedures), there are some shortcomings to the SQLXML 3.0 mechanism. Let's take a look at these.

Microsoft Specific

The most obvious problem with the SQLXML 3.0 support for stored procedures is that they don't provide any sort of type control over the returned values. Instead, the values are always returned as Microsoft-specific object types, either `DataSets` or `XML` elements. In the SOAP response, this information is obviously serialized as XML that can be accessed programmatically by a non-Microsoft platform; however, it involves more work than would be ideal. We'll see how we can encapsulate SQLXML 3.0 web service calls in .NET service calls to provide better functionality along these lines in a moment.

Chapter 14

No Control Over Return Values

There is no way in SQLXML 3.0 to specify that an individual simple value is to be returned. For example, let's say we wrote a stored procedure to return a single customer name given a specified customer ID. The most convenient way to write this service would be as a simple service that takes an integer as an input and returns a string. However, we can't do this directly with SQLXML 3.0. Instead, we need to return a resultset of some kind (either an XML element or a `DataSet`), and then decompose it to pull out the simple value we're interested in. This means that we need more complex and difficult-to-maintain code on the client side. You can return a single value like this with a user-defined function, but then you lose the ability to return multiple individual values (rather than as part of an XML structure in an object array).

Wrapping Services with .NET Services

One way we can get around these limitations of SQLXML 3.0 web services is to wrap them with .NET web services; in other words middle-tier code (written in a language like C#) that exposes functionality as a web service running through IIS. Let's take a look at an example using the `GetCustomerNameByID` stored procedure we set up earlier.

The first step to getting to the functionality we want is to create a Visual Studio .NET web service. Open a new project as an ASP.NET Web service in C# called `sqlWrapper`.

Add a web reference to our virtual name from **Solution Explorer | Add Web References**, as we did for our `soapServiceTest` console. Next, we need to code the body of the .NET web service. In the service, we'll call the SQLXML 3.0 web service (as we did in our console application), decompose the resulting XML, and return the appropriate string value for the name. Replace the `Service1.asmx` source code with the following code (included in `sqlWrapper.txt` in the download):

```
using System;
using System.Collections;
using System.ComponentModel;
using System.Data;
using System.Diagnostics;
using System.Web;
using System.Web.Services;

namespace sqlWrapper
{
    public class serviceWrapper : System.Web.Services.WebService
    {
        public serviceWrapper()
        {
            InitializeComponent();
        }

        #region Component Designer generated code
```

```csharp
      private IContainer components = null;

      private void InitializeComponent()
      {
      }

      protected override void Dispose( bool disposing )
      {
        if(disposing && components != null)
        {
          components.Dispose();
        }
        base.Dispose(disposing);
      }

      #endregion

      [WebMethod]
      public string getCustomerNameByID(int customerID)
      {
        localhost.soap myService = new localhost.soap();
        try
        {
          object[] response =
   myService.GetCustomerNameByID(customerID);
          System.Xml.XmlElement result =
   (System.Xml.XmlElement)response[0];
          if(result.HasChildNodes)
          {
            string customerName = result.ChildNodes[0].InnerText;
            return(customerName);
          }
          else
          {
            // no match found
            return("no match");
          }
        }
        catch (Exception e)
        {
          return("exception");
        }
      }
   }
}
```

Build and deploy this web service to our server using .NET's IIS integration. We now have a web service that returns a simple type (a string) containing the name of the customer whose ID is passed in. Create a new C# console application called `sqlWrapperTest` and add our new service as a web reference. The reference for this will be:

http://localhost/sqlWrapper/Service1.asmx

Chapter 14

Again, if you are not running this service from the local server, include the server name instead of `localhost`. We can now write the following code (in `sqlWrapperTest.txt` in the download) in `Main()`:

```
localhost.serviceWrapper myService = new
localhost.serviceWrapper();
string name = myService.getCustomerNameByID(1);
System.Console.WriteLine("Name: " + name);
System.Console.ReadLine();
```

While this is a simpler form to call from our .NET applications, we can also easily write code in other SOAP-compliant languages (such as Java) to take advantage of this wrapped service.

Summary

In this chapter, we've taken a look at the support for direct SOAP transactions provided by the SQLXML 3.0 libraries running in conjunction with SQL Server 2000. If you are working exclusively in the .NET development environment, you can take advantage of the rich typing provided by these libraries to return XML elements or .NET `Dataset` objects for further manipulation. If you are authoring web services you wish to expose to non-Microsoft platforms, it probably makes more sense to wrap SQL Server functionality in .NET middle-tier web service wrappers, since .NET gives you much better control over the SOAP messages created by web services than SQL Server does directly. While the object types returned by SQLXML 3.0 web services are not the most cross-platform compatible, wrappers can easily be written in .NET to use simple types, and make it easy to share SQL Server data between different programming languages and operating systems.

The next release of SQL Server, code-named Yukon, will provide much better support for web services. Since Yukon will actually embed the .NET CLR, it will be possible to write stored procedures directly in .NET languages like Visual Basic or C# (for more on where SQL Server is headed, please see Chapter 17). With the new tight integration, it will be possible to author more flexible web services that access the SQL Server database directly, thus eliminating the need for a middle tier. This will lead to easier web service creation, and better integration with non-Microsoft platforms.

Bryant Likes

- Benefits and Drawbacks of the Three Client Detection Methods
- Basic Detection
- Client Detection Using SQLXML
- Client Detection Using the SQLXML Managed Classes
- Client Detection Using SQLXML and ADO
- Summary

15

Case Study: Detecting Web Site Clients

In this case study we will look at some methods of SQLXML browser detection that can be used when dealing with three popular browsers (Internet Explorer (IE), Netscape Navigator, and Pocket Internet Explorer). We will begin by briefly discussing what possibilities are available to us in terms of:

- Using XML Templates in SQLXML Virtual Directories
- Using XML Templates with SQLXML Managed Classes in ASP.NET
- Using XML Templates with ADO in classic ASP

The benefits and drawbacks that each method presents will be discussed. Having given an overview of these three methods, we'll then take a closer look at each in turn, considering:

- Building on the SQLXML `nwind` virtual directory that we setup in Chapter 2 by adding templates that can be passed parameters through the use of XSLT stylesheets.
- Creating an ASP.NET web project, which uses the SQLXML managed classes, in conjunction with the `System.Web.HttpBrowserCapabilities` class, to detect the different browser types.
- How to use traditional ADO with the templates we create, within a traditional ASP page.

When you are finished with this case study, you should have an understanding of how to handle client detection in SQLXML and be able to code your own web applications that can provide appropriate HTML code to the various clients that access them.

Chapter 15

Benefits and Drawbacks of the Methods

Before we begin looking at the components of detecting a client and the methods we can use, it will be helpful to quickly discuss some of the benefits and drawbacks of each method.

The first method we will explore is using XML templates in SQLXML virtual directories. This method is by far the least efficient. Our primary goal in looking at it is to get a basic understanding of why client detection is important and we will build the other two methods with the templates we create in the first method. The virtual directory method is simple to create because you only need a text editor and a SQLXML virtual directory. However, since at least one template will have to be run more than once, it's an inefficient means of client detection. The eXtensible Style Language (XSLT) document that we will use in this method is complicated as the HTML for each browser must be included in one XSLT document. The other methods have the option of breaking the XSLT out into separate files, making them easier to maintain and understand.

The other two methods we will look at, namely using ASP.NET and ASP, are more efficient, because the server can detect the client type. This will allow us not only to run the XML templates once, but also to simplify our XSLT documents. Additionally, since the client detection is done on the server, we don't have to worry about client-side issues such as scripting being disabled on the client. The drawback to both of these methods is that you need to have an understanding of additional technologies, though the examples that are given in this case study should be easy to follow, even if you've never worked with ASP or ASP.NET.

Basic Detection

The ability to detect the type of client that is making an HTTP request relies on reading the headers that are sent along with such requests. These headers give the server information about the client, such as what program is making the request and the operating system that the program is running in. This information is contained within a header called `User-Agent`. For example, if we were using Microsoft Internet Explorer (`IE`) 6.0 on a computer running Windows XP, our `User-Agent` header might look like the following:

Mozilla/4.0 (compatible; MSIE 6.0; Windows NT 5.1; Q312461; .NET CLR 1.0.3705)

Based on this string we can determine the type of client we are dealing with. If we were to make the same request using Netscape 4.08 we would see something like the following `User-Agent`:

Mozilla/4.08 [en] (WinNT; U ;Nav)

In cases where the client hitting our site is the Pocket PC, with its Pocket IE version, we need to be able to provide a page suitable for its screen. The `User-Agent` string for a Pocket PC will look similar to this:

Mozilla/2.0 (compatible; MSIE 3.02; Windows CE; PPC; 240x320)

As you can see, the `User-Agent` string is very important for client detection. Some platforms, such as ASP.NET, come with built-in tools that can be used for client detection. We will look at the ASP.NET tools later in this case study.

Client Detection Using SQLXML

So how can we detect the client type from within SQLXML? The reality is that there is no easy way to do this since SQLXML HTTP access, be it via XML templates or URL queries, has no way of passing the request headers to you. In other words, there is no means of directly accessing the `User-Agent` string. However, just because we can't directly access this information from within SQLXML doesn't mean we can't somehow pass it in. The idea here is that instead of relying on SQLXML to get us this information, we simply use some other tool to get the information for us and then pass it to SQLXML. There are two ways that we can accomplish this, and we'll look at each in turn.

Client-Side Scripting

The first method of getting the `User-Agent` string is **client-side scripting**. Client-side scripting involves adding some script (such as JavaScript or VBScript for example) to an HTML page. We then take the value that we obtain using the script and pass it either to the XML template or into the URL in the case of an URL query. As the name suggests the script is run on the client and, as a result, has the advantage of reducing the load on the server. However, if a client doesn't support scripting, or has scripting disabled, a solution relying on client-side scripting will break.

Server-Side Scripting

Server-side scripting uses a script (such as JavaScript or VBScript) to return the `User-Agent` string from the request, in a similar manner to client-side scripting. This string is then passed into an XML template or an URL query. In this case the advantages correspond to the disadvantages of client-side scripting, in other words, since the script is processed on the server, there's no problem if the client doesn't support scripting because the client can't disable server-side scripting. However, as we mentioned above, this does add to the load on the server. This increased load is rarely very large though, since the scripts are generally quite simple.

The Solution to SQLXML Client Detection

In this solution we'll use a client-side scripting detection process, since this is as close to a SQLXML-only solution as we can get. We begin by setting ourselves up with a virtual directory and the templates that will access the database.

Chapter 15

The SQLXML Virtual Directory

The first thing you will need to ensure is that you have the `nwind` SQLXML virtual directory configured, as described in detail in Chapter 2. You will also need to set up a `templates` folder within `nwind` to hold our templates, as described in Chapter 8. Please look back to the relevant chapters if you haven't already configured these items.

Creating the XML Templates

In this example we will use the `Northwind` sample database and the `nwind` and `templates` virtual directories that we already setup. We are going to create two templates: one for the customer login and one for displaying the orders.

Instead of creating a complex solution, we will use a simple drop-down where the customer can choose their name from a list and then log in. The most important part of this template is the client detection. Below is the template itself, which you can save in the `templates` folder as `login.xml`:

```
<root xmlns:sql="urn:schemas-microsoft-com:xml-sql">

<sql:header>
  <sql:param name="browser"/>
</sql:header>
<sql:query><![CDATA[
SELECT '<browser>' + @browser + '</browser>'

SELECT    CustomerID, CompanyName
FROM      Customers
FOR XML AUTO

]]></sql:query>

</root>
```

Chapter 5 covered the creation and use of templates in detail.

The first thing to notice about this template is the `<sql:param>` named `browser`. This is how we are going to pass in the browser information. The actual browser detection code is in the `login.xsl` file that we will look at below. You will also notice that the `<sql:query>` section is enclosed in a CDATA section. This is required since we need to use XML elements in our SELECT statement in order to pass the browser parameter to the XSLT file. You can test this template by opening the following URL in your browser:

http://localhost/nwind/templates/login.xml

Case Study: Detecting Web Site Clients

When you open that URL you should see something like the following:

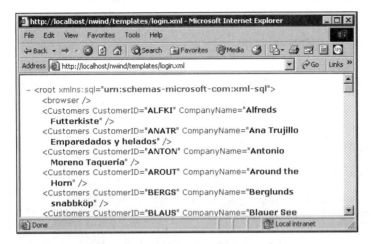

Notice that the <browser> element is empty. You can pass in a browser string by adding a parameter to the URL like this:

http://localhost/nwind/templates/login.xml?browser=myOwnBrowser

When you use the URL with the browser parameter you should see a result like the following:

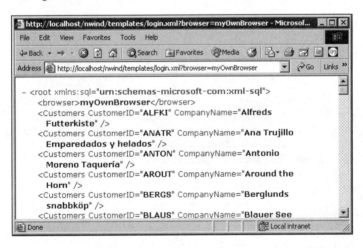

Notice that the <browser> element now contains the value we passed in through the browser parameter. This is important because our XSLT will make the decision about how to create the HTML to be returned based on the content of this element.

The next template (vieworders.xml) is the one used to view the past orders. This template will use a FOR XML EXPLICIT query and will pass in the browser parameter, as well as the CustomerID parameter. Save the following in your templates folder:

437

```
<root xmlns:sql="urn:schemas-microsoft-com:xml-sql">

<sql:header>
  <sql:param name="browser"/>
  <sql:param name="CustomerID"/>
</sql:header>
<sql:query><![CDATA[

SELECT '<CustomerID>' + @CustomerID + '</CustomerID>' +
       '<browser>' + @browser + '</browser>'

]]></sql:query>
<sql:query>

SELECT   1 as Tag,
         null as Parent,
         OrderID as [order!1!ID],
         convert(varchar(10), OrderDate, 101)
         as [order!1!date],
         null as [product!2!quantity],
         null as [product!2!name]
FROM     Orders
WHERE    CustomerID = @CustomerID

UNION ALL

SELECT   2 as Tag,
         1 as Parent,
         Orders.OrderID,
         null,
         Quantity,
         ProductName
FROM     Orders, [Order Details], Products
WHERE    [Order Details].ProductID = Products.ProductID
         and Orders.OrderID = [Order Details].OrderID
         and CustomerID = @CustomerID

ORDER BY [order!1!ID], Tag

FOR XML EXPLICIT

</sql:query>

</root>
```

This template requires that you pass in a `CustomerID`, which, in this case, can be any valid `CustomerID` from the `Customers` table in the `Northwind` database. You can use the following URL to test the template.

http://localhost/nwind/templates/vieworders.xml?CustomerID=VINET

Case Study: Detecting Web Site Clients

When you open that URL you should see something like the following:

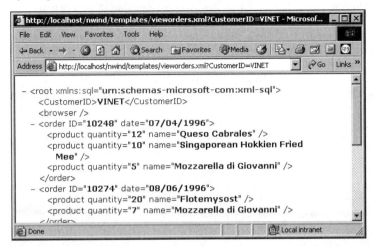

Notice that the `<browser>` element is empty since we did not include a `browser` parameter, but that, as specified in our URL query, the `CustomerID` parameter is `VINET`. We need to pass this to the XSLT along with the browser string. If there is no `CustomerID` passed in, we will redirect the users back to the login page (we'll see how to do this shortly).

> If the `CustomerID` passed in doesn't exist in the database then no records will be displayed.

Now that we have the templates in place we need to create the code to turn the XML results into the appropriate HTML, based on the type of client making the request.

Creating Client Detection Code

The client detection code is fairly simple. We use client-side scripting to grab the `User-Agent` string, and then parse out the string to determine what browser we are using. Then we reload the template but pass in the browser string that we wish to use as a parameter. We can then use the value passed in through this parameter to determine how to render the page using XSLT. Since we are also using the Pocket PC as a client, if the client does not support scripting then we will assume it is the Pocket PC. This may not always be true, but it will be useful for this example. So for this case study we will have three possible clients:

❑ IE 4.0 or greater
❑ Netscape Navigator 4.0 or greater
❑ Pocket PC or scripting is disabled

The first XSLT that we'll create will be the XSLT for the `login.xml` template. This XSLT is fairly complex since we must include the HTML code for all three of our clients: IE 4+, PocketIE, and Non-IE. The XSLT can be downloaded from the Curlingstone website (http://www.curlingstone.com) and you can copy it into the templates folder as `login.xsl`.

Chapter 15

Let's now consider the key sections of our XSLT coding. The `<xsl:choose>` section is used to check the `<browser>` element that we know is passed in by the `browser` parameter. If it's blank, then we need to run some script to check the type of browser. If we have already determined which of our three clients is making the request, then we need to return the appropriate HTML. Below is a code snippet from the XSLT that handles running the appropriate section. The `$browser` variable is filled by the client script and the values in this `<xsl:choose>` section correspond to the values in the client-side script.

```
<xsl:template match="/">

  <xsl:choose>
   <xsl:when test="$browser=''">
    <xsl:apply-templates select="root" mode="detect"/>
   </xsl:when>
   <xsl:when test="$browser='ie'">
    <xsl:apply-templates select="root" mode="ie"/>
   </xsl:when>
   <xsl:when test="$browser='ppc'">
    <xsl:apply-templates select="root" mode="ppc"/>
   </xsl:when>
   <xsl:when test="$browser='nonie'">
    <xsl:apply-templates select="root" mode="nonie"/>
   </xsl:when>
  </xsl:choose>

</xsl:template>
```

The appropriate HTML is returned using `<xsl:apply-templates>` and setting the `mode` attribute. Each `mode` corresponds to a different client. The `ie` mode is the most complex mode and draws some nice borders around the different sections of the page. Before testing this out we need to modify our XML template, adding `sql:xsl="login.xml"` to the `<root>` element as shown below:

```
<root xmlns:sql="urn:schemas-microsoft-com:xml-sql"
    sql:xsl="login.xsl">
...
</root>
```

Once this is done, we can open the template again with IE but this time we should get a formatted web page instead of XML.

> **NOTE:** If you get an error about invalid XML, it is probably because IE has cached the content type, which we have just changed from `text/xml` to `text/html`. Just open a new instance of IE and retype the URL.

440

Case Study: Detecting Web Site Clients

You should get something that looks like the following:

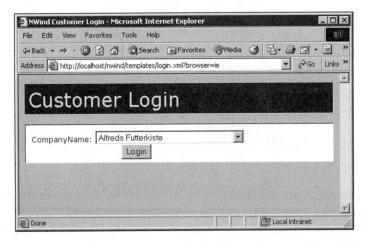

So how did the client detection work? When we first hit the page, we didn't include a `browser` parameter and so the `<xsl:choose>` section ran the `<xsl:when>` where the test was `$browser=''`. This section then output some HTML that contained two things: a client-side script and a meta tag. The client-side script attempts to determine if the client is either IE 4 (or greater) or not. It then reloads the page and passes either `ie` or `nonie` as the `browser` parameter. The screenshot below shows how the same page looks in Netscape 4.08 (the most popular version of the Netscape browser):

Notice that it is missing the nice borders and the background is all gray. We can also hit this same URL with the Pocket PC and it will get its own version of the page as shown below (using the Pocket PC 2002 emulator - http://www.pocketpcdn.com/). Since the Pocket PC uses a version of IE called PocketIE, which doesn't support scripting, it will get the page that is called using the meta tag. The meta tag just tells the browser to reload the page with the URL in the `content` attribute.

441

Chapter 15

Now that we have our login page working with all three clients, we need to add the XSL for the `vieworders.xml` template. This XSLT is also fairly complex as it deals with both client detection and determining if a `CustomerID` was passed in. This XSLT file can also be downloaded from the website and should be saved as `vieworders.xsl` in the `templates` folder.

This XSL works in the same way as the `login.xsl` in that it detects the type of client that is being passed in. One of the key differences is that if either no browser is passed in, or no `CustomerID` is passed in, then the browser is redirected back to `login.xml`. If the browser is passed in then the XSLT loops through the orders and displays them to the user. To test this we need to modify the `vieworders.xml` template as follows:

```
<root xmlns:sql="urn:schemas-microsoft-com:xml-sql"
      sql:xsl="vieworders.xsl">
// rest of code goes here
</root>
```

Once this is done, you should be able to click the Login button on the `login.xml` page and view the orders for that customer. The following screenshots show this in IE 6.0, Netscape 4.08, and PocketPC respectively:

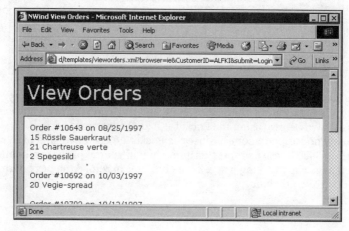

Case Study: Detecting Web Site Clients

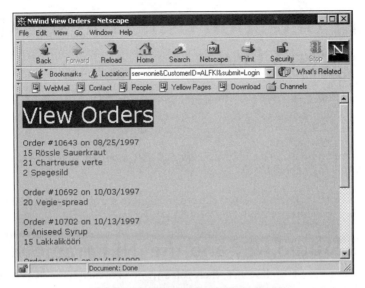

So we now have templates that can detect the type of client making the request and return the HTML specific to that client. This has all been done with XML templates in SQLXML virtual directories.

Drawbacks to Client Detection in SQLXML

The main drawback to performing client detection in SQLXML is that you have to hit the page twice: once to detect the browser and once to render the correct version of the page. This means that your query is being run twice the first time the user hits the page, which could have some serious implications if your site is heavily used. Also, since the browser detection is done on the client, if the client has scripting disabled we can't accurately detect what type of client it is. For example, if you disable scripting in IE and hit the page, you will get the HTML meant for the Pocket PC in our example.

Chapter 15

Client Detection Using the SQLXML Managed Classes

We can use the SQLXML Managed Classes to call our templates from within ASP.NET, which has browser detection built into it. This makes the job of detecting the client much easier, much more efficient, and is the preferred method of dealing with the problem of client detection.

> More information on how to use the SQLXML Managed Classes can be found in Chapter 13.

Before we can use the managed classes we need to set up an appropriate virtual directory and create an ASP.NET project.

VIsual Studio.NET and the .NET Framework

If you have Visual Studio .NET, then you only need to install the .NET Framework on the server you're using; if your virtual directories are on the same machine that has VS.NET installed on it then you don't need to download or install anything and you can skip down to the section that outlines how to setup an IIS virtual directory.

To download the .NET Framework Runtime go to the following URL:

http://msdn.microsoft.com/downloads/sample.asp?url=/msdn-files/027/001/829/msdncompositedoc.xml

At this page you can download the 21 MB redistributable .NET Framework Runtime, which you will need to install on the server that is hosting the sample application.

The rest of this section will be using VS.NET to create the virtual directory and the ASP.NET files. If you don't have VS.NET you can get by with the .NET SDK which can be found at the URL above. You can also download the Web Matrix, which is a free download from http://www.asp.net. With either of these programs you can compile and run the code available from the Curlingstone website.

Creating the Project

Open VS.NET and create a new C# web project called nwind.net, specifying localhost as the server name unless you're using a different server. The create project dialog looks like this:

Case Study: Detecting Web Site Clients

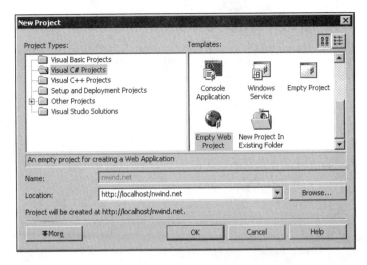

We also need to add a reference to the `Microsoft.Data.SqlXml` namespace. Make sure you select the 3.0 version of the namespace instead of the 2.0 version:

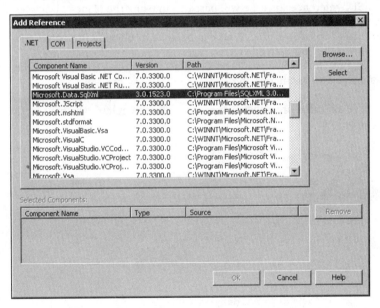

Our ASP.NET project is now ready for us to start adding some files.

ASP.NET Browser Detection

The browser detection in ASP.NET is done using the `System.Web.HttpBrowserCapabilities` class. With it we can determine the browser that is making the request, whether or not scripting is enabled, the operating system, and many other features of the application that is making the request.

445

Chapter 15

SQLXML Managed Classes

The SQLXML Managed Classes allow us to run SQLXML templates in ASP.NET. We can call our template with these classes without any modification. However, since we don't need to detect the client using the XSLT, we'll make some modifications to our templates, beginning with our `login.xml` template as follows:

```
<root xmlns:sql="urn:schemas-microsoft-com:xml-sql">

<sql:query>
SELECT    CustomerID, CompanyName
FROM      Customers
FOR XML AUTO
</sql:query>

</root>
```

Notice we have removed the parameters and the XSLT reference. Since ASP.NET will be detecting the browser type, we no longer need to pass this in. We removed the XSLT reference since we will pass this in using the Managed Classes based on the type of browser. Copy the modified template from above and add it to your project as `login_net.xml`. This can be done by clicking **Project | Add New Item**, and then selecting XML File as the type and changing the name to `login_net.xml`. Then paste the XML above into the XML file using the **Edit | Paste as HTML** menu option.

We have also simplified the `vieworders.xml` template. The new version is shown below:

```
<root xmlns:sql="urn:schemas-microsoft-com:xml-sql">

<sql:header>
  <sql:param name="CustomerID"/>
</sql:header>
<sql:query>

SELECT    1 as Tag,
          null as Parent,
          OrderID as [order!1!ID],
          convert(varchar(10), OrderDate, 101)
           as [order!1!date],
          null as [product!2!quantity],
          null as [product!2!name]
FROM      Orders
WHERE     CustomerID = @CustomerID

UNION ALL

SELECT    2 as Tag,
          1 as Parent,
          Orders.OrderID,
          null,
```

Case Study: Detecting Web Site Clients

```
            Quantity,
            ProductName
   FROM    Orders, [Order Details], Products
   WHERE   [Order Details].ProductID = Products.ProductID
      AND Orders.OrderID = [Order Details].OrderID
      AND CustomerID = @CustomerID

   ORDER BY [order!1!ID], Tag

   FOR XML EXPLICIT

   </sql:query>

   </root>
```

For this template we also removed the browser detection and, since we can check for parameters in ASP.NET, we removed the query that returned the `CustomerID`. The XSLT reference was also removed as it was in the `login_net.xml`. Add this new version of the template to your project as `vieworders_net.xml`.

Plugging in our SQLXML Templates

The next step is to create the ASP.NET pages that will run these templates. To run the `login_net.xml` template we'll use a page called `default.aspx`. To create this click on **Project | Add Web Form** and change the name to `default.aspx`. Once the file has been created, change the view from Design view to HTML view using the buttons just below the page (assuming you haven't changed your VS.NET setup). Go ahead and delete all the HTML code below the first line so that you are left with something that looks like the following:

```
<%@ Page language="c#" Codebehind="default.aspx.cs"
    AutoEventWireup="false" Inherits="_default" %>
```

Notice that there is no real HTML code in this file. The HTML code will be generated by the `default.aspx.cs` page so we don't need any HTML on this page. This page is only used to load the `codebehind` page that will then generate the HTML output.

Next switch to the code view by clicking **View | Code**. You will notice that VS.NET will have generated quite a bit of code for us. Delete all the code that .NET has generated for you and then add the code below in its place:

```
using System;
using System.Web;
using Microsoft.Data.SqlXml;

public class _default : System.Web.UI.Page
{
    private void Page_Load(object sender, System.EventArgs e)
    {
        SqlXmlCommand sxc = new SqlXmlCommand("Provider=SQLOLEDB;"
```

447

Chapter 15

```
        + "Data Source=<server>;User ID=<user>;Password=<password>;"
        + "Database=Northwind");
    sxc.CommandType = SqlXmlCommandType.TemplateFile;
    sxc.CommandText = Server.MapPath("login_net.xml");
    sxc.ExecuteToStream(Response.OutputStream);
}

override protected void OnInit(EventArgs e)
{
    InitializeComponent();
    base.OnInit(e);
}

private void InitializeComponent()
{
    this.Load += new System.EventHandler(this.Page_Load);
}
}
```

> Make sure that you modify the connection string by filling in the `Data Source`, `User ID`, and `Password` fields with the values that are correct for your SQL Server.

If you open this page with the following URL you should get the same XML as we got in the previous method, but without the browser element.

http://localhost/nwind.net/default.aspx

The next step is to modify the XSLT document. Instead of trying to include all the XSLT in one single document we are going to split it out into the three documents below. This makes our XSL easier to understand and to maintain. With the virtual directory method we couldn't specify the XSL based on the client type, but we can do so here using the SQLXML managed classes. The following are the names of the three XSLT files that you should add to your project.

- `login_ie.xsl` - XSLT for IE 4.0 or greater
- `login_nonie.xsl` - XSLT for Netscape or other browsers
- `login_ppc.xsl` - XSLT for Pocket PC devices

You can find these files in the code download for this chapter.

Now that we have the XSLT documents for each of the three clients, we need to modify our code to apply the correct one, based on the client making the request. As mentioned earlier, the detection is done with the `System.Web.HttpBrowserCapabilities` object. The `Page_Load` method from the `default.aspx.cs` file is shown below, with the modifications for applying the XSLT documents:

Case Study: Detecting Web Site Clients

```
private void Page_Load(object sender, System.EventArgs e)
{
  // user code goes here
  sxc.CommandText = Server.MapPath("login_net.xml");
  HttpBrowserCapabilities brows = this.Request.Browser;
  if (brows.Browser == "IE" && brows.MajorVersion >=4)
    sxc.XslPath = Server.MapPath("login_ie.xsl");
  else if (brows.Browser == "IE" && brows.Platform == "WinCE")
    sxc.XslPath = Server.MapPath("login_ppc.xsl");
  else
    sxc.XslPath = Server.MapPath("login_nonie.xsl");
  sxc.ExecuteToStream(Response.OutputStream);
}
```

Once this page has been compiled (using **Build | Build Solution**) we can now browse the `default.aspx` file with any of our clients and get the correct page.

To create the same thing for the `vieworders.aspx` page we need to employ the same method that we did for the `default.aspx` page above, and remove all the HTML below the first line. Here is the HTML source of `vieworders.aspx`:

```
<%@ Page language="c#" Codebehind="vieworders.aspx.cs"
    AutoEventWireup="false" Inherits="vieworders" %>
```

Next we need to switch to the code view and look at the code behind the page, which is similar to our previous coding. The only difference here is that, since we are now passing in a `CustomerID`, we need to pass this parameter to the template when we execute it, using the `SqlXmlParameter` object as shown below. Note that you need to remove all the code generated by VS.NET and then paste in the following code:

```
using System;
using System.Web;
using Microsoft.Data.SqlXml;

public class vieworders : System.Web.UI.Page
{
  private void Page_Load(object sender, System.EventArgs e)
  {
    string custID = Request["CustomerID"] != null ?
      Request["CustomerID"] : "";

    SqlXmlCommand sxc = new SqlXmlCommand("Provider=SQLOLEDB;"
      + "Data Source=<server>;User ID=<user>;Password=<password>;"
      + "Database=Northwind");
    SqlXmlParameter p1 = sxc.CreateParameter();
    p1.Name = "@CustomerID";
    p1.Value = custID;
    sxc.CommandType = SqlXmlCommandType.TemplateFile;
```

Chapter 15

```
      sxc.CommandText = Server.MapPath("vieworders_net.xml");
      HttpBrowserCapabilities brows = this.Request.Browser;
      if (brows.Browser == "IE" && brows.MajorVersion >=4)
         sxc.XslPath = Server.MapPath("vieworders_ie.xsl");
      else if (brows.Browser == "IE" && brows.Platform == "WinCE")
         sxc.XslPath = Server.MapPath("vieworders_ppc.xsl");
      else
         sxc.XslPath = Server.MapPath("vieworders_nonie.xsl");
      sxc.ExecuteToStream(Response.OutputStream);
   }

   override protected void OnInit(EventArgs e)
   {
      InitializeComponent();
      base.OnInit(e);
   }

   private void InitializeComponent()
   {
      this.Load += new System.EventHandler(this.Page_Load);
   }
}
```

Before we can run this page we need to add the XSLT documents. As shown in the code, we need to split the XSLT document into three parts, for ease of reading and maintenance, by creating the following XSLT documents:

- vieworders_ie.xsl – XSLT For IE 4.0 or greater
- vieworders_nonie.xsl – XSLT for Netscape and other browsers
- vieworders_ppc.xsl – XSLT for the Pocket PC

If you look at the XSLT you can see the templates are much simpler than the previous ones, since we can separate the client code out and don't have to deal with client detection. This makes for much cleaner XSLT files and easier debugging. It also means that if we need to add new client types we don't have to modify (and possibly break) our existing XSLT file. Instead we just add a new one and match it to our new client type.

Advantages to Using ASP.NET Client Detection

The main advantage of using ASP.NET is that we don't have to make two trips. We can use the information sent with the request to dish out the right kind of page. In addition to this we can rely on server-side code instead of client-side code, which means it will run regardless of the client's settings. Another advantage is that the user can bookmark the page or e-mail the URL to someone else and it will work even if they are using a different browser.

Client Detection Using SQLXML and ADO

This is a method you can use if you don't have access to .NET. It is almost identical to the method we just used with ASP.NET, except that we have to parse the `User-Agent` string manually, and use ADO instead of SQLXML managed classes. The code looks a little different since you're using both classic ADO and ASP.

Using Classic ADO

Without access to the SQLXML managed classes, we still want to read the template from the file, execute it, and apply the stylesheet to the results. The way this is done is with the `ADODB.Command` object.

The code below should be placed in a file called `login.asp` that you can save in either a new IIS virtual directory or the same `nwind.net` virtual directory that we just created. If you are going to use a new IIS virtual directory you will need to use the IIS management tool. You can use this tool to create a new virtual directory via a wizard that will take you through each step.

```
<%
Response.Expires = 0

Dim sAgent, oCmd, oStream

Set oCmd = Server.CreateObject("ADODB.Command")
oCmd.ActiveConnection = "Provider=SQLOLEDB;" & _
    "Data Source=<server>;User ID=<user>;" & _
    "Password=<password>;Database=Northwind"

Set oStream = Server.CreateObject("ADODB.Stream")
oStream.Open()
oStream.Charset = "ascii"
oStream.LoadFromFile(Server.MapPath("login_net.xml"))

oCmd.CommandStream = oStream
oCmd.Dialect = "{5D531CB2-E6Ed-11D2-B252-00C04F681B71}"

sAgent = Request.ServerVariables("HTTP_USER_AGENT")

If InStr(sAgent, "MSIE") > 0 Then
    ''' Internet Explorer
    If InStr(sAgent, "Windows CE") Then
        ''' Pocket PC
        oCmd.Properties("XSL").Value = _
Server.MapPath("login_ppc.xsl")
    Else
        oCmd.Properties("XSL").Value = _
Server.MapPath("login_ie.xsl")
    End If
```

Chapter 15

```
Else
    oCmd.Properties("XSL").Value = _
Server.MapPath("login_nonie.xsl")
End If

oCmd.Properties("Output Stream") = Response
oCmd.Execute , , 1024

%>
```

> **NOTE:** You must have all the files we created in the ASP.NET section in the same folder (`login_net.xml`, `login_ie.xsl`, `login_ppc.xsl`, and `login_nonie.xsl`). Also, you must modify the reference that points to `vieworders.aspx` and change it to `vieworders.asp`.

This code first creates an `ADODB.Command` object and sets its connection using the connection string. It then creates an `ADODB.Stream` object that we use to load the XML template.

```
Dim sAgent, oCmd, oStream

Set oCmd = Server.CreateObject("ADODB.Command")
oCmd.ActiveConnection = "Provider=SQLOLEDB;" & _
    "Data Source=<server>;User ID=<user>;" & _
    "Password=<password>;Database=Northwind"

Set oStream = Server.CreateObject("ADODB.Stream")
oStream.Open()
oStream.Charset = "ascii"
oStream.LoadFromFile(Server.MapPath("login_net.xml"))

oCmd.CommandStream = oStream
oCmd.Dialect = "{5D531CB2-E6Ed-11D2-B252-00C04F681B71}"

sAgent = Request.ServerVariables("HTTP_USER_AGENT")
```

> Make sure that you modify the connection string by filling in the `Data Source`, `User ID`, and `Password` fields with the values that are correct for your SQL Server.

Once we have read the template file into the stream, we specify the stream as the `CommandStream`. This means the `Command` object will use the stream as the source of its query. The `Dialect` property is required since we are using an XML template as our query. The `Dialect` specifies that `SQLOLEDB` should use `SQLXMLx.dll` to parse the command before sending it to SQL Server.

Case Study: Detecting Web Site Clients

ASP Browser Detection

Since we have to manually parse the `User-Agent` string, our code looks a little different:

```
If InStr(sAgent, "MSIE") > 0 Then
    ''' Internet Explorer
    If InStr(sAgent, "Windows CE") Then
        ''' Pocket PC
        oCmd.Properties("XSL").Value = _
Server.MapPath("login_ppc.xsl")
    Else
        oCmd.Properties("XSL").Value = _
Server.MapPath("login_ie.xsl")
    End If
Else
    oCmd.Properties("XSL").Value = _
Server.MapPath("login_nonie.xsl")
End If
```

This code is fairly simple in that we just use the `InStr` function to look for certain strings in the `User-Agent` string. You can modify it to create a more sophisticated browser detection procedure, but this will work for our purposes here. Once we have determined which of our three clients is making the request, we can specify which XSLT file to use with the XSLT dynamic property of the `Command` object. Note that this is a dynamic property, which means it only exists because we are using the `SQLOLEDB` provider.

Once we have set the XSL property, we then set another dynamic property called `Output Stream`:

```
oCmd.Properties("Output Stream") = Response
oCmd.Execute , , 1024

%>
```

This property specifies where the results should be streamed out to. In this case we want the results to be written to the `Response` object so that they will be returned to the client making the request. Finally, we execute our command passing in `1024`, which is the equivalent of `adExecuteStream`. Since we haven't declared any ADO constants though, we just supply the value.

You should now be able to open the `login.asp` file in all three clients and get the corresponding HTML results. You can use the same code for the `vieworders.asp` page by substituting the XML template filename and XSLT filename. You'll also need to pass a `CustomerID` parameter by inserting the following code before the `IF` statement block:

```
<%
...
oCmd.Dialect = "{5D531CB2-E6Ed-11D2-B252-00C04F681B71}"
oCmd.NamedParameters = True
oCmd.CommandType = 1
```

Chapter 15

```
oCmd.Parameters.Append
oCmd.CreateParameter("@CustomerID", 130, 1, 5)
oCmd.Parameters("@CustomerID").Value = _
Request.Form("CustomerID")
sAgent = Request.ServerVariables("HTTP_USER_AGENT")
...
```

Advantages to Using ASP Client Detection

ASP client detection gives many of the same advantages as ASP.NET. The code is a little more complex, because we have to do our own client detection and use classic ADO. However, we get the benefit of being able to deal with client detection on the server and the user only having to hit the page once instead of twice.

Summary

In this case study we have looked at three methods of browser detection. We began by using standard XML templates, mapped in a SQLXML virtual directory. We saw how client-side scripting involved running queries twice, first to determine the browser type, and then to render the appropriate page for the user. We then migrated the code to both ASP.NET and classic ASP and saw how they created a better method of client detection.

In the latter two methods only a single call was required in determining the browser type and supplying the results of the query, since all the processing was done on the server side. This demonstrates how you can easily start off using pure XML templates to develop your data driven website. Once you have a working site you can then move the templates with little or no changes to either ASP.NET or classic ASP to gain control over things like detecting the User-Agent.

Case Study: Detecting Web Site Clients

Stephen Mohr

- Software You Will Need
- HR and Departmental Databases
- Ideal Business Process
- BizTalk Primer
- BizTalk Messages
- HR Orchestration Schedule
- Department Phone List Schedule
- Testing the System
- Assessing the System

16

Case Study: BizTalk Integration

Microsoft BizTalk Server 2002 allows you to integrate applications through the exchange of structured messages. It is particularly well suited to working with XML documents. If your applications can process and receive messages via one of a number of well-known protocols (HTTP among them), you can orchestrate the operation of several applications to build a distributed system without the need for extensive, complex custom programming. In the ideal case, your integration work is restricted to configuring the BizTalk system through a series of wizards, though in most cases a small amount of custom code is required. The ideal, to which we can approach fairly closely, is to rapidly develop and deploy distributed apps without programming, thereby maintaining flexibility and productivity.

As you have seen before, SQL Server can work with XML messages as well as native-format `recordsets`. SQLXML Updategrams, in particular, should work well with BizTalk, as they allow database updates via XML messages posted over HTTP. To test this theory, we'll build a sample application that allows us to maintain detailed information about a newly hired employee in a HR database, and less detailed information in a phone list database for the department in which he will work. The application will use XML for its representation of employee data and use BizTalk to turn the data into a SQLXML Updategram, which it submits to SQL Server.

Naturally, we could implement this through a Visual Basic application making ADO (or indeed ADO.NET) calls to insert information into the two databases. The advantage of using the ADO route is that it gives us total control over security and transaction boundaries. The disadvantages are that it necessitates a substantial amount of custom code, and requires one application to know about the internals of two databases and have full access to both. In the real world, the departmental phone list database is likely to be owned and maintained by the department itself and not the Human Relations department.

The Human Relations department, in turn, would control its database as well as the application that captures the new employee's information. Working with SQLXML and BizTalk Server, we can isolate the two databases from one another and from the employee intake application. This isolation allows the two departments to use different computing environments, operating systems, and security arrangements. So long as they can access one another using HTTP, the two databases can be integrated. The example is of integration between departments; it could, of course, be between enterprises as well.

Here are the requirements for our system:

- Employee information should be captured in an XML vocabulary that is distinct from SQL Server Updategrams. In other words, employee intake is isolated from the database tier.
- The HR and Department databases are distinct and should be capable of independent maintenance.
- Input of a new employee's information should flow first to the HR database, then to the department where the new employee will be working.
- The Department database should never receive sensitive personal information subject to privacy restrictions.
- All actions following submission of employee information should be automated and subject to tracking.

Then, use of an XML vocabulary for talking about new employees allows us to bring in XML technologies like XSLT for data format manipulation, and to avoid database-specific programming such as ADO. Making the vocabulary independent of Updategrams keeps the client tier independent of the data tier. Should the databases change, we won't need to alter the client application that is used to process new employees. The goal of using BizTalk in conjunction with SQL Server's XML support is to allow us to avoid custom programming entirely. This would increase productivity and flexibility. Wiring together this system should be a matter of configuration only. Let's see if we can reach that goal with our chosen technology.

Software You Will Need

In addition to SQL Server 2000, you will require the SQLXML 3.0 SP1 update and Microsoft BizTalk Server 2002. Both are available for free from the MSDN website.

SQLXML 3.0 SP1 enhances SQL Server's XML capabilities with Updategrams and is available from:
http://msdn.microsoft.com/downloads/default.asp?URL=/downloads/sample.asp?url=/msdn-files/027/001/824/msdncompositedoc.xml.
The download file is 2.7MB.

Case Study: BizTalk Integration

BizTalk Server, Enterprise Edition, is available in a free, trial version from http://www.microsoft.com/biztalk/evaluation/trial/default.asp. The download file is 64MB in size. It requires an instance of SQL Server. In order to specify the business processes we'll discuss shortly, you will also need Microsoft Visio 2000 (or above). Make sure SQL Server and Visio are installed and available prior to installing BizTalk Server. During the installation of BizTalk, four databases will be created for you and an add-in for Visio will be installed. Detailed directions for installing BizTalk are included with the download, although the process is fairly straightforward and wizard-driven.

If you do not wish to manually enter all the BizTalk configurations and create the databases, utility files have been included in the `Utility` folder of the code download so you can rapidly rebuild the sample configuration. The databases may be created by executing the SQL command files `HR.sql` and `Department.sql` using SQL Server Query Analyzer. After executing the commands, be sure to add the user ID under which BizTalk runs to the list of permitted users for the databases. You can use the **BTConfigAssistant** tool included with BizTalk Server to import the file `BTSConfigForSample.xml`, found in the `BTSConfig` folder of the code download. **BTConfigAssistant** is found under the **Messaging Samples** menu in the typical BizTalk Server installation. The import will establish all the configurations we describe later in this chapter, but you will need to edit some of them to reflect the locations of the schedule files and the folder where Updategrams are deposited.

HR and Departmental Databases

Our application needs two independent databases, one representing the Human Relations department's database of employee information, and one representing one department's abbreviated listing of employee information suitable for generating a telephone contact listing.

HR Database

This database, which we've named `HR`, consists of three tables related through an employee ID. We're assuming an ID consisting of an American Social Security number, but we've only typed it as an `nchar` column of length 11, so you can put any sort of unique ID into that column. The first table, `Employees`, represents the employees themselves: name, address, date of birth, and telephone number. Here are the columns:

Field	Type	Length	NOT NULL?	Other
emp_id	nchar	11	NOT NULL	Primary key
emp_fname	char	25	NOT NULL	
emp_middle	char	10		
emp_lname	char	30	NOT NULL	
emp_dob	nchar	10	NOT NULL	

459

Chapter 16

Field	Type	Length	NOT NULL?	Other
emp_sex	char	1	NOT NULL	
emp_race	char	30		
emp_telephone	char	12	NOT NULL	
emp_street1	char	40	NOT NULL	
emp_street2	char	40		
emp_city	char	20	NOT NULL	
emp_state	char	2	NOT NULL	
emp_zip	char	10	NOT NULL	

The emp_dob (date of birth) column is typed as it is because we want to use a date type in the XML, and that type is translated by SQLXML as an nchar column. The next table, Benefits, contains basic information about an employee's benefit elections as indicated by the following columns:

Field	Type	Length	NOT NULL?	Other
bene_id	nchar	11	NOT NULL	Primary key, refers to emp_id in Employees
bene_retirement	char	10	NOT NULL	
bene_medical	char	10	NOT NULL	

The final table, Employment, captures the employee's employment information, including a reference to the employee ID of his supervisor:

Field	Type	Length	NOT NULL?	Other
empl_id	nchar	11	NOT NULL	Primary key, refers to emp_id in Employees
empl_start	nchar	10	NOT NULL	
empl_dept	char	20		
empl_title	char	40	NOT NULL	
empl_salary	decimal	18		
empl_super	nchar	11	NOT NULL	

Case Study: BizTalk Integration

A SQL script that will build this database for you (HR.sql) is found in the code download for this chapter.

Department Database

The departmental phone list database, by contrast, is simplicity itself (simpler than we might like for good database design but ideal for the purposes of our demonstration). It consists of one table, `PhoneList`, with the following columns:

Field	Type	Length	NOT NULL?	Other
dept_id	nchar	11	NOT NULL	Primary key
dept_fname	char	25	NOT NULL	
dept_lname	char	30	NOT NULL	
dept_start	char	10	NOT NULL	
dept_telephone	char	12		

A SQL script that will build this database for you (Department.sql) is found in the code download for this chapter.

SQLXML Configuration

Next, you should use SQLXML's IIS configuration utility to set up two virtual directories, `HR` and `Dept`.

If you need a reminder as to how to configure virtual directories then look back to Chapter 2.

Configure the directories to use Windows Integrated Authentication and associate them with the databases you just set up. At a minimum, allow template requests and HTTP POSTs. Although the documentation warns against the latter, the system will be operating inside the corporate firewall and employs native authentication. Limiting the size of a POST further secures the directory. This can be done on the **Settings** tab of the **Properties** dialog for the virtual directories in the configuration utility.

Set up the HR directory with two subdirectories, `schema` and `template`. Create virtual names, `template` and `schema`, on the **Virtual Names** tab of the properties dialog and associate the names with these subdirectories. Place the map file `employee_map.xsd` from the code download in the `schema` directory. A sample template (`hr_update.xml`) in the code download can be used to test the HR database's SQLXML configuration, while you can test HTTP POSTing with the rudimentary file `HTMLPost.html`, also in the code download. In a fresh installation, you can open Internet Explorer and request the page:
http://yourserver/HR/template/hr_update.xml. You should see the following response:

```
<p:Root xmlns="urn:schemas-microsoft-com:xml-updategram"
        xmlns:p="urn:schemas-wrox-com:xml-updategram" />
```

Chapter 16

At that point, you can examine the tables in the HR database and see that a new employee has been added with benefits and employment details. Resubmitting the HTTP request will yield a page with an error message complaining of a violation of a primary key constraint as you have tried to add the same employee again. The page HTMLPost.html, in contrast, has a form with a hard-coded Updategram in a hidden field. Submitting this form allows you to test the ability to send your own Updategram via HTTP.

Set up Dept similarly, although you can skip the schema subdirectory and virtual name, as the Updategram for that virtual directory will not use a map file. The sample Updategram for this directory is dept_update.xml in the code download.

Ideal Business Process

This is the business process we would like to implement:

- ❏ Receive an Employee XML document from the employee uptake application via BizTalk messaging, using an MSMQ queue or HTTP POST.
- ❏ Pass this message to the HR SQLXML application via BizTalk, using mapping *en route* to convert the message to the Updategram format for that application.
- ❏ Pass the same Employee message to the Dept SQLXML application, again using BizTalk, HTTP, and mapping to departmental Updategram format.
- ❏ Optionally, configure the process to take compensating action, such as sending an e-mail to an administrator if either POST fails.

The basic scheme would look like this:

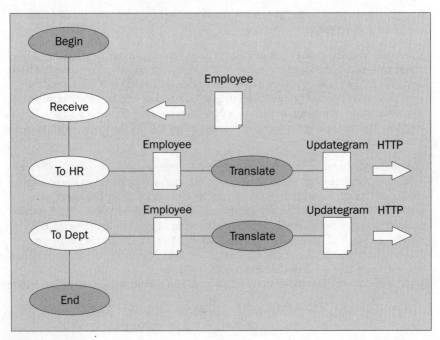

Advantages

This process has some notable advantages over the ADO approach:

- Extreme simplicity. Our process would deal solely with the `Employee` XML format. We would have to define the Updategrams for BizTalk's benefit, but the process itself would stick to the `Employee` vocabulary we have defined for our internal applications.
- We would leverage SQL Server's XML support for our benefit. It would entirely hide the nature of the database storage from our application. Once we fling an Updategram at the database's URL, our application is through with the database. Contrast this to a programming approach using ADO. We wouldn't have to worry about the ADO object model, the database schema, or anything else related to databases.
- We would be well positioned for the future. We could use SQLXML's SOAP support to let our HR personnel do hiring offsite, for example, at a job fair. The employee intake application would be modified to use SOAP and would aim at the `HR` database.

Security Ramifications

If we implemented this process, we would need to make some modifications to security from the typical configuration explained in the SQLXML documentation. If BizTalk Server is not running as a user ID known to the database, we would need to allow anonymous access to the SQLXML site and grant access to the `IUSR_machinename` ID (which is what IIS uses for anonymous access) to the database. You can't do this through the SQLXML Configure IIS Support utility, so you must use the IIS Administration utility. Once you do this, the new security configuration will be reflected in the SQLXML utility.

This is not as dangerous as it might seem. First of all, we are assumed to be operating behind the corporate firewall designed to screen out the worst attacks from the Internet, and completely within the confines of the corporate LAN. If we need external access, we could put the receiving BizTalk machine in a demilitarized zone. The BizTalk machine is isolated from the rest of the corporate network by a much more restrictive firewall. The HR and Dept IIS servers would reside inside this second firewall. The second firewall only allows traffic from the BizTalk machine to the IIS servers. The actual databases, in turn, allow access only from the HR and Dept IIS servers.

> *Naturally, we're assuming that your IIS and SQL Server installations are up to date with respect to service packs, hotfixes, and updates. In addition to running Windows Update and visiting the product pages for the software you have installed, you should make a point of regularly checking the Microsoft security home pages at http://www.microsoft.com/security.*

Finally, secure SOAP access to the HR SQLXML application is strictly for the future when security enhancements now under discussion are part of the SOAP (or XML Protocol) standard. These will include provisions for encryption and digital signing, just the sort of things needed to secure an otherwise anonymous request traveling through the public Internet via the insecure HTTP protocol.

> For more information on security as it relates to future versions of SOAP, see the W3C technical resources at http://www.w3.org/TR, the OASIS site at http://www.oasis-open.org, and the Web Service Interoperability consortium at http://www.ws-i.org.

BizTalk Primer

Let's have a brief bit of review of BizTalk concepts for the benefit of readers who are new to that product. This won't be enough to make you proficient by itself, but it will help you to make sense of the discussion that follows.

BizTalk Server is made up of two services; the **messaging service** and the **XLANG Scheduler**. The former handles the passing of messages between two parties or applications. It is the simplest form of data interchange supported by BizTalk. **Messages** are data documents written in XML or flatfile format. These formats are described in **message specifications**, which are essentially XDR schemas with a little extra information added. The service uses **message definitions** that tell the runtime engine where to look for message specifications. A **messaging port** is a destination; it combines a transport protocol, such as HTTP, an organization or application name, and the URL to which messages will be delivered. One or more **channels** are built on a port. A channel describes what kind of message comes in, what format it should be in when delivered to a port, how it is converted to the new format, and which port takes delivery of the message. A channel is a sort of agreement describing the exchange of messages.

The **XLANG Scheduler** handles the composition, or **orchestration**, of messaging exchanges into a unified process. It takes its name, XLANG, from the name of the XML vocabulary used to describe a process. A process, called a **schedule** in orchestration, is a flowchart in which the basic operations are messaging exchanges. Each such operation, termed an **action**, is implemented by a **messaging implementation**. These implementations are frequently accomplished using the BizTalk messaging service, but may also use MSMQ or COM. Messaging implementations are connected to actions through **ports**. These ports are not the same as the messaging ports we described above, but should be thought of as the connection between a business process and a physical implementation. They specify what kind of data is passed between the messaging implementation and the business process.

First Problem

In an ideal world, the business process described above would be what we implement in the rest of the chapter. Unfortunately, there is a bug in SQLXML 3.0 SP1; an HTTP POST from BizTalk will not be accepted. You can get past security with anonymous IIS access. You can correctly configure the Updategram's MIME type as text/xml by overriding the messaging port default configuration when you set up the channel (about which much more later). Unfortunately, nothing you do will allow your Updategram to reach the database. The ISAPI application used by SQLXML rejects the Updategram as a bad request. Something in the way BizTalk messaging presents HTTP POSTs to SQLXML leads to a breakdown. We will need to devise a workaround for our business process.

Case Study: BizTalk Integration

Revised Business Process

We shall overcome this limitation by breaking the business process into two applications; one for the HR side of the system, and one for the Department side. Here is what the HR business process will do:

- Accept an `HR` Updategram from BizTalk; BizTalk will accept an Employee message and convert it to the Updategram format before passing it to the `HR` application.
- Submit the Updategram to the `HR` database using a scripted COM component and ADO.
- Send the `HR` Updategram to the `Department` application via BizTalk, mapping it to the `Department` Updategram format en route. The `Department` Updategram will be dropped on to disk by BizTalk in a predetermined location monitored by the Department side of things.

See the HR Business Process section later for a diagram.

BizTalk supports a component called **file receive functions**. You use these to monitor a specific directory for the arrival of a particular class of files. In our case, we will monitor the directory specified in the last step of the HR side of things for depositing `Department` Updategrams for the arrival of files with the extension `.xml`. This file receive function will launch the `Department` process, which performs the following tasks:

- Receive a `Department` Updategram from BizTalk.
- Submit the Updategram to the `Department` database using the same script component used in the HR business process.

Happily, the code we require is short, written in VBScript, and can be made sufficiently general-purpose for use submitting Updategrams to any SQL Server database.

BizTalk Messages

The heart of any BizTalk system is its messages. We have three in the system we are describing: the canonical Employee XML format, the `HR` Updategram, and the `Department` Updategram. Let's consider these messages, particularly how we must declare them using the BizTalk messaging tools.

New Employee

The `Employee` message is an XML vocabulary of our own construction that has nothing to do with SQLXML. It is designed to capture a variety of information about an employee. Adding a new employee is accomplished by sending a complete Employee message into the Human Relations system. The **document element** (root) of the message is `<Employee>`. It has a single attribute, `id`, which is designed to be a Social Security Number. `<Employee>` contains four elements: `<Name>`, `<PersonalData>` (for the employee's home address, date of birth, and other information), `<Benefits>` (for medical and retirement elections), and `<Employment>` (for departmental assignment, start date, supervisor, salary, and job title). Here's a sample `Employee` message:

465

Chapter 16

```xml
<Employee id = "123-55-1234">
  <Name>
    <First>John</First>
    <MI>A</MI>
    <Last>Doe</Last>
  </Name>
  <PersonalData dob = "1960-01-01">
    <Home telephone = "215-555-1212">
      <Street1>1234 Main Street</Street1>
      <City>East Knucklejunction</City>
      <State>PA</State>
      <PostalCode>19105-1234</PostalCode>
    </Home>
    <Gender sex = "M"/>
  </PersonalData>
  <Benefits>
    <Retirement>401K</Retirement>
    <Medical>BC-PPO</Medical>
  </Benefits>
  <Employment startDate = "2002-07-04">
    <Department>Engineering</Department>
    <Title salary = "85000">
      Senior Development Engineer</Title>
    <Supervisor id = "123-55-4321"/>
  </Employment>
</Employee>
```

I started my message design by creating an XML schema to illustrate the limitations of BizTalk's message specifications as compared to state of the art schemas. BizTalk 2002 uses an annotated version of the proprietary XDR format. The schema file `employee.xsd` *in the code download makes use of patterns to control the composition of strings, particularly for IDs, zip codes, and telephone numbers. Following this, I created and imported a sample XML instance conforming to the schema into BizTalk to generate the message specification. Even editing the resulting specification, we end up with a specification that is less restrictive than the XML schema version. In particular, the XML schema had patterns constraining the permissible values for Employee and Supervisor ids, as well as PostalCode and telephone values. These are lost going to the XDR-based message specification in BizTalk.*

Messages are specified in BizTalk using the **BizTalk Editor tool**. Since the Editor can be used for non-XML files as well as XML documents, the tool uses the idea of **records** for items that can contain other items, and **fields**, that do not contain nested items. XML messages always use elements to implement records, but fields can be attributes or elements. The following table specifies the `Employee` message type for BizTalk. Any entries that are not specified in this table are left on the Editor's default setting. Items in boldface are records. Records in gray cells contain the records that follow them. The nesting structure of records is:

```
Employee-
        |-Name-
        |     |-First
        |     |-MI
        |     |-Last
        |-PersonalData-
        |             |-Home
        |             |-Gender
        |-Benefits
        |-Employment-
                    |-Title
                    |-Supervisor
```

The document specification for this message type is called NewEmployee.xml and, like all the message specifications, is found in the Docs code download folder for this chapter.

Item	Declaration settings	Reference settings
Employee	Type: Element, Content: Element Only	Specification Name: Employee, Standard: XML
id	Type: Attribute	Required: Yes
Name	Type: Element, Content Element Only	Minimum Occurrences: 1, Maximum Occurrences: 1
First	Type: Element, Content: Text Only	Required: Yes
MI	Type: Element, Content: Text Only	Required: No
Last	Type: Element, Content: Text Only	Required: Yes
PersonalData	Type: Element, Content: Element Only	Minimum Occurrences: 1, Maximum Occurrences: 1
dob	Type: Attribute	Required: Yes
Home	Type: Element, Content: Element Only	Minimum Occurrences: 1, Maximum Occurrences: 1
telephone	Type: Attribute	Required: Yes

Table continued on following page

Chapter 16

Item	Declaration settings	Reference settings
Street1	Type: Element, Content: Text Only	Required: Yes
Street2	Type: Element, Content: Text Only	Required: No
City	Type: Element, Content: Text Only	Required: Yes
State	Type: Element, Content: Text Only	Required: Yes
PostalCode	Type: Element, Content: Text Only	Required: Yes
Gender	Type: Element, Content: Empty	Minimum Occurrences: 1, Maximum Occurrences: 1
sex	Type: Attribute	Required: Yes
Benefits	Type: Element, Content: Element Only	Minimum Occurrences: 1, Maximum Occurrences: 1
Retirement	Type: Element, Content: Text Only	Required: Yes
Medical	Type: Element, Content: Text Only	Required: Yes
Employment	Type: Element, Content: Element Only	Minimum Occurrences: 1, Maximum Occurrences: 1
startDate	Type: Attribute	Required: Yes
Department	Type: Element, Content: Text Only	Required: Yes
Title	Type: Element, Content: Text Only	Minimum Occurrences: 1, Maximum Occurrences: 1
salary	Type: Attribute	
Supervisor	Type: Element, Content: Empty	Minimum Occurrences: 1, Maximum Occurrences: 1
id	Type: Attribute	Required: Yes

Case Study: BizTalk Integration

When you are done, save the specification to the WebDAV repository as `NewEmployee.xml`.

> *The WebDAV (Web Distributed Authoring and Versioning) repository on the server exposes all documents and folders through HTTP. This allows administrators to edit documents from any computer with web access to the BizTalk Server, rather than requiring direct access to the server's file system.*

This creates a message specification, but we have to tell the messaging system about it so that it can use it when processing messages. To do this, go into the BizTalk Messaging Manager utility (accessed via the **Start | Programs | Microsoft BizTalk Server 2002 | BizTalk Messaging Manager** menu) and select **Document definitions**. Then, select the **File | New Document definition** menu item. On the **General** tab of the properties dialog that appears, enter **New Employee** for the name, check **Document specification** and browse to the specification file you just specified. Finally, click **OK** to close and save the information. This makes the message specification available to the BizTalk messaging system.

Updategrams

The other two messages in our system are SQLXML Updategrams. The first, for the `HR` database, is going to update three tables, so a mapping schema is required. The second, for the `Department` database, only affects a single table. In this case, we'll make the attribute names match the table's column names so that a mapping schema won't be needed. As a general rule, it is a good idea to use a mapping schema in order to conceal database table names, but it adds unnecessary complexity to our example. We'll use a mapping schema only when we need to alter the structure of a message; but in production we would always use such a schema, if only to provide security for the table structure.

First, however, we have to deal with another problem introduced by SQLXML 3.0 SP1.

Changes from Prior Releases of SQLXML

Updategrams have always used `<ROOT>` as the document element, but the documentation has been careful to say that any element name is acceptable. Earlier versions of SQLXML allowed you to specify the `urn:schemas-microsoft-com:xml-updategram` namespace URI on `<ROOT>`. Strictly speaking, however, since SQLXML is agnostic as to the name of the document element, `<ROOT>` shouldn't be part of the SQLXML namespace. As of this version of SQLXML, this is enforced.

That wouldn't be a problem, except that BizTalk message specifications currently do not handle multiple namespaces well. In previous versions of SQLXML, you could associate the required URI with the `<ROOT>` element and all would be well. If you do that with this version, the SQLXML ISAPI DLL will reject the message. BizTalk Editor will not allow you to use `xmlns` as a field name, and you cannot specify another namespace below the level of the document element.

Our message specifications, then, will use `<sync>` as the document element. We'll wrap it with the `<ROOT>` element outside BizTalk before submitting the Updategram to the database.

469

Chapter 16

HR Updategram

The nesting of records for this Updategram should look like this:

```
Sync-
    |-after-
        |-Employee-
                |-Benefits
                |-Employment
```

Here are the settings you need in BizTalk Editor to specify the HR Updategram; the table conventions are the same as those used in the Employee table:

Item	Declaration settings	Reference settings
sync	Type: Element, Content: Element Only	Standard: XML, Target Namespace: urn:schemas-microsoft-com:xml-updategram
mapping-schema	Type: Attribute	Required: Yes
after	Type: Element, Content: Element Only	Minimum Occurrences: 1, Maximum Occurrences: 1
Employee	Type: Element, Content: Element Only	Minimum Occurrences: 1, Maximum Occurrences: 1
id	Type: Attribute, Data Type: String, Minimum Length: 11, Maximum Length: 11	Required: Yes
dob	Type: Attribute, Data Type: Date	Required: Yes
gender	Type: Attribute, Data Type: Enumeration, Data Type: Values M F	Required: Yes
first	Type: Attribute, Data Type: String	Required: Yes
mi	Type: Attribute, Data Type: String	
last	Type: Attribute, Data Type: String	Required: Yes
telephone	Type: Attribute, Data Type: String, Minimum Length: 12, Maximum Length: 12	Required: Yes
Street	Type: Element, Content: Text Only	Required: Yes

Case Study: BizTalk Integration

Item	Declaration settings	Reference settings
Extra	Type: Element, Content: Text Only	
City	Type: Element, Content: Text Only	Required: Yes
State	Type: Element, Content: Text Only	Required: Yes
Zip	Type: Element, Content: Text Only	Required: Yes
Benefits	Type: Element, Content: Empty	Minimum Occurrences: 1, Maximum Occurrences: 1
Retire	Type: Attribute, Data Type: String	Required: Yes
Medical	Type: Attribute, Data Type: String	Required: Yes
Employment	Type: Element, Content: Empty	Minimum Occurrences: 1, Maximum Occurrences: 1
start	Type: Attribute, Data Type: Date	Required: Yes
dept	Type: Attribute, Data Type: String	
title	Type: Attribute, Data Type: String	
salary	Type: Attribute, Data Type: String	
report	Type: Attribute, Data Type: String	Required: Yes

After you are finished, save this specification to the repository as hrupdgram.xml. Go into Messaging Manager and configure a document definition with the name hr_update that points to this specification. Again, this is a pointer within the messaging system that lets the system find the message specification at runtime. Note that we have not specified the value for the mapping schema. We'll take care of this during message format mapping.

We also need an XML Schema format mapping, incorporating SQLXML's annotations, to map attributes to columns and elements to tables. We use this map for three things:

- ❑ mapping elements to tables
- ❑ mapping attributes to table columns
- ❑ expressing the relationships between Employees and Benefits, and Employees and Employment.

471

Chapter 16

The `<Employee>`, `<Benefits>`, and `<Employment>` elements are mapped to their respective SQL Server tables with the `sql:relation` attributes as shown below:

```
<xsd:element name = "Employee"
              sql:relation="Employees"
              sql:key-fields="emp_id">
<xsd:element name = "Benefits"
              sql:relation="Benefits"
              sql:relationship="emp_bene"
              sql:key-fields="bene_id">
<xsd:element name = "Employment"
              sql:relation="Employment"
              sql:relationship="emp_empl"
              sql:key-fields="empl_id">
```

The value of the `sql:relation` attribute is the name of the table to which the element applies. The `sql:key-fields` attribute names the table column that is the primary key for the table. Note also the use of the `sql:relationship` attribute for the last two elements. This value points back to a pair of `sql:relationship` elements earlier in the schema that explain how the three tables are related:

```
<sql:relationship name="emp_bene"
                   parent="Employees"
                   parent-key="emp_id"
                   child="Benefits"
                   child-key="bene_id" />
<sql:relationship name="emp_empl"
                   parent="Employees"
                   parent-key="emp_id"
                   child="Employment"
                   child-key="empl_id" />
```

The mapping schema is found in the `hr_map.xsd` file in the code download.

Department Updategram

The final Updategram follows a similar structure. Here is the nesting diagram:

```
Sync-
    |-after-
         |-PhoneList
```

Case Study: BizTalk Integration

Here are the message specification settings:

Item	Declaration settings	Reference settings
sync	Type: Element, Content: Element Only	Standard: XML, Target Namespace: urn:schemas-microsoft-com:xml-updategram
after	Type: Element, Content: Element Only	Minimum Occurrences: 1, Maximum Occurrences: 1
PhoneList	Type: Element, Content: Empty	Minimum Occurrences: 1, Maximum Occurrences: 1
dept_id	Type: Attribute, Data Type: String, Minimum Length: 11, Maximum Length: 11	Required: Yes
dept_fname	Type: Attribute, Data Type: String	Required: Yes
dept_lname	Type: Attribute, Data Type: String	Required: Yes
dept_telephone	Type: Attribute, Data Type: String, Minimum Length: 12, Maximum Length: 12	Required: Yes
dept_start	Type: Attribute, Data Type: String	Required: Yes

Save this specification to the repository as `deptupdgram.xml`, and create a document definition in Messaging Manager under the name `dept_update`.

HR Orchestration Schedule

Orchestration is the term given to the process of ensuring application integration is transparent to designers and developers. A distributed system involves many messages passed between applications, all of which must be passed in logical sequence if the system is to function. Orchestration is the process by which these messages are coordinated as a single system; business processes are implemented in BizTalk as orchestration schedules, and these schedules are built as flowcharts in BizTalk Orchestration Designer (an add-in for Microsoft Visio). Each **action** in the flowchart is a message exchange. An action is represented in a schedule diagram as an unfilled oval. You will implement an action by connecting it to a messaging implementation such as BizTalk. Actions are the basic units by which schedules do things. Such exchanges may be implemented with BizTalk messaging, or may call MSMQ, COM, or scripted COM components directly.

Chapter 16

The BizTalk messaging system will receive an `Employee` message from the client application, reformat it as an `HR` Updategram, launch the schedule, and send it to the Updategram. After receiving the message as its first action, the schedule submits this Updategram to the database using a scripted COM component. Finally, it uses BizTalk messaging to send the Updategram to a file directory for pickup by the Departmental `file receive` function, and intake into the departmental schedule. BizTalk messaging will reformat the message as a departmental Updategram *en route*.

HR Business Process

The orchestration schedule for this business process is depicted in the figure below. Note the flowchart symbols on the left and the message exchange implementations on the right. The boxes on the double line border in between are orchestration ports. These are the specific interfaces between the logical business process and the specific messaging implementation. These ports are not the same as ports in BizTalk messaging. However, when the exchange is implemented with BizTalk messaging, as in the first and last exchanges in this schedule, there will be a BizTalk messaging port that directly corresponds to the orchestration port, so I have found it convenient to use the same name for both.

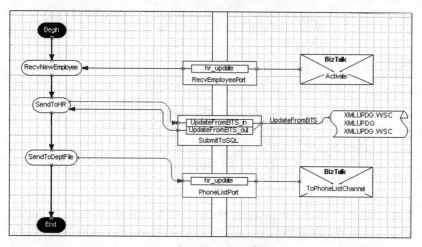

The business process is represented by the action shapes on the left. The **messaging implementations**, the things that actually carry out the intention of an action through some message interchange, are the shapes on the right side of the double border. We'll discuss the messaging implementations in a moment, but we have to build a utility component first.

Updategram Component

Since we cannot use an HTTP POST (through BizTalk messaging) to submit the Updategram, we'll use ADO. I've chosen to use a script component that can be created using the Windows Script Component Wizard. This utility builds a script file that uses some XML conventions to designate a COM interface. At runtime, the scripting engine recognizes these conventions and creates a dispatch interface. Similarly, the operating system recognizes the conventions and allows you to register the `.wsc` script file as a COM DLL so that applications may call the interface just as they would any other COM component.

Case Study: BizTalk Integration

> *If you don't have the Windows Script Component Wizard, then you can download it from http://msdn.misrosoft.com/downloads. The installation file (122KB) can be found by drilling down to the* **Web Development / Windows Script / Component Wizard** *menu. You may register a WSC component by right-clicking on it in the Windows Explorer and selecting* **Register** *from the context menu.*

The details of the ADO object model are beyond the scope of this chapter, but our usage of the ADO API is minimal. You can read more about ADO in *ADO 2.6 Programmer's Reference* (Wrox Press, ISBN 186100463X). If you wish to take advantage of the Microsoft .NET Framework, then you should take a look at *ADO.NET Programmer's Reference* (Wrox Press, 186100558X).

We create a function (exposed as a COM method) named `UpdateFromBTS`. This function takes the core of an Updategram (from the `<sync>` element on down), the name of the database, and the name of the SQL Server instance hosting the database. Here is that function:

```
function UpdateFromBTS(sUpdgCore, sDb, sServer)
    Dim sQuery
    sUpdgram = "<ROOT>" + sUpdgCore + "</ROOT>"
    UpdateFromBTS = ExecSQL(sUpdgram, sDb, sServer)
end function
```

We wrap the `<ROOT>` element around the core (taking care of our SQLXML 3.0 SP1 problem regarding the namespace of this element), then pass it on to the private function `ExecSQL`:

```
function ExecSQL(XMLQuery, sDB, sServer)
    Dim conDb
    Dim cmdXML
    Dim sQry
    Dim strmIn    ' query text
    Dim strmOut   ' query results

    Set conDB = CreateObject("ADODB.Connection")
    With conDB
        .ConnectionString = "DATA PROVIDER=SQLOLEDB;" & _
                            "provider=SQLXMLOLEDB.3.0;" & _
                            "DATA SOURCE=" + sServer + ";" & _
                            "INITIAL CATALOG=" + sDB + ";" & _
                            "INTEGRATED SECURITY=SSPI;"
        .Open
    End With

    Set cmdXML = CreateObject("ADODB.Command")
    Set cmdXML.ActiveConnection = conDb

    Set strmIn = CreateObject("ADODB.Stream")
```

475

Chapter 16

```
        strmIn.Open
        strmIn.WriteText XMLQuery, 0
        strmIn.Position = 0

        Set cmdXML.CommandStream = strmIn

        cmdXML.Properties("xml root") = "ROOT"
        cmdXML.Properties("ss Stream Flags") = 56

        Set strmOut = CreateObject("ADODB.Stream")

        strmOut.Open
        cmdXML.Properties("Output Stream") = strmOut

        cmdXML.Execute, , 1024
        ExecuteXMLQuery = strmOut.ReadText
end function
```

Without going into the details of ADO programming, this function logs into the named database on the specified instance using Windows authentication. It creates a Command object that uses a stream holding the Updategram. The Updategram is submitted by executing the command on the connection. If it works, the value returned by SQL Server is passed all the way back as the return value of the UpdateFromBTS method.

> *The script component is supplied with the code download in the file XMLUPDG.WSC. You can copy that anywhere on your BizTalk computer, then right-click on it and choose **Register** from the context menu.*

HR Messaging Implementations

Now we are ready to specify implementations for each of the actions in our schedule. When we are done, we'll need to create BizTalk configurations to go with two of these implementations, but let's stick with BizTalk Orchestration Designer for now.

RecvNewEmployee

Drag an **Action** shape in the Orchestration Designer on to the left hand side of the screen, below the **Begin** icon, and call it RecvNewEmployee. Link the two shapes together by dragging the node of the **Begin** icon to the node of the RecvNewEmployee icon. This action receives a message from BizTalk messaging, so drag a BizTalk Messaging shape onto the implementation side of the schedule (see the diagram in the *HR Business Process* section earlier). The BizTalk Messaging Binding Wizard, shown in the following screenshot, appears:

Case Study: BizTalk Integration

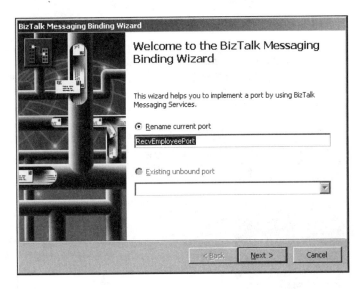

Here are the settings you need to specify:

Tab	Settings
Welcome	Port name: RecvEmployeePort
Communication Direction	Receive
XLANG Schedule Activation Information	Yes

Now connect the RecvNewEmployee shape to the RecvEmployeePort port that was created when you added the BizTalk Messaging shape. The XML Communication Wizard appears. Here are the settings:

Tab	Settings
Welcome	Receive (disabled but set for you)
Message Information	Message name: hr_update
XML Translation Information	Receive XML messages from the queue
Message Type Information	Message type: sync
Message Specification Information	Message Specification: browse to the repository folder (typically Program files | Microsoft BizTalk Server | BizTalkServerRepository | DocSpecs) and point to the `hrupdgram.xml` specification file.

477

Chapter 16

SendToHR

Add this new Action shape to the diagram below the RecvNewEmployee shape, and link them as previously. SendToHR is a bit different, in that it involves instantiating a COM component and calling one of its methods. Drag a Script Component shape onto the message implementations side of the diagram. The Script Component Binding Wizard appears:

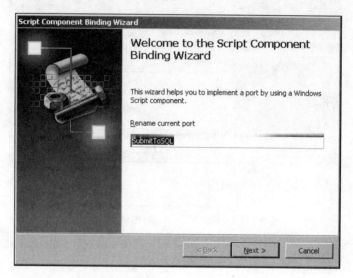

Make the following settings:

Tab	Settings
Welcome	Port name: SubmitToSQL
Static or Dynamic Communication	Static
Specify the script file	Browse to the file XMLUPDG.WSC
Component Instantiation Information	Use the Prog ID XMLUPDG.WSC
Advanced Port Properties	Accept defaults

When you connect the action to the port (by dragging your mouse from the SendToHR node to the SubmitToSQL port node), the Method Communication Wizard appears:

Case Study: BizTalk Integration

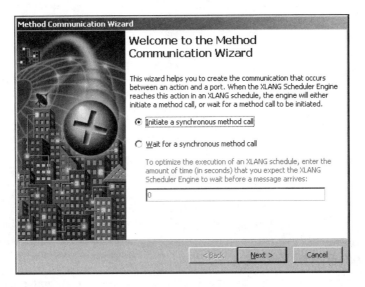

Specify the settings as indicated below:

Tab	Setting
Welcome	Initiate a synchronous method call
Message Information	Create a new message
Message Specification Information	Methods: UpdateFromBTS

SendToDeptFile

This implementation is similar to the first one we performed, although the message direction is outbound. The goal is to send the Updategram out to a directory as a file, for pickup by a file receive function. Add an **Action** shape below the **SendToHR** icon and name it `SendToDeptFile`. Link it to the SendToHR icon as previously. Add a **BizTalk messaging** shape to the right hand side of your diagram and specify the settings as follows:

Tab	Settings
Welcome	Port name: PhoneListPort
Communication Direction	Send
Static or Dynamic Channel Information	Static Channel: ToPhoneListChannel

Now drag the right hand node of the **SendToDeptFile** icon with the mouse and connect it to the left hand node of the **PhoneListPort**. The settings for the XML Communication Wizard are:

479

Chapter 16

Tab	Settings
Welcome	Send (disabled but selected for you)
Message Information	Message name: hr_update (look for the **Add a reference to an existing message** option)
XML Translation Information	Send XML messages to the queue
Message Type Information	Message type: sync
Message Specification Information	Message specification: browse to hrupdgram.xml in the repository

Now all you need do is add an **End** shape below the **SendToDeptFile** Action shape, and connect it to this by dragging the node downwards to complete the diagram.

HR Data Flow

There is one final thing to do, and that is to specify how data is going to flow from the update message into the `UpdateFromBTS` method call. Click on the **Data** tab of the schedule. Message shapes for `hr_update` and `UpdateFromBTS` will have been created automatically. The Updategram is the value for the first parameter of the method call, so drag a connection from the `Document` field of the `hr_update` message to the `sUpdgCore` field of the `UpdateFromBTS_in` message. This will cause the orchestration runtime to transfer the information to the method call automatically. The other two parameters are values we must specify. Double-click the **Constants** shape and click **Add...** on the dialog that appears. Enter `cServer` for the Name, `string` for the Data type, and the servername for Value (the latter is (`local`) for my configuration). Repeat the process, but this time provide the values `cHRDb`, `string`, and `HR`. Now, drag a connection from `cServer` on the `Constants` shape to `sServer` on `UpdateFromBTS_in`, and from `cHRDb` to `sDb`. This fully specifies the parameters for the method call.

When you are finished, the connections on the data diagram will look like this:

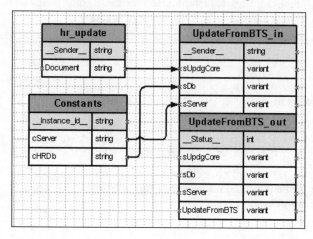

Case Study: BizTalk Integration

When you have finished specifying the data flow, you will be able to compile the schedule to the XML document required by the orchestration server engine by selecting File | Make XLANG NewEmployee.skx from the main menu. This file, NewEmployee.skx, may be placed anywhere on your system. You will need to point to it later when we set up the messaging configuration.

BizTalk Messaging Configuration

By itself, this business process will do nothing. We need to configure the messaging system to support the message implementations in the schedule. The majority of this work will be done in the Messaging Manager. We've already started this process by creating document definitions when we created the message specifications.

Home Organization Applications

The system is defined as a series of application-to-application integrations. BizTalk messaging requires that you have names for your applications. These are strictly logical names. To do this, select **Organizations** in Messaging Manager, double-click on **Home Organization**, select the **Applications** tab, and click **Add...** Add the following names: NewEmployee (representing the employee intake client application), HR (for the HR business process), and DeptPhone (for the departmental business process).

Map Between New Employee and HR Updategram

Before we can set up the first message exchange, in which the Employee message arrives in the schedule as an HR Updategram, we need to specify a map between the two messages. Open the BizTalk Mapper tool and create a new map. This brings up a series of dialogs in which you select the source and destination messages. Select NewEmployee.xml for the source and hrupdgram.xml for the destination. Make the following links by dragging from the source field to the destination field:

Source field	Destination field
id (Employee record)	id
First	first
MI	mi
Last	last
dob	dob
telephone	telephone
Street1	Street
Street2	Extra
City	City
State	State

Table continued on following page

481

Chapter 16

Source field	Destination field
PostalCode	Zip
Sex	gender
Retirement	Retire
Medical	Medical
startDate	start
Department	dept
Title	title
salary	salary
id (Supervisor record)	report

There is one final link to specify. We need to get a value into the `mapping-schema` attribute. To do this, we'll use a scripting function to return a constant value. There really is no input value, but BizTalk Mapper requires one. Since the `id` attribute on Employee will always appear on a message, we can use that. Drop a scripting functoid onto the map area, then drag a link to the functoid from `id`. Drag a link from the functoid to `mapping-schema`, then double-click on the functoid body. Enter the following script code into the body of the `Script` tab, making sure that VBScript is selected, and modifying the file path to reflect the location of the file `hr_map.xsd`:

```
Function MyFunction1 ( p_strParm0 )
    MyFunction1 = "c:\Inetpub\wwwroot\HR\schema\hr_map.xsd"
End Function
```

At this point, you should save the map to the repository as `NewEmployeeToHRUpdategram.xml`. You can use the **Tools | Test Map | Instance XML to XML** menu item to submit a sample `Employee` message (such as `Employee.xml` in the download) to Mapper. A valid Updategram minus the `<ROOT>` element should result.

Receive Port

Messaging configurations in BizTalk are based on **ports**, corresponding to an endpoint of an exchange, and **channels**, a set of configurations representing an agreement about the details of an exchange built on top of a port. A port can be used in multiple channels. To start configuring BizTalk messaging to support our schedule, we need to configure a port that can be used to send messages to the application our schedule represents. You create ports (and channels) using Messaging Manager. From the main menu, select **File | New Messaging Port | To an Application**. The New Messaging Port Wizard appears. Specify the settings from the table opposite:

Case Study: BizTalk Integration

Tab	Settings
General Information	Name: SchedRecvNewEmployee
Destination Application	New XLANG Schedule: browse to `NewEmployee.skx`, Port Name: RecvEmployeePort
Envelope Information	Envelope Information: None
Security Information	Check **Create a new channel for this messaging port** and select **From an application**

The effect of this port is to specify that a message arriving at this port will cause a new instance of the `NewEmployee` schedule to be launched and the message passed to the port `RecvEmployeePort` in the schedule.

Receive Channel

Now we need to specify some additional information to explain what happens when a new employee message, in particular, arrives at the port we just created. The Channel Wizard launched by checking **Create new channel** in the Port Wizard should be configured as stated below:

Tab	Settings
General Information	Name: SchedRecvEmployee
Source Application	Check **Application**, Name: NewEmployee
Inbound Document	Inbound document definition name: NewEmployee (this is the name from the messaging manager document definition, not the specification file)
Outbound Document	Outbound document definition name: hr_update, check **Map inbound document to outbound document**, then browse to the map file in the repository for the Map reference, `NewEmployeeToHRUpdateGram.xml`.
Document Logging	Check **Log outbound document in XML format**
Advanced Configuration	Number of retries: 0

Now we have a channel that, when invoked through the BizTalk APIs, will use our port to send an `Employee` message to the designated orchestration schedule and port after converting the message to HR Updategram format.

483

Chapter 16

Map Between HR and Department Updategrams

The final action of the schedule involves sending a message out to the Departmental application, translating it from the Updategram format for the HR database to the form needed by the Department database. This means another message map, so let's take a brief break from Messaging Manager and return to BizTalk Mapper. Select `hrupdgram.xml` as the source and `deptupdgram.xml` as the destination. Create the following simple links:

Source field	Destination field
id	dept_id
first	dept_fname
last	dept_lname
telephone	dept_telephone
start	dept_start

There are no functoids, and the `mapping-schema` field in the source is not involved. Save the map to the repository as `hrupdatetodeptupdate.xml`.

Port to Department

Returning to Messaging Manager, we can configure a port and a channel to support the action forwarding the Updategram to the departmental application. The settings for the port are as follows:

Tab	Settings
General Information	Name: PhoneListPort
Destination Application	Application, Name: DeptPhone, Primary Transport Address: `file://c:\temp\DeptPhone\%tracking_id%.xml` *(adjust file path to reflect some directory you want to use)*
Envelope Information	Envelope Information: none
Security Information	Check **Create a new channel for this messaging port**, and select **From an application**

Since we expect to be passing many messages through this system, we need to ensure that each message dropped into the directory for pickup by the departmental application receives a unique name. There is a series of macros in BizTalk to add various kinds of information to field names. The macro `%tracking_id%` in the file name specified (c:\temp\DeptPhone\%tracking_id%.xml in the Destination Application tab) for the destination address creates a unique ID – a GUID -- for the base portion of the file name.

484

Case Study: BizTalk Integration

Channel to Department

Now that we have a port for dropping files into the departmental pickup directory, we need to establish a channel to get an HR Updategram through reformatting and into the port. The proper settings are:

Tab	Settings
General Information	Name: ToPhoneListChannel
Source Application	Application: HR
Inbound Document	Inbound document definition name: hr_update
Outbound Document	Outbound document definition name: dept_update, Map inbound document to outbound document, Map reference: browse to hrupdatetodeptupdate.xml
Document Logging	Log outbound document in XML format
Advanced Configuration	Number of retries: 0

If we tested the system right now using the procedure given in *Testing the System*, below, we could use the first channel, submit an `Employee` message, and watch the HR database receive a new row and see a departmental Updategram arrive in the pickup directory. We'll defer gratification for a bit, however, and look at the other side of the system.

Department Phone List Schedule

We're going to pick up the Updategrams deposited by the HR schedule with a file receive function. Before we can configure that, however, we need to have somewhere to put them. We'll use a channel to launch a schedule, as with the HR application, so it makes sense to begin with the business process for updating the department database and back through the messaging configuration into the file receive function.

Department Business Process

The schedule for this is quite similar to the schedule we created for the HR application. We start by receiving a message, then submit it to the database. The schedule looks like the diagram overleaf:

Chapter 16

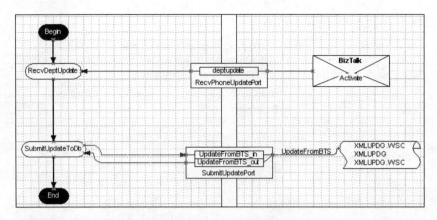

Notice that we are again using BizTalk for the receive action, then reusing the script component to submit the Updategram to the database.

Department Messaging Implementations

The process for implementing the message exchanges uses the same tools and procedures that you saw for the HR schedule. For brevity, then, we'll review the configurations in summary and without substantial comment.

RecvDeptUpdate

The BizTalk Messaging Binding Wizard settings are:

Tab	Settings
Welcome	Port name: RecvPhoneUpdatePort
Communication Direction	Receive
XLANG Schedule Activation Information	Yes

The XML Communication Wizard settings are:

Tab	Settings
Welcome	Receive (disabled but set for you)
Message Information	Message name: deptupdate
XML Translation Information	Receive XML messages from the queue
Message Type Information	Message type: sync
Message Specification Information	Message Specification: browse to the repository and point to the deptupdgram.xml specification file.

486

Case Study: BizTalk Integration

SubmitUpdateToDb

The Script Component Binding Wizard settings are:

Tab	Settings
Welcome	Port name: SubmitUpdatePort
Static or Dynamic Communication	Static
Specify the script file	Browse to the file XMLUPDG.WSC
Component Instantiation Information	Use the Prog ID XMLUPDG.WSC
Advanced Port Properties	Accept defaults

The Method Communication Wizard settings should be:

Tab	Settings
Welcome	Initiate a synchronous method call
Message Information	Create a new message
Message Specification Information	Methods: UpdateFromBTS

Department Data Flow

The data flow diagram is similar to the one for the HR schedule. Create constants cDeptDb (value Department) and cDbServer (for me, this is (local)), and connect them to sDb and sServer, respectively, on the UpdateFromBTS_in message shape. Connect Document from deptupdate to sUpdgCore.

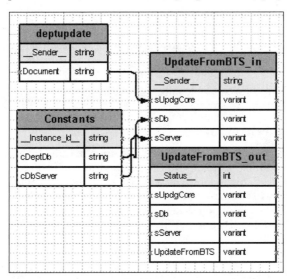

When you are done, save the schedule as PhoneList.skv and compile it as PhoneList.skx.

487

Chapter 16

BizTalk Messaging Configuration

We are closing in on a solution. We need but one more port and channel, followed by a file receive function before we are ready to test our completed system.

Receive Port

Create a new port using the settings from the table below:

Tab	Settings
General Information	Name: RecvPhoneUpdatePort
Destination Application	New XLANG Schedule: browse to `PhoneList.skx`, Port Name: RecvPhoneUpdatePort
Envelope Information	Envelope Information: None
Security Information	Check **Create a new channel for this messaging port**, and select **From an application**

Receive Channel

The channel associated with the port should be configured as follows:

Tab	Settings
General Information	Name: RecvPhoneUpdateChannel
Source Application	Check Application, Name: DeptPhone
Inbound Document	Inbound document definition name: dept_update
Outbound Document	Outbound document definition name: dept_update
Document Logging	Check **Log outbound document in XML format**
Advanced Configuration	Number of retries: 0

File Receive Function

The departmental application is ready, save for one little thing: there is nothing to pick the inbound documents off the disk and submit them to BizTalk. This is where file receive components come in. These are stock components that are part of the messaging system that monitors a directory and submit newly arrived documents to the messaging system. You configure such functions through the BizTalk Server Administration utility.

Case Study: BizTalk Integration

Expand the tree down to the **Microsoft BizTalk Server 2002 | BizTalk Server Group | Receive Functions**. Right mouse click on the **Receive Functions** node and select **New | File Receive Function**. The **Add a File Receive Function** dialog appears. Provide `RecvPhoneList` for the name, ensure the server machine name is filled in for you, enter `*.xml` for **File types to poll for**, and enter the drive and directory you specified for depositing department Updategrams as the value for **Polling location**. If necessary, provide a Windows username and password for the folder. Click the **Advanced** button and enter `RecvPhoneUpdateChannel` for **Channel Name**.

The effect of all this is to have the BizTalk messaging system monitor the directory for the arrival of files with the `xml` extension. When one arrives, it is removed from the directory and submitted to the messaging system using the `RecvPhoneUpdateChannel`. If access to the directory is restricted, the username and password you provided are used to gain access as that user. As we now know, that channel launches the departmental schedule, which submits the Updategram to the departmental database.

Testing the System

If we've done everything correctly, we should be ready to drop a new employee XML message into BizTalk and have it ripple through our distributed system. In lieu of writing a front end for the employee intake function, I've included a utility application I wrote for *Professional BizTalk Server* (Wrox Press, ISBN 1861003293), which also works in BizTalk Server 2002. This utility, depicted in the foreground window below, allows you to browse for a message and submit it to a named BizTalk channel using the BizTalk API, and is included in the code download for this chapter.

If you open `Employee.xml` (or manually enter an `Employee` message) and execute the `SchedRecvEmployee` channel, you can then check the two databases and ensure that the appropriate insertions were made. For a little more nerd-like entertainment, you can watch it all happen in real-time by opening the XLANG Event Monitor application included in the XLANG Samples for BizTalk Server. Start XLANG Event Monitor, then execute the channel and watch the monitor window. The `Employee` schedule will appear in the **Running** Folder, then terminate (moving to the **Completed** folder), followed a second or so later by the `PhoneList` schedule. When that terminates, select one of the schedules in the **Completed** folder and inspect the events. You should see all the actions in each schedule fire in sequence with successful results:

Chapter 16

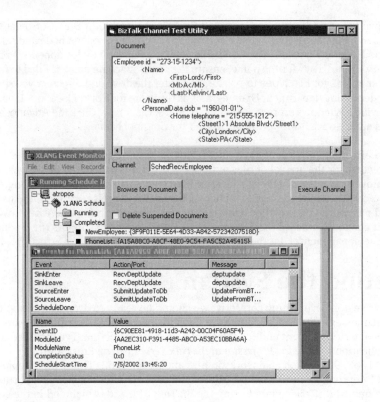

Assessing the System

The system has the virtue of requiring very little code. While we had to point and click through a large number of wizard screens, we are able to modify the behavior of the system at any future time by editing the configuration rather than changing and rebuilding an application. Due to the bug in either BizTalk Server or SQLXML 3.0 that prevents us from using the HTTP POST method for Updategrams directly, we lost some simplicity and ended up with two schedules instead of one. Let's consider the performance and security of this system.

Performance

Let's add up the overhead involved in this solution. First, the XML interface to SQL Server may require more processing than SQL (depending on how the two are implemented). We explicitly accept this potential overhead in order to gain generality and conceal the database schema. Next, any action in the schedules involving BizTalk messaging will require several hits to the BizTalk databases. Calls to our script component avoid this. Finally, the schedules involve some overhead. In this example, the overhead is minimal once the schedules are running. Had they included a transaction (in the schedule, not the database), there would have been additional roundtrips to a SQL Server database, as the XLANG Scheduler serializes schedule state on transaction boundaries.

Case Study: BizTalk Integration

That brings us to another issue: which is faster, BizTalk Server or SQL Server? Will BizTalk flood SQL Server, or will SQL Server be starved for incoming messages? This is largely a comparison of two SQL Server applications. BizTalk Server is largely implemented through stored procedures, albeit highly optimized ones. Our sample deliberately used a fairly simplified database schema, so BizTalk is unlikely to outstrip SQL Server, or even SQLXML. If the SQLXML side involves some complex schemas, though, that side of things could dominate the performance of the two servers.

Now consider the input side of the system. A human user has to enter the information manually, and employees don't join a company, let alone a single department, all that quickly. So unless the manual inputs are queued up somehow and submitted in batch to BizTalk Server -- very big batches -- feeding a single, lonely database, the gating factor in the entire system is the frequency of input. The input is measured in seconds (perhaps minutes) while BizTalk and SQL Server are operating several orders of magnitude faster. It simply isn't worth putting lots of effort into tuning and scaling the back-end until multiple applications are flowing through the BizTalk/SQLXML combination, or until the input of a single application is driven by automated processes.

We actually benefit by having to use ADO code. This is the fastest way to submit Updategrams, faster by far than HTTP POSTs. Although we were unable to post from BizTalk, we can post from script or HTML forms and observe the results. The only way to get the information in faster is to use native Recordsets instead of XML. Going to disk with the department Updategrams imposes the biggest penalty, but it only imposes a delay of a second or so under normal load.

Security

If the application is confined to a properly secured local area network, this system can have very good security. Certainly, it is better than if we used HTTP and anonymous access. The Updategrams are submitted using Windows Authentication, and we can secure the file receive function beyond what we showed above by restricting access to the pickup directory to the user name under which BizTalk is operating. If security on the network is important and we had access to digital certificates, we could use BizTalk's encryption and signing features to secure messages in transit.

Chapter 16

Summary

SQL Server's ability to accept information in the form of XML messages is very useful and enables us to make use of BizTalk Server for application integration. We can support decentralized data management and coordinate updates through the exchange of structured messages. BizTalk, in turn, takes advantage of technologies related to XML to perform message translation, working from specifications provided by the system administrator. We used this feature not only to perform two such translations, but also to filter out sensitive information. The HR system receives such data, but must not pass it on to the departmental application. This information, in fact, never leaves the machine on which BizTalk is running. The translation from the HR Updategram to the department Updategram strips out the sensitive information before it is deposited in the pickup directory. The departmental application could be running its own instance of BizTalk Server, and it would never see the sensitive and personal information provided by the new employee to the HR department.

The match of BizTalk Server and SQLXML is not a perfect one; the bug preventing us from using HTTP updates directly should tell us that more work is required. Until that is fixed, the system is more complicated than it needs to be, opportunities for error recovery are more limited than need be, and we cannot take advantage of SOAP to open up new avenues for submitting employee information. Even so, the technology is good enough to allow IT organizations to rapidly build decentralized and distributed applications without a great investment in development time.

Case Study: BizTalk Integration

Daryl Barnes

- ISO SQL/XML Working Draft (or SQLX)
- Oracle 9I Release 2 (9.0.2)
- W3C XQuery
- Microsoft Next Steps - Yukon
- So What Does all This Mean?

17

The Future – Emergent Technologies

If you have made it this far in the book, then by now you have a pretty clear understanding of Microsoft's approach to the problem of providing XML support in a relational database. It is fair to say that until now the approaches have not been integrated into the core database or DBMS, and that is true for all major database products. This will change in the future, but do not think for one minute it is not worth pursuing an XML extraction strategy today because it will all change tomorrow. XML is here to stay, and its beauty is that, as a format, it is future-proof. Think about it – the more data that is structured in an independent format in your organisation, the easier it will be to map it to standard interfaces in the future. The final sanity check if you are not yet convinced is to ask yourself the following questions:

> *Would ALL the major vendors independently invest so many dollars to develop something that didn't have a future? And would XML be making such a big impact in the open source world?*

This final chapter will take a look at the future of XML, both in the short term (with Yukon, the next SQL Server release), and in the longer term. It is structured as follows:

- ❑ A discussion of the ISO SQL/XML initiative, which is aimed at covering the basic XML to SQL data item mappings.
- ❑ A look at the important aspects of what Oracle offers in terms of XML Support within its latest release, 9.0.2.
- ❑ W3C XQuery. The main subsection of this chapter will take a detailed look at XQuery.

Chapter 17

- An overview of the expected XML functionality in Yukon, a beta of which is due out late 2002 – early 2003.
- So what does it all mean? A realistic look at what is more likely to be a cooperation between XQuery and SQL, rather than a final showdown.

ISO SQL/XML Working Draft (or SQLX)

Although the SQLX initiative is not a W3C specification, other major standards bodies, such as ISO and ANSI, as well as major vendors support it. It is a working group (including Microsoft, Oracle and IBM) aiming to provide a consistent approach to low-level mappings between XML and SQL. It is important to mention it, because the resulting ISO recommendation will compose the bedrock for the way database products handle XML.

Example key areas covered by this Working Draft are as follows:

- Mapping SQL characters to Unicode (and vice versa). For example, SQL_TEXT to Unicode, or < to <.
- Mapping SQL identifiers to XML names (and vice versa). This deals with the issues surrounding the use of characters in SQL identifiers that are not allowed in XML.
- Mapping SQL data types and XML Schema datatypes: the intrinsic linking required when mapping different data types.

From the list above, it can be seen that this work is aimed at the low level plumbing of SQL / XML interoperability. The most important factor to consider is that this initiative addresses the very issues that have to be considered in order to produce industry strength systems. It is vital, for example, that data type mapping is consistent, and that special characters are handled in the same way. This should give you the confidence to see that vendors are taking the prospect of XML handling within relational databases very seriously.

More information can be found at *http://www.sqlx.org.*

Oracle 9i Release 2 (9.0.2)

We will now take a look at the new functionality offered in the latest release of the Oracle Database. We will cover the following:

- A brief introduction to the history of XML support in Oracle.
- An overview of the new integrated functionality on offer.
- Finally, a short look at how Oracle is approaching XQuery.

Oracle and XML Support

Oracle introduced XML support in version 8.x of its database product (as an add-on, just like Microsoft with SQL Server 7). The support consists of an XDK (XML Developer Kit), allowing developers to programmatically handle XML using PL/SQL, Java, C or C++. At a summary level, it is fair to say that up to Version 8.x the approach has been similar to that of Microsoft, although the native API functionality core to Oracle ensured that the detailed mechanisms were slightly different. Things are a little different with Oracle 9i Release 2, available since May 2002, and which we will focus on next, gaining more of an insight into where database support for XML is heading in general.

> The key word in the above sentence is integrated. XML is now central to the Oracle product. This means it shares directly in all of the core functionality you expect from a DBMS as standard.

In the latest version of Oracle, the core integrated functionality offered revolves around the following:

- The introduction of a new data type, namely the **xmltype**. Previously, native XML documents had to be stored as CLOBs (Character Large OBjects).
- Integrated support for XML Schema to provide structure to `xmltypes`.
- Integrated functions to manipulate and extract the `xmltype`.

What's so Good About the Native xmltype?

Storing XML within relational databases has not been an easy task in Oracle until now. The designer or developer has had to decide whether to use some kind of relational or XML extraction mechanism where the data is still stored relationally, or store the XML document in its entirety as a `CLOB`. In simple terms, this means a string of characters that could not be thought of as a structure at all. SQL can only retrieve it as one object and, in order to make it readable, it must be parsed and then processed using the DOM or another XML method outside of the core database. This approach has been acceptable for less critical applications, but most developers consider it to be an inefficient method (and Oracle agreed, hence the introduction of the `xmltype` to allow the DBMS to provide XML data manipulation tools).

The `xmltype` changes all of this. It considers that an XML structure, as defined by its schema, is in reality not much different from a relational table or a database table schema. To put it simply, this means that a data "object" is stored against a data definition in its native form in the database.

Consider the following PL/SQL which creates a table of `xmltype`:

```
CREATE TABLE customerList OF xmltype;
```

Chapter 17

It can be seen that it suddenly becomes very simple to store XML natively in Oracle. The relevant XML document can then be loaded into Oracle by using a SQL `INSERT`, or by using the SQL Loader utility. The `INSERT` below shows the loading of an XML file called `custList.xml` into the `customerList` table:

```
INSERT INTO customerList VALUES (xmltype(getDocument
('custList.xml'));
```

It is also possible to create a table where just one field is of `xmltype`, although it is important to say that unless you assign a schema to the field (discussed below), the XML document is still stored as a `CLOB`:

```
CREATE TABLE customerList(
            custListid NUMBER PRIMARY KEY
            custList xmltype
);
```

And What's So Good About the Integrated Support for XML Schema?

It is important to note that whilst the `xmltype` is readily available for use, it is not optimized until an XML schema has been registered against it. Until that point it is stored as a `CLOB`. Once a schema is assigned, the document is stored internally as an object-relational structure. This means that, because the schema defines the structure, the database can create an internal structure just as for relational tables; this in turn means that we can then validate against it inside the DBMS:

```
...
dbms_xmlschema.registerSchema("CustomerList.xsd",
getDocument("CustomerList.xsd"))
...
```

The PL/SQL extract above shows the `CustomerList.xsd` schema being registered within Oracle. Once it has been registered, tables can be created which map the schema to the `xmltype`:

```
CREATE TABLE customerList OF xmltype
XMLSCHEMA "CustomerList.xsd"
ELEMENT "Customer"
```

As we can see, the `CustomerList.xsd` schema is now mapped to the new `customerList` table. The final `ELEMENT` part of the PL/SQL identifies the root node of the schema so all sub-definitions will be included. Now the schema has been associated, any XML documents that do not conform to the schema (either the data types it defines or the structure) cannot be added.

The Future – Emergent Technologies

What About These Integrated Functions?

Once an XML document is stored within Oracle as an `xmltype`, several functions exist allowing the XML document to be queried using XPath. These functions utilize the inbuilt C parser, so offer an integrated approach and faster retrieval than the creation of a DOM tree for querying.

The `existsNode()` function allows you to test whether a node actually exists; this is obviously very useful for error handling. In the XPath query below, if the node exists then the function would return 1:

```
existsNode('Orders/OrdID[@Code = "ORD123"]')
```

The `extract()` and `extractValue()` functions are very useful for returning XML fragments or different values contained within an XML document respectively:

```
extract(customerList, '//Customer')
```

The function used above would return a node set of all customers and child elements as an `xmltype`, and the function below would return the value as type NUMBER:

```
extractValue(customerList, '//Customer[First_Name = "Fred"]/Age')
```

There is also a function that allows XML elements to be updated using XPath, the `updateXML()` function:

```
UPDATE customerList
SET custList = updateXML(custList, '//Customer[Last_Name = "Hawthorn"]/First_Name/text()', 'Ran');
```

> There are many more functions and methods available than described above. More information can be found at
> http://otn.oracle.com/docs/products/oracle9i/doc_library/release2/appdev.920/a96620/toc.htm

The most important thing to observe is that Oracle has given a large amount of thought to using SQL and XML side by side. All the functions we've seen can be run within SELECT statements, for example:

```
SELECT extractValue(customerList, '//Customer/First_Name')
AS NAME FROM customerList
```

If the XML document has a schema registered against it, then this SELECT would return the data type associated with the `<First_Name>` element.

499

Chapter 17

Oracle and XQuery

Oracle has created an XQuery prototype, conforming to the current Working Draft (we cover the W3C XQuery Working Draft later in the chapter). It comes in the form of JXQI, a Java API for XQuery, and it allows the creation and running of conformant XQueries. In the longer term, this will allow the creation of XQueries directly into Oracle, rather than just using JDBC for data access.

Oracle Summary

We have seen that the latest release of Oracle includes a lot of integrated support for XML, and all signs point to more integration in the future. Fundamentally, Oracle 9.0.2 has introduced the `xmltype`, which can be validated by an XML schema. It has also made it possible to use XPath queries alongside SQL queries.

W3C XQuery

In recent times, XSLT and XPath 1.0 have become the common languages for manipulating and querying XML documents, mainly because they have now been Recommendations for a while. All along it has been recognized that, while they offer an effective way to query XML documents, there remains the need for an approach similar to SQL for relational data, with insert, update, and delete functionality.

There were several initial attempts to promote an XML Query language: XQL, XML-QL being the more prominent. The main outcome of all these early attempts has been to stimulate the production of what exists today in working draft form. The key to the stability of the latest working draft is the XQuery syntax and the core mechanisms that underpin it.

XQuery Working Draft

All W3C works-in-progress go through a set process before they become fully-fledged Recommendations, or activity on them ceases. XQuery is currently at "Working Draft" status, meaning that it must go through Candidate Recommendation status before it can become a full Recommendation. Importantly, this means that it is all still subject to change. It wouldn't be wise therefore to use any prototype technologies based upon it in a production environment. Having said all of that, it is now clear that what does exist is stable and the main components are unlikely to change.

The core XQuery working drafts can be found at these locations:

- XQuery 1.0: An XML Query Language – http://www.w3.org/TR/xquery
- XML Query 1.0 and XPath 2.0 Data Model – http://www.w3.org/TR/query-datamodel
- XQuery 1.0 and XPath 2.0 Functional and Operators – http://www.w3.org/TR/xquery-operators

XQuery and XPath 2.0, XSLT and XPath 1.0 and 2.0

Before we go any further, it must be pointed out for the sake of completeness that the XSLT and XQuery communities have in the past been very "competitively active" when considering each other's approaches. For the observer, the net effect has proved positive because at last it has been recognized that the two can work together very effectively, as we shall see.

XPath provides a base level for querying the node structure of an XML document, while XSLT provides a framework for transforming an XML document into another format (for example, HTML), using XPath to select the elements required and transform them to the required output. This mechanism can be, and is, used to output a required set of data in an XML form from within a DBMS, but it is generally recognized that this is not the best approach for querying:

- ❑ XQuery as a concept works well with the now classic DBMS approach, in that it can be thought of along the same lines as SQL. This is not the case with XSLT.
- ❑ XQuery (beyond version 1.0) has detailed plans to offer insert, update, and delete data manipulation functionality. This can be achieved using XSLT, but it is messy to say the least.

XPath 2.0, which will develop the existing Recommendation XPath 1.0, is being developed jointly with XQuery to ensure that the requirements of XQuery 1.0 are fulfilled.

In summary, XSLT combined with XPath is designed for presentation. XQuery is designed for use in a database environment. It considers aspects such as element constructors, statement nesting, and joins, something that XPath was never meant to do.

> In future, the XSLT 2.0 and XPath 2.0 will provide the best approach for presentation, and XQuery 1.0 combined with XPath 2.0 will provide the best approach to reading and writing XML data.

XQuery Overview

Now we have briefly covered the background of XQuery, let's delve into its core syntax and functionality.

> *The examples that follow are deliberately simple, to aid an understanding of XQuery at a high level. However, Microsoft has an XQuery prototype website where you can see more complete examples (http://xqueryservices.net). It is also possible to download C# managed classes from the same site; these act as an XQuery processor. The W3C have also provided a use-case scenario document (http://www.w3.org/TR/xmlquery-use-cases), with excellent examples/scenarios.*

Chapter 17

As a language, XQuery is purely functional (as opposed to declarative), where a query is made up of one or more expressions. It satisfies a few basic syntax rules and, as we shall see, works quite happily alongside XML in terms of query construction. It defines its operators in the XPath data model the same way that SQL operates on the relational model. XQuery fully conforms to the use of W3C Schema 1.0 data types (because XPath 2.0 does).

For the following examples, we'll use this XML document (cust.xml) as our basis:

```
<?xml version="1.0" encoding="UTF-8"?>
<Customer_List>
    <Customer>
        <Customer_ID>CU001</Customer_ID>
        <First_Name>Fred</First_Name>
        <Last_Name>Simmons</Last_Name>
        <Age>67</Age>
    </Customer>
    <Customer>
        <Customer_ID>CU002</Customer_ID>
        <First_Name>Ran</First_Name>
        <Last_Name>Hawthorn</Last_Name>
        <Age>25</Age>
    </Customer>
    <Customer>
        <Customer_ID>CU003</Customer_ID>
        <First_Name>Louis</First_Name>
        <Last_Name>Simmons</Last_Name>
        <Age>56</Age>
    </Customer>
</Customer_List>
```

Basic Syntax

Syntactically, XQuery is designed to be a human readable format, and in its simplest form it can be pure XPath. (XML syntax and XQuery syntax differ in the type of brackets that are used.) In the example below, an XQuery processor would understand what is meant to be XML syntax with the use of <>, and XQuery Syntax with the use of { }. It is important to note that an XQuery statement is not, however, valid XML.

Here is our first XQuery:

```
<Customer_First_Names>
    <Title>A List of First Names</Title>
    { document("cust.xml")//Customer/First_Name }
</Customer_First_Names>
```

The Future – Emergent Technologies

The query above would return the following output:

```
<Customer_First_Names>
   <Title>A List of First Names</Title>
   <First_Name>Fred</First_Name>
   <First_Name>Ran</First_Name>
   <First_Name>Louis</First_Name>
</Customer_List>
```

In this example, you can see there is still a clear use of XPath when creating an XQuery, and it is clear that XML syntax can be used in the XQuery formulation to help structure the required output. It could be said, however, that with this example we have seen no real advantage over existing mechanisms for querying XML documents, so let's now look at some more detailed examples demonstrating this.

FLoWeR – or FOR LET WHERE RETURN

Other than a basic XPath statement, `For`, `Let`, `Where`, `Return` (or **FLWR**) are the root query expressions in XQuery, rather like the `SELECT` statement in SQL. As with the `SELECT` statement, there are many different ways of using them to construct queries.

`For` iterates sequentially through the relevant nodes in a node set identified in the XPath in order to return the output, whereas `let` initiates a bound variable. It may contain a node-set or a simple data type for possible future reference; the `let` statement is optional.

The example below shows the structure of a `for` query. In essence, the query initially defines the nodeset constraints, before returning the matching values. It can be seen that the `$Customer` variable gets mapped to the `//Customer` nodeset in `cust.xml`. Notice also that the XPath is an integral part of the query:

```
for $Customer in document("cust.xml")//Customer
where $Customer/Last_Name = "Hawthorn"
return
   <Name>
   {
   $Customer/First_Name,
   $Customer/Last_Name
   }
   </Name>
```

Below is the resultant XML from the `for` XQuery. Only one `<Customer>` was returned because of the **where** clause in the original XQuery expression; if the `where` were removed, then all of the relevant nodes would have been returned:

```
<Name>
  <First_Name>Ran</First_Name>
  <Last_Name>Hawthorn</Last_Name>
</Name>
```

503

Now lets have a look at a `let` in action. In this example we will list all of the `Last_Name` elements that appear more than once. Here, we use the inbuilt function `count()` that provides a node count of the chosen node set:

```
for $x in document("cust.xml")//Customer/Last_Name
let $y := document("cust.xml")//Customer[Last_Name = $x]
where count($y) > 1
return
    <Duplicate_Last_Name>
        {
        $x
        }
    </Duplicate_Last_Name>
```

It can be seen that the variable `$x` is created and used again in the `let` and `where` clauses to test whether a surname is duplicated. This is the same as conducting a HAVING test in SQL. Correctly, the output shows that the surname `Simmons` appears more than once:

<Duplicate_Last_Name>Simmons</Duplicate_Last_Name>

To give you a bit more flavor of just how flexible XQuery expression construction is, consider the following nested `for`:

```
<Name_List>
{
for $x in document("cust.xml")
    for $y in $x/Customer
        return
            <Name> { $y/First_Name, $y/Last_Name } </Name>
}
</Name_List>
```

The example above is actually quite simple, but you can really begin to get a feel that XQuery allows very dynamic query construction. Here are the results from that query:

<Name_List>
 <Name>
  <First_Name>Fred</First_Name>
  <Last_Name>Simmons</Last_Name>
 </Name>
 <Name>
  <First_Name>Ran</First_Name>
  <Last_Name>Hawthorn</Last_Name>
 </Name>
 <Name>
  <First_Name>Louis</First_Name>
  <Last_Name>Simmons</Last_Name>
 </Name>
</Name_List>

The Future – Emergent Technologies

As expected, the `for` statements iterated throught the nodesets and output all the relevant nodes. Notice the absence of the `where` clause in this statement: yet another example of the flexibility of XQuery.

FLoWeR and SQL

Having now seen the basic core retrieval statement in XQuery, you are probably thinking that it bears a striking resemblance to `SELECT` statements in SQL. Obviously it is a good thing that they are vaguely related, since it makes the learning curve smoother. There is, however, one fundamental difference in the way an XQuery works (apart from the fact that `SELECT` is the only query command in SQL and FLWR is just a subset of XQuery).

Compare the following outline queries:

SQL:
```
SELECT (the output)
FROM (from here)
WHERE (based on this condition)
```

XQuery:
```
FOR (from here)
WHERE (based on this condition)
RETURN (the output)
```

When a `SELECT` is defined, you initially state what output is required, then you say where from, before finally providing the condition. With a FLWR query you are defining it in a different way. Initially you define your source, then you provide the constraint, before requesting the output.

Even if you have worked with SQL for years, after some reflection you will probably buy into the fact that the XQuery construct is a more logical approach.

Joins

As with SQL, it is quite straightforward to implement join functionality with XQuery. The examples given below show an inner join and a basic outer join, although all outer join types are possible. Consider the following XML (`orders.xml`). We will use this along with the `cust.xml` file shown earlier for the `join` examples:

```xml
<?xml version="1.0" encoding="UTF-8"?>
<Customer_Orders>
    <Customer_Ord>
        <Customer_ID>CU001</Customer_ID>
        <Number_Of_Orders>32</Number_Of_Orders>
    </Customer_Ord>
    <Customer_Ord>
        <Customer_ID>CU022</Customer_ID>
        <Number_Of_Orders>0</Number_Of_Orders>
    </Customer_Ord>
    <Customer_Ord>
```

505

Chapter 17

```
            <Customer_ID>CU043</Customer_ID>
            <Number_Of_Orders>179</Number_Of_Orders>
        </Customer_Ord>
</Customer_Orders>
```

The goal of the inner join below is to extract the customer name and number of orders placed from the separate XML documents where the `<Customer_ID>` element values match, and then output elements from both source documents:

```
<Order_Count>
{
for $Customer in document("cust.xml")//Customer,
    $Cust_Ord in document("orders.xml")//Customer_Ord
where $Customer/Customer_ID = $Cust_Ord/Customer_ID
return
    <Order_Listing>
        {
        $Customer/First_Name, $Cust_Ord/Number_Of_Orders
        }
    </Order_Listing>
}
</Order_Count>
```

There is only one matching `Customer_ID` (`CU001`), so the output from the inner join is as below:

```
<Order_Count>
  <Order_Listing>
    <First_Name>Fred</First_Name>
    <Number_Of_Orders>32</Number_Of_Orders>
  </Order_Listing>
</Order_Count>
```

Let's now consider an outer join. In the following example, the requirement is for a list of all customers, with the number of orders where there is a link. The key is that the output doesn't just consist of elements where the `Customer_ID`s match:

```
<Customer_Order_Count>
{
for $Customer in document("cust.xml")//Customer,
return
    <Customer_Listing>
    {$Customer/First_Name }
        {
        for $Cust_Ord in document("orders.xml")//Customer_Ord
        where $Customer/Customer_ID = $Cust_Ord/Customer_ID
        return $Cust_Ord/Number_Of_Orders
        }
    </Customer_Listing>
}
</Customer_Order_Count>
```

The Future — Emergent Technologies

It can be seen that the `<First_Name>` is returned for every customer, and the nested `for` only outputs where the `Customer_ID`s are the same:

```
<Customer_Order_Count>
  <Customer_Listing>
    <First_Name>Fred</First_Name>
    <Number_Of_Orders>32</Number_Of_Orders>
  </Customer_Listing>
  <Customer_Listing>
    <First_Name>Ran</First_Name>
  </Customer_Listing>
  <Customer_Listing>
    <First_Name>Louis</First_Name>
  </Customer_Listing>
</Customer_Order_Count>
```

If...Then...Else

It is also possible to use the `If...Then...Else` conditional construct within XQuery, providing a very succinct way to further constrain a variable and act on the outcome. The simple example below basically changes the element that is output if the customer's first name is `Fred`:

```
for $Customer in document("cust.xml")//Customer
return
    <Name>
        {
        if ($Customer/First_Name = "Fred")
        then $Customer/First_Name
        else $Customer/Last_Name
        }
    </Name>
```

Core Functions

We have already seen a few of the functions that are available in the examples we've seen so far (for example, `count()` and `document()`). There are many more available to us (See the XQuery 1.0 and XPath 2.0 Functional and Operators document mentioned at the beginning of the XQuery subsection), which allowing automation of commonly required mechanisms, such as mathematical calculation, text retrieval and manipulation, output ordering, and generic selection condition functions. It is also possible to create user-defined functions. Importantly, the functions defined in the Working Draft are not guaranteed to be complete, given the immaturity of XQuery at the time of writing.

It has already been shown how the functions easily integrate into XQuery expressions (see the earlier examples), so consider the following table of major functions that could all be applied just as easily:

507

Chapter 17

Function	Description
count()	Provides a node count for a node-set.
max()	Selects the maximum value in a node-set.
min()	Selects the minimum value in a node-set.
avg()	Selects the average value of a node-set.
sum()	Provides a total for values in a node-set.
contains()	Used when searching and works with text content.
sortby()	Allows an output to be sorted.
empty()	Used to test if a node or node-set is empty.
exists()	Tests whether a node exists.
distinct-values()	Avoids the retrieval of identical nodes.
deep-equals()	Searches 2 node-sets to ensure they are identical (including whitespace).
document()	Accesses the required XML document.
input()	Can be used instead of document() if an XML document is already imported.

Data Types and Validation

None of the examples covered have made use of data types or validation. Many of the functions listed in the previous subsection require either numeric or textual data types in order to work correctly. The supported data types are directly in line with those defined in the W3C Schema Recommendation and, in the Working Draft definition, it can be seen that it is possible to import and validate against a schema. The Working Draft also defines concrete rules for conversion and comparison relating to interoperability between data types. At the time of writing, this area is still very much 'in development' within the XQuery community, however it is fair to say that the basic foundations are sound.

XQuery Future – In the Pipeline

For XQuery to become a true equal to SQL, it would require rigid rules and methods for the ability to insert, update, and delete elements and attributes. Consideration has been given to this and, although it is not expected that this functionality will be an integral part of XQuery 1.0, it will come later.

XQuery Summary

Having read through the basics of XQuery, I hope to have shown that it is pretty solid in its foundations, although there is still some way to go.

The Future – Emergent Technologies

Some W3C standards get started but never really get the momentum to reach Recommendation and are superseded by something else. This won't be the case with XQuery, as it already has support from most major database vendors (relational and XML). It will fit nicely into the database environment and, when used alongside SQL, will work well.

Microsoft Next Steps – Yukon

This book has been focused on the functionality available within SQL Server 2000. It would not be complete without a few paragraphs relating to the next release of SQL Server, codenamed **Yukon** within Microsoft. At the time of writing, it is due for beta release in Q4 2002. First though, let's consider a few significant facts about the support for XML in SQL Server 2000 and SQLXML 3.0 SP1:

- XML data is persisted relationally. It can be persisted as XML, but only as large text objects, so there is no internal way of querying that data, unlike with the latest Oracle release.
- Data can be extracted as XML from a base relational structure, either as a view, via a schema mapping or using SELECT statements with FOR XML EXPLICIT, AUTO or RAW extensions.
- Data can be added from an XML format (albeit stored relationally) using OPENXML, Updategrams, DiffGrams, or XML Bulk Load.
- ADO.NET fully supports the retrieval of XML, and the .NET Managed Classes allow full exploitation of the XML Support.
- XML can be specifically extracted in SOAP or web services format using stored procedures.

It is also fair to say the following about Microsoft:

- Microsoft is committed to .NET. ADO.NET and the SQLXML Managed Classes already show great support for XML; they are therefore likely to receive more attention.
- Microsoft is committed to web services. Therefore XML, SOAP, and web services functionality will remain central to its strategy.
- Microsoft is committed to XQuery. It is possible to say this because of its position on the SQLX group and its prototype XQuery functionality. Also, in the past SQL Server and Oracle functionality have always remained pretty much inline, so the fact that Oracle openly supports XQuery is another sign.

At the time of writing, Microsoft is not making public exactly what will be new with Yukon but, based upon the above, it is reasonable to assume the following:

- Continued support for existing XML mechanisms, because they are effective and they will provide a stepping-stone for existing use of XML with SQL Server.

Chapter 17

- The introduction of an xmltype and integrated functionality to query it with XPath. Microsoft has said publicly that it will include a native xmltype, and it can be deduced that there will be functions similar to those available in the Oracle 9.0.2 `xmltype` implementation.

- Ongoing improvements to the .NET SQLXML Managed Classes. This is an obvious statement because they must improve to support the `xmltype` core functionality.

- Integrated support for XQuery. This is a logical progression given the growing stability of the W3C standard.

- Further enhanced ADO and OLE DB XML features. It is not likely that any enhancements in this area will change the approach to using these APIs, given the way ADO.NET handles relational `DataSets` (with an XML Schema structure) for disconnected `Recordsets`. It is fair to assume that Microsoft will offer functionality allowing developers to handle XML data and relational data in the same way.

So What Does all This Mean?

This chapter has provided a background and broad overview into the way things are heading. We have included this to allow you to make up your own mind about what the future holds. Currently, depending upon who you speak to, you will get a different opinion of what lies in the future. It is likely that a 'relational database addict' would say that XML is just another format and relational databases are far too prolific to ever to be removed from the IT map. It is likely that an 'XML junkie' who lives for hierarchies would tell you that it is only a matter of time before XML is all-pervasive and the future is markup.

Of course, the reality lies somewhere in between, but in general terms it is worth considering the following:

- Today, we are seeing requirements for XML structured data and relational structured data from the same systems. These requirements will only grow over time, meaning that any data store will have to be capable of offering parallel XML and relational interfaces at all levels.

- It all comes down to how the data is organized and stored. At the end of the day, data items stored in 'object locations' according to a database schema are no different from data items that are stored in 'object locations' according to an XML schema.

- SQL is optimal for querying (and inserting, updating, and deleting) relational datasets. The forthcoming XQuery from the W3C is optimal at querying XML documents, but not inserting, updating, and deleting in the current version.

The basic constructs of XQuery allow it to sit nicely with the way SQL operates at a database level; by this I mean that it is easy to envisage T-SQL and PL/SQL support for XQuery in stored procedures, triggers, transactions, and so on.

The Future – Emergent Technologies

In terms of any future database product, it is fair to say that the importance of each format as a 'direct competitor' will dwindle; the focus will be on fitness for purpose. This is a good thing.

> **Currently most indicators point to a side-by-side approach to XML and relational storage and retrieval.**

My final word in this section is to underline some of the sentiments in Chapter 1: the ability to store, extract, update, map, and generally turn data into any format has a massive potential for disorganized design and implementation. Obviously, careful design always needs consideration, but the way vendors are approaching XML support should give us confidence that these problems can be solved.

In this book, we have seen the multitude of ways that XML can be handled using SQL Server 2000 and SQL XML 3.0. Hopefully, with this final chapter, you now have a much clearer picture of what to expect with the next releases and beyond.

Jeni Tennison

- XPath Data Model
- Location Paths
- Variables
- Operators
- Functions
- XPath 2.0 and XQuery

XPath Reference

This appendix provides a quick introduction to, and reference for, XPath 1.0 (http://www.w3.org/TR/xpath). XPath was developed as part of XSLT, the Transformations part of the Extensible Stylesheet Language (XSL), to identify parts of an XML source document so that they could be included in the result of a transformation. XPath is designed to be incorporated into other "host" languages, and indeed it's used in several places:

- ❑ XSLT, where it's used to select nodes to process from an XML document and to evaluate tests and expressions to access values that can be placed in the result of a transformation.
- ❑ XML Schema, in which it's used to select nodes in order to test identity constraints, for example that all elements of a certain type have different identifiers. It is in this context that we mostly see XPath interacting with SQL Server.
- ❑ XPointer, where it's used to indicate nodes to which pointers can point.
- ❑ XForms, in which it provides a mechanism for indicating the nodes within the instance data which are completed through different fields in the form, and for testing the constraints on the values used in the fields
- ❑ DOM (Level 3), in which it provides a quick method of selecting nodes in the DOM tree.
- ❑ XQuery, which takes XPath as its basis to create a query language over a collection of documents or a database (as we'll see later in this appendix).

The distinguishing feature of XPath is its ability to select nodes from an XML document. In this, XPath gives roughly the same functionality as the SELECT statement in SQL. However, selecting nodes from an XML document often involves testing nodes to see if they fulfill various criteria (much as in the WHERE clause of a SELECT statement), so XPath provides an expression language for calculating and testing values as well.

Appendix A

In fact, the basic building block of XPath is an **expression**, which an XPath processor evaluates an expression to return a value. As in SQL, the simplest kind of expression is a literal value, such as a string or number. More complex expressions use **operators** or calls to **functions**. A special subset of expressions is **location paths**, which pinpoint nodes within an XML document.

> You should note that SQL Server 2000 with SQLXML 3.0 does not implement the full set of XPath 1.0 functionality. This appendix covers the XPath 1.0 Recommendation comprehensively, so some of the examples you'll see are not appropriate for use in SQL Server 2000 (although they might be implemented in later versions). The current limitations were outlined in Chapter 8, along with how to use the supported XPath functionality in SQL Server 2000 with SQLXML 3.0.

In this appendix, we'll look at how XPath works and in particular its relationship with SQL and XQuery, as well as providing a quick reference to XPath concepts, operators, axes, and functions. Before we start looking at XPath syntax, we'll take a look at how XPath views an XML document and the data model that underlies the XPath language. We'll then examine the basic syntax of location paths, which enable you to select nodes from an XML document, and more general tests and expressions. We'll then discuss the operators and functions that are available within XPath. Finally, we'll look at the changes that XPath 2.0 is likely to bring and how XQuery 1.0 will use XPath.

Note throughout that XPath, like XML, is case-sensitive: all operators and function names are lowercase and hyphen-separated.

XPath Data Model

Let's start by looking at a simple XML document:

```xml
<?xml version="1.0"?>
<Customer Name="Kevin Williams">
  <Invoice InvoiceDate="2002-06-06T00:00:00"
           ShipDate="2002-07-01T00:00:00">
    <LineItem partIDREF="part1"
              number="8"
              unitPrice="0.4000"/>
    <LineItem partIDREF="part3"
              number="22"
              unitPrice="0.6000"/>
  </Invoice>
  <Invoice InvoiceDate="2002-05-06T00:00:00"
           ShipDate="2002-06-01T00:00:00">
    <LineItem partIDREF="part1"
              number="17"
              unitPrice="0.3500"/>
    <LineItem partIDREF="part2"
              number="39"
```

XPath Reference

```
            unitPrice="0.2500"/>
    </Invoice>
    <Part partID="part2" partCode="Q2653R    ">1-inch widgets
    </Part>
    <Part partID="part3" partCode="A3834G    ">1-inch grommets
    </Part>
    <Part partID="part1" partCode="X1726Y    ">2-inch grommets
    </Part>
</Customer>
```

XPath, like DOM, models an XML document as a tree of nodes. The node tree used by the XPath processor is very slightly different from the node tree used by a DOM processor, but it mostly follows the same pattern. Each important feature of an XML document becomes a node, and these nodes are arranged in a node tree based on the nesting in the XML document, such that an element inside another element becomes its child in the tree. The node tree for the above document will look something like the following:

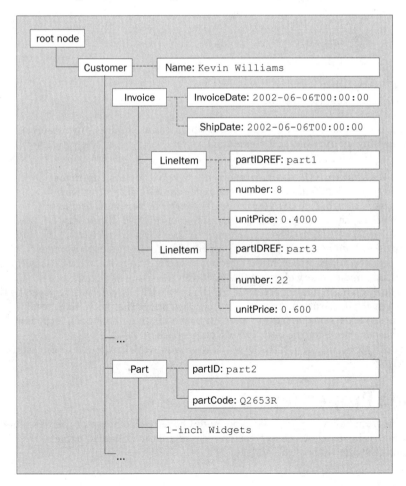

515

There are two things to note in particular about this node tree. First, note that the XML declaration (`<?xml version="1.0"?>`) isn't represented within the node tree; this is because the XML declaration is not part of the content of the document, it's only something used by the XML parser to understand how to parse the document. Second, note that the attributes are set to one side of the main node tree – they are not part of the main nesting structure, although text nodes are.

In this section, we'll look a bit more closely at nodes, and then look at the other kinds of data types that are used within XPath.

Node Types

Nodes in XPath are of the following types:

- root node
- elements
- attributes
- text nodes
- comments
- processing instructions
- namespace nodes

Each document has a single root node, which has as children any top-level processing instructions and elements.

> *Well-formed XML documents can only have one top-level document element, but XPath node trees can represent XML documents with more than one, or with text node children, which enables them to be used with external parsed entities as well as full XML documents.*

The other kind of nodes that are a bit peculiar are the namespace nodes. Namespace nodes represent the binding of prefixes to namespace URIs within the XML document. Every element that is within the scope of a namespace declaration has a namespace node for the prefix-URI association declared by the namespace declaration. As well as namespace nodes that get added from namespace declarations, every element in the XPath data model has an associated namespace node for the built-in XML namespace of `http://www.w3.org/XML/1998/namespace`, which is bound to the prefix `xml`.

Node Properties

Aside from having a particular type, nodes have two common properties that can be accessed within XPath expressions. These are the **expanded name** of the node and the **string value** of the node.

XPath Reference

Not all nodes have an expanded name – it's only relevant for elements, attributes, processing instructions, and namespace nodes. Expanded names in XPath are qualified names: they have a local part (the **local name**) and a (possibly empty) namespace URI derived by resolving the prefix that was used for the element or attribute in the XML document. The expanded names of processing instructions and namespace nodes both consist of the local part of the name only – that is, their expanded names don't have a namespace URI, only a local part.

> *As far as XPath is concerned, namespace URIs are just strings, and two namespace URIs are compared on a character-by-character basis. Although namespace URIs usually look like URLs, XPath processors never resolve those URLs.*

All nodes have a string value. Note that the string value does not have a particular data type – it's just a string. XPath 1.0 does not use information from a schema to tell it the type of a node's value (XML Schema wasn't invented when XPath 1.0 was developed) so, as far as XPath is concerned, all elements and attributes are just strings, not numbers or dates or URLs. This is one of the fundamental differences between XPath and SQL, and something that will change in XPath 2.0 (see later).

The expanded names and string values of nodes are summarized in the following table:

Node Type	Expanded Name	String Value
root node	-	The concatenation of the values of all the text nodes in the document.
element	The name of the element.	The concatenation of the values of all the text node descendants of the element.
attribute	The name of the attribute.	The value of the attribute.
text node	-	The text itself.
comment	-	The comment itself.
processing instruction (PI)	The target of the processing instruction (the content before the first space).	The data of the processing instruction (the content after the first space).
namespace node	The prefix used in the namespace binding.	The namespace URI used in the namespace binding.

Appendix A

Data Types

As we've seen, the values of nodes don't have a particular data type – they are just strings – but XPath does more than just get the values of nodes, it's a full expression language. **Expressions** in XPath are a lot like expressions in SQL: a bit of code that can be evaluated to give a value. Expressions fall into four classes:

- **literal values** – expressions that return a literal value, such as a string or a number.
- **operations** – expressions where two values are combined based on a particular **operator**.
- **function calls** – expressions where several values are passed as arguments to a **function** which returns a value based on those values.
- **location paths** – expressions that return a node-set by navigating an XML document.

Unlike SQL, with its multitude of different data types, XPath expressions can only result in values of four different data types. They are:

- **node-sets** – an unordered collection of nodes, similar to a set of rows returned from an unordered `SELECT` statement.
- **strings** – a sequence of zero or more characters; there's no limit (aside from via processor limitations) to the size of a string, and all strings in XPath are Unicode, just like XML, so you don't have to worry about encodings.
- **numbers** – a double-precision 64-bit floating-point number, including the special values NaN (not a number), Infinity and -Infinity, and positive and negative zero.
- **booleans** – true or false; unlike SQL, XPath doesn't use three-value logic, so there is no "unknown" boolean value.

We won't be going into the details of operators, functions, or location paths here (see later in the appendix), but this section summarizes the different ways of creating values of the different types and the rules about casting between them.

Creating Values

Node-sets can be created in three ways, all of which we'll be seeing in more detail later. The main way of creating a node-set is through a location path (equivalent to a `SELECT` statement in SQL). You can also merge two node-sets to create a third using the union operator (`|`). Finally, the `id()` function, which locates elements based on their ID, also returns a node-set.

You can create literal strings by enclosing the string within either single or double quotes within an XPath expression. For example, both the following expressions create a string whose value is "Kevin Williams":

```
'Kevin Williams'
"Kevin Williams"
```

XPath Reference

There's no way of escaping either kind of quotation mark within an XPath string literal, so if you want to include a double quote within the string, you should use apostrophes to delimit the string and vice versa. If you have to create a string that contains both a double quote and a single quote, you can use the `concat()` function to create it by splitting the string around the quotes. For example, to create a string whose value is ""I'm fine thanks," he replied.", you have to use something like:

```
concat('"', "I'm fine thanks,", '" he replied.')
```

> It's likely that XPath 2.0 will enable you to double-up quotes within literal strings in order to escape them, just as in SQL, so the above string could then be expressed as `'The rules say "this isn''t encouraged"'`.

Strings can also arise from getting the string value of a node, or when you evaluate functions that return strings, such as `substring()` or `concat()`.

You can create numbers in an XPath expression by specifying the number, but numeric literals are a little more restricted than those in SQL. The only characters allowed in a numeric literal are an optional minus sign, the digits 0-9 and the decimal point – you can't specify exponents in XML, nor have an explicit plus sign to create a positive number, nor use a dollar sign (since XPath doesn't have a `money` data type) and, like SQL, you can't use commas within numeric literals. Some example valid numeric literals are:

```
0.40000
14936359
.5
-000014
```

> Technically, the minus sign of a numeric literal is interpreted as a unary minus operator rather than as part of the numeric literal. You could create the number -14 using `---14` if you wanted.

There are also no literals for the special values `NaN`, `Infinity` or `-Infinity`. If you need to create `NaN`, you can do so by turning a non-numeric string into a number using the `number()` function, for example:

```
number('NaN')
```

Infinity and negative infinity can be created by dividing 1 or -1 by 0 using the `div` operator:

```
1 div 0
-1 div 0
```

> If you're using MSXML4, you can also use the MSXML-specific extension functions `ms:number('INF')` and `ms:number('-INF')`.

Appendix A

Numbers can also be created as the result of various numeric operations (such as multiplication or addition) and from function calls, such as `floor()` and `count()`.

There are no literal boolean values in XPath; instead, you can use the functions `true()` to create boolean true and `false()` to create boolean false. Boolean values are also created as the result of evaluating comparisons (such as equals or greater-than) and from some other functions, such as `not()` and `lang()`.

Casting Between Data Types

Unlike SQL, XPath is a weakly typed language, which means that if a value doesn't have the type that it should have to participate in a particular operation or be an argument to a particular function, it automatically gets cast to the correct type. The following table shows the different data types that can be cast to each other (note that none of the other data types can be converted to a node-set).

	String	Number	Boolean
Node-set	Take the string value of the first node in the node-set.	Take the string value of the first node in the node-set, and convert it to a number.	False if the node-set is empty, true if it contains any nodes.
String	-	Interpret the string as if it were a literal number.	False if the string is empty, true if it contains any characters.
Number	NaN becomes 'NaN', positive and negative zero become 0, infinity becomes Infinity, and negative infinity becomes -Infinity. Otherwise, a straightforward string representation with no leading or trailing zeros; integers do not get given any decimal part.	-	False if the number is either 0 or NaN, true otherwise.

	String	Number	Boolean
Boolean	`'true'` for boolean true, `'false'` for boolean false.	1 for boolean true, 0 for boolean false.	-

If you want to force a cast to a particular data type, there are three functions that you can use:

- `string()` to cast to a string
- `number()` to cast to a number
- `boolean()` to cast to a boolean

> The casting rules and methods are a lot more complicated in XPath 2.0 because XPath 2.0 includes a lot more data types than XPath 1.0 – in fact all of those from XML Schema.

Location Paths

The most important kind of expression that you can write with XPath is a **location path**. A location path enables you to select nodes from the node tree that's built from an XML document in a similar manner to how the SQL SELECT statement enables you to select information from a database. The main difference is that while databases have a relational structure, node trees are hierarchical organizations of nodes. While the SELECT statement has to have good support for navigating between tables based on key values, location paths need to enable movement around the node tree based on the structural relationships between nodes. In this, location paths are a lot more similar to file paths (which enable you to navigate a hierarchical structure of directories) than they are to SELECT statements.

Absolute and Relative Location Paths

Like file paths, location paths can be divided into two categories: **absolute location paths** and **relative location paths**. Absolute location paths start from a known location, the root node of the document, and navigate from there, while relative location paths navigate from 'where you are now'. This is known as the **context node**.

You can tell an absolute location path because it starts with a /. A forward slash at the beginning of an XPath represents the root node. The / character is also used in location paths to separate steps in the path, just as it is in file paths. A simple absolute location path, selecting all the `<Part>` elements in the example document we looked at earlier would be:

```
/Customer/Part
```

If you were currently looking at a particular `<Invoice>` element, then you could get all its `LineItem`'s `partIDREF` attributes using:

```
LineItem/@partIDREF
```

Steps

As you can see, each step in a location path identifies the node that you want to step to, in the same way as each step in a file path identifies the directory to which you want to navigate. The basic kind of steps, such as those in the previous examples, name the element to travel to, that element being a child of the node that you're on. So the location path:

```
/Customer/Invoice/LineItem
```

Starts at the root node (it's an absolute path), then steps down to the `<Customer>` element that's a child of the root node (the document element), and then steps down to the `<Invoice>` elements that are children of that `<Customer>` element, and finally down to the `<LineItem>` elements that are children of those `<Invoice>` elements. Note that *all* the `<LineItem>` elements are selected, not just those belonging to the first `<Invoice>`.

Steps can be more complex than this. The general syntax for a step is:

```
axis::node-test[predicate]*
```

Each step is made up of an **axis**, a **node-test** and any number of **predicates**. The axis and node-test are separated by two colons (::), and the predicates come after the node-test, within square brackets. Briefly, the axis specifies the direction in which to travel in the node tree, the node-test specifies what kind of nodes to look for in that direction, and the predicate filters that set of nodes based on some kind of boolean test. Both the axis and the predicates are optional; if you don't specify an axis, you look at the children of a node, and if you don't specify a predicate then all nodes that pass the node test are selected.

Axes

The axes available in XPath reflect familial relationships between the nodes in the node tree. The basic axis, used by default, is the `child` axis, but other axes enable you to move around the node tree with complete flexibility.

Axes fall into two categories: **forward axes** and **reverse axes**. Forward axes travel in **document order** – forwards or down the node tree (such that you encounter nodes that appear after the context node in the XML document) – while reverse axes travel in reverse document order – backwards or up the node tree (such that you encounter nodes that appear before the context node in the XML document). The difference between the two only really comes into play when you're using steps that do things like selecting the first following or preceding sibling of a node.

XPath Reference

A forward axis like `following-sibling` will select the (following sibling) node that's first in document order (the immediately following sibling) while a reverse axis like `preceding-sibling` will select the (preceding sibling) node that's last in document order (the immediately preceding sibling). Basically, whenever you select nodes that are at a particular position along an axis, that position is counted from the context node out rather than always being counted from the start of the document.

The full set of axes is summarized in the following table:

Axis	Direction	Description
`self`	forward	Selects the context node itself
`child`	forward	Selects the children of the context node
`parent`	reverse	Selects the parent of the context node
`attribute`	forward	Selects the attributes of the context node
`descendant`	forward	Selects the descendants of the context node (children, children's children and so on)
`descendant-or-self`	forward	Selects the descendants of the context node, and the context node itself
`ancestor`	reverse	Selects the ancestors of the context node (parent, parent's parent and so on)
`ancestor-or-self`	reverse	Selects the ancestors of the context node, and the context node itself
`following-sibling`	forward	Selects the siblings of the context node (nodes that have the same parent) that follow the context node in document order
`preceding-sibling`	reverse	Selects the siblings of the context node that precede the context node in document order
`following`	forward	Selects the nodes (aside from attribute and namespace nodes) that follow the context node in document order and are not descendants of the context node – those nodes that start after this node ends

Table continued on following page

Appendix A

Axis	Direction	Description
`preceding`	reverse	Selects the nodes (aside from attribute and namespace nodes) that precede the context node in document order and are not ancestors of the context node – those nodes that end before this node starts
`namespace`	forward	Selects the namespace nodes on the context node

Note that because attributes and namespace nodes don't form part of the hierarchy of the node tree, you have to get to them via their parent element (elements are parents of their namespace and attribute nodes, but namespace and attribute nodes are not their children).

Note also that only the `attribute`, `child`, `parent`, and `self` axes are supported when using SQL Server 2000 with SQLXML 3.0.

The XPath 1.0 Recommendation allows you to mix and match different axes within a location path as much as you like, which means that there are always several routes that you can take to a particular set of nodes. For example, if you're on a `<Part>` element at the moment, all the following paths select the `<LineItem>` elements in the document:

```
/child::Customer/child::Invoice/child::LineItem
parent::Customer/child::Invoice/child::LineItem
preceding-sibling::Invoice/child::LineItem
self::Part/preceding::LineItem
/descendant::LineItem
ancestor::Customer/descendant-or-self::LineItem
```

Different routes can take different times to navigate, however. In general, the more nodes that there are on a particular axis, the longer it will take to use that axis. For example, the first path above visits the root node (1), which only has one child, the `<Customer>` element (1 + 1 = 2). The `<Customer>` element actually has five children (2 + 5 = 7), two of which are `<Invoice>` elements, which have two `<LineItem>` element children each, making 7 + 4 = 11 nodes visited in total. On the other hand, in the last path above, the context `<Part>` element has two ancestors (the root node and the `<Customer>` element), and the `<Customer>` element has twelve descendants (two `<Invoice>` elements, four `<LineItem>` elements, three `<Part>` elements and three text nodes that are children of the `<Part>` elements), and it includes itself in the `descendant-or-self` axis, making a total of 2 + 12 + 1 = 15 nodes visited in total.

In general, focusing a search with paths that make one step at a time tends to be more efficient than trying to gather everything together in one step. Avoiding the `descendant`, `descendant-or-self`, `following` and `preceding` axes is a good way of making sure that your XPaths run quickly.

Node Tests

Node tests are ways of identifying the kind of nodes that a particular step should pick up. Text nodes, comments, and processing instructions all have their own node tests, and there's a special node test that matches nodes of all kinds:

Node Test	Description
`node()`	Matches node of all types
`text()`	Matches text nodes
`comment()`	Matches comment nodes
`processing-instruction()`	Matches processing instruction nodes
`processing-instruction('target')`	Matches processing instruction nodes with the given target (name)

> The brackets on these node tests make them look as though they're function calls, but don't be fooled. The brackets are there to distinguish, for example, a node test for text nodes (`text()`) from a node test for elements called text (`text`).

For example, to select all the text node children of the `<Part>` elements in the document, you could use:

```
/Customer/Part/text()
```

To select all the elements, text nodes, comments, and processing instructions in the document, you can use:

```
/descendant::node()
```

> Note again that this doesn't select attributes or namespace nodes, because the `descendant` axis doesn't get to them.

Since elements, attributes and namespace nodes all have names and are on separate axes, they can be selected using a **name test**. The simplest name test is one that specifies the name of the element, attribute, or namespace node. For example:

```
attribute::InvoiceDate
```

selects the attribute called `InvoiceDate` on the context element (an `<Invoice>` element, we'll assume).

You can also use a wildcard as the name test: a `*` means 'any name'. For example, to select all the elements in the document, you could use:

```
/descendant::*
```

Similarly, to select all the attributes on an element, no matter what they're called, you can use:

```
attribute::*
```

One important thing about name tests is that the names are treated as being qualified and are resolved according to a set of namespace bindings that are set before evaluating an XPath. How the namespace bindings get set up depends on the host language of the XPath expression. In XSLT, for example, the namespace bindings are those in place on the element that contains the XPath expression, so you can declare a namespace as normal and use that prefix within the XPath expressions in XSLT. If you're using an XPath in the selectNodes() method in MSXML, on the other hand, you need to have set up the namespace bindings by setting the SelectionNamespaces property before calling the selectNodes() method. It's best to read the documentation for the host language to work out how namespace bindings are set up in that particular context.

The one thing that is fixed about XPath 1.0 namespace bindings, however, is that the default namespace binding (the one with no prefix) is ignored when interpreting the qualified names used as name tests. For example, if you have the step:

```
child::Part
```

this always selects <Part> elements that are in no namespace. If you want it to select <Part> elements in some other namespace, for example http://www.example.com/orders, then you have to associate a prefix (such as ord) with that namespace URI, and use that prefix in the name test:

```
child::ord:Part
```

> One change in XPath 2.0 is that it will be possible to use a default namespace when interpreting element (but not attribute) names. Again, different host languages will have different ways of setting this default element namespace: XSLT 2.0 will probably use an attribute called default-element-ns, while XQuery has a default namespace declaration such as
> default element namespace = "http://www.example.com/orders".

You can combine prefixes with the wildcard * to select all elements (or attributes) in a particular namespace. For example, given that the prefix ord is bound to the namespace http://www.example.com/orders, you can select all the elements in the document that are in the namespace http://www.example.com/orders with:

```
/descendant::ord:*
```

XPath Reference

The following table summarizes the name tests that you can use within location path steps:

Name Test	Description
`*`	Matches all elements, attributes or namespace nodes (as appropriate to the axis)
`local-name`	Matches all elements, attributes or namespace nodes with the given local name (and not in a namespace)
`prefix:*`	Matches all elements or attributes in the namespace associated with the specified prefix
`prefix:local-name`	Matches elements or attributes with the given local name in the namespace associated with the specified prefix

Abbreviations

There are several abbreviations that you can use in location paths, as listed in the following table. Note that not all of them are abbreviations for whole steps:

Abbreviation	Expansion	Description
`.`	`self::node()`	Selects the context node – the node that you're looking at
`..`	`parent::node()`	Selects the parent of the context node – goes up a level in the node tree
`@`	`attribute::`	Shorthand for the attribute axis, such that `@ShipDate` is equivalent to `attribute::ShipDate`
`//`	`/descendant-or-self::node()/`	Shorthand for locating nodes at any level in the document, such that `//LineItem` selects all the `<LineItem>` elements in the document

Predicates

The final (and optional) part of a step is its predicates. Predicates can be used to filter node-sets, either at the level of an entire node-set or on particular steps within a location path.

527

Appendix A

There are two classes of predicates: **logical predicates** and **positional predicates**. Logical predicates are the more general kind, and test any expression, converting it to a boolean to see if it's true or false. Positional predicates hold expressions that evaluate to a number, and test the position of the node amongst the other nodes in the node-set or selected by a step. Basically, if the expression held in a predicate evaluates to a number, then you're testing the position of a node with a positional predicate, otherwise you're using a more general logical predicate.

Logical predicates act like WHERE clauses in SELECT statements in SQL: only nodes that fulfill the logical predicate get selected. For example, to select the <LineItem> elements in the document whose number attribute has a value greater than 20, you can use:

```
/Customer/Invoice/LineItem[@number > 20]
```

Most logical predicates contain comparisons but, if the expression evaluates to a node-set or to a string, it will be converted to a boolean using the casting rules that we looked at earlier: an empty node-set or empty string resolves to false and the node won't be selected. For example, you can select all the elements in the document that have a child element themselves (the <Customer> and <Invoice> elements) using:

```
//*[*]
```

Positional predicates are the same as testing whether the position of a node (as returned by the position() function) is equal to the number specified in the predicate. For example, the following are equivalent:

```
/Customer/Invoice[2]
/Customer/Invoice[position() = 2]
```

> Note that the current implementation of XPath in SQL Server does not support positional predicates. For a workaround for the lack of the position() function, please see Chapter 8.

The 'position' of a node is judged relative to the other nodes selected from the same node in the particular step, in document order, or reverse document order, according to the direction of the axis. For example:

```
/Customer/Invoice/LineItem[1]
```

selects the first <LineItem> element of each <Invoice> within the <Customer> element in the document, so you end up with two <LineItem> elements. If you wanted to select only the first <LineItem> element in the document as a whole, the predicate needs to be on the location path as a whole instead (which you can achieve by wrapping the location path in brackets):

```
(/Customer/Invoice/LineItem)[1]
```

XPath Reference

Alternatively, of course, you could use the `descendant` axis to select all the `<LineItem>` elements at once, as follows:

```
/Customer/descendant::LineItem[1]
```

A useful positional predicate is one that selects the last occurrence of a particular element within a list. This works using the `last()` function to return the position of the last of that particular element type. For example, to select the last `<Invoice>` element within the document, you could use:

```
/Customer/Invoice[last()]
```

You can have as many predicates as you like within a step or at the end of a location path. Each predicate is applied on the results of the previous predicate, so in most cases it's the same as combining the expressions that they contain using and. The exception arises when combining positional and logical predicates. For example, consider the following:

```
/descendant::LineItem[@partIDREF = 'part1'][2]
/descendant::LineItem[2][@partIDREF = 'part1']
```

The first path selects those `<LineItem>` elements whose `partIDREF` attribute has the value `part1`, and then takes the second of them; as long as you have two or more `<LineItem>` elements in the document whose `partIDREF` attribute has the value `part1`, you'll get a node in the result. The second path selects the second `<LineItem>` element in the document, and then tests whether its `partIDREF` attribute is equal to `part1`; you'll only get a node in the resulting node-set if the second `<LineItem>` in the document has a `partIDREF` attribute equal to `part1`.

Variables

We've seen how to create literal strings and numbers, how to create boolean values, and how to create node-sets. The other primary expression in XPath is a **variable reference**, used to substitute the value of a variable into an expression.

Variable references in XPath are expressed as a dollar sign ($) followed by the name of the variable. For example:

```
$number * 2
```

returns the value of the variable called `number`, multiplied by two.

Variable assignment isn't handled within XPath. As with namespaces, the host language of the XPath expression governs the assignment of values to variables. In XSLT, for example, the `xsl:variable` element sets up a global or local variable assignment.

529

Appendix A

In the current Working Draft of XPath 2.0, there are ways of assigning values to 'range variables' when iterating over a sequence, but no general assignment method. Variables can be assigned values in XQuery using the `let` sub-expression within a `for` expression.

Operators

XPath's set of operators is smaller than, though similar to, SQL's and, like SQL, these are 'infix' operators, meaning they come between the operands:

```
operand1 operator operand2
```

As in SQL, brackets can be used to delimit particular subexpressions and control their precedence. Without brackets, the default precedence is used. The following list shows the default precedence of the different operators, from highest to lowest:

- |
- unary -
- *, div, mod
- +, -
- <=, <, >, >=
- =, !=
- and
- or

Note: not all of these operators are currently supported in SQL Server 2000 with SQLXML 3.0.

XPath operators can be divided into four groups: arithmetic, comparisons, logical, and node-set operators.

Arithmetic Operators

The arithmetic operators in XPath are as follows:

Operator	Description
+	Addition
-	Subtraction
*	Multiplication
div	Floating point division
mod	Remainder from integer division
unary -	Negation

The only ones that are different from SQL are `div` rather than / and `mod` rather than %. XPath couldn't use / for division because this character is already used within location paths to separate steps and to indicate the root node. Also note that there is no unary + in XPath.

For all of these operators, both operands are converted to numbers, using the casting rules shown earlier in this appendix, before being used (note that this means that if an operand is a node-set, only the value of the first of the nodes in that node-set is used in the arithmetic). Unlike in SQL, you cannot use + and – on dates, since dates are not part of XPath. Nor can you use + as a concatenation operator; to concatenate strings together, you must use the `concat()` function.

> *In XPath 2.0, when dates and times are introduced, you will be able to use arithmetic operators on dates, times and durations.*

Comparisons

The comparison operators in XPath are as follows:

Operator	Description
=	Equal to
!=	Not equal to
<	Less than
<=	Less than or equal to
>	Greater than
>=	Greater than or equal to

> *If you use the < or <= operators within an XPath that's embedded in an XML document (such as an XML template), then you must escape the less-than sign so that the XML document continues to be well-formed. In other words, use: `&lt;` and `&lt;=`.*

These operators are mainly familiar from SQL, with the exception that != is used for not equal to, rather than <>. Also note that SQL's !> (not greater than) and !< (not less than) are not included in XPath; you can use <= instead of !> and >= instead of !<.

There are three more subtle differences between comparisons in XPath and those in SQL.

The first difference between comparison operators in XPath and SQL is that the <=, <, >, and >= operators all automatically convert their arguments to numbers before performing the comparison. This leads to the slightly strange situation where:

```
'1.0' = '1'
```

Appendix A

is false (since the two strings are not equal) whereas:

```
'1.0' <= '1'
```

is true, since both operands are converted to the number 1 before being compared as equal.

> In XPath 2.0, comparisons will be made based on the data type of the two arguments; strings will be compared as strings (alphabetically), dates as dates and so on. In the meantime, if you're using MSXML4, you can use ms:string-compare() to compare two strings.

The second difference between comparison operators in XPath and SQL is that they can only return true or false – there is no UNKNOWN boolean value. If either argument is NaN, the comparison is always false, even if the test is NaN = NaN. You can therefore test whether a value is numeric by converting it to a number and comparing it to itself. For example, to select those <LineItem> elements whose number attribute is numeric, you could use:

```
/Customer/Invoice/LineItem[number(@number) = number(@number)]
```

The final difference in comparison operators in XPath and SQL arises because node-sets are a data type in XPath. If either of the operands to a comparison is a node-set, then the comparison is carried out between each node in the node-set and the other operands. If *any* of the comparisons return true then the comparison as a whole is true. For example:

```
/Customer/Invoice/LineItem/@number > 20
```

is true because at least one of the <LineItem> elements in the document has a number attribute with a value greater than 20. Thus, comparisons in XPath always work as if, in SQL, the SOME, ANY, or EXISTS operators were being used in the comparison. To perform an ALL comparison – for example, to check whether *all* the <LineItem> elements' partIDREF attributes are equal to part1 – you need to reverse the comparison and use the not() function to negate its result:

```
not( /Customer/Invoice/LineItem/@partIDREF != 'part1' )
```

> XPath 2.0 retains this functionality, but also offers some and every expressions for explicitly testing whether any or all items in a sequence fulfill some condition.

The comparisons discussed above address the comparison of *values*. There are occasions when you might want to compare node identity – to see whether two nodes are the same node. The best way to do this in XPath is to use **set logic**: if you create a union of two node-sets, one containing node $A and one containing node $B, then if they are the same node, the resulting node-set will only contain one node. The expression for testing whether the two nodes $A and $B are the same node is therefore:

XPath Reference

```
count($A | $B) = 1
```

If you want to test whether two node-sets contain exactly the same nodes, you need to use set logic again, this time testing whether there are no nodes that are in $A and not in $B and similarly no nodes in $B that are not in $A:

```
not($A[not(count(.|$B) = count($B))]) and
not($B[not(count(.|$A) = count($A))])
```

Logical Operators

There are only two logical operators in XPath:

Operator	Description
or	true if either operand is true when converted to booleans
and	true if both operands are true when converted to booleans

The missing logical operator, not, is actually available as the not() function rather than as a unary operator.

One thing to note about the logical operators or and and is that the order of the operands matters. If, using or, the first operand is true, then the second operand will not be evaluated, because the processor already knows that the result of the expression as a whole is true. Similarly, if the first operand to the and operator is false, then the expression as a whole is false and the second operand isn't evaluated. This means that you should try to order logical tests so that a complex test is skipped where possible by putting the simpler test as the first operand.

> This behavior differs from SQL, where the order of the conditions tested by a WHERE clause has no effect and the SQL optimizer is free to test them in whatever order makes most sense; XPath 2.0 is likely to adopt SQL behavior.

Node-Set Operators

There is only one node-set operator in XPath:

Operator	Description
|	Creates a union of two node-sets

Intersections and set differences can be carried out with more complex expressions. To find the intersection of two node-sets, $A and $B, you can use:

```
$A[count(.|$B) = count($B)]
```

533

Appendix A

To find the set difference between $A and $B – those nodes that are in $A and not in the node-set $B, you can use:

```
$A[not(count(.|$B) = count($B))]
```

Set intersections and differences will be supported by `intersect` *and* `except` *operators in XPath 2.0; for consistency, the alias* `union` *might be added for the union operator.*

Functions

XPath offers a large set of functions for manipulating strings, numbers, booleans and node-sets, some of which have already been mentioned. To call a function in XPath, use the following syntax:

```
function-name(argument, argument, ...)
```

As well as functions from XPath itself, the host languages of XPath often add their own functions; in particular, XSLT adds several extra functions to XPath. In addition, vendors of XPath processors are free to create their own extension functions. These functions have their own namespace, and when you call them you must use a name qualified by a prefix for that namespace. MSXML, the processor used within SQL Server, defines several extension functions for accessing schema information and to aid in the interpretation of numbers and dates; the namespace for these functions is `urn:schemas-microsoft-com:xslt`.

You must associate this namespace with a prefix, for example `ms`, as described previously, in order to use these extension functions.

The rest of this section lists the XPath, XSLT and MSXML extension functions in alphabetical order.

> **Each function is an XPath 1.0 function, unless otherwise stated. Also, SQL equivalents are only given where they exist.**
>
> **Also remember that the current implementation of XPath in SQL Server does not support all of these functions. See Chapter 8 for a listing of unsupported features.**

boolean()

Syntax:	`boolean boolean(object)`
SQL equivalent:	`CONVERT(bit, object)`
See also:	`string()`, `number()`

XPath Reference

Converts the argument to a boolean value (either `true` or `false`). Usually this is done automatically, for example in logical predicates, so you rarely need to call this function explicitly. About the only time when it's useful is if you want to test whether the value of a node is either non-numeric or 0. For example, to select only those `LineItem` elements whose `number` attribute is numeric and not 0, you could use:

```
/Customer/Invoice/LineItem[boolean(number(@number))]
```

If you didn't use the `boolean()` function in this example, the result of `number(@number)` would be interpreted as a positional predicate, and you would get only those `<LineItem>` elements whose position (within their `<Invoice>` parent) was equal to the value of their `number` attribute.

ceiling()

Syntax:	*number* ceiling(*number*)
SQL equivalent:	ceiling(*number*) (SQL Server extension function)
See also:	floor(), round()

Rounds the argument up to the nearest integer. For negative numbers, this means rounding nearer to 0, so `ceiling(-1.5)` is -1.

concat()

Syntax:	*string* concat(*string, string,...*)
SQL equivalent:	*string* || *string* || ...
	string + *string* + ... (in SQL Server)

Concatenates the strings passed as arguments into a single string. There must be at least two strings to concatenate together. For example, to create a US version of the `InvoiceDate` attribute on the current `<Invoice>`, in the format `MM/DD/YYYY`, you could concatenate together substrings of the `InvoiceDate` attribute with literal / strings as follows:

```
concat(substring(@InvoiceDate, 6, 2), '/',
       substring(@InvoiceDate, 9, 2), '/',
       substring(@InvoiceDate, 1, 4))
```

contains()

Syntax:	*boolean* contains(*string1, string2*)
SQL equivalent:	*string1* LIKE '%*string2*%'
See also:	starts-with()

535

Returns `true` if the string passed as the first argument contains the string passed as the second argument or if the second argument is an empty string, and `false` otherwise. For example, to get all the `<Part>` elements that represent grommets (whose content contains `grommets`), you could use:

```
/Customer/Part[contains(., 'grommets')]
```

count()

Syntax:	*number* count(*node-set*)
SQL equivalent:	COUNT(*node-set*)
See also:	last(), position()

Counts the number of nodes in the node-set passed as the argument. For example, to select only those Invoices that have more than one `<LineItem>` child, you could use:

```
/Customer/Invoice[count(LineItem) > 1]
```

> Another method of doing this is to simply see whether each `<Invoice>` has a second `<LineItem>` – if it does it must have more than one `<LineItem>`: `/Customer/Invoice[LineItem[2]]`. This can be a bit more efficient since the processor can stop looking once it's found the second `<LineItem>` and doesn't have to gather together all of them in order to count them.

current()

Syntax:	*node-set* current()
Defined in:	XSLT 1.0
See also:	the path .

Returns the current node – the node that's currently being processed within the `<xsl:for-each>` or `<xsl:template>` as opposed to the context node, which is the node currently being looked at within an XPath. If a processor supports `current()` outside XSLT, then it's equivalent to getting the context node (with `self::node()` or the shorthand `.`).

document()

Syntax:	*node-set* document(*object*, *node-set?*)
Defined in:	XSLT 1.0

This function opens up another XML document, so in a way it's similar to accessing a separate table using SQL. If the first argument is a string, `document()` returns the node found at the URL specified by that string (usually the root node of a document). The URL is resolved relative to the location of the file containing the first node in the node-set passed as the second argument (which is usually used to resolve the URL relative to the source document). If the second argument is missing, the URL is resolved relative to the XSLT stylesheet in which the XPath is being used. If the first argument is a node-set, then the result is a node-set containing all the nodes that are retrieved by calling the `document()` function with the string values of the nodes in the node-set.

For example, if the `<Part>` elements were listed in a separate, `catalog.xml` document, wrapped in a `<Part>` element, then you could access only those `<LineItems>` that were listed in this catalog with:

```
/Customer/Invoice/LineItem[@partIDREF =
                document('catalog.xml')/Parts/Part/@partID]
```

element-available()

Syntax:	*boolean* element-available(*string*)
Defined in:	XSLT 1.0
See also:	function-available()

Returns `true` if an XSLT processor supports the extension element or new XSLT instruction named by the string passed as the argument. The string should be a qualified name, with a prefix. This function has no purpose outside XSLT.

false()

Syntax:	*boolean* false()
SQL equivalent:	FALSE
See also:	true(), boolean()

Returns `false` – this is simply a way of getting a false value since there are no boolean literals.

floor()

Syntax:	*number* floor(*number*)
SQL equivalent:	floor(*number*) (SQL Server extension function)
See also:	ceiling(), round()

Rounds the number down to the nearest integer. If the number is negative, then it gets rounded away from zero, so `floor(-1.5)` returns −2.

537

Appendix A

format-number()

Syntax:	*string* format-number(*number*, *string*, *string*?)
Defined in:	XSLT 1.0
See also:	number()

Returns the number passed as the first argument formatted according to the format pattern passed as the second argument. The format pattern usually contains # to mean an optional digit, 0 to indicate a required digit, . to indicate the decimal point, and , to indicate a grouping separator. So:

```
format-number(1234.5, '#,##0.00')
```

returns the string '1,234.50'. If the third argument is specified, it gives the name of a decimal format, which in XSLT is declared with the `<xsl:decimal-format>` element, which can define other characters to be used instead of #, 0, , , and ..

function-available()

Syntax:	*boolean* function-available(*string*)
Defined in:	XSLT 1.0
See also:	element-available()

Returns true if the processor supports the function named by the argument string. The string usually includes a prefix to test for the availability of extension functions, such as those available in MSXML. For example, to check that the extension function ms:type-is() is available, you can use:

```
function-available('ms:type-is')
```

generate-id()

Syntax:	*string* generate-id(*node-set*?)
Defined in:	XSLT 1.0

Returns an ID for the first node in the node-set passed as the argument which is both unique and a valid XML ID. If no argument is given, it returns a unique ID for the context node. This ID can be useful because not all nodes in XML documents have identifiers of their own. You can use the generated ID to compare two nodes. For example, to test whether node $A and node $B are the same node, you can use:

```
generate-id($A) = generate-id($B)
```

538

XPath Reference

The unique IDs are not stable – they are different from processor to processor, and even for the same processor operating over the same source XML document at different times. Thus, you can rely on a generated ID to be stable within a particular XPath expression, but not for a particular element to have the same generated ID each time a document is queried.

id()

Syntax:	*node-set* id(*object*)
See also:	key()

Returns the nodes with the XML IDs specified by the argument. If the argument is a string, then it's split up at whitespace, and the function returns all the nodes in the current document that have any of the IDs. If the argument is a node-set, the same is done but with the string values of each of the nodes in the node-set.

You have to have declared an attribute as an ID attribute within a DTD for the id() function to work, and the context node must be in the same document as the nodes that you want to retrieve. For example, if the partID attribute on the <Part> elements in our sample document had been declared in the DTD as being ID attributes, using something like:

```
<!ATTLIST Part
   partID    ID      #REQUIRED
   partCode  CDATA   #REQUIRED>
```

then you could get hold of the <Part> element related to a <LineItem> using the id() function and passing the value of the partIDREF attribute as the argument. For example, to get hold of all the invoices that contain an order for grommets, you could use:

```
/Customer/Invoice[ id(LineItem/@partID)
   [contains(., 'grommets')] ]
```

key()

Syntax:	*node-set* key(*string*, *object*)
Defined in:	XSLT 1.0
See also:	id()

While the id() function always uses the ID attribute on an element to index it, you can use keys to index nodes in an XML document by whatever you want. This is an XSLT addition to XPath, so for other host languages to use it, they must have their own mechanisms for defining keys. The key() function returns the nodes that are indexed by the value specified by the second argument in the key named by the first argument. If the second argument is a node-set, then all the nodes with any of the values are returned.

539

Appendix A

lang()

| Syntax: | *boolean* lang(*string*) |

Returns true if the language of the context node (as specified on its own or one of its ancestors' xml:lang attributes) matches the language specified by the argument. This test is aware of sub-languages and is case-insensitive, so for example lang('en') would return true even if the context node's language was specified as EN-US.

last()

Syntax:	*number* last()
See also:	position(), count()

Returns the index of the last node in the list that's currently being looked at (or the number of nodes that are currently being looked at, depending on how you like to view it). For example, to get the last of the <Part> elements within the <Customer> element, you can use:

```
/Customer/Part[last()]
```

local-name()

Syntax:	*string* local-name(*node-set*?)
See also:	name(), namespace-uri()

Returns the local name of the first node in the node-set, that is, the part of the name after any prefix that there might be. If no argument is passed, then returns the local name of the context node. For example, to get those <LineItem> elements whose partIDREF attribute is equal to either the partID or partCode of a <Part> element in the document, you could use:

```
/Customer/Invoice/LineItem
    [@partIDREF = /Customer/Part/@*
                        [starts-with(local-name(),'part')]]
```

ms:format-date()

Syntax:	*string* ms:format-date(*string1*, *string2*, *string3*?)
Defined in:	MSXML 4
See also:	ms:format-time()

540

XPath Reference

This function formats the date/time string passed as the first argument in the format specified by the second argument, using the locale indicated by the optional third argument (or the locale of the system environment if the third argument isn't specified). The format string can contain the following characters:

Character(s)	Description
M	Month numbers (1-12)
MM	Month numbers in two digits (01-12)
MMM	Month abbreviations (Jan-Dec)
MMMM	Month names (January-December)
d	Day of the month (1-31)
dd	Day of the month in two digits (01-31)
ddd	Day of the week abbreviations (Sun-Sat)
dddd	Day of the week names (Sunday-Saturday)
y	Years without century (0-99)
yy	Years without century in two digits (00-99)
yyyy	Years with century (0000-9999)
gg	Period/era (ignored if there isn't one)

Other characters are included literally within the format string. For example, to format the `InvoiceDate` attribute of the current `<Invoice>` to be something like `6 June, 02`, you could use:

```
ms:format-date(@InvoiceDate, 'd MMMM, yy')
```

ms:format-time()

Syntax:	*string* ms:format-time(*string1*, *string2*, *string3*?)
Defined in:	MSXML 4
See also:	ms:format-date()

This function formats the date/time string passed as the first argument in the format specified by the second argument, using the locale indicated by the optional third argument (or the locale of the system environment if the third argument isn't specified). The format string can contain the following characters:

541

Appendix A

Character(s)	Description
h	Hours using 12-hour clock (0-12)
hh	Hours using 12-hour clock in two digits (00-12)
H	Hours using 24-hour clock (0-23)
HH	Hours using 24-hour clock in two digits (00-23)
m	Minutes (0-59)
mm	Minutes in two digits (00-59)
s	Seconds (0-59)
ss	Seconds in two digits (00-59)
tt	Insert AM or PM
t	Insert A or P

Other characters are included literally within the format string. For example, to format the `InvoiceDate` attribute of the current `<Invoice>` to be something like `12:00 am` you could use:

```
ms:format-date(@InvoiceDate, 'hh:mm tt')
```

ms:local-name()

Syntax:	*string* ms:local-name(*string*)
Defined in:	MSXML 4
See also:	ms:namespace-uri()

The argument string must be a qualified name; this function then returns the local part of that qualified name (the part after the colon). For example, the following would return `date`:

```
ms:local-name('xsd:date')
```

ms:namespace-uri()

Syntax:	*string* ms:namespace-uri(*string*)
Defined in:	MSXML 4
See also:	ms:local-name()

The argument string must be a qualified name; this function then returns the namespace URI that's associated with the prefix of that qualified name.

For example, if the prefix xsd were associated with the namespace http://www.w3.org/2001/XMLSchema, then the following would return http://www.w3.org/2001/XMLSchema:

```
ms:namespace-uri('xsd:date')
```

ms:node-set()

Syntax:	*node-set* ms:node-set(*result-tree-fragment*)
Defined in:	MSXML 3 and 4

Converts a result tree fragment (created by XSLT) into a node-set so that it can be queried further. This function isn't applicable aside from within XSLT stylesheets.

ms:number()

Syntax:	*number* ms:number(*string*)
Defined in:	MSXML 4
See also:	number()

Converts a string into a number. This function is similar to the number() function and the default method of casting strings to numbers, except that it recognizes scientific notation (exponents) and the special strings INF and -INF as representing infinity and negative infinity. For example, to select those <LineItem> elements that have a unitPrice attribute greater than 0.01 (1e-2), you could use:

```
/Customer/Invoice/LineItem[@unitPrice > ms:number('1e-2')]
```

ms:type-is()

Syntax:	*boolean* ms:type-is(*string1*, *string2*)
Defined in:	MSXML 4
See also:	ms:type-local-name(), ms:type-namespace-uri()

Returns true if the context node is, based on the XML schema used to validate the document, of the type specified by the arguments; the first argument is the namespace URI of the type, and the second argument is the local name of the type. For example, to select only those elements in the document that are of the type string in the namespace http://www.w3.org/2001/XMLSchema (the built-in XML Schema type), you could use:

```
//*[ms:type-is('http://www.w3.org/2001/XMLSchema', 'string')]
```

Appendix A

The `ms:type-is()` function uses the type hierarchy defined in the XML schema, so for example if
`ms:type-is('http://www.w3.org/2001/XMLSchema', 'integer')`
is true, then so is
`ms:type-is('http://www.w3.org/2001/XMLSchema', 'decimal')`
, since `xsd:integer` is derived by restriction from `xsd:decimal`.

ms:type-local-name()

Syntax:	*string* ms:type-local-name(*node-set*?)
Defined in:	MSXML 4
See also:	ms:type-is(), ms:type-namespace-uri()

Returns the local name of the type of the first of the nodes in the node-set passed as the argument, or the context node if no argument is passed. For example, to select all the attributes in the document whose type was `date` in any namespace, you could use:

```
//@*[ms:type-local-name() = 'date']
```

Beware of using `ms:type-local-name()` without also using `ms:type-namespace-uri()`, since without qualifying the local name of a type with a namespace, it can mean selecting nodes with types other than those you're interested in.

ms:type-namespace-uri()

Syntax:	*string* ms:type-namespace-uri(*node-set*?)
Defined in:	MSXML 4
See also:	ms:type-is(), ms:type-local-name()

This returns the namespace URI of the type of the first of the nodes in the node-set passed as the argument, or the context node if no argument is passed. For example, to select all the elements in the document whose data type is an XML Schema built-in type, you could use:

```
//*[ms:type-namespace-uri() =
   'http://www.w3.org/2001/XMLSchema']
```

ms:schema-info-available()

Syntax:	*string* ms:schema-info-available(*node-set*?)
Defined in:	MSXML 4
See also:	ms:type-is(), ms:type-local-name(), ms:type-namespace-uri()

Returns true if there is type and other information available about the context node from validation against a schema. This will only be true if MSXML has used an XML schema to validate the document prior to it being queried by the XPath, and if the schema contains information about the node you're looking at. For example, to select all the attributes in the document that have a numeric type (if schema information is available) or that look like numbers (if schema information is not available), you could use:

```
//@*[(ms:schema-info-available() and
      (ms:type-is('http://www.w3.org/2001/XMLSchema', 'decimal')
or
      ms:type-is('http://www.w3.org/2001/XMLSchema', 'float')
or
      ms:type-is('http://www.w3.org/2001/XMLSchema',
'double'))) or
      (not(ms:schema-info-available()) and
      number() = number())]
```

ms:string-compare()

Syntax:	*number* ms:string-compare(*string1*, *string2*, *string3?*, *string4?*)
Defined in:	MSXML 4
SQL equivalent:	CASE
	WHEN *string1* < *string2* THEN −1
	WHEN *string1* = *string2* THEN 0
	WHEN *string1* > *string2* THEN 1
	END
See also:	ms:type-is(), ms:type-local-name(), ms:type-namespace-uri()

Compares the first and second strings passed as arguments to the function alphabetically, and returns −1 if the first comes before the second alphabetically, 0 if they are equal, or 1 if the first string comes after the second. For example, to select all <Invoice> elements from <Customer> elements where the surname sorts after Levinson, you could use:

```
/Customer[ms:string-compare(substring-after(@Name, ' '),
   'Levinson') = 1]
   /Invoice
```

Since different languages have different sort order and, even within a language, there are different ways of comparing two strings, the third and fourth arguments give finer control over the kind of comparison that gets made. By default, the comparisons are case-sensitive, with lower-case counting as being before upper-case letters, using the language of the system environment on which the XPath is being evaluated.

Appendix A

The third argument can be used to specify the language for the comparisons, while the fourth argument can contain either or both of the characters u and i – a u indicates that upper-case should come before lower-case, while an i indicates that it should be a case-insensitive comparison. For example, the following function call will return 0 since Levinson and LEVINSON are the same in a case-insensitive comparison using English:

```
ms:string-compare('Levinson', 'LEVINSON', 'en', 'i')
```

ms:utc()

Syntax:	*string* ms:utc(*string*)
Defined in:	MSXML 4
See also:	ms:format-date(), ms:format-time()

Converts a date/time string to a format that can be used for comparing or sorting dates. The format is based on the xsd:dateTime format, but hyphens are used in place of any missing information. For example:

```
ms:utc('--05-30')
```

returns the string '-----05-30'.

name()

Syntax:	*string* name(*node-set*?)
See also:	local-name(), namespace-uri()

Returns the full name of the first node in the node-set, including the prefix for its namespace as declared in the source document. If no argument is passed, then it returns the full name of the context node. You shouldn't use this function since it relies on the prefix of the elements in the original document, something that should be ignored by namespace-aware applications. Use the local-name() function (combined with the namespace-uri() function) instead.

namespace-uri()

Syntax:	*string* namespace-uri(*node-set*?)
See also:	local-name(), name()

Returns the namespace URI for the first node in the node-set, or an empty string if the node is not in a namespace. If no argument is passed, then it returns the namespace URI of the context node. For example, to select all the elements in the document that are in the namespace http://www.example.com/order, you could use:

```
//*[namespace-uri() = 'http://www.example.com/order']
```

XPath Reference

normalize-space()

Syntax:	*string* normalize-space(*string*?)
SQL equivalent:	TRIM(*string*) (roughly)
See also:	string()

Returns the argument string with leading and trailing whitespace (including tabs, new lines and carriage returns) stripped, *and* (unlike the TRIM function in SQL) any sequences of whitespace converted to single spaces. If no argument string is specified, then it returns the normalized string value of the context node. For example, to select the <Part> element whose partCode attribute (without the trailing whitespace) is A3834G, you could use:

```
/Customer/Part[normalize-space(@partCode) = 'A3834G']
```

not()

Syntax:	*boolean* not(*boolean*)
SQL equivalent:	NOT *boolean*
See also:	true(), false(), boolean()

Returns false if the argument is true, and true if the argument is false. For example, to select all the <Part> elements that *aren't* grommets, you could use:

```
/Customer/Part[not(contains(., 'grommets'))]
```

number()

Syntax:	*number* number(*object*?)
SQL equivalent:	CONVERT(float(53),*object*)
See also:	string(), boolean(), format-number()

This converts the argument to a number; if no argument is given, returns the numerical value of the context node. You don't usually need to use this function because values are converted to numbers automatically if they need to be numbers, for example for comparison using greater-than or less-than or when involved in arithmetic.

position()

Syntax:	*number* position()
See also:	last(), count()

547

Appendix A

Returns the position of the context node amongst the list of nodes that are currently being looked at: those that are selected from the same context node within a particular step. For example, to get the third <LineItem> within the document, you could use:

```
/Customer/descedant::LineItem[position() >= 3]
```

round()

Syntax:	*number* round(*number*)
SQL equivalent:	round(*number*) (SQL Server extension function)
See also:	floor(), ceiling()

Rounds the argument number to the nearest integer. If the number is exactly between two integers, then it rounds up (the same as `ceiling()`).

starts-with()

Syntax:	*boolean* starts-with(*string1, string2*)
SQL equivalent:	*string1* LIKE '*string2*%'
See also:	contains()

Returns `true` if the first argument string starts with the second argument string, or if the second argument string is empty, and returns `false` otherwise. For example, to select all the <Part> elements representing 1-inch parts, you could use:

```
/Customer/Part[starts-with(., '1-inch')]
```

string()

Syntax:	*string* string(*object*?)
SQL equivalent:	CONVERT(nvarchar(*n*), *object*, *n*)
See also:	boolean(), number()

Converts the argument to a string: if no argument is given, returns the string value of the context node. You don't normally need to use this function because values are converted to strings automatically if they need to be strings. One time when it is useful can be when you want to test whether a node has some (textual) content or not. For example, to select only those <Part> elements that have a description (some textual content) you can use:

```
/Customer/Part[string()]
```

This is equivalent to:

```
/Customer/Part[. != '']
```

string-length()

Syntax:	*number* string-length(*string*?)
SQL equivalent:	CHAR_LENGTH(*string*)
See also:	substring()

This function returns the length of the string passed as the argument. If no argument is passed, then it returns the length of the string value of the context node. For example, to select only those `<LineItem>` elements whose `unitPrice` is a whole number of pence, you can convert the `unitPrice` to a number, create a string from it implicitly (which will strip leading and trailing zeros) and see whether the result has only one character after the decimal point:

```
/Customer/Invoice/LineItem
    [string-length(substring-after(number(@unitPrice), '.')) = 1]
```

substring()

Syntax:	*string* substring(*string, number1, number2*?)
SQL equivalent:	SUBSTRING(*string* FROM *number1* FOR *number2*)
See also:	substring-before(), substring-after()

Returns the substring of the first argument string starting from the number passed as the second argument and a number of characters long equal to the third argument number. If the third argument isn't specified, then it returns the rest of the string, to the last character. The first character in the string is numbered 1. For example, to get the `<Invoice>` elements that were shipped in June, you could test a substring of the `ShipDate` (the 6th and 7th characters in the string), as follows:

```
/Customer/Invoice[substring(@ShipDate, 6, 2) = '06']
```

substring-after()

Syntax:	*string* substring-after(*string1, string2*)

SQL equivalent:	SUBSTRING(*string1*
	    FROM CHARINDEX(*string2, string1*) +
	    CHAR_LENGTH(*string2*))

See also:	substring-before(), substring()

Returns the substring of the first argument string that occurs after the second argument string. If the second string is not contained in the first string (which is always the case if the first string is empty), or if the second string is empty, then it returns an empty string. For example, to select the `<Invoice>` elements related to the `<Customer>` if the customer's surname is `Williams`, you could use:

```
/Customer[substring-after(@Name, ' ') = 'Williams']/Invoice
```

Appendix A

substring-before()

Syntax:	*string* substring-before(*string1*, *string2*)
SQL equivalent:	SUBSTRING(*string1* FROM 1 FOR CHARINDEX(*string2*, *string1*))
See also:	substring-after(), substring()

Returns the substring of the first argument string that occurs before the second argument string. If the second string is not contained in the first string, or if the second string is empty, then it returns an empty string. For example, to locate the LineItems of the <Invoice>s that were invoiced on the 6th of May 2002, you could use:

```
/Customer/Invoice[substring-before(@InvoiceDate, 'T') = '2002-05-06']/LineItem
```

sum()

Syntax:	*number* sum(*node-set*)
SQL equivalent:	SUM(*node-set*)

Returns the sum of the values of the nodes in the node-set. If any of the nodes' values aren't numeric, then this function returns NaN. If the node-set is empty, it returns 0. For example, to select only those <Invoice> elements that involve an order of more than 50 items (whose <LineItem> children's number attributes sum to more than 50), you could use:

```
/Customer/Invoice[sum(LineItem/@number) > 50]
```

> You cannot use the sum() function to add together numbers that are computed for each node, for example to locate those <Invoice> elements whose total (the sum of their child <LineItem>s number attributes multiplied by unitPrice attributes) is more than $25.

system-property()

Syntax:	*object* system-property(*string*)
Defined in:	XSLT 1.0
See also:	element-available(), function-available()

Supplies information about the processor that's being used to evaluate the XPath. The argument string specifies the kind of information that's returned. There are three standard arguments:

- xsl:version – the version of XSLT supported by the processor (usually 1.0 in current XSLT processors)
- xsl:vendor – the name of the vendor of the XSLT processor
- xsl:vendor-url – a URL for the vendor of the XSLT processor

Processors can support their own system properties. For example, MSXML supports the system property msxsl:version which returns the version of MSXML that's being used.

translate()

Syntax:	*string* translate(*string1*, *string2*, *string3*)
SQL equivalent:	TRANSLATE(*string1*, *string2*, *string3*) (not supported in SQL Server)

Returns the first argument string with all occurrences of the characters in the second argument string replaced by their corresponding characters in the third string. If a character in the second string doesn't have a corresponding character in the third string, then the character is deleted from the first string. The translate() function is mostly used to change a string from uppercase to lowercase and vice versa (though it can only be used in this way if there's a one-to-one mapping between lowercase and uppercase characters, which isn't the case for all languages). For example, to identify those <Part> elements whose content includes grommets in any case combination, you could use:

```
/Customer/Part[contains(translate(., 'grommets', 'GROMMETS'),
'GROMMETS')]
```

true()

Syntax:	*boolean* true()
SQL equivalent:	TRUE
See also:	false(), boolean()

Returns true – this is simply a way of getting a true value since there are no boolean literals.

unparsed-entity()

Syntax:	*string* unparsed-entity-uri(*string*)
Defined in:	XSLT 1.0

Returns the URI of the unparsed entity whose name is passed as the argument. Unparsed entities are declared within DTDs as a way of pointing to non-XML files, but they aren't very common nowadays.

Appendix A

XPath 2.0 and XQuery

At time of writing, XPath 2.0 and XQuery 1.0 are under development, with their latest Working Drafts dated 30th April 2002. The two languages have to go through at least three more stages (Final Working Draft, Proposed Recommendation and Candidate Recommendation) before they become Recommendations; this is unlikely to happen before the beginning of 2003. The XPath 2.0 Working Drafts are as follows:

- *XQuery 1.0 and XPath 2.0 Data Model* – describes the underlying data model for XPath 2.0.
  (http://www.w3.org/TR/query-datamodel/)
- *XQuery 1.0 and XPath 2.0 Functions and Operators* – describes how the various functions and operators in XPath 2.0 work.
  (http://www.w3.org/TR/xquery-operators/)
- *XML Path Language (XPath) 2.0* – describes the syntax of XPath 2.0
  (http://www.w3.org/TR/xpath20/)

XQuery 1.0 is a host language for XPath 2.0, but shares a lot of its syntax (rather than adopting an XML-based syntax as XSLT does), so the main Working Draft for XQuery 1.0 is the same as the XPath 2.0 Working Draft, but with some portions amended, added, or removed. The XQuery 1.0 Working Drafts are as follows:

- *XQuery 1.0: An XML Query Language* – describes the syntax of XQuery 1.0
  (http://www.w3.org/TR/xquery/)
- *XML Query Use Cases* – provides a range of use cases for XQuery along with examples showing their solutions in the current syntax
  (http://www.w3.org/TR/xmlquery-use-cases)
- *XQuery 1.0 Formal Semantics* – describes XQuery using formal notation
  (http://www.w3.org/TR/query-semantics/)

This section briefly summarises the changes from XPath 1.0 to XPath 2.0 and the additions that XQuery 1.0 makes to XPath 2.0.

XPath 2.0

The changes from XPath 1.0 to XPath 2.0 fall into three main categories: changes to the data model, additions to the expression language, and additions to the function library.

There are two significant changes to the data model in XPath 2.0.

Firstly, the data types of XPath 2.0 mirror those used in XML Schema, with a few slight changes to make processing easier (XPath 2.0 splits `xsd:duration` into `xf:yearMonthDuration` and `xf:dayTimeDuration`, for example) – the `string` data type becomes `xsd:string`, `boolean` becomes `xsd:boolean` and `number` becomes `xsd:double`. Alongside these changes, any of these data types can be included in a **sequence** – a replacement for the XPath 1.0 node-set, in which items *are* ordered. It is possible in XPath 2.0 to have a sequence containing a `xsd:dateTime` and a `xsd:duration`, for example.

XPath Reference

Secondly, the information available about the nodes in the node tree constructed from an XML document is supplemented by information from a schema (usually an XML schema, although it could come from a DTD or from a schema in another language). Each element and attribute has a **type**, which is simply the (namespace-qualified) name of a data type, and a **typed value**, which is the properly typed value of the node, as well as the normal string value.

The large number of data types available in XPath 2.0 mean that new mechanisms must be found for constructing and casting between the various data types. Strings and numbers can still be constructed through literals; in fact, there are several types of numeric literals for creating `xsd:integers`, `xsd:decimals` and `xsd:doubles`. For other data types, in the current Working Drafts, construction is done through dedicated functions named after the data type, such as:

```
xsd:date('2002-06-06')
```

to construct an `xsd:date` with the value `2002-06-06`, and casting is done through a `cast as` expression such as:

```
cast as xsd:date('2002-06-06')
```

to cast the literal string `'2002-06-06'` to an `xsd:date`. It's anticipated that construction and casting will be revisited in the next Working Drafts, so there may eventually be a unified syntax.

XPath 2.0 isn't just aware of the simple data types like dates and tokens, it also knows about the complex types of elements, as declared in a schema. There are therefore mechanisms for casting to complex types, using `assert as` and `treat as`, which cast elements to different types and enable processors to optimise queries.

Types are fairly significant, so there's also a method of testing whether a particular node or value is of a particular type, using the `instance of` expression. For example:

```
/Customer/Part instance of element of type ord:PartType
```

tests whether the `<Part>` elements in the document are instances of the type named `ord:PartType`. Again, it's likely that the syntax of this expression will change in later Working Drafts.

There are several other new expressions, and changes to existing expressions in XPath 2.0:

- Steps in location paths can be **general steps**, containing any expression as long as it returns a sequence of nodes, which makes it easier to do things like accessing nodes in other documents using the `id()` function.
- Location paths can include **dereferences**, which lead from a node containing a reference, to a node to the node that's being referenced.

Appendix A

- Node identity can be tested using the new operators `is` and `isnot`.
- The relationship of two nodes in terms of their relative document order can be tested using the `<<` and `>>` operators or the `precedes` and `follows` operators (there are slight technical differences between them, and only one of the pairs is likely to be retained in later versions of the Working Draft).
- Sequences can be created by separating the items of the sequence with a comma; sequences of integers can be created with the operator `to`. For example, to create a sequence containing the integers 1 to 5, you could use either `(1, 2, 3, 4, 5)` or `1 to 5`.
- Set manipulation can be carried out with the operators `union` (equivalent to `|`), `intersect` and `except`.
- Conditional expressions are included in XPath 2.0 with the syntax `if (condition) then true-expression else false-expression`.
- Simple iterating expressions are included in XPath 2.0 with the syntax `for $var1 in $expr1, $var2 in $expr2, ... return result`. These form the basis of the FLWR expressions in XQuery.
- You can test explicitly whether all or some of the items in a sequence fulfill some condition using the expressions `every $var in $expr satisfies condition` and `some $var in $expr satisfies condition`.

Added to this range of new expressions are a number of new functions:

- Accessors to information about nodes, such as `node-kind()` to find out what kind of node it is, `data()` to access the node's typed value, and `base-uri()` to work out what document the node came from.
- String functions such as `compare()` for comparing strings alphabetically (similarly to `ms:string-compare()`), `ends-with()` to test whether a string ends with another, `normalize-unicode()` to create a Unicode-normalized version of a string, and `lower-case()` and `upper-case()` to convert a string to lowercase or uppercase.
- Regular expression functions such as `match()` to test whether a string matches a regular expression, and `replace()` to replace parts of a string as identified by a regular expression.
- Date manipulation functions for extracting components from a date, which follow the general pattern of `get-component-from-datatype`, for example `get-hours-from-dateTime()` or `get-year-from-date()`.
- Functions for accessing information from qualified names: `get-namespace-uri()` and `get-local-name()` (similar to `ms:namespace-uri()` and `ms:local-name()`).
- Conditional functions: `if-empty()` and `if-absent()` to quickly supply default values when nodes are missing.
- Sequence manipulation functions, such as `index-of()` for getting the first index of a value in a sequence, `distinct-nodes()` and `distinct-values()` for getting the distinct items of a sequence based on node identity or on value, and `insert()`, `remove()` and `subsequence()` for creating new sequences by inserting, removing, or taking a subsequence of an existing sequence.

XPath Reference

- Aggregation functions, such as `min()`, `max()`, and `avg()` for calculating the minimum, maximum, and average value of the items in a sequence.

XQuery 1.0

XQuery builds on top of XPath 2.0 to create a language suitable for extracting information from a large XML document (probably a virtual one constructed from a database) and creating a new XML document from it. In this way it is similar to XSLT, although it does not use XML syntax and is focused on queries over predictable, data-oriented structures rather than the unpredictable, document-oriented structures to which XSLT is suited.

> Please note: Chapter 17 takes a more in depth look at how we might use XQuery in practice.

XQuery both adds to and removes functionality from XPath. For example, it supports only a subset of the axes defined in XPath, namely:

- `self`
- `child`
- `parent`
- `descendant`
- `descendant-or-self`
- `attribute`

On the other hand, it adds constructors such that the result of an expression can be a *new* sequence of nodes rather than a sequence of nodes from the source document. Mostly, node constructors look exactly like the XML that they generate. For example, to create an `<invoice>` element with a `date` attribute of `2002-07-07`, you could use:

```
<invoice date="2002-07-07">
  ...
</invoice>
```

Both element content and attribute values can be constructed based on evaluating expressions by wrapping the expression in curly braces (`{` and `}`). For example, to create an `<invoice>` element whose `date` attribute had the same date as the context `<Invoice>` element's `InvoiceDate` attribute, you could use:

```
<invoice date="{substring(@InvoiceDate, 1, 10)}">
  ...
</invoice>
```

On occasions when elements or attributes cannot be constructed in this way, for example if the element name has to be decided dynamically or an attribute added only under certain conditions, you can use `element` and `attribute` expressions to create them. For example, to create an `<invoice>` element by using the lowercase version of the context `<Invoice>` element's name, you could use:

Appendix A

```
element {lower-case(name())}
{
   attribute date {substring(@InvoiceDate, 1, 10)}
   ...
}
```

XQuery also adds syntax to the XPath 2.0 `for` expression, allowing you to assign values to arbitrary variables as well as the range variables that are used to identify items from the sequences that are being iterated over, and to filter the set of items that are used with an optional `where` clause which is familiar from SQL's `SELECT` statement. For example, to create a `<subtotal>` element for each `<LineItem>` whose referenced `<Part>` is a grommet, you could use:

```
for     $l in /Customer/Invoice/LineItem,
        let $id := $l/@partIDREF,
        $p in /Customer/Part[@partID = $id]
where   contains($p, 'grommet')
return  <subtotal>
            { $l/@number * $l/@unitPrice }
        </subtotal>
```

The `some` and `every` expressions are also expanded to allow multiple sequences to be tested in parallel.

XQuery allows you to sort sequences using the `sortby` expression, for example to get a sequence of `<Part>` elements sorted by the substring after the space in their description in descending order and then by the substring before the space in ascending order, you could use:

```
/Customer/Part sortby (substring-after(., ' ') descending,
                      substring-before(., ' '))
```

As well as the conditional expression and `instance of` expression from XPath 2.0, XQuery has a `typeswitch` expression, containing `case` clauses, that allows you to perform different actions based on the type of an item.

Finally, as XQueries stand alone rather than being embedded in some other language, XQuery defines mechanisms for declaring namespaces, defining functions and importing schemas so that the types they define can be used within the query.

XPath Reference

Andrew Polshaw

- Namespaces for XML Schema
- XML Schema Elements
- Defining and Constraining Types
- Relationships and Null Fields
- Namespaces
- Importing Schemas
- Documentation
- References

B

XML Schema Reference

Since XML is a language designed for representing structured data, it's vital to have some way of defining the structures and data types permitted in a given XML document. Say we have an **instance document** (containing our XML data) and a **schema** (containing the rules that define how it should be structured). We can test the instance document against the schema, and make sure we're dealing with XML that's valid for our purposes.

XML Schema defines one particular way to express schematic rules for XML, and is rapidly becoming the most widely used type of schema on the Web. In this Appendix, we'll take a look at all its most important features, and see how they can be put to use.

Namespaces for XML Schema

Namespaces can be used to distinguish different kinds of data within a single document. Each element in an XML schema document will ultimately be used by a validating parser, telling it what the targeted instance document ought to contain. XML Schema is divided into three namespaces, corresponding to the different purposes of each element or attribute being specified:

- http://www.w3.org/2001/XMLSchema is the most important namespace, defining the **structure** of an XML document and the **data types** it contains. Most of the entries in this Appendix deal with elements and attributes from this namespace.

- http://www.w3.org/2001/XMLSchema-datatypes is a subset of the first namespace, and contains the **defined data types** that can be used with XML Schema. Separating them from structure allows other XML standards (such as XSLT 2.0 and XQuery) to use the same types.

Appendix B

- `http://www.w3c.org/2001/XMLSchema-instance` allows you to specify the **schema location** from the XML instance document.

Remember that these namespaces are just labels, so that an XML parser knows what an instance document's vocabulary relates to – they don't have to be resolvable URLs.

XML Schema Elements

In this section, we'll go through each of the elements within the XML Schema namespace and look at what they do. The `xsd:` namespace prefix applies to all these elements, as specified by the XML Schema Recommendation.

Global Attributes

First, we'll look at the attributes that can be applied to any element within an XML Schema:

Attribute	Possible Values	Description
`id`	Any `xs:ID` type value. Values may not include whitespace or start with a number or punctuation.	Uniquely identifies any element within an XML Schema. Equivalent to the XML DTD `ID` attribute type. You can read a complete definition of this attribute at http://www.w3.org/TR/2001/REC-xmlschema-2-20010502/#ID.
`xml:lang`	Any locale specifier. Takes the form `xx-YY`, where `xx` is a language (for example, `en` for English, `fr` for French) and `YY` a region (`GB` for Great Britain, `US` for the US, and so on).	Specifies a locale (language and region) for the contents of the element. Can be used on any XML node.

<xsd:schema>

The `<xsd:schema>` element serves as the root of any schema document. Its attributes let you define various global settings determining how the schema will be parsed, and therefore control how the instance document will be validated:

Attribute	Possible Values	Description
targetNamespace	Any URI.	Specifies the namespace of the XML instance document you wish to validate. The instance document must contain a matching namespace declaration.
version	Any `token` data type. Normally takes the form of a period-separated number. Cannot include leading or trailing whitespace.	Used to pass a version number of the schema to the reader or XML parser. Equivalent to the XML DTD NMTOKENS attribute type.
elementFormDefault	qualified, unqualified (**default**)	Specified a default value for the `form` attribute (controlling namespace qualification) on element declarations. Covered further in *Namespaces* section.
attributeFormDefault	qualified, unqualified (**default**)	Supplies a default value for the `form` attribute (controlling namespace qualification) on attribute declarations. Covered further in *Namespaces* section.
blockDefault		See Defining and Constraining types.
finalDefault		See Defining and Constraining types.

Appendix B

Everything defined as an immediate child is declared globally. This means that any element declared globally could be the root node of this namespace. However, this isn't really a problem as normally it would make little sense for someone to start an instance document with a different root node, and there is only a requirement for one globally declared element.

A schema file would, therefore, look something like this:

```
<?xml version="1.0" encoding="utf-8"?>
<xsd:schema xmlns:xsd=http://www.w3.org/2001/XMLSchema
            xmlns:test=http://my.schema/version1
            version="1.0"
            targetNamespace="http://my.schema/version1">
    <xsd:element name="rootNode" type="test:contentType" />
    ...
</xsd:schema>
```

> Note that all `<xsd:*>` elements may contain `ID` attributes

`<xsd:element>`

This is used to declare elements that are allowed inside the instance document, along with their respective types.

Below, you can see the various attributes of this element.

The first word in the **Possible Values** column represents an XML Schema data type. If necessary, a fuller description is provided underneath:

Attribute	Possible Values	Description
default	string	If the element does not appear with any content in the instance document, then the value specified here is substituted instead. This is equivalent to the DEFAULT SQL keyword in a CREATE TABLE declaration, where the element is congruous with a column in a table.
fixed	string	Specifies that the contents of this element in the instance document must always be equal to the value specified by this attribute.

562

XML Schema Reference

Attribute	Possible Values	Description
maxOccurs	nonNegativeInteger or unbounded. If attribute omitted, then defaults to 1.	This attribute defines how often this element can occur in its current context/location. It may make sense to repeat elements of the same name one after the other with different contents. If unbounded is specified, then the element can be repeated indefinitely; there is no limit to the number of elements that may occur.
minOccurs	nonNegativeInteger If attribute omitted, then it defaults to 1. 0 is a permitted value for this data type.	This attribute defines the minimum number of times the specified element may appear in the instance document. minOccurs must always be less than or equal to maxOccurs, and vice versa.
name	NCNAME An acceptable name for an XML element, as defined in the XML Recommendation. An NCName type is a non-namespace qualified name; any name permitted for an attribute or element.	This specifies the name of the element being defined here. It must follow the standard rules for XML element names, as defined in the XML 1.0 Recommendation.
nillable	boolean If omitted, defaults to false.	If this attribute is set to true, then the element can be declared NULL. You have to specifically allow NULL values to be able to use them.

Table continued on following page

Appendix B

Attribute	Possible Values	Description
ref	QNAME The namespace qualified name (if qualified) of a globally defined element.	If an element declaration is likely to be used repeatedly throughout a document, then you can declare it as an immediate child of an `<xsd:schema>` element, and refer to it elsewhere in the document. The value of the `ref` attribute points to the `name` attribute of the element to be referenced. This saves entering multiple identical declarations.
substitutionGroup	QNAME	Whenever the element specified by a qualified name in this attribute occurs in the instance document, this and any other element with the same `substitutionGroup` element may be substituted for it instead.
type	QNAME	This specifies the type of the content of this element. Its value can either be one of the data types as already seen, such as `xsd:string` or `xsd:QNAME`, or it can be a user-defined type. If you omit this attribute, then you must define its type by giving this element some content defined in child elements.

Some attributes are missing – `block`, `final`, and `form`. They will be defined later, but first we need to explain substitution.

XML Schema Reference

Anything declared as an immediate child of the `<xsd:schema>` element is declared as global. Being global means it can be referred to anywhere else in the schema document, or even from other documents. A globally declared element or attribute is not specified as a child of another element. This means it can be used anywhere or, more importantly, it can be the root node of an XML document. By convention, you would normally stick the element you intend to be the root node at the beginning or end of the other declarations.

If you have more than one global element in the schema, then any of these elements can be the root node for this namespace and be correctly validated. However, normally only one of these elements is the entry point to the rest of the elements and attributes defined in this schema. This ties in with substitutions. A global element can be inserted anywhere inside any document through use of the `ref` attribute. An example of this is shown below:

```
<xsd:schema xmlns:xsd="http://www.w3.org/2001/XMLSchema">
   <xsd:element name="houseNumber" type="xsd:string" />
   <xsd:element name="street" type="xsd:string" />
   <xsd:element name="town" type="xsd:string" />
   <xsd:element name="zipCode" type="xsd:string" />

   <xsd:element name="Customers">
     <xsd:complexType>
       <xsd:sequence maxOccurs="unbounded">
         <xsd:element name="customer">
           <xsd:complexType>
             <xsd:attribute name="name" type="xsd:string" />
             <xsd:sequence>
                <xsd:element ref="houseNumber" />
                <xsd:element ref="street" />
                <xsd:element ref="town" />
                <xsd:element ref="zipCode" />
             </xsd:sequence>
           </xsd:complexType>
         </xsd:element>
       </xsd:sequence>
     </xsd:complexType>
   </xsd:element>
</xsd:schema>
```

A number of elements in this document haven't been seen yet; however, they are needed to illustrate how substitution works. Normally, the global elements would be much more complex than these if you were going to refer to them through substitution. This schema would validate against an instance document that looked like the following:

```
<Customers>
  <customer name="John Doe">
    <houseNumber>44</houseNumber>
    <street>Electric Avenue</street>
    <town>SpringField</town>
    <zipCode>CA 54554</zipCode>
  </customer>
  <customer>
    ...
  </customer>
</Customers>
```

Appendix B

It would also validate against a document that contained nothing but:

```xml
<houseNumber>44</houseNumber>
```

There is also something else to consider here. If you use a global element in an instance document and the schema has a target namespace, then every global element has to be namespace-qualified. So, say there was a `targetNamespace` attribute with a value of `"http://www.wrox.com/testSubstitution"`, and this namespace was given the prefix `ws:`, then the instance document would need to look like the following instead:

```xml
<Customers xmlns="http://www.wrox.com/testSubstitution"
           xmlns:ws="http://www.wrox.com/testSubstitution">
   <customer name="John Doe">
     <ws:houseNumber>44</ws:houseNumber>
     <ws:street>Electric Avenue</ws:street>
     <ws:town>Springfield</ws:town>
     <ws:zipCode>CA 54554</ws:zipCode>
   </customer>
</Customers>
```

Even though a default namespace has been applied here, each additional global element has to be explicitly qualified. This is a feature explicitly built into the substitution process, so that there can be no confusion as to where the element is from. Remember that each global element can be a root node, so it should be namespace-qualified to make it explicit.

If you use the `substitutionGroup` attribute, then every other element with the same value on their `substitutionGroup` attribute can be used instead of the one referred to. This allows you to group similar elements together. Much of the finer details of this process will be discussed throughout this chapter, but one fact to come away with is that it is generally preferable to define content of an element in a type rather than reuse elements through substitution, just specify the correct type for each element.

<xsd:group>

This element allows you to group elements together so they can be reused elsewhere in the document. Your instance document may allow a set of elements to appear in multiple locations. You can use this element to avoid repeatedly entering these element declarations. The elements must appear inside an `<xsd:sequence>` element, which means the elements must appear in the same order in the instance document as they appear in the schema or an intended `<xsd:choice>` element. This indicates that only one of the elements may appear. The attributes are as follows:

XML Schema Reference

Attribute	Possible Values	Description
name	NCName Any name permissible for elements and attributes.	This names the group so it can be referred to elsewhere in the schema. It must be a unique name in the schema.
ref	QName A namespace-qualified NCName.	This points to a previously declared `<xsd:group>` element. The previous group will either be part of the null namespace, or be namespace qualified. If qualified, then the name must be prefixed with the prefix for that namespace.
minOccurs	nonNegativeInteger Must be less than or equal to the value of maxOccurs. Default is 1.	This sequence or choice of elements must appear more than once if set higher than 1. When set to 0, appearance is optional.
maxOccurs	nonNegativeInteger Must be greater than or equal to the value of minOccurs. It can take a value of unbounded to indicate that there is no limit on the number of times this set of elements repeats. Default is 1.	When set to something other than 1, then sequence or choice of elements may appear as many times as specified by this attribute. If the value is set to unbounded, then it can appear as many times as the XML instance document writer wishes.

This element can be very useful if you are constantly repeating such things as address fields, or employee details, or any number of other patterns. An example of its use is shown below:

```
<xsd:group name="addressDetails">
  <xsd:sequence>
    <xsd:element name="houseNumber" type="xsd:string" />
    <xsd:element name="street" type="xsd:string" />
    <xsd:element name="town" type="xsd:string" />
    <xsd:element name="state" type="xsd:string" />
    <xsd:element name="zip" type="xsd:string" />
  </xsd:sequence>
</xsd:group>
```

This sequence could be referred to elsewhere in the schema document by entering this line in the location where you want this sequence to appear:

```
<xsd:group ref="addressDetails" />
```

Appendix B

If the schema were tied to a specific target namespace, then you would have to stick the relevant namespace prefix before `addressDetails`. The `<xsd:group>` element must be declared globally to be used anywhere in the document, and if it referred to elements via reference (substitution), then the elements must be global, or present in the same context as the group (the same type).

It is rarely if ever preferable to place the `<xsd:group>` element anywhere but as an immediate child of the `<xsd:schema>` element. Also, if your data is normalized, as it usually is if part of a database, then it is unlikely you will ever use this element. This is because you don't want repetition in your normalized XML document, and the `<xsd:group>` element (and `<xsd:attributeGroup>` element, which we'll see later) is a shorthand for introducing repeating elements into your document. It is preferable to have a separate table containing addresses and other repeated items in your database and refer to the relevant data via a foreign key. This mechanism is possible in XML Schema too, which we'll see in the *Relationships and Null Fields* section below.

<xsd:attribute>

Attributes can be declared globally, as with elements, but they are often defined inside `<xsd:complexType>` definitions. The various attributes of the `<xsd:attribute>` element, used to declare the presence of attributes, are shown below:

Attribute	Possible Values	Description
id	ID	Same as for `<xsd:schema>`.
default	string	If the attribute is not present in an instance document, then the parser gives the attribute the value contained here.
fixed	string	Specifies that the attribute must always be the same as the value specified here.
name	NCName	The name is specified here. Attributes follow the same naming convention as elements.
ref	QName	As with element, you can point to a globally declared attribute here, and you must namespace qualify it.
type	QName	As with element, this allows you to specify the type of the attribute. Remember that attribute content can only be simple; attributes cannot contain elements or other attributes.

XML Schema Reference

Attribute	Possible Values	Description
use	One of `optional` (default), or `prohibited`, or `required`	By default, an attribute does not have to appear on an element. However, you can change this. Choosing `required` means that this attribute must always be present in the instance document (although you can use the `default` attribute to work around this). The `prohibited` value, however, states that this attribute must not appear on this element. This can be useful when redefining types, which is explained in *xsd:redefine* later.

Like `<xsd:element>` declarations, `<xsd:attribute>` elements can occur either globally, as immediate children of `<xsd:schema>`, or inside `<xsd:complexType>` definitions. `<xsd:attribute>` declarations appear as immediate children of the `<xsd:complexType>` element.

`<xsd:attributeGroup>`

If you want to group a set of attributes together, because often elements will have similar attributes, you can do so using the `<xsd:attributeGroup>` element. This can be referred to from the inside of an `<xsd:complexType>` element. The `name` and the `ref` attributes shown below are mutually exclusive:

Attribute	Possible Values	Description
id	ID	Same as for `<xsd:schema>`
name	NCName a non-namespace qualified name.	This names the attribute group so it can be referred to from an `<xsd:complexType>` element. An attribute group definition (`<xsd:attributeGroup>` with the `name` attribute) must occur as an immediate child of the `<xsd:schema>` element.
ref	QName a namespace qualified name.	This attribute is used when `<xsd:attributeGroup>` occurs inside a complex type. It cannot be used if the `name` attribute is being used.

569

Appendix B

An `<xsd:attributeGroup>` definition would be used like this:

```
<xsd:schema xmlns:xs="http://www.w3.org/2001/XMLSchema">
  <xsd:element name="showGroups">
    <xsd:complexType>
      <xsd:any>
        <xsd:element name="person1">
          <xsd:complexType>
            <xsd:attributeGroup ref="commonAttributes" />
          </xsd:complexType>
        </xsd:element>
        <xsd:element name="person2">
          <xsd:complexType>
            <xsd:attributeGroup ref="commonAttributes" />
          </xsd:complexType>
        </xsd:element>
      </xsd:any>
    </xsd:complexType>
  </xsd:element>
  <xsd:attributeGroup name="commonAttributes">
    <xsd:attribute name="name" type="xsd:string" />
    <xsd:attribute name="role" type="xsd:string" />
    <xsd:attribute name="age" type="xsd:nonNegativeInteger" />
  </xsd:attributeGroup>
</xsd:schema>
```

Defining and Constraining Types

In the previous sections, the types have been described inside the elements. However, this doesn't have to be the case. We can define them separately if we wish, and it often makes sense to do so. This can be related to how you define data types in SQL Server. You would declare a new type by executing an `EXEC sp_addtype` statement; which would be separate from a `CREATE TABLE`, or other statement. This allows for the separation of types from content, which allows reuse. This separation of types from content is also a feature of object-oriented programming, and many XML Schema features can be related to features such as **inheritance** and **polymorphism**. The point is, if you go to the effort of creating a new type, you don't want to have to create it every time you wish to use it. By defining a type separately from the structures it appears in, you can use it anywhere by just referring to it by name.

So far we have neglected to define two attributes used in `<xsd:element>` and `<xsd:attribute>` declarations: `block` and `final`. These attributes can also be used when defining types, so they will be explained here. The attributes are shown opposite:

XML Schema Reference

Attribute	Possible Values	Description
`block`	`#all`, list of `extension`, `restriction`, `substitution`	In the XML instance document, you can use the XML Schema instance namespace attribute (`xsi:type`) to make use of a different type, which derives from the type that should be used in the instance document. Applying this attribute on an element declaration prevents this from occurring. Using the `substitution` value prevents a type being replaced by substitution. This attribute only occurs on `<xsd:element>` declarations.
`final`	`#all`, or one or more of `extension`, `restriction`, and `union` (`union` replaces `extension` on an `<xsd:simpleType>` element).	If used on an `<xsd:element>` or `<xsd:attribute>` element, it prevents a type from extending or restricting another type by referring to this element or attribute by substitution. If used on a complex type, it prevents a type deriving from this type by extension or restriction. If defined on a simple type, it prevents a type deriving from this type by restriction or union.

These attributes are invaluable for ensuring certain validity constraints in your XML document. There are also two attributes on the `<xsd:schema>` element that specify defaults for these values when they are not present:

Attribute	Possible Values	Description
`blockDefault`	`#all` or list of `extension`, `restriction`, `substitution`	When a `block` attribute is absent from an element declaration, then this attribute defines its default value. This allows you to set a schema-wide policy on what kinds of derivations should be blocked. In other words, when this attribute is present, the XML parser will add a block attribute to any element declaration that does not already contain one, and give it the value specified here.
`finalDefault`	`#all` or list of `extension`, `restriction`	This sets the default of the `final` attribute on all occurrences of an element or attribute declaration.

Appendix B

We need to describe how to define types and we'll start with the `<xsd:simpleType>` element.

`<xsd:simpleType>`

A simple type is a value type with no attributes or elements. Attributes always contain simple content, and element content may be restricted similarly. A simple type can be thought of like data types present in the columns of tables. All data types, such as `varchar` and `numeric`, can be mapped to a simple type. The attributes of this element are discussed below:

Attribute	Possible Values	Description
id	ID	As for `<xsd:schema>` above.
name	NCName	This defines the name of the simple type and when this attribute appears, the element must be a direct child of the `<xsd:schema>` element.

Omitted from this table is the `final` attribute, which was explained at the start of this section. This attribute may contain one additional value different from the other cases we have seen, and this is `union`. This only makes sense when you look at the ways you can extend and restrict types; a simple type may be constrained by `<xsd:restriction>` or `<xsd:union>` only.

`<xsd:union>`

A union is defined as a union of different data types, or increasing the *value space* of a possible type to include the value spaces of all types referenced by `<xsd:union>`. Its attributes are shown below:

Attribute	Possible Values	Description
id	ID	As for `<xsd:schema>` above.
memberTypes	List of QNames A whitespace separated list of simple types.	This element appears as a direct child of the `<xsd:simpleType>` element, and the value space of the type contains the value types of all those specified in the list. Optional.

The simple types that form part of the union may be XML Schema types, or they may be types defined in the schema. They have to be namespace-qualified and the `memberTypes` attribute is required.

XML Schema Reference

<xsd:restriction>

This element restricts a type. Its attributes are shown below:

Attribute	Possible Values	Description
id	ID	As for <xsd:schema> above.
base	QName A namespace qualified type.	This restricts a type that already exists, either as an XML Schema type, or as a type defined in the schema. Required.

A complex type can be restricted to make it a simple type, but not the other way round. However, it would generally be easier just to redefine the complex type, as you see in the next section. It is the restriction of simple types that is really useful. You can restrict a simple (value) type to any degree so that it can contain only valid postal codes, telephone numbers, IP addresses, or any other kind of data. The <xsd:simpleType> attribute defines simple types and is shown next.

<xsd:complexType>

This defines types containing the elements or attributes we've seen so far. It also has other attributes you haven't seen yet:

Attribute	Possible Values	Description
id	ID	The same as for <xsd:schema>.
abstract	boolean The default is false.	This defines a type that cannot be used directly. It can only be extended or restricted, which is shown in the *Redefining Types* section. This can be considered similar to abstract types in object-oriented programming languages.
mixed	boolean The default is false.	XML languages like XHTML require that the content be mixed. In this case, the content may contain text that is mixed up with the elements specified in this type. You see this in use whenever you see HTML inside a <BODY> tag. The text mixed in with the elements has no restriction on its content or length, and there is no way to place restrictions on this content in the current version of XML Schema.
name	NCName	Here is where the complex type can be named. Named complex types must be immediate children of <xsd:schema>. These types are referred to from within the type attributes of <xsd:element> and <xsd:attribute> declarations.

573

As with `<xsd:element>` and `<xsd:attribute>`, this element may also contain a `final` or `block` attribute. Now you will see how to define these complex types. Note that `<xsd:restriction>` can be used to restrict a complex type in the same way as with a simple type.

`<xsd:extension>`

When this is a child of a complex type, it allows you to insert additional content to a predefined or XML Schema data type. Its one attribute is shown below. Like all other schema elements, it can contain an `ID` attribute as well:

Attribute	Possible Values	Description
`id`	ID	As for `<xsd:schema>`, above.
`base`	QName A namespace qualified type.	This element extends a type that already exists, either as an XML Schema type, or as a type defined in the schema. Required.

The main thing you have to be certain of is that the type defined is relevant to the `<xsd:extension>`'s parent element. In addition, both `<xsd:extension>` and `<xsd:restriction>` need to be present inside `<xsd:simpleContent>` or `<xsd:complexContent>` elements. You'll see those in the next section. The various additional schema elements that help extend a type are shown later.

`<xsd:complexContent>` and `<xsd:simpleContent>`

When you are defining complex types, the `<xsd:extension>` or `<xsd:restriction>` elements are normally wrapped in either an `<xsd:complexContent>` or an `<xsd:simpleContent>` element. This is for clarity, and helps solve some ambiguous definitions that may occur. Complex content contains any number of attributes and elements, whereas simple content contains neither. Both may contain an `ID` attribute and an `<xsd:complexContent>` element may additionally contain a `mixed` attribute, which has the same function as that on the `<xsd:complexType>` element, allowing text content to be interspersed with elements.

This is about good design practice. When extending or restricting a complex type, you must wrap the `<xsd:extension>` or `<xsd:restriction>` element in an `<xsd:complexContent>`. When extending a simple type to make it the whole or part of a new complex type, the `<xsd:extension>` element used to make it a new complex type should be wrapped in an `<xsd:simpleContent>` element.

To see this in action, an example of using `<xsd:extension>` and `<xsd:complexContent>` is shown below:

```
<xsd:schema xmlns:xsd="http://www.w3.org/2001/XMLSchema">
    <xsd:element name="Employees">
        <xsd:complexType>
            <xsd:sequence>
```

XML Schema Reference

```xml
      <xsd:element name="manager"
                   maxOccurs="unbounded"
                   type="managerType" />
    </xsd:sequence>
  </xsd:complexType>
</xsd:element>

<xsd:complexType name="employeeType">
  <xsd:simpleContent>
    <xsd:extension base="nameType">
      <xsd:attribute name="name"
                     type="xsd:string"
                     use="required" />
      <xsd:attribute name="ID" type="xsd:ID" />
    </xsd:extension>
  </xsd:simpleContent>
</xsd:complexType>

<xsd:simpleType name="nameType">
  <xsd:restriction base="xsd:string">
    <xsd:maxLength="50" />
  </xsd:restriction>
</xsd:simpleType>

<xsd:complexType name="managerType">
  <xsd:complexContent>
    <xsd:extension base="employeeType">
      <xsd:attribute name="managesOver" type="xsd:string" />
    </xsd:extension>
  </xsd:complexContent>
</xsd:complexType>
</xsd:schema>
```

You can see here how the `<xsd:extension>` elements are extending a complex type by adding attributes. We haven't explained the `<xsd:sequence>` or `<xsd:maxLength>` elements yet. These are explained in the next two sections.

Simple Type Restrictions

You will now see the various elements that can restrict simple types. These allow you to create new simple types of any kind. An enumeration of values is one possible derived type, or a numeric value restricted to or extended by limits other than those already present in the XML Schema Recommendation.

`<xsd:enumeration>`

An enumeration is a number of `<xsd:enumeration>` elements that each specify a possible value. Any attribute or element that implements this type can only contain those values described, and no others. Its attribute is shown below, and it can additionally contain an ID attribute:

575

Appendix B

Attribute	Possible Values	Description
id	ID	As with every other XML Schema element.
value	anySimpleType Anything that can be legally entered into an XML attribute can be entered here.	You will normally place an enumeration inside an `<xsd:restriction>` or `<xsd:extension>` element. If `<xsd:restriction>` is used, then each value entered must be of the type specified in the base attribute of the `<xsd:restriction>` element. If used inside `<xsd:extension>`, then as well as all the possible values of the base type, the values specified in each `<xsd:enumeration>` element may also be present.

The easiest way to show how this works is with an example. Below is an extract of a schema that defines two enumerations:

```
<xsd:simpleType name="payScale">
   <xsd:restriction base="xsd:integer">
      <xsd:enumeration value="1" />
      <xsd:enumeration value="2" />
      <xsd:enumeration value="3" />
   </xsd:restriction>
</xsd:simpleType>

<xsd:simpleType name="age">
   <xsd:extension base="xsd:nonNegativeInteger">
      <xsd:enumeration value="Unknown" />
   </xsd:extension>
</xsd:simpleType>
```

An element or attribute that uses the `payScale` type can only contain the values 1, 2, or 3. One that uses the `age` type must contain any non-negative integer, or the text value `Unknown`.

`<xsd:list>`

A list is a whitespace-separated sequence of words, which may be text (`<xsd:string>`), numbers (`<xsd:integer>`, `<xsd:decimal>`, etc.), or any other simple data type. You can also use derived simple types, like those defined above. We could define a list of ages or pay scales using these types.

XML Schema Reference

Apart from the `ID` attribute, this element has only one attribute:

Attribute	Possible Values	Description
`itemType`	QName A pre-existing data type that of which all members of the list must be a member of	This simple type defines a whitespace-separated list of values, each value being of the type specified in this attribute. You can use a built-in XML Schema type (such as `xsd:string`) or a type defined in the schema. The type must be a simple type – you cannot have lists of elements or attributes.

Unlike the `<xsd:enumeration>` element, which declares that the element or attribute with this type must have one of the contained values, the `<xsd:list>` element declares that the element or attribute must contain a whitespace-separated list of values.

This element does not need to appear inside an `<xsd:restriction>` or `<xsd:element>`, and can be a direct child of an `<xsd:simpleType>` element.

`<xsd:length>`

This is a constraining facet on a data type and, when used inside an `<xsd:restriction>` or `<xsd:list>` type, defines the length of the simple type. It can be used to define the exact number of digits used in a type (useful for credit card numbers, for example). Other than `ID`, it has two attributes shown below:

Attribute	Possible Values	Description
`value`	nonNegativeInteger or unbounded	This specifies the exact length of the type. If this is a child of the `<xsd:list>` element, then it specifies the number of items the list must contain. If it is a child of `<xsd:restriction>`, then it specifies exactly how many characters data of this type should contain.
`fixed`	boolean default `false`	When set to `true`, this fixes the length at the specified `value`, so that any type that derives from this via restriction or union must also be of this length.

577

Appendix B

<xsd:minLength> and <xsd:maxLength>

These elements are related to `<xsd:length>`. Rather than being specific, however, thy specify the minimum and maximum length of a type. By default, the minimum length of a simple type is 0, and maximum length is unbounded. Like all schema elements, these elements may contain `ID` attributes.

Attribute	Possible Values	Description
value	nonNegativeInteger or unbounded	Here you specify the minimum or maximum number of characters a type can contain, or the minimum and maximum number of values in a list type. Required.
fixed	boolean default false	When set to `true`, this fixes the minimum or maximum length at the specified `value`, so that any type that derives from this type must have the same restrictions. Optional.

<xsd:totalDigits> and <xsd:fractionDigits>

These elements only apply to numeric types and they define the length of the whole and fractional components. `<xsd:totalDigits>` specifies the maximum number of digits that can be used in the type, whereas the `<xsd:fractionDigits>` specifies the maximum number of decimal places. Contrary to what might be expected, `<xsd:totalDigits>` does not specify only the whole number part of a number. If a type is said to have 3 total digits, and 1 fraction digit, then values like `1`, `1.9`, `23`, and `45.9` are permitted, but not `103`:

Attribute	Possible Values	Description
value	nonNegativeInteger or unbounded	The total number of digits the number can contain, including fractional digits if this is used on the `<xsd:totalDigits>` element, and the degree of accuracy used if applied on the `<xsd:fractionDigits>` element. Required.
fixed	boolean	When set to `true`, this fixes the total or fractional digits at the specified `value`, so that any type that derives from this type must have the same restrictions. Optional.

XML Schema Reference

<xsd:minInclusive>, <xsd:maxInclusive>, <xsd:minExclusive>, and <xsd:maxExclusive>

When applied to a numeric data type (normally within an `<xsd:restriction>` element, these elements allow you to restrict minimum and maximum range of possible values. These elements have identical attributes to `<xsd:minLength>` and `<xsd:maxLength>`. Here, `<xsd:minInclusive>` and `<xsd:maxInclusive>` specify an **inclusive range** (so the type may also contain the values specified in the `value` attributes), and `<xsd:minExclusive>` and `<xsd:maxInclusive>` specify an **exclusive range** (so the type may not contain the values specified in the `value` attributes).

<xsd:pattern>

This allows you to use a regular expression to define precisely the possible content of a data type. Regular expressions are a way of describing a pattern in data. They have an arcane language, but if you are familiar with Perl regular expressions, then with an XML schema, you already know how to constrain a data type in a much more flexible way than you can using the various XML Schema elements. Other than `ID`, this has only one (required) attribute, shown below:

Attribute	Possible Values	Description
value	An XML Regular Expression.	This contains the regular expression that defines the pattern of the content that is permissible for this data type. Any simple data type can be rewritten as a regular expression because they are very powerful. However, the syntax is very obscure and, unless you are already familiar with it, it is impossible to deduce the pattern it is describing.

The regular expressions that can be used differ from those used by Perl, but other than the differences detailed below, they are identical in every way.

> You can read more about Perl regular expressions at
> http://www.english.uga.edu/humcomp/perl/regex2a.html.

- ❏ XML Schema regular expressions match Unicode, and so are not restricted to those characters in the ASCII set, unlike those used by Perl.
- ❏ ^ is a negation operator in XML Schema regular expressions. In Perl, this character attaches the pattern to the beginning of the text. Patterns specified in an `<xsd:pattern>` element always match the entire text. This also means the $ character, which attaches a pattern to the end of some text in Perl, has no special meaning in XML Schema regular expressions.

579

Appendix B

- XML Schema specifies hexadecimal character references in the same way XML character references are used, rather than \xnn as used by Perl regular expressions. To specify the space character using a character reference, for instance, you would use &#20; instead of \x20. XML Schema has no mechanism for specifying character references in octal.
- \c matches a character that can be used as an XML name; an NCName character.
- \i matches a character that is permitted as the first character of an XML name; a character that can be the first in an NCName type. This is a subset of \c.
- Zero-width assertions, look aheads and look behinds, back references, and non-greedy wildcard operators are not available in XML Schema regular expressions.

We don't have space to explain regular expressions to those who aren't already familiar with them, but an example of a regular expression would be:

```
<xsd:pattern value="(\w+@\w+\.)+[a-zA-Z]{2,5}" />
```

This is an e-mail address pattern that states that there can be one or more letters, numbers, or underscore characters, in any combination, followed by an @ symbol, followed period separated words, ending with between two and five letters. Unless you are familiar, the language is very obscure. If you have the time and inclination to learn this language, however, you will find that you can exactly specify any kind of textual data.

<xsd:whiteSpace>

This element is different from the constraining elements, or facets, shown previously; it specifies what will happen to any whitespace that is present in the XML content passed to the parser to validate against the type this element defines. This can be invaluable for numeric types and those being validated using regular expressions. This element contains one attribute, value, with one of the three following values:

- preserve – This is the default and means the usual XML whitespace collapsing rules apply.
- collapse – When this value is used, all whitespace is replaced with space characters and collapsed in size so that no more than one space character occurs at once. In addition, whitespace at the beginning and the end of the content is removed.
- replace – This instruction just replaces the all whitespace characters with space characters; useful for content that should appear in an attribute.

This facet is used for normalizing the data types. This should not be an issue when retrieving XML data from SQL Server, as the data should be normalized anyway.

XML Schema Reference

<xsd:notation>

This, like the previous element, is different from the usual constraining elements on simple types. In fact, this is often used when defining a complex type. What this does is define a notation for an encoding type specified in ISO 8879. This encoding is the kind used for MIME types in e-mail and on the Web. For example: `text/xml`, `image/jpeg`, `movie/mpeg`, `text/html`. With the first and last encodings, the data can appear as is. With the middle two, the binary data contained in the image or movie has to be encoded using a text-based encoding so that it can be present inside the XML file. This is normally a `Base64` encoding. This would be a good way to store BLOB data in your XML file. The `<xsd:notation>` element can be used as a shorthand to the MIME encoding.

The best way to show how this works is to see it in use. First, here are its attributes:

Attribute	Possible Values	Description
name	NCName Required.	When this name occurs in an attribute in the instance document, the parser knows to refer to this named `xsd:notation` element to see how to deal with this kind of data.
public	string This has to be one of the identifiers present in ISO8879. These follow the format: `image/jpeg`. Required.	This contains the MIME type specified in ISO 8879 so that the parser knows how to deal with data of this kind. Normally, the data would be `Base64` encoded and then placed inside an element with an attribute set to the value contained in name.
system	anyURI This is a path to an application used by the system to view this kind of file. Normally you just enter the name of the executable file and the operating system finds it: e.g. `notepad.exe`. Optional.	This is the path to the application that can deal with this kind of application. This would be used by the application/parser to correctly deal with the data.

`<xsd:notation>` always appears as an immediate child of `<xsd:schema>`, although the data it relates to can appear anywhere. Look at the following example:

581

Appendix B

```xml
<xsd:schema xmlns:xsd="http://www.w3.org/2001/XMLSchema">
  <xsd:notation name="jpeg"
                public="image/jpeg"
                system="iexplore.exe" />
  <xsd:element name="photo">
    <xsd:complexType>
      <xsd:simpleContent>
        <xsd:extension base="xsd:hexBinary">
          <xsd:attribute name="picType">
            <xsd:simpleType>
              <xsd:restriction base="xsd:NOTATION">
                <xsd:enumeration="jpeg" />
                ...
              </xsd:restriction>
            </xsd:simpleType>
          </xsd:attribute>
        </xsd:extension>
      </xsd:simpleContent>
    </xsd:complexType>
  </xsd:element>
```

In an instance document, you could have an element that looks like this:

```xml
<photo picType="jpeg"> ... </photo>
```

Inside this element would be a stream of Base64 encoded (xsd:hexBinary) content. This can then be decoded and viewed in Internet Explorer by the application. Photos of employees could be stored and retrieved as XML in this way.

The xsd:NOTATION type is that which relates to the use of the <xsd:notation> element. In this example, we just allow the "jpeg" value.

Complex Type Restrictions

A complex type, by default, can contain any element and attribute in any order. Apart from <xsd:restriction> and <xsd:extension>, you have seen a restriction on the ordering: the <xsd:sequence> element. There are three ordering restrictions that can be applied, <xsd:sequence>, <xsd:all>, and <xsd:choice>. They all have the following, optional, identical attributes:

Attribute	Possible Values	Description
minOccurs	nonNegativeInteger, default 1	These attributes allow a <sequence> or <choice> to occur zero times, or more than once. minOccurs must always be less than or equal to maxOccurs. minOccurs designates the minimum number of times this sequence or choice may occur in this type.
maxOccurs	nonNegativeInteger or unbounded, default 1	The maxOccurs attribute specifies the maximum number of times a sequence or choice may occur in this type.

XML Schema Reference

<xsd:sequence>

A complex type that is constrained by this element must contain the elements in the order provided by the schema. If `minOccurs` and/or `maxOccurs` are set differently, then the group of elements ordered may be repeated or omitted, depending on the values of `minOccurs` and `maxOccurs`. Here is an example:

```
<xsd:complexType>
  <xsd:sequence>
    <xsd:element name="houseNumber" type="xsd:string"/>
    <xsd:element name="street" type="xsd:string" />
    <xsd:element name="town" type="xsd:string" />
    <xsd:element name="zipCode" type="zipCodeType" />
  </xsd:sequence>
</xsd:complexType>
```

In the instance document, the elements must appear in the order shown above.

<xsd:all>

A complex type constrained by this element may contain the elements specified by its children in any order. `minOccurs` and `maxOccurs` allow repetition or omission in the same way as that used in `<xsd:sequence>`. `<xsd:all>` must be the only child of an `<xsd:complexType>` element; it can be put to good use in various ways. One use is when you want to use optional elements:

```
<xsd:complexType>
  <xsd:all>
    <xsd:element name="name" type="xsd:string" />
    <xsd:element name="ID" type="xsd:ID" />
    <xsd:element name="comments"
                 type="xsd:string"
                 minOccurs="0"
                 maxOccurs="2"/>
  </xsd:all>
</xsd:complexType>
```

In this example, there must exist `<name>` and `<ID>` elements (in any order), but optionally there can be up to two `<comments>` elements, inserted anywhere.

<xsd:choice>

A complex type constrained by this element may contain only one of the elements specified by its children. This element provides an either/or alternative to element content. `minOccurs` and `maxOccurs` define how often this choice occurs.

Below is an example that implements many of the structures and data type constraints seen previously; and the first complex type seen implements `<xsd:choice>` to specify one of many elements:

```
<xsd:schema xmlns:xsd="http://www.w3.org/2001/XMLSchema">
  <xsd:element name="Employees">
    <xsd:complexType>
      <xsd:choice maxOccurs="unbounded">
```

583

```xml
            <xsd:element name="managerial"
                        type="managerType" />
            <xsd:element name="professional"
                        type="employeeType" />
      </xsd:choice>
   </xsd:complexType>
</xsd:element>

<xsd:complexType name="managerType">
   <xsd:sequence>
      <xsd:element name="employee"
                   maxOccurs="unbounded"
                   type="manager" />
   </xsd:sequence>
</xsd:complexType>

<xsd:complexType name="proType">
   <xsd:sequence>
      <xsd:element name="employee"
                   maxOccurs="unbounded"
                   type="professional" />
   </xsd:sequence>
</xsd:complexType>

<xsd:complexType name="manager">
   <xsd:complexContent>
      <xsd:extension base="employeeType" />
         <xsd:attribute name="managesOver" type="manageType" />
      </xsd:extension>
   </xsd:complexContent>
</xsd:complexType>

<xsd:simpleType name="manageType">
   <xsd:list itemType="xsd:IDREF" />
</xsd:simpleType>

<xsd:complexType name="professional">
   <xsd:complexContent>
      <xsd:extension base="employeeType" />
         <xsd:attribute name="reportsTo" type="xsd:IDREF" />
      </xsd:extension>
   </xsd:complexContent>
</xsd:complexType>

<xsd:complexType name="employeeType">
   <xsd:sequence>
      <xsd:element name="Name" type="xsd:string" />
      <xsd:element name="Department" type="xsd:string" />
   </xsd:sequence>
   <xsd:attributeGroup ref="employeeAttributes" />
```

XML Schema Reference

```
    </xsd:complexType>

    <xsd:attributeGroup name="employeeAttributes">
        <xsd:attribute name="employeeID" type="xsd:ID" />
        <xsd:attribute name="salary" type="salaryType" />
    </xsd:attributeGroup>

    <xsd:simpleType name="salaryType">
        <xsd:restriction base="xsd:decimal">
            <xsd:totalDigits value="5" />
            <xsd:fractionDigits value="2" />
            <xsd:minInclusive value="8500.00" />
        </xsd:restriction>
    </xsd:simpleType>
</xsd:schema>
```

The choice in this example simply says that an element chosen as a direct child of the root may be one of <professional> or <managerial>. The <xsd:choice> can occur any number of times, but if it could only be used once, then only one of those elements could occur, exactly once.

Relationships and Null Fields

You need to use an additional mechanism to handle null fields in XML because an element without any content would be an empty string, if it had a type that derived from <xsd:string>, or invalid, if it were some other data type. You have already seen the `nillable` attribute on <xsd:element> and how this permits a null value to exist, but an additional mechanism needs to be implemented in the instance document to actually pass a null value.

Along with the XML Schema namespace, there is also the XML Schema *instance* namespace. This contains a set of attributes that can be used in an instance document, and one of these attributes is `nil`. In the following example XML document, the <extensionNumber> element may contain a null value and it has been given one here:

```
<employees xmlns:xsi="http://www.w3.org/2001/XMLSchema-instance">
    <employee id="EMP001">
        <name>Kate Rusby</name>
        <extensionNumber xsi:nil="true" />
    </employee>
</employees>
```

The definition of the <extensionNumber> element looks like this:

```
<xsd:element name="extensionNumber" type="extNoType" nillable="true" />
```

You have also seen simple relationships with the `<xsd:ID>` type. As long as the value follows the `ID` type character restrictions (no whitespace, no colons, restricted on the first letter), and as long as there is only one identity restraint across the entire data, then this type will work fine for your use. This isn't usually the case, however; you may be representing many tables in your data, where each table has a unique key, occurring in different field columns of different tables.

In addition, most tables have relationships with others, defined by foreign keys. If the keys are auto-incremented values then, when represented as XML, there are likely to be many repeated values. Defining the keys as type `<xsd:ID>`, and the relationship with `<xsd:IDREF>` will not be adequate. Data in XML is structured in a hierarchical way, and XML Schema defines relationships using XPath, which is perfect for uniquely identifying nodes in XML.

The element used for defining the uniqueness of nodes, and where in the XML document they are unique, is `<xsd:unique>`. The element for identifying with what would be a key in a database table is `<xsd:key>` and you use `<xsd:keyref>` to refer to this key, foreign or otherwise.

`<xsd:unique>`

`<xsd:unique>` allows you to define what elements or attributes have to have unique values and where in the document they have to be unique. This element is defined within an `<xsd:element>` declaration and, with its two child elements, `<xsd:selector>` and `<xsd:field>`, allows you to specify what nodes have unique values. In other words, if an attribute or element should be unique within a certain scope, it is specified by `<xsd:unique>` and its child nodes. Each unique value is specified in a separate `<xsd:unique>` element. This element contains only one attribute, shown below:

Attribute	Possible Values	Description
name	NCName	This attribute does not have a purpose, as such, insofar as it relates to data returned from SQL Server 2000. It allows you to uniquely name the uniqueness constraint and is used for readability so that applications like XSLT can get a handle on the uniqueness constraint.

With `<xsd:unique>`, `<xsd:key>`, and `<xsd:keyref>`, the constraining facets are contained in the two children of these elements, `<xsd:selector>` and `<xsd:field>`. In its `<xsd:selector>` child, you specify where the attribute or element has to be unique. Use "/" if you want it to be unique throughout the entire document. With `<xsd:field>`, you say what element or attribute has a unique value. Remember that the XPaths specified with these elements navigate the instance document, not the schema document.

XML Schema Reference

<xsd:selector>

This element allows you to specify with XPath in what set of elements a value is unique. If a node represents data in a particular table or column, then this allows you to specify what this node is. Its required attribute is shown below:

Attribute	Possible Values	Description
xpath	XPath A valid XPath reference.	This is the XPath location relative from the element/node within which the complex type, the `<xsd:unique>` element, is contained. The XPath is a subset of the full XML Path language as defined in XML Path 1.0.

This element appears exactly once inside each `<xsd:unique>` element and contains no content other than that defined in the table. An example use of this element would be:

```
<xsd:selector xpath="professional" />
```

If the `<xsd:unique>` element above were placed inside an `<xsd:element name="Employees" />` element, then this would specify that the `<professional>` child element must have unique content for the `"Employees"` name value. You could just use the value `"."` to specify that the value has to be unique across all children of the `<Employees>` element.

<xsd:field>

This element actually defines the attribute or element that has a unique value inside the XML document. It can occur more than once to specify more complex uniqueness constraints. The attribute it contains is the same as that defined in `<xsd:selector>`. This XPath is relative to the node specified in `<xsd:selector>`.

We will illustrate these uniqueness values by amending the schema shown earlier at the end of the *Defining and Constraining Types* section. You can see the amended schema below:

```
<xsd:schema xmlns:xsd="http://www.w3.org/2001/XMLSchema">
  <xsd:element name="Employees">
    <xsd:unique name="managerUnique">
      <xsd:selector xpath="managerial" />
      <xsd:field xpath="employee/@employeeID " />
    </xsd:unique>

    <xsd:unique name=professionalUnique">
      <xsd:selector xpath="professional" />
      <xsd:field xpath="employee/@employeeID " />
    </xsd:unique>
```

```
        <xsd:complexType>
          <xsd:choice maxOccurs="unbounded">
...
<xsd:attributeGroup name="employeeAttributes">
  <xsd:attribute name="employeeID"
                 type="xsd:nonNegativeInteger" />
  <xsd:attribute name="salary" type="salaryType" />
...
<xsd:simpleType name="manageType">
  <xsd:list itemType="xsd:nonNegativeInteger" />
</xsd:simpleType>

<xsd:complexType name="professional">
  <xsd:complexContent>
    <xsd:extension base="employeeType">
      <xsd:attribute name="reportsTo"
                     type="xsd:nonNegativeInteger" />
    </xsd:extension>
  </xsd:complexContent>
</xsd:complexType>
```

The following XML document will illustrate how uniqueness constraints are defined:

```
<Employees>
  <managers>
    <employee employeeID="1"
              salary="14000.00"
              managesOver="1">
      <Name>Rupert Giles</Name>
      <Department>Library</Department>
    </employee>
    <employee employeeID="2"
              salary="18000.00"
              managesOver="1 2">
      <Name>Jenny Calendar</Name>
      <Department>IT Services</Department>
    </employee>
  </managers>
  <professionals>
    <employee employeeID="1" reportsTo="1">
      <Name>Buffy Summers</Name>
      <Department>Library</Department>
    </employee>
    <employee employeeID="2" reportsTo="2">
      <Name>Willow Rosenberg</Name>
      <Department>IT Services</Department>
    </employee>
  </professionals>
</Employees>
```

In this document, the `employeeID` attribute is unique inside either the `<managers>` or the `<professionals>` element, but not both. The type of each element and attribute is defined separately in the schema, using the methods already described in this appendix.

XML Schema Reference

Here, we have specified two uniqueness constraints. If you remember from our previous discussions, attributes aren't compulsory unless explicitly defined as so in the schema. In this case, only the managers have `salary` attributes. Originally, the `managesOver` and `reportsTo` attributes contained IDREFs, but we have yet to define identity relationships. This is the topic of the next section.

Uniqueness can be specified across a number of nodes. For instance, in a UK postal address, the postcode and house number uniquely identifies each property. Unless you generated a new primary key, then it used to be impossible to specify a uniqueness constraint. However, you can specify more than one `<xsd:field>` restriction. To specify uniqueness across `<address>` nodes, where each address contains `<houseNumber>`, `<street>`, `<village>`, `<town>`, and `<postcode>` elements, you would use a constraint that looked like the following:

```
<xsd:unique name="addressUniqueness">
   <xsd:selector xpath="address" />
   <xsd:field xpath="houseNumber" />
   <xsd:field xpath="postCode" />
</xsd:unique>
```

To summarize, `<xsd:selector>` specifies each node that has to have a uniqueness constraint. The last node specified in its XPath is the node that is unique and is usually mapped to a table in the database. The `<xsd:field>` node specifies the column or set of columns that have unique values.

<xsd:key>

`<xsd:key>` relates to the KEY SQL keyword. As in a database, each key has to be unique and not null. Each `<xsd:key>` element contains `<xsd:selector>` and `<xsd:field>` elements in the same way as `<xsd:unique>`. Say we have a database of employees that contains employee addresses in a separate table, maybe because a number of employees share a flat or house. Using a UK postcode, we might define a key as follows:

```
<xsd:key name="addressKey">
   <xsd:selector xpath="Addresses/address" />
   <xsd:field xpath="houseNumber" />
   <xsd:field xpath="postCode" />
</xsd:key>
```

This ensures that addresses are never repeated. In addition, rather than having to define a separate PRIMARY KEY column, we can store only data that is directly relevant – the address details. Of course, you can specify a PRIMARY KEY by just including one `<xsd:field>` element. The `<xsd:keyref>` element is how you define the relationships.

Appendix B

`<xsd:keyref>`

`<xsd:keyref>` contains an additional attribute to the previous relationship elements, shown below:

Attribute	Possible Values	Description
name	NCName	This uniquely identifies each `<xsd:keyref>` element.
refer	QName. This refers to a previously defined `<xsd:key>` relationship by name.	A previous `<xsd:key>` relationship would have also been given a unique name. If we have foreign keys in a table, then they refer to keys already defined in another table. The same is true for XML. The exact nodes that refer to the node or nodes specified in the `<xsd:key>` relationship are specified in the `<xsd:field>` elements.

If we use the example used for `<xsd:key>`, then we can have a number of address elements that contain just the house number and the postcode. These nodes could be attributes, and they could contain different names; it is irrelevant. In this case, we will use attributes named houseNumber and postCode:

```
<xsd:keyref name="addressKeyReference" refer="addressKey">
    <xsd:selector xpath="//employee/address" />
    <xsd:field xpath="@houseNumber"
    <xsd:field xpath="@postCode"
</xsd:keyref>
```

Recall that the @ prefix is used to refer to attributes in XPath, and // is a wildcard meaning that the node is a descendent rather than just a child. In the case of `<xsd:keyref>`, the `<xsd:selector>` element seems fairly pointless, as we should be able to use a more specific `<xsd:field>`. `<xsd:selector>` is necessary here, however, and it defines the semantic meaning of the relationship. Key references are grouped together if you want to retrieve meaningful data, and `<xsd:keyref>` defines that grouping.

Using a relationship like this on an XML document will allow non-duplication of data, as well as consistent relationships across nodes. It would be possible, for instance, for an XSLT stylesheet to retrieve the addresses referred to in this key reference node and transform it so that it can be displayed in its entirety. Knowing that the data is constrained by uniqueness means that you know that the data retrieved and transformed is the data required.

XML Schema Reference

Namespaces

So far, we haven't been using namespaces in the XML data examples. However, it is likely and preferred that XML data belong to a specific namespace, and that the XML schema will validate data belonging to a specific namespace. We have also neglected to explain one further attribute available on `<xsd:element>` and `<xsd:attribute>` declarations. This is the `form` attribute and it defines how any named element or attribute should be treated; whether or not it is already considered to be part of the namespace specified in `<xsd:schema>`'s `targetNamespace` attribute. This is for ease of use as normally, if you specify a namespace that your schema relates to, you wouldn't want to have to namespace-qualify every element in that schema. This attribute will be explained in this section. First we need to explain how namespaces are dealt with in XML schemas, as there can be complex hierarchies when where to use qualified names is often confusing.

By default, any element or attribute defined in a schema is not namespace-qualified, and so would belong to the null namespace. An exception with attributes is that if the element containing the attribute is namespace qualified, so is the attribute. This changes slightly when the `targetNamespace` attribute is used. The immediate children of the `<xsd:schema>` element are qualified with the same namespace as that specified in the `targetNamespace` attribute.

This difference, with immediate children automatically being part of the target namespace, means that elements and attributes declared through substitution have to be explicitly namespace-qualified in the XML instance document. We cannot just use the `xmlns` attribute in the instance document and assume that they are qualified. This is because, in effect, the element or attribute exists outside the structure of the XML document, defined by the root node. The `xmlns` attribute applies to the element and all its children, but a substituted element or attribute isn't, strictly speaking, a child of the root node. The main reason for this distinction is that the element declaration may not exist in this schema. You will see later how we can import different schemas validating the same or different namespaces. This is important to remember, as it is a source of many XML schema authors' frustrations.

By default, a name given in the `name` attribute of an `<xsd:element>` or `<xsd:attribute>` element is unqualified. The type of the `name` attribute is `NCName`, which is a non-namespace-qualified name. This can cause problems if you want your instance document to be part of a namespace, because only the root node would be namespace-qualified. Generally, it is preferred that elements are namespace-qualified to ensure that they are part of the target namespace. You can change this behavior through use of the `form` attribute on the `<xsd:element>` or `<xsd:attribute>` declaration.

form Attribute

This attribute can take one of two values: `qualified` or `unqualified`, and the default is `unqualified`. When `qualified` on an `<xsd:element>` declaration, then the element must be namespace-qualified to the namespace specified in the `targetNamespace` attribute on `<xsd:schema>`. This is irrelevant on a direct child of an `<xsd:schema>` element, as it has to be namespace-qualified anyway if the `targetNamespace` attribute is present.

Appendix B

It is recommended to set this as `qualified` for elements, as it ties each element to a specific namespace, which can be specified in the instance document.

When `form` is `qualified` on an attribute, it works slightly differently. An attribute is by default part of the namespace of its parent element. This means that even though it is set to `unqualified` by default, then each attribute used is automatically namespace-qualified to that of the element. Setting this to `qualified`, though, means that you have to explicitly give a namespace prefix whenever this attribute appears.

Thankfully, two attributes, `elementFormDefault` and `attributeFormDefault`, are available on the `<xsd:schema>` element. When either of these is set to `qualified`, then whenever `form` is not present on `<xsd:element>` or `<xsd:attribute>` respectively, the `form` attribute is defaulted to `qualified`. Many XML schema authors recommend that you set `elementFormDefault` to `qualified` and omit `attributeFormDefault` for the reasons outlined in the paragraph above: it ties each element and their attributes to a specific namespace that must be specified in the instance document. So, let's see an example of such a schema and instance document:

```
<xsd:schema xmlns:xsd="http://www.w3.org/2001/XMLSchema"
            xmlns:em="http://SQLServer.schema/appendix"
            elementFormDefault="qualified"
            targetNamespace="http://SQLServer.schema/appendix">
  <xsd:element name="Employees">
    <xsd:complexType>
      <xsd:sequence maxOccurs="unbounded">
        <xsd:element name="employee">
          <xsd:complexType>
            <xsd:all>
              <xsd:element name="Name" type="xsd:string" />
              <xsd:element name="Department"
                           type="xsd:string"
                           minOccurs="0" />
            </xsd:all>
            <xsd:attribute name="employeeID"
                           type="xsd:ID"
                           use="required" />
          </xsd:complexType>
        </xsd:element>
      </xsd:sequence>
    </xsd:complexType>
  </xsd:element>
</xsd:schema>
```

An instance document that would validate against this schema is the following:

```
<Employees xmlns="http://SQLServer.schema/appendix">
  <employee employeeID="EMP001">
    <Name>Ian Botham</Name>
  </employee>
  <employee employeeID="EMP002">
    <Department>Snooker</Department>
    <Name>Jimmy White</Name>
  </employee>
</Employees>
```

XML Schema Reference

Importing Schemas

Other schemas can be imported into your schema. This allows you to define data types in one schema, and a structure in another. This can also be useful if, for instance, you have defined the schema for the XML representation of a number of tables in separate schemas. If a JOIN statement is used, then you can reuse those types specified in the separate schemas for each table. It also allows you to derive new types from pre-existing schemas. <xsd:include>, <xsd:import>, and <xsd:redefine> are the three elements that allow you to do this.

<xsd:include>

This element allows you to import the elements of another XML schema. The schema being imported must define elements and attributes in the same namespace as the one used in your schema. Once included, you can refer to a type by its name, or use a substitution group on a globally declared attribute or element. Its required attribute is as follows:

Attribute	Possible Values	Description
schemaLocation	anyURI The location (as a URL) of the schema you wish to include.	This attribute actually specifies the location of the schema. The elements, attributes, and types defined must be of the same namespace as the schema where this element appears. You can use the URL prefix file: to specify a path, or omit the prefix altogether, if dealing with local files.

A common use for this mechanism is to define types separately from the structure of a document. Another possibility is to define structures for different database tables, as long as they are all of the same namespace, a schema can import the schemas for each table that is having data returned from it. <xsd:include> statements are chained, so the parser could continue to include many schemas until there are no more <xsd:include> instructions.

<xsd:redefine>

Because we may not have much control over the design of an included schema, we may want to use pre-defined structures that have different data types from those specified in the schema. With this element, you can redefine a named simple type, complex type, group, or attribute group by entering its definition here. Its one required attribute is shown overleaf:

Appendix B

Attribute	Possible Values	Description
schemaLocation	anyURI URL of the schema being redefined	To be useful, this element will always have content. With it, you redefine a type or group.

\<xsd:import\>

This element allows you to redefine the namespace of a schema. This is especially valuable when using third party schemas. The types defined within the schema can be imported and reused:

Attribute	Possible Values	Description
namespace	anyURI New target namespace – often that of the source document.	This attribute defines the new target namespace of the schema elements being imported so they may become part of the target namespace of the source schema.
schemaLocation	anyURI	This specifies the location of the schema being imported.

Documentation

Schemas have a great facility for documentation. You are free to use an XML comment with your schema (<!-- ... -->), but these are only human readable. Parsers usually ignore these, and their content is unstructured. XML Schema defines the **\<xsd:annotation\>** element for documenting your schemas. These elements can occur anywhere within your schema document and they contain no attributes, other than id. This element contains one or both of <xsd:documentation> and <xsd:appinfo>.

\<xsd:documentation\>

The documentation for the schema or specific schema element is contained here. It can contain any XML content desired, or none at all. This allows XSLT stylesheets to transform the contents of this element, perhaps for presentation in a web browser. There is no restriction on the XML tags that may be used in this element, as long as the fragment is well-formed. It also has a source attribute that enables you to include the documentation in a separate document:

XML Schema Reference

Attribute	Possible Values	Description
source	anyURI	The URI specified here must be a URL pointing to a document that contains any mixture of XML and textual information to be imported into the schema as a child of the `<xsd:documentation>` element. This allows you to keep the documentation for this particular part of your schema in a separate file.
xml:lang	A locale specifier: for example, en-US.	This attribute is not required, and by default it carries the value specified in the `xml:lang` attribute on the `<xsd:schema>` element (if present). It defines the language of its content.

No XML Schema elements can be present inside `<xsd:documentation>`.

`<xsd:appinfo>`

Content inside this element is targeted at parsers and XML applications rather than humans. It can have identical content to the `<xsd:documentation>` element, but you would normally provide additional information or instructions for a parser to read. For instance, you could include the content of another schema language here and any code could read these definitions too, perhaps to provide additional validation or business logic to an XML instance document. This has only a `source` attribute that works in the same way as for `<xsd:documentation>`, and you would normally define its content to be of a different namespace. The content cannot be part of the XML Schema namespace.

This can be used to bring much richer documentation to your schema. As you saw in Chapter 6, you can use it to more closely define relationships between elements and tables. This was implemented through the use of the `urn:schemas-microsoft-com:mapping-schema` namespace in this chapter; but you can define any XML vocabulary you like to do this. Again, an XSLT stylesheet could create human-readable documentation from this schema by, say, transforming these elements into tables.

Varying XML Content

One final detail of XML Schema that needs mentioning is that which defines XML content to be of type `xsd:anyType`. This data type is a global type that states that the content may be anything, as long as it is well formed. The `<xsd:documentation>` and `<xsd:appinfo>` elements used above are of this type, as are others. You can define content in your instance document to be of any or a specific namespace type (perhaps to implement XHTML, or content from another XML schema) by using the `<xsd:any>` element.

Appendix B

<xsd:any>

This element, when included within an <xsd:sequence> or <xsd:choice> declaration, specifies that the XML element content to be included in the instance document is not of this schema, and can be of a specific or non-specific namespace. Its attributes are shown below:

Attribute	Possible Values	Description
maxOccurs	nonNegativeInteger default is 1 and must be greater than or equal to minOccurs. Use unbounded to specify no upper limit.	Specifies how often this content can be repeated. The maximum number of occurrences is specified here.
minOccurs	nonNegativeInteger default is 1 and must be less than or equal to maxOccurs.	The minimum number of times this content can occur.
namespace	One of ##any, ##other, list of anyURI (possibly including ##targetNamespace and/or ##local. Default is ##any.	A whitespace-separated list of namespaces, of which the content can be a part. Optionally, one of the values in the list can be ##targetNamespace, which includes the namespace of the schema; and ##local indicates null namespaced content can be used. Instead of the list, ##any specifies that any XML content can be used, whereas ##other indicates any content other than that of the target namespace.
Process Contents	One of lax, skip, or strict. Default skip.	This indicates how the content should be validated. Using skip means that no validation occurs. If lax is used, validation occurs if possible (schema exists for the content). If strict is used, then a schema must exist for all the content and it has to validate against it.

This could be useful if you are using structures from different tables that are of different namespaces. These structures could be included inside <xsd:any> elements, rather than being imported and redefined.

XML Schema Reference

<xsd:anyAttribute>

As you might expect, this works in the same way for attributes as <xsd:any> works for elements. This, when included in an <xsd:complexType> element, specifies that this type can contain attributes from the specified, or any, namespace. Its attributes are the same as those for <xsd:any>, but do not include `minOccurs` and `maxOccurs`, as attributes can only appear once on an element.

When you use <xsd:any>, the attributes and other child items are obviously included as well. The <xsd:anyAttribute> element allows you to permit just certain attributes. In an XML schema, these attributes would be declared globally. The same goes for the <xsd:any> element above; but remember that all children of this globally declared element need not be declared globally.

The XML Schema Instance Namespace

This namespace is used inside the XML instance document, and allows you to do things like indicate what schema should validate this document. It only contains attributes, and each attribute's function only applies to the element in which it appears (and possibly its children). You can see its attributes below:

Attribute	Possible Values	Description
`nil`	`boolean` `true` or `false`	If present on an element in the instance document, the element has null content, rather than empty content.
`schemaLocation`	List of `anyURI` The first URI specifies the target namespace of the XML schema, the rest the location of the schema document(s).	This is used when referring to an XML schema with a `targetNamespace` attribute present on its <xsd:schema> element. The first URI indicates the namespace of the schema (its `targetNamespace` value). The rest are the URLs pointing to the locations of the XML schema document or documents to validate this document.

Table continued on following page

597

Appendix B

Attribute	Possible Values	Description
NoNamespaceschemaLocation	anyURI The URL of the XML schema document used to validate this instance document.	This is used when there isn't a targetNamespace element present in the schema document. You just specify the URL that points to the XML schema document.
type	QName An XML Schema or defined type.	This allows you to specify that the content of the element is of a different type from that specified in the XML schema. However, the type used must derive from the type that is supposed to be there.

The namespace for the XML Schema instance attributes is shown below, as well as an example of its use on an element:

```
<Employees xmlns:xsi="http://www.w3.org/2001/XMLSchema-
instance">
```

With this namespace, the attributes are prefixed with xsi:. You have seen the xsi:nil attribute before. Also, the next two attributes in the table are used whenever you want to refer to the schema document from the instance document. You choose between them, depending on whether a targetNamespace attribute is present in the schema document(s).

The xsi:type is more interesting. It allows the schema instance document author to specify additional constraints on content. The type must derive from the original type (that is, it must be a restriction of the type that should be present in that element). Two XML Schema types that fall into this category are decimal and nonNegativeInteger. The decimal type is known as a built-in type, and the integer type derives from this (it must have no fractional parts). nonNegativeInteger derives from integer and excludes all numbers less than 0. So, if a <salary> element were defined to contain data of decimal type, you could have the following in the instance document:

```
<salary xsi:type="xsd:nonNegativeInteger">12000</salary>
```

You must declare the namespace prefix for XML Schema and for XML Schema instance in this case.

References

XML Schema Part 0: Primer – http://www.w3.org/TR/xmlschema-0/
XML Schema Part 1: Structures – http://www.w3.org/TR/xmlschema-1/
XML Schema Part 2: Datatypes – http://www.w3.org/TR/xmlschema-2/
XML Schema Instance –
http://www.w3.org/TR/xmlschema–1/#Instance_Document_Constructions
XML 1.0 Recommendation 2nd Edition –
　　　　　　　http://www.w3.org/TR/2000/REC-xml-20001006
Namespaces in XML – http://www.w3.org/TR/1999/REC-xml-names-19990114/
XPath 1.0 Recommendation – http://www.w3.org/TR/xpath

Andrew Novick

- Why is a Query Tool Useful?
- The Query Tool
- Working With the Tool

A Tool for XML Queries

Chapter 13 covers how to write ADO code to work with SQL Server's XML output. We can put this method to work to solve one of the problems associated with querying XML, and produce a tool to help us format our returned XML more usefully.

This appendix firstly explains why our tool is useful, and then goes on to explain how to install and use it.

Why is a Query Tool Useful?

None of the tools provided with SQL Server produces really usable XML output. ISQL won't even handle the Unicode output of XML, as this exchange shows:

```
C:\>isql -E
1> use pubs
2> go
1> select * from authors for XML auto
2> go
Msg 4004, Level 16, State 1, Server ANDREW-FL1ZL914, Line 1
Unicode data in a Unicode-only collation or ntext data cannot be sent to
clients using DB-Library (such as ISQL) or ODBC version 3.7 or earlier.
1>
```

OSQL will accept FOR XML queries, but the results just scroll off the screen and are impossible to read.

One might hope that Query Analyzer would do a little better. Up to a point it does, if you know how to set it up correctly, as we saw in Chapter 4's *FOR XML Query Results* section.

The real secret, however, to making Query Analyzer produce more useful XML output is to use DBCC TRACEON(257) as seen in this query:

Appendix C

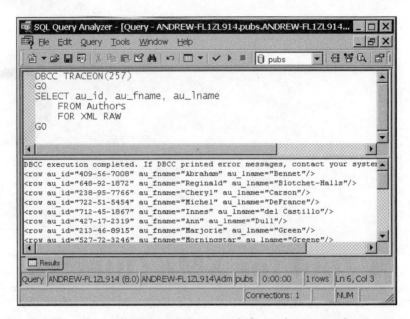

To take effect, the DBCC TRACEON(257) only has to be executed once per session. As with all undocumented TRACE codes, you're warned that it may change at any time without notice. However, in this case there isn't really anything to worry about; by the time it's eliminated there will be a way to get nicer output from Query Analyzer automatically.

As you can see, each row of the XML result starts on a new line. For simple XML, this is very usable; for more complex XML, it's still OK but not ideal. Here's an example:

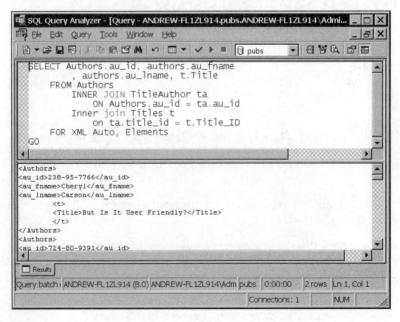

A Tool for XML Queries

That's better. It works most of the time but becomes difficult to read as the XML gets more complex. What I really want to see is XML the way IE displays it; that way I can open and close the element hierarchy to be sure everything is correct. The supplied query tool does it my way.

The Query Tool

You'll find query tool project, SQLXMLQueryTool, in this Appendix's code download. SQLXMLQueryTool is a Visual Basic 6 program written with the standard VB6 controls. It lets you execute FOR XML queries, templates, and XPath queries, and sends the results to a web browser control (the real guts of Internet Explorer) for display.

The source code to SQLXMLQueryTool is provided so that you can modify it to suit your needs. You must have ADO 2.7 and MSXML 4.0 installed in order to use the program. ADO 2.7 (also know as MDAC) can be downloaded from http://www.microsoft.com/data; MSXML 4.0 is installed when the SQLXML 3.0, Service Pack 1, is installed. If you don't have Visual Basic 6, there's a compiled version of the query application and an installation program in **SQLXMLSetup** Directory of the code download.

Working With the Tool

Once you have it set up, the query tool starts with a standard **Data Link Properties** screen that lets you build the connection string. You should choose the "**Microsoft OELDB provider for SQL Server**". It's not possible to choose the SQLXMLOLEDB provider from this screen. The actual provider used will be modified later before running a query. The screen looks like this:

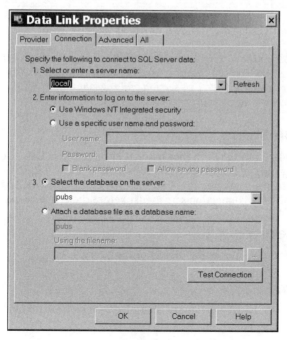

603

Appendix C

These details are saved to the registry. If you don't have permission to write to the registry, then login will fail.

SQLXMLQueryTool's main screen comes up with three tabs. The **Query** tab allows you to write your query and select the options used by the Command object. You can run any of the queries shown throughout the book through this interface. Here it is with a simple query:

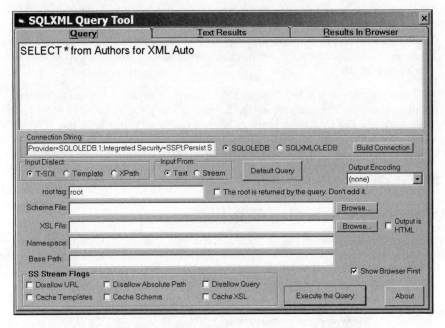

Let's now work through a rundown of what's on the screen.

The fields on the screen correspond closely to the properties of the ADODB.Command object that is used to execute the queries. You should refer to Chapter 13's section on Programming SQLXML with ADO for more on these properties.

Connection String

This section lets us work with the connection screen. The **Build Connection** button brings up the **Data Link Properties** screen to make it easy to write the connection string. The two radio buttons, **SQLOLEDB** and **SQLXMLOLEDB**, are used to modify the connection screen just before the connection is made.

Input Dialect

This group lets you choose the dialect of the query.

Input From

Lets you choose the way the query is handed to the Command object: in CommandText or as a Stream.

A Tool for XML Queries

Default Query

Fills the query area with a sample query in the dialect selected by the **Input Dialect** group.

Output Encoding

This drop down lets you choose which output encoding to set. The default is (none).

Root tag

Unless a root tag is provided, either in a template or in this field, SQL produces an XML fragment instead of well-formed XML. The IE browser control will not display XML fragments, so you should put a root tag in this field. If none is provided, <root> is used as the default, unless the **The root is returned by the query. Don't add it** checkbox is checked, when the root is ignored.

Schema File

The full path to the schema file can be set here. Use the **Browse** button next to the textbox to open a file open dialog for specifying the file.

If you set a base path (see Base Path below), then you only need to specify the filename that can be found at the end of that path.

XSL File

The full path to the XSL file is specified here. Use the **Browse** button next to the textbox to open a file open dialog for specifying the file. **Output is HTML** indicates that the XSL is going to transform the XML into HTML. When it's checked, SQLXMLQueryTool attempts to display the result as HTML instead of XML.

If you set a base path (see Base Path below), then you only need to specify the file name that can be found at the end of that path.

Namespaces

This is where the Namespaces parameter is specified.

Base Path

Allows us to specify a base path (either a file path or a URL) that is used to locate the other files we can specify in the Schema File and XSL File fields.

Show Browser First

Allows us to choose which of the two other tabs is displayed when the query is run. See *Execute the Query* below for more on this.

SS Stream Flags

Used to set the SS Stream Flags that can restrict how files are specified in other parameters and to control caching. See Chapter 13 for details on what each of the flags does.

Appendix C

Execute the Query

When you click the Execute the Query button or press the *F5* key, the query is run and the results are displayed in both of the two Results tabs.

Results in Browser

The Results in Browser tab shows the results the way I want to see them, in an IE browser window:

Text Results

The Text Results tab shows the XML as text, but with indenting based on the element hierarchy. This is also very readable and suitable for anyone who needs to get formatted XML without doing it by hand. Here's a sample:

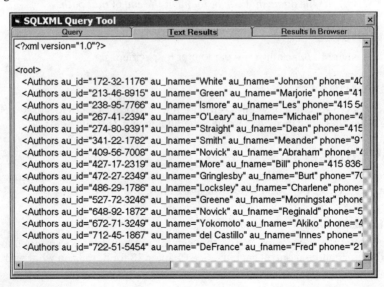

A Tool for XML Queries

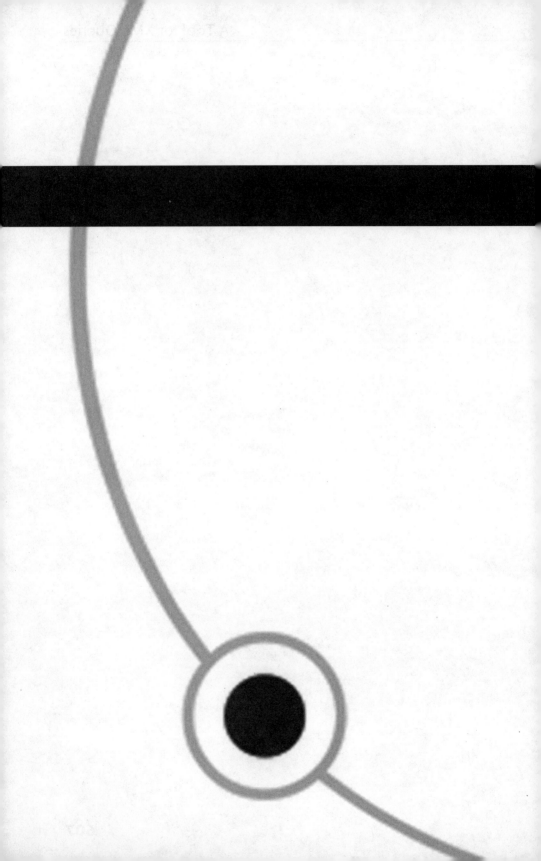

Index

A Guide to the Index

The index is arranged alphabetically in word-by-word order, so that New York would precede Newark. Unmodified entries represent the principal treatment of a topic; subheadings identify specific aspects. Acronyms have been preferred to their expansions as main entries as they are easier to recall and an asterisk (*) indicates variant endings.

A

abbreviations, XPath location paths, 527
absolute location paths, XPath, 521
   STREAM_FLAGS_DISALLOW_* flags, 371
AccessView SQL Server view, 183
ad hoc business approach to handling XML, 24
address information and uniqueness constraints, 589
Administration utility, BizTalk Server, 488
Administration utility, IIS, 463
ADO (ActiveX Data Objects)
   ADO 2.5 can save Recordsets to disk or stream, 385
   ADO.NET differences from, 364, 389
      comparing Recordset XML with DataSet, 393
   browser detection using with ASP, 451
   client-side FOR XML queries, 39
   commands, XML Templates processed as, 37
   converting Recordsets into XML documents, 23
   formatting output with SQLXMLQueryTool, 601
   processing FOR XML queries via, 381
      using SQLXMLOLEDB Provider, 381
   programming XML with, 365-389
      querying with XPath and a mapping schema, 377
      using templates, 375
   saving contents as XML, 385
   SQLXMLQueryTool needs ADO 2.7, 603
   stored procedure using OPENXML and, 388
   submitting Updategrams in BizTalk Integration Case Study, 474
   Updategram approach advantages over, 463
   Updategram performance compared to HTTP POSTs, 491
   Updategrams, applying using, 323
   Updategrams, use with, 38
   use with Visual Basic 6 in programmatic access examples, 364
   using XDR schemas with, 35, 36
   XPath queries using, 202
ADO.NET
   choice between ADO and, 364, 389
   differences from ADO, 389
   programming XML with, 389
      executing a FOR XML query with SqlCommand, 390
      saving DataSets as XML, 392

ADOCreateXMLExample project, 386
ADOFullXML.xml, 387
AdoUpdategram.vbp, 323
Advanced tab, SQLXML VDM tool, 51
<after> element, 292
   see also <updg:after> element.
aggregate functions
   FOR XML NESTED supports, 118
   not usable with some FOR XML queries, 95
aggregating temporary data in SQL Server, 215
aliasing
   column names
      FOR XML EXPLICIT queries, 105
      FOR XML RAW queries, 97
   elements, ignored by FOR XML NESTED, 383, 384
   table names
      FOR XML AUTO queries, 100
      FOR XML NESTED overrides, 118
      schemas for added security, 208
alternate keys
   distinguishing updates from inserts, 218
   fulfillment system example, 243
annotated XML schemas, 145
   annotation technologies, 145
   driving Updategrams with annotated schemas, 295
   layering an XML View over a SQL Server view, 184
   mapping XML to database columns, 331
   supporting multiple actions within one Updategram, 308
   updg:id attribute alternative, 306
   XML views rely on, 173
annotation favors using elements to represent data points, 79
annotation mechanisms, 147
   creating ID-IDREF relationships in XML schemas, 159
   creating XML views, 175
   defining unmapped XML elements, 150
   escaping invalid XML characters, 161
   filtering the data in an XML document, 155
   limiting recursion depths in XML schemas, 167
   mapping attributes to SQL Server columns, 148
   mapping BLOBs, 162
   mapping complex elements to SQL Server tables, 147
   mapping text-only elements to SQL Server columns, 149

annotation mechanisms (continued)

annotation mechanisms (continued)
  specifying a GUID in an XML schema, 166
  specifying identity columns in an XML schema, 165
  specifying relationships between two SQL tables, 152
  specifying unique keys in an XML document, 157
annotation namespace
  attributes tabulated, 168
  XML schemas, 146
anonymous access
  BizTalk Integration Case Study, 463
  security problems with, 46
ANSI (American National Standards Institute) support for SQLX initiative, 496
anyURI data type, XML Schema, SQL Server equivalent types, 221
application integration, BizTalk Integration Case Study, 473, 481, 492
architecture overview of XML support in SQL Server 2000, 20, 31
  diagram, 32
architectures of Web application
  architecture predecessors, 11
archival use
  for XML created from SQL Server, 63
  hybrid design approach suits, 225
arithmetic operators, XPath and SQL, 530
ASP (Active Server Pages) browser detection, 453
ASP.NET
  advantages of, for browser detection, 450
  to run SQLXML templates, 447
assigning variables not handled within XPath, 529
at-identity attribute, updategram namespace, 293, 314, 318
attribute-centric XML
  OPENXML flags property values and, 262
  use by ADO, 393
attributed data elements, 236
attributeFormDefault attribute, <xsd:schema>, 592
attributes
  advantages for representing data points, 78
  annotation namespace, tabulated, 168
  data points as, 235
  mapping to SQL Server columns, 148
  returning overflow column data as, 113
  specifying, with the @ prefix, 193
  updategram namespace, tabulated, 292
  XML schema annotations appear as, 147
  XML Schema instance namespace, 597
audit trails, Windows Integrated Authentication, 123
authentication mechanisms
  security problems from Basic Authentication, 54
  setting, in New Virtual Directory Properties, 46
  web services, 427
Authors.xsd schema, 407
Authors2HTML.xsl stylesheet, 372
Authors4Insert.xsd mapping schema, 409, 410
AUTO mode, FOR XML see **FOR XML AUTO queries.**
axes, XPath, 522
  support for, in SQL Server 2000 with SQLXML 3.0, 208, 524
  tabulated, 523
  XQuery 1.0 subset, 555

B

Base Path property, ADODB.Command object, 370
base64Binary data type, XML Schema
  image/varbinary SQL Server equivalent types, 221
  representing SQL Server binary types, 71, 72, 73
BaseData.xml example document, 256
BasePath property, SqlXmlCommand, 395, 398
Basic Authentication
  security problems from, 54
  setting, in New Virtual Directory Properties, 46
BCP (Bulk Copy Program) compared to XML Bulk Load, 37, 327, 356
<before> element, 292
  see also <updg:before> element.
bigint data type
  SQL Server, equivalent XML Schema types, 222
  use with OPENXML, 256
BINARY BASE 64 argument, FOR XML RAW queries, 98
binary data type, SQL Server, 71
bit data type, SQL Server, XML Schema equivalent types, 220
BizTalk Editor tool, 466
  specifying the HR Updategram, 470
BizTalk Integration Case Study, 457
  accessing the system, 490
  business process, Departmental, 485
  business process, HR, 474
  departmental phonelist database, 461
  file receive function, 488
  HR databask, 459
  ideal business process, 462
    advantages, 463
  messages and the BizTalk messaging tools, 465
  messaging configuration, 481-485, 488
    channel to Deapartment, 485
    home organization applications, 481
    map between HR and Department Updategrams, 484
    map between New Employee and HR Updategram, 481
    port to Deapartment, 484
    receive channel, 483, 488
    receive port, 482, 488
  messaging implementations
    departmental data flow, 486, 487
    HR data flow, 480
  orchestration schedule, Departmental phonelist, 485
  orchestration schedule, HR, 473
    HR messaging implementations, 476
  problem with ideal business process, 464
  revised business process, 465
  security issues, 463, 491
  system requirements, 458
  testing the system, 489
  Updategrams, 469
    Department Updategram, 472
    HR Updategram, 470
BizTalk Mapper Tool, 481, 484
BizTalk Messaging Configuration, 488
BizTalk Messaging Manager utility, 469
BizTalk Orchestration Designer, 473
BizTalk Server 2002
  see also XDR schema.
  needed for BizTalk Integration Case Study, 458
  primer on, 464
  security features, 491

BLOBs (Binary Large Objects)
  mapping to XML schemas, 162
  storing XML documents as, 21, 26
boolean data type, XPath, 518, 520
boolean data type, XML Schema, SQL Server equivalent type, 220
boolean operators, XPath, 198
boolean() function, XPath, 535
  forcing a cast, 521
braces, XQuery delimiters, 502
brackets
  XQuery and XML delimiters distinguished, 502
  left angle bracket, mapping SQL characters to Unicode, 496
browser detection
  see also Detecting Web Site Clients case study.
  basic principles, 434
  using ASP.NET, 445, 450
  using classic ASP, 453, 454
  using SQLXML and XML templates, 435
browsers
  operation, compared to client-server GUIs, 12
  possible corruption of XPath expressions, 199
BTConfig Assistant tool, BizTalk, 459
bug in SQLXML 3.0 SP1, affecting BizTalk, 464, 490
BULK INSERT statement compared to XML Bulk Load, 327, 356
bulk load interfaces, SQL Server
  see also SQLXML Bulk Load. .
  options not available in SQLXML Bulk Load, 357
  SQLXML Bulk Load differences from, 356
BulkLoad property, SQLXML BulkLoad object, 338
business approaches to handling XML
  ad hoc approach, 24
  evaluation criteria, 21
  relational end-to-(near the) end approach, 23
  taking a step back, 25
  XML end-to-end, 21
business processing, location of, 21
business requirements
  detemining database structure, 213
  driving the selection of information from XML documents, 225
byte data type, XML Schema, SQL Server equivalent type, 223

C

caching
  SS STREAM FLAGS property, ADODB.Command object, 374, 375
  XPath queries in templates, 199, 201
caching options
  SQLXML registry settings, 53
  VDM Advanced tab settings, 52
  template and stylesheet caching, 134
caching results and OPENXML limitations, 286
calculations on temporary data in SQL Server, 215
case sensitivity, XML, 148
  columns to XML element mapping, 253
  extends to XPath, 514
  implications for node names, 100, 334

case studies *see* **BizTalk Integration Case Study; Detecting Web Site Clients; inventory example.**
casting
  between XPath data types, 520
  complex types, in XPath 2.0, 553
CDATA blocks
  specifying with FOR XML EXPLICIT, 115
  specifying with sql:use-cdata, 161
cdata directive, FOR XML EXPLICIT queries, 115
ceiling() function, XPath, 535
char data type, SQL Server, 70
character encoding, Output Encoding property, 370
character sets other than UTF-8, 131
charset parameter, 131
CHECK constraints
  adding to SQL Server columns, 237
  DBCC CHECKCONSTRAINTS, 343
  modeling in an XML Schema document, 79
CheckConstraints property, SQLXML BulkLoad object, 342
child elements, modeling as SQL Server tables, 226
circular joins, infinite recursion risk, 167
ClearParameters method, SqlXmlCommand, 401
client detection *see* **browser detection.**
Client Tools, SQL Server 2000, for SQLXML installation, 42
client-server architecture compared to Web application architecture, 11
client-side processing
  dynamic creation of templates, 142
  FOR XML queries, 117-119
    advantages over server-side, 92, 93
    diagram, 92
  posting template queries, 133
  SQLXML Bulk Load, 359
  SQLXMLOLEDB Provider and, 381
  XSLT stylesheets, 373
client-side scripting to access User-Agent headers, 435
client-side web development and URL queries, 121
client-side XML
  using FOR XML queries, 38
  using stored procedures with, 384
ClientSideNestedQueryOnSP project, 384
client-side-xml attribute, <sql:query> element, 142, 383
ClientSideXML processing request, 382
ClientSideXml property, SqlXmlCommand, 396, 399
CLOB (Character Large Objects) alternative, Oracle 9.0.2, 497, 498
ColPattern argument, SchemaDeclaration, 256
column order effect on FOR XML AUTO output, 101
column patterns negate OPENXML flag settings, 263
columns
  identifying information to be represented in XML, 74
  mapping attributes to, 148
  mapping column values, 242
  mapping to XML Schema data types
    inventory example database, 85
  ordering XML on hidden columns, 111
  returning as XML sub-elements, 110

COM interfaces, BizTalk Integration Case
Study, 474
COM objects used by XML Bulk Load, 37
Command object, ADODB, 451, 452
   CommandText property, 367
      assigning templates as strings to, 377
      sending XML to a stored procedure in, 388
      XPath queries in, 378
   Dialect property, 366, 375, 377
   dynamic properties, 453
   extended properties, 368-381
      Base Path property, 370
      Mapping Schema property, 371
      NameSpaces property, 369
      Output Encoding property, 370
      Output Stream property, 375
      OutputStream property, 367
      SS STREAM FLAGS property, 374
      XML Root property, 369
      XSL property, 371
   MinimalExample ADO code, 366
   properties tabulated with SqlXmlCommand equivalents, 395
   SQLXMLQueryTool screen fields correspond to properties of, 604
CommandSteam object, ADODB, 452
CommandStream property, SqlXmlCommand, 395, 397
CommandText property, ADODB.Command object
   assigning templates as strings to, 377
   MinimalExample ADO code, 367
   sending XML to a stored procedure in, 388
   XPath queries in, 378
CommandText property, SqlXmlCommand, 395, 397
CommandType property, SqlXmlCommand, 395, 396
comments within XML Schema, 594
comparison operators, XPath compared to SQL, 531
complex elements
   adding unique key declarations, 157
   mapping to SQL Server tables, 147
   specifying with sql:is-constant, 152
compound keys, sql:key-fields attribute, 158
computed columns, FOR XML RAW queries, 97
concat() function, XPath, 535
   concatenation operator absent, 531
   dealing with quotation marks, 519
conditional constructs, XQuery, 507
conditional expressions, XPath 2.0, 554
Connection object, ADODB, MinimalExample ADO code, 366
ConnectionCommand property, SQLXML BulkLoad object, 336
   Transaction property and, 336, 341
ConnectionString property, SQLXML BulkLoad object, 336
   use in sample script, 335, 354
ConnectionString writing, with SQLXMLQueryTool, 604
constraining types, XML Schema, 570
constraints
   see also CHECK constraints.
   apply while using Updategrams, 302
   modelling enumeration constraints, 238
   ON DELETE CASCADE constraint, 310, 311
   SQL Server, creating to match XML constraints, 237

consumed data, OPENXML, 264
container elements using sql:is-constant attribute, 151
contains() function, XPath, 536
   no SQLXML support, 198
content types
   allowing varying content types in XML Schema, 595
   errors caused by IE caching, 440
   modifying in URL queries output, 130
contenttype parameter, URL queries, 130
context nodes, XPath, 521
count() function, XPath, 536
   including with a rowpattern, 260
   MSXML2 support, 259
   XQuery, 504
CreateParameter method, SqlXmlCommand, 401
cross-platform use
   see also interoperability; Microsoft-specific.
   web services as cross-platform mechanism, 416
currency values
   money data type, SQL Server, 67
   specifying with attributed data elements, 236
current() function, XPath, 536
cust.xml document, using XQuery, 502
   modified to show XQuery joins, 505
custom programming, avoiding, 458
Customer.xsd schema, creating XML views, 176
Customer2.xsd schema, 182
customerElementSchema.xsd schema, 300
CustomerInvoice.VBS script, 352
CustomerInvoice.xsd schema, 178, 351
   using to retrieve XML, 378
CustomerInvoices.xml, bulk loading multiple tables, 348
Customerlist.xml file, SQLXML Bulk Load examples, 330
customerSchema.xml schema, 295, 302, 305
customerSchema.xsd annotated schema, 299
customerSchema2.xsd annotated schema, 308
   applying Updategrams as HTML forms, 321
customerSchema3.xsd schema, 312
customerSchema4.xsd schema, 315

D

dangling elements, 78
data based computing, 10
data flow diagrams, BizTalk Integration Case Study, 480, 487
data formats, changing needs and XML, 9
data interchange and n-tier architecture and, 13
data logging, SQLXMLBulkLoad object properties, 342
data manipulation
   best done within SQL Server, 185, 215
   XML views unsuitable for complex manipulations, 174
data modification see modifying tables.
data points
   mapping to columns, 235
   representation as elements or attributes, 78
Data Source tab, SQLXML VDM tool, 47

<diffgr:before> element

data types, XPath queries, checking with SQL Profiler, 202
data types, Oracle 9.0.2 xmltype data type, 497
data types, SQL Server
   binary type, 71
   built-in types tabulated with their XML schema equivalents, 65
   char type, 70
   datetime type, 69
   decimal/numeric type, 66
   float type, 68
   image type, 73
   mapping to XML Schema data types, 496
   money type, 67
   nchar, nvarchar and ntext types, 71
   real type, 68
   smalldatetime type, 69
   smallmoney type, 67
   sql_variant type, 73
   tabulated with XML Schema equivalents, 219
   text type, 70
   timestamp type, 73
   uniqueidentifier type, 74
   user-defined data types, 237
   varbinary type, 72
   varchar type, 70
data types, XML Schema
   base64Binary type, 71, 72
   converting columns to, 79
      inventory example database, 85
   converting to SQL Server types, 237
   datetime type, 69
   decimal type, 66, 67
   double type, 68
   equivalent SQL Server data types tabulated, 219
   float type, 68
   giving problems with mapping to SQL Server, 223
   hexBinary type, 71, 72
   long type, 73
   mapping to SQL data types, 496
   mapping to XPath functions, 196
   namespaces, 559
   string type, 70, 73, 74
   tabulated as equivalents to SQL Server built-in types, 65
   XPath 2.0 types will mirror, 552
data types, XPath, 195, 518
   casting between, 520
   XPath 2.0, 532, 552
data types, XQuery, 508
database schemas, fulfillment system example, 241
databases
   success of relational databases, 10
   web service support example, 416
   XML aspects relevant to, 13
data-centric XML, 25
   processing with Updategrams, 27
   relational storage appropriate to, 25
   retrieval methods for, 26
data-driven web applications, 11
DataProvider paramter, SQLXMLOLEDB Provider, 383
DataSet class, System.Data, 392

DataSet Objects output method, SQLXML 3.0 web services, 422
datasets, flattened, 421
DataSets, ADO.NET
   changes propagated by SQLXMLAdapter class, 403
   persisting as DiffGrams, 412
   population by SQLXMLAdapter class, 403
   saving as XML, 392
   use DiffGrams internally, 404
date data type, XML Schema
   datetime SQL Server equivalent type, 220
datetime data type, SQL Server, 69
   XML Schema equivalent types, 219
dateTime data type, XML Schema, 69, 219
DBA (Database Administrator) uses of XML, 9
DBCC TRACEON (257) formatting results, 601
dbobject mappings, SQLXML virtual names, 50
debugging
   tools useful for SQLXML problems, 56
   VB6 advantages over VB Script, 345
decimal data type, SQL Server
   equivalent XML Schema type, 222
decimal data type, XML Schema
   decimal SQL Server equivalent type, 222
   giving problems with mapping to SQL Server, 224
   mapping SQL Server decimal/numeric types to, 66
   mapping SQL Server money and smallmoney types to, 67
decimal/numeric data types, SQL Server, 66
default mappings, Updategrams, 297
default namespace bindings, 526
default.aspx page, Detecting Web Site Clients case study, 447
default.aspx.cs page, 448
defining types, XML Schema, 570
Delete1.xml Updategram, 302
Delete2.xml Updategram, 303
Delete3.xml Updategram, 303
deleting data with DiffGrams, 410
deleting data with Updategrams, 302
   deleting multiple rows, 303
   optimistic and pessimistic deleting, 303
delimiters, XQuery and XML, 502
departmental phonelist database, BizTalk Integration Case Study, 461
dept_update.xml Updategram, BizTalk Integration Case Study, 462
deptupdgram.xml Updategram, 472
design methodology
   deriving XML schemas from SQL Server structures, 74
   mapping XML to SQL Server, 224
      identifying relevant information, 225
      mapping data points, 235
      overall relational structure, 226
Detecting Web Site Clients case study, 433
   benefits and drawback of the three methods, 434
   using SQLXML and ADO, 451-454
   using SQLXML and XML templates, 435-443
      creating the client detection code, 439
   using SQLXML Managed Classes, 444-450
Dialect property, ADODB.Command object, 366, 375, 377
   SqlXmlCommand.CommandType corresponds to, 395
<diffgr:before> element, 405, 407

613

<diffgr:errors> element

<diffgr:errors> element, 405
DiffGrams, 404
   compared to Updategrams, 412
   DELETES using, 410
   FOR XML NESTED and, 383
   INSERTS using, 408
   inseting XML data into SQL Server, 40
   limitation for sophisticate processing, 217
   persisting DataSets as, 412
   updating example using, 406
   XML schema annotation technology, 145
directed nature of foreign key relationships, 76
directives usable with FOR XML EXPLICIT, 110-117
discarding information
   storing XML in SQL Server, 225
      fulfillment system example, 241
      fulfillment system example, 241
distributed applications without programming, 457
document element *see* **root element.**
document objects, 20
document() function, XPath, 537
documentation
   SQLXML, 44
   within XML Schema, 594
   XML schema elements for, 153
document-centric XML, 25
DOM (Document Object Model)(Level 3) use of XPath, 513
DOM parsers as standard XML technology, 15
double data type, XML Schema
   float SQL Server equivalent type, 221
   mapping SQL Server float type to, 68
dt:type attribute, XML schema, 116
DTD (Document Type Defintions)
   backward compatabilty requirements, 78, 81
   edge tables and inline DTDs, 282
   role as an XML standard technology, 15
DTS (Data Transformation Services) and SQLXML Bulk Load, 328, 344
DTS Bulk Load Task, 356
duplicate data, removing for database storage, 217
duration data type, XML Schema, 219
Dynamic Properties Tasks, 348

E

edge tables
   omitting OPENXML WITH clauses results in, 279
   simple example, 280
   using with inline DTDs or inline schemas, 282
element directive, FOR XML EXPLICIT queries, 110
   xml directive compared to, 113
element types, problems from reuse, 228
element-available() function, XPath, 537
element-centric XML
   FOR XML AUTO ELEMENTS parameter, 104
   FOR XML EXPLICIT element directive, 110
   OPENXML flags property values and, 262
   use by ADO.NET, 393
   XSL property illustration, 371

elementFormDefault attribute, <xsd:schema>, 592
elements
   data points as, 235
   defining unmapped elements, 150
   distinguishing between with namespaces, 192
   excluding elements from the mapping, 151
   fixed performance overhead for OPENXML parsing, 284
   updategram namespace, tabulated, 292
   use for representing data points, 79
   XPath queries return whole elements, 190
ELEMENTS parameter, FOR XML AUTO, 103
e-mail address patterns, 580
emergent technologies, 495
employee_map.xsd scheme
   BizTalk Integration Case Study, 461
employees.xml sample template, 135
employeesterritories.xml template
   with multiple SQL statements, 138
employeesterritories2.xml template
   with multiple <sql:query> tags, 139
encoding
   text and binary content, 71
   specifying with the Output Encoding property, 370
ENTITIES and ENTITY data types, XML Schema
   varchar/nvarchar SQL Server equivalent types, 222
enumeration constraints, modelling, 238
ErrorLogFile property, SQLXMLBulkLoad object, 339, 347
errors
   exposing runtime errors as HTTP errors, 49
   IE friendly error messages, 54
   overwirtten messages and use of Query Analyzer, 56
   raised by MSXML, catching in OPENXML, 251
   Server: Msg 6603, 252
   Server: Msg 6809, 97
   Server: Msg 6829, 99
   Updategrams, 298
   web services error mechanisms, 423
escaping
   embedded XPath < signs, 531
   FOR XML EXPLICIT directives and, 113
   invalid XML characters, 161
      in URL queries, 131
      OPENXML limitations, 286
   quotation marks
      impossible within XPath strings, 519
   special characters
      XPath queries in templates, 201
every expression, XPath 2.0, 532
   XQuery modification, 556
Example_AuthorUpdate.xml* files, 389
except operator, XPath 2.0, 554
Exec command, running stored procedures, 125
ExecuteNonQuery() method, SqlXmlCommand, 400, 407
ExecuteStream() and ExecuteToStream() methods, SqlXmlCommand, 400
ExecuteXmlReader() method, SqlCommand object, 390, 391
ExecuteXmlReader() method, SqlXml Command, 400
existsNode() function, XPath, 499
expanded names XPath node property, 516

functions, XPath

expressions, XPath, 518
  possible corruption by browsers, 199
  SQLXML conversion to WHERE clauses, 380
  XPath 2.0, 553
extension functions, XPath, 534
external information
  transmitted XML dependence on, 61
  XML created for archiving shouldn't rely on, 63
extract() function and extractValue(), XPath, 499

F

false() function, XPath, 537
  boolean values from, 520
file receive functions, BizTalk, 465, 488
filtering the data in an XML document, 155
  using the OPENXML rowpattern parameter, 258
FIRE_TRIGGERS option unavailable with SQLXML Bulk Load, 357
FIRST_ROW option unavailable with SQLXML Bulk Load, 357
flags, SS STREAM FLAGS property, ADODB.Command object, 374
flattened datasets, raw row formatting output, 421
float data type, SQL Server, 68
  double XML Schema type equivalent, 221
float data type, XML Schema
  mapping SQL Server real type to, 68
  real SQL Server equivalent type, 221
floor() function, XPath, 537
FLWR (For Let Where Return)
  XQuery expressions based on, 503
    XPath 2.0 and, 554
For queries, XQuery, 503, 529, 556
FOR XML AUTO queries
  always run on the server, 49
  ELEMENTS parameter, 103
  one of three server-side options, 94
  server-side processing, 99
    limitations, 103
FOR XML EXPLICIT queries, 104
  adding a second UNION, 107
  cdata directive, 115
  client-side processing, 119
  conversion of time zone offsets, 69
  directives, 110-117
  element directive, 110
  generated by XPath queries, 195
    recursive queries, 205
  hide directive, 111
  ID, IDREF and IDREFS directives, 115
  mapping the inventory database to XML, 86
  modifying data to match the required output format, 60
  one of three server-side options, 95
  serializing Unicode strings, 71
  timestamp conversions, 73
  treatment of NULL values, 81
  using to create an XML document, 82
  vieworders.xml template, 437
  xml directive, 113
  XML views allow tighter control, 174
  XML views less cumbersome than, 88
  XMLDATA argument, 115

  xmltext directive, 112
  XPath queries with mapping schemas, 378, 380
FOR XML NESTED queries, 118
  client-side processing, 383
  client-side XML use, 49
  ClientSideNestedQueryOnSP project, 384
FOR XML queries, 91
  clause removed by SQLXMLOLEDB Provider, 382
  client-side processing
    advantages, 117
    three options available, 118
  client-side XML using, 38
  diagram of processing via ADO, 381
    using SQLXMLOLEDB Provider, 381
  differences between client-side and server-side, 382
  executing with SqlCommand, 390
  introduced, 32
  modes, 33
  nested output formatting and, 422
  OPENXML complementary to, 247
  retrieving results with ADO, 365
  retrieving XML from SQL Server based on, 41
  server-side and client-side compared, 92
  server-side processing
    three options available, 94
    viewing results, 93
  SQL limitations affecting aggregate functions, 95
  URL queries must use, 124
FOR XML RAW queries
  BINARY BASE 64 argument, 98
  client-side processing, 118
  one of three server-side options, 94
  server-side processing, 96
  XMLDATA argument, 98
ForceTableLock property, SQLXMLBulkLoad object, 340
foreign key problem, reused element types, 230
foreign key relationships, 76
  fulfillment system example, 242
  modeling child elements, 226
foreign keys, modeling ID-IDREF relationships, 231
form attribute, <xsd:attribute> and <xsd:element>, 591
format-number() function, XPath, 538
formatting output with SQLXMLQueryTool, 601
forms, HTML, applying Updategrams as, 321
forward axes, XPath, 522
forward slash, XPath absolute location paths, 521
friendly error messages, IE, SQLXML installation troubleshooting and, 54
FROM clause, XPath query equivalent, 190
fulfillment system example, 239
  design goals, 241
  designing the table structure, 241
  identifying relevant information, 241
  mapping column values, 242
function-available() function, XPath, 538
functions, XQuery, tabulated, 507
functions, XPath, 534-551
  calls to, as component of XPath expressions, 514, 518
  full alphabetic listing, 534
  functions not supported by SQLXML 3.0, 208
  SQLXML support, 198
  XML Schema and XDR equivalent data types, 196
  XPath 2.0 new functions, 554

615

future of XML and SQL Server, 495
  XQuery and, 508
future proofing criterion
  ad hoc business approach, 25
  evaluating the recommended design approach, 27
  relational end-to-(near the) end approach, 24
  XML end-to-end design approach, 22

G

gDay data type, XML Schema
  datetime SQL Server equivalent type, 220
General tab, SQLXML VDM tool, 45
generate-id() function, XPath, 538
GET requests, HTTP, applying Updategrams, 319
GetCustomerNameByID stored procedure
  exposing as a web service, 419
  web service example database, 417
  wrapping in .NET Services
    SQLXML 3.0 web services support, 428
GetInvoicesByBillingDate stored procedure
  exposing as a web service, 419
  row formatting output, 421
  web service example database, 417
global attributes, XML Schema, 560
global elements or attributes, XML Schema
  usng as root nodes, 565
gMonth and gMonthDay data types, XML Schema
  datetime SQL Server equivalent type, 220
GROUP BY clauses
  FOR XML NESTED supports, 118
  not usable with some FOR XML queries, 95
GUID (Globally Unique Identifiers)
  creating with Updategrams, 317
  setting ADODB.Command object Dialect property, 366
  specifying in an XML schema, 166
  uniqueidentifier data type, SQL Server, 74
guid attribute , updategram namespace, 293, 317
Guid.xml Updategram, 317
Guid2.xml Updategram, 318
gYear and gYearMonth data types, XML Schema
  datetime SQL Server equivalent type, 220

H

Handler.sql script, 317
<header> element, 293
hexBinary data type, XML Schema
  image/varbinary SQL Server equivalent types, 221
  representing SQL Server binary types, 71, 72, 73
hide directive, FOR XML EXPLICIT queries, 111
hierarchies, XML
  aggregating or repeating data, 62
  modeling, in XML views, 178
  resulting from multiple table joins, 102
  saving with metaproperties, 267, 274
home organization applications, BizTalk, 481
hr_map.xsd schemas, BizTalk Integration Case Study, 472
hrupdatetodeptupdate.xml, 484
hrupdgram.xml Updategram, 471

HTML
  applying Updategrams as HTML forms, 321
  shortcomings, addressed by standardization, 12
HTTP
  access from SQL Server 2000, 34
  applying Updategrams to a database, 319
    using HTTP POST, 322
HTTP requests
  SOAP requests run over HTTP POST, 418
  Updategram performance compared to ADO, 491
  using Updategrams with, 38
  XDR schemas and, 36
  XML Templates processed as, 37
HttpBrowserCapabilities class, System.Web, 445, 448
HttpPostUpdategram.vbp, 322
HTTPS, web service security, 427
human readabilty of XML, 19
hyperlinks, formatted URL query results, 128

I

ID attributes as identifier columns, 80
ID data type, XML Schema
  varchar/nvarchar SQL Server equivalent types, 222
id global attribute, XML Schema, 560
id() function, XPath, 539
ID, IDREF and IDREFS directives
  FOR XML EXPLICIT queries, 115
  values only distinct within a document, 235
identifiers, SQL, mapping between XML names and, 496
IDENTITY columns
  creating record identifiers, 239
  exclusion from XML schema designs, 80
  generating using local variables, 273
  not mapped in OPENXML, 253
  specifying in an XML schema, 165
  SQLXML Bulk Load from a stream object, 355
  values not propagated in SQLXML Bulk Load, 354
IDENTITY values
  capturing when inserting data with Update grams, 311
  propagating with the updg:at-identity attribute, 314
  returning with the updg:returnid attribute, 314
IDENTITY_INSERT setting, 273
  KeepIdentity property, SQLXML BulkLoad object and, 343
Identity1.xml Updategram, 313
ID-IDREF relationships, 77
  creating in XML schemas, 159
  fulfillment system example, 242
  modeling in relational structures, 231, 233
  performance problems from parsing, 78
  representing many-to-one relationships as, 77
ID-IDREFS relationships
  fulfillment system example, 242
  modeling in relational structures, 233
IDREF attributes *see* **ID-IDREF relationships.**
IDREF data type, XML Schema
  unspecificity of, 233
  varchar/nvarchar SQL Server equivalent types, 222
IDREFS attribute, OPENXML limitations affecting, 287
IDREFS data type, XML Schema, SQL Server equivalent types, 222

IE (Internet Explorer)
  Detecting Web Site Clients case study
    sample output from login.xsl, 441
    sample output from vieworders.xsl stylesheet, 442
  display of XML by SQLXMLQueryTool, 603
  error caused by absence of root node, 191
  IE 5+ needed for installing SQLXML examples, 42
  SQLXML problems and friendly error messages, 54
  User-Agent headers for IE6, 434
  viewing FOR XML query results, 94
  viewing inventory example results in, 88
  viewing results from SQLXMLQueryTool, 606
if...then...else constructs, XQuery, 507
IgnoreDuplicateKeys property, SQLXML BulkLoad object, 342, 343
IIS (Internet Information Services)
  see also Virtual Directory Management tool.
  architecture diagram component, 32
  SQLXML installation troubleshooting and, 55
IIS logging, SQLXML debugging tool, 56
image data type, SQL Server, 73
  XML Schema equivalent types, 221
images
  decoding BLOBs with sql:encode, 163
  mapping BLOBs to XML schemas, 162
implicit mappings, Updategrams, 297
importing schemas, 593
indexes, staging tables, 329
infinite recursion, 167
Infinity and -Infinity data types, XPath, 518, 519
inline schemas, 205
inner joins, XQuery example, 506
INNER LOOP JOINS, 269
input streams, CommandStream property, 397
Insert1.xml Updategram, 299
Insert2.xml Updategram, 297
Insert3.xml Updategram, 300
inserting data
  distinguishing inserts from updates, 217
  OPENXML compared to SQLXML Bulk Load, 358
  Updategrams
    inserting multiple rows, 301
    inverse relationships, 317
  using DiffGrams, 408
installing SQLXML, 42
  previous versions not overwritten, 43
instance documents, validating against a schema, 559
instance namespace, XML Schema, 585, 597
InStr function, ASP, searching for User-Agent headers, 453
int data type, SQL Server
  equivalent XML Schema types, 222
int data type, XML Schema
  int SQL Server equivalent type, 223
integer data type, XML Schema
  equivalent SQL Server types, 222
  problems with mapping to SQL Server, 224
interoperability
  different XML document types, 26
  n-tier architecture and, 13
  SQL/XML, ISO Working Draft and, 496
  SQL/XSQL as a possibility, 510
  web services as cross-platform mechanism, 416

intersect operator, XPath 2.0, 554
intranets and URL queries, 121, 122
invalid XML characters *see* special characters.
inventory example database, annotation examples, 147
inventory example, mapping database information
  design goals, 82
  identifying relevant database information, 83
  introduced, 82
  schema specification, 85
inverse relationships in Updategrams, 315
Inverse.xml Updategram, 315
invoice amounts from XML, totalling, 216
IO (Input-Output)
  combining OPENXML rowsets with other data, 269
  OPENXML performance implications, 285
is and isnot operators, XPath 2.0 node identity comparisons, 554
ISAPI (Internet Server API) configuring HTTP access, 34
ISO (international Organization for Standardization) SQL/XML Working Draft, 496
ISQL tool deficiencies in handling XML output, 601
is-xml attribute, <sql:param> element, 141
iterating expressions, XPath 2.0, 554

J

joins
  see also relationships; union.
  between OPENXML and tables, 274
    inefficient query plans from, 270, 286
  effect on FOR XML query examples, 97
  effect on XPath query performance, 203
  forcing using hints, 269
  inner joins, XQuery example, 506
  INNER LOOP JOINS, 269
  modeling in XML views, 177
  outer joins, XQuery example, 506
  structure and nested row formatting, 421
  use within FOR XML AUTO queries, 100
    effect of joining three tables, 102
  using UNION instead of, in FOR XML EXPLICIT queries, 105
  XQuery, 505
JXQI (Java XQuery API), Oracle, 500

K

KeepIdentity and KeepNulls properties, SQLXML BulkLoad object, 342, 343
key() function, XPath, 539
KILOBYTES_PER_BATCH option unavailable with SQLXML Bulk Load, 357

L

lang() function, XPath, 540
language data type, XML Schema
  varchar/nvarchar SQL Server equivalent types, 222

617

last() function, XPath, 540
  positional predicates and, 529
LAST_ROW option unavailable with SQLXML Bulk Load, 357
leastexpensiveproducts.xml template, 136
leastexpensiveproductsxsl.xml template, 140
left angle bracket, mapping SQL characters to Unicode, 496
length constraint, XML Schema, mapping to binary data, 72
less than character, mapping SQL characters to Unicode, 496
let queries, XQuery, 504
linking formatted URL query results, 128
LoadXML method, sp_xml_preparedocument preparation similar, 249
local-name() function, XPath, 540
location paths, XPath, 521-529
  steps, 522
  XPath expression type, 514, 518
locking, DiffGram operation, 408
logical operators, XPath and SQL, 533
logical predicates, XPath, 528
login.xml template, 436
  modified to use SQLXML Managed Classes, 446
login.xsl stylesheet, 439
login_ie.xsl. login_nonie.xsl and login_ppc.xsl stylesheets, 448
login_net.xml template, 446
long data type, XML Schema
  bigint SQL Server equivalent type, 223
  mapping SQL Server timestamp type to, 73
lookup values, 238
  fulfillment system example, 241

M

management reporting example, ID, IDREF and IDREFS directives, 115
many-to-many relationships
  modeling ID-IDREF relationships, 231
  modeling ID-IDREFS relationships, 233
many-to-one relationships, representing as IDREF attributes in XML, 77
mapper, interpreting relationships between tables, 154
Mapping Schema property, ADODB.Command object, 371
mapping schemas
  ADO querying using XPath with, 377
  client-side processing via SQLXMLOLEDB, 382
  BizTalk Integration Case Study, 472
  use by BizTalk Integration Case Study Updategrams, 469
  use with DiffGrams, 407, 409
mappings
  attributes to SQL Server columns, 148
    BizTalk Integration Case Study, 471
  BLOBs to XML schemas, 162
  column values to SQL Server model, 242
  column values to XML, 78
    converting data types, 79
    inventory example database, 85
  columns to XML
    influence of OPENXML flag settings, 263
  columns to XML elements, OPENXML, 253
  complex elements to SQL Server tables, 147
  data points to columns, 235
    creating constraints, 237
    creating record identifiers, 239
    data type conversion, 237
    modeling enumerations, 238
  database information to XML, 59
    inventory example introduced, 82
  elements to SQL Server tables
    BizTalk Integration Case Study, 471
  excluding elements from, 151
  fields between Updategrams, 484
  sample mapping illustrating use of sql:identity, 165
  SQL characters to Unicode in SQLX, 496
  SQLXML virtual names, 50
  text-only elements to SQL Server columns, 149
  Updategram default mappings, 297
  XML and relational data, 18
  XML to database columns, 331
    problems from data type differences, 223
  XML to SQL Server, 213
    design approach, 224-239
    example, 239
  XML to SQL Server data types, 219
  XPath functions to XML Schema and XDR data types, 196
mapping-schema attribute, 295
  adding to root elements as alternative, 297
  updategram namespace, 293
  use with XPath queries in templates, 200
markup characters
  escaping, 161
  protecting with the cdata directive, 115
markup documents, mapping XML to SQL Server, 224
MAXERRORS option unavailable with SQLXML Bulk Load, 357
maxExclusive restrictions, modeling check constraints, 80
maxLength attribute, base64Binary data type, 73
MaxRequestQueueSize registry setting, 53
MDAC (Microsoft Data Access Components)
  ADO 2.7 needed for SQLXMLQueryTool, 603
  MDAC 2.6 or 2.7 needed for installing SQLXML, 42
memory allocation, OPENXML, 33, 248, 283
  SQLXML Bulk Load and, 359
menus.xml template, 205
menus.xsl stylesheet, 206
message specifications, BizTalk, NewEmployee.xml, 467
Messaging Binding Wizard, BizTalk, 476, 486
Messaging Manager utility, BizTalk, 469, 482
messaging service, BizTalk, 464
messaging use of XML, 19
meta data columns
  FOR XML EXPLICIT queries, 104
  OPENXML and edge tables, 279
metaproperties, 252
  see also mp:.
  edge table coolumns as, 279
  namepace and attributes, 266-267
Method Communication Wizard, BizTalk, 478, 487
Microsoft Corporation
  see also BizTalk Server; SQL Server; Yukon.
  advocacy of data based computing, 10
  commitment to XML support, 509

Microsoft Visio 2000
Microsoft Visio 2000
  BizTalk Orchestration Designer, 473
  needed for BizTalk Integration Case Study, 459
Microsoft.Data.SqlXml namespace, 445
  SQLXML Managed Classes and, 40, 394
Microsoft-specificity, SQLXML 3.0 web services support, 427
  overcoming by wrapping as a .NET Service, 430
minExclusive restrictions modeling check constraints, 80
MinimalExample ADO code, 365
mixed-mode documents, mapping XML to SQL Server, 224
mod operator, XPath, not supported by SQLXML 3.0, 208
modeling XML in SQL Server
  mapping column values, 242
  mixed-mode documents, 224
modes, FOR XML clause
  client-side XML, 39
  introduced, 33
modifying tables
  with OPENXML, 271
  with URL queries, 125
money data type, SQL Server, 67
mp:id and mp:parentid metaproperties, 274
mp:xmltext metaproperty, 264
ms:format-date() function, XPath, 541
ms:format-time() function, XPath, 541
ms:local-name() function, XPath, 542
ms:namespace-uri() function, XPath, 542
ms:node-set() function, XPath, 543
ms:number() function, XPath, 543
ms:schema-info-available() function, XPath, 545
ms:string-compare() function, XPath, 532, 545
ms:type-is() function, XPath, 543
ms:type-local-name() function, XPath, 544
ms:type-namespace-uri() function, XPath, 544
ms:utc() function, XPath, 546
MSSQLXML command dialect, 323
MSXML (Microsoft XML Core Services)
  catching errors in OPENXML, 251
  converting Recordsets into XML documents, 23
  MSXML 4.0 needed for SQLXMLQueryTool, 603
  selectNodes() method, 526
  status, availability and updates, 32
  XPath extension functions from, 534
MultiAction.xml Updategram, 309
MultiAction*.xml Updategrams, 310
MultiInsert.xml Updategram, 301
multivalued attributes, OPENXML limitation, 287

N

name attribute, updategram namespace, 293
Name data type, XML Schema
  varchar/nvarchar SQL Server equivalent types, 222
name tests, XPath, 525
  tabulated, 527
name() function, XPath, 546
named parameters, XML Sales By Year stored procedure, 126
name matching, in Updategram default mappings, 298
namespace bindings and XPath name tests, 526
namespace declarations, OPENXML, 252
namespace nodes. XPath data model, 516
namespaces
  see also System.*.
  programmatically-generated namespace prefixes, 193
  specifying in schemas, 191
  SQLXML 3.0 SP1 bug affecting BizTalk, 469
    workaround, 475
  XML Schema, 559, 591
    form attribute and, 591
    instance namespace, 585, 597
NameSpaces property, ADODB.Command object, 369
Namespaces property, SqlXmlCommand, 395, 398
namespace-uri() function, XPath, 546
naming conventions
  ErrorLogFiles, SQLXMLBulkLoad object, 340
  generated IDs, 161
NaN (Not a Number) data type, XPath, 518, 519
narrative documents, mapping XML to SQL Server, 224
nchar data type, SQL Server, XML date types translated as, 460
nchar, nvarchar and ntext data types, SQL Server, 71
NCName data type, XML Schema, 222
negativeInteger data type, XML Schema, 223
nested For queries, XQuery, 504, 507
nested row formatting, XML Objects output method, 421
Nested.xml Updategram, 296
.NET Framework
  DiffGrams, 40
  required for SQLXML installation, 43
  using SQLXML with, 42
  Visual Studio .NET and, 444
.NET Managed Classes, 39
.NET Services, wrapping SQLXML 3.0 web services, 428
Netscape Navigator 4.08
  Detecting Web Site Clients case study, 441, 442
  User-Agent headers, 434
Network Load Balancing, 133
network performance
  OPENXML compared with stored procedures, 279
  server-side FOR XML queries, 96
new features, SQLXML 3.0 Service Pack 1, 34
New Messaging Port Wizard, 482
New Virtual Directory Properties dialog, VDM tool, 44
NewEmployee.skx XLANG file, 481
NewEmployee.xml message specification, 467
NewEmployeeToHRUpdategram.xml, 482
nightmare scenarios, 24
nillable attribute, 81
NMTOKEN and NHTOKENS data types, XML Schema
  varchar/nvarchar SQL Server equivalent types, 222
node properties, XPath, 516
node tests, XPath steps, 525-527

619

node trees, XPath modeling of XML documents, 515
node types, XPath, 516
  expanded names and string values tabulated, 517
nodes
  selection of, as distinguishing feature of XPath, 513
  XPath node identity comparisons, 532, 554
  XQuery 1.0 node constructors, 555
node-set operators, XPath, 533
node-sets, XPath
  comparisons, 532
  creating, 518
  sequences to replace in XPath 2.0, 552
  XPath data type, 518
nonNegativeInteger data type, XML Schema
  equivalent SQL Server types, 223
nonPositiveInteger data type, XML Schema
  equivalent SQL Server types, 222
normalized data avoids need for `<xsd:group>` and `<xsd:attributeGroup>`, 568
normalizedString data type, XML Schema, 221
normalize-space() function, XPath, 547
Northwind sample database
  combining OPENXML rowsets with other data, 267
  Detecting Web Site Clients case study, 436
  modified to show use of overflow columns, 112
  modifying tables with OPENXML, 274
  stored procedure returning XML from, 125
  used for FOR XML query examples, 96
    FOR XML AUTO queries, 100
    FOR XML EXPLICIT queries, 104
  used for SQLXML Bulk Load examples, 354
  used for SQLXML install examples, 45
  used for URL queries examples, 122, 123
NorthwindList.vbs script, 356
NorthwindList.xsd schema, 355
not() function, XPath, 547
  node-set comparisons, 532
NOTATION data type, XML Schema
  varchar/nvarchar SQL Server equivalent types, 221
n-tier architectures, system interoperability and data interchange, 13
NULL values
  applying Updategrams as HTML forms, 322
  expressing in an XML document, 81
  not null columns and OPENXML SchemaDeclaration, 256
  not null columns and OPENXML TableNames, 253
  passing to template queries, 141
  XML Schema null fields, 585
number() function, XPath, 547
  forcing a cast, 521
  parameterized templates and, 201
  use with XPath queries, 196
numbers XPath data type, 518
  creating, 519
numeric values, testing for, with XPath, 532
NumThreads registry setting, 53
nvarchar data type, SQL Server
  equivalent XML Schema types, 221
  SQL Server assumed type, XPath queries, 195
nwind.net project, 444

O

ODBC call syntax, running stored procedures, 127
OLEDBConnection object, System.Data.OLEDB, 391
ON DELETE CASCADE constraint, 310, 311
one-to-one relationships
  designing the tables structure, 241
  modeling parent-child relationships, 227
  representing as parent/child relationships in XML, 77
OPENQUERY, 286
OPENROWSET, 286, 364
OPENXML, 247
  ad hoc business approach and, 24
  ADO sending XML to a stored procedure using, 388
  appropriate to seldom used XML documents, 26
  column patterns, 265
  combining rowsets with other data, 267
  considered a remote scan, 269
  flags property, 262
  FOR XML compementary to, 91
  function syntax, 253
  introduced, 33
  limitations, 217, 286
    caching and statistics, 286
    multivalued attributes, 287
    updating documents, 286
    whitespace and escaped characters, 286
  memory allocation, 33, 283
  parsing an XML document, 248
    example, 250
  performance improvement by storing results in a table, 270
  rowpattern parameter, 258
  SchemaDeclarations, 255
  SQLXML Bulk Load compared to, 358
  using INSERT command with, 146
  using XML to modify tables, 271
  XML Bulk Load compared to, 37
  XML document example, 256
OPENXML-BasicInsert.sql, 271
OPENXML-BasicSelect.sql, 257
OPENXML-FilteringData.sql, 259
OPENXML-Flag8.sql, 264
OPENXML-FlagsPerformance.sql, 263
OPENXML-InsertHierarchicalData*.sql, 274
OPENXML-JoinToTable.sql, 269
OPENXML-MultipleInsertsWithIdentity.sql, 271
OPENXML-PerformanceNodeTest.sql, 284, 285
OPENXML-ReturnOrderBasedOnList.sql, 268
OPENXML-SaveHierarchy.sql, 275
OPENXML-sp_xml_preparedocument-BasicExample.sql, 250
OPENXML-sp_xml_preparedocument-ErrorHandling.sql, 251
OPENXML-sp_xml_preparedocument-MaximumDocumentSize.sql, 284
OPENXML-sp_xml_preparedocument-MemoryProof.sql, 284
OPENXML-sp_xml_preparedocument-TipsForLargeXML.sql, 251

OPENXML-TimestampIssue.sql, 256
OPENXML-VB and OPENXML-VB.Net
  perfromance test, 279
OPENXML-Whitespace.sql, 287
OPENXML-WithTable.sql, 255
operators, XPath, 530-534
  component of XPath expressions, 514, 518
  SQLXML support, 198
optimistic deleting, 303
Oracle
  support for XQuery, 500
  XML support prior to Oracle 9.0.2, 497
Oracle 9i release 2, 496-500
  XML support, 497, 498
    integrated functions for XPath querying, 499
orchestration schedules, BizTalk, 473
  Departmental phonelist, 485
  Updategram component, 474
ORDER BY clause, FOR XML EXPLICIT
  queries, 106
ORDER option unavailable with SQLXML Bulk
  Load, 358
orders.xml document, illustrating XQuery
  joins, 505
orders.xml template, 200
orders.xsd schema, 189
organizational approaches to handling XML, 21
OSQL tool, deficiencies in handling XML
  output, 601
outer joins, XQuery example, 506
Output Encoding property, ADODB.Command
  object, 370
output options, SQLXML 3.0 web services,
  420-423
  DataSet objects, 422
  Single Dataset, 423
  XML objects, 421
output parameters, template queries, 140
Output Stream property, ADODB.Command
  object, 367, 375
OutputEncoding property, SqlXmlCommand,
  395, 398
overflow columns
  ADO query example using, 380
    treatement when run client-side, 384
  SQLXML Bulk Load provision for, 332, 355
  use of xmltext directive, 112

P

paging returned XML with XSLT, 209
<param> element, 293
parameterized stored procedures
  calling using template queries, 138
  calling using URL queries, 126
parameterized templates, 37
  security advantages, 54
  storing Updategrams as, 321
  XPath queries as, 201
parameters, positional and named, 126
parent meta data column, 104
parent-child relationships
  modeling one-to-one relationships, 227
  nested output formatting and, 422
  representing one-to-one relationships in XML, 77
  reuse of element types, 228

parsers, XML, treatment of IDREF attributes, 78
performance criterion
  evaluating the recommended design approach, 27
  relational end-to-(near the) end approach, 23
  XML end-to-end design approach, 22
performance implications
  BizTalk Integration Case Study, 490
  client-side and server-side FOR XML queries, 118
  joins between OPENXML and tables, 274
  problems parsing ID-IDREF relationships, 78
  problems with Updategram use, 311
  problems with XPath in URL queries, 199
  processing added constraints, 237
  saving data using OPENXML compared with stored
    procedures, 279
  server-side FOR XML queries, 96
    network performance, 96
  using OPENXML
    IO effects, 285
    memory allocation, 283
    timings, 284
  workarounds for FOR XML limitations, 95
  XPath queries, 202
  XPath query type conversions, 196
  XPath steps and query performance, 524
performance improvement
  OPENXML, by storing results in a table, 270
  performance optimization
    SQLXMLBulkLoad property for, 340
    XPath, using SQL Profiler, 202
  pre-fetching of critical output, 26
  SQLXML, using registry settings, 53
  using OPENXML rowpattern in place of a WHERE
    clause, 259-260
  using templates for XPath queries, 203
  VDM Advanced tab caching options, 52, 135
persisting transient data
  see also archival use.
  hybrid design approach, 225
  loading XML into a database, 213
pessimistic deleting, 303
pessimistic updating, 305
PhoneList.skv orchestration schedule,
  BizTalk Integration Case Study, 487
Pocket PC
  Detecting Web Site Clients case study, 441, 442
  User-Agent headers, 434
portability advantage of XML storage, 19
position() function, XPath, 548
  not supported in SQL Server 2000, 528
  workaround for lack of SQLXML 3.0 support, 208
positional parameters, XML Sales By Year
  stored procedure, 126
positional predicates, XPath, 528
positiveInteger data type, XML Schema, 223
precedence, XPath operators, 530
predicates
  numeric-valued predicates not supported by SQLXML
    3.0, 208
  XPath location paths, 527
  XPath queries and, 193
    specifying, 194
pre-fetching of critical output, 26
prefixes
  identifying inline schemas with the # prefix, 206
  programmatically-generated namespace prefixes, 193
  specifying attributes with the @ prefix, 193

presentation of data, use for XML output, 20, 62
primary key constraints, SQLXML Bulk Load, 339
primary keys
see also identity columns.
creating record identifiers, 239
processing instructions, 298
processing see data manipulation.
products.xsl stylesheet, 127
products2.xsl stylesheet, 129
Profiler see SQL Profiler.
programmatic interfaces to SQL Server, 363
prohibited characters see special characters.
promoting normalized information, table design, 228, 230

Q

QName data type, XML Schema, 221
queries
see also template queries; URL queries; XPath queries.
formatting results to be user friendly, 88
returning results as XML, advantages, 202
Query Analyzer
error messages
Server: Msg 6603, 252
Server: Msg 6809, 97
Server: Msg 6829, 99
formatting FOR XML results, 364
formatting results using DBCC TRACEON (257), 601
OPENXML rowpattern
compared to the WHERE clause, 259
set operation costs, 262
SQLXML debugging tool, 56
viewing FOR XML query results, 93
viewing inventory example results in, 88
query plan unreliability for OPENXML, 270, 286
query tool see SQLXMLQueryTool.
quotation marks, escaping, 161
impossible within XPath strings, 519

R

rangedemployees.xml template, 137
raw row formetting, XML Objects output, 421
real data type, SQL Server, 68
float XML Schema type equivalent, 221
real estate site example
alternative presentation structures, 63
mapping database information to XML, 60
record identifiers, creating primary keys, 239
recreateTables.sql script, 311
recursion depth limiting in XML schemas, 167
recursive queries, XPath, 203
RecvDeptUpdate messaging implementations, BizTalk Integration Case Study, 486
RecvNewEmployee messaging implementations, BizTalk Integration Case Study, 476
RecvPhoneUpdateChannel, BizTalk Integration Case Study, 489
referential integrity preserved by SQLXML Bulk Load, 357

registry settings
SQLXML performance and, 53
SQLXMLQueryTool needs write permissions, 604
regular expressions and <xsd:pattern> element, 579
Relate.xml Updategram, 306
Relate2.xml Updategram, 307
relating tables
fulfillment system example, 242
modeling many-to-many relationships, 234
relational data and XML, 18
relational databases
success of, 10
support for retrieval as XML, 12
XML aspects relevant to, 13
relational datasets for data presentation, 9
relational end-to-(near the) end approach, handling XML with SQL Server 2000, 23
relational operators, XPath, 198
relational structures, 17
designing, for XML storage in SQL Server, 226
handling child elements, 226
handling ID-IDREF relationships, 231
handling ID-IDREFS relationships, 233
problems in storing XML within, 18
XML and, optimized for different areas, 17
relationships
see also joins; walking through.
designing relational structures for XML storage, 226
determining the XML structure, 77
inverse relationships in Updategrams, 315
specifying relationships between two SQL tables, 152
Updategrams and, 295
XML Schema, 585
relative location paths, XPath, 521
relevant information
identifying, when storing XML in SQL Server, 225
fulfillment system example, 241
'Reluctant Codd Approach', 23
remote data, OPENXML rowsets regarded as, 269, 270, 286
repetition, avoiding with the <xsd:group> element, 566
retrieval of different XML document types, 26
return codes, stored procedures, 423
return values
controlling with .NET wrappers, 429
no control over, in SQLXML 3.0 web services, 428
returnid attribute, updategram namespace, 293, 314
reused element types, 228
reverse axes, XPath, 522
rmenu.xsd schema, 204
root element
adding to FOR XML query results, 94, 109
adding to URL queries output, 130
adding, with SQLXMLQueryTool, 605
defining for SQLXML Bulk Load, 332
example of an unmapped XML element, 150
identifying for XML derived from a database, 75
problems specifying in BizTalk Integration Case Study, 469
workaround, 475
specifying with XML Root property, 369
XMLFragment property, SQLXML BulkLoad object and, 344

root node
  required for IE display of XML, 191, 194
  using global elements or attributes as, 565
  XPath absolute location paths start with, 521
root parameter, URL queries, 124
RootTag property, SqlXmlCommand, 395, 398
round() function, XPath, 548
rowpattern parameter, OPENXML, 258
  extending to set operations, 260
ROWS_PER_BATCH option unavailable with SQLXML Bulk Load, 357
rowsets, OPENXML
  combining with other data, 267
  fixed size and performance overhead, 285
rowversion columns, OPENXML, should use bigint instead, 256
RPC (Remote Procedure Calls) with web services, 416
rules, XML, generated IDs, 161
runtime errors, exposing as HTTP errors, 49

S

salesbyyear.xml template, 138
scalability and client-side processing, 381
scalability criterion
  evaluating the recommended design approach, 27
  relational end-to-(near the) end approach, 23
  XML end-to-end design approach, 22
schema mapping
  setting up for XPath queries, 188
  SQLXML Bulk Load, 330
  SQLXML virtual names, 51
schema objects, data access with XML views and, 180
SchemaCacheSize registry setting, 53
SchemaDeclarations, OPENXML, 255
  column patterns as alternatives, 265
SchemaGen property, SQLXML BulkLoad object, 338
SchemaGen property, SQLXMLBulkLoad object, 332
SchemaPath property, SqlXmlCommand, 395, 399
schemas
  see also annotated XML schemas; database schemas; XML Schema; XSD.
  aliasing tables in, for added security, 208
  edge tables and inline schemas, 282
  example, defining and constraining types, 583
  HTTP access and, 35
  illustrating recursive queries, 204
  inline schemas, 205
  role in SQLXML Bulk Load, 328
    example, 333, 351
  setting up sample schemas for XPath queries, 189
  showing uniqueness constraints, 587
  showing use of the form attribute, 592
  specifying namespaces in, 191
  use in XPath 2.0, 553
  XML schemas compared with XDR, 64
schemas-microsoft-com namespace see urn:schema*.

SCOPE_IDENTITY() function, 271
Script Component Binding Wizard, BizTalk, 478, 487
scripts, access to User-Agent header, 435
scrolling problem, OSQL tool, 601
seconds, treatment by smalldatetime data types, 70
security advantages of SOAP faults, 426
security criterion
  evaluating the recommended design approach, 27
  relational end-to-(near the) end approach, 23
  XML end-to-end design approach, 22
security features, STREAM_FLAGS_DISALLOW_* flags, 374
security issues
  applying Updategrams as HTML forms, 321
  applying Updategrams from a URL, 320
  BizTalk Integration Case Study, 463, 491
    Updategram translations removing sensitive information, 492
  dbobject mappings, 50
  server-side FOR XML queries, 95
  SQLXML, 53
  SQLXML Bulk Load, 359
  template queries, 133
    advantages over URL queries, 132
  transmitting XML data, 61
  URL queries, 48, 54, 122
  XPath queries, 207
    use of templates advisable, 199
  XPath queries in URL queries, 199
Security tab, SQLXML VDM tool, 46
security updates, SQL Server, 463
SELECT statement
  see also FOR XML queries.
  FLWR expression differences from, 505
  FLWR expressions resemble, 503
  XPath queries compared to, 190-198, 513
SelectCustomersByName stored procedure
  exposing as a web service, 419
  web service example database, 417
selectNodes() method, MSXML, 526
self-contained documents
  preferable for data transmission, 61, 62
  XML created for archiving, 63
self-joins
  infinite recursion risk, 167
  recursive queries and, 203
SendToDeptFile messaging implementations, BizTalk Integration Case Study, 479
SendToHR messaging implementations, BizTalk Integration Case Study, 478
sensitive information see security issues.
separating content from presentation, XSLT role, 20
separation of types from content, XML Schema, 570
sequences replace node-sets in XPath 2.0, 552
serializer, interpreting relationships between tables, 152
serializating content, for later presentation, 62
servers, FOR XML AUTO queries always run on, 49

server-side processing
  disadvantages of using SQLOLEDB Provider, 381
  FOR XML queries, 94
    advantages of client-side over, 93
    compared to client-side, 92
    FOR XML AUTO queries, 99
    FOR XML EXPLICIT queries, 104
    FOR XML RAW queries, 96
    security and performance considerations, 95
  OPENXML, 359
server-side script access to User-Agent headers, 435
set logic
  XPath 2.0 new operators, 554
  XPath node identity comparisons, 532
set operations, OPENXML rowpattern parameter, 260
Settings tab, SQLXML VDM tool, 48
setup, SQLXML, 42
  previous versions not overwritten, 43
SGDropTables property, SQLXML BulkLoad object, 338
SGUseID property, SQLXML BulkLoad object, 338
short data type, XML Schema, 223
shredding, OPENXML, 248
simple type restrictions, XML Schema, 575
Single Dataset output method, SQLXML 3.0 web services, 423
smalldatetime data type, SQL Server, 69
smallint data type, SQL Server, 222
smallmoney data type, SQL Server, 67
SOAP (Simple Object Access Protocol)
  see also web services.
  basis for system interoperability and data interchange, 13
  creating a SOAP virtual name, 418
  possible future security enhancements, 463
  potential for using in BizTalk Integration Case Study, 463
  role as an XML standard technology, 16
  role in web services, 415
  web services support in SQLXML, 41
SOAP faults, 423
  security advantages of using, 426
soap mapping, SQLXML virtual names, 51
SOAP Toolkit
  needed for setting up SQLXML web service support, 416
  version needed for installing SQLXML, 43
SoapServiceTest project, consuming web services, 424
Social Security Numbers used as ID, 459
some expression, XPath 2.0, 532
  XQuery modification, 556
sp_executesql stored procedure, 402
sp_InsertOrUpdateCustomer stored procedure, 218
sp_reset_connection stored procedure, 251
sp_UpdateTotalInvoice stored procedure, 216
sp_xml_preparedocument stored procedure, 33
  use by OPENXML, 248
  xpath_namespace parameter, 252
sp_xml_removedocument stored procedure, 33
  OPENXML use, 249
spaces *see* **special characters; whitespace.**

special characters
  escaping invalid characters, 161, 287.
  escaping in URL queries, 131
  escaping in XPath queries, 201
  spaces prohibited within URLs, 124
  SQL identifiers, SQLX mapping and, 496
  tabulated, with appropriate replacements, 131
SQL
  possible interoperation with XQuery, 510
  XQuery similarities to, 500, 501, 502
    FLWR expression differences from SELECT, 505
    FLWR expressions resemble SELECT, 503
SQL ISAPI DLL, configuring HTTP access, 34
SQL Profiler
  effect of data types on XPath queries, 195
  performance optimization of XPath with, 202
  SQLXML debugging tool, 56
SQL Server 2000
  see also Yukon.
  organizational approaches to handling XML, 21
SQL Server Agent Job Step, running VB Script, 335
sql:* attributes tabulated, 168
sql:datatype attribute, 332
  effects on SQLXML Bulk Load table creation, 339
  specifying data types in XSD, 195
sql:encode attribute, 163
  XML schema attributes tabulated, 169
sql:field attribute, 148, 149, 331
  annotating schemas with, 176, 178
  mapping nodes to columns when creating XML views, 175
  XML schema attributes tabulated, 168
sql:guid attribute, 166
  XML schema attributes tabulated, 169
<sql:header> element
  parameterizing template queries, 136
  sql:nullvalue attribute, 141
sql:hide attribute, 169
sql:identity attribute, 165-166
  capturing identity values, 313
  XML schema attributes tabulated, 169
sql:inverse attribute, 169, 315
sql:is-constant attribute
  annotating the schema for the XML views example, 182
  choice of, against sql:mapped, 151
  defining root elements, 332
  introduced, 148
  layering a XML View over a SQL Server view, 184
  unmapped XML elements and, 150
  XML schema attributes tabulated, 168
sql:key-fields attribute, 157, 296
  providing for Updategrams updates, 306
  specifying compound keys, 158
  XML schema attributes tabulated, 169
sql:limit-field attribute, 156
  checking data types for XPath queries, 203
  XML schema attributes tabulated, 169
sql:limit-value attribute, 156
  XML schema attributes tabulated, 169
sql:mapped attribute
  choice of, against sql:is-constant, 151
  excluding elements from, 151
  introduced, 150
  XML schema attributes tabulated, 168

SQLXMLBulkLoad object

sql:max-depth attribute, 168
  recursive queries and, 203
  XML schema attributes tabulated, 170
sql:nullvalue attribute, <sql:header> element, 141
sql:overflow-field attribute, 333
  XML schema attributes tabulated, 169
<sql:param> element
  is-xml attribute, 141
  login.xml template, 436
sql:prefix attribute
  creating ID-IDREF relationships, 160
  XML schema attributes tabulated, 169
<sql:query> element, 37
  client-side-xml attribute, 383
  template queries, 135
    calling stored procedures, 136
    client-side-xml attribute, 142
<sql:relationship> element
  asserting relationships between elements, 153
  asserting relationships between tables, 296
  sql:inverse attribute, 315
  Updategrams perfoming mutliple actions, 309
sql:relation attribute
  annotating schemas with, 176, 178
  BizTalk Integration Case Study, 472
  mapping complex elements to SQL Server tables, 147
  mapping elements to tables when creating XML views, 175
  XML schema attributes tabulated, 168
sql:relationship attribute
  annotating schemas with, 178
  modeling joins in XML views, 177
  specifying relationships when creating XML views, 175
  XML schema attributes tabulated, 169
sql:use-cdata attribute, 161
  XML schema attributes tabulated, 169
<sql:xpath-query> element, 141, 200
sql:xsl attribute
  login.xsl stylesheet, 440
  menus.xsl stylesheet, 206
sql_variant data type, SQL Server, 73
SqlCommand object, ADO.NET
  executing FOR XML queries, 390
SQLCommandClientSide project, 399
SqlConnection object, System.Data.SqlClient, 391
SQLDemoDiffGramWriter project, 405
sqlis3.dll library
  Advanced tab settings, VDM, 51
  configuring HTTP access, 34
SQLOLEDB Provider
  ADODB.Command object extended properties, 368
  architecture diagram component, 32
  server-side FOR XML processing, 92
  XDR schemas part of, 35
  XML Templates parsed by, 36
sqlWrapper project, 428
sqlWrapperTest application, 429
SQLX initiative, 496
SQLXML
  see also Updategrams; Virtual Directory Management Tool.
  architecture, features and versions, 34
  browser detection using with ADO, 451
  browser detection using XML templates
    benefits and drawbacks, 434
    drawbacks, 443

configuring virtual directories with ISAPI, 34
features available in custom setup, 44
installation, 42
  creating virtual directories, 44
  installing SQLXML 3.0, 43
  registry settings, 53
  software requirements, 42
  testing the virtual directories, 52
  troubleshooting, 54
integration with .NET and DNA, 42
Microsoft news group, 55
no direct access to User-Agent headers, 435
programmatic access, 363
security issues, 53
server-side FOR XML support with SQLXML 3.0, 92
SQLXML 3.0 SP1 bugs affecting BizTalk, 464, 469
  workaround, 475
SQLXML 3.0 SP1 needed for BizTalk Integration Case Study, 458
SQLXML 3.0 web services support, 415
  setting up, 416
  shortcomings, 427
  wrapping in .NET Services, 428
supports both XML Schema and XDR annotation, 146
web releases, role in XML support, 31
SQLXML 3.0
  XPath 1.0 functionality not fully supported, 187, 208
SQLXML 3.0 Custom Setup, 43
SQLXML Bulk Load, 37, 327
  see also SQLXMLBulkLoad object.
  differences form other bulk load interfaces, 356
  DTS hosting, 344
  example schema, 333
  functionality not available with, 357
  loading from a stream instead of a file, 354
  loading multiple tables, 348
  OPENXML compared to, 358
  overview diagram, 328
  possible use in ad hoc business approach, 24
  sample script, 345
  stored procedures for batch processing and, 217
  Updategrams compared to, 358
  XML schema annotation technology, 146
SQLXML Managed Classes, 39, 393-404, 446
  architecture diagram component, 32
  can use with client-side FOR XML queries, 119
  Detecting Web Site Clients case study, 444
  improvements expected in Yukon, 510
  integation with .NET, 42
  SqlXmlAdapter class, 402
  SqlXmlCommand class, 394
  SqlXmlParameter class, 401
  XPath queries in, 202
SqlXmlAdapter class, 402
  least flexible of the Managed Classes, 404
SQLXMLAdapterExample project, 402
SQLXMLBulkLoad object
  architecture diagram component, 32
  completing the script, 345
  properties, 336-344
    control over data logging, 342
    error handling, 339
    optimization, 340
    providing connection information, 336
    table creation and deletion, 338
    transaction management, 341
  running the script in DTS, 344
  sample script, 335

625

SqlXmlCommand class, 394
  ExecuteStream method, 400
  methods tabulated, 400, 401
  properties, 395
  using an XPath query, 402
SqlXmlCommandDemo project, 394
SQLXMLDataSetDemo project, 392
SQLXMLDiffgramBeforeUpdate.xml file, 406
SQLXMLDiffgramDelete project, 410
SQLXMLDiffgramDelete.xml file, 411
SQLXMLDiffgramInsert program, 408
SQLXMLOLEDB Provider
  ADODB.Command object extended properties, 368
  architecture diagram component, 32
  benefits of using, 42
  can use with client-side FOR XML queries, 119
  client-side processing and, 381
  DataProvider paramter, 383
  server-side FOR XML support, 92
  XML Schema must use, 378
  XPath queries using ADO, 202
SQLXMLOpenXMLExample project, 388
SqlXmlParameter class, 401
SQLXMLQueryTool, 603
  compared to ISQL, OSQL and Query Analyzer, 601
  Data link Properties screen, 603
  programming techniques used for, 364
  results in a browser window, 606
  text results, 606
srvorder.xsd schema, 192
SS STREAM FLAGS property, ADODB.Command object, 374
  setting, 375
SSL (Secure Sockets Layer), 54
staging tables, SQLXML Bulk Load, 329
standards support
  see also W3C.
  mapping database information to XML, 59
  XML technologies, 13
starts-with() function, XPath, 548
status attributes, modifying tables with OPENXML, 275
steps, XPath location paths, 522
storage media, XML for archiving, 64
storage of different XML document types, 25
stored procedures
  alternative to XPath queries returning large documents, 210
  batch processing using XML Bulk Load and, 217
  client-side FOR XML and, 93, 118
  distinguishing updates from inserts, 218
  executing using URL queries, 125
  exposing functionality as a web service, 419
  output parameters used in template queries, 140
  parameterized stored procedures, 126, 138
  querying, to get XML, 384
  return codes, 423
  saving data using OPENXML compared with, 279
  sp_reset_connection, 251
  sp_xml_preparedocument, 33
    use by OPENXML, 248
  sp_xml_removedocument, 33
  totalling XML data in SQL Server, 216
  using OPENXML, ADO and, 388
  web service support example, 417

Stream object, ADODB, 452
  ADO 2.5 can save Recordsets to, 385
  MinimalExample ADO code, 367
  programming XML with ADO, 365
  providing XML templates in an input stream, 377
  SQLXML Bulk Loading from, 354
STREAM_FLAGS_* constants
  security features, 374
  tabulated, 374
  using absolute paths, 371
string data type, XML Schema
  mapping SQL Server char type to, 70
  mapping SQL Server nchar, nvarchar and ntext types to, 71
  mapping SQL Server sql_variant type to, 73
  mapping SQL Server text type to, 70
  mapping SQL Server uniqueidentifier type to, 74
  mapping SQL Server varchar type to, 70
  varchar/nvarchar SQL Server equivalent types, 221
string values, XPath node property, 517
string() function, XPath, 548
  forcing a cast, 521
string-length() function, XPath, 549
strings, XPath data type, 518
style.xslt stylesheet, creating Updategrams on the fly, 319
stylesheets
  caching, VDM Advanced tab settings, 134
  formatting template query results, 140
  formatting URL query results, 127
SubmitUpdateToDb messaging implementations, BizTalk Integration Case Study, 487
substitiutionGroup attribute <xsd:element>, 566
substitution
  namespace qualification and, 591
  usng the ref attribute, 565
substring() function and substring-after() functions, XPath, 549
substring-before() function, XPath, 550
sum() function, XPath, 550
support for XML in SQL Server 2000, SQLXML 3.0 and Yukon, 509
sync blocks, Updategrams, 38
<sync> element see <updg:sync> element.
system XML files, 25
System.Data.DataSet class, 392
System.Data.OLEDB.OLEDBConnection object, 391
System.Data.SqlClient.SqlConnection object,, 391
System.Web.HttpBrowserCapabilities class, 445, 448
system-property() function, XPath, 550

T

table creation using sql:datatype annotations, 339
table creation and deletion, SQLXML BulkLoad object properties, 338
table structure
  fulfillment system example, 241
  persisting XML transactional data, 215

unbounded data types

table variables
   recommended for OPENXML UPDATEs and DELETEs, 271
   storing results in, to reduce OPENXML IO, 269
   use with OPENXML INSERT example, 272
tableCreation.sql script, 291, 307
TableCreationScript.sql, 330
TableName specification, OPENXML, 253
tag meta data column, 104
taking a step back, 25
targetNamespace attribute, <xsd:schema>
   global elements and, 566
   namespace qualification and, 192, 591
TDS (Tabular Data Stream), 382
TempFilePath property, SQLXMLBulkLoad object, 341
template caching, VDM Advanced tab settings, 134
template mapping, SQLXML virtual names, 51
template queries, 132-142
   advantages over URL queries, 132
   calling stored procedures, 136
   parameterizing queries, 136
   posting dynamically created templates, 142
   security issues, 133
   server-side and client-side templates, 133
   setting up the environment, 133
   settings for additional features, 141
   usage, 135
      not recommended for database administration, 139
      usage guidelines, 132
   using multiple queries, 138
   using output parameters, 140
   using stylesheets, 140
   XPath queries within, 141
TemplateCacheSize registry setting, 53
TemplateExample project, 376
TemplateFromFile project, 377
templates, XML
   accessing data through XMLviews, 180
   accessing XML views using, 180
   applying Updategrams from, 320
   can use with client-side FOR XML queries, 119
   Detecting Web Site Clients case study
      using SQLXML and XML templates, 436
   DiffGrams as, 404
   example including multiple queries, 377
   example with embedded inline schema, 205
   HTTP access and, 35
   retrieving XML from SQL Server 2000, 36
   security advantages of using with parameters, 54
   SOAP faults and, 423
   use for XPath queries, 199
      performance gain from, 203
      security advantages, 199, 207
      using parameters, 201
   using via ADO, 375
TemplateWith2Queries.xml, 377
TemplateWithQuery.xml, 376
temporary data, manipulating in SQL Server, 215
temporary files, role in SQLXML Bulk Loading, 328
temporary tables
   recommended for OPENXML UPDATEs and DELETEs, 271
   storing results in, to reduce OPENXML IO, 269
Ten Least Expensive Products stored procedure, 125
   calling from a template query, 136
   modified to illustrate using stylesheets, 127

text data type, SQL Server, 70
text-only elements, mapping to columns, 149
threading and registry settings, 53
time data type, XML Schema, 220
timestamp columns, OPENXML, should use bigint instead, 256
timestamp data type, SQL Server, 73
timings, OPENXML performance implications, 284
tinyint data type, SQL Server, 222
token data type, XML Schema, 222
tokenizing IDREFS values, 234
tools
   debugging tools for SQLXML problems, 56.
   SQLXMLQueryTool compared to ISQL, OSQL and Query Analyzer, 601
Top Product stored procedure, 140
totalling invoice amounts, 216
transaction data, persisting in SQL Server, 213
transaction isolation levels, INSERTs with IDENTITY columns, 273
transaction management
   differences between Updategrams and SQLXML Bulk Load, 358
   multiple statements within an <sql:query> element, 139
Transaction property, SQLXML BulkLoad object
   ConnectionCommand property and, 336, 341
   IgnoreDuplicateKeys property and, 343
Transaction property, SQLXMLBulkLoad object, 341
transactions
   defined by <updg:sync> blocks, 294
      deleting data with Updategrams, 303
      inserting several rows, 301
   Updategrams performing multiple actions, 307
   XLANG Scheduler and, 490
translate() function, XPath, 551
transmission of data use for XML, 61
   inventory example database, 82
troubleshooting SQLXML installation, 54
   properly set up virtual directories, 55
true() function, XPath, 551
   boolean values from, 520
T-SQL
   see also SELECT statement.
   FOR XML and OPENXML based on, 247
   performance advantages over XPath queries, 202
tuning *see* **performance improvement.**
type attribute, <xsd:attribute>, 195
   XPath data types and, 196
type conversions, XPath queries, 196

U

UDDI (Universal Description, Discovery and Integration), 426
   role as an XML standard technology, 17
UDF (User-Defined Functions) returing errors as SOAP faults, 423
unary operator, XPath not supported by SQLXML 3.0, 208
unbounded data types, problems mapping to SQL Server, 223

627

Unicode
  deficiencies of ISQL tool in handling, 601
  mapping SQL characters to, in SQLX, 496
  SQL Server nchar, nvarchar and ntext types to, 71
UNION ALL statement, OPENXML rowpattern set operations, 260
union operator, XPath, 533
  merging node-sets, 518
  node identity comparisons, 532
  XPath 2.0, 554
UNION statement, FOR XML EXPLICIT queries, 104, 105
  adding a second union, 107
unique keys, specifying in XML, 157
uniqueidentifier data type, SQL Server, 74
uniqueness, 586-590
  defining for nodes, 586
  document illustrating uniqueness constraints, 588
  schema showing uniqueness constraints, 587
unit conversion before transformation, 62
units, specifying with attributed data elements, 236
unmapped XML elements, 150
unparsed-entity() function, XPath, 551
unsigned* data types, XML Schema, 223
Update*.xml files, 304-305
UpdateFromBTS function, 475
Updategram examples
  Delete1.xml, 302
  Delete2.xml and Delete3.xml, 303
  dept_update.xml, 462
  deptupdgram.xml, 472
  Guid.xml, 317
  Guid2.xml, 318
  hrupdgram.xml, 471
  Identity1.xml, 313
  Insert2.xml schemaless Updategram, 297
  Insert3.xml, 300
  Inverse.xml, 315
  mapping hrupdgram.xml fields to deptupdgram.xml, 484
  MultiAction.xml, 309
  MultiAction2.xml and MultiAction3.xml, 310
  MultiInsert.xml, 301
  Nested.xml, 296
  Relate.xml, 306
  Relate2.xml, 307
  Update1.xml, 304
  Update2.xml and Update3.xml, 305
Updategrams, 291
  applying to a database, 319
    as HTML forms, 321
    directly using HTTP POST, 322
    from templates, 320
    using ADO, 323
  BizTalk Integration Case Study, 469
    advantages over ADO approach, 463
    performance helped by ADO use, 491
  BizTalk Server and, 457
  capturing identity values for inserted records, 311
  compared to DiffGrams, 412
  creating GUIDs, 317
  default mappings, 297
  defined, 292
  deleting data with, 302
    deleting multiple rows, 303

  driving, with annotated schemas, 295
  errors, 298
  example, 293
  generating on the fly, 318
  illustrating the use of sql:guid, 166
  illustrating the use of sql:identity, 165
  inserting data with, 298
    capturing identity values, 311
    inserting multiple rows, 301
  inseting XML data into SQL Server, 38
  inverse relationships, 315
  limitation for sophisticate processing, 217
  performing multiple actions, 307
  performing multiple updates, 296
  possible use in ad hoc business approach, 24
  preferable to DiffGrams in most cases, 404
  processing data-centric XML with, 27
  SQLXML 3.0 SP1 bug affecting root specification, 469
  SQLXML Bulk Load compared to, 358
  storing as parameterized templates, 321
  sync blocks, 38
  table constraints apply, 302
  updating data with, 304
    explicitly relating before and after, 307
    explicitly relating records, 306
  using XSLT to create Updategrams as needed, 318
  XML schema annotation technology, 145
  XPath query security problems, 207
updateXML() function, XPath, 499
updating data
  distinguishing updates from inserts, 217
  example using a DiffGram, 406
  updating data with Updategrams, 304
    explicitly relating before and after, 307
    explicitly relating records, 306
    importance of matching elements, 306
updating documents
  different XML document types, 26
  OPENXML limitations, 286
<updg:after> elements, 294
  inserting data with Updategrams, 298
  inserting multiple rows, 301
  updating data with Updategrams, 304
updg:at-identity attribute, 293, 314, 318
<updg:before> elements, 294
  deleting data with Updategrams, 302
  distinguishing updates from insertions, 296
  updating data with Updategrams, 304
updg:guid attribute, 293, 317
updg:id attribute
  explicitly relating records when updating data, 306
updg:returnid attribute, 293, 314
<updg:sync> element, 292, 294
  defining transactions, inserting several rows, 301
  mapping-schema attribute, 295
Upgrade to Version 3 tab, SQLXML VDM tool, 52
URL encoding
  examples for installing SQLXML don't use, 42
  unencoding to return an image reference, 163
  URL queries, 124
URL queries, 121-131
  applying Updategrams to a database, 320
  can use with client-side FOR XML queries, 119
  HTTP access and, 35
  issuing against an XML View, 185

Index

URL queries (continued)
  modifying content types, 130
  returning an entire document, 190
  security issues, 48, 54, 122
  setting up the environment, 123
  specifying namespaces, 193
  testing the virtual directory installation, 52
  usage, 123
  using stylesheets, 127
  version testing and, 55
  XPath queries in, 199
    using parameters, 201
URLs
  accessing XML views using, 180, 183
  applying Updategrams from a URL, 320
  hybrid design approach to XML storage, 225
  web service location in UDDI registries, 427
urn:schemas-microsoft-com:mapping-schemas namespace, 331
urn:schemas-microsoft-com:xml-metaprop namespace, 252, 266
urn:schemas-microsoft-com:xml-sql namespace, 55, 146
urn:schemas-microsoft-com:xml-updategram namespace
  elements and attributes tabulated, 292
urn:schemas-microsoft-com:xml-updategram schema, 358
  SQLXML 3.0 SP1 bug affecting BizTalk, 469
urn:schemas-microsoft-com:xslt namespace
  XPath extension functions, 534
User-Agent headers
  browser detection dependence on, 434
  not directly accessible to SQLXML, 435
  searching for, with ASP InStr function, 453
user-defined data types, 237
  mapping SQL Server money type to, 67
usp_CustomerInvoices stored procedure, 384
usp_Update_AuthorNames stored procedure, 388

V

validation
  instance documents, 559
  not performed by SQLXML, 40
  XQuery, 508
value spaces, XML schemas, 223, 237
varbinary data type, SQL Server, 72
  XML Schema equivalent types, 221
varchar data type, SQL Server, 70
  equivalent XML Schema types, 221
variables, XPath, 529
  parameterized templates and, 201
VB Script
  debugging, 345
  use in SQLXML Bulk Load examples, 329, 335
    CustomerInvoice.VBS script, 352
    DTS hosting, 344
VB_Posting.txt, 142
VDM (Virtual Directory Management)
  see also Virtual Directory Management tool.
  applying Updategrams using HTTP, 319
  configuring HTTP access, 34
  template queries and, 133
  URL queries and, 123

version testing
  SQLXML installation troubleshooting and, 55
vieworders.aspx page, 449
vieworders.xml template, 437
  modified to use a stylesheet, 442
  simplifying for SQLXML Managed Classes, 446
vieworders.xsl stylesheet, 442
vieworders_ie.xsl, vieworders_nonie.xsl and vieworders_ppc.xsl stylesheets, 450
vieworders_net.xml template, 447
views, layering an XML view over a SQL Server view, 183
virtual directories
  see also VDM.
  configuring, in BizTalk Integration Case Study, 461
  creating a SOAP virtual name, 418
  creating in classic ADO, 451
  creating schema objects, 180
  creating when installing SQLXML, 44
    testing the setup, 52
  Detecting Web Site Clients case study
    using SQLXML and XML templates, 436
  securing data access, 207
  setting up, for template queries, 133
  setting up, for URL queries, 123
  setting up, for XPath queries, 188
  setting Updategrams as templates, 320
  SQLXML installation troubleshooting and, 55
  URL queries run against, 121
  web service security and authentication, 427
Virtual Directory Management Tool, SQLXML, 44, 188
  Advanced tab, 51
  Data Source tab, 47
  General tab, 45
  Security tab, 46
  Settings tab, 48
  Upgrade to Version 3 tab, 52
  Virtual Names tab, 50
Virtual Names tab, SQLXML VDM tool, 50
Visual Basic .NET, example FOR XML query, 390
Visual Basic 6
  code to apply an Updategram using ADO, 323
  code to apply an Updategram using HTTP POST, 322
  SQLXMLQueryTool, 603
  use with ADO in programmatic access examples, 364
Visual Studio .NET
  consuming web services, 424
  Detecting Web Site Clients case study, 444
  wrapping web services in .NET Services, 428
volume criterion
  evaluating the recommended design approach, 27
  relational end-to- (near the) end approach, 23
  XML end-to-end design approach, 22

W

W3C (World Wide Web Consortium)
  see also SOAP; XPath.
  standardization, addressing HTML shortcomings, 12
  XML Schema references, 598
  XQuery Working Draft, 500
walking the relationship structure, 76, 80
  inventory example database, 83

Web application architecture
  success of, 11
  technologies and XML role, 12
web farms, 381
Web Matrix, 444
Web references, adding, 424
web services, 415
  see also SOAP. .
  consuming through Visual Studio.NET, 424
  error mechanisms, 423
  exposing stored procedure functionality, 419
  exposing UDF functionality as, 423
  output options, 420
  security and authentication, 427
  setting up in SQL Server 2000 with SQLXML 3.0, 416
  support in SQL Server 2000 with SQLXML 3.0, 415
    shortcomings, 427
  support in SQLXML, 41
  technology convergence and, 13
  UDDI registries, 426
  wrapping with .NET Services, 428
web sites coding using URL queries, 121
  adding hyperlinks, 128
WebDav repositories, 469
well-formed XML, 14
WHERE clauses
  OPENXML rowpatterns preferable, 259-260
  SQLXML conversion of XPath expressions to, 380
  WHERE 1=2 trick, 410
  XPath predicates similar to, 193
whitespace, OPENXML limitations, 286
Windows DNA (Distributed Internet Application Architecture), using SQLXML with, 42
Windows Installer 2.0, installing SQLXML, 43
Windows Integrated Authentication
  audit trails, 123
  BizTalk Integration Case Study, 461
  recommended for template queries, 133
  setting in New Virtual Directory Properties, 46
  using URL queries for intranets, 122
Windows Scripting Host, running VB Script, 335
WITH clause, OPENXML
  edge tables result from not specifying, 279, 281
  introduced, 253
wizards, BizTalk *see* **Messaging Binding Wizard, BixTalk; Method Communication Wizard, BizTalk; New Messaging Port Wizard; Script Component Binding Wizard, BizTalk; XML Communication Wizard, BizTalk.**
wrapping complex types, 574
wrapping web services, 428
WriteXml method, DataSet class, 392
  updating example using DiffGrams, 406
WSDL (Web Service Description Language), 416
  role as an XML standard technology, 17
  soap.wsdl file, 420

X

xblkld3.dll library, 38
XDK (XML Developer Kit), Oracle, 497
XDR (XML Data Reduced) schemas, 35
  annotation compared with XML Schema, 146
  availability of XML schema attributes in, 168
  BizTalk use and deficiencies compared with XML Schema, 466
  creating XML views, 175
  data types mapping to XPath functions, 196
  edge tables and inline schemas, 282
  equivalent to <sql:relationship> attribute, 155
  equivalent to sql:identity attribute, 166
  equivalent to sql:mapping attribute, 152
  replaced by the W3C XML Schema Recommendation, 36
  role as an XML standard technology, 15
  sql:guid not avaiable with, 167
  sql:max-depth not available with, 168
  XML schemas compared with, 64
XForms, 513
XHTML (Extensible HTML)
  role as an XML standard technology, 16
XLANG Event Monitor, 489
XLANG Scheduler
  BizTalk Server component, 464
  transactions and, 490
XLANG, NewEmployee.skx file, 481
XML Bulk Load *see* **SQLXML Bulk Load.**
XML Communication Wizard, BizTalk, 477, 479, 486
XML declararations, distinguishing with namespaces, 191
xml directive, FOR XML EXPLICIT queries, 113
XML documents
  designing the overall structure, 75
    inventory example database, 83
  determining an unknown structure, 282
  document types used in recommended design approach, 25
    storage, 25
  identifying relevant database information, 74
    inventory example database, 83
  main uses of XML documents identified, 19
  mapping to SQL Server
    fulfillment system example, 239
  modifying data to match the required output format, 60
  paging with XSLT, 209
  parsing with OPENXML, 248
    memory overhead, 283
  risks of sharing across presentation structures, 63
  serialising binary content, 71
  specifying unique keys, 157
  storing data from in SQL Server, 213
    distinguishing inserts from updates, 217
  suitability for intended uses, 61
  XPath modeling as a node tree, 515
XML end-to-end approach, 21
XML Objects output method, SQLXML 3.0 web services, 421
  benefits, 422
XML query tool *see* **SQLXMLQueryTool.**
XML Root property, ADODB.Command object, 369
XML Sales By Year stored procedure, 126
XML Schema
  see also data types, XML Schema. .
  defining and constraining types, 570
  documentation within schemas, 594
  elements, 560
  global attributes, 560
  importing schemas, 593

XML Schema (continued)
namespaces, 559, 591
  instance namespace, 585, 597
Oracle 9.0.2 integrated support, 497, 498
reference appendix, 559
  W3C web sites, 598
relationships and null fields, 585
role as an XML standard technology, 15
specification for inventory example database, 85
specifying XPath data types, 195
use of XPath, 513
varying XML content, 595
W3C web sites, 598
<xsd:key> and <xsd:keyref> values, 78

XML Schema Recommendation replaces XDR, 36

XML schemas
annotated schema example, 156
annotation attributes tabulated, 168
annotation compared with XDR, 146
deriving from SQL Server structures
  design methodology, 74
fulfillment system example, 240
generally preferable to XDR, 64
illustrating ID-IDREF relationships, 232
illustrating ID-IDREFS relationships, 234
modeling child elements example, 226
modeling one-to-one relationships, 227
returning, using XMLDATA argument, 98, 115
showing enumeration constraints, 238
showing reused element types, 229
SQLXML and, 40
SQLXML use unusual, 40
structure for XML views example, 182
use of annotated schemas
  annotation namespace, 146
use of annotated schemas by SQL Server and SQLXML, 145
using check constraints, 237

XML templates *see* **templates.**

XML views, 173
accessing data through URLs or schema objects, 180
acessing data using XML templates, 180
  advantages, 181
associating Updategrams with, 294
compared to other access technologies, 173
conversion of time zone offsets, 69
creating, 174
  modeling joins, 177
  modeling tables and columns, 175
FOR XML EXPLICIT queries compared to, 174, 185
layering over a SQL Server view, 183
less cumbersome than FOR XML EXPLICIT queries, 88
limitations arising from use of XPath, 174
modifying data to match the required output format, 60
publishing as schema objects, 180
  advantages, 181
restricted to reading data, 174
serializing Unicode strings, 71
simple example, 181
timestamp conversions, 73
treatment of NULL values, 81
using to create an XML document, 82
XML schema annotation technology, 146

xml:lang global attribute, XML Schema, 560

XMLDATA argument, FOR XML queries
FOR XML EXPLICIT queries, 115
FOR XML RAW queries, 98
generating an inline schema, 282

XMLFragment property, SQLXML BulkLoad object, 342
root element and, 344

xmlHttp object, 322

XMLOverFlow field, 384

XML-RPC
basis for system interoperability and data interchange, 13
role as an XML standard technology, 16

XML-Signature, 359

xmltext directive, FOR XML EXPLICIT queries, 112, 264

XmlTextReaderExample project, 390

xmltype data type, Oracle 9.0.2, 497
equivalent expected from Yukon, 510

XPath, 187
see also expressions; functions; operators.
ADO querying using XPath with a mapping schema, 377
  advantages and drawbacks, 381
  client-side processing via SQLXMLOLEDB, 382
applying expressions to XML views, 179, 183
column patterns, OPENXML, 265, 266
compared to XQuery, 501
complex type restrictions, 582
creating values, 518
data model, 514
  changes from XPath 1.0 to XPath 2.0, 552
data model used by XQuery, 502
data types, 195
distinguishing elements with namespaces, 192
functions, 534-551
importance of understanding flow, 194
limitations of SQLXML support, 187, 208
location paths, 521-529
  abbreviations, 527
  predicates, 527
operators, 530-534
Oracle 9.0.2 integrated functions for querying xmltypes, 499
queries, SqlXmlCommand use, 402
reference appendix, 513
restricting user access with templates, 183
retieving data from SQL Server, 187
risks of infinite recursion in XPath queries, 167
role as an XML standard technology, 15
rowpattern parameter, OPENXML, 257, 258
source of XML views limitations, 174
specifying within template queries, 141
updating requires XPath with a mapping schema, 404
use in SQLXML queries, 187
variable references, 529
XPath 1.0 not fully implemented by SQL Server, 514
XPath 2.0 changes from XPath 1.0, 552
  casting complexity, 521
  casting complexity, 553
  comparisons based on data types, 532
  default namespaces, 526
XPath 2.0 status, 552

XPath queries, 187
ADO and, 202
performance optimization, 202
predicates, 193
recursive queries, 203
security issues, 207
SQLXML Managed Classes, 202
type conversions, 196

631

XPath queries (continued)
  unexpected results, 194
  use in applications, 199
  using templates, 199
    parameters and, 201
    passing to ADO, 202
  using URL queries, 199
xpath_namespace parameter
  sp_xml_preparedocument stored procedure, 252
XpathExample project, 378
XPointer, 513
XQuery, 501-509, 555
  compared to XPath and XSLT, 501
  conditional constructs, 507
  core functions, 507
  FLWR expressions, 503
  integrated support expected in Yukon, 510
  joins, 505
  Oracle support for, 500
  possible interoperation with SQL, 510
  role as an XML standard technology, 15
  use of XPath, 513
  W3C status, 500
  XQuery 1.0 status, 552
XSD (XML Schema Defintion language) schemas see **XML Schema.**
xsd: namespace prefix, XML Schema # nodes, 66
<xsd:all> element, 583
  attributes, 582
  using elements to model data points, 76
<xsd:annotation> element
  asserting relationships between elements, 153
  documentation within XML Schema, 594
<xsd:any> element, 596
<xsd:anyAttribute> element, 597
<xsd:appinfo> element, 595
  asserting relationships between elements, 153
<xsd:attribute> element
  attributes, 568
  attributes listed, 570
  sql:field attribute, 331
  type attribute, 195
  xsd:ID attribute, 332
<xsd:attributeGroup> element, 569
<xsd:choice> element, 583
  attributes, 582
  unsuitable for organizing elements within XML, 75
<xsd:complexContent> element, 574
<xsd:complexType> element, 573
<xsd:documentation> element, 594
<xsd:element> element
  attributes listed, 562, 570
  sql:key-fields attribute, 296
<xsd:enumeration> element, 575
<xsd:extension> element, 574
<xsd:field> element, 587
<xsd:fractionDigits> element, 578
<xsd:group> element, 566
xsd:ID attribute, <xsd:attribute> element, 332
<xsd:import> element, 594

<xsd:include> element, 593
<xsd:key> element, 589
  alternative to ID-IDREF relationships, 78, 81
<xsd:keyref> element, 78, 81, 590
<xsd:length> element, 577
<xsd:list> element, 576
<xsd:maxExclusive> element, 579
<xsd:maxInclusive> element, 579
<xsd:maxLength> element, 578
<xsd:minExclusive> element, 579
<xsd:minInclusive> element, 579
<xsd:minLength> element, 578
<xsd:notation> element, 581
<xsd:pattern> element, 579
<xsd:redefine> element, 593
<xsd:restriction> element, 573
<xsd:schema> element
  adding the annotation namespace, 331
  attributeFormDefault and elementFormDefaultattributes, 592
  attributes listed, 561, 571
  targetNamespace attribute, 192, 591
<xsd:selector> element, 587
<xsd:sequence> element, 583
  attributes, 582
  organizing elements within XML, 75
<xsd:simpleContent> element, 574
<xsd:simpleType> element
  attributes listed, 572
  inventory example database, 85
<xsd:totalDigits> element, 578
<xsd:union> element, 572
<xsd:unique> element, 586
<xsd:whiteSpace> element, 580
xsi: prefix, 598
xsi:nill attribute, 81
xsl parameter, URL queries, 127
XSL property, ADODB.Command object, 371
XSL see **XSLT.**
XSLCacheSize registry setting, 53
XslPath property, SqlXmlCommand, 396, 399
XSLT (Extensible Stylesheet Language Transformations)
  see also stylesheets.
  alternative to XPath recursive queries, 203
  client-side processing, 373
  combined with XPath, compared to XQuery, 501
  creating stylesheets for three possible browsers, 439
  creating Updategrams on the fly, 318
  development of XPath and, 513
  paging returned XML, 209
  role as an XML standard technology, 16
  shortcomings for manipulating data, 63
  using to pass browser infromation, 436
  workaround for lack of SQLXML 3.0 support, 209
  XPath extension functions from, 534
  XQuery 1.0 compared to, 555

Y

Yukon
  expected web service suport, 430
  expected XML support, 509

Index